Philip Norman

Simon & Schuster

RAVE ON
The Biography of Buddy Holly

SIMON & SCHUSTER
Rockefeller Center
1230 Avenue of the Americas
New York, NY 10020

Thanks to the Norman Petty Estate
for use of the Norman Petty letters.

Thanks to Gerald F. Fisher for his assistance
and the use of his photos.

Letters of Harold Orenstein, lawyer for Buddy Holly,
to Norman Petty used by permission.

"American Pie," words and music by Don McLean, copyright © 1971, 1972 by Music
Corporation of America, Inc. and Benny Bird Music. All rights controlled and
administered by Music Corporation of America, Inc. International copyright secured.
All rights reserved. Used by permission.

SIMON & SCHUSTER and colophon are registered trademarks of Simon & Schuster Inc.

Design by Levavi & Levavi

Manufactured in the United States of America

1   3   5   7   9   10   8   6   4   2

Library of Congress Cataloging-in-Publication Data
Norman, Philip, 1943–
Rave on : the biography of Buddy Holly / Philip Norman.
p.   cm.
Includes index.
1. Holly, Buddy, 1936–1959.   2. Rock musicians—United States—
Biography.   I. Title.
ML420.H595N67   1996
782.42166'092—dc20
[B]   96–24543
CIP
MN
ISBN 0-684-80082-9

AUTHOR'S NOTE

This book could not have been written without the help of Buddy's widow, Maria Elena Holly, and his eldest brother, Larry Holley. I am grateful to both for suspending their usual low opinion of would-be biographers and trusting me to write a book that would do justice to its subject at long, long last. I owe a huge debt of gratitude to Trevor Lailey, co-founder of Britain's Buddy Holly Appreciation Society, for opening the first doors to me in Lubbock and Clovis. However devoted, a biographer is only as good as his luck, and I must here record two strokes of luck well beyond the ordinary. The first was enjoying the help and guidance of the meticulous Bill Griggs, Holly archivist and researcher par excellence. The second was making the acquaintance of the remarkable Dr. Jerry Fisher and sharing his insights into the character and motivations of Norman Petty.

Heartfelt thanks also, for their assistance, kindness, and patience, to Tommy Allsup, Tony Barrett of Rockstar records, John Beecher, Kenneth Broad, David Bryce, Jim Carr, Carley Clark, June Clark, Bill Clement, Jerry Coleman, Sonny Curtis, Jack Davis, Murray Deutch, Don Everly, Phil Everly, Jeannie Fisher, Jake Goss, Echo and Ron Griffith, Tommy Hancock, Ben Hall, Ronnie Keene, Buddy Knox, Shirley Kornegay,

Robert Linville, Little Richard, Pansie McGuire, Alice Maddox, Edith Massey, Joe B. Mauldin, Bob Montgomery, Jack Neal, Terry Noland, Des O'Connor, Barbara O'Nions, Harold Orenstein, Bill Pickering, Peggy Sue Rackham, Jimmy Self, Sharon Sheeley, Pappy Dave Stone, Niki Sullivan, the late Bob Thiele, and Gary and Ramona Tollett.

My gratitude, as always, goes to Michael Sissons and Peter Matson for their unfailing encouragement and enthusiasm, and to my wife Sue, the best editor any writer could have.

To the Lailey family, Trevor, Anne, Anne-Marie, and Suzannah
Good companions on the road to Lubbock

CONTENTS

LISTEN TO ME

B uddy Holly is buried almost within sight of the modest street where he was born in Lubbock, Texas. Despite the thousands who have come to visit his grave these past thirty-six years, no tour buses run to it; there are no sonorous-voiced guides, no Disney-style working models nor souvenir stands. His home city may have been slow to recognize his enormous fame, but at least that has prevented any hint of the tacky opportunism with which Elvis Presley is memorialized at Graceland. In death, as in his brief life, Buddy remains untainted by vulgarity.

Those who would do him homage must make their own way by car from the new Civic Center where he is belatedly commemorated by a lanky bronze statue and a "Walk of Fame." You drive past La Quinta Inn along Avenue Q, make a right on to Fourth Street, then another right on to Martin Luther King Jr. Boulevard, which Buddy knew as Quirt Avenue. Beyond the railroad tracks, in a desolate hinterland of granary yards and truck depots, is Lubbock's municipal cemetery. It is wholly typical of this star of uttermost magnitude that his last resting place should be on public land, accessible to any and every visitor.

Lubbock's cemetery is a pleasant place, tranquil and understated in a way that seems hardly Texan yet somehow evokes the spirit of Buddy everywhere you look. In defiance of year-round scorching sun, the interconnecting lawns are kept a fresh spring green. The gravestones are unpretentious and set generously wide apart. Small trees lend dappling shade to vases and pots whose flowers are regularly replenished and arranged with loving care. The only noise is the steady roar of a neighboring grain silo, as huge and somberly magnificent as a medieval cathedral. Beside one newly grassed hillock, a little black and white dog keeps vigil with its nose resting miserably on its front paws. Its air of baffled disbelief that a much-loved voice could be extinguished with such cruel suddenness is doubly appropriate here.

A female clerk in the nearby administration office points out "the Holly grave" with a courteous smile, despite the wearisome familiarity of the inquiry. It lies a hundred yards from the main gate, and beside a dusty roadway where the cars of one or two latercoming mourners are usually parked. There is no fancy memorial, not even an upright stone—just a simple oblong of granite, embedded in the stubby grass. The red dust that blows from the cottonfields, winter and summer, has illuminated the letters of the inscription in dusky orange. This commemorates Buddy under the surname he was born with and would have kept throughout his life had not a typing mistake on his first recording contract decided otherwise:

> In loving memory
> of our own
> Buddy Holley
> September 7, 1936
> February 3, 1959

To the right of the inscription is a bas-relief of a Fender Stratocaster guitar, that once-astonishing two-horned silhouette, set about by musical notes and holly leaves. Across the guitar's granite contours lies a scattering of small coins like so many extra volume knobs in pristine silver and copper. It has become a tradition that the fans who find their way here from all over the world leave behind good-luck tokens of nickels and new-minted pennies, as well as red carnations, plastic crickets, children's drawings of Buddy, and pairs of black horn-rim glasses in case there should be no opticians in heaven.

In the distance, the grain silo temporarily abates its roar, turning up the level of birdsong. The sad little dog still lies and waits. The sun glances off the nickels and pennies, turning them to sparkling treasure under the giant Texas sky whose stillness now might be of conscious remembrance.

☆   ☆   ☆

On a basis of simply counting heads, rock music surpasses even film as the most influential art form of the twentieth century. By that reckoning, there is a case for calling Buddy Holly the century's most influential musician.

Elvis Presley and he are the two seminal figures of fifties rock 'n' roll, the place where modern rock culture began. Virtually everything we hear on recordings and see on video or the concert stage can be traced back to those twin towering icons: Elvis with his drape jacket, sideburns, pout, and swiveling hips; Buddy in big black glasses and buttoned-up Ivy League jacket, brooding over the fretboard of his Fender Stratocaster.

But there is no question as to whom posterity owes the greater debt. Presley's place in rock 'n' roll is no more than that of a gorgeous transient: having unleashed it on the world, he soon forsook it for slow ballads and schlock movie musicals. Holly, by contrast, was a pioneer and a revolutionary, a multidimensional talent that arrived fully formed in a medium still largely defined by fumbling amateurs. In the few hectic months of his heyday, between 1957 and 1959, he threw back the boundaries of rock 'n' roll, gave substance to its shivery shadow, transformed it from a chaotic cul-de-sac to a highway of infinite possibility and promise. To call someone who died at age twenty-two "the father of rock" is not as incongruous as it might seem. What has always set his persona apart from others in the rock 'n' roll pantheon is its air of maturity, sympathy, and understanding. To successive generations of fans he has seemed less like an idol than a teacher, guide, and friend; a "buddy" in every sense of that unassuming yet so comforting word.

The songs he wrote and performed are classics of rock 'n' roll, two-minute masterpieces that remain as fresh and potent today as when they were recorded going on forty years ago. "That'll Be the Day," "Peggy Sue," "Oh Boy," "Rave On"—the titles have become synonyms for a drape-suited, pink-Cadillac Belle Epoque which we have come to regard almost with the same misty-eyed nostalgia as we do the golden years of Hollywood.

His voice is the most imitated, yet inimitable, in rock music. Dozens of other singers down the decades have borrowed its inflection and eccentricities of pronunciation and phrasing. None has ever exactly caught the curious luster of its tone, its erratic swings from dark to light, from exuberant snarl to tender sigh, nor quite brought off the famous hiccuppy catches of breath with which he could fracture even a monosyllable like *well* into six separate, stuttering components. It was a voice able effortlessly to run the whole gamut of pop, from rock 'n' roll in maximum overdrive to thoughtful love songs whose warm intimacy stays in bloom year after year. As I write this, in London on March 6, 1995, the radio is playing a commercial for Home Comfort garden conservatories and storm windows. The jingle is a breath-for-breath copy of Buddy singing "Everyday": as usual, like him yet nothing like him.

One crucial detail above all sets him apart from Presley and the other primal rock genii. Whereas they had all become solo performers by the time they burst on the world, Buddy Holly came to stardom fronting a group, the Crickets, whose guitar–bass–drums lineup was the prototype of every rock band there has been or will be. Unlike Presley and other guitar-toting idols of the period, Buddy was a gifted player, responsible for most of the hypnotic guitar breaks that became a trademark of his records. His playing style is as widely copied as his voice: the moody drama he could conjure from a shifting sequence of four basic chords, his incisive downstrokes, and radiant, ringing solos. The deification of the rock guitarist, the enduring sex appeal of the solid-body guitar, the preeminence of the Fender make—all were set in motion, on the stage of the New York Paramount and the London Palladium, by Buddy and his brown sunburst Stratocaster.

As a songwriter, performer, and musician, he is the acknowledged progenitor of virtually every world-class rock talent to emerge in the sixties and seventies. The Beatles, the Rolling Stones, Bob Dylan, the Byrds, Eric Clapton, Pete Townshend, Elton John, Bruce Springsteen, and many others freely admit that they would never have started to play music without having the way shown to them by Buddy Holly and the Crickets. The uncountable imitators and derivatives of those artists, whether they know it or not, owe the same elemental debt. However rock may have seemed to advance or mutate, one performer above all remains ineradicably part of its spirit and soul. Listen to the newest record by the latest "original" singer–songwriter: you're almost bound to hear an echo of Buddy in there somewhere.

His time on the world stage was pitifully short, lasting only from September 1957, when "That'll Be the Day" became a hit, to the snowy, disillusioned February of 1959. But in those sixteen months he created a blueprint for enlightened rock stardom that every modern newcomer with any pretense at self-respect still aspires to follow.

He was the first rock 'n' roll performer both talented and strong-minded enough to insist on the artistic control his successors now take for granted. He was the first not only to write his own songs but also arrange them and supervise his own studio sessions, directing his backup musicians to his own exacting standards. He was the first to master the studio's technical resources, achieving effects with echo, double-tracking, and overdubbing which to this day have never been bettered.

He was the first rock 'n' roller not to be a simpering pretty boy; to be, in fact, rather homely and weedy-looking, with glasses whose metal half-frames weren't replaced by the familiar librarianish black horn-rims until the very last months of his life. He was the first to make it on solid ability, energy, and personality, attracting a male public as much as a female one; redefining the perception of sex appeal and enviable style much as John Lennon and Mick Jagger would in later years; making rock 'n' roll audiences listen and reflect as well as jive and jump about; endowing teenage fan worship with the grown-up properties of liking and respect.

Whereas other great rock music talents have needed years of trial and error to reach fulfillment, Buddy's took only a few sure-footed months. Just weeks after recording the wonderful but elementary "That'll Be the Day," he was taping "Words of Love," a ballad with which the rest of pop has still only barely caught up. In a time when repetition was believed to be the key to success, each of his releases was utterly different from its predecessor, a policy he maintained even when it began to cost him record sales. He used wacky percussion, such as an empty cardboard box beaten with drumsticks ("Not Fade Away") and hands slapping on denim-clad knees ("Everyday"); extended the vocabulary of the rock 'n' roll guitar to flamenco ("Well . . . All Right") and Hawaiian ("Heartbeat"); and worked with arcanely non-rock sound effects like Hammond organ, celesta, and, finally, massed violins. He rebelled against the apartheid that had hitherto divided white rock 'n' roll artists from black, cutting one track ("Early in the Morning") with a full gospel choir, another ("Reminiscing") with the blues saxophonist King Curtis. He anticipated how the record market of later decades would be dominated by albums rather than singles, and foreshadowed the "Live Aid" spirit of the eighties and nineties, when superstars would form ad hoc duets and even play on one another's records anonymously, just for the fun of it. He was the first pop performer to make the now familiar transition to record producing and talent spotting, and the first with ambition to become a businessman and impresario as well as a creative artist, planning his own publishing company, recording studios, record label, and even retail business almost a decade ahead of the Beatles' "revolutionary" Apple organization.

His death in a plane crash on February 3, 1959, with fellow tour artists Ritchie Valens and J. P. "The Big Bopper" Richardson, is the most famous tragedy in rock history. Numerous songs have been written about it, notably Don McLean's "American Pie," which immortally called it "the day the music died."

It was yet another of Buddy's long series of firsts, darkening rock 'n' roll's brassy face with the twin concepts of death and irony—his career apparently in decline, he had just recorded a song called "It Doesn't Matter Anymore"—and creating the definition of pop musical genius as something tragic, self-consuming, and short-lived. Here, too, imitators were to abound in the years that followed: Eddie Cochran, Patsy Cline, Sam Cooke, Jim Reeves, Janis Joplin, Jimi Hendrix, Jim Morrison, finally even Elvis himself.

But once again, the copies could never quite match the original. There was always to be something uniquely poignant about Buddy's death, a quality both sad and satisfying. For this was no rock 'n' roll wild man, hell-bent on self-annihilation, but an amiable young Texan, whose life seemed to bear not the least taint of scandal; discredit or unkindness; who had recently married and was about to become a father; who took that fatal flight with his two fellow artists only to gain a few hours' rest and get his laundry done.

Desperately sad, of course, to think of such a talent extinguished at twenty-two, when it might have gone on to achieve so much more. But how satisfying to have a hero who can never be made otherwise. For Buddy, unlike Elvis Presley, there has been no grisly unmasking. For him, unlike the Beatles, there has been no bitter, disillusioning anticlimax. For him, unlike Dylan and the Stones, there has been no grotesque, undignified senescence. To his millions of original devotees, and the millions more who join them each year, he is as immaculate and irreproachable as one of his own songs, his sufficient eulogy spoken time and again in the bittersweet regret of "American Pie":

> I can't remember if I cried
> When I read about his widowed bride
> But something touched me deep inside
> The day the music died.

Buddy Holly, in short, is the perfect modern myth.

☆ ☆ ☆

I was sixteen when he died. I can remember for certain that I didn't cry: sixteen-year-olds don't really do that. True to my generation, what touched me deep inside was not much stronger than resigned dismay. So it was over already, even though it had only just begun.

Like John Lennon, Paul McCartney, Mick Jagger, Keith Richards, and Eric Clapton, I was a British boy whom Buddy Holly had rescued from dullness, boredom, and pessimism, and pointed toward a dazzlingly better way. With his tacit encouragement, I took up playing the guitar, nerved myself to perform his songs in public, tasted the heady nectar of applause, even fancied myself endowed with some of his unostentatious charisma. Like first love, first daydreams never quite die. Here in deep middle age, there is still a part of me that longs to wear a high-buttoning suit and a flat, two-horned guitar, and be able to play every twist of the heavenly back-spiraling electric intro to "That'll Be the Day."

But crying is difficult when you have no idea who it is you're crying for. Buddy Holly was my idol, hero, and exemplar, but at the time of his death, like all his other British fans I knew next to nothing about him. If the most brilliant, he was also the vaguest of rock 'n' roll deities. Unlike Elvis, he was accompanied by no marketing campaign, what today we call hype. There were no souvenir badges, no fan magazine interviews, no roles in movies. The few photographs of him that I'd seen all showed him integrated into the Crickets' lineup: tall, lean, smilingly vague. While every breath and tongue-waggle of his singing voice was familiar to me,

I had no idea what his speaking voice sounded like. The only clue was to be found mingled with, perhaps, his most hypnotic molten-silver guitar solo: that soft, encouraging murmur of "Listen . . . listen to me."

In March 1958, he and the Crickets toured Britain (a favor Presley was never to confer), bringing him face to face at last with many of his disciples. His itinerary included Southampton, which is separated by only six miles of choppy water from the Isle of Wight, where I then lived. But I had no money for the ferry fare, let alone a concert ticket. His famous television appearance on *Sunday Night at the London Palladium* was for me just a glimpse: three numbers dashed off at the very end, then he was gone—for good, as it would turn out.

Death is, anyway, an incomprehensible subject to a sixteen-year-old. It really did not seem all that terrible, especially when one listened to Tommy Dee's "Three Stars," the tribute record honoring Buddy, Ritchie Valens, and the Big Bopper together, which painlessly transmuted the fallen earthly stars to brand-new heavenly ones, shining "up towards the north," and added almost cheerfully that Buddy was "singing to God now."

Despite the sadly appropriate title, his last single "It Doesn't Matter Anymore" contained none of the weary resignation it suggested. The voice was as airy and full of optimism as ever, skipping above the unfamiliar pizzicato strings. And how could something that had brought him back to the top of the charts possibly be the end?

To us fifties teenagers, the concept of a posthumous hit record was a completely new one, endowed with fascinating morbidity and voyeurism, like seeing James Dean still alive up on the CinemaScope screen in *Giant* and *Rebel Without a Cause*. After the success of "It Doesn't Matter Anymore," we learned there was still more to come in the form of songs recorded and stockpiled in the months before Buddy's death. For his record company, at least, the fact of his death could be postponed for a while. At the time, the longest we thought it could possibly be postponed was a year, perhaps two.

A month after his death came an LP (as we called them then), *The Buddy Holly Story*, its unusual black and white cover showing a face that I for one had never seen before. Sleekly barbered, pensive and calm, with new, modishly sculpted black glasses-frames, he looked like someone whose career had been just launched rather than just extinguished.

That July came a new single, "Peggy Sue Got Married," a playful sequel to the darkly tom-tomming love chant of December 1957. The Crickets also continued to put out records, admittedly without Buddy leading them on vocal and guitar, but with the same rhythms, the same chord changes, the same blurry "mmm's," "ooh's," and "aah's" as on all his living hits. The Crickets had always seemed such a part of him and he of them that just the rhythms, the chords, the "ooh's" and "aah's" were enough to turn our minds away from the reality yet again.

Nor was it any coincidence that 1959 was the year in which British pop music finally started to amount to something. Cliff Richard became the nation's top rock 'n' roller fronting the Shadows, a group of the same composition as the Crickets, whose lead guitarist, Hank B. Marvin, was as wand-thin as Buddy had been, wore thick black horn-rim glasses exactly like his, and played a Fender Stratocaster. At the year's end, a struggling vocalist named Adam Faith borrowed Buddy's inflection of a single word on "It Doesn't Matter Anymore" ("Buy-bee") and had a No. 1 single with "What Do You Want?," couched in the same shivery pizzicato strings as Buddy's posthumous hit. Repetition of the formula made Adam Faith the first home-grown performer to have three consecutive British number ones.

In the new decade of pop music, Buddy Holly wasn't just there, he *was* the new decade of pop music. Among the rising American generation of pretty-boy crooners, none was more successful than Bobby Vee, who sang with an uncanny tremor of Buddy's voice (he had deputized for him in concert after the fatal plan crash) and who used his vocal style to appeal directly to girls in a way Buddy himself had always seemed too grown-up and well-bred to do. Bobby Vee also recorded and performed with the post-Buddy Crickets, and once again it was almost enough.

Buddy's way, if not his voice, could be anyone's, however flat the emotion or limited the range. Between 1960 and 1963, it notched up fleeting success for John Leyton, Mike Sarne, Joe Brown; there were two unabashed British Buddy clones, Mike Berry (whose "Tribute to Buddy Holly" made the Top 20 in 1961) and the horn-rimmed Buddy Britten. In America, Bobby Vee's impersonation was rivaled by that of Tommy Roe, whose 1962 No. 1 "Sheila" used the same rolling drumbeat and chafing guitar as "Peggy Sue."

One British songwriter, Geoff Goddard, even claimed direct input from Buddy from beyond the grave on the "Peggy Sue"–inspired "Johnny Remember Me," which was a hit for John Leyton in 1961. A devout spiritualist, Goddard claimed to be in psychic contact with Buddy and to have been assured by him that the record was bound for No. 1.

Meanwhile, releases kept on coming from the authentic and irreplaceable voice itself: "Reminiscing"; "Brown-Eyed Handsome Man"; "Bo Diddley"; "Wishing." So regularly were the posthumous singles issued and so vibrant was the presence on them that many began to wonder whether he really was dead after all. There were rumors that the plane crash had been no more than a highly successful stunt to boost his sales, and that he could make a Lazarus-like return at any moment. Another widely circulated story had it that he'd survived the crash, but with terrible disfigurements which prevented him from appearing in public ever again, and that he was now living as a recluse in, of all places, Scotland.

These repeatedly profitable resurrections also focused attention for the first time on Buddy's former manager and producer, Norman Petty, in whose Clovis, New Mexico, studio most of the hits took shape and who shared credit with him as writer of "That'll Be the Day," "Peggy Sue," "True Love Ways," and many more. Producers and managers in the late fifties did not aspire to the celebrity they were later to enjoy, and thus far little had been known of Petty beyond that regularly appearing second surname on Buddy's records. But now he began to be a talking point in his own right. Since many of the tracks left behind by Buddy had been voice-only demos, Petty was having to overdub them with instrumental backing—not by Buddy's Crickets, for some reason, but by a sixties group called the Fireballs. As time went on, these doctored releases seemed to have less and less of the authentic Buddy sound. But we accepted them unquestioningly, presuming that if anyone had Buddy's best artistic and financial interests at heart, it would be his former manager.

The British "Beat Boom" of the mid-sixties is credited with having changed the face of pop music and transformed its audience from an embattled minority to a worldwide movement. In its essentials, though, it was not British at all, but merely Buddy Holly's students coming to maturity.

The Beatles had founded themselves on his vocal style and repertoire. John Lennon and Paul McCartney's vocal harmony, in its first incarnation at least, was a northern English version of Buddy's doubled-tracked solo voice from 1957. The fact that he wrote his own material encouraged Lennon and McCartney to try to do likewise, and so to become the most prolific and successful songwriting team in pop-music history. They acknowledged their comprehensive debt on their 1964 *Beatles For Sale* album with a near-perfect facsimile of "Words of Love," the greatest Holly song never to become a hit during his lifetime.

In 1963, the Rolling Stones transformed themselves from backwoods R&B group to commercial chart-toppers with a pounding, harmonica-ridden version of Buddy's '57 B-side, "Not Fade Away." Britain's third most popular new group were called the Hollies. The fourth most popular, the Searchers, named themselves after the John Wayne movie that pro-vided the inspiration for "That'll Be the Day." The ninth or tenth most popular could have had nothing but holly on their minds when they called themselves the Rockin' Berries. He was there in (bespectacled) Peter and Gordon (who made both the U.K. and U.S. charts with their 1965 cover of "True Love Ways"); in Herman's Hermits (one bespectacled), the Ivy League (named after the style of his suits), the Moody Blues, the Barron Knights, the Fortunes, the Applejacks; in a hundred more who got onto the charts for five minutes, plus thousands more who never made it beyond their local pub or youth club.

He was there, too, in the American backlash—in Bob Dylan's new "electric" voice, the harmony and echo of the Byrds, the chord patterns of new-look attractions like Neil Diamond, Mitch Ryder and the Detroit Wheels, the Fireballs, the Bobby Fuller Four, even the Monkees. He was there in the time of psychedelia and acid, when the smartest thing for any rock star to do was put on a pair of little granny-specs. He was still there in London's Hyde Park in the moon-shot summer of '69, when the hippie multitudes gathered to see rock's first "supergroup," Blind Faith, the least recognizable mutation yet of Buddy's Crickets, whose sacred solitary album included his most brilliant non-hit of 1958, "Well . . . All Right."

For year after crowded year, all that went with this huge creative national debt was the same life story of barest essentials. A nice kid had come out of Texas, made wonderful music, got married, died. It was a legend in the purest sense, carried mostly in the head, passed on from mouth to mouth. Even after all this time, one saw no images of Buddy other than the half-dozen or so familiar ones in photographs and album covers. Few articles were written about him, and those that were merely repeated the same one or two facts. There seemed to be no film clips of him, nor even recordings of his speaking voice.

I had become a journalist with the London *Sunday Times Magazine,* writing extended profiles of major rock and soul figures such as James Brown, Johnny Cash, Stevie Wonder, Wilson Pickett, B. B. King, traveling to interview them in New York, Los Angeles, Memphis, and Nashville. In all that time, though he remained my hero of heroes, I never wrote a word about Buddy Holly, nor even contemplated doing so. My assumption was the one of which every reporter should beware: If there were any story to tell, surely it would have been told already.

In 1972, I interviewed the Everly Brothers, Don and Phil. Though a major revival in rock music and style was then under way in America, it did not yet encompass rock's original stars, all of whom remained in unfashionable obscurity in their native land. The surviving big names, Bill Haley, Little Richard, Chuck Berry, Carl Perkins, Jerry Lee Lewis, Neil Sedaka, and the Everlys, worked mainly in Britain, where the loyalty of their original following remained undiminished.

Both Don and Phil Everly talked at length, and with great warmth, about Buddy Holly, with whom they had toured extensively during 1957 and 1958. Don remembered first meeting him and the Crickets in the basement of an arena in Toronto, and how the badly dressed Texas boys' eyes lit up at the sight of the Everlys' sharp Ivy League clothes. Recalling the Crickets' lack of sophistication in those early days, he added what then seemed a bizarre detail: that at the time, their only publicity picture showed them down in Lubbock, in Levi's and T-shirts, setting tiles on a roof.

Phil Everly's memories were more emotional: he and Buddy had evidently been real friends, not merely joshing companions on the road. "He wrote 'Wishing' for Don and me. It burns me up when I read about 'Wishing' being 'reportedly written by Buddy Holly for the Everly Brothers.' I remember Buddy putting me into bed with a girl one night . . . and how he laughed! But I can remember him in New York, right at the end, playing all his songs for me and asking me why he couldn't get a hit; he was so low. Then he said, 'Will you put me to bed?'"

I was the *Sunday Times*'s "Atticus" gossip columnist in 1975 when Paul McCartney began his secondary career as pop music's most astute businessman with another gesture of homage to his most formative influence. Thanks to the lack of interest in Buddy Holly in America, McCartney's MPL company was able to acquire publishing rights to all Buddy's greatest hits in the United States and Canada for a bargain price, rumored to be less than a million pounds. McCartney also inaugurated an annual Buddy Holly Week of memorial concerts and fan-fests, coinciding with

Buddy's birthday on September 7. In my capacity as Atticus—that is, in no very serious or reverential spirit—I attended the launch of that first Buddy Holly Week, for which McCartney had taken the trouble to fly Norman Petty over from Clovis, New Mexico. At the lavish lunch that marked the occasion, Petty presented McCartney with a pair of Buddy's gold cufflinks, allegedly the very ones he'd been wearing when the plane crashed. I remember thinking it odd that a dead rock 'n' roll star's ex-manager should possess such an intimate souvenir, let alone feel free to hand it out as a PR gesture.

In the late 1970s—when Elvis Costello dominated the post-punk charts, wearing black horn-rims and playing a Fenderish solid-body guitar, and when Linda Ronstadt found "That'll Be the Day" and "It's So Easy" no less accessible to the voice of a country-rock chanteuse—I switched from journalism to writing biographies of pop-music stars: the Beatles, the Rolling Stones, Elton John. My aim was to get behind the mythology and the hype; to turn superstars and legends into creatures of flesh and blood; to discover who and what had made them what they eventually became; to savor all the absurd accidents and wrong turns that led them to their stupendously right destination; above all—and most challengingly—translate the excitement of great pop music into words. When I first thought of applying this formula to the Beatles, friends and editors alike urged me not to waste my time. "It's all been said already," they told me. "Everyone knows everything there is to know."

During my research for all three biographies, Buddy Holly cropped up time and again. I learned the full story of how he had encouraged Paul McCartney and an unhappily bespectacled John Lennon to write their earliest songs on truant afternoons in Allerton, Liverpool; how Holly tracks like "Crying, Waiting, Hoping" and "Mailman, Bring Me No More Blues" bolstered the Beatles' early repertoire in the Liverpool dance halls and helped get them through all-night club sessions in the Hamburg Reeperbahn; how the first record they ever made, at their own expense, was "That'll Be the Day"; how their very name evolved from a desire to resemble Buddy's Crickets.

In the annals of the supposedly hard and unsentimental Stones, he occupied a similarly warm niche. I learned how Mick Jagger still remembered seeing him perform "Not Fade Away" in Woolwich during his one and only British tour; how Keith Richards's original guitar-playing technique was modeled on his; how, to be sure, the name "Buddy Holly" was almost the only one in Creation with the power to soften Keith's vampirelike physiognomy. Later on, I learned how the great flashy four-eyes of seventies rock had acquired the look from the same role model that inspired Hank B. Marvin's horn-rims and John Lennon's (and Roger McGuinn's and John Sebastian's) granny glasses. Reg Dwight, alias Elton John, was born with normal vision but during his schooldays took to wearing black horn-rims in imitation of Buddy Holly, thereby ruining his eyesight forever.

I was as ravenous as ever for information about Buddy but, after all these years, still had almost nothing to chew on beyond that basic formalized fifties legend. The one existing biography, *Buddy Holly: His Life and Music* by John Goldrosen, published in 1975, was a sincere effort by a painstaking, levelheaded fan, but one that sacrificed almost all color and vividness to dry musical analysis. In 1978, America's rekindling appreciation of Buddy's talent was marked by a Hollywood film, *The Buddy Holly Story,* with Gary Busey in the title role. Though a self-evident travesty (Buddy's two fellow Crickets, Jerry Allison and Joe B. Mauldin, were portrayed under fictitious names), it nevertheless became a box-office success and even received an Oscar for score adaptation.

The first real television documentary about Buddy was not seen in Britain until 1986, on the fiftieth anniversary of his birth. The maker was Paul McCartney's MPL, a company by now grown hugely wealthy on the back of its presciently acquired Holly song copyrights. McCartney, deeply offended by the shallow and semi-fictional Hollywood portrayal of Buddy's life, had resolved to employ both his commercial and personal clout to set the record straight.

McCartney's film was shown on BBC 2, in the *Arena* arts program's series on great names of rock 'n' roll. I sat through it spellbound. Here at last was film of Buddy and the Crickets, performing "That'll Be the Day" and "Peggy Sue" on *The Ed Sullivan Show*—the original four of them, all in tuxedos, and featuring a rhythm guitarist who, confusingly, also wore glasses. It was a surprise to see how thin and anemic Buddy looked, especially in those original un-chic half-frames, and how hard he had to work with the indifferent sound system. To the learner guitarist of thirty years previously, a great unresolved question was settled at last: he played "That'll Be the Day" in the key of A, with a capo over the Stratocaster's fretboard to save his index finger the labor of forming a six-string bar.

Here, for the first time, was a walking, talking Buddy Holly, long-necked and almost one-dimensionally thin, summoned for a few impromptu front-of-curtain words with Ed Sullivan; answering his host's perfunctory question about the Crickets' ages in what one always should have guessed must be a huskily melodious tone ("Well, there's two eighteen, one twenty, and I'm twenty-one"), saying "Sir" punctiliously and at the end, rather to Sullivan's surprise, thrusting out his hand to be shaken.

Here was a highway between the Texas cottonfields, and a speeding truck with "Holley Tile Co., Lubbock" printed on its cab. Here were his two brothers, Larry and Travis, reminiscing about his early childhood, and the amiable Sonny Curtis, one of Buddy's first musical partners, remembering him as a teenage bluegrass wizard on a four-string banjo. Here was Jerry Allison, the Crickets' once fair-haired, wolf-eyed drummer, now with a bushy biblical beard, describing him as a student at Lubbock High School, and as an after-hours musician at the seamy 16th and J Club. Here was Vi Petty, Norman's widow, in the tiny studio in Clovis where the greatest hits were made. Here, even, were scraps of conversation between takes: Buddy's voice saying "Are we rolling?" "Can you go like that?" then, commandingly, "Okay, let's do it."

Here were his song publisher, Murray Deutch, and his A&R man at Coral records, Bob Thiele. Here was his "widowed bride," Maria Elena, describing how he proposed marriage to her on their very first date. Here was the apartment building in Greenwich Village where they settled for the few months they were to enjoy together. Buddy Holly in the Village among beatniks and coffeehouses . . . it was a thought somehow almost too exotic to handle.

Here was Tommy Allsup, the lead guitarist he brought in on his final great run of rock 'n' roll singles, and his companion on the last tour. Here was Allsup's account of the cold and misery of it, and the bizarre twist of fate that led Ritchie Valens and the Big Bopper to join Buddy on the fatal flight. Here was Phil Everly, still as impassioned as when we had spoken about his old friend, giving added weight to a thesis tentatively raised in John Goldrosen's biography. This was that Buddy's royalty earnings had been tied up in in some unfair and exploitative way by Norman Petty; that in early '59 Buddy had meant to stay in New York until he got another hit, but was forced out on the road again by the need to provide for his pregnant young wife.

In a one-hour documentary, of course, all these matters could only be touched on with tantalizing brevity. One moment on the soundtrack stuck in my mind as revealing tremendous niceness, tact, and power of understatement on its subject's part. In some rain-sodden far-northern city or other, an interviewer asked Buddy what the weather in Lubbock would be like just now. "Oh, it's not quite this cool," he replied. "And it's a little bit drier."

The new information in the documentary, added to the legend, inspired me to write a play, *Words of Love,* which contrasted the last hours in Buddy's life with the existence of a boy like myself at sixteen, for whom his music is a respite from parental repression and dreary hopelessness. The play was shown on BBC 2 in 1988. That same year, the musical *Buddy* opened in London, combining the usual vestigial life-story with a reprise of all his greatest hits. The show is still playing to capacity audiences seven nights a week, and is taking bookings to the year 2000.

In 1990, a startled British public learned that its new prime minister, John Major, relaxed by listening to Buddy Holly records. But it was not until there had been a bespectacled Buddy Holly fan at 10 Downing Street for nearly four years that the idea came to me at long, long last. Might there be even more to be learned about Buddy than the McCartney documentary had uncovered? Might the way to obtain the facts I had been hungering for since the age of fourteen be to go out and find them? I had vowed never to write another pop music biography, but this was not quite the same as Elton John, the Rolling Stones, and the Beatles. Those books had been motivated by the promise of a good story. This one would be motivated by three decades of love, fascination, and gratitude.

When I mentioned the idea to friends, the general reaction was much as in 1978 when I first thought of investigating the Beatles: "It's all been said. Everyone already knows everything there is to know." That was all I needed to hear.

During the filming of my television play I had gotten to know Trevor Lailey, co-founder of the British Buddy Holly Appreciation Society and an enthusiast since his schooldays. With Trevor, his wife, Anne, and their daughters, Annie-Marie and Suzannah (all three also devout Buddy fans), I traveled to Lubbock in the summer of 1994. Within a couple of days of arriving, I was holding Buddy's Fender Stratocaster. Spread before me on a table lay a selection of his stage clothes: a mustard-colored tweed jacket; a pair of Florsheim "Tuxedo" shoes in black suede with red piping; charcoal-gray slacks, still shiny-seamed from their last dry cleaning in his lifetime. And the real Buddy Holly story was flying at me from every direction, sometimes almost too fast for me to write it down.

PART ONE

BLUE DAYS, BLACK NIGHTS

L ook at a map of the nation-sized expanse that is the state of Texas, move westward from Dallas a couple of hundred miles, then north, and you eventually light upon Lubbock. Far away from all the buzz-names, Houston, San Antonio, Laredo, El Paso, shut away in the narrowing corridor between the Oklahoma and New Mexico state lines that becomes the Texas Panhandle, it proclaims itself as much a backwater as any hot, dry, inland place can be. Its nearest substantial neighbor is Amarillo, 120 miles to the north, where Interstate 40, the successor to famous old Route 66, flings endless silver ribbons of traffic west to Los Angeles and east to Memphis and Nashville. Except for one brief, brilliant period in the late 1950s, the ebb and flow of national events has seemed equally intent on passing Lubbock by.

The town stands, alone and self-contained, on huge vistas of flat farmland. The principal crop is one that has nurtured so much American music and mythology that the foreign visitor, seeing it for the first time, is disconcerted by how ordinary it looks. Surely those meager melting snow-white pods, set in Roman-straight rows of vermilion earth to the horizon, can't possibly be all there is to cotton!

For nine months of each year in these Texas plains, the climate is an ideal one of strong, steady sunshine, hard blue skies, and almost zero humidity. But spring and fall bring more complex, erratic times, when the temperature can drop twenty degrees in a few seconds and ferocious gales called blue northers come sweeping over the high plateaus that extend to Canada, buffeting each unsheltered hamlet in turn with their Arctic onslaught. Other days bring a vague, directionless turbulence—Lubbockites call it "blowin' dust"—when the whirling red grit from the cottonfields stings eyes and nostrils and stains the whole immensity of the sky a delicate rose-petal pink. Most alarming is the tornado season, between April and June, when up to seven of the deadliest black cones, the kind that reach to the ground, can be counted out there at a time, whirling around the cotton and wheat like some ghastly square dance of monsters out of M. R. James. Every year brings its crop of "just fancy that" tornado stories—of hens stripped of every feather; cattle picked up and carried miles across country; straws driven inches deep into wooden telephone poles; entire hamlets hammered flat. In 1970, the biggest tornado ever recorded chose to cleave its mile-and-a-half-wide path with almost geometrical precision right through the center of downtown Lubbock.

In Abilene, 160 miles to the east, you can stand on the main street and instantly visualize the frontier town it once was. But Lubbock has no such romantic origins. First settled in the 1890s well after the Old West was tamed, named in honor of the Mexican War hero Colonel Tom S. Lubbock, it did not become a city proper until shortly before World War I. Apart from cotton, general farming, and some limited light industry, its principal raison d'être is Texas Technical College, founded in 1923, granted university status in the early sixties, attended today by 29,000 students and boasting the largest campus in the country. Texas Tech gives Lubbock the air of an Oxford or Harvard, out there on waving seas of grass. The broad thoroughfare that passes the campus is called University Avenue, lending a vision of gowns and mortarboards to the scene of Buddy's earliest triumphs as a musician. But, despite this whiff of academe, there is never any doubt that you are in deepest Texas, where long-legged men settle at diner counters without troubling to remove their ten-gallon Stetsons, and every other vehicle in the traffic stream seems to be a prairie-dusted Dodge or Chevrolet pickup truck.

From well-watered roadside grass in the downtown area, crosses of many styles signal Lubbock's original claim to celebrity. It possesses more churches per capita than any other city in America. If West Texas is "the Buckle of the Bible Belt," then Lubbock is that belt's first and most deeply worn notch: a place where worship is still as regular and vociferous as in pioneer days, and where notions of good and evil, heaven and hell, have much the same stark simplicity they did a century ago. Here in teeming display can be found all the usual outwardly similar, inwardly irreconcilable banners of Presbyterian, Episcopalian, Lutheran, Church of Christ. Here, as everywhere through the South, Baptists predominate, not as a unified creed but in innumerable, hotly competitive subdivisions: the First Baptist Church, the Second Baptist Church, the Trinity Baptist Church, the Bethany Baptist Church, the Wayne Avenue Baptist Church, the Lyons Chapel Baptist Church. Here, too, churches do not hold themselves aloof from the ebb and flow of secular life but stand along all the busiest commercial strips, sober, one-story temples to God democratically cheek-by-jowl with bright-colored ones to McDonald's, Arby's, and Whataburger. Among the largest and most prosperous of all Lubbock's churches is Tabernacle Baptist on 34th Street, a vermilion hangar of a place that Buddy's money helped to build, where his funeral took place, and where his two brothers, Larry and Travis, are still pillars of the congregation.

To Lubbock, the virtue next to godliness has always been sobriety. In Buddy's time, and right up to 1972, the city was dry; although today one can buy a drink at bars and restaurants, it is impossible to obtain liquor by the bottle within the city limits. When men of a certain age forgather over their long-neck beer bottles, the talk will often turn to those comparatively recent Prohibition days; to famous bootleggers whose congregations were larger than any pastor's; to the speakeasies and joints—and their equally illicit music—that once flourished on the raffish edges of town, beyond the jurisdiction of church elders or police.

The face that Lubbock turns to the visitor has all the Southern virtues of courtesy, helpfulness, and openness, sweetened with that peculiar, slow-smiling Texan charm. "Where y'all from?" is a question people here ask with genuine interest, often on a note of flattering incredulity. They imply you have done them honor to seek them out, across all those tracts of corn and cotton. A sign at the city's threshold, only lately taken down, used to say WELCOME TO LUBBOCK FOR ALL REASONS.

But the courtesy and smiles can have limits, as strictly defined as the city's own, and can vanish with the abruptness of sunshine in the face of a blue norther. "Don't mess with Texas"—a caution printed even on dry cleaners' plastic garment-covers—underlines how carefully it is advisable to tread in some company hereabouts. One must remember not to be even glancingly flippant about God, the Flag, or the Republican Party, nor show too much enthusiasm for contemporary concepts such as feminism or gay pride. One remembers that, despite all those crosses and public texts about forgiveness and brotherly love, this is a part of America where to carry firearms is not merely a constitutional right but the sine qua non of manliness and self-respect. On the subject of brotherly love, one remembers that when Buddy was growing up, and until almost a decade after his death, Lubbock practiced racial segregation that was as stubbornly ruthless as any in Alabama or Mississippi. The old ghetto boundaries remain to this day: blacks to the east of town, Hispanics to the north. A great change of heart has been forced to take place, epitomized by the metamorphosis of Quirt Avenue into Martin Luther King Jr. Boulevard. Even so, there are still some citizens of a certain age who persist in such traditional usages as calling east Lubbock "Colored Town" and a child's slingshot a "nigger-shooter."

☆   ☆   ☆

Off the wide boulevards are intersecting back streets of one-story houses, some showy, some simple, all bound into the familiar idyll of communal front lawns, family-named mailboxes, sprinklers, sunlight and dappling shadow. In its essential ways of life, America has a continuity that makes Britain seem a land of mad flux by comparison. Looking down Sixth Street, where Buddy was born, you feel that little can have changed in sixty years, other than the shapes of the cars parked there.

There is one great change, however, a mystifying one to the fans who arrive here on their circuit of devotion between Buddy's statue and his grave. Number 1911 Sixth Street, where he was brought into the world (at 3:30 P.M. on September 7, 1936), has vanished. The only trace of the house is the grass strip it once occupied, gaping like the cavity of a lost tooth between its former next-door neighbors. There is no alternative but to turn up the photograph taken during the early seventies by that most devoted of all Holly archivists, Bill Griggs. It looks like a fitting enough birthplace for an all-American hero—a narrow wooden dwelling, not much more elaborate than a pioneer cabin, its front door situated at one narrow end, beneath a small slope-roofed porch. The solitary visible decoration are cut-out shapes like playing-card clubs on the window shutters.

Buddy's parents, now also years dead, must likewise be sought in photographs. Here is his father, Lawrence Odell Holley, a tall, black-browed man, thin and sinewy in a way that has almost vanished from these obese modern times, and with a familiar lantern-jawed amiability of expression. Here is his mother, Ella, a tiny, fine-boned woman, barely reaching to Lawrence's shoulder, but a patent ball of fire whose robustness, energy, and humor leap out of the orangey early-fifties Kodachrome. There is a chemistry that attracts lanky and easygoing men to small, feisty women, and in this Buddy was destined to take after his father, although not, alas, with the same reward of a lifetime's happiness and harmony.

L. O., as Lawrence Holley was always called, grew up in Honey Grove, near Paris, Texas, far away to the northeast, near the Oklahoma border. He was twenty-five and working as a short-order cook in nearby Vernon when he met Ella Drake, whose family traced their lineage from the Elizabethan adventurer Sir Francis Drake and whose father was part-Cherokee Indian. The couple married in 1924 and, a year later, moved to Lubbock, a community then in the throes of frenetic expansion around Texas Tech. By the time Buddy arrived in 1936, Ella Holley was thirty-four, and must have believed her childbearing days to be past. She already had two sons, Larry (born in 1925) and Travis (born in 1927) and a daughter, Patricia (born in 1929). But the six-and-a-half-pound baby boy was greeted with joy both by his parents and siblings. He was named Charles Hardin Holley, after his two grandfathers, Charles Wesley Drake and John Hardin Holley. As this seemed absurdly long and formal for a little baby, it was quickly abbreviated to Buddy, a traditional nickname for the youngest boy of a family and one that Ella had always liked. Foreshadowing the indifference it would show to Buddy throughout his short life, Lubbock's morning paper, the *Avalanche,* recorded his birth as that of a girl, weighing eight and a half pounds.

He entered the world in the mid-season Depression years, when America's eastern cities were vistas of weary, work-starved men, its westbound highways teemed with migrant jalopies, and miserably firelit hobo jungles lined its railroad tracks. L. O. Holley kept in work by turning his wiry arms to many trades and by his tireless industry and conscientiousness. "There never was a worker like Daddy," his son Larry remembers. "If folks couldn't pay him, then he'd work for nothing." In Lubbock he had been fortunate in finding a good long-term employer, an entrepreneur named L. D. Thomas, universally known as Little Dog or Pup Thomas. L. O. held down a variety of jobs in Thomas's various enterprises down the years: café cook, tailor in a menswear store, even timekeeper at the boxing ring where Thomas presented nationally famous pugilists such as Max Baer. On Buddy's birth certificate L. O.'s surname is given as Holly, not Holley, and his occupation as "tailor," but his main activity thereafter was working for Pup Thomas's construction company as a carpenter and house framer.

When Buddy was a year old, L. O. moved his brood from the little plank house on Sixth Street to Wolfforth, in those days a rural hamlet, a few miles southwest of Lubbock, where they read by the light of oil lamps, used an earth closet, and burned cow chips for fuel. Over the next twelve years, the family would have five other addresses in and around the city: on Avenue O; on 28th Street; in the Loftland addition beyond east Lubbock; on Acuff Road; then on Mulberry Road. Shortage of money kept them permanently on the move; the one house they owned rather than renting had to be sold after eighteen months.

But despite their straitened circumstances, L. O. and Ella were the epitome of "decent folks," respectable, sober, public-spirited, and, of course, God-fearing. Their church, where L. O. served for many years as deacon, was Tabernacle Baptist, in those days situated at 15th Street and Avenue N. The Tabernacle Baptists are a sect based on an almost 100 percent literal reading of the Bible, yet in matters of teaching and proce- dure set apart from other Lubbock Baptist congregations almost as vehe- mently as from competing denominations like the Episcopalians or the Church of Christ. In common with most Southern churchgoers, Taberna- cle Baptists are expected to pay a tithe from their earnings, usually fixed at 10 percent.

The Holleys might have been "pretty much behind the eight-ball fi- nancially," as Larry now puts it, but thanks to the unremitting sweat of L. O.'s brow and the blessed egalitarianism of the educational system, Buddy lacked few of the ingredients for a classic American boyhood. Like his better-off school friends, he played baseball, joined the Cub Scouts, and entered local fancy dress contests in fancy cowboy clothes, riding on a pony. L. O. had not hesitated to chastise his two older boys with a double-thickness leather razor-strop, but Buddy received no such dire punishment for his juvenile misdemeanors. Most third sons have to resign themselves the existence of "tail-end Charlie" as far as their parents' affections are concerned, but Buddy might have been L. O. and Ella's only child. His tiny, strong-minded mother, in particular, petted, indulged, and watched over him almost obsessively.

Like many devout and self-sufficient Southern families, then and now, the Holleys loved music and were adept at making it, both as an expression of faith and to amuse themselves, their relations, and their friends. Ella sang duets with her twin sister, Allie. Buddy's older brothers performed as a twosome in local hoedowns and talent contests, Larry on violin and piano, Travis on accordion and guitar. Their sister Pat had a sweet singing voice, and at family get-togethers would harmonize with Ella and Allie. The one exception was the head of the family: as Travis Holley remembers, L. O. "couldn't carry a tune in a bag."

When Buddy was five, his parents bought him his first musical instrument, a toy violin. He made his first stage appearance soon afterward when he accompanied his brothers in a talent contest at the schoolhouse in County Line, about thirty miles northwest of Lubbock. Peeved at being "slowed up" onstage by a toddler, Larry smeared grease on Buddy's violin bow so that no one would hear it. But the song he sang so captivated the judges that they awarded him the $5 first prize. "I can see him doing it now," Larry Holley says. "It was that old song that goes 'Have you ever gone sailing down the river of memo-rees?'"

In character, these two elder brothers could hardly have been more different. Travis Holley, though his family thought him "as good-looking as a movie star," was shy and unassuming, while Larry was a tough, humorous character, sharing his father's dedication to hard work but also with an adventuring, roistering bent recalling his famous ancestor Sir Francis Drake. As Buddy grew up, Larry became a combination of surrogate father and role model; whatever his big brother did, he would gamely try, although his nature back then was anything but confident. "He was just an insecure, scared little kid," Larry remembers. "When I'd just got married, Buddy was about ten and my wife and I took him with us on a hunting trip. We slept out in the open, and late at night, you know, the coyotes would get to howling. Buddy crawled into the sleeping bag with my wife and me, right in between the two of us."

The Holleys' quest for cheaper housing outside Lubbock city limits uprooted Buddy from his first elementary school, Roscoe Wilson, at the age of ten, and transferred him to Roosevelt Elementary School in Lubbock County, where he had no friends and to which he had to make a long, wearisome journey by bus each morning. Here music, for him, changed from recreation to salvation. A year later, he began formal piano lessons. His teacher reported him to be a promising pupil with a natural ear, but after a few months Buddy announced that the piano wasn't for him. On the school bus he'd seen a boy named Wayne Maines strumming a guitar and singing. Buddy's parents started him on steel guitar, the kind played on the lap like a zither, but that did not do either: he said he wanted an acoustic "flat-top" model "like the one Travis has." L. O. Holley bought him a cheap Harmony model from a pawnshop; brother Travis, who'd learned to play during wartime service with the Marines, showed him the first one-finger chords; from there on, Buddy was seldom seen without a guitar in his hands. He'd strum and sing in his room, on the front steps of his house, and on the trip to and from school.

For a Texas boy with his first guitar in the late 1940s, there was only one kind of music to play and sing. It was country music (in Texas, more commonly known as Western music), the folk songs of the frontier, ballads of the prairie, the cattle range, and the campfire. Forged inside the circled wagons of the first pioneers, it was music that knew no barriers of age or class. "Country-style" meant family, friends, and neighbors—the community spirit, harmony, and togetherness that were the youthful nation's most cherished virtues. Its quintessential form was the hoedown, barn dance, or jamboree, with hay bales for seats, pies and lemonade set out on red-and-white gingham cloths, fiddles sawing, hens clucking, grandpappies and small children clapping along together. Two Saturday-night radio shows, hugely popular throughout the South in Buddy's childhood, were presented in this homely manner before a live audience: the *Louisiana Hayride,* transmitted by KWKH in Shreveport, Louisiana; and the famous *Grand Ole Opry,* transmitted by WSM from country music's capital, Nashville, Tennessee.

But first and foremost, country was white man's music, as barefaced a declaration of white supremacy as the drinking fountains, lunchrooms, and public benches available to some and not to others throughout the unreformed South. Like their housing, drinking, eating, and transport, black people's music was subject to rigid segregation. The whole panoply of blues genius, from Blind Lemon Jefferson and Robert Johnson to Muddy Waters and John Lee Hooker, was lumped together under the same condescending classification of "specialty" or "race" music, ferociously corralled off from the ears of white people, especially women and children, allowed to be retailed only to black audiences in black-owned clubs and halls, and broadcast only over black-operated radio stations. Country music, with its formality and decorum, epitomized white civilization and refinement to God-fearing Southern minds, just as the blues, with its simplicity, humor, sexual frankness, and insidious rhythm, epitomized every possible nuance of the word "sin."

For all country music's huge popularity, it had barely begun to be commercialized when Buddy came to it at the tail end of the forties. The public at large knew it mainly as incidental music for cowboy movies, warbled by buckskinned heroes like Gene Autry or Roy Rogers and the Sons of the Pioneers. Its single splash of contemporary glamour was Hank Williams, whose idiosyncratic yodeling vocal style managed to suggest youth rather than late middle age, and whose songs, such as "Your Cheatin' Heart," "Hey, Good Lookin'," and "Jambalaya," regularly crossed over from the purely country sphere to become international pop hits. Williams is regarded as the first true pop singer–songwriter, not least for creating an image that was tantalizingly aloof, yet troubled and vulnerable. He was to die of drugs and drink in 1953 at twenty-nine, one of the earliest intimations that fame, wealth, and adulation need not necessarily be beneficial to one's health.

The style of country music varied according to the regional psyche that fostered it. From the eastern South came bluegrass, a frenetically fast and nimble banjo-led sound, popularized far and wide by Bill Monroe and the Bluegrass Boys, and the duo of Lester Flatt and Earl Scruggs, who picked together as competitively as if their banjo and guitar were dueling rapiers. Along the paranoiacally guarded frontier with Mexico, it became chili-flavored Tex-Mex; up around the Louisiana bayous, it took on the accordions and accent of the French colonists to become Cajun; to its detractors it was hillbilly, redolent of remote mountain regions where families still carried on blood feuds with shotguns. The open, windy Texas plains, and the restless energy of its people, had fostered a further zestful subdivision called Western swing, whose chief exponents, Bob Wills and Hank Thompson, fronted groups augmented by brass and drums—and made music specifically for energetic dancing.

The songs Buddy learned to sing and strum as a twelve-year-old were his parents', and grandparents', favorites: sentimental cowboy ballads, folk songs, spirituals handed down from tent meetings on open prairies a century earlier. Like many young people, he was fascinated by Hank Williams and would gamely try to copy the way Williams's yodel pulverized simple words like "do" and "cry" into half a dozen or more breath-jerking syllables on "Lovesick Blues," the jukebox hit of the hour. He admired the same stars that every adult country fan did: Woody Guthrie; Jimmie Rodgers, the Singing Brakeman; Slim Whitman; the Carter Family; Hank Snow, whose train songs were the first in Western music to introduce a driving, finger-snapping beat. "He started learning the banjo, too," Larry Holley remembers. "Seems like he picked that up in just a matter of days."

At his first elementary school, Buddy had made friends with another guitar enthusiast, a plump, rather matronly-looking boy named Bob Montgomery whose parents ran the Gin Café (named after the cotton-processing machine, not the liquor) on the south side of town. Buddy and Bob spent long hours practicing at each other's houses, modeling themselves on bluegrass duos like the Louvin Brothers and Johnny and Jack, whose high tenor harmonies suited their unbroken voices. They even managed to get hold of a wire-recorder, precursor of the tape-recorder, and put down middle-aged country tracks like "Footprints in the Snow," "I'll Just Pretend," and "Take These Shackles from My Heart." At the beginning, and for some time to come, Bob Montgomery seemed the more talented of the pair: he would usually sing lead while Buddy supplied the harmony. "I didn't have any brothers or sisters, and Buddy's two brothers and his sister were much older than he was, so we became kind of like brothers," Montgomery says now. "I don't really remember him having any personality in those days. He was just a scrawny, gangly kid."

When Buddy was thirteen, his family moved back into Lubbock, settling at 3315 36th Street. This meant he could attend J. T. Hutchinson junior high school with many of the city friends he had made at Roscoe Wilson. They included Bob Montgomery and two others who were to be crucial in his early musical development, Don Guess and Jerry Ivan Allison. After school, he found another kindred spirit in Jack Neal, a diminutive seventeen-year-old with a quiet voice and wide smile, then working with L. O. Holley as a carpenter's helper. "At lunchtime, I'd get my guitar out of the car and set and play out in the sun," Neal remembers. "One day, Mr. L. O. Holley saw me and said, 'My boy Buddy plays guitar, too. You all ought to get together.'"

The two boys formed a duo, "Buddy and Jack," and started appearing in the talent shows that continually cropped up in the little towns around Lubbock: Meadow, Whiteface, Abernathy, Levelland. Jack Neal sang lead while Buddy supplied the guitar riffs that are to country music what vegetable florets are to modern haute cuisine: decorative, painstaking, and about as exciting as puréed carrot or tomato. "We started writing songs together, too," Jack says. "Only in those days, you didn't call it that. You just called it makin' up songs.

"Buddy was real quiet and shy—but not all the time. He could be a cutup, too. He loved the car I used to have, an off-yellow and brown '48 Fleetline Chevrolet. 'Cause the only thing Buddy had to drive at the time was his daddy's Dodge flatbed truck. The old Fleetline had a throttle lever and a choke lever. One of Buddy's favorite things to do while we were driving along was to suddenly reach over and pull on the throttle. The car'd leap forward; I'd slap his hand away. Then he'd lean and pull on the choke. That car'd be leaping and jumping down the highway like some ol' firecracker."

☆　☆　☆

In September 1952, along with his friend Bob Montgomery, Buddy began his first semester at Tom S. Lubbock High School. The school is still there on 19th Street, a long biscuit-colored structure, rather Spanish-looking with its formal high windows and terra-cotta roof. It takes only a half-beat of imagination to picture the scene on that scorching fall day: the boys in their crewcuts and Western shirts, the girls in their anklesocks and ponytails; the sunny, uncomplicated faces, the excited but restrained hubbub.

Inside, the long corridors of shiny gray linoleum and the high-ceilinged classrooms are still just as they were in Buddy's time, doubtless wafting the same resiny odor of textbooks and yellow writing tablets. Upstairs in the reference library, a counter assistant obligingly dredges up the year-books for 1953, 1954, and 1955, the span of Buddy's studentship. To anyone educated in Britain during that same era, it is marvelous that a school should make so much of its pupils, recording their evolution in hardback pictorial albums rather than smudgy samizdat magazines and group photographs. Lubbock High's yearbooks are particularly handsome, bound in olive-green cloth, their flyleaves decorated with lariat-twirling rodeo riders.

Here, then, is the Class of '55, which Buddy had joined, commemorated in a page of snapshot-size portraits. And here is "Buddy Holley" at sixteen, scarcely recognizable as the person he will become: chubby-faced, jug-eared, with slicked-flat hair, a rather shy, uncertain smile—and no glasses. He did not start wearing those until his senior year, when one of his teachers sent a note to his parents, urgently recommending them to have his eyes tested. The subsequent examination, by Lubbock ophthalmologist Dr. J. Davis Armistead (another unsung but crucial link in the Buddy Holly story), revealed his vision to be 20/800, four times the minimum requirement for certification as legally blind. His first pair of glasses, unveiled with no visible pleasure or pride in that fall's yearbook, had lightweight plastic frames with an ostentatious zigzag design on the earpieces. These were soon exchanged for half-frames, a classic piece of fifties design which, with their transparent lower area, seemed to give the wearer an additional pair of thick, dark eyebrows.

For the mid-fifties adolescent, particularly in America, most particularly in Texas, wearing glasses meant saying goodbye to any hope of being thought good-looking or interesting, and accepting relegation to a risible subspecies of bookish weakling. The only bespectacled figure in popular culture was Clark Kent, the "mild-mannered reporter" who was the alter ego, and antithesis in every way, of Superman. But that was, alas, not Buddy Holley's only physical demerit. The chubby cuteness of his toddlerhood had given way to almost painful skinniness; though he was tall enough, almost a six-footer eventually, when he turned sideways you could hardly see him. Ever-ready and winning though his broad smile might be, it revealed an extreme case of what were called "West Texas teeth," not only crooked but dulled and stained brown by the region's overfluorided water. It hardly helped that his complexion was good, his face almost free of adolescent spots and blackheads. "He was what today we'd call a nerd," a Lubbock High classmate, Jane Livermore, remembers. "I don't think any of us took him seriously in those days."

At all three of his previous schools, he had been a diligent student and at Lubbock High he kept up the good work. His report cards show a steady stream of A's and B's, though there could be lapses when his guitar beckoned more strongly than homework. His best subject was English: he had been a reporter on his junior high school's newspaper, learning to type in the process, and had once won a decorative pin in an essay competition organized by a paper in Fort Worth. In essays and letters as later in his songs, he expressed himself with unfailing clarity and succinctness. His handwriting was neat and legible, though little like standard American italic. His signature had a particular flourish—almost as if anticipating the autograph-signing to come—with its elongated capital B and H, its long-tailed, slightly wavery d's, l's, and y's.

If resigned never to be the class Adonis, he was fussy about his clothes and grooming. Jerry Allison, who also had followed him to Lubbock High from J. T. Hutchinson, noticed how an indulgent mother provided him with a clean, crisply starched, and flawlessly ironed shirt each day; how his white socks shone and his black loafers sparkled; how even his Levi's always had a knife-edge crease in them. "Buddy's hair bothered him more than anything else," Jack Neal remembers. "It was always real curly, and he didn't care for that. He wanted it to be straight so he could comb it right back. He used to say he'd never have had curly hair like that if his folks hadn't made him wear a toboggan [woolen hat] when he was a little kid."

Music loomed large in Lubbock High's curriculum. The school had two mixed a cappella choirs and a band that performed at sports events, concerts, and assemblies. Buddy joined both choirs, the sophomore Choralaires and the junior–senior Westernaires, but seemed content to remain just another voice among many. The school also cultivated a strong cowboy flavor, naming its students and sports teams "the Westerners" and holding an annual Westerners Round-Up, with suitable dress and music. One Round-Up souvenir program records that Bob Montgomery had written a song called "Flower of My Heart" especially for the occasion. Bob's name figures prominently on the list of "Wranglers" (participants), but Buddy's isn't mentioned.

The drippy, nerdish look of his early teenage years was in fact wholly misleading. Although totally uninterested in organized sports, he enjoyed the outdoor life, going on regular hunting and fishing trips with his brothers and cousins. In August 1952, while on vacation in Colorado, he wrote his sister Pat that he'd enjoyed swimming in both the Pecos River and the Rio Grande, despite the icy coldness of the water.

From his father he had inherited both a versatile practical streak and a capacity for hard manual work belied by his beanpole physique. His eldest brother Larry had augmented the family's meager income by starting a tiling business a couple of years earlier: during school vacations, Buddy would help L. O. on house-framing contracts and go out on tiling jobs with Larry, who taught him to set plain red tiles on roofs and fancy ceramic ones in kitchens and bathrooms. "When I laid tile, I took a lot of care but went real slow," Larry remembers. "Travis went fast, but sometimes used to skimp the work. Buddy could go fast *and* take care."

The principal of his several hobbies was leatherwork. He would make wallets and purses as gifts for his family and friends, hand-tooled with intricate Western-style curves and swirls. He also drew and painted and, as he grew older, became interested in industrial drafting and blueprint-making, an occupation that so suited his neat, painstaking nature that he began to think of it as a possible career.

At Lubbock High, his main extracurricular activity was the Industrial Co-Operative Training club, designed to bring students together with prospective employers from local industries. Buddy and Bob Montgomery were stalwarts of ICT's Chapter 95, which also provided a willing audience for their country music partnership. They would perform at chapter meetings as well as at more formal occasions like the banquet for the Lubbock Real Estate Board. Buddy was elected a vice president of Chapter 95, and also served on its entertainment committee. At parties and barbecues, he would be put in charge of the games: balloon-bursting, pillow-stuffing, and the like.

His nature was genial, considerate, and endlessly obliging, but with an edge of self-assurance, almost cockiness, the result of growing up the adored and petted baby of his family. In particular, his brother Larry remembers, patience was a concept almost unknown to him. "With Buddy, everything had to be right now. If he wanted to write a song, he'd just pick up his guitar and get right on with it. If he felt like doing some leatherwork, even if the family wasn't through with Thanksgiving dinner, he'd go get all his tools and materials and spread them out on the floor. It was almost like he knew he didn't have much time to do all the things he wanted."

For all his gawkiness and glasses, the lottery of teenage romance seemed to have dealt him a winning ticket. At the Roscoe Wilson elementary school, he had met a tiny girl with glossy dark eyebrows, a captivating smile, and the equally captivating name of Echo McGuire. Echo came from a prosperous background: her father owned McGuire's drive-in dry cleaners, and her house on 20th Street, close to the Texas Tech campus, was considerably grander than the Holley family's rented one on 36th. There was also a great religious divide. While the Holleys were Tabernacle Baptists, the McGuires were Church of Christ, a sect if possible even more zealous in its scriptural observances and sterner in its definition of worldly sin. Larry Holley had once dated a Church of Christ girl, but had been forced to break up with her by the extreme disapproval of their respective ministers. "Our two churches just don't see eyeball to eyeball about anything."

Buddy and Echo became friends at Roscoe Wilson, losing touch for the couple of years Buddy's family moved outside the Lubbock school system and he had to transfer temporarily to Roosevelt Elementary. They met up again at Hutchinson junior high, by which time Buddy had begun playing music with Bob Montgomery. Buddy, Bob, and Echo became a threesome, spending long hours playing Ping-Pong together at Echo's house. It wasn't until well into their sophomore year at Lubbock High that Buddy put the relationship into different gear by asking Echo for a date. They went to a football game together, and afterward to the Hi-D-Ho drive-in at College (now University) Avenue and Second Place, which in those days was the favorite meeting place of Lubbock's teenage crowd. From the archetypal round, flat-roofed servery, Hidey burgers, Hidey fries, and Hidey pies were sped to the semicircle of parked cars by carhops in scarlet and white uniforms with military-style pillbox hats. For Buddy and his friends, the favorite evening amusement was what they called "circling the Ho"—driving their borrowed family cars round and round the Hi-D-Ho, exchanging pleasantries or challenges through their wound-down windows, periodically stopping to continue the dialogue over yet another round of cheeseburgers and malts.

Echo was a catch in anyone's terms, barely five feet tall, with an aureole of fluffy hair and a more than usually seductive West Texas drawl. An exceptional student, she quickly joined Lubbock High's honor roll with straight A's. She was also a deeply serious girl who unquestioningly accepted the rigorous teachings of her church, even though it canceled one of teenagerdom's chief pleasures. The Church of Christ used no music in its services and forbade dancing.

Echo's father, O. W. "Mac" McGuire, had initially thought her too young to go steady, but he and his wife, Pansie, were won over by Buddy's respectfulness, good manners, and charm. Though the McGuires were much better off than the Holley's, and Echo had grown up with many luxuries Buddy had lacked, the two families came to be on amicable terms. Even their opposing religious creeds did not present the obstacle that might have been expected. Buddy regularly accompanied Echo to services at the Church of Christ's richly endowed establishment on Broadway, and took part in get-togethers and expeditions organized by its youth group. For her sake, he even gave up Lubbock High's annual prom, where she would have been a scripturally enforced wallflower, instead escorting her to the banquet and entertainment that the Church of Christ provided as an alternative. Echo still has the frothy white formals she wore at two such functions.

Back at her family's old home in 1996, she demonstrates how she'd watch for Buddy from her bedroom window above the neat front yard with its white picket fence. He'd always come in, say hello to her parents, and sit for a while on the ottoman that still stands among the antique vases and marble surfaces in Pansie McGuire's living room. Then Echo and Buddy would set off together in the Holley family car, bound for a football or basketball game, or a session at Lawson's roller rink on College Avenue, near the Hi-D-Ho. Echo owned a horse, a mare named Gypsy, and Buddy and she would go riding together on the Texas Tech campus—which then, as now, encompasses large tracts of open countryside—or hike together in Palo Duro Canyon, a scenic area in the Texas Panhandle, south of Amarillo. Their relationship was easy, humorous, understanding, above all perfectly chaste. As Echo remembers now, "Buddy didn't even kiss me until we'd been going together for a year."

Even in his decorous wooing of Echo McGuire, the impudent and anarchic side of Buddy's nature was apt to break out. She remembers once accompanying him to a Tabernacle Baptist service, with its music and informality so much looser than the Church of Christ's. "The minister was asking for donations for missionary work and he looked at Buddy and said, 'How about you, Buddy? Will you give ten dollars?' Buddy said, 'Do you think I'd be here if I had ten dollars?' I turned several shades of pink and almost crawled under the pew."

The most illuminating glimpse of him as a sixteen-year-old, however, comes down to us in his own words. Early in 1953, his English class at Lubbock High was asked to write an essay titled "My Autobiography." Buddy's effort (written on pages from a jotting pad given out by the

RAVE ON ☆ 45

Morrow Thomas Hardware Co., Amarillo) is mainly a rueful inventory of his current academic and personal problems. However, it reveals in passing that his musical ambitions are already quite serious. There is also a whisper of the personality we recognize from his music—modest, unpretentious, and confiding; doubtful about what the future will bring, but resolved to hope for the best:

> . . . Little did I know what the last nine weeks of my sophomore year held in store for me. This will make the second time I have given my English theme for my test; I got kicked out of Plane Geometry class in the last week of school; I am behind with my Biology work and will probably fail every course I'm taking. At least that's the way I feel. But why quit there? I may as well go ahead and tell all. My father's out of town on a fishing trip, and he is really going to be proud of my latest accomplishments when he gets back. As of now I have these on the list. When I was driving our pickup Sunday afternoon against a hard wind, the hood came unfastened and blew up and now it's bent so that it won't fasten down good. Before I got home, I stopped at a boy's house and he knocked a baseball into the front glass, shattering it all over me. As if that wasn't enough, I had an appointment to apply for a job with a drafting firm yesterday afternoon and when my mother came after me, she let me drive on towards town. I had bought a picture of the choir and she was looking at it. She asked where I was, and I pointed to my picture. Just as I looked back up we hit the back of a Chrysler and tore the front end of our car up. So you see, I hope my father gets to catching so many fish that he will forget to come back for a little while.
>
> Well, that's enough of bad things for a while. I have many hobbies. Some of these are hunting, fishing, leatherwork, reading, painting, and playing western music. I have thought of making a career out of western music if I am good enough but I will just have to wait and see how that turns out. I like drafting and have thought a lot about making it my life's work, but I guess everything will just have to wait and turn out for the best.
>
> Well, that's my life to the present date, and though it may seem awful and full of calamities, I'd sure be in bad shape without it.

It's hard to believe today, tuning one's car radio through teeming bands of steel guitars, violins, and plaintive, Stetson-shaded voices, but in the mid-fifties America possessed not a single radio station devoted exclusively to country music. All it had were general music stations which might or might not feature country in their programming. Even deep down here in its Tennessee–Texas–Louisiana heartland, country could seldom be heard for longer than a couple of hours each day, usually early in the morning to reach the farmers who were presumed to be its main audience. Hence the enormous interstate popularity of the two live radio jamborees, the *Grand Ole Opry* and the *Louisiana Hayride.* Nashville's WSM and Shreveport's KWKH were both clear-channel stations, well apart from their rivals on the dial and supposedly audible for hundreds of miles. But the West Texas plains harbored iron deposits that interfered with radio reception: on Saturday evenings, Lubbock country fans had to cluster close around their crackling sets to catch the precious drafts of sentiment, jollity, and togetherness.

Lubbock's station KSEL had always maintained the usual broad-banded policy of easy-listening pop and talk. In 1953, its general manager and chief announcer was a genial man named Dave Pinkston, known over the air as Pappy Dave Stone. Although subject to the usual prejudice against country music from KSEL's owners and advertisers, Pappy Dave remained convinced of its commercial potential, and strove to give his listeners as much of it as possible. Under his aegis, KSEL acquired its own miniature *Grand Ole Opry,* the *Saturday Night Jamboree,* with local country acts performing to a studio audience. Pappy Dave found a willing ally in his assistant manager and co-star disc jockey, an immensely tall and long-Levi-legged man, known, with impeccable Western logic, as Hi Pockets Duncan. Hi Pockets both emceed the *Saturday Night Jamboree* and did comic monologues as a hayseed character called Herkimer Tornsnoff.

KSEL had recently acquired another disc jockey, Ben Hall from Breckenridge, Texas, a talented country singer and guitarist who played and sang on his own nightly record show. Early in 1953, Hall heard that a license for a new radio station in the Lubbock area was about come up for grabs. Hall had long pined for a station that would play country music exclusively rather than shoehorning it in here and there. Unable to do anything himself on a deejay's salary, he persuaded Pappy Dave Stone to bid for the license on the unprecedented basis of an all-country playlist. Pappy Dave—still alive today, and living on Kissing Camels Drive, Colorado Springs, Colorado—remembers the the incredulous horror of the local businessman he approached to the finance the enterprise. "He said, 'You mean every time I turn on this new station, I'm gonna hear a gittar plunkin'?' I said, 'Yes, that's just what I mean!'"

The new station, KDAV, was established at the southern end of Quirt Avenue, a rural setting that allowed its founders to style its one-story stone shoebox "the KDAV Country Farm." It went on the air in September 1953, transmitting in daytime hours only, "sun-up to sundown," with programs whose names richly reflected the combination of music, talk, homespun humor, and worship: *Sunset Trading Post, Old Camp Meeting, Corral Club, Bethel Chapel, Easy the Janitor.* Both Hi Pockets Duncan and Ben Hall defected from KSEL to join the announcing staff. Pappy Dave Stone insists—and no one has come forward to contradict him— that this was America's first-ever all-country station.

One of KDAV's earliest attractions was an afternoon live music show called *The Sunday Party,* intended to showcase various local country singers and groups. Hi Pockets Duncan combined the roles of disc jockey, talent scout, and entrepreneur, putting on shows in and around Lubbock with the object of finding performers good enough to broadcast on KDAV. In October, he ran across a lanky seventeen-year-old Lubbock High School boy and a smaller, older partner, performing as "Buddy and Jack." Their playing so impressed Hi Pockets that he booked them in a show he was promoting out at the old glider aerodrome. There they acquitted themselves so well that Hi Pockets offered them a fifteen-minute (unpaid) slot on KDAV's *Sunday Party.* They made their debut on November 4, 1955, with four numbers, "Your Cheatin' Heart," "Got You on My Mind," "I Couldn't Keep from Crying," and "I Hear the Lord Callin' for Me."

That first appearance brought such a favorable response from the station's fledgling audience that Pappy Dave Stone gave Buddy and Jack the half-hour *Sunday Party* spot to themselves, renaming it *Buddy and Jack's Sunday Party.* They performed in a tiny room, not much more than ten feet square, with their audience, twenty to thirty strong, watching them from the corridor through a glass partition. Many more people turned up to see the show than could be accommodated, and the overflow would sit outside in their cars, with radios turned to the show going on a few feet away.

No longer did Buddy's classmates regard him merely as an amiable, forgettable nerd. He was a radio star, in the same firmament as Hank Snow, Ernest Tubb, and other great strumming deities of the *Grand Ole Opry.* When he and Jack arrived at KDAV each Sunday, they would find a pile of letters, requesting favorite numbers both from the standards they covered and the songs they had "made up." There would also be straight fan mail, albeit usually addressed to "Jack and Buddy," and from people of their parents' generation. "I think you boys are doing better each week. Keep up the good work..." "...Jack has the best hillbilly voice with the most distinctive style that I have heard among local musicians..." "Buddy, tell your mother hello from me, Loretta..."

For someone with Buddy's technical mind it was thrilling to be given virtual free run of a brand-new radio station, to sit in with Hi Pockets Duncan and Ben Hall as they did their work, observing the complexities of its desk controls, turntables, and large-spooled professional tape-recorders. The most exciting discovery was that KDAV possessed facilities for converting the choicer items it put on tape into the more permanent form of a 78 rpm acetate disc. In other words, the station could double as a basic recording studio.

On November 10, 1953, less than a week after their debut on *The Sunday Party,* Buddy and Jack paid KDAV a nominal couple of dollars to cut a double-sided acetate containing the spiritual "I Hear the Lord Callin' for Me" and Jack Neal's song "I Saw the Moon Cry Last Night." Jack (who hung on to the acetate, and possesses it to this day) remembers how ambition and determination kindled in his junior partner at their first mild taste of celebrity. "He often used to say after that: 'Jack, it's not that I want to be in the lamplight, it's not that I want to be rich. I just want the world to remember the name Buddy Holley.'"

While performing with Jack Neal on KDAV, Buddy also kept up his partnership with his childhood friend and high school classmate Bob Montgomery. Before long, Bob was invited to join Buddy and Jack's *Sunday Party,* as was another ex–J. T. Hutchinson boy, Don Guess, who could play both steel guitar and double bass, and whose triangular, shaggy-browed face was like that of a Steven Spielberg extraterrestrial thirty years before its time. This larger group was known as the 580 Ranch Hands (580 being KDAV's spot on the radio dial). Buddy took on the role of PR man, composing a two-page release in his pains-taking block print, from his family's latest change of address, to be circulated among other local high schools that might offer the group an engagement:

DEAR SIR

WE ARE A GROUP OF HIGH SCHOOL BOYS THAT HAS ORGANIZED ONE OF THE LEADING HILLBILLY & WESTERN BANDS IN LUBBOCK. WE

ARE INTERESTED IN HELPING NEIGHBORING HIGH SCHOOLS TO RAISE
FUNDS AND AT THE SAME TIME RAISE MONEY FOR US TO PAY OUR
WAY THROUGH COLLEGE.

I KNOW YOU WOULDN'T WANT TO LET JUST ANYONE PLAY AT
YOUR SCHOOL, SO IF YOU HAVE NOT HEARD OF US, WE ARE THE 580
RANCH HANDS AND BUDDY AND JACK, AND WE HAVE TWO RADIO
PROGRAMS EVERY SUNDAY AFTERNOON AT 3:15 O'CLOCK AND 3:30
O'CLOCK RESPECTIVELY. THE RADIO STATION WE ARE ON IS KDAV
(580 ON YOUR RADIO DIAL). IF IT WOULD NOT BE ASKING TOO MUCH,
WE WOULD LIKE TO REQUEST YOUR LISTENING TO OUR PROGRAMS
AND SEE IF YOU LIKE US . . .

. . . I KNOW THAT IF YOUR SCHOOL IS LIKE OUR SCHOOL, IT CAN
ALWAYS USE SOME EXTRA MONEY. WE HAVE HELPED QUITE A FEW
SCHOOLS AROUND AUSTIN, TEXAS, TO GATHER MONEY IN THIS WAY
AND THEY ARE QUITE SATISFIED WITH THE RESULTS. IF YOU ARE AT
ALL INTERESTED IN THIS, WE WOULD APPRECIATE IT VERY MUCH IF
YOU WOULD WRITE TO ME, BUDDY HOLLEY
                    3204 1ST ST
                    LUBBOCK, TEXAS

At the time, the idol and role model of most teenage country musicians
in the Lubbock area was a fiddle player named Tommy Hancock, sometime owner of the Glassarama Club and leader of a seven-piece Western
swing dance band, the Roadside Playboys. Adding another junior schoolmate, Larry Welborn, KDAV's group changed their name to Don Guess
and the Rhythm Playboys. On May 4, 1954, temporarily minus Don
Guess, the Rhythm Playboys performed for the distributive education
class at Brownfield High School. The contract for the appearance has
survived—a letter written in Buddy's careful, long-tailed hand, confirming that their fee will be 50 percent of the evening's receipts.

Such paid gigs were rare. The far more usual thing would be for
someone to invite them, and their instruments, to a party or social where
the only rewards, it was mutually understood, would be soft drinks, cake,
and heartfelt appreciation. For Buddy, Bob, Jack, Larry, and Don, the
important thing was being asked to perform. They would play anywhere
—teen clubs, church groups, school halls, in the boxing ring at the center
of Lawson's Skating Rink, or to swell the Saturday-morning trade at
grocery stores like Sewell's Country Market on East Broadway. Ever
eager for an advertising tie-in, Pappy Dave Stone would send KDAV's

outside broadcast truck to put them on the air live, competing for shoppers' attention with special offers on watermelon or hamburger.

For all its many-steepled piety and state of strict prohibition, there was a side to Lubbock as rowdy and boozy as anywhere on the West Texas frontier. With no legal liquor store nearer than Amarillo, 120 miles away, bootleggers did a roaring trade, shipping in beer by the illicit truckload or compounding lethal home brew in backyard stills. The most famous local bootlegger was a man named Frenchy who lived out on Slaton Highway in a cabin with a stuffed two-headed calf on its front porch. The city's music clubs—the Glassarama, the 16th and J, the Cotton Club—had a reputation for being the most violent for miles around. "There's several reasons for that," Tommy Hancock says. "First, the liquor folks were drinking in those clubs was so raw and bad, and they had to drink it back real quick, thinking there might be a raid at any minute. And anyway, country music always does seem to get folks fighting worse than any other kind."

As Buddy's group became better known, they began playing in clubs, even though all of them were too young to be on premises where liquor could be bought. "The 16th and J booked us a lot of times," Jack Neal remembers. "It was a big barn of a place at Avenue J and 16th Street—I think it may have been a church some time before. Trouble there used to come just like a twister out on the plain. One minute it'd be quiet, the next there'd be bottles flying. We'd go on playing and try to calm things down with our music. If we were playing a real jumpy number, we'd cut it to something more mellow, like a two-step."

Inevitably, the boys made their own experiments with the Falstaff bootleg beer that Frenchy sold at a dollar per quart bottle. Buddy downed his share, but never became the serious drinker that most self-respecting West Texans aspire to be. Since childhood, he had suffered mysterious stomach pains for which doctors could find no cause other than "nerves," and which redoubled agonizingly if he overindulged in alcohol or too-spicy food, like the ubiquitous Mexican tamales and taquitos. In common with almost every fifties teenager, he took up smoking at the earliest possible age, choosing Salem cigarettes from the myriad soft-pack brands available. Although L. O. Holley was a heavy cigarette smoker and Larry and Travis both smoked pipes, Buddy was obliged to indulge the habit in elaborately underhanded ways until he became legally entitled to smoke at eighteen. Even then, devout young Baptist that he was, he always took care never to do so in front of his parents or church minister and never, if he could help it, in photographs. Only in rare, unguarded shots can the Salem pack be seen in ghostly silhouette through the breast pocket of his crisp white shirt.

Five musicians and their instruments proved tricky to fit into Jack Neal's '47 Fleetline. Then, on Fenner Tubbs's used-car lot in Lubbock, Buddy and Jack spotted a more commodious vehicle. "It was a '37 Packard hearse, two-tone red and yellow," Jack says. "I had to persuade my dad to stand guarantor if I traded in my Chevrolet, though he told me I was crazy to do it. We used that ol' hearse as a bandwagon and to take us on hunting trips, too. One time, me and my dad and Buddy were heading for Tahoka, Texas, to go duck shooting, and by the side of the road we saw this dead cow with a coyote feasting on it. We turned right around and headed back, and Buddy took a blast at the coyote with the 4.10 shotgun he had. 'Did you hit it?' my dad and I yelled. 'Sure I hit it!' Buddy said, but I don't believe he did. The thing just gave a jump up in the air with the noise, and ran right off into the brush."

Despite the burgeoning talent in their lineup, and their eyecatchingly macabre bandwagon, the Rhythm Playboys never did quite get off the ground. But Don Guess and Larry Welborn were to remain part of Buddy's intimate circle, and with Bob Montgomery, to accompany him to the lower foothills of fame.

In any case, no single group or partnership could satisfy the appetite he now had for performing. He had gotten to know Ben Hall, the dapper, dignified KDAV disc jockey and country singer, when Hall was new in town and still working at KSEL. Buddy admired Hall's musicianship and songwriting abilities, and often backed him onstage, together with Hall's other teenage protégé, steel guitarist Weldon Myrick. Whenever a group found itself short a musician, or invited volunteers for a jam session, Buddy would be straight up there with his guitar slung over his starched sport shirt, and his unfailing, snaggly grin of "Don't mind if I do." To take a random instance, October 9, 1954, found him and Bob Montgomery at the high school in Borger, Texas, still ostensibly preparing for their postgraduate working life by attending a chapter meeting of the school's Vocational Industrial Club. The minutes record that entertainment was supplied by the Borger Metal Trades Hillbilly Band, with Buddy sitting in on guitar.

He had by now switched from acoustic guitar to his first solid-body electric model, a Gibson Les Paul Gold Top. It was a handsome instrument for a high school boy to own: semi-cutaway, with an inlaid fretboard, studded with volume knobs and bearing the signature of Les Paul himself, the great pioneer of electric guitar playing and double-track recording. Buddy had always loved Paul's gentle, fluid "talking guitar" style and the intimate close harmonies he sang with his wife, Mary Ford, and was to be enormously influenced by them when he began to make records of his own.

Around the time he got his Les Paul Gold Top, a kind of music very different from country, bluegrass, and Western swing began itching at Buddy's fingertips. But this was not one that could be played, or even talked about, to his family, his church elders, or his grown-up fans at KDAV's *Sunday Party.* This was black people's blues music, the fatal mixture of pigments which in all correct white Southern minds still produced apoplectically purple contempt, revulsion, and fear.

Since the "race" and "specialty" euphemisms of Buddy's prewar toddlerhood, black music had, in artistic terms at least, taken a major step forward. The postwar migration of rural Southern blacks to Northern industrial cities had produced a new version, very different from the country blues of Robert Johnson and Blind Lemon Jefferson. Amended to "rhythm and blues," it hymned the racier pleasures and pressures of metropolitan life with crudely amplified guitars, braying saxophones, and a driving drumbeat. It was performed by solitary voices no longer but by groups who, rather like urban street gangs, cultivated a unified personality and named themselves with eccentric and self-mocking collective nouns: the Drifters, the Moonglows, the Spiders.

From the beginning, R&B had attracted a following among white teenagers who, on their side of the racial divide, had nothing more visceral to listen to than big bands and crooners. Nineteen fifty-four was the first year that America's mainstream music industry awoke to R&B's dollar-earning potential. Formerly segregated artists, such as Antoine "Fats" Domino from New Orleans, and the Drifters with their sighing, twittering lead vocalist Clyde McPhatter, began to infiltrate the white airwaves and score hits on the white charts.

Buddy and his cronies were by then already longtime surreptitious listeners to R&B radio shows, beamed across the cottonfields from stations far away in the teeming hothouse of southern Louisiana. To add to the sense of something forbidden and deviant, the disc jockeys who played

R&B were generally not allowed on the air until late at night. Buddy's secret circle of addicts used to listen in one or another of their cars, partly to avoid parental interference and partly because a car radio's DC current provided better reception of long-distance signals. "You'd have to put the antenna right up," Ben Hall remembers. "Even then, the signal often used to fade, and you'd have to turn the car around to make it louder. You'd keep turning the car this way and that through the number, the way people today keep turning the portable aerials on their TV sets."

Buddy loved R&B, with its driving drumbeat, so unlike the restrained amble of country music, and the raucous electric guitar breaks constructed around chords and chiming pairs of strings rather than single notes. His great favorite was Hank Ballard and the Midnighters, a Chicago group who combined raunchily tongue-in-cheek songs about the same recurring character, Annie ("Work With Me Annie"; "Annie Had a Baby"; "Annie's Aunt Fanny") with intoxicating half-chord guitar licks. Buddy also had a taste for the hardcore urban blues of Muddy Waters, Elmore James, and Howlin' Wolf, whose stylish plectrum downstrokes served as a counterpoint to anger or mordant humor, and for Lonnie Johnson, whose voice was deceptively mild, and who picked guitar notes as soft as kittens' paws as he sang about syphilis, alcoholism, and murder.

Many white teenagers in the South during this period enjoyed black people's music in the abstract without feeling obliged to treat black people in the flesh as human beings on the same level as themselves. Buddy had grown up in a city of rigid segregation, most of whose Bible-quoting men and women would have felt physical nausea as well as moral outrage if ever compelled to share a lunch counter, bus seat, or drinking fountain with a black person. For all his mildness and tolerance in other directions, L. O. Holley was a man of his time and place, and might well have contemplated the use of that double-thickness leather razor-strop had he ever learned what his youngest son was listening to after midnight.

With his usual impatience, Buddy blanked out the social and academic consequences of playing R&B music, and with his usual all-out thoroughness set about educating his voice and fingers in it by every possible means. On nights when he and his group were not playing country and bluegrass, he would lead them determinedly across Lubbock's racial frontier, to the ghettoized sector east of Avenue A. "They had little cafés and joints over there, where Buddy loved to sit and listen," Jack Neal remembers. "Sometimes it'd just be someone's yard or front porch. There'd be

one guy with a guitar, another with a horn, and usually barbecue cookin'
in a pit. You could get a sandwich for fifty cents."

Inevitably, Buddy got talking to these amateur bluesmen, asking them
about the chords and single-string licks they played. Under their good-
humored tutelage, the wispy, bespectacled white boy began to develop a
guitar style as lean and aggressive as any to be heard from T-Bone Walker
or Leadbelly. Most important, he discovered that the language of music
makes race irrelevant. From here on, Buddy Holley wanted no truck with
Southern apartheid and, in his own way, would do much to chip away at
its foundations. As an act of domestic subversion, he even named his cat
after the black hero Booker T. Washington.

At the end of 1954, though he was barely twenty, Jack Neal decided to
get married. Faced with new grown-up responsibilities, he told Buddy
regretfully he could no longer play on KDAV's *Sunday Party.* His place
was taken by Bob Montgomery and bass player Larry Welborn, though to
preserve continuity the trio called itself Buddy and Bob. "Kay-Dave" was
by now so much a second home that they gave it as their address on their
business cards.

The station was also important for the increasing role of its general
manager, Pappy Dave Stone, and its star deejay, Ben Hall, as entrepre-
neurs and concert promoters. From 1954 on, Stone and Hall staged regular
country music spectaculars at Lubbock's Fair Park Coliseum, a covered
arena recently built for the annual South Plains agricultural fair. They
also developed close ties with the Cotton Club, an establishment which,
atmospherically as well as geographically, was as far as could be imagined
from its glamorous namesake in New York. The Lubbock Cotton Club
was a place of no frills and little refinement, a 1,400-square-foot ex-
military Quonset hut with an awesome reputation for bootleg booze and
brawling. Unlike Fair Park Coliseum, it lay outside the city limits, and so
could allow black and white spectators to mingle as equals. The two
venues in tandem made Lubbock a worthwhile stop for the major country
stars and the multi-act tours promoted by the *Grand Ole Opry* in Nashville. On the northwesterly swing from Dallas to Amarillo or Albuquerque, everyone who was anyone could be guaranteed to pass through,
sooner or later.

Through the good offices of Pappy Dave Stone, Buddy and Bob would
get the opening spot on the country spectaculars KDAV presented at Fair
Park Coliseum and the Cotton Club. Their set might be brief and barely

heeded, but at least it allowed them backstage to mingle with their country idols, like Ferlin Husky and Tommy Collins. Country music then had a tradition of informality, and the stars were usually accessible and friendly to the gawky local boys who plied them with questions about the music business. One who went out of his way to encourage and advise them was Marty Robbins, a rising talent still half a dozen years away from his cowboy classic, "El Paso." Robbins was much impressed by Buddy's singing and also by his skill at leatherwork. "Buddy made Marty a bill-fold," Larry Holley remembers. "He liked it so much, he wrote saying 'Can you make me a hundred more to give away as gifts?'"

Every dollar Buddy and Bob earned from playing and from vacation jobs as carpenter's helpers with L. O. Holley was poured into financing demos of their songs, either at KDAV or at Nesman's Recording Studios in Wichita Falls, a drive of over a hundred miles. It was at Nesman's, for example, that they cut "Flower of My Heart," the song written by Bob for their high school Round-Up, together with other tracks of a doleful cardiological nature: "Door to My Heart," "Soft Place in My Heart," "I Gambled My Heart."

Late in 1954, having long been their unofficial manager, Hi Pockets Duncan proposed that he take on the job officially. As Pappy Dave Stone remembers, it was an offer inspired less by thoughts of personal gain than annoyance at the way the boys still often found themselves conned into playing for nothing or next to nothing. Buddy was so short of cash at Christmastime that he had to pay for his $11.70 class ring (the one he hoped Echo McGuire would wear on a chain around her neck) in two installments of $3 and $8.70. Every entrepreneur who takes on a group of teenage musicians claims to have only their interests at heart, but in Hi Pockets' case it was true. The contract he made with Buddy and Bob promised that if they ever became famous outside the Lubbock area, he would give up all managerial claim on them.

Although Jack Neal and Don Guess were no longer in the lineup, they continued to hang around with Buddy, Bob, and Larry, sitting in on guitar and steel respectively whenever the spirit moved them. By the year's end, this same easy companionability had turned the duo-named trio into a quartet. The new recruit was Sonny Curtis, a farmer's son from Meadow, a few miles north of Lubbock, who brought with him impressive talents and antecedents. Two of his uncles had formed the Mayfield Brothers, a well-known bluegrass act, and one in addition had played with the revered

Bill Monroe's Bluegrass Boys. Though two years Buddy's junior, Sonny was proficient on violin and guitar, a good singer and an aspiring songwriter, and he possessed the almost unheard of distinction of having appeared on local television.

A mutual friend arranged for him to come in to Lubbock and meet Bob Montgomery. "I sat waiting in Bob's folks' place, the Gin Café; I remember it was kind of a cloudy, sandstormy afternoon. Bob arrived home on the school bus, then we got in the car and went straight over to Buddy's house. We skipped all the small talk, took our instruments out, and got right to playing. I was accepted into the group right there and then.

"At that time, they were still playing mostly bluegrass. Buddy had a banjo—a four-string, not the five-string that bluegrass people use—and he played the mandolin some, too. With him and Bob, it was like playing cowboys and Indians, seeing which one of them could pick faster, Buddy trying to be Earl Scruggs and Bob trying to be Lester Flatt." But when Buddy switched to guitar, Sonny noticed a different style altogether, infused with the blues and R&B influences he had been absorbing through every pore. "I was getting into jazz at that time. I was studying under a jazz guitarist and learning real difficult chords. But Buddy wasn't too interested in chords. He cared more about the feel of it."

The first gig Sonny played with them was at a school near Austin where Bob Montgomery's uncle was superintendent. Bob's mother drove them all down in her open pickup with one riding alongside her, the others lounging on a mattress in the back.

Sonny, too, loved black music, and soon became a confederate in Buddy's secret listening sessions. Their favorite source was KWKH in Shreveport, the *Louisiana Hayride* station which after dark changed character as radically as Jekyll into Hyde, putting out a blues and R&B show sponsored by Stan's Record Shop and hosted by a black-sounding white deejay named Frank "Gatemouth" Page. "He didn't come on until midnight," Sonny remembers. "So I'd go to Buddy's house to spend the night, and at midnight we'd creep out into the drive, get into his folks' car, turn on the radio, sit back in the front seat, and listen . . . to Elmore James . . . Howlin' Wolf . . . Lonnie Johnson. Boy, was he terrific!"

Sprawling back on the leatherette bench with the churchy stillness of Lubbock all around them, and those hot, angry, hilarious sounds pouring from the dashboard's glimmer into their bloodstream, Buddy and Sonny would be torn between bliss and despair. For there seemed no way on earth that two white boys could get to be a part of such music.

☆　☆　☆

Toward the end of 1954, together with other radio stations throughout the Southwest, KDAV received a new single from a small record label in Memphis, offering an elixir that none before had ever dared concoct. One side was a country song, "Blue Moon of Kentucky," written by the bluegrass giant Bill Monroe; the other was an R&B song, Arthur "Big Boy" Crudup's "That's All Right, Mama." The big, breakable 78 rpm disc bore a label decorated with the two-tone rays of a rising sun; the name on it was "Elvis Presley."

It was clearly meant to be country music—otherwise, why would it have been sent to KDAV? But the voice was like none ever heard in country: not measured and melodious but urgent and breathless, high when it should be low, low when it should be high, hitting notes sideways instead of straight on, reducing one of country's most sacred images to an insistent, almost clownish mumble of "Blue moon, blue moon, blue moon." It was, in short, and unbelievably, somebody white singing in the style of somebody black.

Elvis at that point was not yet twenty, a year and three-quarters older than Buddy. Although he hailed from an exotically different city and state, his background was similar to Buddy's in several essential respects. Born in Tupelo, Mississippi, the son of poor migrants, Elvis too had been brought up in a devout fundamentalist sect, the First Assembly of God, and had been performing in public since early childhood. The great edge he possessed was having grown up in Memphis, a city that is to urban blues what New Orleans is to jazz, and one whose more relaxed interracial atmosphere allowed a white boy open access to its famous music quarter, Beale Street. He had been spotted by Sun Records as an eighteen-year-old truck driver, using the studio's record-your-voice booth to sing a birthday greeting to his mother. To his first professional session he brought the phrasing and body language he had absorbed first from black gospel choirs, then from Beale Street's R&B dives. Sun's boss, Sam Phillips, was prescient enough to let the kid do it his way.

Combustible as this stylistic cocktail was, it did not make Elvis notorious overnight. Quite the contrary, he made his initial impact on the middle-aged country audience, who accepted him as one of their faction, reassured by the endorsement of radio stations like KDAV. Though the term "rock 'n' roll" did exist by then, it was not even mentioned in connection with Elvis at the very beginning. Billed, with deliberate imprecision, as "The Hillbilly Cat" or "The King of Western Bop," he toured in conventional country spectaculars and appeared on the *Louisiana Hayride*.

Thanks to their friendship with KDAV's Ben Hall, Buddy and his group received an early preview of Elvis's debut record. "Buddy loved this new sound, like we all did," Hall remembers. "But it was mysterious to us. All we had was this name, 'Elvis Presley.' We had no idea where he came from or what he looked like."

They found out on January 2, 1955, when Elvis appeared in a country show promoted by KDAV at Fair Park Coliseum. Buddy was still two weeks away from being prescribed his first pair of glasses, but even his unassisted 20/800 vision could not miss the moment when the Hillbilly Cat first exploded on to the stage. Forty years on, Sonny Curtis can still picture the dazzling vision. "He had on an orange sport coat, red pants, white bucks. Tell you what, boy, he looked like a motorsickle headlight comin' right at you!"

The local boys, with their neat poplin shirts and pressed blue jeans, sat mesmerized by this performer in brilliant Technicolor whose every song tore down the ancient laws and customs of country music and trampled them under white buckskin shoes. Instead of staying rooted to center stage, as even Hank Williams always had, the Hillbilly Cat bobbed and ducked and wove continually, twisting his midriff, buckling at the knees, flinging out his arms and jerking his head so that a spray of his oily hair flopped over his pale, sullen face. Instead of picking the respectable country guitar slung around his neck, he beat on it with his hands, spun it by the fretboard, or pushed it contemptuously behind his back; instead of articulating the words that respectable country fans hungered to hear, he mumbled and slurred them with almost drunken irreverence; instead of smiling cordially upon all ages, he grimaced, glared, pouted, sneered, smirked, and smoldered in a manner that did not spell "barnyard" half so eloquently as it spelled "bedroom."

If the Texans had initially felt disposed to laugh at this extraordinary burlesque, their minds were soon changed by the sheer wicked joy of the music, and also by something even more alien to normal country music practice. While the grown-up portion of the audience watched in speech-less horror, the normally undifferentiated teenage portion reacted with roaring delight, the girls in particular forgetting the starchy decorum required of a mid-fifties Southern miss, and bouncing up and down in their seats, screaming in the strangest mixture of pleasure and anguish.

From that moment on, Buddy's group abandoned bluegrass music and adopted a role model very different from Lester Flatt or even Earl Scruggs. "The day after Elvis left town, we turned into Elvis clones," Sonny Curtis says. "And we was bookin' out as an Elvis band."

It helped to have a leader with a draftsman's eye that could instantly render down the new style to its essential blueprint. Elvis camouflaged himself with a traditional country trio, backed only by a lead guitarist, Scotty Moore, and a stand-up bass player, Bill Black; as yet even he had not dared include the giveaway R&B touch of a drummer. In total contrast with the vocalist's unbridled lunacy, Scotty Moore played an angular and stylish guitar riff, invented by the doyen of country pickers, Chet Atkins: starting as an upward slide along the thickest bass string, it then leapt crosswise to make pairs of treble notes swing and knock against each other like windchimes. And Bill Black did not pluck his bass fiddle in the usual discreetly muffled way, but belabored it with a foreground-grabbing *thunk-thunk-thunk* or slapped the amazed old spinster silhouette percus-sively with the flat of his hand.

So Sonny Curtis put his fiddle aside, took up his big Martin D-28 acoustic guitar, and mastered the Scotty Moore riff. Don Guess gave up steel guitar and played slap bass in the Bill Black style. As for Buddy himself, the transformation was as complete, and astonishing, as chrysalis into butterfly. Sonny Curtis remembers how Buddy's singing voice seemed to change in an instant, soaring from the drab husk of that re-strained, even rather self-conscious country tenor; initially just copying the Hillbilly Cat's tricks of intonation and phrasing but soon hitting on a repertoire that was all his own. Physically, too, his stage presence was transformed. "Buddy had never moved around much up till then," Sonny remembers, "In country, you just stood still and did your thing. But after seeing Elvis, there was no holding him. Soon as he picked up a guitar, he was way out front and all over the place."

On February 13, Elvis returned to Fair Park Coliseum as part of a country show that starred Jimmie Rodgers Snow, Charlene Arthur, and the Duke of Paducah. Elvis's fee, for him and his two backup musicians, was $75. The day was a Sunday, the show began promptly at 4 P.M., and this time the local group who opened for the out-of-towners was Buddy and Bob. KDAV's Ben Hall had just acquired an 8mm movie camera and one of the first places he and his wife tried it out was backstage at the Coliseum that day. Here is the first-ever movie sequence of Elvis, the famous features poignantly carefree and unused, laughing and joshing with his two avuncular sidemen, Scotty and Bill. A little apart, not wishing to intrude but tickled pink to be there, are the Lubbock boys: Buddy in his half-frame glasses, a smart blue sport coat, and matching shawl-collar shirt; beside him the rubicund Sonny Curtis and the E.T.-faced Don Guess.

"When we saw the way Elvis was onstage, we couldn't imagine what he'd be like as a person," Sonny Curtis says. "But he was real nice and quiet and unpretentious, just sitting by himself with a Coke." After the show, its country headliners were besieged by autograph-hunting fans, but Elvis could leave through the front entrance, bothered by no one.

Over the next nine months, Elvis returned to Lubbock several more times, and that reverent posse of local boys was never far away. When he appeared at the Cotton Club on April 29, they had to be content with seats in the audience, but when he returned to Fair Park Coliseum on June 3, Buddy's group once more was the warmup act. They had done the same earlier that evening for Elvis's (unpaid) appearance on the back of a flatbed truck at the gala opening of the Johnson-Connelly Pontiac showroom at Main Street and Avenue O. Before long, they were on friendly enough terms to be driving Elvis around Lubbock on a tour of what sights the city could offer. Jack Neal, who also went along, remembers that Elvis had nothing special to do afterward, so they invited him to the movies. They all trooped off to the Lindsay theater together to see *Gentlemen Prefer Blondes,* starring Marilyn Monroe and Jane Russell.

According to Larry Holley, Elvis had been so lonesome on the night of his first Lubbock appearance that Buddy volunteered to find him a date. "It was just to go around with," Larry stresses. "Buddy wasn't fixing him up or anything." However, it is recorded that the girl in question accompanied Elvis to his next gig, in Odessa, Texas. Now in her fifties, and still living in Lubbock, she has always firmly declined to reminisce about the matter.

Elvis expressed friendly enthusiasm for Buddy and Bob's music, and promised to use his influence to get them a booking on the *Louisiana*

Hayride. Taking him at his word, they all piled into Buddy's parents' car, a Hudson Hornet, and drove the thousand miles to Shreveport, expecting to be welcomed with open arms. But on their arrival at the *Hayride* studio, they were told Elvis was out on tour again, and the show's producer hadn't even heard of them. As Bob Montgomery recalls, "We couldn't even get through the door."

All this time, Buddy was still a senior at Lubbock High and—in theory, at least—studying hard to complete the courses necessary for his graduation in May. He was also still going steady with Echo McGuire, the five-foot-nothing beauty whose surname adorned Lubbock's principal drive-in drycleaning establishment. Though Echo preferred not to wear his class ring around her neck in time-honored style, there was no doubt about the depth of their relationship. A gifted seamstress, she tailored shirts for Buddy to coordinate with her dresses; he had made a Western belt with "Echo" printed on the back to encircle her twenty-four-inch waist; one of his Western boots bore the initials BH, the other EM. After graduation, they planned to marry; indeed, they seemed so happily engrossed in each other that some of their friends suspected they might already have become secretly engaged.

Buddy loved Echo deeply and sincerely, and strove with all his might to live up to her high ideals and devout religious convictions. As their relationship had deepened and his fascination with rockabilly music intensified, he had found himself increasingly leading a double life of bootleg liquor and boogie with Bob, Larry, and Sonny by night and devoutness and teetotalism with Echo by day. About this time there occurred another of the periodic moves by local businessmen to end prohibition in Lubbock. Buddy and Echo were among a group of Christian students who went around collecting signatures for a petition—successful, as it turned out—to keep their city dry.

Echo loved Buddy just as much as he loved her, and was more than ready to brave the displeasure of her church, for even contemplating "marriage out" to a Tabernacle Baptist. But of late the serious-minded young woman had begun to worry about just what kind of married life she could expect with Buddy, she whose inflexible religion forbade her even to dance. As her mother, Pansie McGuire, recalls: "She said, 'I can't go with him into those clubs, Mother, and I don't want to spend half my life sitting at home and waiting for him.' "

In mid-1955, Elvis Presley threw away the last remaining fig leaf of country music by adding a drummer, D. J. Fontana, to his backup band. Among *Grand Ole Opry* and *Louisiana Hayride* purists, the outrage was roughly comparable to a modern rock star's being exposed as a child-molester. And in Lubbock, Texas, the former Hillbilly Cat's faithful aco-lytes, sightseeing guides, and movie companions once again followed the revolutionary blueprint to the letter.

The only possible drummer for the Buddy and Bob group was sixteen-year-old Jerry Ivan Allison—even then known to his friends with orotund Southern formality as J. I.—whom Buddy had first met in junior high. Slightly built and pudgy, with the triangular face and slanted eyes of a Burmese cat, J. I. was three years Buddy's junior but so academically gifted as to be only just behind him at Lubbock High. Since those first schoolyard encounters, he had developed into a gifted percussionist and was currently the undisputed star of a country group named Cal Wayne and the Riverside Ranch-hands, with whom Buddy sometimes sat in at dives like the 16th and J Club.

J. I. Allison and his drums were on board when Buddy, Bob Montgom-ery, and Larry Welborn returned to cut more demo records, at their own expense, at Nesman's studios in Wichita Falls during the late spring of 1955. They came away with two tracks, Elvis Presley's "Baby, Let's Play House," and a number called "Down the Line" that Bob had composed in his head while driving to see his girlfriend in Albuquerque. Listened to with hindsight, it is very much R&B in bluegrass style, with still-traditional close-harmony voices taking turns in its frantic "Go! go! go!" refrain. But Buddy's guitar solo is a straight lift from a new record at the top of the charts, Bill Haley's "Rock Around the Clock."

Hi Pockets Duncan, their long-legged saint of a manager, had recently taken a furlough from KDAV to try his hand at running a Western swing hotspot called the Clover Club just outside Amarillo. The Clover Club thus became a regular gig for Buddy and Bob as well as somewhere they could always find a free meal and words of encouragement in Hi Pockets's reassuring deep-velvet drawl.

Whatever Buddy's parents thought about his sudden abandonment of country music, they too remained tirelessly supportive. The Holleys' new home, 1906 24th Street, was always open to his friends as a rehearsal hall, flophouse, free café, and now, too, as a permanent parking space for Jerry Allison's drums. When L. O. Holley bought a new car, a black and white '55 Oldsmobile, he virtually gave it to Buddy's group as a bandwagon on condition that Buddy help keep up the payments. Around this time, his doting mother wrote proudly to a friend that he was now giving several shows a week in the Lubbock area, as well as continuing to appear on KDAV's *Sunday Party,* and sometimes shared as much as $40 an appearance with his sidemen. However late he rolled home in the Olds, Ella would always be waiting up for him with peanut-butter sandwiches and milk, and his cat, Booker T. Washington, on her lap, avid to hear everything about the night's gig and how well he had gone over.

His brother Larry, the member of the family who knew him best, happened to be off on a three-month tiling job in Arizona during this whole Elvis changeover period. When Larry returned home he was amazed to see what a great leap Buddy had made, both in musicianship and self-confidence:

"I had gotten a contract to work on a new school here in Lubbock, and I had to go down to San Angelo to pick up a load of tiles. I rented this big eighteen-wheeler flatbed truck to carry 'em in, and took Buddy along with me. I'd never driven a rig that big, and I had to learn how on the way. Buddy drove it some, too. He'd never chicken out of anything I was going to do.

"We got to San Angelo too late in the day to pick up the tiles, so we went into this place to get a hamburger. We thought it was a diner, but it was really more of a colored joint. It was the deadest little old place you ever seen, and in the corner of it there was a black combo getting ready to play that evening. Buddy got to watching them real intently, then he went up and started talking to 'em, and of course they could tell he was a musician 'cause he knew their lingo. So these guys said, 'Hey, man, how about playing us a number?' and Buddy, who'd been dying to, says, 'Don't mind if I do!'

"Well, he picked up that guitar and hit the chords, and it made a clean sound, like it was a different instrument. He played 'em that song 'Sexy Ways,' that he'd heard Hank Ballard do. While he's playing, people start crowding around him, and I see the owner get on the phone, and then more and more people start coming in. Suddenly the little old joint isn't dead anymore. Buddy made the whole place come alive!

"Then I saw him again in a thing they called 'the Battle of the Bands' at the Tower theater here in town. I was way at the back, and there was a bunch of crazy kids in front of me, shouting and yelling and stepping on paper cups to pop 'em. There'd been a lot of real good-looking singers up on that stage and when it was Buddy's turn to come on, all these kids started laughing at him and yellin' out things at him, like 'Ol' Turkeyneck.' I was starting to get real aggravated about it all. But Buddy came from the side to the center in one movement without seeming to move his feet at all, and hit his guitar, and that whole crowd went hog-wild."

☆ ☆ ☆

On May 27, the Lubbock High School class of '55 lined up in their gowns and mortarboards to receive their diplomas. Buddy was among them, albeit only by the skin of his teeth. A month earlier the school principal, Floyd Honey, had written to L. O. Holley warning that his son might not qualify for graduation because of consistently poor grades in solid geometry. So, for a few nights at least, the Les Paul Gold Top had to be put aside in favor of set-squares, protractors, and compasses.

That spring was a customarily brilliant and busy one in an America where every day still represented another measurable step toward perfection. The U.S. Supreme Court had just ordered the Southern states to end racial segregation, although neglecting to specify a date when this should come to pass. The Salk vaccine had been pronounced effective against polio, thus removing another deadly disease from the ever-shortening list. In movie houses across the continent, audiences sat transfixed behind their red and green 3-D glasses, periodically ducking to avoid the express trains, Grand Prix cars, and Apache tomahawks that seemed to fly out of the screen into their faces. Ike was in his White House, Ricky loved Lucy, a dollar was a dollar, and Pepsodent toothpaste made you wonder where the yellow went. To be sure, in the whole VistaVision expanse of progress, stability, enlightenment, and shiny chromium plating, the only unsightly blot was this thing called rock 'n' roll.

Though horrifically novel and unspecific to adult whites, the term had of course been familiar for years within America's parallel black culture. From earliest blues days the twin verbs "to rock" and "to roll" had meant to dance, have sex, or enjoy oneself uninhibitedly. Postwar R&B had teemed with double-entendre invocations of one or the other, from Roy Brown's "Good Rockin' Tonight" to Big Joe Turner's "Shake, Rattle and Roll." The first tautologous coupling of the two is generally agreed to have taken place in 1952: Alan Freed, a white disc jockey on WJW in Cleveland, Ohio, realized that as many white teenagers as black were listening to the R&B music he played and, to banish racial distinction from his late-night show, renamed it *Moondog's Rock 'n' Roll Party.*

Its evolution into a music, and a movement, began a year earlier, when a country musician named Bill Haley, from Chester, Pennsylvania, had a minor hit with an R&B-flavored song called "Rock the Joint." For all his respectable, pudgy whiteness, Haley sang with the humorous ebullience usually found only in black performers; for a time, indeed, his record company encouraged the misconception by issuing no publicity photographs of him. In 1955, his song "Rock Around the Clock," already once released, was used on the soundtrack of *The Blackboard Jungle,* a film about delinquent teenagers at a New York City high school. Its raucous theme produced uproar among teenagers wherever *The Blackboard Jungle* was shown: from all over America—and, subsequently, Europe—came reports of demented screaming, wild cavorting in the aisles, and wanton vandalism of seats. "Rock Around the Clock" stayed at No. 1 on the charts for twenty-two weeks and Bill Haley and his group, the Comets, were catapulted to international stardom. Thus did the term "rock 'n' roll" achieve wide currency, linked—as it would prove, irredeemably— with visions of adolescent rebellion and riot.

This initial phase, from mid-1955 to early 1956, can be classified as rock 'n' roll's Phony War. Hysterical outbreaks of juvenile fan-worship might be distasteful but they were hardly new, having occurred in the twenties over silent movie stars like Rudolph Valentino and in the forties over crooners like Frank Sinatra. Against such sex-saturated icons, Bill Haley cut an unthreatening figure with his chubby cheeks, receding hairline, and query-shaped kiss curl. The general adult view was that, like Sheikh movies and swing before it, rock 'n' roll was a fad which would quickly pass.

Throughout that first year, Bill Haley and the Comets were the only visible white rock 'n' roll stars. The rest were mainly R&B performers, like Fats Domino and Johnny Otis, who had honed their styles for years around the blacks-only "chitlin circuit," and now for the first time tasted the heady mixture of white audiences and serious money. In the R&B tradition, there were also vocal groups: the silky-voiced Platters; the multi-harmonizing Penguins, whose "Earth Angel" had sold 2 million copies by the beginning of 1955. From New York came the Teenagers, fronted by a vivacious boy soprano named Frankie Lymon, and from the Chess label in Chicago, a spindle-shanked young man named Chuck

Berry—sometimes alternatively known as Berryn—who sported a thin moustache like a 1930s tango champion, played a cherry-red guitar down around his knees, and sang about the real life of attending high school, dating girls, and driving cars, with a clear enunciation and darting wit not heard in black music since the days of Louis Jordan. From the kitchen of a Georgia bus station came a youth baptized Richard Penniman but known since infancy as Little Richard, a wild-haired, wide-eyed, drape-suited whirling dervish whose shriek of "Awopbopaloobopalopbamboom!" would take the new culture to its delicious, driveling apotheosis.

As jukeboxes blared, new employment spread, profit margins quintupled, and factories and pressing plants worked overtime, the moral debate continued to rage. Young performers who, to a man (for they were all men), had been raised by devout Christian families and learned their first performance skills in church, were denounced from pulpit and pamphlet as emissaries of the devil. In particular, the spectacle of such as Little Richard, Chuck Berry, Bo Diddley, and Fats Domino wearing good clothes, driving expensive cars, and being treated as heroes by white boys and girls caused anguish below the Mason-Dixon line. As one typical ad hoc moral guardian, the North Alabama White Citizens Council, noted of rock 'n' roll with quivering, quasi-literate disgust: "It is sexualistic, unmoralistic, and brings people of both races together."

"NOTICE! STOP!" ran another leaflet distributed to restaurants and stores throughout the South: "Help save the Youth of America. Don't buy Negro records. If you don't want to serve Negroes in your place of business, then don't have Negro records on your jukebox or listen to Negro records on the radio. The screaming, idiotic words and savage music of these records are undermining the morals of our white youth in America. Call the advertisers on radio stations that play this type of music and complain to them . . . " Black rock 'n' roll stars on tour in the South routinely faced the affront of segregated theater audiences; in many cities, white and black musicians could not share the same bill; hotels, motels, and restaurants could with impunity refuse service to blacks. Had it not been for the rapid rise of the fast-food outlet in this era, there would often have been nowhere for them to get a meal on the road.

The piety and conservatism of Lubbock had not inhibited its two radio stations from swiftly moving with the times. KDAV was now the Elvis Presley station, proud of its role in bringing the Hillbilly Cat to West Texas. Despite having alienated the pure country audience, Elvis was still not classified as a rock 'n' roll artist. Yet another new term, "rockabilly," had been welded from "rock" and "hillbilly" to keep him in the approximate domain of hay bales and hoedowns. The same term defined the other young white performers now following Elvis from the Sun label: Carl Perkins, Johnny Cash, even a recruit from Wink, West Texas, named Roy Orbison. KDAV's arch-rival KSEL, by contrast, had moved from easy-listening pop to all-out rock 'n' roll, spiced by hardcore blues and R&B. It also had acquired a formidable new weapon in the airwaves war: a hotshot teenage disc jockey named Jerry Coleman, whose *Hi-D-Ho Hit Parade,* sponsored by Lubbock teenagers' favorite drive-in ("Don't just say 'Hello,' say 'Hi-D-Ho'") went out between 9 and 11 every night.

Jerry Coleman became aware of Buddy Holley as "a real ugly young guy in glasses" who was infatuated with R&B stars like the Drifters and Smiley Lewis and loved to hang out at KSEL, when he wasn't performing over at KDAV, watching the hyperactive "Jerry-bo" at work. "I'd put him on the air sometimes, talking about the records I was playing," Coleman remembers. "And I'd go see the group play at the Cotton Club. Boy, that place was rougher 'n a stucco bathtub. That was the kind of place where they'd stab you goodnight! At six o'clock, you'd see the bouncers wrapping gauze around their hands so as not to injure them when they started hitting folks. One time, two bouncers had a fight, and one bit off the other's ear!"

Graduation from Lubbock High School, which should have been an exciting threshold, instead seemed to have left Buddy in limbo. Despite all that assiduous wooing of local employers through ITC's Chapter 95, he had not, after all, found a well-paid white-collar job in the drawing office of some local company like Panhandle Steel. Nor had he carried out his second long-nurtured life-plan, that of going straight from graduation ceremony to church, to marry his sweetheart Echo McGuire. Thanks to the combination of her academic record and high spiritual seriousness, Echo had won a place at the Christian university in Abilene, a hundred miles east of Lubbock. Buddy and Echo were still pledged to each other, and kept constantly in touch. But, as his family—especially his mother—noticed, a light seemed to have gone out of his life.

During that first rock 'n' roll summer, with Echo in Abilene and his classmates dispersed to college, traineeships, or the armed forces, the only conventional work Buddy could find was as a casual laborer. Between tiling jobs, his elder brother Larry was building the house on 17th

Street, West Lubbock, that he occupies to this day. Buddy spent most of the sweltering June days stripped to the waist, digging out foundations for Larry's storm cellar and helping lay the tile floor in the front hall.

His KDAV mentor Pappy Dave Stone was now bringing black rock 'n' roll acts to Lubbock—not to Fair Park Coliseum, where the city's segregation laws would have caused difficulties, but to the geographically immune Cotton Club. Buddy was there with J. I. Allison or Sonny Curtis every Saturday night as the rackety stage unveiled yet another magical presence once available only via car radios after midnight: Fats Domino with his gently rolling bulk and tiny Oriental face; Ivory Joe Hunter, a dignified man of forty-one, bemused at suddenly finding himself a teen icon. For Buddy, the greatest excitement of all was seeing Little Richard swagger out with his baggy suit and wild Medusa mop, and open his mustachioed Clara Bow lips to unleash ear-shattering, heavenly mayhem.

Offstage, he was just as spectacularly outrageous, garlanded with chunky gold jewelry, reeking of cologne, and comporting himself in a manner for which the term "screaming camp" had yet to be invented. This concatenation of all the South's most hated taboos—blackness, effeminacy, and rock 'n' roll—made Richard prey to constant official persecution and harassment. His debut appearance at the Cotton Club was brought to a premature halt by Lubbock's police department on the excuse that it was causing fights outside. In Amarillo the previous night, he had been arrested for "vagrancy," despite having $1,200 in cash in his suitcase. In El Paso the following night he would be arrested again, this time for failure to carry his draft card.

Meeting Richard in the Cotton Club's communal band room, Buddy was captivated, as many others would be, by the self-knowing wit that leavened his preposterous vanity and promiscuity. At this point in his career, Richard traveled with a stripper named Lee Angel, whose bust measured fifty inches and whom he encouraged to have sex with any of his fellow performers who fancied her. He also freely admitted being attracted to men, and boasted of his ability to masturbate "seven or eight times each day." As for his conversation, an ear-assaulting, almost schizophrenic mixture of the sacred and profane, well might Richard himself affirm that while other young men may have majored in math at high school, he "majored in Mouth."

Buddy was to spend many hilarious hours in his company and, after a later Cotton Club gig, invited him home to dinner, blissfully unmindful of L. O. Holley's inevitable reaction. "When Buddy's Daddy saw who his son had brought home, he wouldn't let me in," Little Richard writes in his memoirs. "But Buddy told his Daddy 'If you don't let Richard in, I'll never come back to this house again.' So they let me in, but they weren't very happy. I'll bet they washed them dishes I ate off about 20 times after we'd gone." Ella Holley later confirmed that L. O. truly had been reluctant to admit Richard to their home and that, as a compromise, dinner was a barbecue in the backyard.

Buddy's summer of marking time coincided with J. I. Allison's high school vacation and the two began spending long hours together, J. I. to some degree filling the void left by Echo. In addition to their love of rock 'n' roll, Buddy and he had every other taste in common: cars, motorcycles, hunting, guns. J. I. had a lazily humorous wit and love of wordplay that appealed to Buddy; despite his squat build and poor complexion, he was also enviably successful with girls. Apart from rehearsing with the group still called Buddy and Bob, they spent hours practicing as a duo at each other's house, Buddy singing and playing guitar, both rhythm and lead, J. I.'s energetic drumsticks filling in every other crack. "They were *the* perfect combination," a fellow musician who'd known Buddy since Sunday school days remembers. "Just the two of them could make a bigger and better sound than my whole band."

J. I. Allison was more than willing to kick against authority wherever it might raise its head. But for all Buddy's seeming quietness and shyness, he could be rash and reckless in a way that even J. I. sometimes found alarming. Such was his blithe disregard of traffic tickets that at one point, in late 1954, the City of Lubbock was at the point of issuing a warrant for his arrest. A classic Buddy toe-curler occurred when he was driving the band to a gig at the South Plains Fair, the annual showcase for local agriculture and industry. "A cop pulled us over for speeding," J. I. later remembered. "If it'd been me, I'd have said, 'Sorry, sir, won't do it again.' But Buddy gets real argumentative with this cop, like, 'Hey, I'm on my way to do something that's going to benefit this county, and now you want to give me a ticket.'"

Like many teenage boys, Buddy went through a phase of aggressiveness toward his parents, so much so that his brother Larry had to take him aside and say, "They're my parents, too, and I don't think you should talk to them that way." With most adolescents, such an elder-brotherly dressing-down would have been counterproductive. But Buddy was mortified to think he'd upset L. O. and Ella, and vowed to be nicer in the future.

J. I. discovered, too, that despite Buddy's outward good nature and love of laughter, he had a dark and strange and unknowable side. In the middle of the most enjoyable get-together with his cronies, he would suddenly get up and, without a word to anyone, go out to the family Oldsmobile and drive away. Next day, when the others saw him, he would be back to his old genial, easygoing self; if they asked where he'd been, he just grinned and said, "For a drive." In fact, he might have gone hundreds of miles alone to Dallas or Carlsbad, New Mexico, nonstop and often through the night.

They knew he was missing Echo, worrying about what handsome young Christians she would be meeting in Abilene, struggling to reconcile his ambitions in music with being the kind of person she required as a husband. That autumn of 1955, she gave him a copy of a currently celebrated religious novel, inscribing it in a way that left no doubt about her faith in his deeper spiritual qualities: "Dearest Buddy, I hope you will receive as much inspiration from this book as I have. I also hope it will help you to see things more clearly after carefully reading it and comparing it with your Bible. Love always, Echo." The book had a title that now seems horribly prophetic: *Must the Young Die, Too?*

But at night, as Buddy pounded his Les Paul gold top in some club or hall outside Lubbock's ring of godliness, Abilene and Echo could seem very far away. He discovered with incredulity how rock 'n' roll banished his physical shortcomings in the eyes of the opposite sex; how his scrawny build, his too-curly hair, his "West Texas teeth," even the hated half-frame glasses were all instantly magicked away as soon as he leapt onstage and started cutting up like Elvis or Little Richard. Girls screamed for him just as loudly as they did for the out-of-town rock 'n' rollers and, after every show, clustered around him in equal numbers, ready and willing for any late-night adventures he might suggest. "Buddy was sure no little plaster saint like people try to make out," his deejay friend Jerry Coleman remembers. "He was an average hard-on good ol' American boy. He liked pussy as much any other guy his age. He ran his traps, the same way all of us did."

Little as might be happening in his life, he remained buoyant, optimistic, confident to the point of cockines. He was sure that, although his only regular gig might be at a windswept local radio station and his management no more influential than a kindly local deejay with high pockets, he was destined, sooner or later, to be gathered up by the same blue norther that was already whirling Elvis, Little Richard, Fats Domino, and Chuck Berry into the big time. "There was never any question in Buddy's mind that he was going to make it," Bob Montgomery says. "The rest of us thought he deserved to, but none of us could see how he was going to do it."

☆　☆　☆

On October 14, 1955, Bill Haley and the Comets appeared at Fair Park Coliseum, supported by Jimmie Rodgers Snow and Buddy, Bob, and Larry. Traveling with the show was a Nashville agent named Eddie Crandall, whose clients included Marty Robbins, that longtime fan both of Buddy's music and leatherwork. Crandall was impressed by Buddy's performance and watched him carefully the following night when he opened another KDAV-sponsored show, headlined by Elvis Presley and featuring rockabilly newcomers Johnny Cash and Floyd Cramer.

Elvis, two months earlier, had acquired a new manager, a former carnival huckster and municipal dog-catcher named "Colonel" Tom Parker—who, indeed, was destined to develop rock's great founding genius as a cross between a fairground freak and a captive poodle. Crandall knew Parker well and suggested to him that there might be as promising a new client in the boy from Lubbock, Texas, as in the one from Tupelo, Mississippi. The Colonel said he was too busy with Elvis to launch another newcomer but agreed that Buddy had possibilities and suggested Crandall himself should take a shot at promoting him.

On December 2, Crandall wrote to Pappy Dave Stone: "Dave, I'm very confident I can do something as far as getting Buddy Holly [sic] a recording contract. It may not be a major but even a small one would be beneficial to someone who is trying to get a break. . . . Col. Parker suggested I try and help Buddy as he's pretty well tied up, and with your friendship I'll try my darndest to help him. Marty Robbins also thinks Buddy has what it takes. So all we can do is try, OK?" The same day Pappy Dave received the letter, a telegram arrived from Crandall requesting a demo of four original songs by Buddy posthaste, and urging, "Don't change his style at all."

By mid-January 1956, Crandall was on the telephone with exciting news. He had taken Buddy's demo to a Nashville talent agent named Jim Denny, who specialized in booking acts for the *Grand Ole Opry* show and also owned a publishing company called Cedarwood. Denny was prepared to offer him a songwriter's contract with Cedarwood and also to try to get him a record deal.

The moment was a providential one. Nashville's recording industry was just then awakening to the challenge being offered to it as "Music City, USA" by the Sun label in Memphis. In the race to make up ground, the RCA Victor label had forged ahead, buying Elvis Presley's contract from Sun, in a deal brokered by Colonel Tom Parker, for a staggering $35,000 plus a Cadillac. The two other major labels with operations in Nashville, Columbia and Decca, were both now frantically seeking young rockabilly stars of their own. Jim Denny could not interest Columbia in Buddy, but was able to persuade Decca's Nashville director of artists and repertoire, Paul Cohen, to offer him a contract.

To the Lubbock boys, unaware of all the background politics and machinations, it was a breakthrough in spades. Decca was a hugely powerful and prestigious label, boasting country music greats like Red Foley, Kitty Wells, and Ernest Tubb "the Texas Troubadour," as well as the single extant white rock 'n' roll star, Bill Haley. Of no small assistance in exploiting Haley's monopoly was the fact that Decca controlled roughly 40 percent of the jukeboxes in America.

The snag was that Paul Cohen wanted just Buddy; he did not want Bob Montgomery, the other half of the musical partnership that had existed since their elementary school days. The painful choice between loyalty and ambition was one Buddy did not have to make, however, since Bob instantly and amicably stood aside. He had always been far too deep-dyed a country musician to feel comfortable with rock 'n' roll, and was to go on to his own fulfilling career as a songwriter and, later, a music publisher. Hi Pockets Duncan, too, behaved with a gentlemanliness hard to imagine today, immediately honoring his long-standing pledge to relinquish all managerial claim once Buddy was on the road to success.

Paul Cohen's offer, however, was a long way from guaranteeing that. Like every other major record label at that moment, Decca was auditioning dozens of young singers in the frenetic rush to come up with another mumbling moneyspinner like Elvis. Cohen expressed no wild enthusiasm about Buddy, and promised no commitment to making him a star nor investment in developing him beyond the costs of a recording session early in 1956.

Buddy himself had no doubt the great moment had arrived for which he had been actively preparing since the previous spring. He had long been itching to trade in his Les Paul Gold Top for a classier instrument and the previous April, at the Adair music store in Lubbock, had found one classy beyond his dreams. Fender solid-body guitars even then were nothing new: it was in 1948 that the electronics wizard Leo Fender marketed his revolutionary prototype, the Broadcaster. But to most guitarists, especially ultraconservative country ones, the idea of a guitar that had no acoustic resonance, and was entirely dependent on amplification to give it voice, belonged in the same daunting sci-fi realm as the H-bomb, 3-D films, and the research into space travel going on at Houston and Cape Canaveral.

That made it all the more remarkable that Adair's had got hold of a Stratocaster, the latest and most expensive Fender; on the market barely a year, named for the new age of space travel, and the perfect craft to explore the virgin galaxies of rock 'n' roll. Fortunately the Adair salesman, Clyde Hankin, was a friend of Buddy's and a guitar buff who had once given him lessons. Buddy had already been allowed to savor the contoured snugness of the Stratocaster's black-to-brown sunburst body against his, testing the new freedom its double-cutaway shape gave to fingering in the high treble register, experimenting with volume changes between its three electric pickups. He loved everything about it except the tremolo lever, worked in the palm of the strumming hand, which bore down on all six strings at their root, or bridge, dragging a note or chord into drawn-out, shivering echo. In the hard, all-downstroke style Buddy had learned from R&B soloists, he preferred all his notes to be ringingly clear and clean.

As a recording star in Elvis's footsteps, he knew he would also need clothes very different from his usual starched white shirts, Levi's, and loafers. The price tag for this combined musical and sartorial makeover, when he added it up, far exceeded the modest savings he had managed to accrue from music and manual labor, so as always in time of emergency he turned to his eldest brother. "He came to me and said, 'Larry, I know good and well I could make it if only I had me a decent guitar and some decent clothes,'" Larry Holley remembers. "I said, 'Make it as what?' He said, 'Why, make it in the music business.' So I said, 'Okay, how much do you need?,' thinking he was going to say about fifty dollars. But Buddy says, 'How about lending me a thousand dollars?'

"Well, I was pretty amazed, because that was a pile of money back then, but I reckoned he knew what he was about, so I scraped up the thousand bucks from somewhere. And he bought some of the gaudiest clothes you ever did see! I wouldn't have worn 'em to a bullfight! There was a red coat . . . a chartreuse sport jacket . . . some suede shoes that were blue. Then he brought over the guitar and showed it to me. I said, 'How much did you give for that?' and he said, 'Four hundred.' I was flabbergasted. 'Four hundred dollars for a guitar!' I said. 'You can get one for fifty at Huber's.'"

To accompany him and the Stratocaster on their triumphal entry into Nashville, Buddy recruited the two backup musicians who had crossed over with him from country to rock 'n' roll: guitarist Sonny Curtis and slap-bass player Don Guess. Naturally he also wanted Jerry Allison on drums, but J. I. had now returned to Lubbock High for another semester and even he dared not play hooky on such a scale. The three traveled in Buddy's family's black and white '55 Oldsmobile, with Guess's bass strapped to the roof.

The producer to whom Decca had assigned Buddy was Owen Bradley, a veteran in the country music field who ran his own studio on Music Row, Nashville's famous boulevard of publishing and recording establishments. An ex-military Quonset hut, not much less cavernous and spartan than the one that housed the Cotton Club back in Lubbock, it bore the wholly appropriate nickname Bradley's Barn.

From the moment the Texas boys walked into Bradley's Barn, on January 26, 1956, chill disillusionment set in. To begin with, Buddy was informed that his backing group did not measure up to the requirements of professional recording. To augment Sonny and Don, Owen Bradley had brought in two session musicians, Grady Martin on rhythm guitar and Doug Kirkham on drums—both highly accomplished, but self-important and condescending to the young out-of-towners as only Nashville session men can be. To make matters worse, Buddy was told that singing and playing guitar simultaneously, as he'd been doing since the age of nine, was contrary to recording practice. Sonny Curtis, therefore, had to take charge of the Fender Stratocaster while its owner stood at the heavy stand-mike, his long arms dangling uselessly beside him, feeling as naked as if he'd forgotten to put on his Levi's.

There were also difficulties about the material to be recorded. Of the original songs Buddy had submitted to Paul Cohen, the A&R man chose only "Don't Come Back Knockin'" and "Love Me," both of them written in collaboration with a Lubbock girl named Sue Parrish. Two numbers by other writers were added to the list: "Midnight Shift," by Earl Lee and Jimmy Ainsworth, an uptempo number featuring the sportive Annie of Hank Ballard's R&B hits; and "Blue Days, Black Nights," written by Buddy's disc jockey friend Ben Hall and taught to him by ear one hot afternoon in the sheltering shade of the KDAV building.

All four titles were recorded in a single evening session at Bradley's Barn, starting at 7:15 and finishing at 10:15. To give Owen Bradley due credit, he made no attempt to turn Buddy into something he wasn't or cramp his style. "Blue Days, Black Nights" bears comparison with any of his later work, a well-crafted if rather staid country song, performed with a skipping lightness of touch, yet total sincerity and involvement. But on the other three tracks, Buddy shows palpable tension and lack of confidence, reflecting his own uncertainty about what Decca expected of him. Even the slap-bass beat and saucy lyrics of "Midnight Shift" produced little more than an exhibition of how well he could mimic Elvis. (So familiar was this impersonation around the Holley home that when L. O. Holley first heard Elvis on the radio he remarked innocently, "That boy sounds just like Buddy.")

As if to underline Decca's vagueness of purpose, the contract that eventually came through on February 8, 1956, spelled Buddy's surname Holly instead of Holley. Since Holly seemed to have a more professional, showbizzy ring to it—and since any objection would doubtless have produced further glitches in Decca's administrative machinery—he decided to let it stand. Paul Cohen had also requested some biographical details for publicity purposes, and on March 2 Buddy sent off a neatly typewritten letter that reads more like the résumé of an aspiring invoice clerk than of a rock 'n' roll singer: "I started taking music lessons on the violin at four years old and won an amateur contest when I was five. I also took lessons on the piana [sic] but as I didn't care for these instruments, I discontinued studying them . . ." The signature on the letter shows he had not yet fully adjusted to his new persona: "Appreciatively, Buddy Holley."

☆ ☆ ☆

Throughout that February and March of 1956, as Buddy anxiously watched the mailbox and listened for the phone, only one sound seemed to come from America's jukeboxes, radios, and speeding, shark-finned cars. It was the first single to be released from Elvis Presley's Nashville sessions, a song called "Heartbreak Hotel," which combined a classic X-rated R&B style with the self-dramatizing angst of a lovelorn white street punk. In January, Elvis had made his first national television appearance, performing two songs on the CBS network's *Stage Show*, hosted by former bandleaders Tommy and Jimmy Dorsey. The resultant deluge of complaints from viewers about his voice, hair, face, clothes, above all, his "obscene" bodily mannerisms was promotion the canny Colonel Tom Parker could not have bought. By mid-March "Heartbreak Hotel" had become the first record ever to reach No. 1 simultaneously on all three record charts: pop, R&B, and country.

No one in Decca's A&R department was under any illusion that a similar whirlwind had been unleashed at Bradley's Barn. After several weeks' agonized waiting, Buddy was informed that his debut single would be the Ben Hall song "Blue Days, Black Nights," coupled with "Love Me." Catchy and polished as the A-side was, it clearly stood no chance in the "Heartbreak Hotel" league. But Buddy's optimism remained buoyant. As proof of his high hopes for "Blue Days, Black Nights," he spent hours in painstakingly tooling a blue and black leather overjacket for his Gibson J45 acoustic guitar, stamping his new name in bold white capitals on the body, and his initials in medieval calligraphy, flanked by miniature guitars, on the shoulder strap.

Thanks to his new status as a Decca recording artist, he had been offered his first professional tour: a week on the road with Faron Young's *Grand Ole Opry* show, visiting spots as breathtakingly far afield as Tulsa, Oklahoma. With him he took his Decca sidemen, Sonny Curtis and Don Guess, although once again not J. I. Allison, who was still fumingly imprisoned in high school. They were billed as "extra added attractions" along with Tommy Collins and Carl Perkins. The pay was $10 a day each, plus room and board.

A last-minute hitch arose when Don Guess, who did not own his own double bass, was unable to borrow one as he usually did for the group's one-night appearances. Then Buddy remembered a Lubbock High boy named Terry Noland who rented a bass from the school for $2 a semester. "He called up the high school, saying he was my dad and needed to speak to me urgently," Noland remembers. "I got pulled out of history class to take the call . . . only to discover that it's just Buddy, wanting me to let him have this bass. The voice that he'd put on as my dad couldn't have been that good because while we were talking, my teacher picked up an extension phone and listened in on us. Boy, did Buddy get an earful for that!"

The Texas trio did not travel on the tour bus with the country stars, but had to follow behind in the Holley family's '55 Olds. "We had to drive hundreds of miles, and never got much sleep between gigs," Sonny Curtis remembers. "To stay awake late at night, we used to tell each other ghost stories. Buddy had some pretty good ones about the Mark of the Beast from the Book of Revelations. Sometimes we all used to get so scared that no one wanted to ride in the back seat of the car. We all used to squash up together in front.

"We'd gone on the road pretty much unprepared, without any stage uniform like the other bands had, or even a name to call ourselves. When we stopped off in Oklahoma City, we went to a haberdasher's and bought some white pants and two shirts each, a blue one and an orange one. So when we went onstage that night, we told 'em to announce us as the Two-Tones." For the Lubbock boys, the biggest thrill of the tour was when one of its stars, Tommy Collins, rode with them in the Olds. "We was flipped out about that," Sonny says. "Riding down the road with a guy who made records! And, because we had our subsistence paid, we could order steaks all the way."

Buddy spent the tour on a wave of extrovert high spirits that frequently embarrassed the polite and civilized Sonny. "When we went into a restaurant, Buddy would fill up all the water glasses to different heights, and start playing tunes on them. I remember once we all went to see this movie *Wuthering Heights,* with Laurence Olivier and Merle Oberon. There's a line in it, 'If you come over to my house, I'll let you hold my hand beneath my fan.' Buddy leans back in his seat, throws out his arms, and says 'Ha-ave *mercy!*' Well, the whole place just broke up."

The release of "Blue Days, Black Nights" in April brought Buddy's spirits down to earth with a crash. Decca spent nothing on promoting the record and organized no publicity beyond a few handout pictures of Buddy tense and unsmiling in his half-frame spectacles, clutching his acoustic guitar defensively to his chest. With no indications to the contrary, the record was treated as pure country. *Billboard* magazine's country & Western reviewer gave it a good rating and also had the acumen to spot the rock 'n' roll singer trying to get out: "If the public will take more than one Presley or [Carl] Perkins, as it well may, Holly stands a strong chance," *Billboard* concluded. Apart from that provided by KDAV-Lubbock, radio airplay was never other than desultory. Buddy was clearly grasping at straws when he wrote to a booking agent a few weeks later: "I have talked to some friends that were traveling up around the northeastern part of the country, and they said my record was very popular around Washington DC and through Missouri." Decca's final estimate of sales was 18,000 copies, which at the standard 2.5 percent royalty rate—and after deducting the publisher's 50 percent—meant that Buddy and his two co-writers, Ben Hall and Sue Parrish, would have shared about $225.

The horribly unflattering Decca publicity photographs made one thing abundantly clear. No one who aspired to be like Elvis Presley could possibly go on being seen in glasses. On the Faron Young tour, Buddy tried leaving them off while he was performing, but with his 20/800 vision could barely see his fellow musicians, let alone the audience. During one show, he dropped his guitar pick and had to crawl around the stage looking for it with his nose only a couple of inches from the floor.

On May 14, the day after he returned from the tour, he went to his ophthalmologist, Dr. J. Davis Armistead, and announced that he wanted contact lenses. This further miracle of fifties consumer technology had at the time been available only for a year or two, and was something more usually associated with fashionable city women than with beanpole young Texans. The hard lenses of 1956 were hugely expensive and, by modern standards, enormous and unwieldy, as tricky to insert under the eyelid as miniature magnifying glasses. Buddy paid $125 for the lenses prescribed for him by Dr. Armistead, but found them so uncomfortable, he could wear them only for about ten minutes each day.

On July 22, he was back in Nashville for a second Decca recording session at Bradley's Barn. School was out, so J. I. Allison could take the place of the session drummer, Doug Kirkham. Buddy had persuaded Owen Bradley to let him, rather than an outsider, play rhythm guitar, so now at least he would be backed by the same band on record as on stage. For further moral support, his cast-off partner, the generous-spirited Bob Montgomery, had also driven up from Lubbock in the jam-packed black and white Olds.

The tracks on this session were angled far more to rock 'n' roll and mainstream pop. There was a Buddy song, "I'm Changing All Those Changes"; a Don Guess song, "Girl On My Mind"; a Sonny Curtis song, "Rock Around with Ollie Vee" (named after an old black woman who helped Sonny's mother with housework); and "Ting-A-Ling," a bluesy number by the future head of Atlantic Records, Ahmet Ertegun. Almost by way of an afterthought, there was also Buddy's first casual attempt at songwriting in partnership with Jerry Allison.

A week or two previously, they had been to the State theater in Lubbock to see *The Searchers,* the darkest and most complex of all John Ford Westerns, starring Buddy's hero John Wayne, for once playing a character who was not wholly good or admirable. The searchers are a posse in pursuit of Indians who have kidnapped two white girls. Throughout the picture, whenever anyone asks Wayne's character, Ethan Edwards, whether he's ready to abandon the chase or is otherwise discouraged, he growls the same laconic response: "That'll be the day."

It became a catchphrase among Buddy's circle, though none was quite as good at reproducing Wayne's slurry monotone as Buddy himself. "A little while after we saw the movie, we were over at my house," J. I. later remembered. "Buddy had a tune in his head, and he said, 'Hey, why don't we two write a song?' I said, 'That'll be the day.' He said, 'Hey, that's a good idea.' " The song was knocked off in less than half an hour, with the two improvising alternate lines and Buddy stirring in a jangly guitar riff borrowed from one of his favorite R&B records, Hank Ballard and the Midnighters' "Switchie Witchie Titchie."

Owen Bradley was perfectly willing for a new original song called "That'll Be the Day" to be added to the morning-long session. But even at the nineteenth take, the result was hardly exciting. Buddy sang it without any backup chorus, in a just-too-high key that robbed his voice of its normal range, suppleness, and humor. The cavernous echo that Bradley added was obviously intended to create the same dramatic, angst-ridden atmosphere it had for Elvis Presley's voice on "Heartbreak Hotel." But here it merely emphasized the unsteadiness of Buddy's delivery and the unsympathetic ambience of Bradley's Barn.

Though Buddy got along with Owen Bradley well enough, the more crucial rapport with Decca's A&R director, Paul Cohen, had failed to materialize. The protocol of recording in 1956 was quite clear: A&R men were God Almighty, and singers followed their instructions to the letter in humble gratitude. But Buddy had been cutting records on his own initiative since early boyhood, and had his own strong and clear-cut ideas about how his music ought to sound. Moreover, when it came to protecting his work, as he saw it, from the indifference of Nashville's ruling elite, his usual Texan courtesy and respectfulness went out the window. Jim Denny, his publisher at Cedarwood Music, several times found himself called on to act as peacemaker in hot disputes between Buddy and Paul Cohen. Yet for all that, and his unspectacular results to date, Decca still felt Buddy had something, and told him to come back to Nashville for a third session later in the year.

All through the high summer months, as Buddy helped Larry lay tiles or worked on house-framing jobs with his father, there was still nothing to see or hear but Elvis, Elvis, Elvis. Instead of blowing over as predicted, rock 'n' roll was raging stronger than ever, but now with something that had not been there in the simple, cinema-smashing days of 1955: it was simple, straightforwardly unpleasant juvenile delinquency no longer, but juvenile delinquency packaged with neon-bright glamour and soaked to the eyebrows in sex.

The cohesion of American family life, its chief pride for a century and a half, was gone forever. To the young generation, Elvis was a rock 'n' roll hero in their own image at long last—an idol more dangerously fascinating than Marlon Brando in *The Wild One,* more tantilizingly unfathomable than James Dean in *Rebel Without a Cause;* the incarnation of all modern teenagerdom's volatile moods, randy energy, and tumultuous self-pity. To their parents, he was a specter of disruption and subversion more terrible than any conjured up by the late McCarthy era; a figure of blatant physicality not shut away in a burlesque house as tradition demanded, but able to penetrate and defile any home with his too-oily hair, his too-long sideburns, his too-garish clothes, his too-sullen face, the too-effeminate twirls of his too-loose head, shoulders, legs, and hips, but worst of all, the too-suggestive forward jerks and thrusts of his far-too-tautly-enclosed crotch. The dim realization that both his material and performing style derived from "Negro music" reactivated all the horrified superstitions and complexes of the white race concerning the sexual powers of the black one. So that was what rock 'n' roll and its new mumbling, glowering figurehead were about! Initiating clean-cut young American manhood and pure young American womanhood into the mindless, shameless rhythms that promoted rutting rituals in the jungle!

The War Between the States, ninety years earlier, was hardly more bitter and unrelenting than that which Elvis had started between America's teenagers and their elders. High schools and colleges, the Federal side, poured forth virulent anti–rock 'n' roll propaganda in the form of pamphlets and even films, showing how to recognize the rebel "enemy within": the males by their sideburns and blue jeans, the even more reprehensible females by their ponytails and ankle bracelets. Elvis himself could have been Robert E. Lee, reincarnated with hair-dye and a pout. And as any armchair psychologist could have predicted, the more furiously adults condemned, deplored, and ridiculed Elvis, the more ardently teenagers formed lines to buy his records and flocked, shrieking, to his concerts. After the monster success of "Heartbreak Hotel," RCA Victor took the unprecedented (and unrepeated) step of releasing seven of his songs simultaneously, thereby keeping him at No. 1 on the charts every single week from August to December. Meanwhile, the media pursued him back and forth across the country, as if he were some ghastly erotic evangelist, faithfully reporting from each new city-gone-berserk where demented girls had besieged his dressing room, obliterated his car, tried to tear the clothes from his back, or kissed him until his mouth bled.

Buddy as a rule was too wrapped up in his music and hobbies, and far too restless, to sit around watching television. But on September 9, even he was anchored before the flickering gray and white screen to see Elvis's first appearance on CBS's *Ed Sullivan Show*. Sullivan was the most unlikely of all TV music hall hosts, a former gossip columnist and sportswriter with hunched shoulders, a long-jawed, misanthropic face, and a rasping voice with which he managed to make even his best-known guests sound like denizens of outer space. Compelled to exploit the ratings opportunity that rock 'n' roll presented, he barely troubled to conceal his personal disgust for the music, introducing Elvis with a self-absolving wave of the hand and the words "America . . . judge for yourselves."

That night of September 9, Elvis performed four numbers: "Don't Be Cruel," "Hound Dog," "Love Me Tender," and Little Richard's "Rip It Up." He drew an audience of 54 million, setting a record that would stand until February 1964, when another reluctant wave of Ed Sullivan's hand introduced the Beatles.

The ensuing national furor signaled open season on rock 'n' roll musicians and fans wherever they should chance to be found. In October, Lubbock's morning paper, the *Avalanche,* published a picture of Buddy playing with his group at the Cotton Club, as if that were a wholly new and noteworthy circumstance. The faces of the musicians and the dancers below them were blacked out in the style of currently notorious scandal magazines like *Confidential* and *Whisper.*

The city's evening *Journal* followed up the story on October 22 by interviewing the rock 'n' roll player whom Lubbock still hardly realized it had in its midst. Headlined YOUNG SINGER IS LUBBOCK'S ANSWER TO ELVIS PRESLEY—BUDDY HOLLY PACKS 'EM IN, the article broke the ten-month-old story of Buddy's Decca recording contract and mentioned his remarkable drawing power on weekends at venues like the American Legion Youth Center. *Journal* readers were no doubt relieved to learn that their homegrown rock 'n' roller resembled Elvis only in the most superficial way, and in private conducted himself with a restraint and decorum entirely appropriate to the City of Churches. While Buddy confessed to playing music in "fancy" sport coats, he emphasized that he never wore such garments offstage, not even "for publicity purposes."

A better reporter could have truffled out some more interesting facts: for instance, that Buddy was by now such a star in the Lubbock area that his brother Larry, the tough ex-Marine, had to go to gigs with him, to keep him from being mobbed and to stave off occasional attacks by envious boyfriends of the girls who screamed for him. Or that the one-time high school nerd whom no one took seriously had become a figure of such glamour and magnetism that the Hi-D-Ho drive-in employed him to attract teenage customers by performing on its circular flat roof.

On November 15, Buddy had his third and, it would prove, final session for Decca in Nashville. This time at Bradley's Barn, Don Guess was the only one of his band allowed to take part; the rest were session men, including Floyd Cramer on piano and E. R. "Dutch" McMillin on tenor saxophone. The most promising track was agreed to be "Modern Don Juan," a lackluster composition by Guess and Jack Neal. "Modern Don Juan," with another Don Guess song, "You Are My One Desire," was released December 24, a date that amounted to marketing suicide. This time, Don, Jerry Allison, and Sonny Curtis received billing on the record: not as the Two-Tones, much to their chagrin, but as the Three Tunes. Once again, *Billboard* reviewed the song as country, and gave it mild praise, but this time sales were negligible.

Relations between Buddy and Paul Cohen, meanwhile, had deteriorated beyond repair. Infuriated by Buddy's refusal to kowtow, Cohen told him flatly that he didn't have the kind of voice that could ever sell pop records and, to a third party, referred to him as "the biggest no-talent I ever worked with." For all Buddy's buoyancy and native stubbornness, he had no choice but to concede defeat by Nashville's music mafia. It was mortifying, but no real surprise, when, early in January 1957, a letter arrived from Decca, terminating his contract.

So was this to be the zenith of his career as a rock 'n' roller—floodlit on the Hi-D-Ho's roof, singing and playing his heart out to a semicircle of parked cars while the carhops in their scarlet tunics and pillbox hats scurried to and fro under his feet with orders of Hidey burgers, Hidey fries, and Hidey pies?

PART TWO

LOOKING FOR SOMEONE TO LOVE

Clovis, New Mexico, is some ninety miles to the northwest of Lubbock, a two-hour drive in a modern small car under modern speed restrictions. Although Route 84 is no longer the undivided two-lane blacktop of Buddy's era, its milestones and incidental sights remain much the same as he would have seen from behind the wheel. On your left are infinite cotton- and wheatfields; to your right run the banked-up tracks of the Sante Fe Railroad. Shabby one-street towns along the way—Shallowater, Sudan, Muleshoe—vainly attempt to beguile the eye with bargain gas prices, real estate offices, trailer parks, junkyards, and silver grain elevators as huge and fancy as Las Vegas casino-hotels. Occasionally a freight train swings into view to relieve the monotony; half a mile or so of boxcars, hauled by squads of dark blue locomotives, each with SANTA FE emblazoned on it in gold Victorian script.

At the state line, the time zone changes from Central to Mountain, setting clocks and watches back one hour. You can thus proceed to Clovis, six miles farther on, with the pleasant illusion that your journey from Lubbock took only half the time you thought. The view may appear much the same as back in Texas, but do not suppose you are anywhere half so candid and straightforward. Even to native Westerners, New Mexico is an enigma, the so-called Secret State whose vast interior deserts are thickly planted with top-secret nuclear research establishments, elite military bases, missile pads, and legends of close encounters with UFOs.

Were it not for Buddy Holly, Clovis would be known merely as a relic of America's great railroad age. Originally named Riley Switch (after the man who once dwelled there, switching trains from one line to another), it grew up in the late nineteenth century as the railhead for herds driven in mainly from a huge ranch in the Texas Panhandle called the XIT and said to have been as big as the state of Rhode Island. Even the city's mellifluous European name—that of a fifth-century Frankish monarch and a character in Saki's short stories—was bestowed by the scholarly daughter of a railway official stationed there. It reached its zenith in the early 1900s as a rail terminal for livestock, freight, and passengers, and, later, a staging post for the first transcontinental air journeys, which originally were made jointly by train and plane.

That busy, purposeful era was already fading when Buddy first came here in the mid-fifties, and now has practically vanished. All that remains of the once splendid passenger terminal is the Harvey House hotel, where travelers would once alight from the 20th Century or Superchief to lunch or dine at their leisure. The once bustling freight depots and repair shops have been closed or been ruthlessly downsized. Looking along cobbled Main Street, with its washed-out colors and permanent air of weekend quiet, you would not think that much of anything goes on in Clovis anymore. Even the ripe odor from the remaining active stockyards has something nostalgic, at night a little ghostly, about it.

Before 1957, other than in railroad schedules, Clovis had only one substantial claim to fame. Just south of the city is the archaeological site which, in the late forties, yielded up the earliest evidence of human habitation in the Americas. This 14,000-year-old culture is known for short among prehistorians as Clovis Man. We have come to disinter another species of Clovis Man, however—one that may date from a more recent era, but is hardly less mysterious and unfathomable.

At 1313 West Seventh Street his neat blue sign still rears over the sidewalk as if half-hopeful of enticing passing trade: NORMAN PETTY in two diagonals of white script, RECORDING STUDIOS in businesslike capitals. Below are two flat-roofed yellow buildings, picked out in vermilion, nestling in lush foliage and connected by a short strip of wire-fenced garden. The larger, two-story building to the right has a decorative facade on which spreading greenery partly obscures the raised letters NOR VA JAK MUSIC INC.

In the smaller, single-story building, to the left, the studio where Buddy created his greatest music is preserved intact, its period fittings and artifacts as fascinating to the modern eye as any pristine cave paintings or unplundered pharaoh's tomb. Here is the tiny reception area with its serried rows of framed Gold Records, and the old red and white vending machine that dispensed Coca-Colas in thick green sculpted bottles, 10 cents apiece. Here, beyond, is Norman Petty's control room with equipment still in place: the black-boxed, silver-studded Ampex tape-recorder; the lathe that used to convert Buddy's tapes into demo discs. Here are glass-fronted cabinets containing headphones, maracas, and recording wire, and Petty's own gray leather armchair pushed up to the veiny black work surface with its heavy-based RCA microphone.

And there, through the glass, the studio itself, a place no bigger than an average-size living room, where Buddy made "That'll Be the Day," "Peggy Sue," "Oh Boy," "Not Fade Away," "Words of Love," "Listen to Me," "Love's Made a Fool of You," "Heartbeat," "It's So Easy," and every other classic track, bar one or two. Pushed up to the lefthand wall is the Baldwin grand piano that played the rolling bass solo on "Think It Over"; opposite is the celesta that tinkled through "Everyday." Here is the heavy stand-mike Buddy used on every session, and the Fender Pro amplifier into which he used to plug his Stratocaster. Amazing to see how small is its yellow cabinet and compare its 20-watt capacity with the almost 4 million watts needed to project the Rolling Stones' stage version of "Not Fade Away" in 1995.

Down a short passage from the studio is the kitchen where Buddy and the Crickets would wolf down inter-session snacks, and the room with two dark-blue-covered beds, folding out into four, where they would sometimes snatch a couple of hours' sleep after dawn. No mummy's tomb was ever packed more densely with relics than is this long-unused guest suite with iconography of the mid-fifties: lamps with hand-stitched vellum shades, supported on twists of gold and black; fish-shaped clocks; narrow-necked vases of dark blue Murano glass; sets of fancy iron fire tongs; swan-necked black cats; pomanders in the shape of straw-hatted donkeys; gilt-racked sets of coaster mats; sage-green Picasso-print curtains; top-of-the-line Grundig valve radios and radio-record players; splayed white table- and chair-legs and orange synthetic leather.

The two-story building across the yard houses the apartment where Petty lived with his wife, Vi, and his elderly parents, and the loft space where Buddy's father and brothers built the echo chamber that was to be used with such effect on "Peggy Sue." At the rear is the barbecue area where Norma Jean, the Pettys' secretary–bookkeeper, would serve picnics of taquitos, and the white truck—Air Force blue in Petty's time—that used to take his cocktail lounge trio to its engagements and that Buddy, an incurable car nut, frequently drove.

Inside this bizarre little compound, almost everything a pop record could ever say was definitively said between February 1957 and the summer of 1958. It is all now history as distant as Clovis Man; yet, in common with all thrilling archaeological sites, one has a sense of life interrupted rather than extinct. The fish-shaped clocks, the swan-necked cats, the dime-slot Coke machine, the Fender Pro amp, all seem to await a crunch of Oldsmobile tires on the forecourt, a yell of Texan laughter, a clatter and ruffle of drums being set up, then a voice, melodious but commanding: "Okay . . . let's do it."

☆　　☆　　☆

Our particular species of Clovis Man left behind such contradictory evidence of his existence, and took such pains to cover his tracks in all crucial areas, that building up a definitive archaeological profile would, in the ordinary way, be next to impossible. You can talk to a dozen people who knew Norman Petty well, and from each vantage point see a totally different character. To some, he was a technical wizard whose inspired know-how shaped raw talent into glossily finished genius; to others, he was simply a button-pusher who happened to be in the right place at the right time. To some, he was a model of generosity, altruism, and square dealing; to others, a shameless opportunist, cheat, and thief. To some, he was the person who made it possible for Buddy Holly to come alive; others feel he could hardly be more to blame for Buddy's death if he'd gone out into the Iowa snows with a machine gun and pointed it straight into the sky.

The many photographs of himself that Petty left behind are scarcely more illuminating than the autobiographical symbols and effigies scratched on stone by the Clovis Man of 14,000 years earlier. Most of these date from his own years as a performing musician, the kind of glossy portrait meant to be displayed on scalloped boards outside cocktail lounges and supper clubs with TONITE printed slantwise in one corner. The face is a blandly good-looking one, its well-oiled hair forming a slight peak, its cheekbones curving with the symmetry of a ventriloquist's dummy's, its complexion airbrush-smooth, its butterfly bow perfectly tied. The expansive smile is professional rather than humorous, and kindles no corroborating warmth in the eyes, which are narrow, opaque, and calculating.

Here is a later study, taken at the height of the Buddy Holly era, when Petty (it's easy to forget) was himself still barely into his thirties. He is turning around from his wall-mounted Ampex recorder, wearing what looks like a short-sleeved shirt but what those who knew him say was more likely a one-piece jumpsuit in cotton or voile. He looks—and no one denies he was—meticulous, efficient, quiet, and polite. One can almost smell the antiseptic fragrance of aftershave and hand lotion that hung around him even in New Mexico's most punishing summer heat, and hear the softly mellow voice, full of long, reflective pauses, that Buddy did so often over the studio intercom. Can this really be the same creature Buddy's brother, Larry, is talking about in a Lubbock coffee shop, rubbing his arms as if to ward off an attack of goosepimples? "During World War Two, when I was with the military over on Saipan, I remember falling asleep one night in a foxhole with water up to my chin. Over there, you know, you get snails, measuring about ten inches to a foot across. When I woke up in the foxhole, there was this giant snail crawling right across my face. . . . Well, I tell you, I used to get just the same kind of feeling when I was around Norman Petty."

It so happens that our investigation into modern Clovis Man has turned up an archaeological find even richer than his crowded sarcophagus on West Seventh Street. By January 1959, when Buddy set out on that fatal tour of the blizzardy Midwest, he had fired Petty as his manager and record producer and begun legal action to recover the supposedly substantial sums in recording royalties that Petty had been "holding" for him. In the face of this lawsuit, to reassure himself that his business dealings could stand impartial scrutiny Petty turned over all the correspondence and financial records relating to Buddy and the Crickets to his banker in Clovis, with instructions to retain them for the three years required by the Internal Revenue Service, then destroy them.

But the banker did not destroy the papers and, after Petty's death in 1984, passed them on to a former friend and associate of the Petty family, who possesses them still and has agreed to open them for our inspection. We can, therefore, shine a light onto the innermost cave walls of our modern, secretive Clovis Man. We can examine contracts, ledgers, and tax returns, read lawyers' angry letters and telegrams; go through receipts for Buddy's guitars and clothes; handle the tickets and boarding passes for his famous British tour in 1958; see the canceled checks for his cars, dental work, and wedding ring; even read the heartbreakingly polite last letter he sent to Petty a couple of weeks before his death. To the self-seeking professional biographer, hungry for the "real" Buddy Holly story, it is a wildly exhilarating experience. But to the one-time English schoolboy, whose adolescence Buddy both brightened and soothed, it is horribly sad.

As is so often the case with those who cloak themselves in ostentatious secrecy, there was little about Petty's life that could be called exotic or dangerous. His father, Sydney, had been a migrant from the Oklahoma oilfields, stricken with tuberculosis and seeking a cure in New Mexico's high altitudes. Norman Eugene Petty was born in Clovis in May 1927 and brought up on the same spot where his studio complex later stood. The two-story building used to be a garage–gas station, run by a once more hale and vigorous Sydney and his wife, Margaret; the studio building was originally a small general store, run by Margaret's sister, Eula, and her husband.

Despite its busy railroad life, Clovis in the 1930s was a small, close-knit community, more village than city. Sydney and Margaret Petty were prominent local characters who made their garage a community focal point straight out of a *Saturday Evening Post* cover by Norman Rockwell. In addition to repairing cars, Pa Petty, as he was universally known, fixed domestic appliances, radios, and cameras; Ma Petty kept the books and pumped gas out front, in addition to raising a brood of four. Besides Norman there were two daughters, Edith and Shirley, and an older boy, Billy, who died at eighteen of leukemia—the same disease that would claim Norman at the age of fifty-seven. After Billy's death, both Ma and Pa Petty, but especially Ma, doted excessively on their "Normie."

Both parents were enthusiastic amateur musicians, Pa Petty playing the harmonica and Ma playing guitar at regular get-togethers with their neighbors. As a small boy, Normie astonished his parents by climbing up onto a piano stool and picking out tunes, such as "Under the Double

Eagle," after hearing them only once. As well as being able to play anything instantaneously by ear, he had such abnormal sensitivity to tone and pitch that he was soon getting lucrative work as a part-time piano tuner. A friend remembers: "He'd walk into a hall or a room before a concert, look around it once, and say 'An octave up from middle C, about F sharp, there's a dead spot.' When they checked it on the piano, he'd always be right. And if he ever heard a bad note, it almost brought him out in a rash."

His technical ingenuity also revealed itself when he was very young. His sister Shirley remembers how, when he was only eight or nine, he wired a microphone into the family radio so that he could broadcast his own shows through its speaker. In his teens he became a disc jockey, presenting a twice-daily program called *Musical Mailbag* on Clovis's station, KICA. He formed his first musical group, the Torchy Swingsters, and would record them on a wire-operated machine to see how to polish up their performance. He also invested his savings in a disc cutter, the only one in the Clovis area, and developed a profitable sideline in recording greetings from servicemen to their families and putting local politicians' campaign messages on disc, for broadcast by the area's radio stations.

At Clovis High School, he met a curly-haired, buxom girl named Violet Ann Brady, a carpenter's daughter who lived only a block or two away from the Petty garage. A year younger than Norman, Vi was an accomplished classical pianist, good enough to play duets with the school's director of music, and able to read—and write—the notes that Norman played by ear. He had never before shown much interest in girls, but Vi's skill on the piano, her talent as a singer, the impressive fact that her uncle had been a professor of music at the University of Oklahoma all helped create a bond. They began dating when he was eighteen and she seventeen; they continued to go steady while Petty did his military service in Norfolk, Virginia, and Vi completed her musical studies at the University of Oklahoma; in 1948, when he was twenty-one and she twenty, they married.

The marriage was cemented by a successful artistic partnership. Shortly after dropping out of Eastern New Mexico University, Petty had formed a musical trio consisting of himself, Vi, and a friend named Jack Vaughn, a former pro baseball pitcher. Petty played organ, Vaughn played guitar, Vi played piano and sang in the lush mid-forties big-band style of

Dinah Shore and Margaret Whiting. They were a self-contained unit, voyaging far and wide in a smart blue truck, always accompanied by Speedy, the Pettys' doted-on black chihuahua.

This was the era of pre-rock pop music, of Guy Mitchell's "Red Feathers," Rosemary Clooney's "Come On-a My House," Kay Starr's "Wheel of Fortune," Frankie Laine's "Jezebel." The Norman Petty Trio never made the premier league, but carved out a profitable niche. They recorded on the Columbia label and had two hits: one in 1954, a close-harmony vocal version of Duke Ellington's "Mood Indigo" (which Ellington himself publicly praised), the other in 1957, an instrumental written by Petty, "Almost Paradise." Petty, too, could sing, but chose to do so only rarely. One of the few surviving examples on record is a version of Hank Williams's "Jambalaya," in which he makes the Creole-accented call to "crawfish pie" and "ol' fruit jar" for "son-of-a-gun" highjinks on the bayou sound about as seductive as an impending dental checkup.

Recording for a major label, even one so large and prestigious as Columbia, was an unhappy experience for Petty. His technical perfectionism was affronted by the sloppiness with which his trio's sessions were often conducted, and the poor acoustics and reproduction quality grated against his fastidious musical ear. Most of all he hated the way that recording sessions were ruled by the clock. When a track had used up its scheduled studio time, finished or not, the A&R man would often simply shrug and let it go out as it was.

The royalties from "Mood Indigo" in 1954 helped Petty to realize his ambition of building a studio where, as well as recording his trio to his own exacting standards, he could be his own producer and engineer, and even cut the master copies of his own records. The studio duly took shape on West Seventh Street, Clovis, on the site of his Aunt Eula's old store, helped by a mortgage taken out on the adjacent family garage. Petty invested in state-of-the-art technology, ordering one of the new Ampex reel-to-reel tape-recorders, the type developed in Germany during World War II and until the early fifties used principally as a tool of the U.S. military. Petty's Ampex was only the second to be supplied for music recording, the first having gone to the guitar wizard Les Paul.

Elsewhere he had no choice but to use the primitive studio equipment of the day. His Altec single-channel recording board, for instance, was light-years away from modern custom-built, multitrack desks. A bulky gray object shaped rather like a Gladstone bag with thick black switches and single Geiger-counter dial, it was standard equipment at most radio and television stations. Where Petty could excel was in the acoustics of his single, small recording space, whose curved walls reflected sound to and from one another to infinity, ensuring no distortion or dead spots in any part of the room.

At first the studio was used exclusively by Petty's own trio for rehearsing and recording between extended spells on the road. Petty had developed close links with that ubiquitous New Mexico employer, the United States Air Force, and as time went on, more and more of the trio's live appearances were at USAF bases like White Sands or Las Cruces—lucrative, undemanding engagements that could last up to two months each as they moved around the various officers' and NCO clubs. If the trio had a concurrent recording commitment, Petty would take along his Ampex machine and, with the Air Force's indulgence, rig up an improvised studio in the corner of some officers'-club lounge. With the studio, he also established a music publishing company, Nor Va Jak Inc., formed from his trio's names, Norman, Violet Ann, and Jack. He continued to record local politicians' campaign messages, supplied the Air Force with packaged music programs, and also worked out of 1313 West Seventh as a professional photographer, covering weddings and civic functions.

No children came along to disrupt this industrious existence. Although the Pettys were still only in their mid-twenties, they always maintained they were too busy for the distractions of parenthood. While they were undoubtedly fond of each other, their friends believed their marriage to be primarily a professional relationship—that Norman had married Vi to secure assets for his trio: her keyboard skills; her singing voice; the fact that she could read music, and so could write out the lead sheets.

And Vi Petty, for all her assured musicianship and warmly sensuous singing voice, was a troubled, vulnerable soul. Her mother had suffered from schizophrenia and had to be institutionalized for several years during Vi's childhood. She herself manifested all the symptoms of the disease in its low-level, episodic form: hyperactivity, anxiety, squirrel-like acquisitiveness, chaotic disorganization. She was completely under Petty's control: he chose the gowns and shoes, even the hairstyles, she wore for her appearances with the trio. In their photographs together, Petty usually has a hand on Vi's shoulder in an almost conscious gesture of keeping her down. Between musical engagements, Vi let Norman take care of all business matters and spent most of her time working in the flower garden she had established around the studio and lavishing affection on Speedy, their chihuahua, and a long-haired cat named Squeaky.

The first outsider to cut a demo record at Petty's studio was a pixie-faced country singer named Jimmy Self, with his group the Sunshine Playboys. Thanks to the contacts Petty had built up in the East Coast music industry, he was subsequently able to get Self a record deal with Elvis Presley's future label, RCA Victor. Word of this success quickly spread among other local musicians, and Petty found himself with a waiting list of singers and groups wishing to avail themselves of his studio's perfect acoustics and his own engineering expertise. The Western Union clock, accurate to the millisecond, that hung on his control-room wall was the least used item of Petty's equipment. Remembering how his own creativity had been stifled by clock-watching, he did not rent his studio facilities by the hour, but instead charged a flat fee for recording each song. The musicians could thus feel free to hone and polish their compositions without constant fear of someone calling "Time." To maintain creative flow at the maximum, there was a kitchen with a well-stocked refrigerator where they could eat, rather than dispersing to restaurants, and a comfortable living room–bedroom where they could relax, or go to sleep.

All this was not quite the openhanded philanthropy it might appear. Petty, in fact, operated on much the same contingency basis as do beady-eyed modern lawyers. If any record made in his studio, with his help and expertise, and networked through his New York contacts, turned out to be a success, it was understood that he'd expect the lion's share of its profits, taking some of the composer's royalties even if he had not written a word or note of it, and also publishing it via his Nor Va Jak company. In his defense, Petty argued that he was gambling time and money; that in the East Coast music world, appropriating a writer's credit was a standard A&R man's perquisite; and that anyway, most of the songs were unlikely ever to earn a cent.

Musicians also had to accept that recording at Norman Petty's studio meant a suspension of their normal manners and customs. A regular and vociferous worshiper at Clovis's Central Baptist Church, Petty did not allow drinking or swearing on the premises and, though he could not actually ban smoking, frigidly disapproved of that also. He kept a Bible near him at all times and, after a particularly good take, was apt to suggest that the musicians put down their instruments, form a circle, join hands, and offer up an impromptu prayer of thanksgiving.

The dawn of the rock 'n' roll era initially made little impression on Petty, even though two of its earliest pioneers materialized under his very nose. Early in 1956, a wispy, chinless teenager named Roy Orbison, from the tiny hamlet of Wink, Texas, came to Clovis with his group, the Teen Kings, to make several demo tracks, including a rock 'n' roll number called "Ooby Dooby." Orbison subsequently moved on to join the rockabilly stable of Sun Records in Memphis along with Elvis Presley, Carl Perkins, and Johnny Cash; he had a minor hit with "Ooby Dooby," but was not to achieve international success until turning to high-decibel ballads like "Only the Lonely" in 1960.

Later in 1956, Petty's studio and engineering services were booked by another West Texas group, the Rhythm Orchids, who had recently appeared in concert with Elvis Presley and been advised by him to get in on the ground floor of rock 'n' roll. The Rhythm Orchids produced their own demo tracks, which included a song called "Party Doll" written by their singer, Buddy Knox, a handsome youth who'd grown up on a farm in Happy, Texas. Since the studio drummer, David Alldred, alias Dickie Do, could not muster a full kit, the beat for "Party Doll" was produced by pounding drumsticks on a cotton-filled cardboard box.

Petty recognized that the Rhythm Orchids had potential, but the lyrics of "Party Doll" (which included the refrain "I'll make love to you") offended his religious sensibilities and he preferred not to try to market "a dirty song" among the New York record companies. He was to rue this decision for, having released a single locally at their own expense, the Rhythm Orchids were offered a deal by a brand-new East Coast label called Roulette. Instead of marketing them as a group, Roulette cleverly conjured two separate hit-making vocalists from their lineup. "Party Doll" by Buddy Knox, with its catchy box-bashing beat, went to No. 1 in March 1957; "I'm Sticking With You," by his colleague Jimmy Bowen, reached No. 11 a month later.

Despite Petty's growing reputation throughout the Southwest, the menage at 1313 West Seventh Street continued to be a picturesque one. His parents' garage was still in business in the building next to his studio, with Pa Petty repairing cars, Ma pumping gas out front, and the couple living in a ground-floor apartment at the rear. Ma also oversaw the studio accounts, and was even empowered by her son to sign checks on his behalf with a shaky counterfeit "Norman Petty" that only such a tolerant hometown institution as the Clovis National Bank would have honored. The fifth member of the household was Petty's secretary–bookkeeper, Norma Jean Berry, a one-time local journalist who'd originally come to the studio to do a newspaper story about him and, somehow, never left. Muscular of build and masculine of dress, with a deep, gruff voice, Norma Jean was devoted to Petty, and the faithful, unquestioning executor of his every command.

Petty's rather effeminate looks, his fastidious manners, his addiction to strongly scented toiletries, his taste for collarless shirts decorated with little elephants—above all, the fact that the raw material of his business was relays of young men—inevitably produced rumors that he might be homosexual. Even wilder speculation was generated by the burly figure of Norma Jean, who conformed in almost every way to the stereotype of the "butch" lesbian and whose relationship with the Pettys was clearly far more than simply clerical. Intermittent gossip had it that Vi Petty and Norma Jean carried on a lesbian relationship; that Norma Jean and Norman Petty had once had an affair; even that the three participated in ménage-à-trois sexual acts. The truth appears to have been that all three, for different reasons, were virtually sexless, and that Norma Jean clung to the Pettys as her surrogate family.

If Petty was not gay, he certainly behaved like someone with a similar deep, dark secret, continually baffling even so close a personal and business associate as his original country music protégé, Jimmy Self. "I knew Norman for something like twenty-five years," Self says. "And every day I spent with him, I seemed to find out something new about him."

Partly as a result of living with the frantic and chaotic Vi, Petty developed a parallel secret life that would have done credit to a Soviet spy or fugitive Nazi war criminal. "When Norman was working with musicians in the studio, he'd be there all the time, taking care of every detail," Jimmy Self remembers. "But in between sessions, he'd disappear completely. He had hideouts all over town, some of them offices for corporations he'd set up without telling Vi, with their own phone numbers, stationery, and checkbooks. Norman would be in one of these secret offices, doing gosh-only-knows-what, for hours on end. Sometimes we'd find he'd just taken off to New York, the West Coast . . . even to Europe. The first Vi knew about it would be when he'd call her up, saying "I'm in L.A." or "I'm in London.""

So may we begin to construct an archaeological profile of modern Clovis Man: technically brilliant but creatively mediocre; a visionary in some respects but in others a blinkered, small-town wheeler-dealer; ostensibly a self-effacing, boffin and backroom-boy, yet with a ravening ego, watchful for any chance to use the talent of the young musicians who passed through his hands for his own profit and advancement; in his own tiny sphere, a figure of absolute power, surrounded by people who never challenged his authority and judgment, and thus able to dwell in his own moral universe, beatifically convinced that in all his dealings, however questionable, he was the very soul of reason and rectitude.

And let us not forget, very, very mean. Petty was never frugal especially not with himself, and was capable of generosity to his wife, parents, and friends. But he was one of those people who value money beyond any power or luxury it can buy and who suffer real anguish when forced to part with it. The various local friends and acquaintances persuaded to work at the Petty studio as session musicians or backup singers mostly had to resign themselves to doing so for free. Among these were two brothers, John and Bill Pickering, who sang as a duo and had known Petty since high school. "Norman would always be as nice as pie," Bill Pickering remembers. "He'd talk to you, encourage you, praise you, and feed you—I mean real good food, steaks and everything. But he'd never give you a dime."

Dr. Jerry Fisher, who worked as an engineer for Petty in later years, believes him to have been a classic case of arrested development: "Norman missed a crucial stage in his evolution: he went straight from being a baby to being an adult. That explains his sexlessness. Like a child, he regarded everyone else as there to validate and accommodate him. Like a child, all he wanted to do was play with his toys, his studio and his equipment. He couldn't—and didn't—deal with anything which got in the way of that. How else could a businessman and impresario like Norman claimed to be let his mother sign his checks? All his life he was just 'Baby Norman.'"

One day toward the end of January 1957, Jimmy Self was at the Petty studio, recording a radio spot for a local politician, when he noticed yet another group of young musicians rehearsing in the studio area. "Their leader stood out because he wore a maroon shirt and because his legs were so long that his Levi's flapped above his ankles," Self remembers.

"And he wore glasses, which was kind of unusual to see on a young musician in those days.

"Norman forgot what we were working on and said, 'Oh, gosh, I have to go and see that guy, Buddy Holly. I'm going to record him.' I said, 'Norman, he doesn't look like he can afford it.' 'No, he can't,' Norman said. 'So I guess I'm going to have to finance him.'

"I said, 'He plays great guitar, Norman. But I don't think he'll ever make a singer.'"

☆ ☆ ☆

Buddy had known about the Norman Petty Recording Studio since his earliest semipro country music days. In March 1954, Don Guess had written him an enthusiastic four-page letter from El Paso, suggesting that their then group, the Rhythm Playboys, try out this new place in Clovis the next time they scraped up enough to finance a demo. Instead, as their style mutated through bluegrass to rock 'n' roll, the habit stuck of using KDAV or Nesman's studio in Wichita Falls. It was not until the early spring of 1956, between his first two sessions for Decca in Nashville, that Buddy finally decided to see what the Petty studio had to offer. Backed by Don, Sonny Curtis, and J. I. Allison, he cut six of his own compositions, "Baby, Won't You Come Out Tonight," "I Guess I Was Just a Fool," "Because I Love You," "I'm Gonna Set My Foot Down," "I'm Changing All Those Changes," and "Rock-a-Bye Rock." According to Petty, Buddy hoped to persuade Decca to let him record for them in Clovis rather than at Bradley's unsympathetic barn in Nashville.

The person who aroused Petty's interest at that first session was not Buddy but his group's second featured guitarist, the chubby and personable Sonny Curtis. It so happened that the guitarist in Petty's own trio, Jack Vaughn, had just announced his resignation, thereby putting many lucrative Air Force bookings in jeopardy. A couple of days later, Sonny was surprised to get a phone call from Petty asking him to return to Clovis on his own. "Norman invited me up to that apartment he had above the garage, and gave me cookies and milk. I'm sitting there, eating these macaroons, feeling as uncomfortable as a hog upstairs. Norman's telling me that if I'll be in his trio, he'll buy me my own electric guitar and I'll be headed for the big time, and I'm thinking 'Hey! Great gig, man!'

"Then he takes me across to the studio for an audition, and I realize that if I joined up with him, I'd have to spend my life playing slow old things like 'Honeysuckle Rose.' Buddy begged me not to quit as well, so I turned it down. And after that, I don't believe Norman liked me until the day he died."

The thought of Petty as a possible savior did not seriously cross Buddy's mind until the end of 1956, after his second Decca single had flopped and he was knocking around Lubbock, resigned to the idea that his contract would be terminated any day. In the tight, mutually supportive circle of West Texas rockabilly, he had become good friends with the Rhythm Orchids and Roy Orbison, and from both quarters had heard how recording at Petty's studio had been a kick-start to bigger and better things. Further encouragement came from his old Sunday-school classmate Terry Noland, who now worked with Larry Welborn in a group called the Four Teens, but whose distinctive voice and good looks had inspired Petty to promote him as a solo singer. Noland remembers Buddy riding up to his house on a motorcycle, sunk in gloom over the Decca business. "I said, 'Why don't you go see Norman? He's got me a recording contract. Maybe he can get you one.'"

Amid the encircling despondency, that January of 1957 contained one bright spot. Back in hopeful 1956, when Buddy and the Two-Tones still enjoyed the prestige of Decca recording artists, a concert promoter named A. W. Bamford had signed them up for their second professional tour, a major road show featuring Hank Thompson, Wanda Jackson, Hank Locklin, Mitchell Torok, and Cowboy Copas, and visiting fourteen cities scattered through Arkansas, Louisiana, Georgia, Alabama, Tennessee, and Florida. The entire bill was country with the exception of Mitchell Torok, who had a novelty hit single titled "When Mexico Gave Up the Rumba to Do the Rock and Roll." But at least Buddy's group were featured artists rather than just fill-ins, though they also had the job of backing other acts on the bill. Afterward, in his usual punctilious way, Buddy wrote to the promoter, apologizing for the fact that they'd been "a little green," but saying he thought the experience had helped them.

In fact, the Hank Thompson tour saw the end of the quartet that had struggled so hard to make it on the Decca label. When they returned home, both Don Guess and Sonny Curtis decided to quit. Don had never been able to afford his own bass fiddle, and the one on loan from Lubbock High School had been so badly knocked about by traveling on car roof racks that its scroll was now completely broken off. And Sonny, despite his genial nature, was miffed by Buddy's growing tendency to play lead guitar as well as sing. Offered another tour, this time with the country giant Slim Whitman, he jumped at the chance and went out on the road, destined for his own glory as a performer and songwriter, but never to play in a group of Buddy's again, at least not during Buddy's lifetime.

As a replacement for Don Guess, Buddy turned to Larry Welborn, who had played bass for Bob Montgomery and him back in schoolboy country days on radio KDAV. Larry agreed to fill in, but was not always available for gigs since he also was still playing rhythm guitar in the Four Teens. There was also the problem of finding a new guitarist content to play rhythm chords in Buddy's—and the Stratocaster's—lengthening shadow. The solution materialized in nineteen-year-old Niki Sullivan, who happened to turn up with his brand-new semi-cutaway cello guitar at one of their living-room jam sessions. A distant cousin of Buddy's—though they only found this out much later—Niki had much the same lanky build and also wore glasses, albeit with slightly more modish transparent frames. He did not consider himself musically talented and was amazed to be asked to join Buddy's group without any kind of serious audition.

At the tail-end of January, with the Hank Thompson tour behind him and no other prospect ahead, Buddy returned to the Norman Petty Studio with Jerry Allison and Larry Welborn. This time they recorded just two tracks: Chuck Berry's "Brown-Eyed Handsome Man" and "Bo Diddley," the only song a composer ever had the hubris to name after himself. Black rock 'n' roll performers had by this point become resigned to the taming and homogenization of their songs by bland white balladeers like Pat Boone. Buddy's interpretations both respected the originals and lifted them to his own plane of humor and exuberance.

By now, the cold-eyed, not-quite-handsome man watching through control-room glass had ceased to be merely an impassive technician. "I was amazed at the intensity and at the honesty and sincerity of [Buddy's] whole approach to music," Petty remembered afterward. "Of course, it was completely foreign to what I had known. . . . Our trio had played mainly in hotel dining rooms and country clubs. And so to see someone so honest and so completely himself was super-refreshing. He wasn't the world's most handsome guy, he didn't have the world's most beautiful voice, but he was himself."

Vi Petty, too, who had initially thought the quartet "real gangly" in their T-shirts and Levi's, was impressed by their professionalism as well as charmed by their old-fashioned politeness. The end result was everything Buddy had hoped. Petty told him to write a couple of new songs, bring his group back at the end of February, and they'd work on putting together a single.

The crucial factor in getting the Rhythm Orchids their deal with Roulette Records had been the sister of their guitarist Donnie Lanier, a glamorous girl named Tuddie who worked as a shoe model in New York and mixed socially with Roulette's boss, the gangsterlike Morris Levy.

Donnie's other sister, June Clark, also had the face and figure of a mannequin, but had opted to stay in Lubbock, get married at sixteen, have a son, and work at the cosmetics counter of the Hull drugstore. In early 1957, June, too, found herself being drawn into a Lubbock music scene that suddenly seemed full of burgeoning talent. June's cousin Gary Tollett was also a singer, ambitious to follow the Rhythm Orchids onto the Roulette label. On February 21 Gary booked a recording session at the KDAV studio, recruited his wife Ramona and June Clark as backup singers, and asked June whether she could find a drummer and a guitarist to accompany them. "I was advised to call Jerry Allison, who said he'd do the session, and did I mind if he brought his own guitarist along?" June remembers. "And the guitarist he brought was Buddy Holly."

The session went well, producing tracks that did ultimately help Gary Tollett to a recording contract on a subsidiary of Roulette. As a quid pro quo, Gary and his wife offered to be backup singers for Buddy's session at the Petty studio, four days hence.

The problem immediately arose of where to rehearse this new, augmented group. Both Buddy's and J. I.'s parents had always made their living rooms freely available, but even they were likely to balk at the presence of six people. Then June Clark made a fateful suggestion. With her husband James and herself both out at work all day and their eleven-year-old son, Carley, at school, their house on Second Place was empty but for June's grandmother, Ada. "And we had this big den with not much furniture in it, which I told them would be great as a rehearsal room."

Buddy, meantime, had been running through the dozen or so songs he had written and recorded over the past year, and arguing with Jerry and with Larry Welborn about which might be the most commercial. They kept coming back to the least promising outtake from Buddy's second Decca session, the song he and Jerry had knocked off in half an hour, inspired by John Wayne's laconic catchphrase in *The Searchers*. Even though its title now seemed an all-too-apt commentary on Buddy's struggle to succeed, they decided to try again with "That'll Be the Day."

Over four days of intensive rehearsal in the Clarks' den, the song underwent drastic revision. Where the Decca version had been strained and over-echoey, this one was lower in key and a little slower, allowing Buddy's voice to be both more relaxed and more polished, hinting at rather than showing off the gymnastics of which it was capable. His word-fracturing hiccup was used only once, but to effect, transforming an otherwise clichéd bridge: "Well, you give me all your lovin' and your tu-(hic)-urtle-dovin'." The Stratocaster moved to the foreground with a janglier version of the Hank Ballard intro, and a middle solo, borrowing the two-note bass riff from another Decca outtake, "Ting-A-Ling." The most crucial new element was the background chorus of Gary and Ramona Tollett and the new rhythm guitarist, Niki Sullivan, chiming with Buddy's voice on the refrain, then supplying a blurry undertow of "ooh" and "aah" that owed something to R&B but even more to the choirs that could be heard in any of Lubbock's numerous churches.

In the late afternoon of February 24, 1957, a bright red '55 Cadillac bowled along the two-lane blacktop from Lubbock to Clovis, beside the hotel-size grain elevators and the tracks of the Santa Fe. The Caddy was Buddy's latest bandwagon, largely financed by his brother Larry—and destined to be returned to Furrs Auto, "shot" inside six months. With the barely restricted speeds and tolerant police of those days, the game was to maintain an average speed of 90 mph–plus so that, with the hour gained at the New Mexico border, they would reach Clovis at the same time, or even a couple of minutes before, they had left Lubbock. On this momentous trip, Larry Holley also went along to do the driving and keep order as best he could. "Buddy and Jerry together were quite a handful," he remembers. "They'd holler or make signs at guys in other cars, then the other guys'd chase us, wanting to fight. I'd have to get out there and calm things down. One or two times, I'd end up having a fight myself."

At the last moment during rehearsals, Buddy had come up with another new song to submit to Norman Petty, a jaunty country-flavored number called "I'm Looking for Someone to Love." He still had not finished it when they set off for Clovis and, Larry remembers, spent most of the journey in the back seat with his guitar, vamping lines that were a light-hearted comment on his own emotional predicament: separated from Echo McGuire, wondering who she might be dating in Abilene, "playing the field" himself in preemptive retaliation, but unable to stop "thinkin' of you." When they crossed the train tracks that mark the state line with New Mexico, he was still stuck for a final verse. "The bump-bump of our tires over the railroad tracks gave me an idea," Larry remembers. "I said, 'Why don't you use that saying of Uncle Henry Drake's: "Drunk man / Streetcar / Foot slip / There you are"?' Buddy says 'Yeah, that might do pretty good.'"

Recording sessions at the Petty studio could not begin until late evening, when Ma Petty had closed the gas pump on the forecourt outside and trucks had ceased to rumble along West Seventh Street. Buddy and his six-person ensemble spent the first three or four hours purely in rehearsal, the first-comers noting with surprise that Petty's control desk did not overlook the studio but was set sidelong to it, as if to remove all distraction from the exercise of his hypersensitive ears. By the time Petty was in his gray leather chair, ready to flip the switch on his Altec board for take one, "I'm Looking for Someone to Love" had superseded "That'll Be the Day" as the A-side of the projected single. With more churchy backup vocals by the Tolletts and Niki Sullivan, and Buddy's wild, two-chiming rockabilly guitar break, it seemed to have everything, not least the virtue of being brand-new rather than a tarted-up outtake. In the light of what Petty was later to claim about his creative input, it's worth noting Gary Tollett's observation: "When we started, Buddy had the whole arrangement worked out. All Norman did was set up the microphones."

They worked on "I'm Looking for Someone to Love" for the greater part of the session, ending up with a jaunty, polished rockabilly romp that tailed off in the mock-melancholy "Waaa" of an old-fashioned glee club. Not until almost 3 A.M. did they finally get around to "That'll Be the Day." "There was a party atmosphere by that time," Tollett remembers. "We were having fun, not concentrating real hard, like we had with 'I'm Looking for Someone to Love.' At about the fourth take, Norman said 'okay, that's it.' I couldn't believe we had a finished record. I thought it was more like a demo he could send to New York to show some record company what potential the song had."

For the free use of his studio, his technical expertise, and his flawless ear for pitch, and for the East Coast connections he would now bring into play, Petty demanded the customary quid pro quo. Not only must "I'm Looking for Someone to Love" and "That'll Be the Day" be published by his Nor Va Jak company, giving him 50 percent of their publishing revenues, but his name must appear on both songs as a co-composer. No matter that Buddy had finished "I'm Looking for Someone to Love" before even reaching Clovis that day, no matter even that "That'll Be the Day" had been written by Buddy and J. I. Allison months before Petty agreed to take them on, and had already been recorded for Decca with their two names as the sole composing credit.

Petty's argument was blandly simple, as Niki Sullivan remembers: "He said that people in the music industry knew him because of his trio, so record companies and disc jockeys and people would be more likely to take an interest if they saw the name 'Norman Petty' instead of just some unknown kid from West Texas. And anyway he claimed he had helped to write the songs in a way, by getting them to sound right in the studio and making suggestions all along the line. Buddy didn't care; he was just delighted to think that the songs were going to be published, and that someone like Norman believed in him and was going to push him in New York. And Norman told us that was the way it always happened. We had no choice but to take him at his word."

What cannot be gainsaid was the acuteness of Petty's ear. Untutored though he was in rock 'n' roll, he instantly realized that the polished and catchy "I'm Looking for Someone to Love" was not half so strong a track as the casually dashed off "That'll Be the Day." Before the song could be offered on the open market, however, two ticklish contractual matters needed resolving. The first was that Buddy had co-written "That'll Be the Day" while under contract to Jim Denny's Cedarwood publishing company, which gave Cedarwood an automatic, preemptive claim on the new version's publishing revenues, if any. Petty later talked Denny into trading his 50 percent of "That'll Be the Day" for full rights in another, much less valuable Buddy song, "Think It Over" (which Denny must have done with extreme resentment many times afterward).

A more serious problem was that although Decca had never shown the slightest desire to release their inferior version of "That'll Be the Day," Buddy was still bound by his contract with them not to rerecord any of the material from the Nashville sessions for a period of five years. On February 28, with the new Clovis version already four days in the can, he made a long-distance call from Jerry Allison's parents' house in Lubbock to Milt Gabler, vice president at Decca, New York, hoping that, since Decca seemed to have no further use for him, they might release him from this lingering obligation. But Gabler was not available, and Buddy had no choice but to plead for clemency with his old adversary, Paul Cohen. For mysterious reasons, the call was taped at Buddy's end; one can thus share the instant crushing of his hopes, the change in Cohen's manner from indifference to suspicion, and the obvious discomfort of a good Baptist boy trapped into telling a lie:

COHEN: No . . . anything you made for Decca, even if they never released . . . You can't make it for five years for anyone . . .
BUDDY: Hm, well . . . okeydokey then. I guess that . . .
COHEN: Don't feel bad about it.
BUDDY: I can't hardly keep from it, Paul . . . It seems sorta a heck of a way to do a guy . . .
COHEN: You haven't made any of these yet, have you? I mean cut 'em for anybody?
BUDDY: No, sir.
COHEN: Well, before you do, let me know. Maybe we can work out something . . .
BUDDY: Well, we was wanting to just about any time now.
COHEN: Huh?
BUDDY: We was wanting to cut a master like you said on our own, pay for it ourselves and see if we could sell it to somebody.
COHEN: Let me hear it first . . .

Petty was equally incensed by Decca's dog-in-the-manger attitude, and offered a solution of appealing deviousness. If "That'll Be the Day" were to be marketed as the work of a group, like the Inkspots or the Platters, and the credits did not mention Buddy's name, chances were that Paul Cohen might never realize he was the vocalist. One of Buddy's favorite R&B groups was the Spiders, and a few nights later he, J. I. Allison, and Niki Sullivan sat in J. I's bedroom, going through the entymological section of an encyclopedia in the hope of finding some other creepy-crawly with which to baptize themselves. They thought, prophetically, of the Beetles, but discarded it when J. I. protested that he didn't want to be named after "a little black bug you'd step on." Eventually they decided on the Crickets, liking the definition of a cricket as "an insect romantically referred to as making music by rubbing its hind legs together."

☆   ☆   ☆

The initial reaction to "That'll Be the Day" was anything but encouraging. And, for a while, it appeared that Norman Petty's much-vaunted New York connections were not so very much help after all.

An early, resounding slap in the face came from the Roulette label, which had not yet had its two hits with Buddy Knox and Jimmy Bowen of the Rhythm Orchids and had no wish to take a chance on a second group from faraway West Texas. Knox tried to soften the disappointment by suggesting that the Rhythm Orchids might record a cover version of "That'll Be the Day." But, while appreciating that kind thought, the less successful of the two Buddys was determined it would be his rendering the public heard first.

Actually, Buddy Knox, Jimmy Bowen, and a good many others around the West Texas music scene wondered whether Roulette's indifference to the Crickets might not have something to do with their name. "Everyone kept telling us what a dumb thing we'd decided to call ourselves," Niki Sullivan remembers. "It was kind of embarrassing even for the people who had to introduce us on shows. 'What, crickets? Like the bug?' they'd say. 'Are you guys really serious?'"

Petty, meanwhile, was having no better luck with Columbia, the label on which his own trio recorded. Columbia's head of A&R was the orchestra leader Mitch Miller, a bald, black-bearded cross between virtuoso and vampire, famous for his singalong albums and for the oracular pronouncement "Rock 'n' roll is just a passing fad. I give it six months." It proved of no help whatever that Petty was on friendly terms with Mitch Miller—nor even that the Miller orchestra's big 1955 hit had been "The Yellow Rose of Texas." The singalong Prince of Darkness hated "That'll Be the Day," and advised Petty not to waste his time by offering it elsewhere.

After Miller's rebuff, Petty gave up on record companies and decided to try the more roundabout music publishing route that had won Buddy his original break in Nashville. Petty's Nor-Va-Jak company had for some years had a tie-in deal with Peer-Southern Music, a New York publishing firm with an international reputation and an impressive, though largely non–rock 'n' roll catalog. Traveling to New York, where he maintained both an office and an apartment, Petty called on Peer-Southern's general manager, a stocky, humorous man named Murray Deutch. "He brought me this demo, which he said nobody wanted, and asked me if I could do anything to help," Deutch remembers. "That was Norman all over. He only came to you when he needed you. I'd done business with him for a number of years, he fed me some good songs, but I can't say there was any warmth between the two of us. Warmth wasn't something you got with Norman Petty. He was the kind of a guy who'd give you ice in the wintertime."

On hearing "That'll Be the Day," however, Murray Deutch's frostiness evaporated. "I could tell immediately that it had something totally special. Rock 'n' roll . . . rockabilly . . . whatever it was, I just flipped out for it." A deal was instantly struck. Deutch agreed to take over the job of getting the Crickets a record deal; in exchange, Peer-Southern Music would receive half the publishing rights to "That'll Be the Day" and "I'm Looking for Someone to Love."

Murray Deutch was well known as an expert talent-spotter, having brought, among others, the era's top black vocal group, the Platters, into the Peer-Southern fold. But even with Deutch behind it, "That'll Be the Day" continued to run into blank walls. Larry Newton, the head of A&R at ABC Records, passed on it without a qualm, as did Jerry Wexler, the usually unerring creative genius behind the Atlantic label. "Even to this day, whenever I meet Jerry, he always comes up with the same line," Deutch says. "'You were right, you bastard!'"

The one response that was anything like positive came from Bob Thiele, head of A&R for the Coral label and husband to one of Coral's main female singing attractions, Teresa Brewer. Ironically, Coral was a subsidiary of Decca, the company which—unknown to Murray Deutch —had already run Buddy through the X-ray machine and rejected him. Thiele, likewise, had no inkling of this unhappy past history, since Coral functioned quite separately from the main Decca label, as well as at a considerably lower level of prestige.

Though primarily a jazz enthusiast, Thiele was not anti–rock 'n' roll and had already worked with another pioneer country-rock act, Johnny Burnette. But Coral's roster consisted largely of mainstream and exceedingly square pop names like Debbie Reynolds, the McGuire Sisters, the Lawrence Welk Orchestra, and Thiele's wife, Teresa Brewer. While agreeing with Murray Deutch that "That'll Be the Day" had an unusual and compelling sound, he knew he could expect trouble from his superiors if he were to attempt such a radical departure from Coral's house style. "But

I knew Bob liked the song, so I kept on and on at him," Deutch remembers. "'Bob—get outta here! Go press a thousand copies! How could that hurt anyone?'"

When Thiele played "That'll Be the Day" to a flock of senior Decca executives, the reaction was unanimously hostile. The jury did not include Paul Cohen; consequently, no one present had the faintest idea that the lead voice of the Crickets belonged to a solo singer whom their organization had unceremoniously dumped a few months earlier. Still less was it dreamed that the song itself had already been recorded for the Decca label, and was legally prohibited from being shopped around in this revamped version. It was as theoretically brand-new material that it made Decca's high-ups wince. The company's president, Milt Rachmil, warned Bob Thiele that to market such a noise would not only damage Coral's image but also have all its greatest treasures, like Debbie, the McGuires, and Larry Welk, up in arms.

With Murray Deutch still good-humoredly riding him, Thiele came up with a solution that would respect the sensitivities of his superiors and still give "That'll Be the Day" a crack at the charts. A Decca subsidiary label even more marginal than Coral was Brunswick, once famous as the mouthpiece for Bing Crosby, but now catering mainly to the unfashionable and barely profitable jazz market. Thiele proposed to release "That'll Be the Day" on Brunswick, thus keeping Coral's precious image intact, and pressing only a hyper-cautious 1,000 copies. "They agreed to let me do it, but no one else in the company thought it was really serious," Thiele remembered. "It was more like 'Oh, Bob wants to do this. Let him get his kicks.'"

That this whole tortuous saga should have been compressed within less than three weeks gives some idea of the frenetic pace at which the record business operated in the rock 'n' roll fever of early 1957. "That'll Be the Day" and "I'm Looking for Someone to Love" had been recorded on February 25; by March 19, Norman Petty had Bob Thiele's written agreement to purchase the two master recordings on Brunswick's behalf for a $100 advance. It was the kind of derisory sum that most labels would have paid an unknown, but the royalty rate itself, just over 2 cents per record sold, was generous in the circumstances. Many newcomers in that era would have received 1 or 1.5 cents, and been ecstastic about it.

The four Crickets summoned to Clovis for the signing ceremony were not, however, the same four who had recorded "That'll Be the Day." On

March 3, bass player Larry Welborn had been unable to make a $65 gig at the Elks Club in Carlsbad, New Mexico. To take his place, Buddy had borrowed the Four Teens' bass player, a diminutive, round-faced sixteen-year-old named Joe B. (for Benson) Mauldin. Compared with Welborn and the departed Don Guess, Joe B. was anything but a wizard on bass. His great virtue was that he had his own instrument, and didn't have to rent or borrow one each time a gig came up. It was to bring that impressive piece of furniture into the Crickets, more than for the sound Joe B. was likely to conjure from it, that Buddy asked him to replace Larry Welborn permanently.

"Buddy was real confident about the way things were going," Joe B. remembers. "He told me the group had just made a record—they were headed straight for the big time. Of course, I'd heard that one so many times before. I said 'Oh yeah? How long d'you think it'll take you?' Buddy said, 'How long'd it take Elvis?' "

So Joe B. agreed to become a Cricket, on the condition that it not interfere with his day job as a butcher's assistant at a Lubbock supermarket.

The Bible that never lay far from Norman Petty's right hand played its part in the contract signing. J. I., Niki, and Joe B., like Buddy, came from devoutly religious families, and all readily accepted Petty's suggestion that they each pay 10 percent of their earnings, the customary tithe, to their respective churches. Before the signing, Petty placed his hand on the Bible, the four Crickets laid their hands on top of his, and all joined in a silent moment of thanksgiving and prayer for the future.

The signatures were then ceremonially appended: "Jerry Allison," "Niki Sullivan," "Joe B. Mauldin," the latter somewhat bemused at thus receiving shares in a record on which he hadn't played. But not "Buddy Holly." To keep Decca in the dark about his involvement for as long as possible, Buddy's name did not appear on the Crickets' first contract. So far as Bob Thiele knew at this stage, the group consisted of three young men named Allison, Sullivan, and Mauldin. Buddy accepted his anonymity willingly enough, still nervous that Paul Cohen or some other Decca high-up would realize he had broken his original contract with the company and veto the release of "That'll Be the Day." But it was a decision that would cause him much trouble and grief in months to come.

☆   ☆   ☆

Between the signing of the contract and the release of the record there was to be a wait of almost three months. During that time, Buddy and the Crickets did little else as a group but record at the Petty studio, under Petty's supervision and at his expense. Whatever faults history may impute to Clovis Man, shortsightedness was not among them. Convinced now of Buddy's potential, he was prepared to go on investing time and resources in him, whether or not his debut single became a success.

Barely a fortnight after recording "That'll Be the Day," and before the faintest breath of good news from New York, Buddy, J. I., and Niki scooped up their new bass player, Joe B. Mauldin, from his supermarket butcher's counter and hurtled out along Route 84, as usual trying to make it to Clovis a couple of minutes before the time they'd left Lubbock. Under Petty's supervision they began working on a song called "Maybe Baby," written—or at least started off—by Buddy's mother ("Just to prove I can write a song, too") and destined to be an international hit more than a year into the future.

Petty's motives were, of course, hardly altruistic. Having chanced on yet another bright recording prospect, he was not about to let him slip through his fingers the way Buddy Knox and Jimmy Bowen had a few months earlier. Giving young Buddy Holly and his group free studio time, cutting master discs from their tapes, feeding them generously, even occasionally letting them stay overnight in the musicians' dormitory room, all cost Petty little enough in real terms. As he accurately sensed, this atmosphere of openhanded hospitality impressed the young Texans deeply, especially after their Nashville experience, binding them to Petty's studio with ties more inescapable than any formal contract. For, as their new producer confided to his friend Jimmy Self in an unguarded moment, he could "almost smell dollar bills here."

Yet there is no doubt that Petty genuinely liked his four new protégés and in their company became a person very different from the cool, detached technician who normally occupied the gray leather swivel chair. Indeed, the exhilaration of working on early tracks like "Maybe Baby" and another new Buddy composition, "Last Night," had the effect of making Petty positively frisky. Though only nine years older than Buddy, he took to addressing the Crickets as "boys" and characterizing himself as "Papa Norman," as if he were some grizzled Hemingway figure or garrulous old-timer in a John Wayne Western. This could be interpreted as another subtle way of underlining his authority, and of giving weight to his ban on drinking and cussing, his abhorrence of cigarette smoking, and his ever-ready recourse to corroborative passages in the Scriptures. To his friend Jerry Fisher, it was yet another symptom of arrested development. "Treating Buddy and the others like children was easier than having children of his own. And they could all be kids and play games together."

With Buddy, he had a special rapport from the beginning. Despite Buddy's youth, there was a maturity about him that the older professional musician recognized and respected. Accustomed though Petty was to having things his own way in the studio, he would always ask Buddy for his views on how a song should be arranged and engineered, adopting Buddy's ideas and deferring to his objections. The lanky Texan in his simple Levi's and T-shirt and the chubby-faced New Mexican in his effete lounging clothes also had more in common than might at first meet he eye. There was, for example, that habit of getting up abruptly from among a crowd of friends or colleagues and disappearing for hours on end—Buddy on his solitary nighttime drives, Petty to his various secret bolt-holes around Clovis. "The two of them were bound to hit it off well," says Jimmy Self. "They were both perfectionists—and both loners."

Even on days when Petty was not working with them, Buddy, J. I., Niki, and Joe B. would still make that clock-cheating drive to Clovis and hang out at the studio, sprawling on the couch in its tiny reception area, feeding dimes into the red and white Coke machine and gossiping with Petty's gruff-voiced secretary, Norma Jean Berry, or wandering around the grassy compound where the Petty Trio's blue truck awaited its next foray to White Sands or Las Cruces and Vi Petty tended her strawberry bed in dungarees and bandanna, as ever lost in a world of her own. Clovis Man's recently excavated paperwork reveals that Buddy took advantage of one visit to have the group's long-suffering red Caddy looked over by Pa Petty in the adjacent family garage. Norma Jean, the former journalist, also took what would be the Crickets' earliest publicity photographs, in their white T-shirts looking more like Pa's supernumerary mechanics than rock 'n' roll hitmakers-in-waiting.

In partial payment of their mounting debt to Norman Petty, they became the studio's unofficial house band, backing other West Texans who came to cut demos, such as their friend Gary Tollett, country singers Billy Walker and Jim Robinson, and Jack Huddle, a personality from local television. And if any visiting group was short a lead guitarist, Petty had only to glance at Buddy and he'd be on his feet with his affable "Don't mind if I do!" Many a mundane rockabilly song that never came within a mile of the late-fifties charts would have a Buddy solo gleaming out of it like a diamond in oatmeal.

The Holley family naturally had been growing curious, and not a little uneasy, about this new benefactor their baby boy had discovered across the state line. West Texans are traditionally suspicious of New Mexicans, regarding them as scarcely less weird and unpredictable than the extraterrestrial beings reputedly given to crash-landing among them. But one meeting with Petty was sufficient to reassure L. O. and Ella that Buddy could not be in safer, more responsible hands if his recording sessions were supervised by their minister at their own Tabernacle Baptist Church. L. O. was particularly impressed—"mesmerized," Larry Holley says now —by Petty's dapper appearance, his air of influence and importance, and the devout Christian sentiments with which his conversation was liberally sprinkled.

Petty also showed keen interest in the tiling firm Larry had started and for which L. O., Travis, and Buddy periodically worked. Indeed, it would not be long before the Holleys discovered Papa Norman's knack of turning everyone around him into dedicated, unsalaried employees.

At Petty's studio, the feature most noticeably lacking was a "live" echo chamber—i.e. one to which he had instant and unlimited access via his Altec board during sessions rather than depending on the taped echo effects that had made Buddy's Nashville version of "That'll Be the Day" sound so artificial. Until now, all the studio's output, including "That'll Be the Day" mark 2, had been one-dimensionally dry; if he needed a more cavernous sound, Petty would transfer his recording equipment to a movie theater called the Lyceum in downtown Clovis.

A few weeks after recording "Maybe Baby" and "Last Night" with Buddy and the Crickets, Petty began building an echo chamber to his own design in the A-frame attic space above the family garage. Larry Holley, accompanied by L. O. and Travis, drove over from Lubbock with a truckload of tiles, remnants from various contracting jobs, and laid them on the attic floor as a highly effective means of soundproofing. It did not occur to Papa Norman to offer payment for their hours of labor, nor would the Holleys have dreamed of accepting any. "We figured it was the least we could do," Larry says, "because of all that Norman seemed to be doing for Buddy."

☆   ☆   ☆

Petty's own oft-repeated definition of Buddy in this period was "a diamond in the rough." From that, history was to infer Petty's own crucial role as a cutter and polisher of precious stones that but for him might never have come to light. The truth is that Buddy's talent developed at its own momentum, and at a speed that makes the maturing of John Lennon and Paul McCartney, half a dozen years later, seem slow by comparison. More often than not, by the time the diamonds reached Clovis, they would be fully fashioned and polished; all Petty had to provide was the setting.

Those long solitary drives provide our best clue to the sudden, huge forward leap in Buddy's talent. Before he began recording in Clovis, he had been used to writing songs with one or more partners: Jack Neal, Bob Montgomery, Don Guess, Sue Parrish. But the songs he brought to Norman Petty from March 1957 onward were generally his work alone, and drew on emotions far deeper than any he would ever have revealed to his friends as they sat around together, tinkering with words and chords. L. O. Holley was later to recall how song ideas would often come to Buddy in the middle of family dinner and how, with familiar impulsiveness, he'd jump up from the table, get into his old red Caddy, and roar off into the night. Two or three hours later, he would return, go straight to his room, and pick up the Gibson with its blue and black Western-tooled leather case. Out on the highway, en route to Abilene or Amarillo, a whole new song—its words, its chords, its entire arrangement—would have worked itself out in his head.

In early 1957, of course, rock lyric writing was in its infancy. Teenagers at that time bought records to dance to, not listen to, which explains why so many primal rock 'n' roll classics, if not pure gibberish, were simple declarations of how mind-explodingly wonderful the music itself was. Most of the songs that fed the record industry were still the work of middle-aged Tin Pan Alley hacks with no liking for rock 'n' roll and the lowest possible opinion of their public's intelligence. Such were the insatiable demand and the minuscule supply that one could achieve a million-selling hit by shoehorning a two-four beat and the word "rock" into such a hoary old chestnut as "Comin' Through the Rye." To be sure, some inspired rock 'n' roll songwriters, white as well as black, had emerged by 1957, notably Chuck Berry, Carl Perkins, and the New York–based partnership of Jerry Leiber and Mike Stoller. But these tended to be in their mid- or late twenties: young enough to be caught up in the teenage revolution, mature and sophisticated enough to comment on, even gently satirize, the culture it produced.

Buddy was only twenty and, thus far in his life, nothing much had happened to him. For a creative muse he could not draw on the neon excitement of Chuck Berry's Chicago or Leiber and Stoller's view down Broadway: only horizonless wheatfields and cottonfields, the lawns and churches of Lubbock, the archetypal young American's life cycle of high school, dating, movies, and drive-ins. It was when he stopped pretending otherwise, when he found the nerve, the encouragement, and the space to be himself, that raw talent suddenly blossomed into fully formed brilliance.

The era of profound or meaningful rock lyrics was still far in the future. Buddy wrote about what his peers expected him to: falling for girls, pursuing girls, winning girls, losing girls and feeling blue. If simple or predictable, his lyrics were always accomplished, phrased with the neatness of the schoolboy journalist he had been, adding up with the logic and precision of the draftsman he had almost become. From Hank Williams first, then the Chicago bluesmen, and finally Elvis, he had learned that words were less important than what the singer put into them. In the perfect aural environment of Norman Petty's studio—and with no one waiting to call "Time" on the Western Union clock—he began to use his voice with ever more adventurousness and audacity, refining the ebullient tongue-waggles, pulverized vowels, swooning sighs, and word-fracturing hiccups that would become his multitudinously imitated trademark.

While the lyrics he wrote and performed were never remotely autiobiographical, they were always suffused with his personal characteristics: friendliness, modesty, humor, and what can only be called instinctive good taste. Most have the same quality as that English essay he wrote as a high school sophomore, on sheets torn from a hardware company scribbling pad. Beneath the ostensible high spirits and self-confidence can be felt a qualm of insecurity, a fear that the sunny dream he has expressed may not turn out as he hopes, but a resolution to hope for the best and keep smiling regardless.

Finding a producer with Norman Petty's peculiar combination of talents and obsessions had, creatively speaking, been a lucky break in a million. In 1957, the number of independent record producers could be counted on the fingers of one hand. Even rarer, especially in far-flung places like New Mexico, were studios well enough equipped to supply major record labels with fully finished masters that could be put straight into production. Buddy therefore would be spared all the bureaucracy and conformity to house style that had made his Decca sessions so miserable.

What Petty gave him was a place to make records in peace and at his own pace, free of distraction and interference, and working to his personal standards rather than committee or corporate ones. In the 1990s this is something any pop musician of original talent takes for granted; four decades ago, it was unprecedented.

Teaming with Petty was important in another crucial respect. For all his dedication to country first, then rock 'n' roll, Buddy had never shut his mind to other musical styles. He enjoyed classical music, and his record collection included all the mainstream greats like Frank Sinatra and Ella Fitzgerald. Nor, unlike the other Crickets, did he find the staid cocktail lounge music of the Norman Petty Trio laughably old-fashioned; he respected the trio's polish and professionalism, listening attentively to their records to see what might be learned from them. Later on, when one of the trio's own recording sessions for Columbia fell due, Buddy joined them on rhythm guitar to demo a sub-Mantovani composition by Petty called "Moondreams." These soft, sweet drafts of mainstream pop played as much a part as the high-octane input of Elvis and Little Richard in lifting Buddy's talent into the stratosphere.

By late spring of 1957, the kindergarten simplicity of "That'll Be the Day" already seemed light-years in the past. April 5 saw the taping of a song originally inspired by Mickey and Sylvia's "Love Is Strange" and already tried out in various styles, one of them featuring Norman Petty on organ. But the final version was Buddy on his own—or rather, Buddy performing with Buddy, since both his vocal and guitar were double-tracked, and the most attentive listener was never to know, still less care, that there had been anyone else in the studio.

"Words of Love" would have been a remarkable production in any era, but is the more remarkable for having been created in the very eye of the rock 'n' roll hurricane, when the only resonance expected from people's music was soulless, one-dimensional uproar. The double-tracking technique itself was nothing new, having been a feature of Les Paul and Mary Ford records since the early fifties. But the aural cloning process had never before, and has never since, created an effect quite like this. Buddy's lead and descanting voice are so much in the foreground that they seem to whisper directly into one's ear. The words are of tender adoration edged with uncertainty ("Tell me love is real . . ."), the dual voice humming confident affirmation in the same breath as it wistfully seeks reassurance. The Stratocaster features not in its usual showoff solo but as a leitmotif that intensifies the two-minded mood, its rhythm track firmly rippled downstrokes, its lead a tearful Hawaiian phrase, dissolving into icy-sharp, windchiming single strings.

The B-side could hardly have been more of a contrast. Just before the session, Petty had received the demo of a song called "Mailman, Bring Me No More Blues," one of whose three writers, "Stanley Clayton," was the pseudonym of Coral Records boss Bob Thiele. Buddy did not have to be persuaded of the wisdom in cutting a song by the man who'd given the Crickets their record contract. And the number itself, a traditional twelve-bar blues, was in the nature of a challenge: "See what your boy can do with this" had been the A&R man's patronizing message to Petty. Clearly, Thiele doubted whether Brunswick's new signee had the talent to perform anything beyond elementary rock 'n' roll.

By the time "Words of Love" had been polished to Buddy's and Petty's satisfaction, there remained only the predawn tail-end of the session to work on "Mailman, Bring Me No More Blues." To give it an authentic blues feel, and also the lift of professional musicianship, Petty got his wife out of bed to augment the Crickets on piano. Buddy by this time was almost dropping with fatigue, but still managed a bravura performance, his single-tracked voice as soaked in schmaltzy melodrama as his double-tracked one previously had been subtle and restrained. Standing at the keyboard of the Baldwin grand in her hair curlers, robe, and slippers, Vi rolled out a raunchy twelve-bar figure that would not have disgraced Fats Domino. After that first, go-for-it take, the mellow voice over the studio intercom told them it would do just fine.

The two-sided master subsequently mailed to Bob Thiele in New York demonstrated beyond argument that here was something more than just the grunting mouthpiece of a rock 'n' roll group. A singer who could perform a complex love song in one breath and a raucous adult blues in the next did not deserve to be hidden away on Brunswick, but could safely be elevated to the Coral label to join the rarefied likes of Debbie Reynolds, Teresa Brewer, and Lawrence Welk. With "That'll Be the Day" still awaiting release under the Crickets' name, Thiele proposed that "Words of Love" would come out on Coral under Buddy's name alone.

Behind the apparent compliment to Buddy lay hardheaded commercial logic. In 1957, the career of a new rock 'n' roll attraction was reckoned in only months, or even weeks. Having a group and a solo-singer–plus-backup who were identical and interchangeable gave Thiele a double bite at the cherry. Teenagers who liked groups might buy the Crickets' records, those who preferred solo singers might buy Buddy's "own-name" ones; more gullible or tone-deaf souls might not even realize the same vocalist was featured, and buy both. It was also a ploy to grab extra seconds of vitally important radio airtime: a disc jockey might well play a Crickets record and a Buddy Holly one on the same program where he could never dream of playing two by the same performer. Talented solo singers emerged from groups commonly enough, but no one before had supposed that a group and its lead vocalist might enjoy successful careers in parallel. (After Buddy and the Crickets, there was not to be another example until the mid-sixties when similar double exposure was created for the Four Seasons and their singer, Frankie Valli.)

Buddy's signing to Coral under his own name, on May 16, 1957, also had the effect of resolving the awkward situation created by his original Decca contract. The main Decca label now recognized Bob Thiele's new solo artist as the same Buddy Holly who'd had two unsuccessful singles with them a year earlier and was legally bound not to rerecord any material from their sessions until 1961. That contract had clearly been breached by his new version of "That'll Be the Day," even though he sang it anonymously within a group. On the other hand, since the rerecorded version was to be issued by one of Decca's subsidiary labels, the organization could hardly be said to be the loser. Even so, there were some angry corporate mutters inside Decca, even talk of legal proceedings against Buddy, until Bob Thiele successfully pleaded the futility of such a course. In return for being released from the old contract's five-year clause, and not being sued, Buddy had to waive his right to any royalties from the Nashville version of "That'll Be the Day."

His relief at the sorting out of the contractual mess and his elation at his solo Coral signing was tempered by unease at being so clearly set apart from the other Crickets, especially from his best friend, J. I. Allison. Norman Petty had already made the tentative suggestion that, as lead singer and instrumentalist as well as principal songwriter, Buddy could claim a larger share of the group's earnings than J. I., Niki, and Joe B., or even get away with paying them a wage as mere sidemen. "Buddy almost got mad over that," Niki Sullivan remembers. "He told Norman we were all part of the team, and we all had to get the same equal share."

☆   ☆   ☆

"That'll Be the Day" was released on May 27, 1957. Buddy and the Crickets had not been told in advance of the release date, and discovered it was finally in the stores only by pure accident. "Buddy was helping me on a tile job," his brother Larry remembers. "We were out at the new city–county health unit, putting down these big green tiles, and he was real depressed, saying how he and the others had cut their record six weeks ago, and they'd heard nothing more from the record company and couldn't find out anything from Norman about when it was supposed to come out. He said, 'Larry, I know good and well I could make it,' and I said, 'Well, you and the guys had your chance. I lent you money for a guitar and clothes and all. Looks like maybe that's it.'

"Later on, we were working inside, and Buddy was still real blue, so I said, 'Why don't you call the guy in New York direct and just ask him? You got his number, don't you?' So we went to Mother's and Buddy called up the record company. And the guy there says, 'Hey, baby! They're playing your record on the streets of New York City!' So Buddy says, 'Well, can you send me five hundred dollars? 'Cause I'm broke!'"

The first test for any new record in 1957, whether rock 'n' roll, country, pop, or calypso, was what the music trade press thought of it. The era of music magazines with a general readership, let alone a specifically youthful one, had still barely dawned. The two all-powerful arbiters were *Billboard* and *Cash Box,* both of which spoke mainly to the industry itself—and neither of which, as their flat, jaded prose indicated, could muster a single reviewer under the age of about forty. Even so, *Billboard*'s capsule notice of "That'll Be the Day" on June 10 was generally favorable: "Fine vocal by [the Crickets] on a well-made side that should get play. Tune is a medium beat rockabilly. Performance is better than material." The B-side, "I'm Looking for Someone to Love," was described with slightly more warmth ("bright, vigorous treatment") and received the same lukewarm 72 out of 100 rating.

A new rock 'n' roll act making its debut that summer faced formidable competition indeed. Not only America but now Britain and most of Europe were gripped by Elvis Presley mania. The mumbling million-sellers continued to congest the tops of all the charts, their titles a shorthand summary of the havoc being wrought on family life across the hemispheres: "Too Much" . . . "All Shook Up" . . . "Paralyzed." But if the shrieks of teenage girls were still as appalling as ever to grown-up ears, they also were now recognized as a force to move the giant mills of American industry. A name that, a year ago, had seemed almost too bizarre to articulate had unleashed a marketing and merchandising bonanza on a scale hitherto known only to the Walt Disney Corporation. Thanks to a thousand and one spinoff deals by Colonel Tom Parker, the Elvis handmaiden could display her master's supercilious likeness on her blouse, her jeans, her purse, her bobby socks; she could buy Elvis cosmetics, with lipstick shades including Tutti-Frutti Red and Houn' Dog Orange, even play her 45s on an Elvis record player upholstered in the same blue suede as his famously untouchable shoes.

The world's fascination was heightened by the contradictory images Elvis himself presented to the media. It was the same paradox that had astonished Buddy and his friends backstage at Lubbock's Fair Park Coliseum: the shameless, posturing rabble-rouser of the concert stage was in private a shy, modest Southern boy, amazed and shocked that people should find his performing style objectionable and anxious to reassure them that he meant no harm to anyone. If not yet dubbed "the King," he could already claim undisputed status as a form of deity. For the New York opening of his first film, *Love Me Tender,* in 1956, ecstatic crowds filled Times Square to watch the covers ceremonially drop from a guitar-toting, sideburned effigy, forty feet high.

No such ambiguity surrounded Little Richard, whose outrageous performances were equaled, if not surpassed, by his behavior offstage, and whose sparkle-suited, piano-punishing, whooping figure seemed to exult in its power to jangle grown-up sensibilities literally beyond endurance. The clergy- and media-led equation of rock 'n' roll with unbridled sex had been confirmed in 1956 by *The Girl Can't Help It,* a movie in glorious Technicolor rather than the dingy black and white of previous rock exploitation pictures, and starring the "blonde bombshell," Jayne Mansfield, whose gigantic, pointed breasts resembled a dead heat in a zeppelin race. Intended as a satire on rock 'n' roll, the picture somehow turned into a celebration of it, perhaps the best ever created on celluloid. The most memorable sequence shows Mansfield tripping top-heavily along a city street while Richard performs the title song in voice-over: at the combined assault of gigantic breasts and lip-smacking soundtrack, milk bottles explode as if in spontaneous orgasm and the spectacles of a male onlooker splinter in their frames.

The Girl Can't Help It featured cameo performances by other rock 'n' roll hitmakers of the hour, such as the Platters and Fats Domino, plus a gaggle of rising newcomers. Here was seventeen-year-old Eddie Cochran singing "20 Flight Rock" with knocking knees and a guitar slung around his neck, for the moment looking and sounding like nothing more than yet another Presley clone. Here was a former merchant seaman named Gene Vincent, partially disabled by a motorcycle accident and with a misshapen palate that gave his singing voice a tremulous castrato pitch. For hardcore rock 'n' roll fans, the film's highlight was Vincent performing a piece of sublime gibberish called "Be-Bop-A-Lula" with his backup group, the Blue Caps (strictly speaking the prototype rock 'n' roll band, though too indefinite and charmless and disheveled under their matching workman-style caps to inspire any direct imitators).

The fact that Elvis was already turning to slow ballads and beginning to carve out a career in Hollywood, together with the dying fall of Bill Haley and his Comets, seemed to indicate that rock 'n' roll's detractors could have been right: maybe it was just a nine days' wonder after all. Certainly, what had begun to dominate the charts by mid-1957 was not rock 'n' roll so much as rock-flavored pop, sung by young whites who mirrored the clean-cut high school image of their audience. The two newest chart arrivals, Ricky Nelson and the close-harmonizing Everly Brothers, were devastatingly good-looking boys with a dewy, unused air that in each case belied long experience in the business. Nelson had started as a child actor with his parents, Ozzie and Harriet, on their television sitcom. The Kentucky-born Everlys, Don and his younger sibling Phil, had begun singing together as toddlers on their parents' country music radio show.

That spring the Everly Brothers had their first No. 1 with "Bye Bye Love." Ricky Nelson was climbing fast with his cover version of Fats Domino's "I'm Walkin'." On the strength of his cameo in *The Girl Can't Help It,* Eddie Cochran had made No. 18 with a sugary teenage idyll called "Sittin' in the Balcony." Yet week after week, on *Billboard*'s Top 100 chart, there still was no sign of "That'll Be the Day" by the Crickets. Only one nice thing had happened to the song; yet another first for Buddy, though of little comfort in the circumstances. A black R&B group, the Ravens, had snapped it up through Norman Petty's publishing partners, Peer-Southern Music, and covered it as the B-side of their new single, "Dear One."

While everyone else seemed to be going places, the only road that stretched before Buddy Holly and the Crickets was the two-lane blacktop to Clovis. Two more future classics, "Not Fade Away" and "Everyday," were already in the can at Petty's, with no idea yet if there would ever be a chance to release them. Both songs exemplify the way Buddy's music evolved in the studio, and how off-the-cuff improvisation—and even outright plagiarism—could be transmuted into something unique. "Not Fade Away" originally belonged to the second category. Largely written by J. I. Allison, it borrowed the shuffling stop–start beat of "Bo Diddley," which Buddy had demo'd six or seven months earlier. Another idea was cribbed from that much-envied Buddy Knox hit, "Party Doll," J. I. forsaking his drums and beating out the staccato rhythm with sticks on an empty cardboard box. Petty's artful use of volume and echo gave the song a fragile, almost haunted quality: Buddy might be singing it alone in the center of some wide Texas plain while his and Niki's dubbed backup voices and the thumping box are borne faintly on the wind.

"Everyday," by contrast, was all Buddy's own, a love song of a delicacy and purity reminiscent of Tudor madrigals, and imbued with his special mixture of confidence, uncertainty, and steadfast hope. Among the instruments standing around Petty's studio was a celesta, a distant cousin to the harpsichord whose tinkling notes most familiarly signified time passing or autumn leaves falling in radio soap operas. In a break from rehearsing "Everyday" with straightforward Crickets backup, Buddy went over to the celesta and began fooling around on it. The dainty, old-fashioned sound, Petty realized, exactly matched the mood of the song. Vi Petty was summoned to work out a formal arrangement, though her spouse made it clear that he'd be the one playing on the record. As she tried it through, J. I. Allison sat nearby, beating an extempore rhythm with his palms on the knees of his jeans. "That sounds pretty good, too!" Petty said. So J. I.'s knee-slapping percussion joined the celesta in an almost nonexistent accompaniment that gave Buddy's voice maximum scope to work its alchemy on hitherto unelastic one-vowel words:

Love like yours will surely come my way
A-hey
A-hey-hey.

With "That'll Be the Day" still nowhere on the charts, Buddy had switched his hopes to "Words of Love," his first own-name release for the Coral label, twinned with "Mailman, Bring Me No More Blues." As with "That'll Be the Day," the publishing rights had been channeled by

Petty's Nor Va Jak company to Peer-Southern in New York, who put "Words of Love" on the open market for anyone who wished to make a cover version. And as with "That'll Be the Day," it was snapped up by another group, in this case the Diamonds, who instantly recorded it as a follow-up to "Little Darlin'," their No. 2 hit of the previous March. The Diamonds' unsubtle, unimaginative "Words of Love" appeared on the charts June 20, the very day that Buddy's original version was released, thereby virtually guaranteeing its eclipse.

Though "Words of Love" had seemingly joined "That'll Be the Day" in oblivion, Norman Petty's confidence appeared unshaken, and Buddy and the Crickets were allowed to keep on recording. On June 30, 1957, when the temperature in Clovis stood at 106 degrees, they returned to Petty's for a session destined to last three days and nights and, among other things, create a rock 'n' roll goddess.

J. I. Allison's current date was a seventeen-year-old Lubbock High junior named Peggy Sue Gerron. Sharply pretty, with an hourglass figure and short blonde hair, she played alto saxophone and and also twirled a drum majorette's baton in the school's Ruritanian-uniformed marching band. Though Buddy's graduation from Lubbock High now seemed an age ago, he would still occasionally sing and play guitar at the school's assemblies. "The first time I met him I was on my way to the band room," Peggy Sue remembers. "Buddy came rushing through the door so fast, he almost knocked me over. As he went on, he called over his shoulder, 'I'm real sorry I don't have time to stop and apologize.'

"Then a few days later, Jerry said to me, 'Would you come out on a double-date with me and my best friend?' When he came by my house to pick me up, there was Buddy sitting in the back seat of the car with his girl, Echo. When he saw who I was, he laughed and said to Jerry, 'I've already overwhelmed your Peggy Sue.' The four of us double-dated quite a few times after that. Echo wasn't allowed to dance, so Buddy and I would dance together. He was a real good dancer, very graceful. And he always made me laugh."

Among the new songs that Buddy brought to Clovis on June 30 was one he'd originally called "Cindy Lou"—Cindy after his sister Pat's small daughter, and Lou after Pat's middle name—which already featured in the Crickets' stage repertoire, played to a light Latin beat. As they began rehearsing, J. I. warmed up, as percussionists often do, with a pounding, cymbal-less paradiddle beat on his snare drum. Buddy liked the sound

and suggested they use it on "Cindy Lou," even though the noise re-
bounded so fearsomely off the acoustically perfect walls that Petty had
J. I. and his drum kit moved out to the tiny reception area, in company
with Norma Jean's vacant desk and the red and white Coke machine.

After several attempts, the new tempo still did not seem quite right
and, as a spur to his banished drummer, Buddy agreed to drop "Cindy
Lou" as a title and substitute the name of J. I.'s girl. With this change of
vision, from toddler in pigtails to svelte high school majorette, the song
finally cohered. In a flash of inspiration, Norman Petty flicked his new
echo chamber's control switch off and on continually, so that J. I.'s paradiddles sounded like two drummers pounding out a dark, undulating
voodoo beat against Buddy's relentless plectrum-clicking downstrokes.
Rudimentary, undeveloped words heightened the trancelike effect, proph-
esying the disco and rap age that would follow almost thirty years later.
About this mythic Peggy Sue, the words revealed nothing other than that
she made her moody paramour feel "blue," yet still love her "with a love
so rare 'n' true." Where she came to life was in the ever-changing shades
and shifts of Buddy's voice, her name repeated over and over like a
mantra—now murmured in tongue-tied bashfulness, now stretched to a
six-syllable schoolyard taunt ("Sue-oo-oo oo-oo oo"), now hiccupped as
if it brought on acid indigestion ("Uh-oh, Peg-gy!"), now sighed in rap-
ture, now transmuted into a ringing four-chord eulogy, the simplest, most
infallibly nerve-tingling solo in all rock 'n' roll.

That weekend saw a record heatwave in Clovis, with temperatures
rising to 107 and dust storms gusting to 90 mph. One can visualize it
almost like the opening sequence of a black and white B movie: a huge,
lowering sky; rattling store signs and whirling tumbleweed; faint sounds
of rock 'n' roll magic drifting from that air-conditioned, alcohol-free
bunker on West Seventh Street.

By the time Buddy and the Crickets started back for Lubbock, at 3
A.M. on July 3, three more tracks had joined "Peggy Sue" in the can.
"Listen to Me" was a new Buddy song in the same wistful mood and
call-and-response style as "Words of Love," but with dramatically heightened echo on his double-tracked vocal and guitar. "Oh Boy" was a tear-
'em-up rock 'n' roll number, recently sent in to Norman Petty on spec by
a young writer from Levelland, Texas, named Sonny West, who'd gotten
the idea from seeing cheerleaders jumping up and down at a college
football game. "I'm Gonna Love You Too" was a frisky rockabilly throw-

back on which the Crickets found themselves augmented from an unex-
pectedly appropriate quarter. As the last notes of the playback died away,
a real cricket, which had somehow found its way into the echo chamber,
gave a reverberant double chirrup. Since the noise happened to be exactly
in beat, they decided to let it stay.

Although Buddy's contractual difficulties with Decca had been resolved, he was still not quite free of worries arising from his false start
the previous year. There remained a residue of disagreement with Cedarwood, the Nashville publishing company whose owner, Jim Denny,
had got him his original Decca contract in exchange for signing him as a
songwriter. Technically Buddy was no longer bound to Cedarwood, but
he was afraid they might find some reason to claim a share in the new
songs he was now turning out so prolifically. To prevent Denny from
realizing just how abundant was the crop, Petty suggested that Buddy
publish some under a pseudonym. He chose one formed from his own
real first and middle names, Charles Hardin.

"Not Fade Away," "Everyday," and "Listen to Me" bore two writer
credits, Charles Hardin and Norman Petty. It was what had already happened to "That'll Be the Day," despite its having been written months
before Petty had even met Buddy and the Crickets; what had also happened to "Maybe Baby"—and, for that matter, to "Oh Boy," the composition of young Sonny West in Levelland, who still did not even know that
Buddy and the Crickets had recorded it.

Buddy himself seemed quite unconcerned by the continual appearance
of Petty's name on songs that, more often than not, were Buddy's own,
unaided work. He accepted that without Petty's studio, engineering expertise, power, light, food, beds, toilet facilities, and running water, the songs
would have been stillborn; that Petty's name on a record label really and
truly would increase its chances of airplay; that for all these manifold
benefits, giving up a share of his publishing royalties was no more than
fair. "It wasn't just to Norman," Larry Holley says. "Buddy'd give a song
away to anyone. 'Cause he knew he could write a new one every night."

Most times, as a track evolved, Petty would make a suggestion that
proved crucial, usually about instrumentation and arrangement, sometimes about tune and lyric, very occasionally both together. His most
significant contribution, J. I. Allison has said, was the bridge in "Peggy
Sue" where Buddy switches to a minor key to sing "Pretty pretty pretty
pretty Peggy Sue." For that, Petty took half the song, giving the other half

to Jerry for providing its hypnotic paradiddle beat. Buddy received no credit, even though he had written the song and even specified what kind of beat J. I. should play.

Although the "second division" Crickets, Niki Sullivan and Joe B. Mauldin, had no ambitions to become composers in their own right, both frequently contributed ideas to Buddy's songs which, as Buddy himself was the first to say, entitled them to some share in the publishing royalties. Unable to keep track of who (apart from himself) had contributed what, Petty would dole out writer's credits in a totally arbitrary way, conceding that the apportionment might not be strictly accurate, but saying at least this way everyone would get a piece of the action. Niki and Joe B. both claim to have contributed to "Maybe Baby," but neither found himself listed as writer with Buddy and Petty. Their consolation prize was an undeserved credit (along with Petty's) on "I'm Gonna Love You Too." "Well . . . All Right," a much later song, 18-karat Buddy through and through, ended up with Joe B.'s name on it as well as Buddy's, J. I.'s, and, of course, Petty's.

After "Peggy Sue," the most bizarre example of this grab-bag method involved J. I. Allison, who wrote most of the lyrics for "Not Fade Away" only to find them attributed to Charles Hardin / Norman Petty. Lines like "My love is bigger than a Cadillac" are as hard to identify with Petty as they are redolent of J. I.'s quirky wit. Yet he was talked into giving up his share of the song, a fact he bitterly resents to this day.

☆　☆　☆

The suspenseful midsummer months of 1957 also produced an interlude not even hinted at in the few formalized stanzas of the Buddy Holly legend. Something happened to Buddy so devastating as to make even his career as a rock 'n' roll star—if he really and truly was to have one—seem unimportant by comparison. He fell head over heels in love with June Clark.

In the recording studio Buddy might show maturity, authority, and self-command way beyond his years, but outside in the sunshine again, he reverted to being an ordinary young man, not yet twenty-one and as emotionally unformed, confused, vulnerable, impulsive, and foolhardy as anyone else his age in that time. Apart from the tension of waiting and hoping, there was a particular reason he should have been so susceptible at this particular moment; why, in his own lighthearted words, he was "lookin' for someone to love."

Echo McGuire, his longtime sweetheart, the tiny, radiant girl he had been planning to marry since they were together in high school, was fading gradually but inexorably from his life. Their enforced separation when Echo went to Abilene's Christian University had been bad enough. But in the autumn of 1956, her church had formed a missionary group to found a new college in York, Nebraska. Echo's fine academic record and her sparkling social skills made her a natural choice to join this group of pioneers.

Her unofficial engagement to Buddy had continued nonetheless: they phoned and wrote regularly, and at the end of the year Buddy had made the daunting eleven-hour road trip to Nebraska to see her. How much he missed her, he confided to no one: not his best friend, J. I. Allison; not even his mother. But Echo was clearly the inspiration for all those love songs composed on solitary nighttime drives, with their chaste innocence, their prevalent moods of pining and uncertainty, their repeated attempts to convince an unnamed third party ("Listen to me, hear what I say") that true love always wins through in the end.

While keeping Echo's image like a chaste altar in his mind, however, Buddy had the normal sex drive of any heterosexual male just out of his teens. During Echo's absence, he had dated numerous, far less respectable girls and, by the age of twenty, was fully sexually experienced. Older women, too, tended to find his combination of energy and vulnerability highly attractive: according to Niki Sullivan, Buddy even enjoyed a brief fling with Petty's wife, Vi. "We were over at the studio early in the evening, around seven o'clock. Norman had totally disappeared, the way he often did. Buddy suddenly comes and tells us that Vi's phoned over and invited him to their apartment. So he got washed and shaved and went over there. He wasn't gone all that long, and when he came back he could hardly believe what had happened. Neither could we. But we said, 'Cool.'"

Admittedly the story contradicts everything else known about Vi: her scrupulous Christian upbringing, her unassertive, anxious nature, the al- most zero sexual quotient in her relationship with Clovis Man, most of all, her delicate mental state. "For the kind of episodic schizophrenic Vi was," the Pettys' friend Dr. Jerry Fisher says, "it would have been impos- sible for her even to contemplate having sex with anyone but Norman."

But Niki Sullivan is adamant. "Buddy was never a braggart about that kind of thing. If Buddy said it happened, it happened."

Away from Clovis, Buddy, J. I., Niki, and Joe B. spent most of their time rehearsing and hanging out at the home of their main Lubbock friends and supporters, James and June Clark. James Clark, universally known as Nig, was a wholesale supplier of snack foods to stores and supermarkets. He and June were themselves only in their late twenties, young enough to be rock 'n' roll fans, yet old enough to seem like surrogate parents in this time of tense uncertainty, offering Buddy and his group sympathy and sanctuary that even their own long-suffering families could not.

June had married Nig when she was only sixteen, and had an eleven-year-old son, Carley, for whom the Crickets' almost live-in presence was undiluted bliss. "They were always real nice to me," Carley Clark remembers now. "They'd take me along with them to gigs, in places like Dumas and Littlefield, riding in that red Cadillac of theirs. I remember on one trip, the wind blew Joe B.'s bass right off the roof and we had to go back along the road, looking for it. They had their own special logo which they called "Pa," like a circle with two feet, painted on the side of the car. They'd draw it on notes and letters, too; it was like a secret sign, a lucky charm to help them get a hit."

Despite the Crickets' air of four Texas Musketeers, one for all and all for one, tensions and personality clashes were developing within the group. They had spent more than three months living in one another's pockets for days and nights on end, in alternating moods of euphoria and disappointment. They were all broke, and under varying degrees of pressure from their families and friends to forget this silly rock 'n' roll and settle down to some real work. As the scorching weeks dragged on, and "That'll Be the Day" still did not even make it into the Top 100, nerves frayed and tempers boiled over.

Their newest recruit, at least, caused little disruption. Joe B. Mauldin might not be God's gift to bass playing but he fitted perfectly into the lineup, being even-tempered, humorous, obliging, and, most important, endlessly willing to follow wherever stronger characters led. "Anything anyone else wanted to do was fine with Joe B.," Buddy's brother Larry says. "He was just like a bump on a log."

But Niki Sullivan, Buddy's third cousin by marriage, was a very different proposition, strong-minded, outspoken, and far tougher physically than his lean face and glasses made him appear. Niki was beginning to resent having been pressed into the Crickets when they clearly had so little use for him. He had sung backup vocals only twice, on "That'll Be the Day," and "Not Fade Away," and with Buddy's Stratocaster filling every crack, his duties as rhythm guitarist were virtually nonexistent. On the "Peggy Sue" session Niki had not played at all. When Buddy changed from singing and playing rhythm to his ringing chord solo, he found he didn't have enough time to flip the Stratocaster's tone-control switch. So on the final take Niki had to kneel by his side, waiting to do it for him.

"I remember a lot of fights with Niki," Carley Clark says. "He and Jerry Allison never did seem to like each other. And Niki made Buddy lose his cool a few times, too. I saw one real bad tiff at our house where the two of them would have come to blows if my dad hadn't gotten in between them and told them to stop. I can hear Buddy's voice now saying, 'Okay . . . but only because this is your house, Nig.'"

That Buddy should have fallen headlong for June Clark was no great surprise. Both emotionally and professionally he was at low ebb: his records still getting nowhere; Echo hundreds of miles away; the songs on which he'd lavished such passionate care simply gathering dust in Norman Petty's vaults. June was a highly attractive woman, slim and wavy-blonde, with snub features and big eyes glancingly like those of Brigitte Bardot, the French sex kitten. Her job on the cosmetics counter at Hull's drugstore gave her an aura of glossy, nylon-crisp untouchability. But in fact she was the very opposite: down-to-earth, warm, fun-loving, and switched on to everything that Buddy and his friends considered most important.

For all her goods looks and sophistication, June, too, stood in dire need of love and consolation. Her marriage to Nig Clark was not a happy one; she persevered with it only for Carley's sake. Filling the house with young rock 'n' roll musicians had seemed no more than an innocent distraction. But she found herself increasingly drawn to Buddy for his charm, his kindliness, his single-minded ambition, and the dark, lonely depths in him that now and then revealed themselves. "I knew he liked me because he was a normal young guy," June says now. "But the thing he always wanted to do most when we were together was just talk to me."

They began a risky, on-the-wing romance, stealing kisses over coffee cups in the kitchen, with the other Crickets, Nig, and Carley only a few feet away in the den. To further complicate matters, June had begun to suspect that J. I. Allison was also sweet on her. "I felt I should tell Buddy that, because Jerry was his best friend. Buddy acted like we were the only two grown-ups involved. 'Jerry's young,' he said. 'He'll probably get over it.'"

June had been prepared for a superficial flirtation. But the intensity of Buddy's feelings began to alarm her. Forgetting the need for discretion, he phoned her constantly, and also took to hanging around the drugstore where she worked. "He wouldn't even pretend he'd come in to buy anything. He'd just stand there staring at me while I waited on customers, till it got to be really embarrassing and unnerving."

Afraid that Nig would discover what was going on, she told Buddy they must cool down and underlined the point by going away from Lubbock for a few days. "When I got back, Buddy's brother Larry came by the house and told me Buddy was in a terrible way and he wanted to see me. We met in the parking lot at the drugstore. Buddy asked me to leave Nig and go away with him. He said if I would, he'd do anything—break up the Crickets, even forget about trying to make it in the music business."

In an attempt to defuse the situation, Larry Holley persuaded Buddy to go with him on a fishing trip to Colorado. But even that didn't succeed in taking Buddy's mind off his troubles. While they were away, the pop music charts produced yet another sensation: a wailing, puppy-love song called "Diana," sung by its composer, sixteen-year-old Paul Anka.

"One day in this little Colorado town, we passed a record store and there was Anka's picture in the window, and a caption saying how 'Diana' was shooting up the Top Ten," Larry Holley remembers. "After that, Buddy couldn't keep his mind on catching fish at all. 'I know I can beat this Paul Anka kid,' he kept saying. 'I *know* I can beat him.'"

☆　☆　☆

Exactly why "That'll Be the Day" took so long to get onto the charts never has been satisfactorily explained. For most rock 'n' roll classics, success has appeared soaringly effortless: for this one, it entailed a footslog up Mount Everest, fighting headwinds and blizzards every inch of the way.

The blend of sounds, which seems unimprovably right to modern ears was an unusual, even eccentric one in mid-1957. Though the electric guitar might be the quintessence of rock 'n' roll, no chart hit up to then had featured one quite so heavily and uproariously. And the voice sounded unlike that of a potential teenage idol, being totally lacking in sexual suggestiveness, self-pitying angst, or any other clue that its owner belonged to the same generation as Elvis, Ricky, Eddie, Don and Phil. The parents of 1957 might believe their teenage children to lack all discrimination, but in fact they were already showing themselves to be deeply conservative and suspicious of change. The novel sound of "That'll Be the Day" and the difficulty of pigeonholing it—not quite dance tune, not quite love song, not quite fast, not quite slow, not funny yet not quite serious—were factors rather more likely to make a failure than a success.

In a continent as vast and disconnected as North America was thirty-nine years ago, a new single could not be expected to break everywhere simultaneously unless it bore some established name—ideally that of Elvis Presley—and was accompanied by a massive advertising and promotional blitz. For an unknown act like the Crickets, the best their record company could hope for was regional breakout—success in a single state or city that a fair wind might fan outward to other cities and states. Not only the geographical size of the continent but its cultural and ethnic diversity stacked up the odds against conquering every one of the "territories" where records were bought. What might delight sun-kissed Californians might be totally lost on the weatherbeaten denizens of the far Midwest. What might be rejected by New England sophisticates might go down a storm around the Great Lakes or beside the Gulf of Mexico. Regional breakout in just one or two of the possible key markets would have shown Coral-Brunswick a decent profit. But it would not have made Buddy Holly a star.

The essential stepping-stones to regional breakout were disc jockeys on local radio stations. The odd thing about "That'll Be the Day" was that initially it received very little airplay, yet despite this lack of vital exposure and endorsement it could be seen to be selling steadily, if not spectacularly. Part of the reason may have been the Ravens' cover version on the Argo label, which had been extensively played on black stations. It's entirely possible that some people heard the Ravens' version on the radio, then went out and bought the Crickets'. Since the Crickets' faces were unknown, and their lead singer's voice had a timbre which, to 1957 ears, seemed more black than white, few of these misdirected customers can have thought it worthwhile to demand a refund. To compound the confusion, there was also a black group called the Crickets, whose existence had been unknown to Buddy and company when they picked out their name from Jerry Allison's encyclopedia. People buying the wrong group, as well as people buying the wrong version of the song, undoubtedly contributed to these puzzlingly respectable sales.

The much-despised Hollywood movie version of Buddy's life offers a cartoon version of how "That'll Be the Day" finally achieved regional breakout. A disc jockey in Buffalo, New York, adores the record so much that he barricades himself in his studio and plays it nonstop over the air until his employers break down the door and restrain him. The scene contains a germ of truth: "That'll Be the Day" did show a surge in the Buffalo area after a disc jockey named Tom Clay, working under the pseudonym Guy King on WGR, took to playing it not around the clock, but with unusual frequency—every fifteen minutes or so. A still more spectacular surge came from the Philadelphia area, thanks mainly to the enthusiasm of deejay Georgie Woods on the city's leading black station, WDAS. Bob Thiele remembered being at a Decca sales conference in Cincinnati and hearing, to his amazement, that Philly had just sent an order for 16,000 copies.

Many other regional disc jockeys began to show genuine enthusiasm for "That'll Be the Day," once they'd worked out which "That'll Be the Day" it was and whether the black or white group named the Crickets was performing it. And even more were willing to enthuse for a price. In the American music industry of 1957, bribing disc jockeys to give preferential treatment to this or that new release was a natural and normal part of the marketing process. Buddy and the Crickets were left in no doubt that some payola, at least, had helped their record along. Niki Sullivan remembers a figure of $200 being mentioned. "It was kind of reproachful . . . like, 'You guys have just cost me two hundred bucks.'"

With orders still mounting steadily, the Decca organization finally began to put some promotional muscle behind their new discovery. Buddy and the Crickets were summoned to New York to meet their label boss, Bob Thiele, and their publisher, Murray Deutch, and make a personal appearance at one of the Manhattan record stores where they were selling best. Buddy made his first-ever flight from Lubbock's old Regional Airport in one of the elderly propeller planes with which Trans World Airlines then served such remote outposts. "It was an old military plane, a C-47, I think," Niki Sullivan remembers. "The ride up to New York was pretty rough. But we could care less! We were all on top of the world."

The size and garish splendor of New York City, as it honked and sizzled in the summer heat of 1957, took the four young Texans' breath away. "We were too young be be frightened," Sullivan remembers. "But we kept saying the same thing over and over: 'Man! Did you ever see so many people in one place before!'" They checked in to the Edison Hotel, between 46th and 47th Street, west of Broadway, and spent a couple of days being introduced to executives and marketing men at Coral-Brunswick and wandering the streets and avenues in a state of pop-eyed wonderment, visiting famous tourist spots like Jack Dempsey's Broadway restaurant and sampling their very first big-city cocktails (bourbon and Coca-Cola). Their innocent high spirits and old-fashioned Texan courtesy so charmed the dour Bob Thiele that he threw a party for them at his home in upstate New York, introducing them to his wife, Teresa Brewer, and other stars of the Coral label, including Steve Lawrence and Eydie Gormé.

By the end of June, sales had reached 50,000 copies—still far short of a national hit, but evidence that, after more than a month, the record had eventually begun to move. A congratulatory wire from Murray Deutch reached Clovis while Buddy and the Crickets were grabbing some sleep during the scorching, dust-stormy weekend of the "Peggy Sue" session. "Norman woke us up to tell us," Niki Sullivan remembers. "We were all so tired, we could hardly be bothered to listen to him." Next day, at Petty's suggestion, they made two jingle-size versions of "That'll Be the Day," one personalized to Deutch, the other to Bob Thiele at Coral-Brunswick. Buddy's improvised vocal bubbled with gratitude for his visit to Bob Thiele, "the Brunswick record compa-nee," and the man who had started the ball rolling. "That was Norman's idea," he sang amid a chorus of rebel yells from the others. "Ooh-ooh, that was Norman's idea."

On July 15, *Billboard* carried a full-page advertisement for current releases on the Coral label by Debbie Reynolds, the McGuire Sisters, Teresa Brewer, the Dick Jacobs Orchestra, and Don Cornell (who had made a deeply square cover version of "Mailman, Bring Me No More Blues"). At the bottom was a thumbnail picture of Buddy, Jerry, Niki, and Joe B., under the legend "Breaking on Brunswick." Bob Thiele also quickly exercised his option to renew their contract, offering what seemed a stunningly higher advance—$600—for the master of "Peggy Sue" and "Everyday."

The growing buzz around the Crickets also brought an offer from an

East Coast promoter to book them on their first-ever national tour. Head-lined by Clyde McPhatter and featuring Otis Rush, Edna McGriff, Oscar and Oscar, and the Hearts, the show was to open at the Howard Theater, Washington, D.C., on August 2, moving on to the Royal in Baltimore and finally to the Apollo in New York.

Buddy and crew, in other words, were the victims of a misunder-standing. The bill they had been invited to join otherwise consisted en-tirely of black singers and groups and was to play at black theaters at the heart of inner-city ghettoes where white people could no longer even walk in safety. The dearth of publicity photographs in advertisements for "That'll Be the Day," the record's raw R&B sound, and the existence of that black vocal group with the same name had all proved a fatal combina-tion. The tour promoters believed they were hiring the black Crickets, not the white ones.

Nonetheless, Buddy, J. I., Niki, and Joe B. unaminously agreed to take the booking. They knew what they might be walking into, but were prepared to risk it in exchange for their first exposure on the national tour circuit. Buddy, in particular, was supremely confident of his power to win any audience over, and laughed off the idea that their fellow performers might regard them with as much hostility as did disappointed paying customers. "We'd always gotten along so well with the black acts that played the Cotton Club, and been so into their music," Joe B. Mauldin says. "We were always in the front row, cheering, every time they came through town."

Although Norman Petty had been the Crickets' constant adviser, as well as their producer and engineer, for the past five months, it was not until this point that he officially became their manager. According to J. I. Allison, Petty was not seeking the job and, as their success began to snowball, told them they'd better find a manager to handle it all. At which point Buddy looked at him, aghast, and said "Heck, Norm—*you're* our manager!" Niki Sullivan confirms that Petty did not want the job; pro-testing that he knew little of the rock 'n' roll business and that, with his commitments in Clovis, he'd be unable to travel with them on tour. But Buddy overruled him with words to the effect: "You've brought us this far. We're not going with anyone else."

Petty's immediate concern was to outfit them for the tour they insisted on making, despite his own deep reservations, three weeks hence. Until now they had been little concerned with their image as a group and possessed no stage uniform to speak of, usually going out to gigs in the same unmatched sports clothes, Levi's, T-shirts, or Bermuda shorts they wore to studio sessions. For the immaculate, fastidious Clovis Man that would not do at all; nor would the Technicolor pseudo-cowboy threads that Elvis Presley had made the standard rock 'n' rollers' wardrobe. On July 8, Petty met Buddy and the Crickets in Lubbock, escorted them to the S & Q menswear store on Broadway, and helped them select a stage wardrobe more appropriate to his own trio's milieu of cabarets and air force officers' clubs: boxy, pale gray suits, white linen jackets, gray slacks, plus white shirts, ties, shoes, and socks.

He also opened an account on their behalf at the Clovis National Bank, where he himself had been a customer for many years. Into this, they understood, would go their joint income, after deduction of Petty's 10 percent management commission and the 10 percent tithe to each of their respective churches in Lubbock; from it would be paid the bills for their clothes, instruments, recording sessions, and traveling expenses.

The complete records of this "Buddy Holly and the Crickets" account are among Clovis Man's recently unearthed papers—account books, receipts, and every single canceled check, helpfully filled in with the purpose of its encashment. We can see that the account was opened on July 24, 1957, with a deposit of $500. The first withdrawal, a day later, was $175, "For payment on Buddy's automobile."

The signature on the sage-green check is that of Norman Petty. Since Buddy and the Crickets clearly would be away from Clovis a great deal of the time, but bills would constantly come in, it seemed sensible to give their manager power of attorney over their collective bank account, with authority to deposit all their income and write checks for such disbursements as might be necessary.

☆　☆　☆

This moment when his fame was about to dawn may also have brought the darkest episode of Buddy's brief life. If it truly did happen, it was not so very dark, goodness knows; hundreds of young men down the centuries have found themselves in the same predicament and behaved no better and no worse. It is shocking only in the context of the Buddy Holly legend, which promulgates a chastely shining, one-dimensional saint rather than a being of flesh and blood.

For many years a story has circulated around Lubbock that, just as Buddy's long-delayed breakthrough finally seemed about to happen, he almost wrecked it by getting a Lubbock girl pregnant. On my first visit to his hometown in late 1994, I talked to two of his close friends who are convinced the story is true. One of them prefers not to be named; the other was the Crickets' rhythm guitarist, and Buddy's cousin, Niki Sullivan.

According to Niki, the young woman had been at Lubbock High with Buddy and was dating him around the time the Crickets got together and found their way to Norman Petty's studio. It was, Niki says, a casual and purely physical relationship. "Buddy and she were just two kids, hot for each other. They had nothing in common. There was no way they could have gotten along in a real relationship." The second source claims to have dated the same person, and, like Buddy, to have "gone all the way" with her. "She was a flighty little thing . . . as wild as a peach orchard boar!"

Niki Sullivan says he was there when the girl broke the news of her condition to Buddy. "We were at the Hi-D-Ho drive-in in Lubbock. Buddy and she in the front of the car, I and a couple of others were in the back, drinking beer. Suddenly she started to throw up. Buddy was real pissed at her, you know, like 'How could you do that in my car!' And then this girl says, 'I can't help it, I'm pregnant. And you're the father!' At that Buddy hit her. I mean, hit her real hard, so that she jerked forward and hit her head on the windshield. I can still hear the smack it made against the glass."

Such brutality might seem wildly out of character for Buddy. But the sad truth is that in the male-dominated late fifties—especially in a place like West Texas—even kindly and well-disposed young men saw nothing reprehensible in hitting their girlfriends. Having no special feelings for this particular young woman, possibly even rather disliking her, Buddy no doubt would have seen her pregnancy as a deliberate plot to ruin his life. And, indeed, it would have been the end of everything. In a community such as Lubbock, extramarital pregnancy was the worst of all social disgraces. For someone raised in the Scriptures the way Buddy had been, abortion could not be an option, even if he knew how to procure one. The only way of saving his family and his church from public disgrace would have been to grit his teeth and marry the girl. Instead of soaring with the Crickets, he would be tied to Lubbock by diapers, mortgages, and monthly payments; instead of a rock 'n' roll star, he would have to turn into an adult.

"The situation in the car quickly quietened down," Niki Sullivan remembers, "because behaving that way wasn't Buddy's style. That was the reaction of a man faced by something he did not need in his life at that point. He wanted to make it so bad . . . God, he wanted it so bad. And when someone wants something that badly, and suddenly thinks he's going to be stopped from getting it, it's understandable that there's some kind of physical release."

His usual confidant and savior in times of trouble was his brother Larry. But Larry Holley says now that he knew nothing about any of this. According to a close family friend, Buddy's mother was the one who found out after mistakenly opening a letter from the girl to him, repeating her accusation. His parents rallied to his side, visiting the girl's family and convincing them that a shotgun marriage to Buddy would create more problems than it solved. Between the two families a plan was hammered out to save them from public scandal, albeit one reeking of the sexual inequity of those times. The young woman would go away from Lubbock to have the baby, and then put it up for adoption. Buddy would be absolved of responsibility, and could continue with his career as planned.

Niki Sullivan also claims to have been with Buddy at his one subsequent meeting with the baby's mother. "It was later in the year, when we were on tour. We came through Texas and passed near the unmarried mothers' home where she'd been sent to have the baby. We stopped the car and Buddy got out by himself and walked over to the wire fence that ran around the place. The girl came along on the other side of the fence and the two of them stood there for a few minutes, talking through the wire. Then Buddy got back into the car and we drove away. He didn't talk about what had happened, and he never mentioned it afterwards."

The story has just one flaw. The person named by several knowledgeable sources as the mother of Buddy's illegitimate child is adamant that she knew him only slightly and certainly never dated him. She got married before Buddy allegedly made her pregnant, and her children—by the same husband—were girls. The trail stops here. But one of my sources is sure that a baby was born to her and Buddy and that it was a boy. We are left with no more than a tantalizing thought: Somewhere in the United States at this moment there may be a man in his early forties who has no idea that he's Buddy Holly's only son.

☆   ☆   ☆

On July 28, 1957, Buddy and the Crickets took the evening TWA flight from Amarillo to New York, little suspecting how long it would be before they saw the West Texas plains again. The current week's *Billboard* listed "That'll Be the Day" as a "best buy," though it still had not broken into the magazine's Hot 100. Petty had had to go to Florida but was flying up to join them in New York the following day. Meantime, each had been provided with a list of his fussily detailed instructions:

> Be at the Amarillo Air Terminal Sunday evening at least by 6:30 to check reservations and to check baggage. Take enough cash along to pay for excess weight and meals between flights. Take about $30–40 cash . . . the rest in travelers' checks. Be sure to take all available identification for each member of the group.
>
> Sign only engagement contracts and nothing more. Take extra sets of guitar strings and drum sticks, head etc. Take out floater insurance for entire group with everyone's name on the contract. Be sure to pack records with clothes to take on trip. Take all available clean underwear and other articles for use on trip.
>
> When you get to New York, take a cab directly to the Edison hotel and check in there. We will see you about noon of that day.
>
> Get at least two dozen Dramamine tablets and take one tablet at least 15 minutes before departure. Make out trip insurance to your parents. Take at least 25 feet of extension cord. Take small [shoe] shine kit for trip. Toilet articles of your choice. Get telephone credit card and carry with you. Take a small Bible with you and READ it. Get hotel credit cards or at least make application for same. Be sure to get and keep receipts for all money spent. Be sure to send money back to Clovis for bank account.

On arrival at the Edison (where they had now risen to the grandeur of a $27.70-per-day suite), they found a telegram awaiting them: "Congratulations and welcome to the big city. See you a little bit later. Papa Norman."

The "black tour," as it has come to be known among Holly aficionados, turned out better than anyone had dared hope. Although understandably bemused by their presence, the Crickets' fellow performers showed them no hostility or resentment; on the contrary, headliner Clyde McPhatter and most of the others went out of their way to be helpful and encouraging.

For opening night at Baltimore's Royal Theater, Papa Norman was on hand to support his boys and, if necessary, arrange a rapid evacuation. There was admittedly a moment of stupefied silence from the audience when the emcee announced "The Crickets" and the curtain went up to reveal four white faces, two of them bespectacled, above four brand-new boxy, pale gray suits. Then Buddy hit his Stratocaster and went straight into overdrive, as was his wont; by the first chorus, if it took even that long, the whole house was with the pick in the palm of his hand. The rest of the week went equally well, even though Buddy suffered an attack of laryngitis midway through and, on a couple of nights, was unable to sing at all. Niki Sullivan took over the lead vocals with no noticeable drop in applause level.

Week two, at the Howard Theater, Washington, was equally successful. Word had spread by now that, although these Crickets might be white, they could give the black ones at least a run for their money. As an additional boost, the summit of Everest had come into sight at long last. On August 12, "That'll Be the Day" entered *Billboard*'s Hot 100 at No. 65. Next to the chart, ironically, was a Chess-Checker record company display ad for the Ravens' competing cover version. Buddy's bill from the Ambassador Hotel shows how modest were his celebrations: "Room, $5.31 . . . LD phone $1.54 . . . Phone, 20¢ . . . Restaurant, $4.29 . . . Restaurant, 16¢."

The Apollo, New York, promised no such easy capitulation, however. Standing on 125th Street in the heart of Harlem, it had not presented a white performer on this stage since the "mixed" orchestras of the jazz and swing era. Fortunately for them, the Texans had not been forewarned of the Apollo crowd's peculiar ruthlessness, expressed most forcefully at a weekly Talent Night which reduced even performers from the immediate neighborhood to palpitant wrecks. Still less did they appreciate that Harlem was a place where white people did not walk, let alone seek lodgings. Arriving for their week's engagement, they cheerfully registered at the Hotel Theresa, directly opposite the Apollo, at 125th Street and Seventh Avenue, where a week's stay for all four, including extras and taxes, cost $76.65.

A good-luck telegram from Murray Deutch, "Congratulations and welcome back. I know you will knock them dead," contained more wishful thinking than certainty. Although everyone in the Apollo's audience knew exactly who and what they were, especially now "That'll Be the Day" was on the charts, a frigid silence greeted them as the curtain went up. "There was this big lady, about four-hundred pounds, sitting right in front," Niki Sullivan remembers. "Before we could hit a note, she hollered out, 'You better sound like the record!'"

It was the last place on earth where Buddy's "y'all" Texas charm could be expected to work its usual magic. And, indeed, the first couple of shows went as badly as they possibly could. Except for "That'll Be the Day," the audience seemed indifferent to the Crickets' original songs; apathetic silence changed to spasmodic booing and the creative heckling for which the Apollo was, and still is, famous. It might have ended catastrophically but for Buddy's equal mastery of a far more acceptable type of material. "When we just couldn't get through with our own stuff, Buddy turns around and says 'Ah, the hell with it, let's give 'em "Bo Diddley,"'" Niki remembers. "He started cutting up and jumping around, giving it everything he had." If the Apollo's audience is pitilessly intolerant of failure, it also famously respects courage and chutzpah. The Texans finished their set amid wild applause and shouts for more, which were repeated at every show for the rest of the week.

On August 23, ever the punctilious correspondent, Buddy wrote to his father, at work on a building job in Wichita Falls: "We finished playing the Apollo last night, and it sure feels good to know that we can relax for a few days. . . . We are staying downtown now, at the Forrest hotel, so you can drop a card here if you have time. . . . There's not much else to tell except that we found out last night that we had sold half a million [of "That'll Be the Day"] as of Wednesday night. Everyone says it should sell at least a million."

Big-time engagements were now coming thick and fast. Also on August 23, Buddy and the Crickets traveled to Philadelphia to appear on a brand-new rock 'n' roll television show called *American Bandstand*, fronted by a dapper young ex-sportscaster named Dick Clark. It was the first network show to reproduce the atmosphere of a teenage hop and the first to regard teenagers' opinions about the music as worth taking seriously. That simple formula would make it the longest-running pop music show on American television and Clark himself, unchangingly boyish and brush-topped, one of the most spectacular American triumphs over Father Time.

The most crucial factor in "That'll Be the Day"'s final ascent, however, was the approval and endorsement of the great Alan Freed. On the strength of his claim to have invented the term "rock 'n' roll," the one-time Cleveland disc jockey had become the most influential figure in American popular music. Age thirty-five, with corrugated hair, bulbous eyes, and a voice like congealing molasses, Freed sold himself with consummate skill to his youthful audience as the one and only adult in creation who truly understood their music and them. As a deejay, he combined immaculate taste with unusual strength of mind: he always played the original records of black artists in preference to the bland white cover versions, and was fired from his own rock 'n' roll TV show rather than yield to the sponsor's demand not to see black boys and white girls dancing together.

But as well as coining "rock 'n' roll," Freed also coined a fortune from it, appearing as himself in a succession of exploitation movies like *Rock Around the Clock,* putting his name on innumerable songs as a quid pro quo for plugging them, and promoting live shows at the Brooklyn Paramount Theater that produced box-office grosses not seen since the Frank Sinatra mania of the late forties.

From August 30 to September 5, the Crickets were added to Freed's "Holiday of Stars" spectacular at the Brooklyn Paramount, co-starring with Little Richard, Larry Williams, the Del Vikings, the Cleftones, Mickey and Sylvia, and "the Alan Freed Orchestra" (yet another nice little earner for Moondog), featuring black instrumental aces like Sam the Man Taylor and saxophonist King Curtis. The pay was musicians' union scale, which, after deductions and Papa Norman's commission, came to just over $1,100 between four, for what the contract termed "a minimum of 29 shows in any one week."

The marathon rock 'n' roll shows put on in American theaters and arenas during the late fifties were closer to old-fashioned nonstop vaudeville than anything in the modern concept of a rock concert. At the Brooklyn Paramount and its higher-prestige counterpart in Manhattan there would be five, sometimes seven shows a day, the first at 11 A.M., the last at 2 the following morning. For a one-dollar ticket the rock 'n' roll fan got up to twenty acts, most of them with a record in the current Top 10, followed by a schlock Western or detective movie, the management's way of clearing the house between shows. The lines would stretch twice around the block, corralled by barricades and squads of mounted police dressed in the old-style flap-over tunics that made them look like Edwardian chauffeurs. Despite all these discomforts and provocations, trouble among the mixed-race crowd was virtually unknown.

With such a gigantic program to get through, each act would be onstage for only a few minutes, enough to blast out their current hit, its B-side, and, maybe, an upcoming release. The age of specialized sound systems and dramatic light shows was not to dawn for another decade or so. Performers used the house microphones and lights, augmented by their own puny guitar amplifiers. Vocalists and singing groups enjoyed the backing of the Alan Freed Orchestra, but a self-contained vocal/instrumental group like the Crickets had to fill the massive stage and dominate the huge, shrieking vault all on their own. They were thus compelled to develop a stage presence far more energetic and spontaneous than the synchronized swaying and finger-snapping of vocal ensembles like the Diamonds and the Cleftones.

Buddy sang in a sidelong posture at the principal—often only—stand-mike, his left leg planted firmly forward as if he were about to take a stride on a roller skate. In the wilder rock 'n' roll numbers, he would start to cut up—not with the self-conscious slinkiness of those who borrowed their body language from Elvis, but in a cheerfully self-mocking way, swinging his Stratocaster around on its strap, snarling, whooping, and rebel-yelling, crouching double to sing a chorus into the low-level mike beside Joe B. Mauldin's bass fiddle, even slithering across the stage on his knees, to the detriment of his new stone-gray slacks.

Joe B., so unassuming elsewhere, matched Buddy in onstage mugging and clowning, at some moments keeling over so far with his bass that he would be playing it virtually parallel to the floor. Niki Sullivan stood away to Buddy's left, compensating for his inaudible rhythm guitar by moving around a lot and conscientiously mouthing the backup "ooh's" and "aah's." J. I. Allison, who seemed to have grown several inches since leaving Lubbock as well as losing the worst of his teenage acne, belabored his undersize drum kit with his self-satisfied, feline half-smile. Though none of the four could be called good-looking in the conventional (i.e., Presley) sense, they performed their three-song set amid a bedlam of feminine shrieks and squeals as mindless and undiscriminating as newborn babies', as unrelenting as a Texas blue norther, as palpable and impenetrable as a brick wall.

They had all been excited at the prospect of a reunion with Little Richard, their old backstage crony at Lubbock's Cotton Club, now at the apogee of outrageousness and extravagance. But even knowing him as they did, the Texans were dumbfounded by the manner in which Richard said "Hello again."

"He called all four of us up to see him in his dressing room at the Paramount," Niki Sullivan remembers. "When we walked in, Richard was there with his girlfriend, Angel, and Larry Williams [a Little Richard soundalike, soon to record 'Bony Moronie']. Richard was masturbating and giving head to Angel while Larry Williams made love to her from behind. None of them took any notice of Buddy, J. I., Joe B., and me, standing in the doorway. They just carried right on with what they were doing.

"Through the window we could see straight across the street, where there was some kind of hospital or institution for the elderly. When Richard had finished what he was doing with Angel, he fastened his robe, walked over to the window, and looked over to this home or hospital or whatever it was. I mean, its windows were full of these old people in bathrobes, with doctors and nurses looking after them. 'Oh, gee,' Richard said, 'I wonder if the folks over there would like me to go and witness [hold a religious meeting] with them.'"

This is the origin of the scene in Richard's own memoirs where Buddy allegedly joins him in sex with Angel, then runs straight onstage to perform, still with a gaping-open fly.

In fact, during that week at the Brooklyn Paramount, Buddy had a more complex sexual agenda to pursue. For June Clark had given in to his pleas and flown up from Lubbock with her son Carley, on the pretext of visiting her shoe-model sister Tuddie. Buddy and June were reunited under the camouflage of a party for Buddy Knox; after that, Tuddie lent them her apartment on West Tenth Street. When Tuddie needed to be at home, they would meet to make love at a nearby apartment hotel.

Fearing that J. I. might also be sweet on June, Buddy was careful to keep his liaison secret from his best friend. But Niki and Joe B. knew all about it. "One afternoon, Buddy took the two of us with him when he went to meet June," Niki says. "We had to wait outside the apartment for him while the two of them got it on."

The strained relations between Niki and Jerry had seemed to improve of late, especially since J. I.'s eighteenth birthday, on August 31, when his fellow Crickets threw a surprise party for him at their hotel. A commemorative snapshot shows the four of them kneeling like schoolboys against one of two single beds in a tiny, chaotic room. Spread on the coverlet before them is a miniature birthday cake, ringed by an elaborate pattern of colored candies. Below, more candies are arranged in neat capital letters to spell out the birthday boy's middle name, IVAN.

But a couple of nights after Buddy's assignation with June, trouble between Niki and J. I. broke out again. Niki admits that he was in a hyperactive and aggressive state, having been forced to give up smoking to please Papa Norman. "Jerry and I were shouting at each other and, to get back at him, I blurted out that Buddy had met June and what they'd done. It was dumb, I admit. Jerry got real mad and we had an all-out fistfight. I got him good above one eye; I mean it swelled up real big. Right after that, we had to go up on to the Paramount's roof and have pictures done for our first album, *The Chirping Crickets*. They had to retouch the shot to try to hide Jerry's swollen eye, but you cold still see it. You can see it to this day."

What even Niki did not know was that Buddy's infatuation with June had grown even more intense during the weeks he had been away from her. "He told me time after time that it wasn't just a crush—that he wanted to have a permanent relationship with me," June says now. "I seriously thought about it, because I did have feelings for him. But in the end, I realized I could never leave Carley.

"The last time we were due to be together [in New York], just before he left on that first big national tour, we ended up just talking on the phone. Buddy told me again that he wanted me to leave Nig and go away with him. I kept saying I couldn't because I had a little boy. It went on for about an hour, him begging, me saying no I just couldn't. In the end, there was nothing else to do but just hang up. I took Carley back to Lubbock, and I never saw Buddy or spoke to him again."

☆ ☆ ☆

The rollercoaster was picking up speed every second. From the Brooklyn Paramount, Buddy and the Crickets went straight into a nationwide multi-act tour put together by New York's most powerful rock 'n' roll agent, Irving Feld of the General Artists Corporation. Called "The Biggest Show of Stars for 1957," it also featured Chuck Berry, Fats Domino, Paul Anka, the Everly Brothers, Frankie Lymon, the Drifters, LaVern Baker, Clyde McPhatter, Johnnie and Joe, the Spaniels, and the Bobettes. The tour opened in Pittsburgh on September 6, the day before Buddy's twenty-first birthday, and continued virtually without a break, through September, October and November.

These so-called package tours were designed by hardheaded impresarios like Irving Feld with a single objective: to carry hitmakers to the largest possible audience during the brief span of favor that they could be expected to enjoy. Even the hyperbole of the show's title reflected this hasty opportunism—i.e., it may be the biggest show of stars for 1957, but don't expect too many of them to be still around in 1958. Wages were minimal: Buddy and the Crickets between them received $1,000 a week, out of which they had to pay all their expenses on the road. Like everyone else, they did not do it for the money but for the prestige, the exposure, and the additional record sales they might generate by performing "That'll Be the Day" and "Peggy Sue" in approximately sixty cities throughout the United States and Canada.

Being on the road with a rock 'n' roll show in 1957 was nothing like the movable feast of luxury and debauchery it would become during the sixties and seventies. The whole enormous troupe of artists were packed into a single bus, with a second one for the full orchestra that traveled with them. The itinerary consisted mostly of one-nighters, planned with a blithe disregard of geographical logic. The opening ten-day stretch, for instance, took them from Pittsburgh southeast to Richmond, Virginia, then northeast to Annapolis, Maryland, south to Norfolk, Virginia, northwest to Cincinnati and Columbus, Ohio, east to Hershey back in Pennsylvania, north (by air) over the Great Lakes to Toronto and Montreal, south to Syracuse and Rochester, New York, and Baltimore, Maryland.

The hundreds, sometimes thousands of miles between each night's venue, seldom left enough time for the performers to go to a hotel after their show. As often as not, they would be herded straight back on to the bus in their stage clothes to drive through the night and most of the following day. "If you're eighteen to twenty years old, the way most of us were, you can live that kind of life," Joe B. Mauldin says. "You'd climb up into the luggage rack and go to sleep—and sleep like a baby, usually. Those things mean nothing when you're on tour with Chuck Berry . . . Fats Domino . . . girls screaming for you and asking for autographs. It's all one big adventure."

Among this gaggle of hyped and hyperactive young males, vice and self-indulgence were miraculously absent. Drinking was minimal and drug use almost unknown, among the performers at least; on one of the Canadian legs, Frankie Lymon's manager was busted for marijuana possession. The punishing schedule allowed few opportunities to take advantage of the girls who mobbed them after each show. Between the different acts, big and small, black and white, there was an almost total lack of jealousy and competitiveness. On the marathon interstate journeys, if not playing cards on suitcase tops they would all jam together. "We didn't need booze or drugs," Niki Sullivan says. "We were all on a natural high. The Drifters used to sit there at three in the morning and sing 'How Deep Is the Ocean' with beautiful a cappella harmony that still brings a lump to my throat when I think of it. Now, what makes guys sing for no money, at three in the morning?"

The black performers, being a little older and more experienced, tended to look after the white newcomers. LaVern Baker, the only female star on the bill, acted as den mother, sewing buttons back onto stage suits if they came adrift. Chuck Berry is not usually considered a generous or unselfish figure, but to the Crickets on that tour—especially to their diminutive bass player—he was kindliness itself. "Chuck was a super guy," Joe B. remembers. "If ever you asked his advice about something, he'd say, 'Well, come on, let's sit down and talk this through.' He and Fats Domino were following the bus in their own cars, and Chuck invited me to ride in the beautiful Cadillac he had, and did everything he could to set me straight on the music business.

"Fats Domino was a sweet guy, too, but if you ever went too deep with him, he'd just talk to you in the titles of his songs. Like, after a show, he might say, 'How are you fellers getting to the next town?' We'd say, 'On the bus, Fats,' hoping he might offer us a ride in his car. 'So how are *you* getting there?' But Fats would just give a big smile and start clicking his fingers and singing 'I'm walkin', yes, indeed, I'm walkin'.'"

Understandably, the most immediate rapport that Buddy and the Crickets struck up was with the Everly Brothers. "We were all from the South, we'd all started out in country music," Phil Everly says. "It was like belonging to a fraternity."

Don Everly remembers first meeting the Texans backstage at the Forum in Montreal. "They were really friendly, funny guys, and they all had on these gray suits which you could tell had been bought in Texas. Phil and I were maybe six months ahead of them career-wise, and were already into Ivy League clothes, like the jackets with buttons right up the front, the pants with the little belt in back. As soon as Buddy saw what we were wearing, he looked at the other three, gave his big grin, and said, 'Let's go shop!'"

The Everlys' music, strongly guitar-accented, clearly articulated, and devoid of smut, had much in common with Buddy's. But whereas the Crickets provided their own accompaniment, the Everlys had to hire musicians at each venue. And while Buddy wrote his own songs, Don and Phil depended on outside writers, principally the husband-and-wife team of Boudleaux and Felice Bryant. "Phil and I had never thought of going around with a self-contained group like that," Don Everly says. "It made them seem real independent and solid against the world. They even had a kind of private language they spoke, through having grown up together. Yeah, we were supposed to be the big-timers, but we envied them in a lot of ways, even though they were so brand-new to the business and had all kinds of rough edges. Like, at that time, the only publicity picture they had was of the four of them back in Lubbock, in T-shirts and Levi's, setting tiles on a roof."

Buddy became a close friend of both brothers, even though they were very different characters within their perfect vocal harmony, the elder Don tractable and humorous, the younger Phil high-strung and fastidious. Don remembers Buddy's neat and methodical ways, in contrast to the general slovenliness of most performers on the road. Emulating his brother Larry, as always, and unmindful how bizarre an accessory it was for a rock 'n' roll star, Buddy had recently bought himself a meerschaum pipe. "I remember him bringing out this crazy pipe, the kind you saw old men in leather shorts smoking in Bavaria or Switzerland," Don Everly says. "He showed us all the special way you had to hold it, so as not to spoil the finish of it. And he had a special little case to carry it in."

Even with rock 'n' roll names as big as Chuck Berry and Fats Domino, the racial attitudes of the South remained inflexible. En route from Atlanta to New Orleans, police flagged down the two tour buses and segregated them, putting all the white performers on one and all the blacks on the other. For the shows in Columbus, Georgia; Chattanooga, and Birmingham, the white performers had to drop off the bill because local ordinances forbade blacks and whites to appear on the same stage. "Some other places where we played used to hang a big curtain down the middle of the auditorium," Joe B. Mauldin remembers. "The whites would be sitting on one side of it, the blacks on the other."

Life on the road held risks for white performers, especially the better-looking ones. Local boys whose girlfriends had screamed too loudly for this or that onstage dreamboat would sometimes form impromptu revenge gangs. "Security," that indispensable feature of modern rock star life, was virtually nonexistent in 1957. "I remember coming out of the theater, just to cross the street to my hotel," Don Everly says. "This big group of guys came after me, got hold of me, and picked me up bodily. They just carried me for three or four blocks like a sack of potatoes, with no idea what to do with me, until some of the people from the show caught up with us and rescued me. It was one of the most frightening experiences of my life."

"Buddy and the Crickets never seemed to alienate the guys the way Donald and I did," Phil Everly says. "But if it ever came to a fight, Buddy was never one to duck out. One time down in Florida, we were all going along a street, and I somehow got separated from the others. Suddenly I realize there's this whole group of young guys closing in all around me. I turned around, looking for help, and saw Buddy running—I mean really sprinting—along the sidewalk to help me. He faced up to this whole gang of guys . . . and they backed off. Seriously, he was ready to take on the whole group."

The life of a rock 'n' roll sensation like the Everlys may have looked enviable from the outside, but on the inside it was a fakir's bed of insults and belittlements. "Everyone used to say the same thing to us," Phil remembers. "'Do you kids realize how lucky you are to have gotten this far?' And 'What are you going to do when rock 'n' roll blows over?' Fear and guilt, that's what we were conditioned by."

Don agrees: "The thing always pressing on your mind was 'Where's our next hit coming from? How in the world are we going to pull it off again? And again after that?' It used to make you real close and secretive about all your ideas. Buddy was under the same pressure as all the rest of us—even more as time went on. But he never had that secretive, looking-over-your-shoulder attitude. I remember him playing a new song of his called 'Maybe Baby' and asking us what we thought of it. He'd suggest ideas that were right for Phil and me—he even wrote a song especially for us. He was the most generous person with his music I've ever met in this business."

On September 23, four months after its release, "That'll Be the Day" stood at No. 1 on both the pop and R&B charts, making it the top-selling single across the United States. On *Billboard*'s Hot 100 chart, which combined retail sales with radio and jukebox play, its highest place was

No. 3. There, to his chagrin, Buddy did not after all beat Paul Anka's "Diana."

"Peggy Sue," coupled with "Everyday," had come out under Buddy's name alone on Coral on September 20, and was now breaking nationwide in the way usually reserved for Elvis Presley records. The main Decca label also hastened to cash in on the name it had spurned nine months previously, and released Buddy's inferior Nashville version of "That'll Be the Day" (on which he'd been forced to give up his royalty entitlement) coupled with the Sonny Curtis song "Rock Around with Ollie Vee." This obvious attempt to dupe teenagers into buying the dud version of "That'll Be the Day" rather than the good one made Buddy angry and unhappy, but he was powerless to do anything about it. Further releases from those unhappy sessions with Owen Bradley were to shadow his successes on Brunswick and Coral until the Bradley's Barn inventory was exhausted, early in 1958.

For a rock 'n' roll act with a hit single in 1957, the next step was to release a long-playing record, still not generally known as an "album." Like so much else, it symbolized the anxiety of record companies to make the most of success that could not be expected to last. An LP usually bore the name of the hit single that had preceded it and—far from any notion of showcasing the performer's range or versatility—was seen as a way of making teenagers buy the same song all over again, at three or four times the price. A contract had already been made with Bob Thiele for Brunswick to put out the Crickets' first LP before the year's end. The problem was that they didn't have enough suitable material stockpiled in Clovis to provide the dozen or so tracks needed, and they would be on tour until the end of November.

Norman Petty solved the difficulty in characteristic fashion. Petty's trio also happened to be on the road, playing a weeklong engagement at Tinker Air Force Base, just outside Oklahoma City. When "The Biggest Show of Stars for 1957" stopped off at Oklahoma City, Petty borrowed the lounge of the Tinker officers' club and set up his Ampex tape machines there. On the night of September 29, after the Norman Petty Trio had finished their performance, Buddy and the Crickets arrived at the officers' club and a recording session was held in this improvised studio. It produced four new tracks of releasable standard: "You've Got Love," Roy Orbison's "Empty Cup," a new version of "Maybe Baby," and "Rock Me My Baby," a Buddy performance of typically innocent charm, its lyrics combining two nursery rhymes, "Hickory Dickory Dock" and "Rocka-bye Baby."

Buddy and Niki Sullivan finally realized they were distant cousins when "The Biggest Show of Stars" played the Heart of Texas fair in Waco on October 2. "There were only thirty-five people in the audience," Niki remembers. "Seventeen of them were Buddy's relations, who'd come over from the Lubbock area to root for him, and the other eighteen of them were relations of mine. That audience of thirty-five got one hell of a show—and there was one hell of a family reunion afterwards."

☆   ☆   ☆

Bob Thiele's decision to separate Buddy's name from the Crickets and give him a parallel solo career had originated purely as a marketing ploy. But in Buddy's orderly and logical mind, it created yet another working blueprint. Following the pattern set by "Words of Love," his own-name releases on Coral would tend toward the adventurous and experimental, while his output with the Crickets on Brunswick would be straightforward rock 'n' roll crowd-pleasers.

On this basis, the Crickets' follow-up to "That'll Be the Day" presented something of a problem. In 1957, one rule governed the sequel to a million-selling hit: it must sound as identical to that hit as was humanly possible. And among all the tracks stockpiled by Norman Petty in Clovis and at Tinker Air Force Base there was no obvious "That'll Be the Day 2." The nearest in atmosphere was "Oh Boy," by the two young Texas writers Sonny West and Bill Tilghman, which Buddy and the Crickets had recorded on the same scorching, sandstormy June weekend that produced "Peggy Sue" and "Everyday." The problem was that in the distant days of early last summer, no distinction had existed between "Buddy Holly" tracks and "Crickets" tracks. Fans who bought the Crickets' second release would naturally expect it to sound like the work of a vocal group once again.

It was, of course, a simple matter to dub background vocals onto Buddy's solo track. Unfortunately, Gary and Ramona Tollett, the husband-and-wife duo who had done such a good job for "That'll Be the Day," were no longer available. And although Buddy's three fellow Crickets all had voices of a sort, they were quite unable to reproduce the Tolletts' moody harmonies. Petty solved the problem by recruiting an outside vocal group named the Picks, comprising his Clovis school friends John and Bill Pickering and a mutual acquaintance, Bob Lapham. Between July and October, while Buddy and the Crickets were still on the road with "The Biggest Show of Stars for 1957," the Picks overdubbed backing vocals on "Oh Boy" as well as four tracks for the impending LP, "Maybe Baby," "An Empty Cup," "You've Got Love," and "Rock Me My Baby."

"Oh Boy" is the most brazen of all the Crickets' greatest hits, a turbo-charged rock 'n' roll racer which from its opening motor-roar of "All my love, all my kissin'" never slips from metal-pressing overdrive. Buddy's vocal is an innocently amorous war-cry, so full of excitement and joie de vivre, you feel he is not addressing any girl nor anticipating any tryst in particular but, rather, standing with his Stratocaster on some hilltop and, like a well-tailored young coyote, exhilaratedly baying at the moon.

"The Biggest Show of Stars for 1957," meanwhile, had reached California prior to heading north through Oregon and Washington and up into Canada once again. Reflecting the new state of the record charts, major changes in the bill had been made by the pragmatic Irving Feld. Out went the Spaniels, the Bobettes, and Johnnie and Joe; in came the Crickets' old Texas friends and rivals Buddy Knox and Jimmy Bowen, the Rhythm Orchids, and Eddie Cochran.

When Buddy and the Crickets performed "Peggy Sue" at the Memorial Auditorium, Sacramento, on October 18, the song's pertly pretty blonde inspiration was in the audience. Peggy Sue Gerron had left Lubbock High to finish her education at Sacramento's Bishop Armstrong Catholic Girls' School; with old-fashioned courtesy, her beau, J. I. Allison, had written to her mother for permission to invite her to the show. Though Peggy Sue had heard the hit bearing her name many times over the radio, she still had to keep pinching herself as, for the first time, she heard Buddy perform it live. When she went backstage later, she was amazed to discover how much J. I. had shot up. (This is needle-free 1957 remember; we are referring to J. I.'s sudden, mysterious increase in height.)

Eddie Cochran, the major new addition to the bill, was fresh from *The Girl Can't Help It,* selling a million copies of "Sittin' in the Balcony," and riotously touring Australia with Little Richard and Gene Vincent. A husky nineteen-year-old, born in Minnesota but transplanted to California, he combined Presleyesque looks, backswept hair, and plum-in-mouth mumble with talent on lead electric guitar that, some say, surpassed even Buddy's. He was a prodigious womanizer, a hard drinker, and a firearms nut, collecting historic Western guns like the Derringer and Buntline Special, and perfecting a fast draw that would have done credit to Wyatt Earp.

Cochran and Buddy had everything in common, except the drinking and fast draw, and over the next year were to become more like brothers than friends. By the time "The Biggest Show of Stars for 1957" had left Canada for Denver, they had turned their adjacent hotel rooms into a communal hangout for themselves and their bands. Interviewing Cochran after the Denver concert, deejay Freeman Hover of KCSR asked about "the good guitar music" coming from the next room. "That's Buddy Holly and the Crickets," Cochran replied. "They've just stolen my baritone ukelele . . ."

Hover then interviewed Buddy and J. I. Allison while Cochran sat nearby, flourishing a new pipe he'd bought that evening (another pipe-smoking rock 'n' roller!) and commenting with approval how "sophisticated" it made him look. After thanking the denizens of Denver, in his huskily polite fashion, for buying "That'll Be the Day," Buddy asked permission to put in a plug "for Eddie Cochran, settin' over there, so contented-like. He's starrin' in a picture that'll be out soon. . . . He said he might be able to arrange it for the Crickets to appear in that picture . . . And so we've been buddyin' up to him . . . gettin' in as good as we can!"

"The Biggest Show of Stars from 1957" wound up its three-month journey at the Mosque in Richmond, Virginia, on November 24. On November 27, Brunswick released the Crickets' "Oh Boy," coupled with the six-month-old "Not Fade Away." Four days later, Buddy, J. I., Niki, and Joe B. were back in New York City for the ultimate acknowledgment of their arrival in the show business first division. They had been booked by CBS to appear on *The Ed Sullivan Show*.

Their appearance, on the Sunday evening of December 1, went out live, coast to coast, but was also preserved on primitive black and white videotape. By comparison with Elvis Presley's appearance a year earlier —and with the Beatles' seven years later—the occasion was decorous. The Sullivan show's main attraction was not rock 'n' rollers but the All-America football team. Arrayed in black, shawl-collared tuxedos,

Buddy and the Crickets had two spots, playing "That'll Be the Day" in the show's first segment and "Peggy Sue" in the second. Whereas they had merely lip-synched on *American Bandstand,* they were expected to give a bona fide performance here, albeit with their sound turned down to a paranoically low level.

The result, preserved for posterity in grainy, distorted gray and white, gives little idea of their true impact onstage. To compensate for the restricted volume, both numbers are played much faster than one is used to hearing them. Assailed by ritual shrieks from the studio audience, Buddy looks a more unlikely rock 'n' roll idol than ever, with his rumpled hair, wispy half-frame glasses, and anemic smile. Around his neck, like some priestly regalia, hangs the V-shape of a newfangled body mike; for all that, the sound quality is atrocious, robbing his voice of all color and expression, reducing his guitar breaks to a wiry scrabble. Cutaway shots show rubicund, shiny-eyed little Joe B. on bass, working hard at looking as if he's working hard; Niki Sullivan (whose guitar was not even plugged in) mouthing inaudible background vocals; J. I. Allison, coiled behind his drums like a sleek, self-satisfied cat. Each song is rounded off by an intrusive blast from the studio orchestra, to which Buddy synchronizes a stiff little bow from the waist.

Their host, the mighty Ed Sullivan, proved well up to form as the sworn enemy of rock 'n' roll and all who espoused it. Hunched of shoulder and heavy of jaw, and wearing a sharkskin suit that looked as if it had the coathanger left in it, Sullivan took customary pains to make his young guests feel anything but at home. Under the conditions of live television at that time, Buddy and the Crickets had to play with the great man standing just off camera, only a couple of feet from his namesake Niki. At one point in mid-number, Niki heard him give a satirical hiss of "Go, Tex!"

The moment when Buddy is called back for a brief front-of-curtain interview, as the others hastily remove their equipment, likewise reeks of metropolitan condescension: let's give this hick a break and see if he can string two words together. Buddy's charm and fluency are all the more impressive for his obvious surprise that Sullivan should pick this of all moments to start being friendly.

". . . Where do you come from? Lubbock, Teck-suss?" Sullivan asks, managing to make it sound like the name of some remote North Atlantic atoll.

"Lubbock, Texas, yes sir," Buddy nods.

"Do you go to school down there?"

"Well, we did, till we got out of high school, finally."

"And after high school you started playing together?"

"Yes sir, that's right."

"And were you a big hit from the start, or has it been sort of a long . . . ?"

"Well, we've had some rough times, I guess you'd say," Buddy admits with a grin. "But we've been real lucky, gettin' it this quick."

"Texas . . . nice to have you up here," Sullivan concludes, accepting the unscheduled handshake Buddy offers him—little guessing how drastically he will revise that opinion within the space of a month.

☆　☆　☆

If the Crickets had expected a heroes' return to Lubbock on December 4, they were disappointed. Awaiting them at the airport were no screaming girls, no brass bands, no reporter and photographer from the Lubbock *Avalanche,* no local dignitaries to present them with the keys to the city. Buddy had planned a triumphal homecoming, arriving at his parents' house on 39th Street in a hired limo, resplendent in one of his new Alfred Norton tuxedos. But alas, he did not warn Ella and L. O. in advance and when he got there, both of them happened to be out. As many a star before him had learned, and many have since, nothing brings one down to earth quite so unceremoniously one's hometown.

The day after their return to Lubbock, Niki Sullivan announced he was quitting. The reason he gave was total exhaustion after three months of nonstop touring, from which there was still to be virtually no respite over the approaching Christmas holiday. But in truth, Niki's ninety days as a Cricket had almost all been unhappy and uncomfortable, as well as musically null and void. Being at loggerheads with J. I. Allison made him odd man out, since Buddy invariably sided with Jerry and little Joe B. followed the majority in everything. By the end of the "Biggest Show of Stars" tour, Niki had felt totally isolated by the others' hostility and teasing—so much so that on the final day, when he took the tour bus microphone to bid farewell to his new friends the Drifters, he almost broke down in tears.

Nowadays, such a defection from a group at the peak of its success would be headline news. Back in 1957, however, the national media took no interest in such things; even the Crickets' fans barely knew any of their names but Buddy's. Inside the music business, however, Niki's prestige stood high enough to win him a recording contract with the Dot label. Over the next few years he was to release several records under his own name and also front a band called Soul Incorporated, before gravitating from rock 'n' roll into the electronics industry.

Niki Sullivan's attempts to extract some kind of compensatory payoff from Norman Petty ought to have forewarned Buddy about the process of getting down to any kind of financial brass tacks with Clovis Man. Accompanied by his father, Niki went to Petty seeking for details of the Crickets' earnings thus far, optimistically anticipating the quarter share that Buddy had insisted each member of the group receive. "We asked to see the books twenty-two times, but Norman always had some excuse. 'Oh, they're not at the studio right now . . .' 'They're being audited.' My dad was right in what he said the first time he ever met Norman. 'Son, *never* trust a businessman who keeps a Bible on his desk.'"

Worn down by Petty's evasions, Niki settled for a payment of $1,000, his share of the proceeds from "That'll Be the Day" and one-third writer's royalties from "I'm Gonna Love You Too." Though a trickle of royalties was to reach him over the years, he says it never came anywhere near a quarter what "That'll Be the Day" was eventually worth. Nor did his church receive the promised tithe. "As I always say, Jesse James wasn't killed in the eighteen-eighties. He was still alive in Clovis, New Mexico, until the nineteen-eighties."

There was initially some talk of replacing Niki with Sonny Curtis, that stalwart of Buddy's pre-Crickets lineup. But Sonny now had a flourishing career of his own, and in any case the gap was purely a cosmetic one, since Buddy and J. I. between them generated all the power, and more, necessary for stage appearances. Even so, their decision to carry on as a trio was an adventurous one. A three-man vocal/instrumental lineup was unknown in rock 'n' roll to that point, and in the decades since, has cropped up only rarely: Cream and the Jimi Hendrix Experience in the sixties and the Police in the post-punk seventies are among the few other notable examples.

No one could pretend that Niki was greatly missed when the new streamlined Crickets convened at Norman Petty's studio on December 19 to work on two tracks for unspecified future use. One was "(You're So

Square) Baby I Don't Care," a Leiber–Stoller song performed by Elvis Presley in his film *Jailhouse Rock,* now given a far quieter, subtler treatment with softly revving rhythm Stratocaster, and the cardboard-box percussion technique of "Not Fade Away." Buddy's vocal acknowledged his debt to the King, though it was now in a style completely his own that he sang "You're s' square" in a soft, sighing register, then plunged into the sub-basement for "Baby I don't care." The second track, "Look at Me," was a gently hiccuppy ballad, credited to "Buddy Holly / Norman Petty / Jerry Allison," and typically blending self-confidence with uncertainty.

Here once again Petty decided that piano rather than guitar accompaniment was called for, and Vi was summoned from her boudoir to provide it. Standing at the Baldwin grand in her robe and slippers, the fidgety, flighty woman as usual metamorphosed into a calmly intuitive musician. Her rolling bass solo under Buddy's knowing yet wistful voice makes one of the most charming mixtures ever to emerge from Clovis Man's electronic melting pot.

The main consequence of Niki Sullivan's departure from the Crickets was to change the all-for-one-and-one-for-all manner in which the group had previously divided their earnings. Norman Petty had at last persuaded Buddy to acknowledge that, as a hitmaker under his own name as well as lead vocalist, lead instrumentalist, and principal songwriter, he deserved more than the equal fourth share he'd taken up to now. Henceforward, he was to receive 50 percent of record royalties and concert earnings; while J. I. and Joe B. received 25 percent each.

This was purely notional anyway, since their combined earnings went directly to Petty to be paid into the Buddy Holly and the Crickets joint bank account. Though Buddy, J. I., and Joe B. all had personal checking accounts at Lubbock banks, almost nothing ever came into these, and even less went out. Every bill they incurred, collectively and personally, was sent directly to Petty—retailers and suppliers of the late fifties really were that trusting!—and settled by Petty, using his power of attorney on their Clovis National Bank account. The checks covered, among other things, session fees to the Picks vocal group, installment payments on Joe B's double bass, repair work on Buddy's car at the Petty family garage, telephone calls, and regular disbursements of pocket money to each of the Crickets—for instance, $600 on October 25, the check made out "To: Mrs. L. O. Holley. For: Buddy."

Exactly how much he had earned thus far was the last thing on Buddy's mind at this point. All that mattered was the excitement of seeing his music leap onto the charts, and the intoxication of having ready cash to spend. In New York, his new friends Don and Phil Everly had taken his sartorial image in hand, introducing him to Phil's menswear shop on Third Avenue where all the rock 'n' rollers went for Ivy League clothes. Buddy, Jerry, and Joe B. all were now faultlessly collegiate in long, thin tweed jackets with vertical stripes, thin lapels, and four buttons up the front; shirts with pin-fastening collars; cuffless, back-belted trousers; shoes with side buckles instead of laces; and rakish little narrow-brimmed hats. "We taught 'em about going to dinner in restaurants, too, instead of just grabbing a hamburger," Don Everly says. "And going to nightclubs instead of just to a movie. They caught on to all of that real quick."

The boy who'd grown up in near-poverty, and spent almost all his early life in Levi's and T-shirts, turned into a voracious shopper, with a natural homing instinct for the best in everything. It had not taken Buddy long to discover that the classiest menswear in New York was not to be found at Phil's but at Alfred Norton on West 50th Street. Clovis Man's paper treasure trove includes receipts for Buddy's spending sprees at Alfred Norton: bills for $150 stage tuxedos, $8.95 cummerbunds, ties at $3.50 or $1.50 apiece, and the $45 dark blue blazer with anchor-emblazoned gilt buttons which—after the Strat—was his proudest possession. His waist measurement is given, unvaryingly, as 29 inches. The salesman, always the same one, is named as "Frank."

Don and Phil Everly claim credit for planting the seeds of the biggest image change of all. "We both kept on at Buddy to do something about his glasses," Phil says. "Those things he had, with the half-frames, were the same ones he'd been wearing since high school. Donald and I both told him, 'Hey, look, you've proved that a guy who wears glasses can make it in rock 'n' roll. So why be ashamed of the glasses? Why not make them a real upfront statement, like, 'Okay, I wear glasses, and here they are'?"

Back home in Lubbock on that pre-Christmas visit, Buddy continued his determined metamorphosis from gawky provincial into smooth and seamless star. At the Everly Brothers' prompting, he had also been to a fashionable men's hairdresser in Manhattan to have his unruly dark curls styled in a permanent wave. But the results did not look or feel right and, as soon as he got home, he went to Jake Goss, the no-frills Lubbock barber who had cut both his and his father's hair for many years. "I took the wave out and gave him a more natural look," Goss remembers. "But he never did decide the way he wanted to have his hair fixed." After hair in the self-improvement blueprint came those disfiguringly snaggled and fluoride-stained West Texas teeth. On December 14 and again six days later, Buddy visited Lubbock dentist Clifford E. Fisher and had his front teeth encased in gleaming caps: subsequently, the Buddy Holly and the Crickets account was debited by $596.

Also on December 20, as a reward to himself for the hours of discomfort under Dr. Fisher's drill, he called at the Stewart-Meadors Chevrolet dealership in Clovis to collect the 1958-model car he had picked out for himself two days earlier. It was an Impala V8 two-seat coupe in symbolic coral pink. Norman Petty subsequently made the $300 downpayment from the Buddy Holly and the Crickets account, negotiating a $721 discount on the car's $3,648.55 list price and paying off the balance within the month. At first, the Impala's "Powerglide" automatic transmission gave trouble, refusing to shift out of low. The day after picking up the car, having already racked up 188 miles, Buddy took it to a Lubbock Chevrolet dealer and had the fault rectified (at a cost of $2).

Only his family and a few close friends knew why Buddy was especially anxious to cut an impressive figure around Lubbock this Christmas. Echo McGuire would also be home for the holidays from her college in Nebraska. At some point out on the road these past three months, Buddy's infatuation with June Clark had faded and he'd realized he was as much in love with Echo as ever.

When "The Biggest Show of Stars for 1957" had performed at the Civic Auditorium in Omaha on November 4, he had tried to phone Echo at her school and ask her to come and see him, but, to her distress, the message hadn't reached her. At a later stopover in the Black Hills of South Dakota, he'd had a present specially made for Echo: a gold charm necklace spelling "Buddy Holley" in tasteful italic script. His use of his real surname rather than its world-famous mutation was highly significant. He wanted to reassure Echo he was still the same person she'd met all those years ago at Roscoe Wilson Elementary School and gone skating and hiking and praying with; that whatever might have happened to each of them in the intervening months meant nothing, and they could go on from here together just as they'd always planned.

But it was not to be. At college in Nebraska, Echo had fallen in love with a fellow student, a lanky, humorous farm boy from Missouri named Ron Griffith, whose studiousness and Christian ideals matched her own. When she returned home to Lubbock that Christmas of 1957, Ron came with her.

"I intended to tell Buddy about it face to face," Echo says now. "But somehow we never did manage to get together." Ron has a different memory, however. "I'm sure he did come by your house one time. Seems like I waited there while you and Buddy went to get a Coke." In any case, the moment when Echo broke it to Buddy that her feelings for him had changed, and that Ron Griffith was now the person with whom she wanted to share her life, came while they were talking on the telephone.

Buddy's brother Larry, always the one best able to read Buddy's heart, thinks he carried a torch for Echo all the brief remainder of his life. Her mother, Pansie McGuire, is equally sure of it. "Every song he wrote was for Echo before they parted and after, too. People might say, 'Well, why didn't he ever mention her by name?' but to me that was just like Buddy. He thought that maybe the songs might be recorded by other people someday, and he didn't want Echo's name passed around among a lot of musicians as if she belonged to anyone."

Echo married Ron Griffith in Lubbock on St. Valentine's Day, 1958. After leaving college in Nebraska, she studied at the University of Montana, then both she and her husband became teachers. During the early years of their marriage, Ron says, he knew that Echo still loved Buddy. But she was destined never to see him or hear from him again.

Buddy never did find an opportunity to give Echo that custom-made gold necklace spelling out "Buddy Holley." "After they split up, Buddy sent it to Mother" Larry says. "I guess he couldn't bear to look at it again."

☆   ☆   ☆

Over that Christmas season, "Peggy Sue" under Buddy's name reached No. 3 on the charts, while "Oh Boy" under the Crickets' climbed steadily toward its eventual peak of No. 10. Buddy, Jerry, and Joe B. had gone straight into another Alan Freed stage show, the "Holiday of Stars," this time at the prestigious Paramount Theater in midtown Manhattan. With them on the gigantic bill were their new friends the Everly Brothers, plus Fats Domino, Paul Anka, Danny and the Juniors, and a new piano-punishing sensation from darkest Louisiana named Jerry Lee Lewis. Their triple chart success had sent their price soaring to $4,200 for the ten-day engagement.

On December 28, they made the most bizarre of all their television appearances, performing "Peggy Sue" on *The Arthur Murray Party,* a show hosted by the doyen of ballroom dancing and his wife, Kathryn. Heaven knows what prompted the Murrays to add rock 'n' roll to their usual program of old-fashioned formation waltzes and foxtrots, but spots on prime-time television shows were not so numerous that any could be lightly turned down; besides, the fee offered was a handsome $2,000. Buddy and the Crickets were introduced as "rock 'n' roll specialists" by Kathryn Murray, a gowned and bejeweled woman with the clipped pseudo-British voice of a Park Avenue socialite, but evidently quite amiable and tolerant for all that.

"Now, whatever you may think of rock 'n' roll," she admonished strict-tempo zealots all over the nation, "I think you have to keep a nice open mind about what the young people go for; otherwise, the young ones will think you don't understand them." Buddy, J. I., and Joe B. then did their stuff on a cleared section of dance floor—Buddy darting the odd incredulous look at the others—while a line of girls in stiff ball gowns stood behind them, one or two daring to sway fractionally with the drumbeat.

On New Year's Day 1957, Buddy had had nothing to look forward to but a torn-up Decca contract and a country-and-Western tour, playing backup to Hank Locklin and Cowboy Copas. Twelve months later to the day, he had three records on the charts; his name was known across America and was beginning to reverberate around the world; everyone seemed to be talking about rock 'n' roll's latest "overnight sensation."

Tours stretched solidly ahead, to ever more distant and thrilling locations. From the New York Paramount, Buddy and the Crickets set off on another GAC road show, "America's Greatest Teenage Performing Stars," with the Everly Brothers, Paul Anka, and Danny and the Juniors: a seventeen-day swing through North Carolina, Virginia, Maryland, Pennsylvania, and Ohio. On January 27, they were to join Anka and Jerry Lee Lewis for two shows in Honolulu, the whole package then flying on for a weeklong tour of Australia. Buddy and the Crickets were to receive $6,000 and be guaranteed "100 percent" billing: their names in the largest-size type in all advertisements.

On January 25, in a few snatched hours between packing and un-
packing, Buddy had his first-ever recording session in New York. For the
first time, the moving spirit was not Norman Petty, but Bob Thiele of
Coral-Brunswick. "Buddy had been saying how he'd like the two of us to
work together. So I booked him a session at Bell Sound Studios, and got
Milton de Lugg, the orchestra leader, in as producer, with extra session
men, like Al Caiola on guitar," Thiele remembered. "We had a vocal
group, the Jivetones, in on it, too. Petty, I know, got really uptight, thinking I was moving in on his boy. To be diplomatic, we had to let him
be there as backup pianist. All the time, I could feel the vibrations of
jealousy."

The session was prompted mainly by a song Buddy couldn't wait to
record, "Rave On," written by the same young partnership that had come
up with "Oh Boy," Sonny West and Bill Tilghman. "We'd sent it to
Norman, as usual—and, as usual, when it came out in published form, it
had his name added to it," Sonny West remembers. "Norman's original
plan was for a group called the Big Beats from Dallas to record it. But
Buddy said, 'No way. I've *got* to have this song.'"

The Bell session showed Buddy's ability to turn out first-class work at
top speed, despite the pressure and fatigue of continual touring. The first
half of the six-hour session was used to record tracks by the vocal group,
the Jivetones. Between 10 P.M. and 2 A.M. two songs were completed:
"That's My Desire," a ballad Frankie Laine had recorded in 1947, and
"Rave On."

"Rave On" is for many the ultimate Buddy Holly vocal, combining as
it does a mood of total rock 'n' roll abandon (its first word, "Well," is
pulverized into six syllables) with a delivery of relaxed economy and
elegance. It is the first uptempo Buddy number not to feature a strong
guitar motif, instead employing heavy bass, a descanting jazzy piano—
played by Norman Petty—and backup vocals with the threatening "walla-
walla" chant of comic-book redskins on the warpath. Despite the one-
third writer's cut he had ritually appropriated, Petty had reason to feel
chagrin. For here was proof that Buddy did not need his studio, nor any
specific one, to work short-order magic.

On January 26, the day before he and the Crickets flew to Honolulu to
join the Paul Anka/Jerry Lee Lewis Australian tour, there was another
major TV engagement to fulfill. In recognition of the growing chart
success of "Oh Boy," they had been invited back for a second appearance

on *The Ed Sullivan Show.* The original plan had been for the Picks to appear also, performing the record's overdubbed backup vocals. "Norman never paid us a cent for doing that session," Bill Pickering says. "And we never got any credit on the record label. But Buddy liked what we'd done so much that he sent us the money to fly up to New York for the Sullivan show. Then at the last minute we were told that the musicians' union wouldn't let us go on."

Despite a $500 hike in their fee (from $1,500 to $2,000), being Ed Sullivan's guest proved no pleasanter for the Crickets in early 1958 than it had been in late 1957. First, their scheduled two numbers were cut to one, then Sullivan requested them not to play "Oh Boy," as he considered its lyrics too "raunchy." Buddy, however, insisted it had to be "Oh Boy" or nothing. Sullivan was compelled to give in, but took revenge in characteristic fashion, muffling his star guests' introduction with a spoken promo for Mercury automobiles, "the performance champions of 1958," then deliberately mangling their name into "Buddy Hollered and the Crickutts."

The staging this time was considerably more polished and dramatic. Buddy was shown under a bright spotlight, standing astride his guitar-spiky shadow, with only occasional side glimpses of J. I. and Joe B. America could thus see all the more plainly what a change had come about in the shy out-of-towner who'd sirred Ed Sullivan so gratefully a month earlier. In place of the conventionally cut dark tuxedo was a long, pale, high-buttoning Ivy League jacket; in place of rumpled curls was the neat wavy wedge that his hometown barber, Jake Goss, had devised; in place of discolored and irregular teeth, a gleaming, symmetrical smile. Most transformingly of all, the high school nerd's half-frame glasses had been replaced by a pair of black horn-rims whose outsize square frames, far from seeking to minimize their existence, proclaimed it defiantly, even triumphantly. On yet another shopping spree a couple of days earlier, Don and Phil Everly had carried their point at last.

And in place of wonderment was devilment. Ed Sullivan's secondary revenge had been to have the Crickets' sound turned right down. On the video recording, Buddy's hand keeps darting to the Stratocaster's volume knob in a vain attempt to get more power. He retaliates by cutting up on "Oh Boy" as never before: making it even more frantically fast; stretching it out with an unscheduled second chorus; at the guitar break, wheeling around to show his new sleekly coiffed, high-buttoned, and horn-rimmed profile, and giving a mischievous coyote howl at the spotlight-moon.

The sequence ends with a cut back to Ed Sullivan, amid the audience's delighted applause, smiling with the conviction of a man whose toenails are being extracted with red-hot pliers.

PART THREE

IT'S SO EASY

T he 1950s in Britain are regarded as a golden age of full employment, low crime, social cohesion, and steadily accumulating prosperity, an era like none before, and none since, when life for everyone seemed to be getting better every day. A world war had been won and a monstrous tyranny overthrown, chiefly (we were assured) by our collective fortitude and self-sacrifice. A brand-new, shyly smiling young queen sat on the throne, and the whole nation seemed as one in striving to earn her good opinion. Public transport was clean and efficient, letters traveled swiftly, taxation was low and food cheap; no beggars could be seen nearer at hand than Spain or Italy. In the whole length and breadth of our aptly named United Kingdom it was hard to find a street that could not be walked in perfect safety at any hour of the day or night.

To the young, however, this did not feel like enviable security, but suffocating dullness. The chaos and cruelties of history might all have been eradicated, but so, apparently, had all its excitement, passion, color, and surprise. One felt one had been born at the very end of the line, with everything settled, tidied, and squared away, and nothing whatsoever left to look forward to. The prewar eras, with their distinctive character and costume and unrationed plenty, lay far behind; the future, with its promise of space travel and scientific marvels, had not yet begun to reveal itself. The present was humdrum, predictable Eternity.

A decade after Victory in Europe, the ethos of wartime still exerted an all-powerful grip. The stereotypical British hero was Jack Hawkins or John Mills in one of the period's numerous black and white war films, clean-cut, pipe-smoking, unshakably modest and reserved, sinking U-boats in the Atlantic or outfoxing Rommel in North Africa. Wartime austerity and self-denial lived on in the disgusting food, and in the monochrome dreariness of the streets. Cars came in two colors, black or beige. Women's fashions were subdued enough; for a man to stand out even slightly from the clerical gray mass meant instant condemnation as a hoodlum or a homosexual. This was the era when a journalist from a national newspaper went to interview a Cabinet minister but was turned away because the minister couldn't face conversing with someone who wore yellow socks.

America lay an inconceivable way off, a destination for none but the rich and famous, reached as commonly by ocean liner as by the scarcely less opulent Comet jets of the British Overseas Airways Corporation. It was a landscape familiar to all from twice- or thrice-weekly cinema visits, yet enduringly opaque and mysterious; a country about which we knew for certain only that it was in every way the opposite of ours: its cities of towering glass, not heaped bomb rubble; its houses long and white, not narrow and dingy; its people warm, spontaneous, and generous, not stand-offish and penny-pinching; its refrigerators immense, its steaks overlapping the plate; its nomenclature bizarre; its cars multi-finned; its footballers helmeted; its police armed; its suits shiny; its vegetation lush; its coffee black; its sunshine unquenchable.

Despite the cataclysmic disruption of the Second World War, mid-fifties Britain remained essentially a Victorian society, still founded on a rigid class system, a respect for authority and seniority, a consensus of self-discipline and self-control. Youth lived under much the same constraints as it had half a century earlier, obeying the Victorian nursery precept of being seen and not heard. The "teenager," long recognized in America as a potent economic force, was still barely noticed in Britain, where the only ones permitted to enjoy their teenage years were the small minority granted a university education. The majority went directly from childhood to adulthood at the age of about seventeen, metamorphosing overnight from school uniforms to print frocks and twinsets like their mothers' or tweed jackets, gray flannel trousers, and manly briar pipes like their fathers'.

Before 1955, Britain's older and younger generations derived their entertainment from broadly similar sources. There remained a few variety theaters, not yet quite annihilated by the movies. The omnipotent medium of popular music, as well as of drama and light entertainment, was radio, in those days totally noncommercial and the monopoly of the government-supported British Broadcasting Corporation, which voluntarily censored and diluted its output in accordance with the Calvinistic prejudices of its founder, Lord Reith. Television had two channels only: one the BBC's, the other shared by brand-new commercial (known as "independent") companies, all dedicated to emulating the BBC, both in quality and conservatism. The main haunt of youth was the dance halls, where forties-style big bands featured pale imitations of American crooners like Eddie Fisher and Dick Haymes. A tiny intellectual fringe passionately argued the merits of traditional over modern jazz; a still smaller one, usually in beards and sandals, followed American folk music and blues.

The culture was an almost wholly passive one, based on watching, listening, and impotently admiring. Britain's long and rich tradition of amateur music-making seemed to have reached a full stop around 1930. Music had come to be regarded as an obscure, elevated science, like mathematics or medicine, which none but professors and experts should seek to create. The only musical instrument generally taught to children was the piano. At my own school, music lessons consisted of standing in a circle and mindlessly beating on kiddy-size tambourines and triangles. Singing was something one did only under the direst sufferance, in church or at end-of-term concerts. To the introverted, self-conscious British schoolboy of 1955, few torments were as purgatorial as being made to stand up before an audience and give any kind of performance.

For all the furor that rock 'n' roll created in America, everyone over there knew where it came from, spiritually as well as geographically. At the heart of the garish new sound was a time-honored American virtue: the all-out energy, attack, and commitment that F. Scott Fitzgerald defined as "willingness of the heart" and that had already produced Hollywood, the Broadway musical, and, for that matter, American sport and American politics.

The one thing notably absent from every section of British society in 1955 was willingness of the heart. All that most adult Britons knew for certain about rock 'n' roll was that it outraged every modest and downbeat virtue that the British Empire had epitomized for five hundred years. Only a very few, on the intellectual fringe and in "the business" itself, recognized the colliding elements of country, blues, and R&B. The rest heard a cacophony so impenetrable, it might just as well have been beamed down from some hostile planet. This is not mere hyperbolic hindsight: in that first devastating glare of noise, Elvis Presley and his fellow perpetrators really did seem not quite human. I remember seeing early film of a shock-haired, mad-eyed Little Richard, and being surprised when, at the end of his song, he bowed and smiled at his audience in the conventional way.

In Britain, unlike America, the rock 'n' roll controversy did not originally focus on race. Steeped though we were in the racism of our dwindling Empire, a distinction had always been made between our own, growing West Indian immigrant population and black Americans who as jazzmen, entertainers, or sports personalities were generally viewed with fascinated respect. To be sure, the first rock 'n' roll scapegoat in Britain was a white man, Bill Haley, and what the resultant uproar brought into ghastly relief was not our racial attitudes but our still rigid and rampant class system. Rock 'n' roll was seen as a working-class aberration, like alcoholism or wife-beating, which it was the duty of their betters—politicians, clergymen, Fleet Street editors—to discourage at every possible opportunity. The riots that had accompanied screenings of *Rock Around the Clock* allowed the stigma of criminality and vandalism to be attached to anyone who admitted liking it. Its earliest and most visible devotees were the teddy boys, young artisans who defied the nation's rigid dress code by sporting Edwardian jackets with velvet collars, string ties, and drainpipe trousers, and who were known to carry on sartorial discussions with the aid of razors, knuckle-dusters, and bicycle chains. The Jive, a dance step familiar since the thirties, now souped up to rock 'n' roll's slap-bass beat, was outlawed by dance halls throughout the country (including my father's on the end of Ryde Pier). Even the new juvenile taste for Italianate cappuccino bars was viewed with suspicion and dread. It was perhaps the ultimate achievement of British Establishment paranoia to have made even frothy coffee seem dangerous!

Teenagers in the several class gradations above teddy boys and teddy girls—lower-middle, middle, upper-middle, lower-upper—remained largely unmoved by the first wave of rock 'n' roll, I myself was one such, in the lower reaches of lower-middle. My friends and I accepted our parents' and teachers' judgment that it was nothing but an ear-affronting confidence trick; that rock 'n' roll singers could not really sing and only pretended to play their guitars; that six months from now, the whole ludicrous, dishonest, unhealthy fad would have blown over.

Between Bill Haley and Elvis Presley, Britain had experienced a smaller but no less influential musical insurrection. Around 1954, the "trad" jazz musicians Ken Colyer and Chris Barber introduced us to skiffle, onomatopoeically named American folk music of the Depression era, when people could afford no better instruments than guitars, harmonicas, and kazoos, and would beat out a primitive "skiffling" rhythm on jugs, washboards, and one-string basses made from an empty crate and a broomstick. The Chris Barber band's banjo player, Tony Donegan (renamed Lonnie in honor of Lonnie Johnson), broke away to form his own skiffle group and had a huge hit with "Rock Island Line," a train song which, unprecedentedly, ricocheted back across the Atlantic to become an American No. 1.

Skiffle was a socially acceptable version of rock 'n' roll, glamorous in its American accent and references, yet without rock's taint of lewdness and subversion. Best of all, its glamour could be re-created, more or less, by anyone with access to a kitchen cupboard. The chronic self-consciousness and lockjaw of British youths instantly melted away. All over the country, in middle-class grammar schools as well as proletarian youth clubs, amateur skiffle groups materialized under rough-hewn collective names (the Nomads, the Hobos, the Quarry Men) to patter out the work-song repertoire of Woody Guthrie and Jimmie Rodgers on acoustic guitars, tea-chest basses, and washboards. After decades of anonymity in folk music and dance bands, the guitar became an object of thrilling glamour, something every young British male, however previously unmusical, longed to wear around his neck. True to national character, it wasn't long before the papers were announcing a countrywide guitar shortage.

Commercially, the skiffle craze lasted barely eighteen months. By late 1957, Lonnie Donegan, its only substantial talent, was already moving into the sphere of comedy and music hall; the handful of other groups who had won recording contracts simply disappeared. Behind them they left thousands of amateur skifflers, equipped with guitars, basses, and drums and with a newly awakened hunger for performance, but no idea what to do now. Then, out of nowhere, someone came along to show them.

☆   ☆   ☆

In Britain, unlike America, "That'll Be the Day" was an immediate success. Within a couple of weeks of its release, in mid-September 1957, it was in the Top 20; by early October it had reached No. 1, cleaving through rival U.S. imports like Pat Boone's "Remember You're Mine," Charlie Gracie's "Fabulous," the Everly Brothers' "Wake Up Little Susie," and domestic hits like Lonnie Donegan's "Dixie Darlin'," Jim Dale's "Be My Girl," and Johnny Duncan and the Bluegrass Boys' "Last Train to San Fernando."

American rock 'n' roll hits in those days came from so far away and were around so short a time that, with a few exceptions, British record-buyers paid minimal attention to the name on the label. Collective nouns tended to denote vocal groups: the Crickets therefore were initially thought to be of the same genre as the Inkspots and the Platters, presumably black, probably an amalgam of males and females in the prevailing style. An additional small stir of interest came from the special resonance of "cricket" to English ears—not the nocturnal insect-buzz of warm climates, but the white-clad summer game still in those days a synonym for gentlemanliness, restraint and fair play.

Today, any pop record that has reached No. 1 assails the ears unavoidably from every quarter. But in the Britain of 1957, even a hit as big as "That'll Be the Day" had to be sought out with some tenacity. The airwaves were the monopoly of the BBC, whose popular music service, the Light Programme, had banned American rock 'n' roll since the first Bill Haley riots. Other than buying the record, there were only two ways of getting it in earshot. One could pay sixpence for a barely audible version on the jukebox at some frighteningly low-class espresso bar. Or one could wait until after 7 P.M. and then tune to Radio Luxembourg, away in almost equally inconceivable Europe, which transmitted an evening program of record shows hosted by English disc jockeys, with American-style station IDs and commercials. Reception was often patchy and punctuated by strident voices speaking in French, Flemish, German, and Dutch. Endlessly retuning the radio's faint-lit dial, ears pressed close to its woven loudspeaker fabric, rock 'n' roll fans were like a Resistance against hostile occupation, struggling to pick up forbidden messages of comfort and encouragement.

It was on Radio Luxembourg that most young Britons first heard the name Buddy Holly, early in December 1957, when "Peggy Sue" began rolling out of the multilingual static. Although nowhere near as bizarre a name as "Elvis Presley," it still struck oddly on our ears with that ungainly double y; the "Buddy" as American as dungarees and drugstores, the "Holly" so English-Christmas-card. Mystery hung in the air from the very beginning: we learned that Buddy Holly was lead singer of the Crickets, but that he'd recorded "Peggy Sue" as a solo performer, even though "Oh Boy," the Crickets' follow-up to their great autumn hit, was also concurrently climbing the charts. So had he left the group and been replaced by another vocalist? Or had he left, then had second thoughts and rejoined the lineup?

Another oddity was hearing the Luxembourg announcer describe him as "the songwriter Buddy Holly." In 1957, the only songwriters British people knew about were middle-aged men who sat in Tin Pan Alley garrets, penning the umpteenth rhyme of "June" with "moon." The voice, too, with its low pitch and air of control, suggested someone more mature than the usual scowling rock 'n' roll whelp, which in those days inevitably meant a black performer. I remember thinking he might perhaps belong to the elder-statesman class of disc jockey, like Alan Freed in America and our own Pete Murray and David Jacobs.

If hearing American rock 'n' roll was difficult, obtaining any data about its performers was next to impossible. National newspapers offered minuscule coverage of the pop-music scene, and that in a tone of middle-aged facetiousness; there was virtually none on daytime domestic radio; television had but a single pop show, the BBC's *Six-Five Special,* presented in the spirit of a youth club social and featuring exclusively feeble home-grown talent. The two specialist music papers, *Melody Maker* and the *New Musical Express,* owed their first duty to mainstream pop and jazz—and, anyway, were not sold by the vast majority of newsstands throughout the country. As with all underground movements, information circulated chiefly by word of mouth. Especially if you lived outside London, rock 'n' roll was a series of brilliant rumors, some absurdly far-fetched, others even more absurdly true.

Around January 1958, three stories about Buddy Holly began circulating among Maquisard groups throughout Britain's rock 'n' roll Resistance. First, that he was not black, like Fats Domino and Little Richard, as had been widely supposed, but as white as Elvis Presley, Charlie Gracie or Paul Anka; second, that, in defiance of all pop-music (and most show-business) precedent, he wore glasses; third, that, besides fronting the Crickets and being a songwriter, he confounded our parents' allegations of poor or nonexistent musicianship among rock 'n' roll stars by playing all his own electric guitar solos. The glasses added to the whiteness gave his maturity a different slant: now he had the aura of some brainy Sixth Form student, mastering each department of rock 'n' roll like so many examination honors.

What had chiefly made "That'll Be the Day" such an instant British hit was an electric sound more ravishingly metallic than the country's guitar-besotted teenage boys had dreamed possible. Elsewhere, the guitar seemed to be fading from American rock 'n' roll. Elvis Presley had given up wearing one as an essential performance accessory, and his records no longer featured those jaunty Sun-era solos by Scotty Moore. On more and more new transatlantic imports, the lead guitar was displaced by hammering piano or squealing chicken-sax. But Buddy Holly records always provided the clanging, jangling uproar that adolescent Britons now hungered for almost sexually; alone of all the rock 'n' roll aliens, he seemed to us consistent, reliable, concerned with giving us what we wanted.

Hero and icon though Elvis was, he had always been remote and unknowable. To the ten thousand learner guitarists and would-be vocalists throughout Britain, his records were as mysterious as they were sublime, the voice fused to its instrumental backing by a process which baffled the ear. All other American rock 'n' roll presented the same implacable mystery, tantalizingly hinted at by exotic label names like Atlantic and Liberty, penned like a genii in glistening grooves of the new, small-size and "unbreakable" 45-rpm discs, unreachably locked away inside the rose-tinted visor of the jukebox.

But with Buddy Holly, in and out of the Crickets, one could instantly see how he did it. All his songs were written in major keys, A, E, D, which translated into simple three-finger guitar chords, and all followed the four-chord twelve-bar blues sequence every skiffler could play. Only a few audacious souls had ever dared try to imitate the way Elvis sang. But everyone could, and did, copy Buddy. The straightforward key and lowered pitch of his voice allowed the most untuneful, and the most bashful, to sing along without looking or feeling like an idiot. Exotic as was the origin of that voice, wild and many-hued as it could be in certain moods, it seemed not so very different from our one-dimensionally reserved and cautious British ones. Anyone could get an echo of "That'll

Be the Day," at least in his own head, by lowering the chin, gritting the teeth and murmuring from the gills through lips as rigid as a ventriloquist's.

Elvis lyrics, if not garbled beyond comprehension, could be blushmakingly coy: "Treat me nice . . . Love me tender . . . Let me be your teddy bear." But Buddy's were clear, simple, neat, self-controlled, and never too serious, consistent in every way with the precious dignity of the average British fifteen-year-old. For those unwilling to venture quite so far, there was always the background chorus of "ooh," "aah," and "ba-ba-ba," which lost nothing if the tongue stayed firmly in the cheek. In Britain, his most influential early song was "Maybe Baby," released under the Crickets' name in March 1958: a simpler-than-ever blueprint for singer, guitar, and backing vocals, scanned and rapidly mastered in living rooms, garages, youth clubs, and Boy Scout huts from John o' Groats to Land's End. At a plectrum stroke, all those bereft and directionless skiffle groups turned into busy, ambitious rock 'n' roll bands.

Not even the hostility and apathy of Britain's domestic media had prevented the aliens from beaming into our midst. They came via the cinema, in black-and-white "exploitation" films like *Rock Around the Clock; Rock, Rock, Rock;* and *Disc Jockey Jamboree,* whose flimsy storylines were excuses for strings of cameo appearances by Bill Haley and the Comets, Freddy Bell and the Bellboys, Fats Domino, Buddy Knox, and Jerry Lee Lewis, all introduced by Alan Freed in his role as The One Adult in the World Who Understands. Elvis, of course, was everywhere —on magazine covers, cinema posters, bubblegum cards; there was even a spoken communique from The King ("Hi, this is Elvis Presley, speaking from Hollywood . . .") counseling his subjects to remain steadfast in the face of persecution and ridicule.

Yet almost four months after "That'll Be the Day" had jangled its way into our dreams, we still had no clear idea what Buddy Holly looked like. Advertisements for his records appeared without photographs; there seemed to be no fan club to write to for information or autographs; by early 1958, the only picture of him I'd seen was the blurry group shot on the cover of "Oh Boy" in sheet-music form (still an important market then), pinned just too high for my myopic vision in the window of Ryde's only record store.

Then, at long last, the *Chirping Crickets* LP came along to open our eyes. Released in America in November 1957, it did not appear in Britain until the New Year and didn't swim into my personal ken until some time early in March. At 30 shillings ($2.00), an LP was a precious rarity, less for playing than passing around a reverent group to be studied as an art object in its own right.

How we stared at, and even reverently stroked, that garish one-dimensional jacket! "The Crickets" was printed in white capitals with "Chirping" interposed in jiggly yellow ones, between condescending quotation marks. Underneath, four figures in identical, high-buttoning pale gray suits were outlined against a garish blue background, smiling broadly (little did anyone suspect the fistfight that had preceded their photo session on the Brooklyn Paramount roof) and cradling the bodies of two brown guitars between them. Even then, identification was not immediate, since *two* of the figures wore glasses. Some instinct told us that Buddy was the one second from left, in half-frames, not transparent rims; the tallest of the quartet, with the longest neck, the darkest hair, the widest smile, the neatest V-shape of thin gray lapels, red tie, and white shirt.

On the back of the record were liner notes as sparse yet suggestive as Japanese haiku. Little was vouchsafed other than that the supporting Crickets, the makers of those plangent background harmonies, so we all devoutly believed, were named Jerry Allison, Niki Sullivan, and Joe B. Mauldin (which I and my friends misread as "Maudlin," the way the British pronounce "Magdalane") and that all four came from an unimaginable place called Lubbock, Texas. To me, the name was almost onomatopoeic, evoking a picture—not inaccurate, as it would one day prove —of Western saddles, dusty with hard riding.

As much as anything he sang or played, Buddy's appearance on the *Chirping Crickets* cover was a revelation. It showed that to play rock 'n' roll you did not have to be a bespangled Technicolor freak—you could be turned out conservatively enough to satisfy the most exacting parent, vicar, or teacher. You did not have to be a pouting dreamboat like Elvis or like our own, troubled Elvis-clone, Terry Dene. You could be thin, hollow-faced, a little goofy; you could even be a foureyes! By what he was no less than what he did, he put the music into everyone's reach.

Until then, rock 'n' roll had been aimed principally at girls. It was something that made girls scream while their boyfriends stood by, fuming with impotent jealousy. Buddy Holly may not have been the first rock 'n' roller British boys liked, but he was the first they could admit they liked.

Even the few misguided souls in my class at school who professed not to like his records, and called his voice "anemic" or "rare" (an Isle of Wight term for bizarre) found it hard to resist his clothes. "Ivy League" was an incomprehensible term to us, merely creating a Christmas-carol juxtaposition with "Holly." What that high-fastening coat with its two slanted lefthand pockets suggested to us were Edwardian hacking jackets, and the upper-class London "Guardee" look that went with chukka boots, string-backed driving gloves, and Austin-Healy sports cars. All over Britain, tailors were deluged by orders for high-buttoning suits. Schoolboys who could not afford that (like myself) made do by pinching our serge blazer lapels together around the level of the breastbone.

I cannot put this strongly enough. We had been born into a world utterly without style. Now, in the same moment, we had been told that it existed, and shown how to acquire it for ourselves. To our newly awakened senses, everything connected with Buddy Holly seemed stylish. The British Decca company, for inscrutable reasons, chose to release both the Crickets' and Buddy's own-name songs on a hybrid label called Vogue-Coral, thereby awakening unconscious echoes both of the famous glossy fashion magazine and one of Britain's classier chocolate selections (Cadbury's Vogue). To our struck-awake ears, even the recurrent alphabetical trio of names in brackets under his best song titles, "Allison-Holly-Petty," belonged to the same casually elegant corporate identity.

To the nation of learner guitarists, Buddy was like a teacher and guide, moving them on kindly but firmly with each new song he released; endlessly producing new patterns for the few chords they knew; showing what different effects could be produced by the same chords played with more difficult shapes higher up the fretboard; opening their ears and guiding their fingers to the subtler emotional suggestion of minors and sevenths. The hundreds of ex–skiffle groups all over the country subsisted entirely on his repertoire, rushing to grab each fresh blueprint as it became available, following his specifications to the smallest hiccup. In Liverpool, two truant schoolboys named John Lennon and Paul McCartney sat for hours in each other's living rooms, playing over his songs on their two guitars, then trying to write similar-sounding songs of their own. The myopic Lennon had always hated his own thick-rimmed glasses; now, like thousands of other British nerds—or, as we said, "weeds"—he discovered a positive cachet in having things on your nose that got foggy over hot tea.

Not every Vogue-Coral secret was instantaneously shared. Among his huge guitar class, very few could puzzle out how to play the intro to "That'll Be the Day"—or, indeed, muster an amplifier powerful enough even to come near reproducing it. One exception was a younger schoolmate of Paul McCartney's named George Harrison, who had joined his and Lennon's group, the Quarry Men, early in 1958. Soon afterward, they scraped up enough money to finance their first demo at a studio in central Liverpool. The song they chose to perform was "That'll Be the Day," with John doing a more than passable job of copying Buddy's voice and George struggling to match that sublime lead guitar.

Buddy Holly gave British boys something else, too, something we barely realized at the time and could only fully appreciate years later. Our late-fifties vocabulary did not contain words like "upbeat" or "positive." Yet it seemed to us that this vague, bespectacled, high-buttoned being understood, and sympathized with, the peculiar hell of being us, and from his distant hemisphere was sending messages of comfort and hope.

☆　☆　☆

The handful of American rock 'n' roll stars whom British teenagers had seen in the flesh thus far had mostly been a severe disappointment. The first to be brought over—by sea rather than air—were Bill Haley and the Comets, in February 1957. After docking at Southampton, they traveled to London by special boat train, with crowds lining the tracks in the manner normally reserved for state funerals. At Waterloo station, they were greeted by 3,000 shrieking fans in what one newspaper dubbed "the second Battle of Waterloo." Alas for Haley, with his roguish kiss-curl, double chin, and hideous plaid jacket, he looked more like a kiddies' entertainer than a revolutionary leader in whose name a hundred provincial cinemas had been trashed.

Everyone assumed that Elvis Presley would soon follow in his footsteps, to face the same probable moment of truth. But Elvis was never to perform in Britain, a fact that kept his legend untarnished here for more than two decades, and that was always put down to brilliant intuition by his manager, Colonel Tom Parker. Not until after Elvis's death, in 1977, did a different explanation emerge. The downhome Southern colonel was in fact a Dutchman named Dries van Kuijk, who had entered America illegally in the early thirties. He had refused to take Elvis abroad for fear that the U.S. Immigration Service would discover his own real identity and refuse to readmit him to America.

The prospect of seeing Elvis on British soil receded even further early in 1958 when the King was drafted into the United States Army. The military authorities had offered a soft billet as a forces entertainer, but Colonel Parker in his wisdom ordained otherwise: Elvis must go through the same punitive barbering and boot camp as any other unlucky young recruit. Convinced that rock 'n' roll could not last much longer, and that he had dredged all he possibly could out of it, the Colonel had decided to change the billing of his carnival freak, from rabble-rouser and scandal-maker to patriotically meek and submissive all-American boy. So rock 'n' roll was deprived of its first guiding light, and Elvis was launched on the downward path that would take him through third-rate movies and the Las Vegas cabaret circuit to drug addiction, obesity, bulimia, glaucoma, incontinence and death.

The original importers of rock 'n' roll into Britain were kindred spirits of Colonel Parker, old-fashioned variety agents whose personal revulsion and bafflement were outweighed by a primordial urge to supply what the public demanded. The only way rock 'n' roll could be staged was as a part of music hall or vaudeville. An American teen idol, accustomed to Alan Freed's twenty-act road shows, would find himself in Britain playing plush old Victorian theaters throughout the foggy Midlands and North, in company with jugglers, trick cyclists, and performing dogs.

For a visiting rock 'n' roller, as any overseas star, the plum television booking was Associated Television's *Sunday Night at the London Palladium,* a variety show transmitted live from the legend-encrusted theater of that name on Argyll Street. Here, the top of the bill shared the limelight not only with jugglers and performing dogs, but with an audience-participation game called "Beat the Clock," so boisterous that its contestants had to wear protective overalls. The top of the bill then had roughly seven minutes before the credits began to roll and the show's entire cast appeared on a revolving platform, interspersed among high-plumed showgirls and giant letters spelling SUNDAY NIGHT AT THE LONDON PALLADIUM.

Such was the unreal context in which Britain's nine million Sunday-night television viewers were invited to compare rock 'n' roll's substance with its shadow. *Sunday Night at the London Palladium* had already brought us Johnny Ray (thumbs down), Pat Boone (qualified thumbs up), and Charlie ("Fabulous") Gracie, who provoked a murmur of delighted approval by actually being able to pick out a rudimentary boogie-woogie figure on his huge, shiny cutaway cello guitar.

Britain's most famous impresarios during the late fifties were the brothers Leslie and Lew Grade, who between them ran a theatrical agency handling most of the top names in domestic film, theater, and television. Lew Grade was also head of the company that owned Associated Television (ATV) and numerous variety theaters, including the London Palladium, hence ATV's audience-hogging Sunday-night spectacular. On February 7, 1958, Leslie Grade wrote to New York booking agent Mannie Greenfield:

Dear Mannie,

Thank you for your very nice letter of February 4 and I am delighted to have such a good report from you on Buddy Holly and the Crickets. You can rest assured that we shall look after them and, of course, Norman Petty and his wife, and make them feel at home here.

The modern rock concertgoer, accustomed to superstar sets of two hours and more, will smile at Leslie Grade's anxious caveat:

I have a little bit of a problem about the time of the act, and would definitely like them to do approximately 25 minutes—would you please try and get them to do this. You know how it is here, they [British audiences] expect the top of the bill to do a long act and if they did less than 23, 24 or 25 minutes the public would be very disappointed, so please do what you can . . .

"And, of course, Norman Petty and his wife"? Could this be the same self-effacing technician who had hesitated to become the Crickets' manager for fear he would be unable to spare enough time from recording sessions to accompany them on the road? Now that they had become a world-class attraction, and the road led to destinations more alluring than Pittsburgh or Oklahoma City, things were rather different. If trips to Hawaii, Australia, and Europe were on offer, Petty naturally had no intention of being left behind twiddling knobs in Clovis.

His management style would nowadays be described as "hands-on," but back then was best summed up in the phrase "hands off." Petty and

Petty alone, in his view, provided everything his boys could possibly need: he was their A&R man, producer, and publisher; he received and banked their income, settled all bills on their behalf from their joint bank account with his power of attorney, and doled out their day-to-day living expenses and pocket money. Anyone who offered the least threat to this creative and administrative monopoly, especially where Buddy was concerned, received the full ice-cave treatment from Clovis Man. Bob Thiele of Coral-Brunswick and Murray Deutch of Peer-Southern Music, those two crucial figures in the success story thus far, were constantly aware of Petty breathing down their necks for fear they might get too close to his "diamond in the rough."

"Buddy used to come to Bob and me for advice about this and that," Deutch remembers. "We both liked the kid and wanted to do all we could to help him. But Norman hated that. Whatever was going on with Buddy, he always had to know all about it. He was like a cross between a headmaster and a traffic cop."

But even Petty, that consummate control freak, realized the need to maintain good public relations with Buddy's record company and East Coast song publishers. When sales of "Peggy Sue" reached 1 million copies, Thiele and Deutch were invited to Clovis to give Buddy his Gold Record in a ceremony at the Petty studio. For their arrival at the city's tiny airport, Petty arranged an extravagant welcome ceremony including a full brass band, and formally presented each of them with a cowboy-style ten-gallon hat.

The urbane New Yorkers considered the brouhaha put on for their benefit more than a little absurd, and found the menage at the studio where the hits originated bizarre in the extreme. Like many others, they took Norma Jean Berry to be the butch lesbian she appeared, in her jeans and shapeless cowboy shirt, and wondered if Vi Petty might not be of the same persuasion since she and Norma Jean seemed always to be together. If that was not sufficient to make the visitors uncomfortable, Petty's expansive welcome quickly proved to have limits. "At mealtimes, you felt you had to struggle to get a glass of milk," Murray Deutch remembers. For Deutch, however, the trip had one worthwhile result. When he returned East he took with him the demo of a song called "Sugartime" by a young Texan named Charlie Phillips, featuring Buddy on lead guitar. Over the next year, despite its "suggestive" title (sugar = sex), it became an international smash, with cover versions by the McGuire Sisters and

Guy Mitchell in the United States and Alma Cogan and Jim Dale in Britain.

On January 27, the day after "cutting up" on *The Ed Sullivan Show,* Buddy and the Crickets left New York by Trans World Airlines to join "The Big Show" tour in Hawaii and travel on with Paul Anka and Jerry Lee Lewis to their week of concerts in Australia. With them went Papa Norman, garlanded with the cameras which, after recording equipment, were his consuming passion.

For most of the trip, indeed, Petty behaved less like a manager than a tourist, filming extensive 16mm color sequences which survive to this day among the treasures of his New Mexico mausoleum: Here is Buddy on arrival at Honolulu International Airport, evidently tickled pink as a smiling hula girl drapes a lei around his long neck; here he is with J. I. and Joe B., splashing like schoolboys in their hotel pool, and smiling and waving from afar in three horribly travel-creased white linen jackets. Here is the first color still shot of the new Buddy—perhaps the most poignant ever taken—on the balcony of his hotel room, a wand-slim figure in dark slacks and open-necked white shirt, gazing unsmilingly through thick black horn-rims out over the Pacific as if some terribly sudden and sad premonition has struck him.

Both of that night's two concerts at Honolulu's Civic Auditorium drew capacity crowds of 5,000. Though Paul Anka was the hit of the night, Buddy wrote to his sister Pat that the Crickets had gone over "better than I thought we would." The next morning, an Air Force friend of Petty's gave them a guided tour of Pearl Harbor, where many buildings still bore the scars of Japan's surprise attack in 1941. Then it was straight aboard a Pan American Constellation for the 6,000-mile overnight journey to Sydney. The Constellation's first-class passengers enjoyed the luxury of Pullman-style sleeping berths, but Buddy and friends were traveling tourist class. Modern rock stars on uncomfortable long-haul flights alleviate their boredom by getting drunk, snorting cocaine, insulting fellow passengers, and screwing compliant stewardesses in the toilets; among "the Big Show's" cooped-up superstars, the only disturbance was sporadic pillow fights.

In those days of propeller planes, trans-Pacific flights had to stop for refueling at the tiny island of Canton, midway between Hawaii and Fiji. As the flight neared Canton—in what, with hindsight, can only seem like a chilling augury—one of the Constellation's engines developed valve trouble, the plane had to make a hurried landing, and the flight was delayed several hours while the fault was repaired. J. I. Allison wrote home to his parents that even at midnight as they hung around the tiny island airstrip, it was "hotter than the john down at Frankie's drive-in on a July day. . . . They have some fine Australian beer here," J. I. continued, "but since the [schoolboyish hieroglyphic for Petty] is with us, we can't drink any."

Unnoticed on the far side of the world, Australia was also in the throes of internecine warfare between a brash, novelty-hungry young generation —harder-drinking even than Texas teenagers—and a conservative older one whose idea of good music was "Waltzing Matilda." Capitalizing on the huge Australian record market, and the dearth of homegrown talent, several major American rock 'n' roll names had been there ahead of Buddy, notably his friends Little Richard and Eddie Cochran, whose tour with Gene Vincent had caused spectacular riots at Newcastle, New South Wales, the previous fall.

The elements on this tour seemed even more combustible. Jerry Lee Lewis had just seen his second single, "Great Balls of Fire," leap onto the world charts and was established as the most balefully brilliant piano man that even rock 'n' roll had ever seen. A pasty Louisiana boy with corrugated blond hair and a permanent lopsided sneer, he combined the hammering energy of a World War I machine-gun nest with a remorseless one-note voice and an air of complete disdain for his audience. Jerry Lee did not play pianos so much as ravish them, pounding their keys with his heels as readily as his hands, kicking their innocent stools viciously across the stage to stand and pound in a palpitant heap of Jell-O–red drape suit; finally climbing atop them to take an overview of his ravening devotees while he passed a comb disdainfully through his uncoiling golden locks.

Only a tour bill of the late fifties could have featured Jerry Lee Lewis alongside a puppy-love heartthrob like Paul Anka, at the time still riding a huge wave of popularity after "Diana." Like those of wrestlers, their nicknames foreshadowed conflict to come: "the Killer" versus "the Boy Millionaire."

With three Australian hits to their credit ("That'll Be the Day," "Oh Boy," and "Peggy Sue" had all reached No. 2), Buddy and the Crickets were the tour's headline act and had been guaranteed their name in the largest type on all concert posters and programs. But in Sydney, the tour promoter, an expatriate American named Lee Gordon, came to Buddy and said that Jerry Lee Lewis was demanding his name in bigger type than anyone else's. Buddy would have been fully within his rights to threaten to pull out unless the billing stayed as it was. Instead, sympathizing with the promoter's plight, he came up with a genially pragmatic solution: Jerry Lee could be billed in the biggest type, but in return Buddy and the Crickets would get extra money. (As it turned out, most of the posters show Paul Anka's name towering over everyone else's.)

The troupe did shows in Sydney, Melbourne, Brisbane, and Newcastle, and also gave a charity performance at Melbourne's Nurses Memorial Centre which later was aired as a radio program sponsored by the Colgate-Palmolive company. Newcastle's city fathers, in particular, breathed a thankful sigh when the expected repetition of the previous year's Little Richard riots failed to materialize, no matter how hard Jerry Lee Lewis strove to incite them. Despite massive competition from Jerry Lee and Paul Anka, not to mention Australian rock 'n' roll star Johnny O'Keefe, the *Melbourne Herald* spoke for all in calling Buddy "the undoubted star of the show." Chippy Australian journalists who interviewed him found him engaging and unpretentious; one described him afterward as "the perfect representation of the American parson—ascetic, serious, dignified . . ."

A taped interview survives between Buddy and Australian disc jockey Pat Barton, backstage at Newcastle Stadium while Jerry Lee Lewis was murdering yet another piano out front. Barton asks about Elvis Presley's imminent career as an Army conscript—and, in passing, reveals just how unimpressive a road manager the camera-laden Petty was turning out:

BARTON: Norman Petty . . . now where does Norman Petty fit into the picture?

BUDDY: He's our manager and our recording engineer and just about the whole works.

BARTON: How old a man is he? He's not in Australia with you, is he?

BUDDY: Yes, he's sitting right over there.

BARTON: Oh, is he? Well, it's just Norman, is it?

BUDDY (to Petty): He'd like to talk to you if you would. [A strange reversal: a star arranging an interview for his manager!]

BARTON: Um, what's the picture as regards rock 'n' roll, say with Presley in the Army? Does that alter things, do you think?

BUDDY: Well, I don't think it alters anything real outstanding in the music business. Presley will probably be a little unpopular for a while, but I think he'll come back into it, into his own after he gets out.

BARTON: You don't think somebody will step into his shoes, like from the ranks . . .

BUDDY: No, I don't think anybody . . .

BARTON: Like Buddy Holly or Jerry Lee Lewis?

BUDDY: No, I don't think so.

On the road, Buddy's humor and good nature did much to defuse the explosive incompatability of his fellow headliners. He admired the precocious songwriting talent of Paul Anka and, with his usual open-heartedness, changed from bitterly envying Anka to suggesting they might write songs for each other. Though quiet and orderly himself (and bound by Papa Norman's no-drinking/smoking/cussing rule), Buddy was completely unshockable: the worst that Jerry Lee could do in the drinking and hell-raising department was nothing Buddy hadn't seen a hundred times before at Lubbock's Glassarama or 16th and J Club. One evening, at minutes to showtime, the Killer was discovered in a local bar, in no condition to walk, let alone maul a piano. Buddy was the one who took him back to the troupe's hotel, flung him into a shower, and sobered him enough to go onstage.

February 2 was spent in transit from Sydney to Brisbane for the two shows at the Cloudland Ballroom that night. As Buddy gazed down past the blur of propellers to the azure continent, how could he possibly have visualized driving snow on an Arctic cold Midwest midnight, or known that there was exactly one year left?

The journey home included another stop-off in Hawaii for a show at Honolulu's Kaiser Hotel. Buddy and the Crickets arrived back in Lubbock via Braniff Airlines on February 10. There was just time to squeeze in a recording session at Clovis before they left on a weeklong "The Big Gold Record Stars" tour of Florida with Jerry Lee Lewis, Bill Haley, the Everly Brothers, and the Royalteens, then went straight on to begin a month of concerts in Britain. Other young performers faced by such a murderous schedule would have told their manager where to stick his cameras—but not Buddy and the Crickets. They had no idea how long this amazing rollercoaster ride would last, and were determined to make the most of every dizzy second.

The sessions in Clovis, between February 12 and 19, 1958, produced another fistful of finished diamonds: "Fool's Paradise," "Tell Me How," "Take Your Time," and another gift-wrapped blueprint to Britain's ex-skifflers, "Think It Over." Also present was a male vocal trio called the Roses, who had sung on Buddy's session with the Norman Petty Trio and now were to supply background vocals as if by the Crickets. Though the Roses rehearsed with Buddy, Jerry, and Joe B., their vocals were dubbed in later. For "Take Your Time," Petty played Hammond organ and, on the strength of contributing a single line to Buddy's lyric ("heartstrings will sing like a string of twine") was able to claim a 50 percent writer's credit as opposed to the one-third he took on "Think It Over," "Tell Me How" and "Fool's Paradise."

One whole night in addition was given to developing J. I. Allison as a solo performer. Under his middle name, Ivan, J. I. recorded "Real Wild Child," a song he had picked up from the Australian rock 'n' roller Johnny O'Keefe (and which was destined to be a hit for Iggy Pop almost a quarter of a century later). The Ivan session featured Buddy and the Roses on backing vocals, a substitute drummer, Bo Clarke, taking J. I.'s place, and Petty playing a finely tuned selection of water-filled wine-glasses.

The pièce de résistance, put into the can on the very first day, owed its inspiration to Little Richard, who would whip audiences to further frenzy between numbers by self-congratulatory cries of "Well . . . all right!" Buddy turned the phrase into a gentle love song infused with all his special quality of patience and optimism and his developing ability to make personal sentiments into universal ones. "Well, All Right" is a riposte to all the criticism and condescension that teenagers faced from their elders in the rock 'n' roll fifties—and have in every decade since. The setting is as adventurously simple as that of "Everyday": Buddy plays flamenco-accented acoustic guitar, with only a plashing cymbal for company. The mood is not one of youthful anger and defiance but of maturity before its time: calm, stoical, steadfast in affirming its "dreams and wishes." The intimacy in the voice could equally be that of lover or elder brother. Girl or boy, you can imagine you and he are alone together, gazing into the fire and seeing a bright future when the young will "live and love with all our might," which could almost be a prophecy of the sixties' hippie culture.

On the "Big Gold Record Stars" Florida tour, the Everly Brothers were top of the bill and closed the show, preceded by Buddy and the Crickets and Jerry Lee Lewis in that order. As was his wont, the Killer pulled out every foot-pounding, piano-mountaineering, comb-wielding stunt to throw Don and Phil's pretty-boy duet into total eclipse. The Everlys still had no permanent backup band and relied on the promoters to provide them with musicians; a different set at each gig. "When we got to this one place in Florida, we found the promoters had hired us three high school kids who could hardly play a note," Phil Everly says. "We literally could not take them onstage with us. So there we were with Jerry Lee working the audience over before us, and no band.

"When Buddy heard about the problem, he and the Crickets volunteered to be our backup group. Jerry Lee did his worst, left the audience stomping and cheering like maniacs, but we had some guys behind us who could give them something every bit as powerful. I always say it was only by the grace of God and Buddy Holly that Don and I managed to come through that night."

We can hear just how exhausted Buddy was in a scrap of conversation caught on tape in Clovis, just after he'd tried for the umpteenth time to get his tongue around Petty's clumsy "heartstrings will sing like a string of twine." The husky Texan voice slurs almost to unintelligibility, but still doesn't snap.

"Boy . . . I just cain't get on it, Norm . . . page just blurs. Cain't even see the words, lookin' right at 'em. Been through it so many times it's . . . you know, it's a circle—tightens up and catches up with itself, and another time comes 'fore it's time to sing this one." The complaint is defused by an audible smile. "That's what's gettin' me so bad—it's the concentration."

"Take your time," a feminine voice which could be Vi Petty's, or J. I. Allison's in falsetto, tells him over the intercom.

Buddy breaks into his familiar snuffly laughter and promises he'll "beat the crap" out of the elusive lyric this time. His composure restored, still audibly smiling, he gives the signal for the right-on take to come: "Let's go . . ."

☆ ☆ ☆

Thanks to Norman Petty's assiduous filmed record, we can share Buddy's first sight of London, on February 27, 1958: a low-lying, murky expanse, still undisturbed by a single skyscraper or tower block, with the Thames curling through it like a faint bronze serpent. We can be with him, looking from seat number C2, tourist class, as British Overseas Airways flight 582 taxis up to the single-story terminal at what was still called London Airport rather than Heathrow: another marathon trek through the clouds safely over.

The party that disembarked that morning, stiff and disoriented after its overnight transatlantic flight, numbered five in all. As well as Buddy, Jerry, Joe B., and Papa Norman, his movie camera permanently clamped to his eye, there was also Vi Petty, still bemused by this almost unprecedented act of sharing on her spouse's part. He had decided to bring Vi along without consulting his "boys," who were not best pleased to find her added to their retinue together with a plethora of fussy little grips and vanity bags. Even the usually quiet and tractable Joe B. remembers wondering whether Petty or they would be paying for this extra plane ticket and hotel accommodation. "But we didn't say anything. And Vi sure was thrilled to be there."

They had arrived at the threshold of a typical British March, bitingly cold, with frequent rain and an enveloping Stygian gloom, often little lighter at midday than at dawn or dusk. Buddy, Jerry, and Joe B. felt the shock particularly, having just left the secure warmth of wintertime Florida. Their matching black shortie raglan raincoats may have looked wonderfully stylish to British eyes, but would afford little protection in the four dank, chilly weeks that lay ahead.

Britain's pop charts, however, provided the warmest of welcomes. "Maybe Baby" under the Crickets' name, coupled with "Tell Me How," was climbing rapidly toward its eventual high of No. 4. "Listen to Me" under Buddy's name, coupled with "I'm Gonna Love You Too," was No. 16. The *Chirping Crickets* LP was cutting a swath through the exiguous album chart, finally to peak at No. 5. All this was in marked contrast with America, where "Maybe Baby" had made only No. 16 and "Listen to Me" and *The Chirping Crickets* both failed to chart at all, despite enthusiastic trade press reviews. In gigantic America, with its myriad radio stations, there was felt to be too much Holly and Crickets music in circulation already. But tiny Britain, with a single domestic radio service and one nocturnal interloper from the Grand Duchy of Luxembourg, clearly could not get enough of it.

The party had reservations at the Cumberland Hotel, Marble Arch, where a comfortable room cost just over £3 ($5.00) per night, plus an extra 9 pence (less than 15¢) if, as Buddy did, you wanted the luxury of a bedside radio. The era of rock stars being trapped in their hotels by screaming girls was still far in the future. Buddy, Jerry, and Joe B. could walk the wintry West End streets in perfect safety, recognized by almost no one. The only publicity organized by British Decca was a press reception at a Soho club, the Whisky A Go Go, where, in a small triumph of addle-brained PR, America's Crickets were ceremonially confronted with two English national-team cricketers, Denis Compton and Godfrey Evans. The Crickets' bafflement was as nothing compared to that of the cricketers; nonetheless, Compton and Evans posed for photographers, showing Buddy how to hold a bat and take up guard at the wicket, while J. I. and Joe B., in their uniform V-neck sweaters, crouched together in the slips.

The road show that the Grade Organisation had put together around them could not have been more bizarrely different from the touring rock 'n' roll menageries back home. In the continuing dearth of native rock talent, British teenagers had to rely on conventional big bands and vocalists from the crooner era for most live versions of current chart hits. Buddy, J. I., and Joe B. thus found themselves the only rock 'n' roll act on a variety bill that could just as well have taken the road in the late forties. Its backbone was the thirteen-piece Ronnie Keene Orchestra, which combined swing classics like "In the Mood" and "Woodchopper's Ball" with items "for the kids" like "When the Saints" and "The 6-5 Special Jive." There were also the Tanner Sisters, a bubble-haired, taffeta-gowned duo modeled on the Andrews Sisters, and balladeer Gary Miller, soon to enjoy his one and only chart success with "The Story of My Life." The emcee was a new young singer–comedian named Des O'Connor.

Buddy and the Crickets' headliner status was proclaimed by a crudely drawn cartoon cricket on the cover of the souvenir program sold at each venue. To placate Leslie Grade, they had worked up a twenty-five-minute performance from among ten possible numbers listed in the program: both current chart-toppers and lesser-known tracks like "Mailman, Bring Me No More Blues" and "Rock Around with Ollie Vee." Mystifyingly (or perhaps not), this list also included the Norman Petty Trio's 1957 hit, "Almost Paradise."

The opening show was on Saturday, March 1, at the now-vanished Trocadero cinema in the Elephant and Castle neighborhood, just south of the Thames. "The place was packed to the rafters," bandleader Ronnie

Keene remembers. "It was obvious that no one had come to see us, or any of the other British acts. We were just the cannon fodder. Still, we weren't booed: they listened to us and clapped politely. But when Buddy and the Crickets were announced, the whole place erupted. At that moment, I realized it was all over for musicians like me. This was the future.

"They had hardly any power—only the house mikes and that one little amp, which Norman Petty carried onstage for them. The bass player, I remember, wasn't even amplified. But they still managed to make as much noise as the whole of my thirteen-piece orchestra."

For British teenagers, the wonder of the occasion was not merely seeing Buddy and the Crickets in person at long last but discovering that, unlike previous such visitors from across the Atlantic, they were able to reproduce the sound of their records in live performance. "They got a terrific reception," Ronnie Keene remembers. "But it wasn't crazy, jiving-in-the-aisles stuff, the way it had been when Bill Haley came over. You could tell that the kids were really listening." The critics from the jazz-biased music press were equally impressed. Keith Goodwin in the *Melody Maker* summed up the general view: "This is rock 'n' roll like we've never heard it before in Britain."

Buddy's stage persona was the very opposite of what had been expected: not cool, serious, and grown-up, but friendly, funny, and unpretentious. He introduced each song with wisecracks about how "pathetic" the Crickets' playing was, and clowned and mugged and threw his lanky, high-buttoned body around the stage with an abandon none had dreamed that horn-rimmed rock 'n' roll swot capable of. It seemed to matter not at all that in live performance his songs were shorn of the plummy background vocals that Petty's imported trios, the Picks or the Roses, had overdubbed on the records. Despite J. I.'s and Joe B.'s evident muteness, British fans stubbornly voted them No. 1 in a poll for the year's top vocal groups.

"After the show, there must have been three hundred kids waiting outside the stage door," Ronnie Keene remembers. "We literally couldn't fight our way through them. But it was all very orderly. The kids seemed to take their cue from Buddy and the Crickets. They were very nice and courteous, and the kids were the same in return."

The next day, a Sunday, they moved from south to north London, giving two shows at the Gaumont State cinema, Kilburn, whose exterior is a scaled-down facsimile of New York's Empire State Building. A member of the audience, Philip Bergman, can visualize to this day how Buddy "literally exploded onto the stage." Into the same evening they also somehow crammed the appearance on Associated Television's *Sunday Night at the London Palladium,* which was part of their contract with the Grades. They found themselves taking part in a special gala marking the show's 100th edition, with Bob Hope, the ballerina Dame Alicia Markova, and actor Robert Morley. There was also the ritual interlude of audience-participation games, as usual so maddeningly drawn out that a confused Buddy later wrote to his parents that he'd just done "a show called Beat the Clock."

Waiting to see him that night was the whole of his nationwide guitar class, crouched over the bluish sixteen-inch screens of Pye, Cossor, or Ferguson television sets. Up in Liverpool, John Lennon and Paul McCartney both had their noses practically touching the screen. I watched at my father's pale blue Formica bar at the end of Ryde Pier, half a mile out at sea, where television reception suffered from the Morse-code signals of passing ocean liners.

Cudgel my memory as I may, those intrusive *dit-dit-da*'s from the *Queen Mary* and the *Mauretania* still break up the black and white memory of seeing Buddy Holly in live performance. All ATV supplied was a straight-on view of the Palladium stage, containing three rather lonely-looking tuxedo-clad figures, a double bass, a drum kit, and a single amplifier. One could hardly see Buddy's guitar, let alone what his fingers might be doing on its fretboard. The sound on all three numbers, "That'll Be the Day," "Peggy Sue," and "Oh Boy," was atrocious: his spot barely seemed to have begun when the gold-tasseled curtains swept shut again amid a blare from Jack Parnell's pit orchestra, and Robert Morley came waddling back to tell another plummy English joke. I also search my memory in vain for any picture of Buddy on the revolving platform, waving goodbye in company with Bob Hope, Markova, and high-plumed Palladium showgirls.

Sunday Night at the London Palladium was not videotaped, as *The Ed Sullivan Show* and even *The Arthur Murray Party* had been, nor even recorded except by fans on reel-to-reel machines in their twilit living rooms. The sole mementos of the occasion are the famous black and white photographs of Buddy in mid-song on the Palladium stage, one of which would be used as a poster for the world-hit musical he inspired thirty years later. Today, posters all over the London Underground reveal what one missed on that fugitive night of March 2, 1958: the look of faint, wholly understandable anxiety on the big-spectacled face; the immaculate tuxedo but slightly rumpled dark curly hair; the Stratocaster's narrow machine head with its six tuning pegs all in one row; the long, bony fingers shaping a D major.

Neither Lew nor Leslie Grade bothered to meet the young stars of their tour before it left London for the provinces. In later years, when the transmogrified Lord Grade was asked to reminisce about Buddy Holly, he would remove his trademark Havana cigar from his mouth and blankly reply, "Who?" Liaison with the Grades' office was handled by David Bryce, now a senior figure in Cliff Richard's organization. There was also a road manager named Wally Stewart, an elderly, red-faced man in a flapping gabardine raincoat, whose roadie duties were confined to driving the tour bus and taking care of the baggage.

The three weeks of one-nighters were as punishing, and as haphazardly planned, as any all-American road show's: from London southwest to Southampton; due north to Sheffield, Stockton-on-Tees, and Newcastle-on-Tyne; south on an illogical zigzag through Wolverhampton, Notting-ham, Bradford, Birmingham, and Worcester; back to outer London for shows in Croydon, East Ham, and Woolwich; eastward to Ipswich; north again to Leicester, Doncaster, Wigan, Hull, and Liverpool; back to outer London again for a single night, in Walthamstow, then southwest to Salis-bury, Bristol, and briefly over the Welsh border to Cardiff.

If the distances to be traveled between concerts were vastly smaller than in America, the incidental discomforts were far greater. Here were no dependable roadside motels with standard king-size beds and gleaming "sanitized" bathrooms; only English provincial "grand" hotels, where en suite baths were still a rarity, bedrooms were often heated by shilling-in-slot electric meters, and restaurants stopped serving dinner around 9 P.M. The hotel bills for Buddy's party record a spartan diet of melon, pork chops, and fried plaice, invariably accompanied by Coca-Cola and—thanks to Papa Norman's presence—without the slightest mention of alcohol. The inclusive cost for Buddy, Jerry, Joe B., and the Pettys seldom exceeded £10 a night.

Although Buddy had a cold for most of the tour, his spirits remained unflaggingly high. "I used to sit next to him on the bus," Ronnie Keene remembers. "He was a lovely lad . . . lovely. There were no big-star affec-tations about him at all. He used to talk to the boys in my band just as if he was one of them." Joe B. Mauldin remembers how they would burrow under the bedclothes in their unheated rooms, and huddle in hotel lobbies, where there would usually be a coal fire. All three of the Texans were buoyed up against the cold, damp, and fatigue by the ecstatic welcome they received everywhere they went, and the fascination of being in a country so comprehensively different from theirs. Jerry Allison still remembers the novelty of leaving his shoes outside his hotel room at night and the next morning finding them not only not stolen, but polished to a high shine.

J. I. had special cause to feel elated: in Australia he had told the others he intended to marry the inspiration for Buddy's first solo hit, Peggy Sue Gerron. "He used to ask me what it was like to be married," David Bryce remembers. "He was particularly worried about what to do if he woke up on his honeymoon with smelly breath."

Norman Petty's tireless filming provides fascinating glimpses of Buddy Holly and the Crickets meeting Olde England. Here they are, with the Pettys, standing on a bridge over the River Cam having stopped off en route to or from Ipswich to look at Cambridge University. Another sequence records the stopover in Salisbury, Wiltshire, at the half-timbered Old George hotel ("Built around 1320," the letterhead of their bill announced), where, Vi Petty would recall, "the ladies fixed us hot chocolate and we drank it in front of the fireplace." Late as it was, Buddy sat down to dash off another letter to his parents: "Norman and Jerry are sitting over by the fireplace (this is a neat, quaint old place). Norman was telling about a dream [in which] all his teeth fell out . . ." Des O'Connor, the show's emcee, had been feeding Buddy jokes to tell between numbers each night, and in this note to L. O. and Ella Buddy proudly recorded that he was sometimes getting bigger laughs than O'Connor. "He was a naturally funny guy," O'Connor remembers. "When hotels were overbooked, I sometimes used to have to share a room with him, and I always had the job of getting him up in the morning, because an early riser Buddy was not. One day, he was so slow, I just got hold of his feet and pulled. 'Don't do that, Des,' I heard this Texan voice say from under the bedclothes, 'I'm tall enough already.'"

Birmingham provided another sightseeing break. Discovering that it was the primary place where Britain's still prestigious and individual Morris and Austin cars were produced, the car-mad Buddy begged to be allowed to visit an automobile factory. On March 10, his party received a guided tour of what were then the British Motor Corporation's plant and showrooms at Longbridge. Petty took the opportunity to order an Austin-Healy deluxe coupe to be shipped back to Clovis. In Clovis Man's documentary treasure trove—along with hotel bills, plane tickets, baggage claim checks, and bright green BOAC boarding passes—is a list of the Austin-Healy's luxurious (for Britain) extras: overdrive, heater, hard top, wire wheels, push-button radio. The total price, including shipping charges, was £996.5 shillings, or $2,303.94.

Abetted by his squirrelish spouse, Petty shopped assiduously throughout the tour. On March 18, while passing through Manchester, he visited the cloth mill of Donald Shearer & Co. on Lower Mosley Street and ordered suit lengths of worsted wool to be dispatched to Clovis in five duty-saving "unsolicited gift parcels," addressed to himself, Buddy, Jerry, Joe B., and Vi (which possibly never reached their destination, since Shearer's salesperson took down the address as "Clovis, Quebec, Canada.") A memo also survives from a Grade employee, deputed to reconnoiter Piccadilly fine china dealers on the Pettys' behalf: "Royal Crown Derby do not make their Vine pattern in any smaller article than a five-inch fruit saucer . . . which is sold at 20 shillings each. . . . I saw a very lovely floral design, in round or rectangular shapes, selling at about 12 shillings each for the smallest size . . ."

If rock 'n' roll left a questionable impression on Denis Compton and Godfrey Evans, cricket had made a lasting one on Buddy. During one of the tour's London interludes, he asked a friendly journalist, Keith Goodwin of the *Melody Maker,* to teach him more about the English sporting ritual his group's name unintentionally suggested. No cricket is played in England in March, but as usual in winter, a national team was on tour (cricket tours long predate rock 'n' roll ones) in Australia. Obligingly Goodwin took Buddy to one of the "news theaters" then numerous in the West End, tiny cinemas showing only newsreels and cartoons. Fortunately the current week's newsreel included an extended cricket sequence and Buddy sat through it, fascinated.

But by the end of the tour's second week, with a second chilly northward foray looming ahead, even his spirits began to droop. "We're getting a little bit tired of England," he admitted in a postcard to his sister Pat. "It's awfully cold over here. Seems like it could never get summer here . . . Well, so long for now. Love, Buddy."

March 18 found him in Wigan (pronounced "wiggan"), the Lancashire industrial town whose name has inspired English music-hall jokes since far back into antiquity. Before the night's two concerts at the Ritz cinema (a last-minute substitution for the St. George's Hall in nearby Blackburn), Buddy's party checked in to Wigan's mock-Tudor Grand Hotel. The desk clerks were two local girls, Barbara Bullough and Jo Burroughs. Both were lively and attractive, especially Barbara, with her big dark eyes and rather Latin-looking cupid's-bow mouth. As might be expected, both took special pains to ensure that their VIP guests were comfortable. "We got on really well with them," Barbara remembers now. "It helped that my parents had been to America a lot, so I knew to say 'sidewalk' instead of 'pavement.' One thing I do recall, though, is that I didn't like Norman Petty."

Buddy was instantly and obviously smitten with Barbara. "He asked me if I was going to the concert that night, and I said I hadn't thought of it. He said, 'You MUST come, and went off and made all the arrangements. I had no idea about rock 'n' roll—I'd been brought up with classical music —but I thought the show was wonderful. I remember what a thrill went through the place when Buddy came onstage.

"I still lived with my parents, and had strict instructions not to be home too late. We lived a little way out of town and by about 11 o'clock my last bus had gone, so Buddy asked if he could see me home. He seemed such a sweet, person that I said 'Yes.' Our house was at the end of an unpaved lane, so the taxi had to stop on the main road and Buddy walked me to my front gate. We talked . . . and cuddled and kissed . . . then he asked me if I'd go on the rest of his tour with him. I liked him a lot, but I knew my father would never stand for something like that, so I had to say no. Then he asked me if I'd come and see him play again when he was in Liverpool, and we said good night."

Savor the moment for another second: Buddy Holly in Wigan in his too-thin black raincoat and his side-buckled shoes, walking the well-bred Lancashire lass down the unpaved lane to her front gate, giving her a chaste good-night kiss, then returning, alone, in the ratty local taxi, past cobbled streets of dark factory chimneys and back-to-back houses, still "lookin' for someone to love." The bill from the Grand Hotel, Wigan, is slightly different from others preserved among Clovis Man's relics: it has the names "Barbara" and "Jo" and a row of X's for kisses handwritten on it. Next to each of the Crickets' names is typed an admiring "Oh Boy!"

Barbara Bullough kept her promise to go to Liverpool and see Buddy when he appeared at the city's Philharmonic Hall two nights later. "He'd told me 'Just say you're Barbara from Wigan and they'll let you in.'" She talked to Buddy backstage, but wasn't able to catch his performance. Nor, to their chagrin, were two of his greatest Merseyside fans. Neither John Lennon nor Paul McCartney, impoverished art student and schoolboy respectively, could afford the price of a ticket, and so had to rely on more affluent friends for descriptions of Buddy's suit and guitar, and what chords his fingers might have been shaping. For both John and Paul, his presence in Liverpool was thrill enough; more important, it kick-started the band they themselves had formed the previous summer. Deciding to emulate Buddy's group and name themselves after an insect, they came up with "the Beetles." Pun-loving Lennon changed it to "Beatles," after what was then called "beat" music and stuck to it tenaciously despite mirthful protests from all sides (much the same as had assailed Buddy and J. I.) that no group with such an idiotic name could ever hope to be successful.

The last stop on the tour was the Gaumont cinema, Hammersmith, West London, on March 25. As Buddy and J. I. Allison were resting between the evening's two shows, Joe B. entered the dressing room in a mood of unwonted braggadocio, flourishing a large cigar he said he intended to smoke as a ceremonial farewell to Britain. Both his colleagues loudly vetoed this plan to fill the place with noxious fumes. What the Buddy Holly legend has always termed "a friendly scuffle" but was in fact quite a serious Texas brawl erupted, with Buddy and J. I. both trying to pin Joe B. down and wrest the cigar from his grasp. As they were rolling and grappling on the floor, Joe B.'s forehead jerked up and smashed against Buddy's mouth, knocking the caps from his two upper front teeth. With minutes to showtime, the only way of camouflaging the naked stumps was to paste chewing gum over them. When the three finally came offstage, amid the usual rapturous applause, Norman Petty told them he'd never seen them give a worse performance.

Earlier that last day, they had fulfilled their only other British television commitment, performing "Maybe Baby" on Jack Payne's *Off the Record* for the BBC. Payne was a former dance band leader whose surname well summarized his character; nonetheless, as a showcase for rock 'n' roll, his program was a considerable improvement on *Sunday Night at the London Palladium*. I watched it at my grandmother's flat, a squalid place

192 ☆ Philip Norman

used mainly to store the candy and cigarettes she sold from her seafront kiosk. Buddy lip-synched his latest British hit without great animation, against a madly contemporary backdrop vaguely resembling a line of outsize turnstiles. At least this time I could see the Stratocaster plainly, although the plainer I saw it, the more implausibly flat and body-hugging it became, less like a guitar than the attachment for some futuristic vacuum cleaner.

I didn't know then that *Off the Record* had been videotaped and that Buddy and the Crickets had actually left Britain three days earlier. Nor can I say I was very upset by his departure: after so many good reviews, he'd obviously be back again before long. All that mattered was rushing to my own cheap Hofner guitar; trying to pick out the "Maybe Baby" intro for myself and discovering that, yet again, he'd made it easy for me.

☆　☆　☆

Only three days after the end of their British tour, Buddy and the Crickets were on the road in America yet again. This sightseeing opportunity, though, held no allure for Papa Norman, who returned to Clovis with his rolls of exposed film, his many pounds of excess baggage, and his wife. Free now to drink, smoke, and cuss as they pleased, Buddy, J. I. and Joe B. joined Alan Freed's "Big Beat Show," a forty-four–day circuit of Eastern and Midwestern states, featuring Jerry Lee Lewis, Chuck Berry, Danny and the Juniors, Frankie Lymon, Screamin' Jay Hawkins, the Diamonds, Larry Williams, Billie and Lillie, the Chantels, the Pastels, Jo-Ann Campbell, Ed Townsend, and the Alan Freed Orchestra, and destined to be more spectacularly chaotic than any rock 'n' roll excursion since the dawn of Haley and Presley.

On Freed's customary mixed-race menu, the battle for the fans' attention waxed fiercer than ever. Danny and the Juniors were a finger-snapping —but otherwise barely animate—white teenage vocal group whose "At the Hop" was to become the top-selling single of 1958. Screamin' Jay Hawkins was a stage extrovert more uproarious and outrageous than even Little Richard; a one-man Rocky Horror Show twenty years too early who greeted his audience by climbing out of a coffin, and performed his solitary hit, "I Put a Spell on You," and other goodies like the much-banned "Constipation Blues" with the harrowing vocal effects of a poorly soundproofed abattoir.

Buddy, about age nine, with
his mother, Ella (right),
grandmother, and sister Pat.
Courtesy of the Holley family.

Buddy, age fifteen, already an auto nut.
Courtesy of the Holley family.

Buddy at Lubbock High in his first pair of glasses.
Courtesy of the Griggs Collection.

*Buddy and his first love,
Echo McGuire.*
Courtesy of the
Griggs Collection.

*Echo wearing the Western
belt Buddy made for her—
and his high school ring
around her neck.*
Courtesy of Echo Griffith.

Hi Pockets Duncan, the gentlemanly Lubbock deejay who became Buddy's first manager.
Courtesy of the Griggs Collection.

The day in 1955 that changed Buddy's life: The newly launched Elvis Presley meets his Lubbock fans. Buddy is on the extreme right of the picture.
Courtesy of Steve Bonner.

*Buddy flight-tests the new Stratocaster with steel guitarist Don Guess (left),
bass player Larry Welborn (far right), and the "wonderfully envy free" Bob
Montgomery.*
Courtesy of Kevin Terry and the Griggs Collection.

Buddy, J. I. Allison (left), and the new bass player, Joe B. Maudlin, give it their all in the den at June and Nig Clark's Lubbock home. Courtesy of the Griggs Collection.

June Clark, the older woman with whom Buddy had a tempestuous affair during 1957, pictured at the El Morocco nightclub in New York. Courtesy of June Clark.

Clovis Man and wife.
Courtesy of Gerald F. Fisher.

Norman Petty: "A bad note could bring him out in a rash."
Courtesy of Gerald F. Fisher.

*The Pettys and their bookkeeper, Norma Jean Berry, in the guest suite
at their West Seventh Street studio compound.*
Courtesy of Gerald F. Fisher.

Petty listens to a playback.
Courtesy of Gerald F. Fisher.

Vi Petty writes lead sheets, guarded by ceramic gnome and real-life Chihuahua, Speedy. Courtesy of Gerald F. Fisher.

Joe B., J. I., Niki Sullivan, and Buddy, the "real gangly" quartet that first recorded with Petty. Courtesy of Gerald F. Fisher.

Buddy and J. I. Allison
interviewed by deejay Freeman Hoover
in their hotel room on the road with
"Biggest Show of Stars" for 1957. One
of the rare occasions when Buddy
allowed himself to be seen smoking.
Courtesy of Freeman Hoover.

Buddy, with original half-frame glasses and West Texas teeth, meets Canadian deejay Red Robinson.
Courtesy of Red Robinson.

Buddy in Decorah, Iowa, during the bumpy "Summer Dance Party" tour, July 1958.
Courtesy of Linda Roed.

Barbara Bullough (right), the British hotel receptionist who allowed Buddy to see her home. "He was the perfect gentleman."
Courtesy of Barbara O'Nions.

Buddy and Maria Elena on tour, 1958.
Courtesy of the Holley family.

December 1958: Despite pressing financial worries, Buddy keeps up a cheerful front with Phil Everly in Phil's room at the Park Sheraton Hotel, New York. Courtesy of the Griggs Collection.

Buddy and his protégé Waylon Jennings find something to laugh about in a photo booth a few days before his death. Courtesy of the Griggs Collection.

Ritchie Valens at the Kato Ballroom. Buddy intended to take his career in hand when they returned to New York.
Courtesy of Dianne Cory.

J. P. Richardson, "the Big Bopper," at the Kato Ballroom, Mankato, Minnesota, on January 25, 1959, eight days before the fatal charter flight.
Courtesy of Dianne Cory.

Poster for Buddy's last appearance.
Courtesy of Elwin Musser, the *Mason City Globe Gazette.*

Investigators probe the wreckage of N3794N.
Courtesy of Elwin Musser, the *Mason City Globe Gazette.*

The tone of the "Big Beat" tour was set on opening night, March 28, at the Brooklyn Paramount theater. Chuck Berry and Jerry Lee Lewis each regarded himself as top of the bill and demanded to be recognized as such by closing the show. Called on to arbitrate between the two grappling brontosaurus egos, Alan Freed ruled that Berry had the greater seniority. Consigned to the next-to-last spot, Jerry Lee was later to take revenge with a piece of performance art that would have upstaged the Second Coming. In the midst of pounding out "Great Balls of Fire," he produced a gasoline-filled Coca-Cola bottle, gave his piano a liberal dousing, set a match to it, and continued hammering while his keyboard blazed around his forearms like a backyard bonfire. Finally sauntering offstage, amid pyromaniacal shrieks of ecstasy from the audience, he gave Chuck Berry a satiated smirk and murmured what has gone down in history as "Follow that, nigga!" but was more likely "Follow that, Killer!"

The tour was, at least, less fatiguing than earlier ones since many of the journeys between its one-nighters being by air rather than over-crowded bus. However, the planes provided were very different from Pan Am Constellations—usually ancient DC-3s that took the air as laboriously as flying elephants and bucked and rattled alarmingly in the frequent turbulence. At Cincinnati, Ohio, came a further unheeded reminder of mortality: on the day the "Big Beat" troupe arrived, a helicopter crashed to the north of the city and its pilot was killed. But Buddy did not mind flying—quite the contrary: he adored it, hanging on and grinning through the worst shake-ups like a schoolboy on a fairground ride while his seat companions blanched and reached for airsickness bags. Danny Rapp, the lead singer with Danny and the Juniors, remembered afterward how much he adored shooting craps on these flights, and how recklessly he threw his money around, betting as much as $500 on a single roll of the dice.

In the nightly spotlight-snaffling contest between Chuck Berry's duck walk, Screamin' Jay Hawkins's coffin, and Jerry Lee Lewis's grievous bodily harm to grand pianos, Buddy, J. I., and Joe B. more than held their own. It did not even seriously break Buddy's stride when the tour bus was broken into during a meal stop in St. Louis, and his Stratocaster was stolen, along with several of J. I. Allison's drums. He went on to Canada, using a substitute guitar while an SOS call was routed via Clovis to Manny's music stores in New York. An identical brown sunburst Strat was flown out to him, arriving in time for the concert in Waterloo, Iowa, a week later.

The May portion of the tour ended in mayhem for which Buddy and the Crickets bore no responsibility and during which they were relieved to take a back seat for once. When "The Big Beat Show" performed at Boston's Arena on May 6, the whole city seemed to have assumed the persona of Jerry Lee Lewis. Rioting erupted outside: a nineteen-year-old sailor was stabbed, fifteen other people were injured, and there was widespread mugging, looting, arson, and vandalism. Trouble also broke out inside the Arena, apparently instigated by conservative Boston-Irish youths who objected to seeing white and black performers using the same stage. When Chuck Berry came on, he was pelted with garbage from the gallery and had to take refuge behind his drummer. Police and security men waded in, clearing the hall and making dozens of heavy-handed arrests, mainly among those who had been innocently dancing in the aisles. The city's Mayor, John Hynes, banned all future such shows, while district attorney Garrett Byrne castigated Alan Freed for inciting what he called "rock 'n' roll paganism."

The Boston riots sent a wave of renewed anti-rock fervor coursing through America's Establishment. No less a figure than the director of the FBI, J. Edgar Hoover (whose penchant for wearing ladies' frocks no one then suspected), gave his opinion that as well as being godless and lewd, rock 'n' roll was part of the Communist plot to undermine Western freedom and democracy. Boston district attorney Byrne indicted Alan Freed under an archaic statute for "inciting a riot" and "conspiring to overthrow the Government." Though the charges were later dropped, it proved to be the first step in Freed's sad and undeserved decline. Three pending "Big Beat" stops—in Troy, New York, New Haven, Connecticut, and Newark, New Jersey—were canceled by fearful municipal authorities. While Freed was broadcasting his radio show on New York's WINS, his Newark co-promoter, enraged by the ticket sales that had been lost, appeared at the station with a handgun, threatening to kill him.

The "Big Beat" tour's canceled dates included its final one, in Newark, New Jersey, and Buddy and the Crickets flew home a couple of days earlier than expected. It was a journey that saw their first mild but decisive act of rebellion against Norman Petty. Each of the three had always wanted a Harley-Davidson motorcycle; since they had with them a substantial part of their tour earnings, several thousand dollars in cash, Buddy suggested stopping off in Dallas, buying a Harley each, and riding the 300 miles west to Lubbock like Marlon Brando's gang (the Beetles) in

The Wild One. The insurrection did not lie in acquiring these costly new toys, which Petty doubtless would readily have done for them, using his power of attorney over their collective bank account. It lay in acting on their own initiative rather than, as usual, letting Petty get them what they wanted via one of his many Clovis business friends with a cat's cradle of concessions and discounts. It lay in holding on to money rather than meekly handing it over; in rejecting, however mildly, Papa Norman's 100 percent control.

As things turned out, it was not Harleys they bought, but English motorcycles, at that time considered among the world's best. "At the Harley-Davidson place, the salesmen were real unfriendly," Joe B. remembers. "They didn't believe we really had the money to buy bikes that expensive." Furious, the trio hopped a cab and went straight to Ray Miller's Triumph dealership, where, within a very few minutes Buddy had blown $3,000 in cash on an Ariel Cyclone (registration: CNLF4510) for himself, a Triumph Trophy for J. I., and a Thunderbird for Joe B., plus jeans and denim jackets and jockey caps emblazoned with Triumph's winged emblem. Thus mounted and equipped, they set off westward for Lubbock, like a scene from *Easy Rider,* happily unaware that a wave of ferocious rainstorms and mini-tornados was currently battering West Texas. "None of us had ever ridden bikes that powerful before," Joe B. says. "And on the journey it came on to rain real hard. We got soaked through, and had to stop and buy ourselves more new sets of Levi's."

When Jerry Lee Lewis returned home to Ferriday, Louisiana, that same week, he was given a civic welcome by the mayor and the Chamber of Commerce, driven through the streets in an open Cadillac, and presented with the keys to the city. Lubbock, by contrast, remained seemingly unmoved by Buddy's international triumphs and the fact that he had made its name as well as his own familiar to record buyers from Sydney to Stoke-on-Trent. Lubbock City Council announced no Buddy Holly Day to match the Jerry Lee Lewis Day being celebrated on the Killer's home turf. Even Buddy's old high school offered no gesture of pride or approbation to its world-famous graduate; both the city's daily papers, the morning *Avalanche* and the evening *Journal,* maintained an almost eerie silence about his achievements.

Puzzled and annoyed though Buddy was by Lubbock's indifference, it had its undoubted advantages. When he came home, as now, exhausted by constant travel and performance, he could escape completely from the pressures of stardom, go hunting and fishing with his brothers, play with his nephews and nieces, and hang out with friends like Bob Montgomery and Jerry Coleman at old haunts like the KSEL studios and the Hi-D-Ho without being mobbed and pestered for autographs. He might have turned records into gold and trodden the boards of the London Palladium, but at the Holley family's modest home at 1305 39th Street he was still just Buddy, the baby of the family, expected to show the same respect as ever to his father, do whatever his tiny, feisty mother considered to be for the best, keep his packs of Salems well hidden, and worship with his family in their pew at the Tabernacle Baptist Church.

One of his first acts after "That'll Be the Day" became a hit had been to repay his brother Larry that whopping thousand-dollar loan for his first Stratocaster and stage wardrobe. Anyone else who'd ever lent him money or given him credit was paid back, often in double measure. Now that Buddy was rich, or thought he was, his extravagant generosity became a byword among his family and around town. "Whenever a group of us from the family would go on a fishing trip, he'd buy us everything we needed to fish, all brand-new," Larry remembers. One day as Buddy sat in a shoeshine parlor, the young man who was buffing his boots happened to admire the expensive wristwatch he was wearing. Buddy slipped off the watch and held it out, saying, "If you like it that much, take it."

The one Lubbock institution that did show an interest in Buddy was his local draft board. On May 28, 1958, he received a letter summoning him to a medical examination to determine his fitness for military service. There was, however, not the remotest likelihood of Buddy's following Elvis Presley into the Army. His 20/800 vision automatically disqualified him, with strong support from the stomach condition that from here on would be formally referred to as his ulcer.

Barely two weeks after riding into town incognito on his Ariel, he was back at Norman Petty's studio to cut three new tracks with the Crickets, augmented by the Roses vocal trio and an additional lead guitarist named Tommy Allsup, a twenty-six-year-old Western-swing musician from Lawton, Oklahoma. Tall, swarthy, and slow-spoken. Allsup had originally come to Clovis to back a singing group. Though his agile single-string technique seemed the very opposite of Buddy's chordal "rhythm lead," it had the same freshness and directness, and Petty had asked him to stick around and try his hand on the Crickets' next session.

The first two songs featuring Tommy Allsup might have been consciously chosen to represent Buddy's own emotional state at this point: one was called "Lonesome Tears," the other "It's So Easy (to Fall in Love)." And, as in his nature, brightness and optimism outweighed introspection and self-pity. While "Lonesome Tears" is just a routine B-side, "It's So Easy" stands among the best things he ever recorded, perhaps the nearest rock 'n' roll has ever come to pure aural sunshine. As in the blues' call-and-response style, two-line verses alternate with a sinuous treble riff, the guitar jaunty and confident, the voice ruefully—and, it would seem, prophetically—owning up: "Here I go, breaking all o' the rules."

The second pearl of the batch was "Heartbeat," written by Buddy's old friend Bob Montgomery, a Latin-accented ballad made to sound almost Hawaiian by Tommy Allsup's swooping steely riff and tearful tremolo. The lyric contained another of Norman Petty's slushy lines ("Why does a love kiss stay in my memory?"), for which he claimed the same 50 percent writing share he had on "It's So Easy," though, for some reason, he allowed Buddy sole credit for "Lonesome Tears."

At Petty's, too, Buddy came down to earth—and appeared happy to do so. The international star reverted to working musician, a pro for whom the good of the music itself was more important than personal pride or vanity. Tommy Allsup was a fine guitarist whose playing gave the Crickets' sound an extra dimension; therefore Buddy was delighted to have him, and ceded him the lead spot without jealousy. Remarkably for a twenty-one-year-old, especially in that era of throat-ripping competitiveness, he was keen to spot and encourage new talent, and unselfish in using his time and energy—and, later, his money—to help struggling musicians, even though they might well become his rivals on the charts. He was still pushing J. I. Allison as a solo performer, under J. I.'s alter-ego of "Ivan," and was proud beyond measure, Peggy Sue remembers, when Ivan's first release, "Real Wild Child," made the outer reaches of the charts. On June 6 in Clovis, the big-time star once more reverted to session man, playing backup guitar for a young folksinger named Carolyn Hester, whom Petty had recently sold to the Coral label and whom Buddy had dated, platonically, in New York. With bass player George Atwood, they recorded Buddy's song "Take Your Time," Hester's own "A Little While Ago," and two with real holly and berries attached, "Christmas in Killarney" and "Hurry, Santa, Hurry."

On visits home, Buddy always sought out Bob Montgomery, that wonderfully envy-free figure from his country music days who had stood aside so selflessly when destiny seemed to beckon from Nashville. Driving around Lubbock together, they revived the Buddy and Bob partnership by co-writing two songs, "Love's Made a Fool of You" and "Wishing," which Buddy, with his usual creative generosity, decided were far better suited to the Everly Brothers than to himself. Instead of the usual rough demo, he made finished studio versions of the songs to sell them to Don and Phil, backed by Tommy Allsup on lead guitar, bassist George Atwood, and drummer Bo Clarke, and with his vocal double-tracked to underline how perfectly custom-made for the brothers' seamless harmony each was. Don and Phil Everly loved both tracks, especially "Wishing," but were prevented from recording them by political difficulties with their regular songwriters, Boudleaux and Felice Bryant. The net result was two more future Buddy Holly evergreens which, despite his best intentions, no one else could have sung quite that way.

Otherwise on this extended furlough, he hung out mainly with J. I. and Joe B., riding, tinkering with, and posing for pictures beside their new English motorcycles. A color home movie, taken by J. I.'s brother James, shows them skylarking like truant schoolboys on the grass outside the Allison home. Buddy, in an unlikely outfit of butcher-striped sweater, dark glasses, and Hell's Angel peaked cap, parodies a biker's duel with J. I., brandishing a miniature penknife.

Even Buddy's huge appetite for performing and perpetual motion had been more than sated by the past year. When the offer of yet another tour came in, which would have meant curtailing their time off in Lubbock, he showed no hesitation in refusing it. The normally easygoing and un-driven J. I. was cast in the unfamiliar role of drill sergeant, protesting that such offers might not be around forever and that they should soak up every dollar they could, while they could. Buddy said they owed it to themselves to take a rest, have fun, and ride their new motorbikes. If J. I. wanted money for a new Cadillac, he added grandiosely, then *he*'d buy him a Cadillac. Enjoying their health and youth was more important than just piling up money, he argued, and J. I. has never forgotten the words with which he drove his point home: "What if you died tomorrow?"

The prodigious run of success on the American charts was now definitely over, though in Britain it continued at full throttle. The glorious "Rave On," released under Buddy's name on May 20, made only No. 37 in America but spent fourteen weeks in the British Top 20, peaking at No. 5. "Think It Over," under the Crickets' name, failed to make the U.S.

Top 20 but reached No. 7 in Britain. The pattern was repeated by Buddy's first own-name LP for Coral, *Buddy Holly,* which failed to chart in America but reached No. 8 in Britain, notwithstanding the widespread puzzlement created by its cover. This was a head-and-shoulders portrait of Buddy, wonderfully stylish in burgundy collared jacket and pin-fastened shirt, but minus his black horn-rims and revealing a decided squint. So did this performer wear glasses or didn't he? To compound the mystery even further, some later liner notes for this album and *The Chirping Crickets* misprinted the name of his home city, informing data-hungry British boys that "Buddy Holly was born in Bullock, Texas . . ."

For any other performer in that time, the response to declining record sales would have been a hurried return to well-tried earlier formulas. But Buddy knew no way but forward. On June 19, he was back in New York for his second recording session there. This time, the venue was Decca's studio at the Pythian Temple building on West 50th Street. The producer was Dick Jacobs, a conductor whose lush string orchestra recorded for Coral and who had recently replaced Bob Thiele as Coral-Brunswick's director of A&R. Instead of J. I. and Joe B., Buddy's backup musicians were high-powered Eastern session men, including saxophonist Sam the Man Taylor from Alan Freed's stage band. Also in attendance was a female gospel group, the Helen Way Singers.

The session was ostensibly to record two cover versions. Another up-and-coming singer–songwriter, Bobby Darin, had been about to defect to Brunswick from the Atco label, and under Dick Jacobs's supervision had already recorded two of his own songs, "Early in the Morning" and "Now We're One," as his debut single. Unfortunately, Darin's last Atco release, "Splish-Splash" (a novelty number mentioning rock 'n' roll hero-ines Miss Molly and Peggy Sue), had turned out to be a huge hit. Atco now understandably refused to let him defect to another label, and the two tracks he had cut for Brunswick were unreleasable.

Buddy's version of "Early in the Morning" is less rock 'n' roll than spiritual and, as everyone involved must have known full well, stood no earthly chance on the pop charts of mid-1958. What it proved—most significantly to the hard-nosed Dick Jacobs—was that Buddy could per-form grown-up gospel and soul as brilliantly as he could adolescent rock and pop; that if rock 'n' roll were to disappear tomorrow, here was a real singer, fit to rank in his own fidgety, hiccuppy way with Frank Sinatra, Dean Martin, or Johnny Mathis.

The lyrics of "Early in the Morning" contain an unwitting reference to some of Buddy's most fervent British standard-bearers in the following decade. It's like a moment of clairvoyance when he sings, and the gospel choir echoes, "Oh, a rollin' stone don't gather no moss . . ."

☆   ☆   ☆

Whenever Buddy and the Crickets were in New York, they always made a point of calling on Murray Deutch, the tersely affable executive vice president of Peer-Southern Music, who had originally coerced Coral-Brunswick into taking a chance on "That'll Be the Day." Outside Deutch's office was a small reception area where visitors emerging from the elevator were greeted by a petite young woman with coiled-up dark hair, a heart-shaped face, and an alluring Hispanic accent. The young woman's name, one destined to be inextricably linked with Buddy's from here on and ever after, was Maria Elena Santiago.

Maria Elena was born near San Juan, Puerto Rico, on January 7, 1933, the daughter of a detective in the San Juan police department. Her mother, a nurse, died when she was seven and, with her father out on police business at all hours, Maria Elena had to learn to take care of herself and her brother, Miguel. After her father had remarried and been widowed a second time, he decided the best future he could give her was to send her to finish her education in America.

Puerto Rican immigrants to America in the late forties and early fifties generally faced racial prejudice and ghettoization little different from that endured by blacks. But Maria Elena was luckier than most of her compatriots in New York. After lodging initially and not very happily with a sister of her father's, she moved in with her mother's unmarried sister, Provi Garcia, a high-powered woman who ran the Latin American division at Peer-Southern Music and had an apartment on Tenth Street in Greenwich Village.

Provi's job involved frequent trips abroad, and Maria Elena became a kind of secretary-companion, packing her aunt's suitcases, buying her clothes, occasionally acting as hostess at cocktail parties for Peer-Southern writers and performers at the apartment. Toward the end of her schooldays, she also took a job as a translator for Spanish-speaking patients at St. Vincent's hospital, and ended up in charge of a clinic there. Though she pursued a busy social life, frequenting fashionable restaurants and mingling with creative, cosmopolitan people, it was always with her strict spinster aunt as chaperone. Indeed by the age of twenty-five, Maria Elena now insists, she had never had a date with a young man, let alone been kissed by one. She was highly attractive, accustomed to organizing other people, chic, worldly, and sophisticated, but also conventional, self-contained, and rather lonely.

She had originally wanted to be a dancer, but that ambition fell by the wayside as she became more and more involved in Aunt Provi's world. When a vacancy for a temporary, Spanish-speaking receptionist occurred at Peer-Southern, Maria Elena joined the company and, before long, had graduated to the vestibule outside Murray Deutch's office. It was here that she first met Buddy, one morning in June 1958.

"He came in with Jerry and Joe B. and said they had an appointment with Murray. I said, 'Have a seat; he'll be with you in a moment,' and they sat down beside my desk. While they were waiting, Buddy tried to get me into a conversation and, of course, I tried to be polite. I didn't even know who he was at that time. And then the three of them started kidding around. Jerry wanted to ask me out, and then Joe B. said, 'No, *I'm* going to be the one taking her out.' But of the three, the one I really hit it off with right away was Buddy. The first moment we looked at each other, it was like, boom. He asked me out to lunch, but I had to say no. At Peer-Southern we were strictly forbidden to go on dates with people who came into the office."

Nothing further might have happened but for Murray Deutch's secretary, Jo Harper, who had previously run Norman Petty's New York office. "At lunch, the two of us would usually go downstairs to Jack Dempsey's," Maria Elena says. "But on this day Jo said, 'Why don't we go to Howard Johnson's for a change?' I said, 'Oh God, that place is always full, you have to wait in line, and we only have one hour for lunch.' Jo said, 'I assure you you won't have to wait in line.' When we got to Howard Johnson's, Buddy was waiting in a booth with the two Crickets—and Norman Petty came later, too. Buddy had spoken with Jo beforehand and made her promise to bring me there.

"They put me in the middle with Buddy on one side of me and Joe B. on the other. Joe B. was trying to grab my hand under the table. But Buddy made it very clear to both him and Jerry, 'Whoa, wait a minute, she's not going out with either of you guys. Don't waste your time. She's going to go out with me. And I'm going to marry her.' I thought that was just part of their kidding around."

By the end of lunch, Buddy had asked Maria Elena to have dinner with him that same night. "I told him I'd have to convince my aunt and that it would be tough because I wasn't allowed to go on dates and—though I didn't say this—because she wouldn't like the thought of me going out with someone who was a musician. She worked with musicians and liked them, but she knew the kind of lives they led. And, of course, rock 'n' roll musicians were worst of all in the eyes of older people like her. The only person I had ever been allowed to go out with, other than her, was her secretary, Margie. But I kept on pleading all afternoon, and Provi was phoning around the company, to Murray Deutch and all kind of other people, checking on Buddy. Eventually, she said, 'Okay, you can go, but you have to be back by midnight. Don't drink anything, come straight back to the house, and be careful because these musicians are all crazy.'

"Buddy called me about three or four times during the afternoon to see how it was going with my aunt. He had told me he was staying at the Edison Hotel on Forty-second Street and the last time he called, I said I could meet him but I didn't get off work until 5:30 so it couldn't be until around 6:30. He said, 'Please make it before then,' because he had to go to a radio station in the early part of the evening to do some live interview-jingles. I couldn't even go home to change or anything. I went out to a store and bought a new sweater and cardigan to wear, and I refreshed myself in my aunt's office, which had its own powder room and shower. I had never rushed so much in my life! I started to walk from the Fifties to Forty-second Street, then I managed to grab a taxi. As I came up to the hotel, Buddy's limo was just pulling away. But, luckily, he saw me. So he stopped the limo, jumped out, and came over and paid off the taxi and put me in the limo."

After recording his radio jingles, Buddy got rid of J. I. and Joe B. and took Maria Elena to dinner at P.J. Clarke's saloon. P.J.'s cozy wood-paneled interior—famously displayed in the film-noir classic *The Lost Weekend*—has always been a hangout for Manhattan's show business and media elite. Over steak (for Buddy) and veal (for Maria Elena), they discovered a rapport that transcended their different ethnic origins, their hugely dissimilar upbringings, even the four-year gap in their ages. "It's hard to know why you hit it off with someone and feel as comfortable with them after a few minutes as if you've known them all your lives," Maria Elena says. "But that's the way I felt—like it all had happened before, like I knew him for years already. And Buddy told me he felt the same, which was more unusual for him. Sure, he liked people, but he never was one to be out there with somebody right away. It always took him a while to warm up to someone.

"In a way we were both similar types of people, both a lot older than our years. I had had to grow up quickly because of having to look after my brother first, then my aunt. And Buddy was the same way, a young man of twenty-one but going on fifty, the way he thought, the way his mind worked. I always say he was an old soul.

"He told me all about Lubbock and his father and his mother, all the personal things in his life and his family. He was very funny and light-hearted in the way he talked, but when he told me about his music and what his intentions were in his career, he was completely serious. He told me that he didn't write music just for himself, but that he wanted everyone to be able to enjoy it, and that he intended to go right to the top in show business, and nothing was going to stop him.

"While we were having dinner, Buddy got up from the table and said, 'I'll be right back.' I thought he just gone to the boys' room, but when he came back he had both his hands behind him. He brought out a red rose and said, 'This is for you. And I have something to ask you. Would you marry me?' I thought, 'Oh my God! My aunt was right. These people are insane!' Of course I thought he was joking or just handing me a line to make me feel nice, but deep inside of me I was hoping that it was true, because I fell in love with that man right away.

"But I pretended to take it very lightly. I said, 'When do you want to get married? Now? Or when we finish dinner?' He said, 'You think I'm kidding, don't you? But I'm very serious. As a matter of fact, tomorrow before I leave New York I want to talk to your aunt.' I said, 'Oh, you do? Then you be there at our apartment at nine in the morning!' Again, here I go, saying these things, thinking, 'He'll never show up. When he gets to his hotel, he'll forget all about it.'

"But nine o'clock next morning, the concierge in our building calls up and says, 'There's a young man called Buddy Holly here to see you and your aunt.' It was a Saturday, and Provi was still in bed. The night before when I got home, I hadn't mentioned anything about what had gone on to her, only that I had a nice evening. At first Provi thought Buddy had just wanted to pay a social call on her after taking me out. But he was very straightforward about the whole thing. He told my aunt, 'I'm here because Maria Elena and I, we want to get married. I asked her last night. Didn't she tell you?'"

No one who knew Buddy would have been much surprised by any of this. The same impetuous nature was at work which, nine months earlier, had been ready to break up the Crickets if June Clark would leave her husband and run away with him. His chaste brief encounter with Barbara Bullough, the Wigan hotel clerk, had further underlined how desperate was his search for someone to assuage the heartbreak of losing Echo McGuire.

And Maria Elena was a bewitchingly attractive young woman, especially to one of Buddy's peculiar susceptibilities: a mixture of big-city sophistication and almost quaintly old-fashioned decorum, of doll-like femininity and evident strong-mindedness, humor, and resilience. She was also very nearly as tiny in stature as Echo—and his mother. Like L. O. Holley before him, gangly Buddy was irresistibly drawn to a small woman of large character whom he might appear to shelter and protect but who in effect would manage and motivate him as well as guard him (and his name, after he had gone) with the ferocity of a terrier.

But even for Buddy, never inclined to wait for anything or anyone, this was an all-fired hurry. Undoubtedly it weighed with his competitive nature that his best friend, J. I. Allison, although three years his junior, was already engaged to Peggy Sue Gerron and planning a midsummer wedding. In a few months he himself would be twenty-two, an age when most young men of his era and background expected to be married and starting a family. It's almost as if he sensed in some way that the sands were already running out, and he had only weeks, days, and hours to enact his urgent destiny. Maria Elena has never forgotten his answer when a bewildered Aunt Provi asked whether it wouldn't be wiser to wait a little before rushing into marriage: "I don't have time," Buddy told her.

Amazingly, the stern Spanish American lady capitulated at once, agreeing to give them her blessing. "I still don't understand how it happened, after she'd always been so strict with me and not wanted me to go out with musicians," Maria Elena says. "If she'd been against it, I would have had to listen to her. But she just asked me, 'Is this really what you want?' I said, 'Yes,' and she said 'Okay. I think you people ought to wait and get to know one another better. But if that's what you want, go ahead.' She figured that if she tried to stop us, we'd just do it anyway."

A jubilant Buddy then went to the phone and broke the news to his family in Lubbock. Knowing their youngest son as they did, L. O. and Ella Holley were not totally astounded to hear that he'd found himself a wife in New York. "He was just lookin' to get married, any way, any how," his brother Larry says. "Jerry was about to do it, and Buddy didn't want to be left behind. And I knew he'd been real heartsick since it all ended with Echo. He was lonesome, he needed someone . . . and Joe B. wasn't going to fill the bill."

For all that, the Holleys' blessing was even less likely than Aunt Provi's had been. Indeed, even West Texans as decent and good-hearted as L. O. and Ella found two reasons for deep disquiet in Buddy's news. First, Maria Elena was Puerto Rican and so of the same ethnic origin as Lubbock's despised Mexican underclass. Second, and even more explosive, being of Hispanic origin must mean she was a Roman Catholic. To the Holleys' Tabernacle Baptist Church, it had been heresy enough when Larry briefly dated a girl from the Church of Christ. What Buddy was now proposing could bring heaven literally crashing down around their ears.

L. O. and Ella Holley flew up to New York at once, and in obvious consternation. At the sight of Buddy's new fiancée, however, all their misgivings melted away. "Buddy's father and I hit it off, boom, right from the beginning," Maria Elena says. "He was a very sweet, easygoing kind of man. His mother was different—she was the one who directed traffic in that family. But they both made me feel welcome right away. They said Buddy had found a gorgeous girl. They thought I was a little doll with my clothes, my accent. They made me feel like I was something breakable."

Buddy's two fellow Crickets also knew by now that the Peer-Southern receptionist whose hand they had competed to grab under the table at Howard Johnson's four days earlier was to become Mrs. Charles Hardin Holley. Despite the obvious implications for their Three Musketeer brotherhood, J. I. Allison and Joe B. Mauldin closed ranks around Buddy as loyally as would the Beatles, a decade later, when John Lennon introduced Yoko Ono into their midst. J. I. could sympathize with the religious difficulty since Peggy Sue's parents were also Roman Catholics, and were pressuring him to convert before they'd agree to the marriage. Accustomed to doing everything together, Buddy and J. I. began planning a double wedding ceremony. And Joe B., the bump on a log, as usual went along with the majority. "I was pretty surprised by the suddenness of it," he says now. "But if it was going to make Buddy happy, I was for it one hundred percent."

The sole opponent of Buddy's marriage plans was the one that might have been predicted. His manager-producer. Norman Petty had been present at the fateful Howard Johnson's lunch, and even then had shown spinsterly unease at Buddy's flirtation with Maria Elena. Perhaps naively, Buddy had hoped for Papa Norman's felicitations along with the rest. Instead, with uncommon forthrightness, Petty told him he was making the worst mistake of his life, one that could have only disastrous consequences for his career. Rock 'n' roll stars of 1958 simply did not get married, or even have visible female companions. The teenage girls who bought their records did so largely in the belief that they were unattached, fancy-free, and so, at least theoretically, available to each and every one of their fans. With Maria Elena's demure silhouette, Petty saw Buddy's worldwide sales visibly start to evaporate. He saw, too, the end of his master jeweler's control over that globally profitable diamond in the rough. "Norman never liked me from the very beginning," Maria Elena says. "He saw the danger in me. He knew the problems I was going to cause him. He knew I was going to take over. In his mind, Buddy was his and nobody else's."

In fact, Buddy had started to rebel against Papa Norman's rule a good while before he met Maria Elena. On that first dinner date at P.J. Clarke's, she remembers, he talked at length about his various dissatisfactions with Petty's management. He complained about how little publicity he seemed to get in comparison with other rock 'n' roll chart-toppers, the result of Petty's stinginess and failure to appreciate the growing importance of image and PR. Despite knowing how much Buddy longed to be in movies, Petty had made no effort to push him that way—indeed, had turned down an offer for the Crickets to appear with Eddie Cochran in *Go, Johnny, Go!*, deciding in typically oracular fashion that "it wasn't right" and "better things would come later." "The only photographs they had were the ones taken by Norma Jean [the Petty studio bookkeeper]," Maria Elena says. "Buddy had always trusted Norman and believed in his judgment. But when he got to New York and started talking to people there, he realized how backward Norman was."

He was also beginning to chafe against Petty's total control of his and the Crickets' income, and the necessity of going to Clovis, cap in hand, for everything he needed in order to live the life of a rock 'n' roll star. At the beginning, when they had been on the road for months at a time, it had seemed only sensible to let Petty be the conduit for their earnings from performing, recording, and publishing, banking the money in their collective account and settling all their bills with his power of attorney to write checks on their behalf. But ten months on, what had been a system to spare them anxiety and boredom increasingly looked like a means of keeping them from the money they had worked like galley slaves to earn.

Admittedly, Petty had never been tight with the funds he administered on their behalf and would generally sign a check (or let Ma Petty forge his signature) for anything Buddy or J. I. or Joe B. asked, even though it frequently made his bookkeeper, Norma Jean Berry, raise her eyebrows in despair. Soon tiring of his '58 Impala two-tone coupe, Buddy exchanged it for a powder-blue Lincoln with a rear window that could be automatically raised and lowered. To his growing guitar collection had lately been added a luxurious Guild F-50 acoustic model ($275 plus $67.50 for the deluxe plush-lined case). He and Joe B. also had gone in on a motorboat to use in their waterskiing sessions on Buffalo Springs Lake, a few miles outside Lubbock. "We'd been to see a movie that had people using jet-skis," Joe B. remembers. "The next day, we went out to look for some jet-skis of our own, but wound up buying a ski boat complete with skis, harness, lifejackets, everything. That was the kind of impulsive thing Buddy would do."

Yet Petty, while allowing these liberal, even reckless inroads into the Buddy Holly and the Crickets account, was mysteriously reluctant to discuss precisely how much it had accumulated to date, beyond assuring Buddy, J. I., and Joe B. earnestly that the sum was far smaller than they might imagine. This was surprising news to a group that had already had two million-selling singles and roughly calculated that, at a two-cent royalty, Coral-Brunswick alone must owe them $20,000 ($200,000 by today's values), never mind the hits in Britain and Australia, never mind the earnings from their tours and television appearances and from BMI (Broadcast Music International), the agency that collected fees for radio airplay on their behalf.

While unable to deny that they were due sizable sums, Petty kept on stressing the slowness with which record companies, in particular, paid out artists' royalties. All these months after "That'll Be the Day" and "Peggy Sue" had gone gold, the money from Coral-Brunswick still had not come through—or so he said, implied, or otherwise led them to believe. As for the $1,000 a week they had so religiously sent home from lengthy tours like "The Biggest Show of Stars for 1957," it had almost all been swallowed up by travel expenses, clothes-buying sprees at Alfred

Norton, session fees for the Picks and the Roses, musicians' union dues, car payments, and long-distance calls.

By mid-1958, even unassertive Joe B. Mauldin had begun to ask about his share of the money and to tire of Papa Norman's equivocations. "I'd go to him on a Friday and say, 'I'm going in to Lubbock and I need some money for a new set of tires.' Norman would say, 'I'll get you the tires, but go get 'em at Montgomery-Ward, not at Sears or Firestone.' 'I need some cash in my pocket, too,' I'd tell him. But there was always some excuse, like Norma Jean's already gone home or there are no more spare checks left in the checkbook."

At P.J. Clarke's that first night, Buddy had also told Maria Elena how it irked him to have to go to Petty for everything, and about the accumulated royalties Petty must now be sitting on. Since her Aunt Provi was a senior executive at Peer-Southern Music, Maria Elena had no difficulty in finding out for herself how Buddy and the Crickets' publishing royalties were paid over. Aunt Provi confirmed that everything was channeled via Petty and his company, Nor Va Jak. "I could tell from the beginning that something wasn't right," Maria Elena says. "I made it a condition of my marrying Buddy that he get this whole situation resolved. I told him, 'I don't want to sit around all the time, waiting for handouts from Norman Petty. If you want us to be married, you have to get your finances in order.'"

Unaware how the tide was already running against him, Petty fought to keep Buddy all his with tactics that revealed an entirely new side of this normally discreet subtle and underhanded Clovis Man. "He tried to break us up," Maria Elena says. "He told Buddy not to marry me because I was a whorish kind of woman, that I'd slept with all kinds of other men who'd come in to Peer-Southern. Buddy knew that wasn't true, of course. He got so mad, he wanted to leave Norman right there and then."

Angry and defiant though Buddy might be, Petty's financial coils still bound him hand and foot. Buddy's own personal bank account in Lubbock did not have enough in it even to buy Maria Elena an engagement ring. He therefore had to suffer the humiliation of asking Petty for the money with the slurs against his fiancée still ringing in his ears. Petty, to his equal chagrin, could not refuse—although, Maria Elena remembers, he tried to talk Buddy into buying something cheap. The check drawn on the Buddy Holly and the Crickets account that June 19 and signed by Petty reads, "To: Gift Mart Jlrs Inc. $515 For: Ring—engagement."

With no royalty payout in prospect, the quickest way of raising money for the new commitments Buddy now faced was to forget what he'd preached to J. I. Allison about taking it easy and enjoying themselves, and go out on the road again. Fortuitously, just before he'd met Maria Elena the General Artists Corporation had offered a ten-day tour through the upper Midwestern states of Illinois, Michigan, Wisconsin, Indiana, Minnesota, and Iowa.

Billed as "The Summer Dance Party," and set to begin July 4 in Angola, Indiana, this was an excursion very different from GAC's normal multi-star spectaculars. Many of the venues were not theaters or arenas but ballrooms; Buddy and the Crickets were the only big name involved, and took with them their own warmup act, a four-man, sax-blowing Western-swing band recruited and fronted by Buddy's stand-in lead guitarist Tommy Allsup. The remainder of each night's bill was to be filled by local singers and groups. Instead of the usual bus, the seven-man troupe provided their own transport, Buddy, J. I., and Joe B. traveling in Buddy's new Lincoln, Tommy and the three Western-swing bandsmen in a yellow DeSoto station wagon representing a further major disbursement ($3,981) from the Buddy Holly and the Crickets account.

Buddy had wanted Maria Elena to accompany him on the tour, but here, at least, Aunt Provi insisted that old-fashioned propriety be observed. So while Provi flew off on business to Argentina, Maria Elena remained in New York to shop for her trousseau with some money Buddy had left behind for her.

That "The Summer Dance Party" got off to a shaky start we know from subsequent correspondence between GAC's Chicago office and Harry K. Smythe, owner of Buck Lake Ranch, Angola, Indiana. As the cartoon drawings around its rustic letterhead indicate, Buck Lake Ranch was a family resort with a boating lake, a picnic area, horseback riding, and a children's amusement park, as well as live music and dancing for teenagers. Two weeks later, Harry Smythe was still fuming about the disruption that "The Summer Dance Party" caused to his Fourth of July program.

... In answer to your letter of July 14 regarding the CRICKETS and BUDDY HOLLY. We are very sorry but at no time have we ever lied to you. We gave you the facts in our previous letter and again we repeat that if the seven-piece orchestra was here, why was it necessary for Buddy

Holly and two members of his band to borrow instruments and drums from an Act we had booked on the Show that day? Truthfully, Buddy Holly was going nuts, wondering where in hell the other four men were, because they had all left Texas together and this was their first date, and they hadn't rehearsed together . . .

. . . I don't give a dam what Buddy Holly or New York or George [sic] Petty says, or anyone else, we were charged for seven men and and only three appeared for the three Shows, and at no time were they prepared to present the seven men on the Stage during the entire day or evening. To me, this is the case that has been quite evident throughout our season this year. THE CUSTOMER IS NEVER RIGHT, IT'S ALWAYS THE ARTIST WHO'S RIGHT. Frankly, I'm dam sick of it and it will be a long time before I'll ever buy a GAC act again.

Best wishes

Buddy, J. I., and Joe B. tried to dress as for a summer ball, in dark blazers and white slacks. Joe B. no longer played his stand-up bass, having switched to one of the new Fender electric bass guitars. Buddy gave such valuable endorsement to the Fender company that they had donated two new Stratocasters and two amplifiers, one for him, the other for Tommy Allsup. A couple of days into the tour, their station-wagon trailer was burgled and one of the Strats and an amp disappeared. "That meant that, until we could get a replacement, Buddy and I couldn't play in the same group," Tommy Allsup says. "I'd open with the Western-swing guys and then pass over the Strat to Buddy for his set with the Crickets."

The seven-man, two-act format proved an awkward one all along the line. Some promoters were interested only in putting Buddy and the Crickets onstage and refused to pay the swing band's fee, despite having signed a contract for them. And it felt strange to a threesome to a group that had appeared at the London Palladium only five months earlier to find themselves now playing for glorified teen hops at campground venues like Buck Lake Ranch.

This was the part of America where Buddy was to travel to his death, under horribly similar festive billing, in just a little over six months from now. Free of its winter snow and biting cold as the Midwest was in early July, placid and safe as the woodlands and lakes must have appeared to him, there were times when one might almost have thought they were trying to warn him off. After a waterskiing session on Cedar River near

Waterloo in his nemesis state of Iowa, J. I., Joe B., and he tried to balance on some half-submerged logs and all three slipped off into the water. While swimming alone in a lake near Wausau, Wisconsin, on July 13, Buddy was overcome by fatigue and had to struggle to reach the shore. He played that night's show at Rhinelander's Crystal Rock ballroom in a state of obvious exhaustion, only perking up when the audience shouted for "Rave On." During the intermission, a group of fans went to look at his car in the parking lot and found him asleep in the back seat.

On this tour, in open defiance of Norman Petty, the performance money was not sent back to Clovis, but shared among Buddy, J. I, and Joe B. on the spot. "Buddy collected the money from the promoters each night and kept it in the glove compartment of his car," Tommy Allsup remembers. "We'd be going down the road and Jerry Allison would say 'Hey, I need some money.' Buddy would open up the glove compartment, get out a handful of bills, and pass'em back." Neat and methodical as ever, Buddy kept a scrupulous record of their daily gas consumption and casual expenses, backed up by receipts for even the most microscopic amount: "July 9: Standard Service, Waterloo, Iowa, gas $4.90, 1 pair sunglasses, $1.00, tax 2¢, total $5.92. July 11: Ruckdashel Co., Duluth, Minnesota, check and adjust power brakes $5.00, Jerry Schmidt mechanic; Duluth and Superior Bridge Co. 50¢."

Carrying around such a large sum in cash held obvious risks, even in the law-abiding Midwest, and to a Texan raised as Buddy had been, there was only one possible source of security. With the wad of large-denomination bills in the Lincoln's glove compartment lay a German-made .22-caliber pistol he'd recently bought secondhand from Tommy Allsup. Buddy knew very well how to handle the .22 and, as Joe B. remembers, was not at all averse to demonstrating his quickness on the draw. "Right after we'd gotten paid one night, there was a problem in the parking lot. Some headlights came up behind us real close and wouldn't let us back out of our space. Buddy reached into the glove compartment, buzzed down the Lincoln's automatic rear window, turned around, and pointed his gun through it. Those headlights just disappeared!"

PART FOUR

LEARNING THE GAME

O n July 22, 1958, tiring of the difficulties being put in the way of their engagement, J. I. Allison and Peggy Sue Gerron eloped from Lubbock to Honey Grove, in East Texas (where Buddy's father had been born and raised), and were married by J. I.'s Uncle Raymond, who, conveniently, happened to be the local Baptist minister.

Buddy knew nothing of the plot beforehand and was a little put out when J. I. triumphantly called him up the next morning. For the past month he had been counting on his best friend to go to the altar in company with Maria Elena and himself. To make amends, J. I. and Peggy Sue offered to delay their honeymoon until after Buddy's wedding and make a foursome of that instead. "Buddy asked me where I wanted to go," Peggy Sue remembers. "I said, 'Somewhere warm, with white sand. How about Acapulco?' He laughed and said, 'I'll take care of it.'"

At the beginning of August, Maria Elena Santiago flew from New York to Lubbock to become Mrs. Charles Hardin Holley. The original plan had been for her Aunt Provi, or another aunt, to go with her as a chaperone, but as it turned out, she made the journey by herself. Buddy met her at the airport and drove her to the Holley home, where she was to spend the week prior to the wedding. L. O. and Ella gave her the warmest of welcomes, insisting that she call them "Dad" and "Mother" and showing her off proudly to their family, friends, and neighbors. "I found I didn't need a chaperone," she remembers. "It was all very proper. I had my own room, completely separate from Buddy's."

The expected religious tug-of-war did not materialize after all. Although Maria Elena had been brought up a Roman Catholic, she was not especially religious and Buddy escaped the usual stringent demands made by the Catholic Church of Protestant marriage partners. He did not have to be married by a Catholic priest nor promise his children would be raised in their mother's faith. And the Holleys' Tabernacle Baptist Church, though liking Catholicism least of almost anything in the doctrinal spectrum, waived its objections in view of Buddy's celebrity and the generous donations it received from him. Indeed, in an impressive charm offensive, he even managed to talk his pastor, Ben D. Johnson, into performing the ceremony.

This took place at the Holley home on August 15, a day when Lubbock was gripped by heat in the high nineties. Maria Elena wore a white sheath dress and a veil; Buddy wore a dark suit, a broadly striped tie, and sunglasses. Only close family members, Buddy's fellow Crickets, and the new Mrs. J. I. Allison were present. With most rock 'n' roll stars, a manager who doubled as record producer might be expected to count as "close family," but Norman and Vi Petty were conspicuous by their absence.

The solemnities over, J. I. Allison went to a record player in the next room and put on the B-side of Buddy's latest single, "Now We're One." The newlyweds posed for photographs in front of the family television set, Buddy now grinning at the camera in his wildly out-of-character Mafioso shades, now leaning down to his tiny, unveiled bride to steal a kiss. As a gesture of appreciation to his church for making things so easy, he then wrote Pastor Ben D. Johnson a check for $100 on his personal bank account.

The double honeymoon in Acapulco, which had sounded such a fun idea in theory, turned out to be hard going for everyone concerned. Despite their absorption in their respective brides, Buddy and J. I. could not resist a sneaking desire to hang out together in the way they had for years around Lubbock and on tour. And while they might be soulmates, their brides, all too clearly, were anything but. To twenty-five-year-old Maria Elena, eighteen-year-old Peggy Sue seemed gawky and provincial and given to embarrassing displays of high spirits. To Peggy Sue, Maria Elena seemed forbiddingly adult, formal and self-contained. "She was sophisticated, worked in New York, and wore fashionable clothes. I'd only just hung up my can-can petticoats."

They had booked rooms at the luxurious Las Brisas hotel, but on checking in were disappointed to find that it didn't overlook the ocean. After a couple of nights, following an incident that Peggy Sue prefers to keep for her own promised memoirs, they transferred to an oceanfront establishment, El Cano. Among the watersports offered was Buddy's favorite, waterskiing, and he instantly rushed off to rent a high-speed motorboat. "But Maria Elena didn't want to try," Peggy Sue remembers. "And Jerry had trouble with his ears, and couldn't go under water. So Buddy ended up teaching me to water-ski." That cannot have helped an atmosphere which even happy-go-lucky J. I. was later to describe as "uncomfortable" and "weird."

For much of the time, Buddy's high spirits kept the party going. "One night at a club we watched a man demonstrating matador passes," Peggy Sue remembers. "Later, when Buddy got up to put some music on the jukebox, he did a perfect imitation of this man. He was so deft and graceful in the way he moved, he could have been a matador himself."

But toward the end, even he seemed downcast by the tense atmosphere and the fear that Maria Elena might not be enjoying herself as much as he'd hoped. "He and Jerry and I were in the hotel restaurant one evening, waiting for Maria Elena to come down and join us for dinner," Peggy Sue remembers. "Time passed, she still didn't show, and Buddy got more and more agitated. Eventually he went off to the house phone to call her up in their room. After a while, he came back and said, 'She's not coming down for dinner after all. She's going to have it up in the room.' He looked tense and stressed the way I'd never seen him before."

To prevent a boycott of Buddy's records by grief-stricken female fans, the marriage was not publicized in any way, and everyone present at the wedding was solemnly sworn to secrecy. Keeping such a secret in 1958 was admittedly not very difficult; newspapers as yet took little interest in the private lives of celebrities apart from a few jet-set figures like Aly Khan and Porfirio Rubirosa, and a handful of Hollywood stars like Elizabeth Taylor and Marlon Brando. Even so, there were scandal sheets that might have made unpleasant capital of a rock 'n' roll big name embarking on a "mixed" marriage, as Brando had done not long previously. Hence Buddy's worldwide public would know nothing of Maria Elena's existence until after she had become a widow.

Married or single, Buddy had always intended to keep Lubbock as his base, and had gone so far as to draw up plans for a house he intended to build there. But with Maria Elena's advent, the blueprint changed: the Lubbock house would be for his parents, and his occasional use. His new wife's home, New York City, was the only possible place to settle down.

☆ ☆ ☆

Fortunately, Buddy could begin married life with some real money in his pocket at last. Early in August, Peer-Southern Music disgorged $28,338 in publishing royalties in five separate checks. Clovis Man's bank records show a substantial payment to each Cricket on August 11 from the Buddy Holly and the Crickets account: $3,887.93 to Buddy, $1,453.82 to J. I. Allison, $4,877.48 to Joe B. Mauldin. On August 26, Buddy received another check, for $14,467, bearing the notation "From record royalties. To Church," but made out in his name.

In seeking their first home in Manhattan, it was natural for the new Mr. and Mrs. Holly to gravitate to the downtown area where Maria Elena had lived since her schooldays. At Ninth Street and Fifth Avenue, just around the corner from Aunt Provi's apartment, they found the Brevoort, a chic new apartment building on the site of a house once occupied by Mark Twain. An apartment was available on the fourth floor and in a premium corner position: one bedroom, living room, dining room, and wraparound outside terrace. Though the monthly rent was $1,000 (many times that by today's values), Buddy took it without hesitation.

Two or three blocks from the Brevoort, Greenwich Village was in full late-fifties flower with its jazz joints, coffeehouses, and antique shops: a colony where the artless "beat" of rock 'n' roll had come to define all manner of complex, intellectual things; where the Beat novelist Jack Kerouac and the Beat poet Allen Ginsberg nightly declaimed their edgy, free-form works to saxophone accompaniment; where the fashionable young of both sexes wore shapeless black clothes and dark glasses and styled themselves "beatniks"; and where age-old jazzmen's terms like "dig," "jive," and "cool" now punctuated earnest espresso-fueled discussions about Camus and Sartre. October's surprise hit single, "Tom Dooley" by the Kingston Trio, had given folk music the same brief hour of high fashion in America that skiffle previously enjoyed in Britain. Every hip bar and club in the Village now had its own resident folksinger– guitarist, male or female, seated on a high stool and strumming to a circle of rapt, deathly white faces.

To Maria Elena, the sights and sounds of Greenwich Village were familiar enough. But Buddy's experience of New York until now had been mainly confined to uptown hotel suites. He found it endlessly fascinating to explore this brownstone- and tree-lined quarter, below the Stonehenge rim of silver skyscrapers, where everything was low-rise, jumbled, and heterogeneous, manners were free and easy, and the wildest eccentricity —even that of being a transplanted West Texas rock 'n' roller—was absorbed into the scene without question.

All that marred the excitement of setting up house with Maria Elena and exploring his new neighborhood was the continual disappointing news from the charts. "Early in the Morning," released as a solo Buddy Holly single in July, had not reached the Top 20 in America and only just scraped in in Britain. "It's So Easy," released under the Crickets' name in early September, ironically proved too complex for its intended au- dience, failing even to make the U.S. Top 100 and becoming the first Holly product not to enter the British Top 20, although in Australia it got to No. 8.

Buddy was not alone in feeling his fortunes start to slip. Over the previous six months, one after another supernova in the rock 'n' roll firmament had come crashing to earth. Elvis Presley, shorn of his kingly sideburns, was polishing his army boots at Fort Hood, Texas, about to be shipped to West Germany as part of NATO's armored bulwark against the expected Soviet onslaught. The ever-unpredictable Little Richard had forsaken rock 'n' roll without warning halfway through his 1957 Austra- lian tour. Seeing Russia's Sputnik satellite shoot through the night sky, he interpreted it as a summons from God, threw the largest of his diamond rings ceremonially into Sydney Harbour, and went off to train as a minis- ter. Jerry Lee Lewis's first British tour had disintegrated in chaos after journalists discovered that his wife, Myra Gale, was only thirteen years old, and his first cousin as well, and that he'd had two wives before her. So much for the more wholesome impression of American rock 'n' rollers that Buddy and the Crickets had left behind them.

For someone with Buddy's canny eye on the market, prospects did not look very bright either. Rock 'n' roll in 1958 was, if anything, even more of a social outcast than it had been in 1956. In the wake of the Boston riots and a highly publicized jeremiad from the evangelist Billy Graham, more and more radio stations throughout Middle America, deciding it wasn't worth the trouble, were sanctimoniously cutting their rock 'n' roll output. Those who had accused the music of cynically duping and manipulating its young audience were starting to find hard evidence to back up their claims. Late 1958 saw the first faint media rumblings about a practice that had always been rife in the music industry but that during the rock 'n' roll era had become even more shameless and blatant: the bribing of disc jockeys to push one new release in preference to others. It was a heaven-sent opportunity for the Establishment to take vengeance on figures like Alan Freed and Dick Clark who had so long and defiantly encouraged the nation's children to behave like yahoos. The so-called payola scandal would grow into the Watergate of its day, culminating in a Senate investigating committee and the satisfying public disgrace of several prominent deejays, Freed among them.

Rock 'n' roll had been around for three years, a prodigious run for an American fad. Now it seemed to be suffering the fate of the Hula Hoop, dance marathon, and pogo stick before it: people wanted something new. Among recent hit singles, only a handful still had the authentic rock 'n' roll voice, undiluted by subtlety or self-consciousness. The majority were ballads, like the Platters' "Twilight Time" and the Everly Brothers' "Dream," or hymns to teenage self-pity like Jody Reynolds's "Endless Sleep," the Four Preps' "Big Man," and Ricky Nelson's "Poor Little Fool." There had been a brief craze for Latin-flavored instrumentals, like Perez Prado's "Patricia" and the Champs' "Tequila," and a summer-long spate of comedy records, Bobby Darin's "Splish-Splash," the Coasters' "Yakety-Yak," Sheb Wooley's "Purple People-Eater," and David Seville's "Witch Doctor," prefiguring the ghastly Chipmunks.

Most crucially, the definition of glamour and sex appeal in pop singers had begun to change. A new breed of teenage heartthrob was emerging, no longer greasily coiffed in the Elvis style, but neatly brush-topped and trim about the ears; no longer lip-curlingly subversive, but soft-centered, simpering, and ingratiating. Whereas Elvis had been a superb vocalist with coincidentally devastating looks, many of these newcomers were young men who'd won recording deals on the strength of their prettiness alone, and whose vocal efforts would not have been releasable without artful enhancement by studio engineers. The chart sensations of the hour were Frankie Avalon, an eighteen-year-old Italian American like a sawed-off Sinatra, whose "De-De-Dinah" had lately sold a million, and Dion and the Belmonts, a New York vocal quartet named after an avenue in their native Bronx, who purveyed a saccharine teenage version of the street-corner doo-wop style. The Top 10's flavor changed from raw spirit to warm milk. As if anticipating investigative tribunals of the future, record companies now cast around for product that suggested the polite, the respectful, and the law-abiding.

Buddy naturally was disappointed by his run of misses, but he did not allow it to depress him. As always, half a dozen new songs and a hundred new ideas were germinating inside his tousled head. Sooner or later, he had no doubt, he'd come up with the right blueprint to take him back to the top. Other rock 'n' roll originals poured scorn on teenage crooners like Frankie Avalon, but not Buddy: he bought all the new hit records and listened to them in his usual analytical way to see what he could learn from them. The normal reaction for a performer in eclipse is to grow secretive, introverted, and misanthropic as he struggles to plot his way back to the limelight. But Buddy remained as open-heartedly generous with his music as ever (witness the trouble he took over his two demos for Don and Phil Everly) and as unselfishly energetic in bringing on new talent he considered promising.

In 1958, few pop singers even dreamed of turning themselves into businessmen and impresarios, but by the time he settled among the Greenwich Village beatniks, Buddy was well on the way to becoming both. That autumn, he set up a recording and publishing company called Prism, which he intended to be the focus of his developing parallel career as a talent-spotter and producer.

Moving to New York did not mean he had cast off Texas and forgotten his boyhood roots in country and rockabilly music. Quite the opposite: Prism's chief objective was to tap the huge reservoir of West Texas musical talent and give a helping hand to some of the numerous young singers he had heard and admired on his trips home. Buddy Holly might not figure significantly in Lubbock's scheme of things, but he was planning to put his hometown on the musical map as firmly as Nashville or Memphis. The original plans he had made for a house in Lubbock developed into a recording studio and office complex that would serve as a command center for Prism as well as a new home for his parents.

The studio was to be designed on much the same lines as Norman Petty's, with the very latest in equipment and stay-over accommodation for musicians. Under the original plan, indeed, Petty was to run it in tandem with his Clovis establishment. And, ever conscious of how L. O. Holley had worked a backbreaking lifetime without ever having owned a business, Buddy took care that the blueprint should include a record store "for Daddy to take care of." This blueprint for a multifaceted music company, not controlled by the usual soulless middle-aged money men but fired by youthful energy and idealism, has more than a whisper of the Beatles' Apple organization, ten years in the future.

Lubbock's top radio station was no longer KDAV nor KSEL but KLLL, situated on the top floor of the Great Plains Life Insurance building, the city's highest high-rise, and operated by three ebullient brothers, Larry, Sky, and Slim Corbin. With a format designated as hillbilly rock, the station had stolen thousands of listeners from KDAV and KSEL, and now fielded the area's top team of disc jockeys, among them, Slim and Sky Corbin, a "gospel jock" called Mr. Sunshine, and Buddy's old mentor and manager, Hi Pockets Duncan. By the fall of 1958, "K triple L" had hubris enough to advertise in *Cash Box* magazine, boasting of the West Texas recording stars who were its supporters and regular visitors, like Terry Noland (Brunswick), the Four Teens (Challenge), Sonny Curtis and Niki Sullivan (Dot). To Buddy, in particular, KLLL became almost the home-away-from-home KDAV had once been; when in Lubbock, he was always stopping by to chat with the Corbins or Hi Pockets on air or give a spontaneous live solo performance. He even recorded a set of promotional jingles to the tune of some better-known Holly songs, including:

Everyday,
It's a-gettin' better,
Gettin' more cards and gettin' more letters.
Ev'rybody
Wants to tune our way.

The newest recruit to the KLLL airwaves was a snakily handsome young man of twenty-one named Waylon Jennings, from Littlefield, thirty miles west of Lubbock. Despite his huge local popularity as a disc jockey, Waylon had ambitions to turn his preternaturally deep voice from announcing to singing. Buddy had been his idol since KDAV *Sunday Party* days, and now, in bull sessions around the KLLL mike, the two struck up a firm friendship. At Hi Pockets Duncan's suggestion, Buddy became Waylon's mentor, advising him on the wardrobe and hairstyle an aspiring performer should have, and promising him help in getting his musical career off the ground.

Despite the rift with Norman Petty over his marriage, and the growing creative pull of New York, Buddy continued to record in Clovis and, optimistic as always, to hope things with Papa Norman would sort themselves out. Petty remained a co-director of the nascent Prism organization, along with Ray Rush of the Roses vocal group, and had agreed to sell Buddy some recording equipment for Prism, notably one of his treasured Ampex tape-recorders.

On September 6, Buddy was back at Petty's studio, playing guitar for a singer named Jerry Engler in a late-night session that ran into the first hours of Buddy's twenty-second birthday. Three days later, he was there again with J. I., Joe B., and yet another audacious new sound effect. Buddy had been an admirer of the R&B saxophonist King Curtis since they'd traversed the country together on Alan Freed's "Biggest Show of Stars for 1957." The father of the braying "chicken sax" style, Curtis had since contributed memorably manic solos to several rock 'n' roll classics, notably the Coasters' "Yakety Yak." Ignoring the convention that white and black musicians did not usually record together—and prefiguring the "two-tone" lineups of the 1980s—Buddy persuaded Curtis to come from New York to Clovis in exchange for his air fare, accommodation, and a $100 studio fee.

On September 10, Buddy, the Crickets, and King Curtis recorded two tracks, "Come Back Baby" and "Reminiscing." The latter featured Buddy's voice alone and exposed in the way it had been on "Mailman, Bring Me No More Blues": stretching, hovering, and swooping to the point of self-parody; at times not singing so much as mimicking the breathy, nonchalant tenor riffs that shadowed it.

Curtis then joined Petty's two house musicians and the Roses on Waylon Jennings's first recording session, financed by Buddy in his debut as a producer for his own Prism organization. The resulting two tracks, on which he also found time to play guitar, were Waylon's compositions "When Sin Stops" and "Jole Blon," a song in Cajun dialect (i.e., "Jolie Blonde") first popularized by Harry Choates in the mid-forties. No one having any idea how to pronounce the Cajun lyrics, let alone what they meant, Waylon had to bluff his way through a rough phonetic version.

Though "Jole Blon" would not take him anywhere near the late-fifties charts, it was the first vital step in the evolution of a future country music giant. Buddy's taste as an A&R man would eventually be vindicated when the song became a hit for Gary "U.S." Bonds in 1980.

The clock-cheating drive from Lubbock to Clovis was now no longer made, at 100 mph–plus, by three carefree young bachelors, laughing, singing, and hurling empty Falstaff bottles at mailboxes along the way. Buddy naturally wanted to have Maria Elena with him while he cut his records. Like the Beatles when John Lennon brought Yoko Ono to their "white album" sessions, J. I. Allison and Joe B. Mauldin pretended this was no problem. But, like Paul, George, and Ringo, they were privately hurt and mystified that an outsider—and a woman—should thus disfigure their creative brotherhood.

As Maria Elena sat in the control room, she could feel freezing hostility from all sides. Clovis Man, of course, could not overtly object to her presence, but he made his disapproval plain with the subtlety of a scalpel. Even the normally good-natured and timid Vi joined in, making fun of Maria Elena's Hispanic accent with Norman Jean Berry. "Whenever I said anything, both of them would laugh and imitate the way I spoke. Vi said it was all in good fun; they thought my accent was cute. But I didn't find it funny. I said to them, 'At least I can speak your language. You can't speak mine.'" Despite herself, she could not repress a twinge of sisterly compassion for Vi. "Norman paid no attention to her. She had no say-so. She was not asked anything—she was just told. The poor woman was just kind of existing in that weird atmosphere."

To fastidious Maria Elena, the studio itself was a strange and uninviting place, even though Ma and Pa Petty's garage had now been replaced by a frontal facade displaying the Nor Va Jak logo. "That place where Buddy recorded was old . . . dilapidated . . . ooh, it was horrible!" To her deep dismay, as Buddy's session ran late, she realized she was expected to stay overnight in the communal bedsitting room behind the studio. Even more ominously, Norma Jean, the Pettys' bookkeeper, now seemed to be showing interest in something more about her than her accent. "This woman who looked just like a man kind of took a fancy to me. She kept saying, 'Oh, you're so nice . . . you're so petite,' and trying to paw me. I wouldn't go to sleep in that back room. I just sat there. In the end, Buddy and I went out and got some sleep in the car."

In New York Buddy acquired a second young protégé, a singer named

Lou Giordano whom he'd met through Joey Villa of the Royalteens. Convinced of Giordano's potential, Buddy helped get him a contract with Brunswick and also gave him a newly written song, "Stay Close to Me." Giordano's debut session took place at Beltone studios on September 30. Buddy and Phil Everly co-produced, also playing backup guitars on "Stay Close to Me" and contributing a falsetto chorus to the B-side, "Don't Cha Know."

Two days later, Buddy appeared with the Crickets on Alan Freed's *Dance Party* television show to lip-synch his imminent own-name single, "Heartbeat," / "Well . . . All Right." He and the Moondog then had a brief conversation that has survived on tape. It's poignant to listen in on their warm, civilized exchange—so very different from modern pop interviews—and realize how desperately close each now was to the edge of the abyss:

FREED: . . . What have you been doing and where have you been?

BUDDY: Well, we haven't been working all summer, Alan. We've been kinda loafing and taking it easy and running around some. Enjoying what we hadn't enjoyed for the whole year previous with all the work.

FREED: Boy, you worked hard that year, Buddy.

BUDDY: So, uh we're getting ready to start in with some new work now.

FREED: You're going on tour again?

BUDDY: I think so, uh-huh.

FREED: Buddy, we had a lot of fun, we did a lot of flying.

BUDDY: Yeah, we sure did . . . We just got into town the other day in Cincinnati, you remember when we landed there and, uh, the helicopter had crashed that day we got in there?

FREED: I think we rode every kind of airplane imaginable.

BUDDY: (laughing) Uh-huh, we sure did.

FREED: Those DC-3s were really something.

BUDDY: [mimics racketing motion] With the oomp-oomp!

FREED: Oh boy, without the seatbelts we'd have been right through the top, that's for sure.

BUDDY: We sure would.

FREED: Buddy, we've had a lot of fun together, and I hope we're going to have a lot of fun together in the future . . .

☆   ☆   ☆

The huge mixed-race rock 'n' roll road shows of the past two years were similarly on the decline, and those that survived reflected the shrinking market and the prissy shape of things to come. The upcoming tour Buddy mentioned to Freed was a GAC presentation lasting only sixteen days instead of the customary three months, and billed with overt revisionism as "The Biggest Show of Stars for 1958—Fall Edition." Apart from Buddy and the Crickets, the white acts on the program—Frankie Avalon, Dion and the Belmonts, Bobby Darin, Jimmy Clanton, and Jack Scott—were a bland and lightweight crew, especially when compared to seasoned black performers like Clyde McPhatter, Bobby Freeman, and the Coasters. After rehearsals at New York's Nola Studios, the show opened October 3 in Worcester, Massachusetts, moving on, with the tour planner's usual illogicality, to one-nighters in Connecticut; Quebec and Ontario; Indiana; Ohio; Pennsylvania; New York State; Virginia and North Carolina.

Gone, never to return, was the Crickets' world-beatingly simple, self-sufficient stage lineup of Joe B. on bass fiddle, J. I. on drums, and Buddy on vocals and rhythm-lead guitar. To match the competition of Frankie Avalon and Co., a more ambitious presentation was felt to be needed. So big, genial Tommy Allsup, the new lead-guitar voice of "Heartbeat" and "It's So Easy," was invited to make his second tour as an extra Cricket. Into the live lineup, too, came the Roses, the male vocal trio whose churchy "ba-ba-ba's" and "fa-la-la-la's" Norman Petty had overdubbed on tracks like "Think It Over" and "It's So Easy." The Roses' leader, Robert Linville, remembers the lavishness and care with which Buddy chose stage outfits at Alfred Norton for him and his two colleagues, David Bigham and Ray Rush: light gray blazers, black slacks, black velour vests, gray-and-black–striped ties.

The final unprecedented addition was that of a wife. Buddy would not think of making the tour without Maria Elena and, tenaciously pursuing the double honeymoon idea, urged J. I. to bring Peggy Sue along also. But Peggy Sue—wisely, as it turned out—preferred to stay in Lubbock, flying up to join them when they returned to New York. Clearly it was impractical for Maria Elena to travel on the bus, so she and Buddy followed behind in his second new car of that year, a taupe Cadillac 60 Special sedan. J. I., Joe B., and Tommy also traveled separately in their communally owned DeSoto station wagon.

To preserve the illusion of Buddy's bachelorhood, Maria Elena was introduced to people as the Crickets' secretary. If she had ever cherished any illusions about the glamour of rock 'n' roll tours, these were quickly shattered. "There were no roadies to do the work in those days. We had to carry all the luggage ourselves, set up and dismantle the equipment. I had to wash shirts . . . underwear. The food was terrible. Buddy had told me about his gastric problem, that a doctor in Lubbock had told him his stomach lining was prone to ulceration. I'm sure a lot of that came from the awful greasy food he had to eat on those tours."

As usual on a tour of one-nighters, the acts were paid individually by the promoter at each venue. Maria Elena took over the job of collecting the money, a role for which her forthright, businesslike nature suited her well. The one or two occasions when a local showman tried to short-change Buddy revealed his doll-like Puerto Rican bride to be a woman of formidable temper. Following now-standard procedure, the earnings were not sent back to Clovis but kept—by Maria Elena—in a plaid hold-all known as the "Scotch bag" and doled out to the others in regular install-ments. The discovery that the bag also contained a .22 pistol did not disconcert Maria Elena. "With all that cash, it was necessary for security. A lot of the performers in those days used to carry guns."

One awkward consequence of her sheltered Manhattan upbringing was that Maria Elena had never learned to drive. After performing to the limit every night, Buddy also had to pilot their Cadillac the hundreds of miles that frequently lay between engagements. Toward the end of the tour, even his usual rock-like steadiness behind the wheel began to falter. On Octo-ber 20, he was flagged down by police and accused of speeding. "Buddy was tired and on edge," Maria Elena remembers. "He didn't think he had been speeding and he got mad, so the police took him off to the station—just left me in the car at the side of the road. When they realized who he was, they brought him straight back again.

"One time when we were on our way to a concert, he was so exhausted that he could hardly keep his eyes open. But we couldn't stop, we *had* to be there at a certain time, so Buddy told me I'd have to drive, even though I'd never driven a car in my life before. He said, 'It's real easy, you just point the car down the highway and hold the wheel steady . . .' To make it even more scary it was at night . . . there were huge trucks coming up behind us all the time. Buddy told me, 'If the trucks honk their horns, don't worry; if they want to pass you, let them pass you.' He let me do it for a few minutes to be sure I was all right, and showed me on the map where we had to make a turnoff, so that I'd know in time to wake him up.

Then the poor soul went to sleep in the back, and I kept that car straight on . . . straight on. I found out very quickly that when you have to do something, you do it."

Traveling separately in the Cadillac with his wife isolated Buddy from J. I. and Joe B. and heightened their feeling that Maria Elena had filched him from them, that she was all he cared about now, and they had been relegated from blood brothers to mere subordinates. Although now a married man himself, J. I. was still only nineteen and primarily interested in having fun, if not with Buddy then with his willing follower Joe B. Since groupies and drugs were still almost nonexistent pleasures of the road, having fun meant one thing only. "We'd sometimes be drunk in the morning," J. I. has since admitted, "and stay drunk all day." This slackness and lack of professionalism infuriated Buddy; there was an angry scene and the two miscreants, genuinely sorry, promised to "tighten up a little bit."

In New York they were joined by Peggy Sue, fresh from Lubbock, full of the thrill of seeing Carnegie Hall for the first time, and convinced that Buddy and the Crickets would appear on its hallowed stage before long. With the masculine condescension of that era, a day's shopping was arranged for the two Cricket wives. Peggy Sue remembers that Maria Elena spent much of it complaining to her about J. I.'s behavior on the tour. That evening the two married couples were to have dinner at Mama Leone's Italian restaurant, one of Buddy's favorites, and then attend a movie premiere. The outing went badly for Peggy Sue: at Mama Leone's she broke the clasp of a new evening purse she'd bought only that day. Then, as they walked to the movie theater, she caught one of her stiletto heels in a subway grating and snapped it off. "I was terribly embarrassed —I wanted to run straight back to our hotel. Jerry and Maria Elena were both really irritated with me for making such a fool of myself, but Buddy just laughed and said it didn't matter and I certainly wasn't going to miss the premiere. So I walked into the theater in my stocking feet. I can't remember now which movie we saw, except that it had an elephant in it."

Back in the autumn of 1957, when rock 'n' roll still swept all before it, a Canadian disc jockey named Red Robinson had put a prophetic question to the jukebox sensation of the hour: "Buddy, if trends change, would you hop on the trend . . . or would you just give up?"

"I'd hop on the trend," Buddy replied without a second's hesitation.

"You would?"

"Uh-huh. Because I'd prefer singing something a little bit more quieter, anyhow."

Now, a year later, one could say he was about to hop on the trend toward softer music if that would restore him to the charts. But Buddy, being Buddy, still could not help staying miles ahead of the pack.

The idea had originally come from Norman Petty, almost four months earlier. Long anticipating the decline of rock 'n' roll, Elvis Presley, Pat Boone, and many others had hedged their bets by recording slow ballads that verged on the mainstream. But even Elvis had never dared to mix his technique with the archetypal easy-listening sound of a string orchestra. When Petty suggested that Buddy might be the first to make this radical leap into convention, he refused to entertain the idea at first, but came around to it during the summer, especially after hearing that, in common with other major record labels, Decca was cutting down on rock 'n' roll output. One day just before their relationship began to nosedive, as they sat together in an airport lounge, Buddy turned to Petty with a grin and said, "Norm, when are you going to arrange my string session?"

Dick Jacobs, Coral-Brunswick's new head of A&R—and a successful orchestra leader in his own right—had proved more than willing to try Buddy in this new medium. The session finally took place on October 21 at Decca's Pythian Temple studios, with Jacobs presiding both as producer and conductor. As a consolation prize to Norman Petty for being thus comprehensively supplanted, one of the three songs to be recorded was his composition "Moondreams," which Buddy had demo'd with the Petty trio in Clovis a year and a half earlier. The other two were "Raining in My Heart" by the Everly Brothers' songwriters Boudleaux and Felice Bryant, and yet another so-called Buddy Holly–Norman Petty joint effort, "True Love Ways."

A couple of hours before the session was due to start, Buddy burst into Dick Jacobs's office carrying his guitar case and waving a piece of paper. "He told me it was a new song that Paul Anka had just written specially for him, called 'It Doesn't Matter Anymore,' and it had to be in the session," Jacobs recalled afterward. "I said okay, and called my copyist in and we wrote the lead sheets from Buddy's version of the song on his guitar. Because time was so short, we could only do the very simplest arrangement, with pizzicato parts for the violins."

When Buddy walked on to the studio floor promptly at 7:30 that evening, he found Jacobs and Coral had done him proud. Awaiting him was an eighteen-piece orchestra, including eight violins, two violas, two cellos, and a harp. As well as string players recruited from the New York Symphony Orchestra and NBC's house orchestra, there were top session men like guitarist Al Caiola and Abraham "Boomie" Richmond, formerly of the Benny Goodman band, on tenor saxophone. It was also to be the first time Buddy had ever been recorded in the new, high-status medium of stereo.

Watching the proceedings, their mutual antagonisms temporarily on hold, were Maria Elena Holly, J. I. and Peggy Sue Allison, Joe B. Mauldin, Norman and Vi Petty, and Jo Harper from Peer-Southern Music. At the last moment Paul Anka joined them, curious to see what would happen to the song that had been snatched out of his hands so unceremoniously a few hours earlier.

Having never met a rock 'n' roller before, let alone been asked to perform with one, the string players from the New York Symphony were more than a little cynical and supercilious about the task at hand. Dick Jacobs remembered afterward that Buddy faced them at a stand microphone, like the vocalist with some old-time swing orchestra. But Peggy Sue is sure that he sang with headphones on, inside an isolation booth. "I was sitting right beside it. I could see Buddy's face through the glass. He seemed tense at first. But after a moment, I saw him smile at me."

The superciliousness of the orchestra vanished when the rock 'n' roller performed "It Doesn't Matter Anymore" perfectly in his very first take. Although from the same bravura pen that had written "Diana" (and later would write "My Way"), it turned out to be pure Buddy: a lament for lost summer love, mixing anguish and playfulness in its exclamations of "Buy-bee," "Golly-gee," and "Whoops-a-daisy," its bridge ending with a long downhill "oo" vowel that cried out to be hiccupped in half. Buddy adjusted his wide-awake Texas voice to the medium of written notes and gliding bows as if he'd worked in it all his life, instinctively toning down his vocal acrobatics to meld with the Straussian lilt of the plucked violins and the tiffling snare drum. As the last notes died away, there was very nearly a burst of applause. Jacobs remarked that if they went on like this, the session could wrap inside an hour.

In fact, it took only three and a half hours to complete the three remaining tracks, "Raining in My Heart," "Moondreams," and "True Love Ways." All were slow, reflective ballads without a hint of beat, and Buddy sang them completely straight, banishing all clicks and hiccups from his voice, drawing only on its warmth, its conviction, its gentleness, its ability to address the listener personally and privately. Everyone at Pythian Temple that day agreed that Buddy's treatment of Felice and Boudleaux Bryant's "Raining in My Heart" to be the high spot of the session. Only his mother, Ella, picked "True Love Ways" as the evergreen track, though even she could not dream what an imperishable standard it would become. Written ostensibly for and about Maria Elena, its stupendous charm lies in its mixture of intimacy and universality. While speaking directly and uniquely to Buddy's young wife, and looking forward to the life ahead of them both, it is also a message to all "those who really care," as ever counseling patience, hope, and trust in the benignity of Fate.

☆   ☆   ☆

On October 28, Buddy appeared on *American Bandstand,* lip-synching his new own-name single, "Heartbeat." J. I. and Joe B. Mauldin then joined him to mime the Crickets' current single, "It's So Easy." Although they did not know it at the time, this was to be their last performance together.

Buddy's mind was now firmly made up as to the direction his career should take in this increasingly chill and uncertain post–rock 'n' roll hiatus. He had decided to fire Norman Petty as his manager and sever all creative links with the tiny studio in Clovis whose sound no one seemed to be buying any more. He would get Petty to release the royalties accumulated in the Buddy Holly and the Crickets bank account and use his share to finance his manifold ambitions both for his own music and other people's.

Having that sizable lump sum behind him was essential to the game plan he had worked out. It would allow him to stop dissipating his time and energy on concert tours and instead stay put in New York with Maria Elena, exploring new directions in his music with Dick Jacobs, establishing his profile with the media, finding and developing talent for his Prism organization, and using the Big Apple's matchless creative resources to get himself back onto the charts.

This did not mean the end of the Crickets, however. When Buddy first revealed his intentions to J. I. and Joe B. during their last tour, he had made it clear that he wanted the three of them to continue recording and performing together. J. I. and Joe B. by now fully shared his resentment at the withholding of their royalties and were in just as rebellious a mood with Papa Norman. They enthusiastically accepted Buddy's proposal that they confront Petty as a group, force him to release their money, then fire him by unanimous vote and take off for New York together, as of old.

The undoing of this strategy was foreshadowed in a jokey exchange with Dick Clark on *American Bandstand:*

CLARK: Are you going back to Lubbock, Texas, or where's home . . . ?

JOE B.: Well, home is Lubbock, Texas, and I'll be going back just as soon as I can get a plane out of New York.

CLARK: Does that hold true of everybody, Buddy?

BUDDY: No, I've got my car up here, Dick, and I'm gonna have to take about a three-day journey getting there . . .

As things turned out, both J. I. and Joe B. made the journey back to Lubbock by air, arriving several days in advance of Buddy. From long habit the two drifted over to Clovis and, during conversation with Petty, news of the impending showdown leaked out. No doubt they had felt some misgivings about the role they would play in Buddy's new life, and the familiar sights and scents of Clovis Man's West Seventh Street cavern —Vi in her flower garden with Speedy the chihuahua; Norma Jean at her reception desk; the almost hypnotic fragrance of their producer's British Sterling aftershave lotion—must have eroded their resolve still further.

In any event, it took Petty only a very short time to talk them out of their pact with Buddy and convince them to remain with him. He told them they'd hate New York; that small-town boys like them would never fit in with the music scene there; that, in weeks rather than months, they'd come running home with their tails between their legs. If they continued to be guided by Papa Norman, on the other hand, they could still have a career as the Crickets without Buddy, as good as or even better than before. As J. I. Allison remembered afterward, Petty spiked these inducements with a subtle threat, reminding them that he still controlled their money and that, if they insisted on following Buddy, "there was no telling what might happen."

When Buddy arrived at his parents' home with Maria Elena on November 2, after their three-day car journey, he was greeted by the news that J. I. and Joe B. had gone to Clovis without him and were now safely in

Norman Petty's pocket. His mother later told his brother Larry of his furious reaction. "She said Buddy stormed out of the house, got into his car, and went straight over to have it out with Norman then and there. She said he was mad enough to fight."

Maria Elena went along, too, determined this time not to tolerate Petty's silky condescension toward her. "Buddy walked in to the office and told Norman they had to talk. Norman said, 'Okay, we'll talk,' then he looked at me and said, 'You go out and visit with Vi while Buddy and I talk business.' I told him, 'Whatever you have to say to Buddy, you say in front of me.' And Buddy said the same thing."

In all these months, Buddy, the Crickets, and Petty had never gotten around to signing a formal management contract. Buddy thus was spared the experience of young pop stars in later eras, for whom the price of freeing themselves from their managers would often be an arm and a leg. He could simply say "You're fired" and walk away. Petty, indeed, offered surprisingly little resistance to losing his diamond in the rough, merely shrugging and saying that if that was what Buddy really wanted, so be it.

Other than recording agreements, all that existed on paper was Buddy's writer's contract with Petty's publishing company, Nor Va Jak, which had grown wealthy both from publishing Buddy Holly songs and from Petty's appropriation of writers' credits. "Peggy Sue," Buddy's great solo tour de force, did not even have his name on it as co-composer, but had ended up credited to Petty and J. I. Allison. When Petty refused to change the billing, Buddy was forced to lodge a formal claim with Broadcast Music International, the agency that collected royalties on songwriters' behalf. According to Larry Holley, the long-agreed-to trade-off for allowing Petty's name to go on so many songs was that Buddy would receive a half-share in Nor Va Jak. When Petty was reminded about this during their confrontation, he pretended total amnesia on the subject. But— apparently content with his piece of "That'll Be the Day," "Oh Boy," "Not Fade Away," "True Love Ways," and all the others—he agreed to cancel Buddy's writer's contract.

What Petty flatly refused to do was pay over the accumulated royalties from the Buddy Holly and the Crickets bank account that Buddy was depending on to finance his solo career in New York. As always, Petty claimed to have scrupulous fairness and correctness on his side. He said that no money could be released to Buddy until a full accounting had been carried out and J. I.'s and Joe B.'s proportionate shares of the recording and publishing income had been calculated. Even when Petty's desktop Bible obliquely entered the argument, he remained implacable. "Buddy needed money to tithe our church, too, and he told Norman that," Larry Holley says. "But Norman told him, 'Don't worry, I'll tithe *my* church instead.'"

By the end of the meeting, Buddy was extremely angry and even the usually composed and ice-cool Clovis Man had begun to show signs of passion. His parting shot, allegedly, was words to the effect: "You'll starve to death before you see a penny of those royalties!" Petty himself, to the end of his days, vehemently denied ever having said such a thing. Possibly he did not mean it as the vindictive threat it appears, but a warning that Buddy's new career plans would end in disaster. Both Maria Elena Holly, who was there, and Buddy's brother Larry, who saw him immediately afterward, corroborate the phrasing.

Buddy returned from Clovis more upset and depressed than his wife, even his family, had ever seen him. He still couldn't believe that, despite the strategy they'd agreed to so carefully together, J. I. and Joe B. could have let themselves be talked out of their agreement, thus giving Petty a firm excuse to continue witholding the money. He was convinced that once he got hold of J. I. and Joe B. and talked to them himself, the whole thing might still turn out to be a ghastly misunderstanding.

"Buddy went straight to Jerry and said, 'What is this?'" Maria Elena remembers. "Jerry said that he and Joe B. didn't want to come to New York because they wouldn't fit in there. But the real reason was that Norman had told them if they went with Buddy, I would be the one deciding everything, and they'd have no say-so. Norman convinced them that they didn't need Buddy, that they were the real nitty-gritty of the Crickets. He'd bamboozled those two boys into doing what they did. Buddy tried to convince Jerry that Norman wasn't looking out for their interests, only his own. But, of course, they didn't listen. Norman was a good talker. He filled their heads with so many ugly things that the boys got scared.

"Buddy was devastated. He could not believe Jerry would let himself be talked into something like that. The two of them had been like brothers. And he knew that Norman was lying to these kids—that on their own they weren't going to do anything out there, and they were just being used by Norman to try to harm him. When we came back to the house that night, Buddy cried. He really cried his eyes out."

Buddy made one last attempt with J. I. a couple of days later when they bumped into each other at a café on Main Street, Clovis. Peggy Sue, who was sitting with her nineteen-year-old husband, well remembers the painful encounter. "Buddy asked Jerry if he was really sure about what he was doing. Jerry said that, as far as he could tell at that moment, he was. Buddy said, 'The person I really worry about in all this is Joe B.' 'Don't worry,' Jerry told him. 'I'll take care of Joe B.'"

With typical magnanimity, Buddy agreed to let J. I. and Joe B. continue to perform and record on Brunswick as the Crickets while he worked under his own name only on Coral. "He came to me and said, 'They want to go on with the name. What do you think?'" Maria Elena remembers. "I told him, 'Sure, let them have it. You don't need it. You can make it on your own.'"

Personal appeals to Petty about his money having failed, Buddy's only recourse was to see a lawyer. Back in New York, his new aunt-in-law, Provi Garcia, arranged a consultation with Peer-Southern Music's legal advisers, but as Peer-Southern royalties figured in the dispute, their lawyers could not represent Buddy. It so happened that his great friends the Everly Brothers were already involved in legal proceedings, for not dissimilar grievances, against their manager, Wesley Rose. Don and Phil recommended Buddy to their attorney, Harold Orenstein, a specialist in the often tortuous business and personal affairs of famous musicians, whose client roster also included Pat Boone, Ray Charles, Benny Goodman, and Erroll Garner (and who, in later years, would engineer a costly divorce between the Rolling Stones and that ultimate manager of the next generation, Allen Klein).

On November 5, Coral released what Buddy intended to be his last own-name product from the Norman Petty Studio, "Heartbeat," coupled with the acoustic, future-gazing "Well . . . All Right." For this magnificent double A-side, as we would call it nowadays, the reception was only marginally warmer than it had been for the last Crickets release, "It's So Easy." "Heartbeat" / "Well . . . All Right" did at least make the U.S. Top 100, but thereafter could manage only a laborious ascent to No. 83. In Britain, where Top 20 placing was all that counted, it stayed firmly shut out in the cold at No. 30.

To make matters worse, his three closest friends in the business seemed to be doing as well as before, or even better, in the post–rock 'n' roll charts. The Everly Brothers' hits had continued through the summer with "Bird Dog" and "Devoted to You"; that December they were to reach No. 2 with the inaptly titled "Problems." Eddie Cochran had ceased copying Elvis and hit on the mixture of wry social comment and Buddy-simple acoustic chord sequences that produced his September million-seller, "Summertime Blues." Just what was it that Eddie, Don, and Phil knew but he didn't?

On November 24, Buddy's lawyer, Harold Orenstein, wrote to Norman Petty, very clearly under instruction from his new young client not to strike too hostile or combative an opening note:

Re: Buddy Holly

Dear Mr. Petty:

As Mr. Holly has undoubtedly told you, he has retained me generally to act as his counsel in all matters affecting his activities as a musician and composer.

So that I may properly advise Mr. Holly, I will need all agreements, books, records and tax returns affecting his business. I understand that you have this material and will appreciate your sending it to me.

Mr. Holly has further asked me to advise you that he wishes immediately to cancel the power of attorney which he has given to you.

I would particularly appreciate your sending me all copyright registration certificates, publication agreements, mechanical licenses, agreements between Mr. Holly and any co-author of any song in the writing of which he collaborated, agreements relating to Mr. Holly's personal appearances and agreements, if any, between Mr. Holly and the other members of "The Crickets" or yourself. We should also like at the earliest possible moment a complete statement of account with respect to any moneys which you have received on behalf of Mr. Holly and a check to Mr. Holly's order for the full balance of any moneys due to him. Mr. Holly is about to engage in certain business enterprises in which he will need any available funds.

Since we are now nearing the end of the year, you will understand that there is some urgency in connection with my request.

Mr. Holly asked me to send you his personal regards when I wrote to you and I add my own.

Petty replied on November 28:

Dear Mr. Orenstein:

Congratulations to you as you take over the affairs of BUDDY HOLLY. He is an outstanding talent and since he is so confident in your abilities . . . the two of you should enjoy great success.

Please be advised that books and tax records are being prepared now for BUDDY HOLLY & THE CRICKETS and as soon as the audit is complete . . . as I informed Buddy when he was in Lubbock . . . the complete information concerning all money and all monies due Buddy will be forwarded to you.

As to other agreements . . . there were no written ones between Buddy and me nor between Buddy and The Crickets . . . only verbal agreements in which all of the boys came to a mutual understanding. Bookings . . . you will find a complete list of such bookings at General Artists Corporation there in New York. Buddy has some of the contracts and some of their TV contracts which I have never seen . . . so complete information you request can be obtained only from GAC. Buddy received all money due him and the boys and made disbursement of same. He sent some checks here for deposit and we will send you a list of them. He paid out the remainder of their earnings and should have knowledge of how the money was spent. I received some record royalty checks for them and statements of these royalties will be sent to you at your expense of duplication and upon your request. However, you may obtain this information directly from Decca Records in New York and Buddy can then find out all the information as to the codes and rates of payment. All checks which I have received for them have been placed in an agency account . . . upon advice from the Treasury Department and our accounting firm. Buddy will be paid his share just as soon as the above-mentioned audit is complete. As to agreements with Buddy as a writer . . . all such agreements are in New York, retained by MELODY LANE PUBLICATIONS in our behalf. You may obtain this information directly from them since they keep all contracts and records for our firm.

I trust this information will be to your satisfaction. If I can be of further assistance, just let me know.

One can imagine Buddy's shock when his lawyer showed him this letter. For months he had supposed, and been led to believe, that his and the Crickets' income was flowing into an account under their name, that Petty's hold over their money was simply by power of attorney and that termination of that power would make the funds accessible to them. But here was the truth at long, long last, if not yet fully spelled out: their recording royalties had not been banked under their name but under Petty's. The "agency account," alluded to with such delightful vagueness, was in fact one of Clovis Man's warren of one-man corporations, the Norman Petty Agency Inc. Even without the excuse of conducting a full audit of Buddy and the Crickets' earnings, Petty could sit on the money for as long as he liked.

To Maria Elena, when Buddy showed it to her, the letter bore out everything she had suspected both about Petty's financial duplicity and the shambolic, semi-detached way he had managed the second hottest act in rock 'n' roll. Yet Buddy, ever optimistic, continued to hope that the dispute would be resolved quickly and amicably, that his back royalties would come through by Christmas—even that, once these financial arguments were disposed of, he and Petty would be able to resume some kind of limited artistic partnership. Petty remained a codirector of Buddy's Prism Record Company, along with Ray Rush of the Roses vocal group. On December 3, Rush dropped out of the company and was repaid his $3,500 stake. But Buddy continued to regard Petty as a future general manager of the studio complex he planned to build for Prism in Lubbock.

All his hopes were now concentrated on the first release from his October 21 orchestral session, "It Doesn't Matter Anymore" and "Raining in My Heart." With "Heartbeat" / "Well . . . All Right" still getting airplay, a new Buddy Holly solo single clearly could not appear until early in the new year, 1959. Meanwhile, as his lawyer locked horns with Clovis Man, he settled down with Maria Elena to their new life among the Greenwich Village beatniks.

Like that of a rock 'n' roll star, life in the Village went on around the clock. A five-minute walk from their apartment at the Brevoort took Buddy and Maria Elena into its raffish, restless heart. The two would spend hours wandering streets that remained crowded long after midnight, then sit over espresso into the small hours at intellectuals' hangouts like the Bitter End and Café Bizarre. "Buddy loved those places . . . the strange clothes the people wore, the poetry readings, the way they talked to one another," Maria Elena remembers. "And he loved the freedom, the way everyone was allowed to do their thing. Late at night, if we couldn't sleep, we'd get up and go out in our pajamas. We'd roll them up so that no one could see them under our coats."

Most of all he loved the music that drifted enticingly from every other doorway—not only blues and folk joints but "serious" jazz venues like the Village Gate and the Blue Note, where modern colossi such as Thelonious Monk, John Coltrane, and Cannonball Adderley wove their complex tapestries with ferocious cool, buttoned into the sternest of Ivy League suits. The Hollys' favorite haunts were the Village Vanguard, Johnny

Johnson's, and Café Madrid, where there was live flamenco guitar music. "Buddy was curious about everything," Maria Elena says. "He'd sit up there with the musicians, asking them, 'How do you do that?' After that, he decided he wanted to learn to play finger-style flamenco guitar, so we found a neighbor of my aunt's who could give him lessons."

Despite the smallness of their $1,000-a-month apartment, the newly-weds found they could coexist happily and comfortably. In the center of the living room, Buddy had set up the Ampex tape-recorder he'd bought secondhand from Norman Petty. Pending the establishment of his Prism company, Buddy was using the Ampex to tape rough versions of the several new songs he'd written in New York. Maria Elena got used to hearing him jump out of bed, rush into the living room, and pick up his guitar to try out yet another idea that had popped into his head. Aunt Provi, who lived only a block away, had a piano at her apartment, and he would often drop by and use it during the hours when she was at the office.

The list of things he planned to do, when his money finally came from Petty, grew longer and longer. In common with a prescient few, he recognized that the future of pop music lay as much with albums as with singles, and was determined to be out there in the 33 rpm vanguard. As soon as he'd become proficient on flamenco guitar, he wanted to make an album of Latin American songs, symbolizing his love for Maria Elena and his commitment to her culture. At various times that winter, he talked of making a jazz album, a Cajun album, even an album of classical pieces.

After the happy experience of the King Curtis sessions, Buddy was on fire with eagerness to build more such bridges between white rock and black soul. His dream was to make an album with Ray Charles, the only black singer equally at home in blues, rock, ballads, or country. The concept of a duet album—let alone one co-starring a white and a black performer—was unheard of at that time. In the eighties and nineties, when Paul McCartney recorded "The Girl is Mine" with Michael Jackson, Elton John teamed with Dionne Warwick and Stevie Wonder played harmonica behind Annie Lennox, Maria Elena was ruefully to remember Buddy's idea all those years before. "While we were in L.A., we even went to Ray Charles's house to try to see him, but his people told us he was away on tour. Buddy never got another chance to see him."

For all this sophisticated big-city life, Buddy kept to the simple and absolute religious beliefs with which he had been raised. Indeed, dwelling among the Village's modish atheists, existentialists, and nihilists brought a powerful resurgence in his spiritual motivation. It troubled him that two years as a rock 'n' roll headliner had not enabled him to "do God's work" in accordance with his boyhood vow to the Tabernacle Baptist Church. High on his list of pressing projects was one intended to reaffirm his personal faith as well as carry him into yet another sphere from which white musicians were traditionally excluded. He planned an album of gospel music, on to which he hoped to inveigle the greatest of all female gospel singers, Mahalia Jackson.

Maria Elena was the sounding board for all his ideas, and an invariably positive force. To her, Buddy confessed his long-cherished dream of following Elvis Presley and Eddie Cochran into the movies—but real movies with real acting, not just Alan Freed–style rock exploitation flicks. Long hours in coffeehouse candlelight were spent discussing his two great screen idols, James Dean and Anthony Perkins. "Buddy talked a lot about writing scores for movies, too," Maria Elena remembers. "And he told me how much he admired Anthony Perkins and wanted to be like him. I said, 'You want to be like Anthony Perkins, then get out there, get involved.'" So, with her encouragement, Buddy registered for classes at Lee Strasberg's Actors' Studio, where Dean and Marlon Brando had learned the Method technique. In preparation for possible TV specials in the future, he also decided to take formal dancing lessons. Maria Elena, who'd once hoped to be a professional dancer, offered to teach him and choreograph some movements for him to use onstage. "We thought we could begin, just the two of us, in the apartment. I said, 'I'm going to teach you how to dance to Latino music.' Buddy said, 'I want to learn how to do the rumba.'"

His most pressing need was for a new manager to guide him not only through an uncertain new year, but also the uncharted waters of a fast-approaching new decade. At different times, he thought of Don Costa, who'd masterminded Paul Anka's huge success; of Irving Feld, who'd staged those mammoth road shows for the General Artists Corporation; even of Murray Deutch of Peer-Southern Music, a staunch friend and adviser to him and the Crickets from the very beginning. Flattered though Deutch was by Buddy's offer, he declined it. "I couldn't think of a better way to spoil our good relationship. I told him, 'Buddy, I don't want to be your mother, your father, your banker, your rabbi . . .'"

Meantime, he and Maria Elena did the job between them as best they could. One great consolation for the falloff in record sales was the sizable fan mail he still received, forwarded to the Brevoort from Clovis or Coral Records. His followers in Europe had learned by now about his going solo from the Crickets, and many now wrote with evident dismay to ask whether the parting was permanent. Buddy replied to all the letters personally, saying he hoped to get back with the Crickets at some future date, writing a neat "Ans" on the front of each envelope as he dealt with it. Another pressing task on his list was the organization of a fan club to establish proper relations with these thousands of intimate strangers.

In the absence of professional advice, he continued to work on his image with only his own instinctive good taste as a guide. He had recently acquired a new pair of glasses, with modishly blunt-cut black plastic Faiosa frames, found for him in Mexico by his ever-attentive Lubbock ophthalmologist, Dr. J. D. Armistead. Dr. Armistead also brought him back a second pair, of identical design but in dark-brown tortoiseshell. Buddy had lenses fitted to the black pair by New York opticians Courmetts & Gaul and asked his optometrist there, Dr. Stanger, to keep the tortoiseshell pair on file for him.

The new glasses were ready in time for his first publicity photographs as a solo performer. Appalled by the low standard of his pictures with the Crickets, Maria Elena sent him to Bruno, then New York's top show business photographer. Bruno's flattering lens—helped by an unaccustomed layer of makeup—softened the angularity of Buddy's face, removed all taint of myopia from the eyes inside the ultra-contemporary squared black frames and reduced his usual happy grin to a pensive, almost enigmatic smile. For some shots, he exchanged his pin-collar shirt and herringbone jacket for a chunky ribbed sweater in the style of Greenwich Village cognoscenti. The session went so well that he arranged with Bruno to return for a second one: another eager appointment destined never to be kept.

Perhaps the most sadly ironic feature of these final months was the interest Buddy suddenly developed in light aircraft. His brother Larry had been taking flying lessons down in Lubbock and was about to qualify as a pilot. As always, anything Larry did was an irresistible spur to Buddy. On November 5, just before returning to New York, he'd had his first (and, it would prove, last) flying lesson with the Champs Aviation Service at Lubbock airport. The aircraft used was a Cessna 175, wing-registration N9274B. Larry sat in on the lesson, during which Buddy's instructor deliberately stalled the Cessna's engine and let it drop sickeningly to earth for a few seconds before calmly straightening it out again. "Afterwards, I told Buddy he'd had a thirty-minute lesson," Larry remembers. "'Man,' he said, 'that stall seemed to last for thirty minutes!'"

Another of Buddy's schemes—once he had his money—was to buy his own aircraft and pilot himself across country from one concert appearance to the next. But this was something he did not mention to his wife. Maria Elena had been terrified of small planes since her childhood, when a family friend had flown her mother and herself in one from San Juan to St. Thomas in the Virgin Islands. On a later flight over the same route, the plane had crashed and its pilot and some friends of Maria Elena's parents had all died.

Grounded for the present in Apartment 4H at the Brevoort, Buddy kept himself as busy as always, drawing, painting, and refining blueprints he'd made for the house and recording studio that were to be Prism's Lubbock headquarters. He also designed furniture for the apartment, notably a cabinet for his stereo equipment, which was then constructed in modish white Formica.

Maria Elena, by her own admission, was not much of a cook, but fortunately cheap restaurants abounded in their neighborhood. Buddy enjoyed cooking—simple things like fried chicken, steaks, and potatoes —and, to show him how much she loved him, Maria Elena took an occasional stab at it. "One of Buddy's favorite things to eat was fried okra. I'd never even seen fried okra before I met him, but I thought I'd make some for dinner. I bought the okra, but I went ahead and boiled it first, and it came out horrible. I told Buddy, 'I made fried okra for you but it just came out a big lump. I don't know what I did wrong.' The minute he saw it he laughed and said, 'I know what you did wrong.'"

With his new taupe Cadillac and immaculate Alfred Norton clothes, his neighbors at the Brevoort took him to be as affluent as anyone in the building. And, indeed, Buddy continued to spend money as if all accounts could still be forwarded directly to Papa Norman. Early in December, little dreaming how fast time was now running out, he treated himself to a new wristwatch, an Omega set with diamonds and engraved with his name and the date. One evening, as he and Maria Elena were leaving a club with Phil Everly, he handed Phil a hundred-dollar bill to pay a check of about $8. Mistaking the bill for a ten in the Stygian gloom, Phil airily told the waiter to keep the change. "But when Buddy realized what had happened, he just laughed," Phil remembers.

In fact, his financial situation was growing desperate. Petty continued to withhold his record royalties, claiming that J. I. Allison's and Joe B. Mauldin's share of the payout still had not been calculated. The lump sum in publishing royalties he had received at the time of his wedding had long since evaporated, as had his earnings from the October tour. With neither savings nor income for the forseeable future, and $1,000 a month to find for rent alone, he had been forced to accept financial help from Maria Elena's Aunt Provi. "We didn't have a red cent," Maria Elena admits. "My aunt was paying for everything. Buddy felt bad about taking money from her, but she told him, 'Look on it as a loan. You can pay me back when you get your money from Norman.'"

As Christmas loomed, and still no check materialized from Clovis, Buddy decided there was only one sure, quick way to put some cash into his pocket. He must forget his resolve to stay in New York until he'd cracked the problem of getting a hit record; he must go out on tour again.

His first call was to GAC, the agency that had booked almost all his domestic tours with the Crickets. Despite his fear that they would be less interested in him as a solo act, GAC quickly came back with what seemed a providential offer. Early in the new year they had scheduled a three-week tour of the same Midwestern territory covered by Buddy and the Crickets' "Summer Dance Party" the previous July. Although slightly more ambitious than its warm-weather namesake had been, this "Winter Dance Party" still reflected the shrinking scale of rock 'n' roll road shows. Opening on January 23, 1959, it featured just four other acts: Ritchie Valens, the Big Bopper, Dion and the Belmonts, and Frankie Sardo. Still, it was work, and Buddy jumped at it, agreeing to provide his own supporting musicians in place of the Crickets.

Maria Elena says she disliked the sound of the "Winter Dance Party" from the beginning. "It was not the right thing for someone like Buddy to be on—it was a tour for beginners. I pleaded with him not to go. I said, 'You don't need to; this is not a tour for you.' He said, 'Yes I do; I need to bring some money in. I'm not going to continue to ask your aunt to lend us money. It's time for me to go to work, no matter what it is.' We had some kind of argument about that. He said 'It's only a three-week tour . . . and I'll bring some money back.' With Buddy, once he made up his mind, that was it."

Everything was arranged by December 14, when he wrote to his old Lubbock friend Terry Noland, full of plans for composing and recording together: "I'm leaving on tour January 23rd, so I hope you'll be here before then as I would like to be at your next session. However, that tour doesn't last but three weeks and I'll be back in New York by the middle of February."

As December drew on, an old friend came in to town. Eddie Cochran was appearing in the Manhattan Paramount's Christmas show (from which Buddy this year was conspicuously absent) and staying at the Park-Sheraton hotel across from the theater. With him was a dark-haired, forceful seventeen-year-old named Sharon Sheeley, who'd become a part of the Everly Brothers' West Coast circle during "The Biggest Show of Stars for 1957" tour, the previous fall. She had gone on to write a hit single, "Poor Little Fool," for Ricky Nelson and transfer her affections from the married Don Everly to the determinedly unattached Cochran.

Buddy spent an afternoon with Don and Phil Everly and his protégé Lou Giordano, hanging out in Cochran's room at the Park-Sheraton. "From Eddie's room, you could hear the sound of the show going on in the Paramount across the street," Sharon Sheeley remembers. "Eddie would stay up there until the end of the act that was on right before him. He had it so perfectly timed, he could walk over to the Paramount, put on his guitar, and step out onstage at the exact moment the emcee announced him."

To both Cochran and Phil Everly, Buddy confided his frustration at the drawn-out wrangle with Norman Petty over his money, and his mystification that neither "It's So Easy" nor "Heartbeat" had made the charts. "He wasn't suicidal about it," Phil remembers. "I guess you could say his pride was a little hurt, but he was determined to get back up there again. That's why I was surprised when he told me he was going out on the road again. The last I heard, he'd decided to stay in New York and work on his records until one of them went Top Ten."

For a time it looked as if Eddie Cochran might co-star with Buddy on the "Winter Dance Party." "Buddy asked him to go," Sharon Sheeley remembers. "And those two always found it hard to say no to each other. But then Eddie got an offer to be on *The Ed Sullivan Show* early in February, and Buddy said, 'Yeah, sure, man, that's much more important.'"

Most unusually for him, with his nervous stomach, Buddy had a couple of drinks that December afternoon in Eddie Cochran's hotel room. He and Phil Everly had a long-standing agreement that if one got snockered, the other would make sure he reached home safely. So it was Phil who, later on, found a cab, pushed Buddy's long frame into it, and delivered him back downtown to the Brevoort and Maria Elena. "He had a professional tape-recorder set up in the middle of his living room," Phil remembers. "He played me about six new cuts that he'd put down, just as demos, accompanying himself on acoustic guitar. They all sounded great to me."

These last recordings Buddy would ever make were called simply "Songs" on the Scotch Magnetic Tape box that housed them, but are known to posterity as "the Apartment Tapes." Any other young songwriter set down in the heart of Greenwich Village might well have been carried away by its intellectual pretensions, its cosmopolitanism, its wackiness. But Buddy, wherever he was, knew only how to be Buddy. Sitting alone with his Gibson J200, four floors above the coffeehouses and jazz clubs, he created songs that were as simple, open, and honest as the West Texas plains that had nurtured him. Worried and uncertain as he was about his personal situation, in songs he could still be humorous, philosophical, and optimistic in his old familiar way; still adopt the role of adviser, comforter, and sympathetic friend when those were the very things he himself needed the most. Never did he speak more plainly, honestly, and intimately than when he believed his audience to be slipping away.

On December 3, he had recorded "That's What They Say," a song about waiting for love, written in his usual hopeful, wistful mode, and "What to Do," a plea for guidance in the numb aftermath of being jilted. One of the ideas running through his mind was to make the high school heroine of his biggest solo hit a recurrent character like Annie in the Hank Ballard songs. So, on December 5, he'd taped "Peggy Sue Got Married," a sequel as light-hearted as the original had been darkly serious, turning the Allisons' brazen nuptials into a "rumor from a friend" that the singer is almost too thunderstruck to repeat.

On December 8, he had recorded "That Makes It Tough," a lament poised between wailing country and growling blues, whose seeming despair, as ever, yields to irrepressible stoicism. On December 14, he had recorded "Crying, Waiting, Hoping," another simple but flawless blueprint, instantly comprehensible to all those boys clutching their Hofners against their school blazers somewhere beyond the Atlantic. On December 17, he had recorded "Learning the Game," a fragile ballad whose sad reflection on "hearts that are broken and love that's untrue" seems to distill the sad experience of a lifetime far longer than twenty-two years.

The slow, measured strum of his guitar has a quality that is almost hymnlike. His voice sounds faraway and lonely, as if Fifth Avenue and the Village vanished and obliterating snow and ice already stretch all around.

☆　　☆　　☆

"I tell my blues they mustn't show," he had sung on the B-side of his new orchestral single. And when he took Maria Elena home for Christmas— the last time he would ever see his mother and father, or Lubbock— Buddy put on a determinedly upbeat and confident front. As far as his family knew, he was a star still at the pinnacle of success, and with money to burn.

"They brought back a whole mess of Christmas presents with them," Larry Holley remembers. "Buddy looked like some kind of New York playboy, 'stead of the little knucklehead we remembered, running around in his jeans." It seemed to Larry that Buddy now spoke more slowly and carefully, as if to sound less like a Texan, more like a native New Yorker. "His speech seemed like he was taking on the tone of a foreigner just a little bit. Trying to be more of a gentleman type 'stead of a rogue. He was spreading it all on a little thick. I think he blew just about all the money he had on coming here to impress us."

A color home movie silently commemorates that Christmas Day family gathering in L. O. and Ella's living room. Children play with their new toys on the carpet; in the foreground, Larry turns around, smiling, with his pipe. Maria Elena, small and vivacious in a dark cocktail dress, hands out expensively wrapped gifts from the pile she and Buddy have brought from New York. Buddy himself sits away to the left, almost painfully stylish in his yellow shirt, black vest, and Slim Jim tie, delving into the present on his knees with small-boyish eagerness.

Many of his old Lubbock cronies still found it hard to believe that he was married and that everywhere he went, Maria Elena now had to go too. The more urbane of Buddy's brother musicians, like Sonny Curtis and Terry Noland, had no problem with the new Mrs. Holly, nor she with them. But simpler "good ol' boys" who had known Buddy since their schooldays were at a loss to understand how he could have fallen for a

Puerto Rican four years his senior, and a New Yorker to boot, instead of some nice West Texas girl.

As blissfully happy in his marriage as Buddy declared himself, there were some who felt that Maria Elena's powerful personality somewhat overwhelmed his; that she organized his life altogether too efficiently, damping down his high spirits and spontaneity, forcing him to concentrate on business matters, lawyers' meetings, and paperwork. During a trip to Clovis, the Hollys had lunch with Jimmy Self, who'd been at the Petty Studio when Buddy first auditioned there. Remembering the ebullient, impulsive young Texan of those days, Self was disconcerted to see how Buddy even allowed his new wife to choose his food for him, rejecting his favorite Mexican dishes for salad, "because of his ulcer." L. O. Holley declared that, on the contrary, Maria Elena had made Buddy his own man instead of the overgrown baby of the Holley family eternally tied to his mother's apron strings. But there were others who doubted whether, a few months from now, he would find this kind of highly organized domesticity quite so charming.

One of the few old friends who saw Buddy tête-à-tête on that final visit was Jack Neal, his original playing partner on KDAV, and the first to whom he'd confided that he wanted the world to remember his name. Jack remembers sitting with Buddy in the Cadillac outside their old teenage haunt, the Nite Owl restaurant, and hearing about his Prism organization and his plan to build a recording studio in Lubbock. To prove this was more than just a pipe dream, Buddy had already bought the land where the studio was to be built and had contracted with his father for the construction of a six-room, brick-veneer house with four bathrooms. He also planned to have his own record label—named Taupe, after his new Cadillac's gray-brown designer shade—for the string of younger protégés he planned to develop. "He said 'Jack, there's a real mess of talent here in West Texas, if only it could get a start. I want to do something to help them along. Then he laughed and said, 'Maybe I can make *you* a star, too!'"

Despite the continuing deadlock with Norman Petty over his royalties, Buddy also drove to Clovis and called at the Petty studio. His friend Bob Montgomery was now working there as an engineer, and Buddy wanted Bob to be involved with Prism, possibly running the company's publishing division in New York. An encounter with Petty himself was unavoidable, but, according to Jimmy Self, the two conversed quite amiably. However,

Buddy made no attempt to see J. I. Allison and Joe B. Mauldin, who were both by that time living in Clovis. Mulling over their defection at a distance, his initial forbearing sadness had turned to anger. "He was mad with J. I. and Joe B. for what they'd done," a friend remembers. "He wanted to kick their asses."

A condition of joining GAC's "Winter Dance Party" was that Buddy recruit—and pay—backup musicians to take J. I.'s and Joe B.'s place. As a symbolic break with the recent past, he had decided on a four-man lineup: himself, lead guitar, bass guitar, and drums. A lead guitarist, at any rate, was easily found. Tommy Allsup, now working with a band in Odessa, Texas, jumped at the chance to tour with Buddy again. In another Odessa club, playing with Ronnie Smith and the Poor Boys, he found Carl Bunch, a young drummer with a faint look of J. I. Allison as well as almost comparable energy and style. Though Bunch had regular employment with Ronnie Smith's group, Buddy was allowed to borrow him for the three weeks of the tour.

To play bass guitar, he wanted Waylon Jennings, the young KLLL deejay, whose recording debut he had sponsored the previous fall. In vain did Waylon protest that his instrument was guitar and that he didn't own a bass nor have the slightest idea how to play one. Buddy swept all his objections aside, promising to buy a bass guitar for him and tutor him, somehow or other, before January 23 when the "Winter Dance Party" hit the road.

As on previous trips home, Buddy's most carefree hours were spent hanging out at KLLL with Waylon, the Corbin brothers, and the other jocks. On one visit, he wrote a new song, "You're the One," dashing it off in fifteen minutes, then recording it on the station's acetate machine with Waylon and Slim Corbin providing handclaps. Another day, he appeared on a KLLL remote broadcast from the Morris Fruit & Vegetable Store. It was his first live show in Lubbock since becoming famous, and he was uncharacteristically nervous about it; he felt guilty about losing touch with the audience that had nurtured him, and remembered only too well the special impatience and hypercriticality of West Texas music fans. He need not have worried; Lubbock flocked to see him along with the pumpkin and cranberry specials at Morris's, and cheered him as if he'd never been away. Buddy enjoyed the occasion so much that he agreed to let Slim Corbin organize a formal "homecoming" concert for him the following summer.

Even Larry, who could usually read him like a book, received no inkling of the worries gnawing at him. One afternoon, he came over to Larry's house, the one he'd help to build in the early summer of 1957, while "That'll Be the Day" was still footslogging up the charts. Seated on the sofa, he played and sang "Raining in My Heart," which even hardboiled Larry thought "one of the purtiest tunes I ever heard." The show of heedless affluence was kept up to the very end. Before leaving his parents' home on New Year's Eve, never to return, Buddy produced his checkbook and grandly wrote the Tabernacle Baptist Church a check for $800.

On January 5, Coral released "It Doesn't Matter Anymore"/"Raining in My Heart." That same week, Buddy received some New Year tidings that all but erased his anxiety over his new single from his mind: Maria Elena told him she was pregnant.

She admits now that it was her own diagnosis, unconfirmed as yet by any doctor but no less certain for that. "If you're a woman and you're pregnant, you *know!* We hadn't been trying to have a baby. It was an accident; it just happened. I didn't want to have a child, because it was going to interfere with all the projects we had starting out. But Buddy was elated about it. I told him, 'If I have a baby, that means I won't be able to travel around with you like you want me to.' But he said, 'No, that'll be fine. The baby can come with us.'"

They agreed to delay breaking the news to their respective families until Buddy's return from the "Winter Dance Party" tour. "He said, 'When I get back, we'll go to Lubbock together and tell Mother,'" Maria Elena remembers. "I knew already it was going to be a boy. Buddy told me, 'It'll be just as nice if it's a girl,' but I told him, 'I know it's a boy.'"

The pregnancy promised not to be an easy one: Maria Elena already felt unwell most of the time, and had begun to suffer extreme bouts of morning sickness. For that reason, allied to shortage of money, they did little to celebrate her twenty-sixth birthday on January 7. Knowing how much she loved flowers, Buddy brought her an extravagant bouquet. They also opened some champagne, and Maria Elena persuaded him to take a few sips, even though it usually disagreed with his nervous stomach. To her distress, he felt ill afterward; his stomach had more reason than ever these days to be nervous.

On January 8, he sat down at his typewriter and wrote Norman Petty the politest and most tactful of reminders about the still unfinished business between them:

Dear Norman:

I will appreciate it if at your earliest convenience you will send me the writer's contract that I had with you and the cancellation of same as per our agreement during the month of November.

I have been waiting for you to send it but as I have not received it yet, no doubt you have forgotten to mail it.

My lawyer has informed me that he has already gotten in touch with you urging settlement of the matter pertaining to my money. I am sure that you will do your utmost to bring this matter to a satisfactory climax.

> Thanking you in advance, I remain
> Yours truly
> Buddy Holly

But the temperature of the dispute was already rising. True to his promise, Petty had very quickly found "a new guy" to front the Crickets in Buddy's place. The new discovery was Earl Sinks, a curly-haired eighteen-year-old from Levelland, Texas, with a vague resemblance to James Cagney and a voice superficially like Buddy's, though with little of its acrobatic variety and none of its inner warmth. Papa Norman was satisfied, however, and already had Sinks recording with J. I. Allison and Joe B. Mauldin as if no disruption had ever taken place. On January 9, he wrote to Isabelle Marks, an executive at Coral Records:

Dear Miss Marks:

Please be advised that Buddy Holly is no longer a Cricket, as of the first of the year.

All new recordings by The Crickets will feature the new lead voice. Buddy will be heard only on his Coral recordings.

Best regards for the new year.

Letters had been flowing between Buddy's legal advisers and Petty at regular intervals since late November, yet still without unlocking the lump sum in royalties which, as a father-to-be, Buddy would need more urgently than ever. Harold Orenstein had by now handed over the case to his associate George Schiffer, who on January 12 wrote patiently yet again:

Dear Mr. Petty:

Thank you for your letter of January 3, 1959.

We are somewhat concerned by its contents since we had thought that as Buddy's personal manager you had substantially complete books concerning his income and expenses.

With respect to his income from personal appearances, Buddy tells me that since last August the bulk of the money received was disposed of. We cannot, of course, evaluate that accounting since we have received no written records concerning it.

With respect to record income, Buddy indicated that his understanding of the division differs substantially from that set forth in your letter. He understands that you are to retain 10 percent as full compensation for your services and that he is to receive 77 and a half percent of the remainder (from which he makes his contribution to his church). It may be, of course, that I misread your letter; I think that this point should in any event be clarified.

We would appreciate it if you would supply us with all of the facts, figures and statements which you may have available, even if they are not complete, as quickly as possible. We particularly want to know what funds you are presently holding for Buddy and what arrangements have been made with respect to his tax liability for 1958 and 1957 if any.

With respect to Buddy's music writing, we still do not have the list of compositions which we requested or the accounting from NOR VA JAK which will also be essential. We also require copies of Buddy's contracts with NOR VA JAK.

In view of Buddy's manifold activities and the many problems which have to be resolved, it might be convenient if we could discuss the situation. Will you be in New York at any time in the near future? If so, I will be very glad to meet you at your convenience.

That same day, Schiffer learned of Petty's announcement to Coral that "Buddy Holly is no longer a Cricket, as of the first of the year." Buddy, it is true, had told J. I. and Joe B. that they could continue working as the Crickets without him. But his lawyers were not about to let him give away the name on two of his three biggest hits. And Petty's high-handed tone was one calculated to make any self-respecting attorney see red. George Schiffer immediately fired off an indignant rebuke via Western Union:

STRONGLY OBJECT TO YOUR LETTER OF JANUARY 9 TO CORAL RE-
CORDS. BUDDY HOLLY HAS FULL RIGHT TO USE THE NAME "THE
CRICKETS" AND WILL CONTINUE TO USE THAT NAME. STRONGLY OB-
JECT TO MISLEADING USE OF THE NAME IN CONJUNCTION WITH
SINGER OTHER THAN HIMSELF. LETTER FOLLOWS. PLEASE BE AD-
VISED THAT IN VIEW OF THE FACT THAT YOU NO LONGER REPRESENT
MR HOLLY YOUR ATTEMPT TO GIVE INSTRUCTIONS TO CORAL RE-
CORDS REGARDING HIS FUTURE RECORDING IS UNWARRANTED AND
UNAUTHORIZED.

The next day, January 13, Isabelle Marks gave Petty equally short shrift
on behalf of Coral:

Dear Mr. Petty:

We are in receipt of your letter of January 9 in which you advise us that
Buddy Holly is no longer a Cricket.

Our contract covering the performance of the Crickets is with Buddy
Holly, Jerry Allison and Joe Mauldin. We must insist that the performances
by the Crickets be with the individuals who are parties of the contract and
we cannot accept any substitutions.

Petty replied to George Schiffer on January 14:

We acknowledge receipt of your telegram dated January 13, 1959, and
naturally immediately conclude that there is a misunderstanding by Buddy
Holly if he is of the opinion that he is "The Crickets." The original
"Crickets" consisted of Niki Sullivan, Joe Mauldin and Jerry Allison.

By an instrument dated December 14, 1957, Niki Sullivan relinquished
all his interest in "The Crickets" and in all previous recordings designated
or labeled "Buddy Holly" or "The Crickets" in consideration of the assignment to him of ten percent of all monies received for one recording on
Brunswick Records of "That'll Be the Day" by "The Crickets."

It would seem obvious that Buddy Holly was never actually a member
of "The Crickets." All personal appearances, all recordings and any other
artistic presentations by Buddy Holly with "The Crickets" were usually
billed and shown to be two separate entities, that is "Buddy Holly and The
Crickets."

We feel constrained to advise therefore, in behalf of "The Crickets,"
who now consist of Joe Mauldin, Jerry Allison and a new member, that

Mr. Holly is definitely not at liberty to use the name "The Crickets" in any artistic presentation without their express written consent.

Brunswick's original agreement with the Crickets for "That'll Be the Day" had indeed borne only the names of J. I. Allison, Joe B. Mauldin and Niki Sullivan. But that had been mere subterfuge to conceal Buddy's presence in the group from Brunswick's parent company, Decca. Subsequently, his contractual difficulties with Decca had been sorted out and his name had been appearing on all the Crickets' Brunswick contracts since October. The wording on this or that concert poster was quite irrelevant: what had happened, as Clovis Man well knew, was that Buddy had developed two parallel careers, one as lead singer with the Crickets, the other as a solo singer backed by them. J. I. and Joe B. had not been "two separate entities" but a single entity under two names. Remembering the cohesion and camaraderie that had taken them around the world together, it's hard to understand how the other two could have been parties to such a breathtakingly untrue allegation.

Petty's letter crossed with one from Schiffer, following up his telegram:

It is quite clear that Buddy has as much right, and probably more, to the use of the name "The Crickets" as the other two boys. He has no intention of surrendering his rights. It would not be proper for the boys to use another singer with the group under the name "The Crickets" because the name and reputation were built primarily on Buddy Holly. It is he who was responsible for the bulk of their success and he who obtained the bulk of the rewards.

From my limited knowledge of the commercial situation, I believe that Buddy can continue to use the name to some good effect, but that no reputable record company and no reputable booking organization would accept the subterfuge of substituting another singer for Buddy in a group to be called "The Crickets." Even if such arrangements could be made, it would seem to me not desirable for either group that there be another group with the same name concurrently working.

So as to avoid further complications and any possible loss of income either to the boys or Buddy, I think that we should resolve the above mentioned matter and the accounting as quickly as possible, if necessary by meeting.,

Please let me hear from you concerning these matters at your earliest convenience.

That same day, Schiffer wrote to Isabelle Marks at Coral:

As you know, Buddy Holly has an interest in funds which become payable to "The Crickets" pursuant to the agreement between them and Coral even though he is not a party to that agreement.

Accordingly, the notification which we previously sent you was intended to apply to royalties becoming due on account of "The Crickets'" records on which Mr. Holly performed. It will be satisfactory to us if the entire royalty for such records is held by you for the time being. In no event should any part of it be paid to Mr. Petty instead of to Mr. Holly since, as you know, Mr. Petty no longer represents Mr. Holly.

George Schiffer's patience with Clovis Man was starting to wear thin. On January 16 he wrote:

Re: Buddy Holly and "The Crickets"

Dear Mr. Petty:

In view of your failure to respond satisfactorily to our numerous letters requesting an accounting and payment of the sums due to Mr. Holly, demand is hereby again made for the immediate payment of all sums presently held by you which belong to Mr. Holly, together with a full accounting and copies of all contracts between Mr. Holly and the other members of The Crickets, between Mr. Holly and you and between Mr. Holly and NOR VA JAK.

Also on January 19, Schiffer wrote the Clovis National Bank:

Gentlemen:

Norman Petty, formerly manager of Buddy Holly, received substantial sums of money in his fiduciary capacity, which sums beneficially belong to Mr. Holly. As attorneys for Mr. Holly, we learned that some or all of these funds may be deposited in your bank.

Please be advised that all of Mr. Petty's powers to deal with the property of Mr. Holly or to represent him have been terminated and that Mr. Petty is not empowered to make deposits or withdrawals of funds belonging to Mr. Holly or otherwise to deal with any matter with or to enter into any transaction concerning Mr. Holly or his property.

The bank's reply, on January 19, showed predictable solidarity with a valued local customer:

We are in receipt of your letter of January 16 concerning Mr. Buddy Holly and Mr. Norman Petty his personal manager.

We do not have an account in our bank for Mr. Holly. Money that has been deposited here is under the heading of Norman Petty Agency Inc. and we cannot honor any signature other than Mr. Petty's.

We have been unable to contact Mr. Petty personally, but his office manager says that all royalty checks that came in were made payable to Mr. Petty or the agency.

You realize we are acting only as a depository and know nothing further about any fund belonging to Mr. Holly.

That same day, Petty's secretary, Norma Jean Berry, wrote to George Schiffer:

Dear Mr. Schiffer:

We acknowledge receipt of your letters of Jan. 12, 1959 . . . Jan. 14, 1959 . . . and Jan. 19, 1959, the last arriving today containing contracts for the signatures of Jerry Allison and Joe Mauldin [for their October 28 appearance on *American Bandstand*].

Please be advised that Mr. Norman Petty has not seen any of these letters as he has been out of town since last Thursday, Jan. 15th, the day on which the first of the above mentioned letters arrived.

Mr. Allison and Mr. Mauldin are also out of town this week and will not be available to examine the contracts you sent until this coming weekend, at which time Mr. Petty will also return to Clovis.

Thus were more days allowed to run out.

☆   ☆   ☆

Buddy had arranged for his new band to spend a week rehearsing with him in New York before the January 23 start of the "Winter Dance Party" tour. Tommy Allsup and the drummer Carl Bunch checked in to a local hotel, but Waylon Jennings, as Buddy's special protégé, was invited to stay at his apartment. All three of the Texans were deeply impressed by

Buddy's Manhattan lifestyle, Tommy in particular by the Brevoort's valet parking service.

These few days were all Waylon had to pick up the rudiments of the brand-new Fender bass guitar Buddy had bought for him. He remembered later that when he arrived in New York, Buddy simply handed him copies of *The Chirping Crickets* and *Buddy Holly* albums with a grin and told him, "Here's my songs. Learn 'em." Kind-hearted Tommy came to his aid, teaching him enough basic rhythm patterns to get by. Not a word was said to any of the band about Maria Elena's being pregnant.

Two weeks had now passed since the release of "It Doesn't Matter Anymore." Though widely played and praised by deejays and admired by Buddy's fellow musicians, it still had not appeared in the *Billboard* Hot 100. "That was really worrying Buddy while we were rehearsing for the tour," Tommy Allsup remembers. "He couldn't figure out why, whatever he did, the hits seemed to have dried up for him."

Along with the consoling blueprints for Prism and the Taupe record label, another new plan took shape in Buddy's mind. If America didn't want him, then he'd return to the country that had given him so unexpected a hero's welcome the previous March. "He'd talked to GAC about going back to England," Tommy says. "That was another reason for doing this 'Winter Dance Party' deal for GAC. Afterwards, he was coming back to New York for two weeks, then going off on a six-week European tour."

Maria Elena concurs: "He was always talking about how much he liked England, what a welcome the people had given him over there. After his recording studio in Lubbock was established, he wanted to open studios in other cities—either L.A. or London. The L.A. smog hurt his throat, so he decided on London. He said there was so much talent in England that no one seemed to be interested in developing. 'You'll love it over there,' he kept telling me. 'You'll love it.'"

Ever conscious of Buddy's precarious finances, hospitable Aunt Provi had the whole band to dinner at her apartment. Another night, Maria Elena made another of her forays into cooking. "I had a book that had Spanish recipes. I decided to fix steaks with rice and red beans and a salad. I went ahead and did the rice, and that didn't come out too bad. But I forgot I'd put the red beans on the stove, and they all burned and got stuck to the bottom of the pan. As we were eating, I could see the look on Waylon's face when he tasted these horrible burned beans. But Buddy was kind of kicking him under the table and saying, 'Mm, isn't this wonderful?' He wouldn't hurt my feelings for anything."

Between rehearsals, Buddy continued to tape songs on the Ampex in his living room, accompanying himself on acoustic or electric guitar, sometimes with Waylon or Tommy Allsup sitting in. The society of fellow pickers from his home state seems to have lifted his spirits, for the second phase of the apartment tapes are noticeably less melancholy and introspective than the first. They include Little Richard's "Slippin' and Slidin'," the Coasters' "Smokey Joe's Café," even an old vaudeville song, a favorite of his mother's, "Wait Till the Sun Shines, Nellie." One version of "Slippin' and Slidin'" was recorded at half-speed, suggesting that Buddy intended it to be a chipmunk-voiced comedy number. Another day he recorded his version of "Love Is Strange," the Mickey and Sylvia song that had inspired his double-track masterpiece "Words of Love." Preserved at the beginning of the tape is the sound of Tommy Allsup knocking at the apartment's front door.

There were also frequent trips uptown to West 57th Street to confer with his lawyer, George Schiffer, not only about the continuing non-appearance of his record royalties, but now, too, about Petty's stupefying claim that Buddy had "actually" never been a Cricket. Schiffer's advice was that a lawsuit against Petty now seemed inevitable, but on January 20, he made one last try to resolve the dispute informally:

Re: Buddy Holly and "The Crickets"

Dear Mr. Petty,

I am most surprised by the content of your letter of January 14, 1959. Not only have numerous recordings been made with "The Crickets featuring Buddy Holly" but Buddy has always been treated by the public as one of The Crickets. I might add that he, in terms of his share of receipts, owns a good deal more than half of that name.

In any event, and without regard to possible technicalities, there can be no question but that Buddy has rights in the name at least equal to those of the other boys. The position which you take is, to my mind, not only unwarranted in law or fact, but unfair. Coupled with your failure to account for the large sums of money which you are now holding on behalf of Mr. Holly, your taking this position represents, to my mind, the first step in what may prove to be a long and unnecessary disagreement.

I understand that you will be coming to New York very soon. Since we would still like at least to try to adjust this whole matter amicably, I would appreciate your calling me for an appointment as soon as you arrive in New York. Should you fail to do so, you will leave us no alternative but to take steps to enforce such legal remedies as Mr. Holly may have available.

Don and Phil Everly were still using the same law firm in their battle with their ex-manager, Wesley Rose. One afternoon as Don and Phil arrived at the firm's office for a conference, they met Buddy coming out. The brothers asked whether the dispute with Petty was anywhere near a resolution and Buddy replied gloomily in the negative. They agreed to meet as soon as possible after the Everlys' forthcoming Australian tour.

Despite its cozy suggestion of fur-wrapped sleigh rides and hot chocolate, Maria Elena still had dire misgivings about the "Winter Dance Party," and was determined to travel with Buddy and watch over him as she had on his October tour. The prospect of the Midwest in midwinter did not daunt her; as a New Yorker, she was well used to blizzards and below-zero temperatures and, indeed, positively relished cold weather. But Buddy would not hear of it. She was still suffering daily bouts of nausea that three weeks on the road could only aggravate. "He said I had to take things easy," she remembers. "I needed to find a doctor to take care of me through the pregnancy. And there were lots of things for me to do in New York."

The arrangements Buddy made to cover his absence were as meticulous as always. While Maria Elena continued organizing his fan club and personal PR, Aunt Provi was to seek out material for his projected album of Latin American music. One song that he definitely planned to use, for obvious reasons, was "Maria Elena," a breeze-soft ballad destined to be an instrumental hit for Los Indios Tabajeras in 1963. He also got in touch with Niki Sullivan, the original fourth Cricket whose conflicts with J. I. Allison were now, perhaps, a little easier to understand. Having heard nothing from Buddy since December 1957, Niki was amazed to be phoned by him and asked to join the songwriting partnership he planned to form with Paul Anka. According to Tommy Allsup, Buddy also asked GAC for an advance on his tour earnings to leave behind as a contingency fund for his pregnant wife. But Maria Elena herself says they remained totally reliant on Aunt Provi, both for day-to-day necessities and money in the bank to pay the whacking monthly rental of their apartment.

Despite the veiled threats now coming from Papa Norman, there was no question in Buddy's mind about the billing of his new band. On January 22, he recorded a spoken promo to be sent to radio stations along the "Winter Dance Party" route: "Hi, this is Buddy Holly. The Crickets and I are really happy to be coming your way on the 'Winter Dance Party.' We certainly hope to see all our old friends and to be making some new ones, too. Also, I hope you like my latest Coral release, 'Heartbeat.' See you soon."

He tried to reassure Maria Elena that the three weeks would soon pass, that before she knew it they'd be back together again, strolling the Village streets with pajamas under their raincoats or having dinner at their favorite table at Café Madrid. But she remained deeply unhappy and uneasy about letting him go off without her. "I got so that I couldn't even listen when Buddy and the others were discussing the tour," she remembers. "Waylon said to me later, 'It's amazing how strongly you were against the whole thing.'"

On the night before Buddy's departure, as she lay beside him for the very last time, Maria Elena had a singularly vivid and upsetting nightmare. "It was like I was standing by myself in a big, vast, barren area, like a farm. I didn't know where I was or how I got there. And then all of a sudden I could hear noises, like shouting, and it got closer and closer. In the distance I could see all these people, running, running, running, and shouting, 'They're coming! Hide! They're coming.' These people were desperately trying to run away from something. They were coming toward me like cattle in a stampede and I knew I would be trampled, but I couldn't move. I was standing there like I was glued there. But they all ran past me and one person, I remember, said to me as they went past, 'Run! Run!'

"Then I can hear this terrible noise, whoosh, really loud, like a storm coming in, and then a rumble, and then I look and I see this big ball of fire coming out of the sky like a comet, headed straight for me. I try to move but I still can't move and I think, 'Oh my God, this thing's going to kill me.' Then, for some reason, I start running, but I know it's too late and this thing's going to crush me. Then I hear this horrible noise on top of me and then passing me, and ahead of me I hear a crash and see a huge explosion. I could see a hole with black smoke coming out of it and I went up to it and tried to look in, but all you could see was a big black hole.

"That's when I woke up, and Buddy woke up and told me he'd had a dream, too. He dreamed he was flying in a plane with me and his brother Larry, and they'd landed on top of a building. Larry had wanted to leave me there. He said: 'On our way back we'll pick her up.' Buddy said, 'No, wherever I go, she goes.' But Larry convinced him that it was not going to be too long and I should just wait there. So Buddy had to leave me, but he said to me, 'Wait right here and I'll be back to pick you up.' He was upset that he'd left me. He held me and he was crying, really crying.

"We were both dreaming the same dream at the same time. And there was so much that came true if you put two and two together: Buddy leaving me . . . an airplane crash . . . on a farm. . . . It was like someone saying something to me, but I didn't listen. I still feel bad at times that I didn't listen."

They were both in a state of deep distress the next morning as Buddy finished his packing. His wardrobe, immaculate as always, showed what a deep impression English tailoring had made on him during his brief visit to London. Rather than a tie, he now preferred an ascot, or dress cravat, knotted inside the fur shawl-collar of a pale brown leather shortie overcoat, styled after the smoking jackets of Pall Mall clubmen. Maria Elena had recently bought him a set of polka-dot ascots in various dark colors with matching breast-pocket handkerchiefs. He carried his toilet articles in a handsome brown leather overnight bag with a zip-up side compartment where he kept his .22 pistol. To make the bag more comfortable to carry, he'd bound its handle with white adhesive tape.

When it was time to leave, he found that Maria Elena had also packed a suitcase and had it waiting by the front door. "I told him that I was feeling fine, that the morning sickness had gone away, but he knew that wasn't true and he wouldn't let me go with him. He was as upset about saying goodbye as I was. But he was determined to get that money.

"I kept saying to him, 'I don't want you to go, I don't want you to go.' One thing I always have in my mind, and that I'll always regret, is that I wasn't more determined, that I didn't insist more. Because I know that if I'd gone with him, Buddy would never have taken that plane."

☆　☆　☆

The "Winter Dance Party's" two other headline acts were newcomers to the pop business, each illustrating how unpredictable was the formula for chart success on the cusp of 1958–59.

In Ritchie Valens, aka Richard Valenzuela, a teen idol had at last emerged from America's vast and varied Hispanic culture. A seventeen-year-old Californian of Mexican–Indian ancestry, Valens was a prolific songwriter and a talented guitarist, singing in a flamenco-high voice that belied his stocky build and rather sullen looks. His debut single, "Come On, Let's Go," had been a minor U.S. hit the previous autumn and reached the British Top 10 in a cover version by Tommy Steele. In December, he had seen both sides of his second single leap simultaneously onto the American charts: one, a puppy-love ballad called "Donna," the other a fiesta-happy torrent of pidgin Spanish called "La Bamba."

As great a contrast with Ritchie Valens as Hardy with Laurel was twenty-eight-year-old J. P. Richardson, "The Big Bopper," a bulkily built deejay-turned-vocalist from Beaumont, Texas. In September, Richardson had made the Top 10 with "Chantilly Lace," a telephone monologue to a prospective date, picturing her decked out in that whipped-cream style of French lace "with a purty face and a ponytail, hangin' down." Rock 'n' roll thus far had not produced a purely comic performer—at least not one consciously so—and the Bopper more than filled the bill with his outsize Stetson and ankle-length fur coat, his expression of pop-eyed lasciviousness, his growly-bass catchphrases "Hel-lo, Bay-bee!" and "You *know* what I like!"

The other two acts on the bill had been chosen to supplement what otherwise would have been a rather meager diet of sex appeal. Fourth in precedence were Dion and the Belmonts, the New York vocal quartet whose peach-fuzz doo-wop harmonies belied their evolution from Italian street gangs in the Bronx. Bottom of the bill was Frankie Sardo, another Italian American, short on vocal ability but irresistible to most females under eighteen.

After a brief rehearsal period in Chicago, the tour opened on January 23 at George Devine's Million Dollar Ballroom, Milwaukee. Most of the subsequent shows were to be at ballrooms of the type that Buddy and Tommy Allsup had played on the "Summer Dance Party," in the same kind of small towns bordering on scenic lakes or forests. But now the lakes were frozen solid and the forests in the grip of a winter that made even New York's seem mild by comparison. The states of Minnesota, Wisconsin, and Iowa were bound into one immense, featureless tundra, bombarded by incessant blizzards, littered with abandoned cars and struggling snowplows, swept by wicked winds like voices moaning out of some vast echo chamber. Temperatures as low as those of deepest Siberia, thirty degrees below zero, were by no means uncommon.

On the "Winter Dance Party's" black and yellow poster, "Buddy Holly and the Crickets" appears at the top with a small inset picture of Buddy, flanked by Ritchie Valens on the left and the Big Bopper on the right. Since none of the other acts had backup bands, Tommy Allsup, Waylon Jennings, and Carl Bunch acted as sidemen for the whole show. The three were outfitted with Buddy's usual fastidiousness in black jackets and gray slacks, with ascots instead of ties. Performing in a line, with their clerkly dress and solid guitars, Buddy, Tommy, and Waylon provided the first inkling of how every guitar "beat group" would look in the first half of the next decade.

Buddy's nightly set mixed his own songs with rock 'n' roll classics such as "Be-Bop-A-Lula" and "Whole Lotta Shakin'," and country songs from his teenage years, like "Salty Dog Blues." He seemed more concerned with having fun than pushing "Heartbeat" and "It Doesn't Matter Anymore," even though both were included. He began each performance alone on the stage, an immaculately coiffed and tailored figure, strumming his guitar and singing another big hit of the hour, Billy Grammer's "Gotta Travel On." For Buddy, doubtless, the lyric echoed his feeling that his long fallow period was nearing an end and he'd soon be up and running again; with hindsight it has a sadly different resonance.

GAC had drawn up the itinerary in customary haphazard fashion, scheduling appearances in the order they were booked and with blithe disregard of geographical logic. The result was a continual crisscrossing zigzag in and out of three states, with each one-night stand separated by distances of up to 400 miles. This would have been fatiguing enough in summer; in the Midwest's sub-Arctic January, it was purgatorial. As often as not, after their show there would be no time for the "Winter Dance Party" troupe to check in to a hotel; instead, they would be herded straight back onto their bus for a nonstop journey lasting through the night and most of the following day to reach their next gig on schedule.

The transportation provided on earlier GAC tours, while never the lap of luxury, had at least always been reliable. But in these days of shrinking margins, rock 'n' roll promoters were out to save every penny. The contract for bussing the "Winter Dance Party" through the Siberian Midwest had gone to a charter company offering cut-rate prices and a fleet to match. The bus in which they started their journey lasted only a few hours on the icy highways before grinding and sputtering to a stop. The fault proved beyond the ability of any local mechanic to repair, and the whole troupe had to disembark, unload their equipment themselves, and huddle in what warmth they could find while their road manager, Sam Geller, contacted the charter company and a substitute vehicle was found.

The second bus proved little better than the first and, likewise, had to be replaced after barely a day's travel. A third was summoned up, but it, too, quickly fell by the wayside—as did a fourth, a fifth, and, unbelievably, a sixth, and a seventh. They were indeed a sorry load of clapped-out junk, with engines unequal to the appalling road conditions, and heaters which barely mitigated the ferocious cold that seeped through their ice-blank windows. Each long wait for yet another replacement in the middle of snow-drifted nowhere put additional strain on an already stressful itinerary, cutting into the musicians' vestigial rest periods, condemning them to longer and longer spells on the move as their black driver, murmuring prayers for the health of his latest carburetor, struggled to make up lost time. After the fifth or sixth breakdown, the only replacement that could be found was a yellow school bus with hard metal seats. But its heater was, at least, noisily efficient.

Rock stars of today would not put up with such conditions for five minutes. But rock stars of 1959 were an infinitely hardier, more philosophical breed. With amazing good grace, the "Winter Dance Party" troupe allowed themselves to be decanted into one rattletrap vehicle after another; resignedly hunkering down in their thin coats for another six or seven hours with poor or nonexistent heat; keeping up their spirits with card games and jam sessions even when fingers grew almost too numb to deal the next hand or shape a guitar chord. However bad the weather and chaotic the schedule, no one even thought of "blowing out" the tour. They considered themselves to be in show business as much as in rock 'n' roll and, as everyone knew, the show must go on.

At each nighttime oasis of colored neon and polished dance floor, they were greeted by an audience numbering between 1,000 and 1,500, many of whom had driven almost as far, through weather just as atrocious. To these Wisconsin, Minnesota, and Iowa teenagers, locked up in their hibernating communities for months on end, live entertainment of any kind was an event little short of miraculous. As cold and exhausted as the musicians felt, it was hard not to respond to the wild welcome they received each night by playing to the limit.

Common adversity bonded the five acts together: despite the difference in their styles, all soon became friends. Five of the ten performers— Buddy, Tommy Allsup, Waylon Jennings, Carl Bunch, and the Big Bopper —were country boys from the Southwest, which made for unanimity in humor and outlook. Only Dion and the Belmonts, the cliquish and self-contained New Yorkers, held themselves slightly aloof. "They seemed a little bit like foreigners to the rest of us," Tommy Allsup remembers.

The Big Bopper kept everyone feeling "real loose, like a long-neck goose" with his constant stream of jokes and deejay wordplay. J. P., or "Jape" as the others called him, overflowed the stage each night in his big Stetson and a tentlike leopardskin jacket he called Melvin. As well as a hilarious performer, he was a talented songwriter, having written "Running Bear" for Johnny Preston as well as "Chantilly Lace" and its follow-up, "Big Bopper's Wedding." The previous April, on his home station, KTRM in Beaumont, he had set a new world record for being continuously on the air, spinning discs and wisecracking for 122 hours, 8 minutes —an achievement proudly engraved on the back of his wristwatch. For all his outrageous flirting, he was a devoted family man and, like Buddy, soon to be a father.

The Bopper had been booked to open in cabaret in Las Vegas straight after the "Winter Dance Party," and was racking his brains for visual gimmicks to grab his audience's attention like the huge "Hel-lo, Bay-bee!" at the start of "Chantilly Lace." Over needlessly cold beers in a wayside bar one night, Tommy Allsup and Waylon Jennings came up with a suggestion. "We knew a midget in Hobbs, New Mexico, who played the bass and sang real well," Tommy remembers. "So we called him up from where we were and fixed for him to be in the Bopper's Vegas act. The idea was for the emcee to announce 'the Big Bopper' and then for this little guy to come running out on to the stage."

Even though the Bopper was six years his senior, Buddy seemed the elder statesman of the party in his chunky new Faiosa glasses and fur-collared coat. To his teenage co-stars, he was a self-controlled, abstemious figure who preferred to be alone in his hotel room—when there *was* a hotel room—rather than joining the others to shoot the bull down in the bar or coffee shop. Because of his stomach condition, he now ate little and cautiously, and drank no alcohol, not even beer. Since his marriage, he had also given up smoking, although that resolution proved impossible to maintain on the endless bus journeys when everyone around him lit up all the time and the flare of a match provided significant extra warmth. A set of snapshots taken in a wayside photographic booth show him with Waylon Jennings, flourishing a cigarette and sticking out his tongue like a defiant schoolboy.

He was obviously missing Maria Elena, about whom he talked continually to Waylon and Tommy Allsup. But he was exhilarated, too, by the reception he got onstage every night and the realization he could still pull off a first-class performance without the security blanket of J. I. Allison and Joe B. Mauldin wrapped around him. "He wasn't uptight, the way he'd been on the 'Summer Dance Party,'" Tommy remembers. "He felt really good about being free of Norman Petty. He was always talking about the plans he had: the new studio . . . his European tour. He just seemed like he was about to explode."

He had been mildy apprehensive about working with seventeen-year-old Ritchie Valens, a chart-topper as precocious in early 1959 as Paul Anka had been in late 1957. Ritchie certainly looked the consummate young punk in his frilly turquoise satin shirt and silver-studded black bolero and vaquero pants. But he showed none of the abrasive arrogance the Boy Millionaire had at his age. "He was a great kid," Tommy Allsup says. "He'd grown up being like a father to the younger kids in his neighborhood, playing guitar for 'em, singing to 'em, telling 'em stories. But he wasn't one of those who know it all. He asked questions all the time. He wanted to learn about everything."

Ritchie looked up to Buddy in much the way Buddy had once looked up to Elvis. He played a sunburst Fender Stratocaster exactly like Buddy's, and had included yet another passing homage to "Peggy Sue" in his song "Ooh, My Head." Such hero worship is not always gratifying, especially if one's fan and disciple happens to be doing better on the charts than one is oneself. But Buddy was as incapable as ever of resenting another musician's success. He admired the chunky teenager's multifaceted talent and warmed to his high spirits and appetite for life. From their long chats on icy-windowed buses evolved yet another plan for the golden age that was to begin as soon as this slushy, shivery tour had ended. Ritchie would join Waylon Jennings and Lou Giordano on Prism Records and Buddy would produce his sessions personally.

Although Buddy had mentioned his dispute with Norman Petty to Waylon and Tommy, neither guessed the anxiety it was causing him, especially since he had not said a word about Maria Elena's pregnancy. Twice a day, at least, he would struggle to a pay phone and place a long-distance call to her in New York, hoping there might be further news about his royalties from George Schiffer at Harold Orenstein's office. "He'd call me around noon from the road, then at night from the place where they were playing," Maria Elena remembers. "That was how I met Ritchie Valens: Buddy introduced us over the phone and said he was going to produce him and that Ritchie would be coming to stay with us in New York. When Buddy went onstage, he'd get Ritchie to hold the phone, so that I could hear him singing 'True Love Ways.' I always knew he was singing that one just for me."

The news from George Schiffer, relayed by Maria Elena, was of further delay and complication. Back in the distant days of late 1957 when the Crickets first became a hot attraction, they had hired a New York agent named Mannie Greenfield to work for them in the several managerial areas where Norman Petty had neither experience nor the inclination to acquire it. Greenfield had proved a valuable ally, getting them their first exposure on national television and arranging their tour of Britain through his good friends Lew and Leslie Grade. The agreement had been a verbal one only, and in the autumn of 1958, just before Buddy's parting from J. I. and Joe B., a dispute had arisen over the rate of commission they had promised Greenfield. They said it was 5 percent of all fees he negotiated on their behalf. Greenfield claimed the figure was 5 percent of all their performance earnings during the period he represented them.

Though Buddy had made the original deal with Greenfield, Petty had always worked in friendly cooperation with him and it was to Petty, as the Crickets' manager, that Greenfield addressed his complaint. In January 1959, having obtained no satisfaction after almost four months, Greenfield began legal action against Petty, claiming $10,000 in unpaid commissions. New York law provided that when one party in a lawsuit resided outside the state, all monies in contention could be attached, or frozen, pending resolution of the case. On January 23, the day the "Winter Dance Party" kicked off in Milwaukee, Greenfield's lawyers served a writ of attachment on Coral-Brunswick Records, suspending payment of further royalties to Buddy Holly and the Crickets. The same was done to Peer-Southern Music and its sister company Southern Music in respect to publishing royalties.

Coral-Brunswick had in fact already suspended payment of all Crickets and Buddy royalties at the request of Buddy's lawyer, George Schiffer. On January 26, as Buddy sat in yet another frozen, fainthearted bus, en route to Fournier's Ballroom in Eau Claire, Wisconsin, Petty dictated a plaintive letter to Coral-Brunswick's Isabelle Marks about the company's decision to cooperate with Schiffer. He contended it was wrong to withhold royalties due the Crickets in a legal dispute involving Buddy since, by failing to sign the group's original Brunswick contract, Buddy had legally never been a Cricket.

He was also anxious to correct what he called "the misapprehension" that the Crickets' royalties from Brunswick and Buddy's from Coral were merely channeled through him to their collective bank account and administered by him under power of attorney. The agreement he had made with Coral-Brunswick in March 1957 governing the sale of their record masters stipulated that all record royalties were to be "paid to the order of Norman Petty and statements rendered to him." This explained why the bulk of Buddy's earnings were not in the Buddy Holly and the Crickets account, as he'd believed all these months, but in that of the Norman Petty Agency, for Petty alone to disburse as and when he felt inclined.

The following day, January 27, as Buddy was en route to the Fiesta Ballroom in Montevideo, Minnesota, George Schiffer finally managed to get Petty on the telephone. Petty tape-recorded their conversation and had the recording transcribed by Norma Jean; its eight closely typed pages are among the relics in Clovis Man's cave. After elaborate opening pleasantries, Schiffer renews his efforts to set up a face-to-face meeting with Petty, inquiring whether he has plans to visit New York in the near future. Petty replies that he doesn't, but invites the lawyer to come and see him and the "beautiful country" in New Mexico. He insists that he doesn't want to be "hard to get along with" and agrees to give Schiffer what facts and figures he can over the telephone. His tone when referring to Buddy is that of a long-suffering adult, discussing some illogical, overdemanding child. He says that Buddy, "while an outstanding talent does have a tendency to want to make contracts and then get out of them," citing the contractual problems with Decca and Cedarwood publishing which he, Petty, had had to sort out before Buddy could begin recording in Clovis.

About the money owed to Buddy he is surprisingly forthcoming and precise. He tells Schiffer that Buddy's total earnings from Coral-Brunswick are in the region of $70,000. Groping for the relevant papers on his desk, he is more specific still: the checks from the Buddy Holly and the Crickets account he has signed on Buddy's behalf total $33,215.53, leaving a balance to be paid of $35,926. He claims that Buddy still owes J. I. and Joe B. $10,000 in performance fees and that a further $10,000 has been put aside, with Buddy's consent, in case they should have to pay out in the Mannie Greenfield case.

Speaking to Schiffer as one man of the world to another, he portrays Buddy as a feckless, chaotic, and even dishonest character who kept back all the Crickets' performance money instead of paying it into their account, spending lavishly on himself, gambling intemperately, and willfully refusing to garner a single receipt to be offset against income tax (an untruth refuted by the bulging folders of receipts that probably lie directly in his sightline). He continues aggrievedly that Buddy isn't the only one to be owed money; he himself hasn't yet been paid the $2,000 for the Ampex tape-recorder and microphone he sold Buddy secondhand the previous autumn, even though he's holding some $7,000 for Buddy as start-up funds for the Prism organization. "Technically [Buddy] has stolen equipment as far as my insurance company is concerned, if we wanted to get nasty." He then rather pointedly asks Schiffer where Buddy is at this moment:

SCHIFFER: He's out of town and he's moving around a bit. I can get in touch with his wife. She's . . .

PETTY: Well, I would appreciate you finding out because I would like to dispose of this immediately.

SCHIFFER: Yes, but it may be . . . as I say . . . you might probably . . . I mean this is a relatively small matter.

PETTY: Now let me ask you this . . . Our lawyer here is contending like you that the boys are entitled to the name . . . The Crickets. Now we have instructed Billboard and the other magazines not to accept the name The Crickets until this thing is settled. . . . I don't believe it is fair on your behalf to assume you already have the name The Crickets when neither one of us knows for sure. Probably we'll have to take it to court to decide, which is all right with us.

SCHIFFER: Well, you see, that's something else again which I think we should discuss in person because I'm not sure of anything at the moment except what Buddy has told me and what I can see from the sharing arrangements and what I know of the history of The Crickets. Buddy was the most important man in there.

PETTY: According to Buddy.
SCHIFFER: Beg pardon?
PETTY: According to Buddy.

Schiffer complains that, despite repeated requests, he still has not received a full list of Buddy's compositions published through Nor Va Jak. Petty promises to forward a copy of every relevant contract. He then tries to persuade Schiffer not to insist on the freezing of the royalties from Coral-Brunswick. But Schiffer affably stands firm. Petty's only weapon of reprisal is the mild, polite little note that Buddy had sent him December 8:

PETTY: Oh, Buddy was asking about his writer's contract, so you can tell him . . . You know, the personal writer's contract with us.
SCHIFFER: Yes.
PETTY: Well, I prefer to leave that status quo, too, until we get some of these matters solved.

On Friday, January 30, the "Winter Dance Party" bus chasséd down the frozen highway to play the Laramar Ballroom in Fort Dodge, Iowa. When Buddy called Maria Elena that lunchtime, she had to break it to him that, after almost four weeks, there still was no sign of "It Doesn't Matter Anymore" in *Billboard*'s Hot 100. Buddy made a brave show of not being worried, telling her it would probably turn out to be another sleeper like "That'll Be the Day." But inwardly he resigned himself to having missed yet again. That night, close to despair, he called his friend Eddie Cochran, who was recording in the enviable warmth of California. "Eddie came back from the phone really concerned," Cochran's soon-to-be fiancée, Sharon Sheeley, remembers. "He said that Buddy sounded really down and thought it was all over in the charts for him. I think Eddie was the only friend he had who was close enough for him to be able to admit something like that. And Eddie, of course, wouldn't hear of it. 'Don't be a fool,' he told Buddy. 'You're the best there is. You'll be back up there again soon.'"

The following night, the "Winter Dance Party" played the National Guard Armory in Duluth, Minnesota. Among the 2,000 fans who had paid $2 each to be there was a scrawny teenager named Bobby Zimmerman from the nearby town of Hibbing. In a few months, he would change his surname to Dylan in homage to Dylan Thomas, sign with Columbia Records, and begin his turbulent metamorphosis into rock's greatest poet, preacher, and satirist. Between the young Bob Dylan and the young Buddy Holly there is almost uncanny similarity: both started out as unprepossessing country boys, both had unstoppable energy and self belief, both had girlfriends named Echo (in Dylan's case, Echo Helstrom). The critic Greil Marcus has noted how indebted was Dylan's raucous, malleable phrasing to Buddy's, especially on primeval rock 'n' roll numbers like "Midnight Shift." As for Dylan himself, through the eras of his perpetual self-reinvention, almost the only memory he has ever admitted to is seeing Buddy onstage that snowy night at the Duluth Armory. "Buddy was great," he told a *Rolling Stone* interviewer in 1980. "Buddy was fantastic."

It seemed that conditions for the "Winter Dance Party" could get no worse, but still they did. In the early hours of Sunday, February 1, the troupe was traveling from Duluth to Appleton, Wisconsin, a journey of 300 miles, in their eighth bus since leaving Milwaukee. As it toiled up a hill on Route 51, in the midst of the "Great North Woods" mentioned in Dylan's "Tangled Up in Blue," the vehicle just died. A piston had gone through the engine block. The performers were marooned for several hours in pitch darkness with no heat, an outside temperature of 30 below, and a real danger of being attacked by bears. The only warmth that could be obtained came from hip flasks and setting fire to newspapers in the aisle.

Yet, somehow or other, they managed to stay cheerful. Buddy and the previously standoffish Dion formed a friendship by huddling under the same blanket and swapping stories of their respective boyhoods in West Texas and the Bronx. Dion has since said that Buddy was one of the very few musicians he ever looked up to. The streetwise New Yorker was also impressed to learn that the brown leather overnight bag Buddy had stowed in the rack above their heads had a .22-caliber pistol concealed in its side pocket.

When a police truck finally came to their rescue, Carl Bunch, the drummer in Buddy's band, was found to have severely frostbitten feet and was removed to the Grand View Hospital just across the Wisconsin border in Ironwood, Michigan. The others were ferried by car to the nearby town of Hurley, where the only place they could find a hot meal, the Club Carnival, refused service to their black bus driver. The afternoon's matinee performance at the Cinderella Ballroom in Appleton was canceled; while their bus was fitted with a new engine, Buddy and some of the others went on to the next stop, Green Bay, Wisconsin, via the Chicago-Northwestern Railroad.

Even the hospitalization of the troupe's only professional drummer did not stop the "Winter Dance Party" that evening at Green Bay's Riverside Ballroom. Several of the other musicians, Buddy included, were more than passable drummers, and the various acts were already well used to mixing and matching. Among the backstage crowd that night was a local photographer named Larry Matti, whose famous portfolio records the cheery scene in all too living color: Here is Ritchie, in flamenco turquoise, silver, and black, caught in a nest of piled-up chairs. Here is the Bopper, crew-cut and leopardskin-clad, with a maidenly Green Bay girl on each arm, still clowning indefatigably despite an obvious heavy head cold. Here is Buddy, looking less like a rock 'n' roller than some classical violinist with his fur-collared coat and red polka-dot ascot. Another backstage photographer snapped him ready to travel on yet again, cradling his leather overnight bag so that one can see the white adhesive tape around its handle.

The whole company was at the lowest possible ebb, riddled with coughs and sniffles, and, by now, dirty and scruffy as well as exhausted. Eight days of virtually nonstop travel had left no time to have their stage outfits dry-cleaned and their shirts and underwear laundered. The day after Green Bay, February 2, had originally been blank on the schedule, allowing a few hours to get thoroughly warm, have their laundry done, and catch up on lost sleep. That respite had now vanished, thanks to a late booking by the Surf Ballroom in Clear Lake, Iowa. Clear Lake lay only about a hundred miles northeast of Fort Dodge, where they had performed three nights earlier: arranging the dates in logical sequence would have given them an easy journey, punctuated by a night's rest. Instead they were now faced with a 350-mile journey along hazardous roads from the easternmost edge of Wisconsin, across eastern Minnesota, into northern Iowa. And still there was to be no letup. On the following night, February 3, they were booked to appear at the National Guard Armory in Moorhead, Minnesota, 400 miles northwest of Clear Lake. To be in Moorhead by the early evening of February 3 meant setting off directly after their Clear Lake show—in other words, yet another through-the-night marathon on an underheated, unreliable bus.

The journey from Green Bay, Wisconsin, to Clear Lake, Iowa, took most of the daylight hours of Monday, February 2. There was time only for a brief stop at an Army surplus store where, fearing a repetition of the North Woods incident, the Big Bopper bought himself a well-padded sleeping bag. Buddy, as usual, seized the chance to phone New York. "When he got back on board the bus, he was really upset," Tommy Allsup remembers. "He said 'When this tour's over, I'm going back to Clovis and I'm going to kick Norman Petty's ass. I'm going to get my money out of that studio, one way or the other.' "

There was yet more bus trouble en route, and the "Winter Dance Party" did not reach Clear Lake until around 7 P.M., less than an hour before the first of the two shows they were scheduled to give that evening. Clear Lake proved to be the smallest and remotest venue on the tour yet, a wooded hamlet scattered along the shores of the 3,600-acre lake for which it was named. During summer, the lake made the town a popular resort, swelling its minuscule population six- or sevenfold. In the premature darkness of Monday, February 2, it revealed little but an expanse of pack ice ringed by shut-up vacation chalets half-buried in snow. Almost the only lights in the town emanated from the Surf Ballroom, a one-story building in the usual hangarlike style, looking across the highway to the icebound lake.

According to Tommy Allsup, the idea of chartering a plane occurred to Buddy on the way to Clear Lake. The 400-mile onward journey to Moorhead, a night and a day's hard grind by road, would take a light aircraft only two and a half hours. Fastidious about his clothes and grooming as Buddy was, he hated having to recycle his shirts and go onstage with pants not faultlessly pressed. He also urgently wanted to continue the phone conversation that had so upset and angered him that afternoon. Flying to Moorhead would get him there sixteen hours before the following night's show at the Armory: he could sleep in a comfortable bed instead of on a hard bus seat, be warm instead of half-perished with cold, have his laundry and dry cleaning done, and get back on the phone with George Schiffer and Maria Elena.

It was not such a tremendous brainwave for Buddy to have had. On previous tours, he'd flown thousands of miles in every kind of plane, from Pan Am Constellations to rickety DC-3s. The past week's Antarctic odyssey had shown that Midwesterners routinely used aircraft to avoid the frightful conditions on the ground. For the "Winter Dance Party" show in Kenosha, Wisconsin, for example, the emcee, Jim Lounsbury, had come in from Chicago by small plane, a Beechcraft Bonanza. The idea had special appeal now that Buddy had caught the flying bug and intended to qualify as a pilot and crisscross the country in his own Cessna. Admittedly, the snowy night sky over Clear Lake did not look promising for air travel. But once he got an idea in his head, he did not easily let it go.

The glacial expanse of Clear Lake might be heart-shiveringly bleak. But inside the Surf Ballroom, the welcome was even more fervent than usual. Something like 1,300 rock 'n' roll fans had gathered for the "Winter Dance Party," driving on well-chained tires from all over Iowa and points far afield in the neighboring states of South Dakota, Nebraska, and Illinois. As its name suggested, the Surf had little to do with north Iowa scenery: the interior was designed to suggest a Florida beach club, with green-upholstered booths fringing the enormous maple dance floor, and a vaulted ceiling of tropical sky blue on which a projector threw illusions of lazily drifting clouds. Nor was the foot-stomping, petticoat-whirling throng an exclusively teenage one. The Surf's manager, an affable thirty-nine-year-old named Carroll Anderson, liked to promote a family atmosphere, and encouraged parents to accompany their children by letting them in for nothing.

The night's emcee was Bob Hale, a disc jockey on KRIB in nearby Mason City. Hale was struck by the high spirits and good humor of the "Winter Dance Party" troupe, despite the punishing all-day journey they'd just had and the even more punishing all-night journey that lay ahead. Ritchie Valens was euphoric, having just been notified that his song "Donna," written for his high school sweetheart Donna Ludwig, had earned a Gold Record by selling a million copies. Dion and the Belmonts were humming and doo-wopping their next release—and first big hit—"Teenager in Love." Playful arm-wrestling took place for the benefit of a reporter from the *Clear Lake Mirror.* Autographs were signed with customary patience and friendliness; fans who had forgotten to bring autograph books went away with "Ritchie Valens," "The Big Bopper," or "Buddy Holly" written on their hands. Bob Hale found the three stars to be all "warm, classy young men."

As soon as he arrived at the Surf, Buddy asked the manager, Carroll Anderson, what were the chances of chartering a plane to Moorhead that night. It turned out that there was an airport at Mason City, only two miles east of Clear Lake, and that its facilities included a charter and air-taxi company, Dwyer's Flying Service. Anderson knew the proprietor, Jerry Dwyer, personally, and offered to phone him and try to book his services on Buddy's behalf.

Dwyer proved not to be available, however, and Anderson was referred to another pilot with Dwyer's Flying Service, Roger Peterson. Peterson had been at work all day and was supposed to be taking the next day off, but in that era, especially in the Midwest, "flying service" meant what it said. He agreed to take the assignment, despite at that stage not knowing the identity of his passenger or passengers. Buddy's destination, Moorhead, Minnesota, had no airport, but there was one at Fargo, North Dakota, only about ten miles to the west. It was arranged that Buddy would report to the Mason City airport straight after his second performance at the Surf some time around midnight.

The aircraft Peterson would be using had space for three passengers. To defray the fee of $108, Buddy looked among the "Winter Dance Party" for fellow travelers. Dion DiMucci has since said he was one of the first to be offered a seat on the plane for a third of the cost, $36. But he balked at parting with what seemed an enormous sum, the amount his whole family back in New York spent on rent each month. The logical arrangement, quickly reached, was that Buddy should be accompanied by his two remaining band members, Tommy Allsup and Waylon Jennings. The plane would also carry the entire troupe's backlog of dirty laundry, which could then be dealt with in time for the following night's show. The plan also suited the hard-pressed road manager, Sam Geller, who had had to deal with inefficient promoters as well as unreliable buses. Reaching Moorhead a day early meant that Buddy could visit their next venue, the National Guard Armory, and make sure all the arrangements there were in order.

Some time that evening, he called Maria Elena from the pay phone in the Surf's lobby. She remembers him telling her how relieved he was she hadn't come with him on the tour, that it was cold and miserable and chaotic, and conditions seemed to be getting worse all the time. "He mentioned that they were having problems with the bus, and that whenever they arrived anyplace, there was a big mess-up, and so the man who was in charge of the tour had asked if he would go on ahead and check things out. I said, 'That's not your place; why do you have to do that?' But knowing Buddy as I did, he just couldn't stand to see things not done properly. He wanted to fix things right away. And besides, people on the bus were getting sick and he was afraid he might get sick, too."

Maria Elena remembers that he hinted he might fly, but, knowing her fear of small planes, did not say it was to be by charter. "He said, 'I'm going to see if I can get another method of transportation.' I said 'Well, get a commercial flight and get up there.'"

One of the more poignant of the legends clustering around Buddy's final hours concerns the two estranged Crickets, J. I. Allison and Joe B. Mauldin. During the previous week, while the "Winter Dance Party" was trekking through the Midwestern snows, J. I. and Joe B. had been in Clovis, working at Norman Petty's studio with "the new guy," Earl Sinks, taking Buddy's place on vocals, both of them seemingly content for Petty to lay claim to the Crickets' name on their behalf by saying that Buddy had never legally belonged to the group. As legend has it, J. I. and Joe B. were themselves now growing suspicious of Petty and bitterly regretting taking his part rather than Buddy's. Both have since claimed that the breakup was amicable and that Buddy had left the door open for a reunion at any time. "That's what he used to tell us," Joe B. Mauldin says. "'It only takes a phone call.'"

According to legend, it was on this very last night of Buddy's life that his two old friends chose to make that phone call, anxious to bury the hatchet and re-create their old lineup. Early in the evening of February 2, they called Maria Elena in New York and asked her where Buddy was. "They thought I was unhappy with them for going with Norman instead of with Buddy. But I was the first to say how delighted I was that they wanted to get back together. Jerry told me later that they phoned the Surf Ballroom, but it was very noisy and the person who answered couldn't get hold of Buddy, or he'd already left. So they phoned ahead to the next place and left a message for him to call them back. But, of course, he never got the message."

It's certainly possible that J. I. and Joe B. were attempting to reach Buddy simply in the name of friendship, nostalgia, and regret. But the principal message from Clovis that Buddy never received was an impersonal and threatening one, arising from legal dispute over a trademark. Petty's correspondence a few days hence would make mention of "letters and cablegrams which were sent on Monday, February 2, after we learned that Holly was on tour with a group he called The Crickets."

Backstage at the Surf Ballroom, meanwhile, Tommy Allsup and Waylon Jennings both were under pressure to give up their places on the Fargo flight. The Big Bopper went to work on Waylon with all the pop-eyed pathos at his command. For someone of his bulk, the bus rides had been especially uncomfortable and, despite his new sleeping bag, he was dreading that night's twelve- or fourteen-hour trip back up half the length of Minnesota. To add to his discomfort, the head cold he'd been nursing over the past few days was developing into full-blown flu. Reaching Moorhead early would allow him to see a doctor and get a shot of antibiotics that might keep the symptoms at bay for the tour's remaining week. Waylon good-heartedly agreed that the Bopper's need was greater than his. Young and strong as he was, and still intoxicated by being on tour for the very first time, he could face another night on the bus with equanimity.

Ritchie Valens angled for Tommy Allsup's seat, pleading that he'd never flown in a small aircraft before. This was true—but entirely of Ritchie's own choosing. Two years earlier, while he was attending Pacoima Junior High School in the San Fernando Valley, two aircraft had collided directly above the school, crashing down onto its premises and killing two students. Ritchie himself, by chance, had been away from school that day, attending his grandfather's funeral. He'd since had recurrent nightmares about the incident, and vowed never to go up in anything less than a commercial airliner. Tonight at Clear Lake, for some reason, that nagging phobia evaporated. He, too, had a cold, and would have suffered on another all-night bus ride. He needed the spare hour or two in Moorhead to get his hair cut. And anything planned by Buddy and Jape could hardly be other than a great adventure.

Tommy, however, refused to give up his seat on the plane, having an urgent need of his own to be in Fargo ahead of schedule. A registered letter from his mother was at Fargo post office, awaiting collection. Flying up would give him ample time the next day to collect his letter as well as get his dry cleaning done. But Ritchie refused to take no for an answer, and throughout the evening kept riding Tommy with the same question: "Are you gonna let me fly, guy?"

Above the murky ice floes of Clear Lake that night, one thing at least was crystal-clear. Ritchie Valens might have the nation's hottest single; the Big Bopper might have created the No. 1 catchphrase of the hour; Dion DiMucci might be the new, foxy face of rock 'n' roll. But it was someone else who had brought 1,300 people here through the snowdrifts of three states. Bob Hale, the deejay-emcee, was always to remember what an electric thrill ran through the huge ballroom when he announced Buddy Holly. "The reaction was fantastic—just one big surge."

Buddy opened his set, as usual, alone on the stage, slenderly immaculate in his space-age black frames and red polka-dot ascot, strumming the brown Strat that seemed like an extra limb and singing the Billy Grammer hit he liked so much: "I've laid around and played around this old town too long . . ." There was, to be sure, a restless, even impatient air about him that night, as several onlookers would later testify. At the beginning, he made little attempt to woo or amuse the big semicircle of upturned faces before him, bounding from one song to the next with only a husky "Thank you" in between.

Most of his greatest hits were there, the titles now deleted from jukebox menus and radio playlists, milestones that had come almost too quickly on the short, blinding highway of his fame. Each one had its special memories: the cold February night in Clovis, with Larry Welborn and the Tolletts, when they'd got "That'll Be the Day" right at long last . . . the sound of Norman Petty's voice and the smell of his hand lotion . . . Vi working in her flower garden, watched by Squeaky the chihuahua . . . the "Peggy Sue" session, with dust storms raging outside and J. I. Allison playing paradiddles in the lobby alongside the red and white Coke machine . . . the real cricket chirping in the echo chamber on "I'm Gonna Love You Too" . . . the Apollo theater . . . the Brooklyn Paramount marquee . . . Little Richard wanting to "witness" with the old folks . . . Eddie Cochran and his pipe . . . "Oh Boy" and Ed Sullivan . . . *The Arthur Murray Dance Party* . . . "Maybe Baby" and England, half-timbered hotels, shilling-in-slot gas meters, and kissing a girl in Wigan . . . Who knows what visions may have passed before those outsize glasses, glinting under the placid summer sky of the Surf's light show? It would later seem to more than one of his companions that he played and sang with special intensity, almost as if sensing this was a farewell performance.

Good humor and joie de vivre could not long be kept at bay, however. For the finale of Buddy's set, Ritchie and the Big Bopper joined him onstage—an ad hoc trio fated never to dissolve—and the three joined in a hilarious, none-too-expert version of "La Bamba." It's hard to see how Buddy's last number on earth could have been more in character: unenviously singing someone else's song, with a big smile on his face.

The show ended just before midnight, leaving only a few minutes for the three fortunate plane passengers to extricate themselves from autograph-hungry fans, change from their stage suits into everyday clothes, and get out to the Mason City airport. Rather than waste time calling a taxi, Carroll Anderson, the Surf's ever-helpful manager, had offered to drive them there himself. It was only now that Waylon Jennings told Buddy he'd given up his seat on the flight to the Big Bopper. "Well, I hope your ol' bus freezes up," Buddy joked, prompting a riposte that Waylon was to spend almost four decades wishing he could unsay.

"Well, I hope your ol' plane crashes," he grinned back.

Buddy and the Bopper took their seats in Anderson's station wagon, which was backed up to the Surf's stage door, a few yards from the communal band room. Also in the vehicle were Anderson's wife Lucille and eleven-year-old son Tom, who had asked to go along for the ride. Emcee Bob Hale and his wife were there, too, despite the freezing conditions and flurrying snow, to see the party off.

The third person on the flight, Tommy Allsup, was still somewhere inside attending to details which, in later eras, would be left to half a dozen roadies. The plane was too small to carry his and Buddy's Stratocasters, so they had to be put on the bus, where Waylon had promised to keep a special eye on them. "I came out and put my satchel full of dirty shirts in the back of the station wagon," Allsup remembers. "Buddy was in front and the Bopper was in the second seat. Then Buddy asked me to go back to the dressing room and check that we hadn't left anything behind. Because a couple of days before, Carl Bunch, our drummer, had left his clothes bag hanging somewhere. And I needed to double-check that our amps had gotten safely on to the bus.

"When I went back inside, Ritchie was still there, signing autographs. He said, 'Are you going to let me fly, guy?' and I said, 'No.' 'Come on,' he said, 'let's flip a coin for it.' I don't know why, because I'd been telling him 'no' all evening, but I pulled a half-dollar out of my pocket. I've never understood what made me. It was like the solo on 'It's So Easy'; it just happened. I flipped the fifty-cent piece and said, 'Call it.' Ritchie said 'Heads,' and it came down heads."

According to other bystanders, the silver face of Benjamin Franklin that foreshadowed his death was greeted by Ritchie as the first real stroke of luck in his seventeen-year life. "Hey!" he exulted. "That's the first thing I ever won!"

Tommy Allsup returned to the station wagon and laconically retrieved his bag from the back seat. "I said, 'Ritchie'll be here in a minute—he's going to go,' and Buddy said, 'What are you talking about?' I said, 'We just flipped a coin, I lost, and he's going to fly in my place.' Then I asked Buddy if, when he got in to Fargo, he'd pick up the registered letter from my mom that was waiting for me at the post office there. 'It's got a check in it,' I said, 'and if I go up on the bus, I may not have time to get it.'

"Buddy said, 'Yeah, I'll pick it up, but they won't let me have it unless I show them your ID. Give me your driver's license.' They were needing to be away to make the flight, so, rather than waste time hunting through my wallet for my driver's license, I said, 'Here—take my wallet.' I held it out to Buddy and he stuck it inside his coat."

☆   ☆   ☆

Mason City's municipal airport in those days was a stark, windswept place comprising a scattering of hangars, a rudimentary passenger terminal, and a control tower of strictly limited technological competence. In air-traffic terms, Mason City ranked only as an "omni station," meaning that it did not possess radar, but put out an omnidirectional beam, which incoming aircraft had to locate and lock on to by themselves.

Such life as could be found at the Mason City airport in early 1959 derived largely from Dwyer's Flying Service and its proprietor, Hubert J. ("Jerry") Dwyer. Dwyer's fleet of six charter planes generated most of the airport's employment; he also bought and sold aircraft ("Your friendly Cessna dealer") and held the license for the tower's fixed-base ground-to-air radio. A rugged, short-spoken individual, Jerry Dwyer already had little cause to bless the Iowa weather. A tornado in the district some years earlier had all but wiped out his business. By the beginning of 1959, he'd just about built it back up to where it was before.

Dwyer had spent that Monday evening of February 2 at a Chamber of Commerce meeting in Mason City. Arriving home around 9:30, he learned from his children's babysitter that Carroll Anderson of the Surf Ballroom had been trying to reach him to book a flight for "three entertainers" after their night's show. As the babysitter had not known how to reach Dwyer, the inquiry had been referred to his employee, Roger Peterson. Peterson was out when Dwyer called his home, but his wife confirmed that he'd accepted the charter to Fargo. Dwyer left word for Peterson to call him if he needed help with getting the chosen aircraft out of its hangar, as there was another one parked in front of it.

Folks in northern Iowa are no less devout than those in West Texas. Dwyer drove over to pick up his wife from a church meeting and, at 10:10 P.M., retired to bed. Around 11:30, he got a phone call from Peterson, who did need help in getting the plane out. Conscientiously, Dwyer rose, dressed, and drove to the lonely little airport complex. There, at 11:45, he rendezvoused with his pilot, a young man with the Midwest's archetypal Scandinavian looks, fair-haired rubicund and just twenty-one years old.

Since receiving the Surf's call, Peterson had been in regular touch with the control tower, checking weather conditions there and at Fargo and the forecasts for the rest of the night. Though hardly good, the weather was not severe enough to curtail flying, especially not in this hardy part of the world. The temperature was 18 degrees with light snow flurries, winds gusting at 38 mph, a cloud ceiling of 4,000 feet, and visibility between 6 and 10 miles. At Fargo, 400 miles to the north, conditions were about the same; however, Mason City's controller had just received warning of a weather front expected to move into the Fargo area around 3 A.M., the flight's estimated time of arrival. After delivering his passengers, Peterson had planned to fly straight back to Mason City. But, with deteriorating weather conditions in prospect, Dwyer told him he should be prepared to stay in Fargo overnight.

After giving the chosen aircraft a thorough inspection, Dwyer and Peterson rolled it out of its hangar onto the snowy forecourt. It was a single-engine Beechcraft Bonanza—the same make and type as had delivered the "Winter Dance Party's" emcee to their Kenosha gig—jauntily striped in red and white with a V-shaped tail and the wing registration N3794N. It was a long way from brand-new, having been manufactured in 1947 and acquired fifth- or sixth-hand by Dwyer in July 1958 after eleven years' continuous service, with something like 1,200 flying hours to its credit. However, Dwyer's team maintained it well: it had received a major overhaul on January 2 and, since then, had logged only about 40 hours in the air. Three days previously, a local sheriff's deputy had taken it up for a spin and pronounced it to be in first-class mechanical order.

The Bonanza was fueled from Dwyer's private gas pump, and Roger Peterson climbed into the cockpit and started the propeller to warm it up. Despite his youth, Peterson seemed more than equal to the task ahead. He had been flying since the age of seventeen and had qualified as a private pilot in October 1955, as a commercial one in April 1958, and as an instructor only a week before tonight. He had logged a total of 710.45

flying hours, 318 as an air-taxi driver and 37.35 night-flying as pilot in command. Two hundred of these flying hours had been logged in the past ninety days, without mishap or incident. Of all Dwyer's charter planes, Peterson knew the red and white Beechcraft Bonanza best: it had been bought specifically for him to use and he had so far flown something over 130 hours in it. He was an easygoing, personable, and—as we can already deduce—obliging young man, frequently praised by passengers for his care and consideration. Jerry Dwyer deemed him "experienced and very competent."

But there were things about Roger Peterson that would have caused his passengers extreme disquiet had they known of them. He suffered from "a hearing disability" in his right ear—or, in plain speech, was partially deaf. Such a handicap obviously had serious implications for a flyer's coordination and sense of balance. Yet the civil aviation authorities of the day had seemed curiously unperturbed about it, allowing Peterson to ascend the ladder from private pilot through commercial pilot to instructor with no sanction worse than a "waiver," or official acknowledgment that his senses were partly impaired, in the margin of his license. Whether any of those whom he ferried across Iowa or taught to fly in the skies above Clear Lake would have endorsed that waiver is highly debatable.

Flying by day in clear weather, with the Iowa wheatfields stretching to infinity all around, Peterson was a skilled, careful, cool, and confident pilot. But when he flew at night or was enveloped suddenly by cloud or fog, an alarmingly different personality revealed itself. On the tests in flying by instruments alone that had punctuated Peterson's career, his instructors had rated him "below average." The tests by their nature simulated emergency in the cockpit: a sudden blank-out of all visibility, demanding instant change from reliance on one's senses to total cool-headed accuracy in reading and correlating half a dozen different gauges and dials. At such moments of controlled crisis, Peterson invariably re-acted badly, suffering attacks of panic and disorientation, muddling and misreading his instruments, failing to tune and use his radio properly and follow air-traffic-control procedures, even on occasion letting the aircraft slip out of his control and go into "diving spirals to the right."

Vertigo, the nauseous, tingling horror of finding oneself in a high place, is the very last malady from which any pilot should suffer. But it was a term frequently used in connection with Roger Peterson. Just the previous month, he'd taken yet another instrument test and failed: his instructor then had been worried by his "false courage," proneness to vertigo, susceptibility to distraction, and tendency to become "upset and confused" and to "let the plane get away from him." Along with the hearing-disability waiver, his license bore a notation that in instrument reading, "holder does not meet night-time requirements."

Thirty-seven years ago, the regulations governing pilots' rest periods were far less stringent than they are today: in rural Iowa, they barely existed at all. On the evening that Roger Peterson was approached to make an after-midnight flight, he had already been up between seventeen and eighteen hours. He had spent a strenuous working day, from 8 A.M. to 5 P.M., on aircraft maintenance inside Dwyer's hangar, eaten dinner at home, then gone to Mason City for a Jaycee (Junior Chamber of Commerce) meeting, which was where Carroll Anderson contacted him. Dwyer's chief mechanic, Charles E. McGlothlen, had been with Peterson at the meeting and had lent him his car to go to the airport and check the meteorological reports. About 9:30, McGlothlen and his wife had got together with Peterson and his wife of four months, DeAnn, for coffee and pie at the Petersons' home. McGlothlen would later testify that when they parted around 10 P.M., Peterson did not seem tired and that he'd been "in a very good mood all the time."

The night's weather conditions en route to Fargo certainly would have presented no problem to any pilot of all-around competence, like Jerry Dwyer. But to one with Roger Peterson's peculiar handicaps, they were ominous in the extreme. The front moving in on North Dakota might bring with it blizzards, fog, or extensive cloud. To avoid flying by instruments alone, which he was unqualified as well as deeply reluctant to do, Peterson would in effect be racing the front to Fargo. Even the relatively good weather around Mason City offered warning and hazard, or should have, to him. The cloud ceiling had by now lifted to 6,000 feet, but for most of its journey the Bonanza would need to maintain an altitude of at least 7,000 feet. Peterson thus faced the options of climbing through the cloud ceiling, which again would mean flying by instruments, or remaining dangerously below it. Any one of these considerations should have been sufficient for Jerry Dwyer to send Peterson home to his young wife and take over the charter himself. But it didn't happen.

Around 12:40 A.M., Carroll Anderson's crowded station wagon crunched to a stop outside Dwyer's Flying Service. Not until the "three entertainers" walked into Jerry Dwyer's office did he realize his clients weren't middle-aged musicians from the dance bands the Surf usually presented, but nationally famous rock 'n' roll stars. The gruff charter boss had no love of teenage music, and expected rock 'n' rollers to be as the media portrayed them: unruly, disrespectful louts who, at this late hour, could be expected to be blind drunk into the bargain. Instead, he found himself greeting "three real nice kids," good-humored and high-spirited but polite, full of gratitude for his firm's effort on their behalf and without the smallest taint of booze on their breath. Young Roger Peterson, for his part, was elated. A devout rock 'n' roll fan, he particularly admired Buddy, but was equally thrilled to shake hands with Ritchie Valens and the Big Bopper and contemplate having all three to himself up in the air for the next couple of hours.

There was almost a party atmosphere in Dwyer's office as each passenger paid his $36 fare and tickets and receipts were written out. Buddy was in especially good spirits and looking forward to the flight even more than was the triumphant Ritchie. He spent some minutes discussing small planes with Dwyer, mentioning that his brother Larry had qualified as a pilot three weeks previously and that he himself intended to do the same and buy himself a Cessna. On the wall hung a map of the United States with a pencil attached to it by string. In the remaining couple of minutes before their flight was called, each star in turn traced the distance from Mason City to his home turf, Ritchie's in the San Fernando Valley, the Bopper's in Beaumont, Texas, Buddy's in Lubbock. Alas, they were closer than they knew.

The dirty laundry they were taking to Fargo on their bus-bound colleagues' behalf, added to their own satchels and suitcases, made an unusually large amount of baggage for a three-passenger flight, forty-two pounds in all. Though his night's obligations were already more than discharged, Carroll Anderson lingered to lend a hand in loading the luggage compartment, situated midway in the belly of the plane. The overflow, including J. P. Richardson's guitar, was packed into the cockpit. Halfway through the loading process, Buddy realized that he'd left his leather overnight bag in Anderson's station wagon and had to run back to retrieve it. The passengers were on the point of boarding when a car drew up; it was full of fans, female and male, who'd been among the Surf's audience and wanted to say "Thanks for the show." Many rock 'n' rollers, buttonholed in subzero temperatures at 1 A.M., would have found it difficult to respond with any grace. But these three cheerily waved back and shouted, "You're welcome."

Jerry Dwyer, too, had come out of his office to watch the party board. In common with all light aircraft, the Bonanza's cockpit had a single access door, on the right-hand side. Dwyer was later to remember that Ritchie and the Big Bopper climbed in first, taking the double rear passenger seat. By mutual tacit agreement, the privilege of riding beside the pilot, in the front righthand seat, went to Buddy. It stuck in Dwyer's mind that, palpably eager to be off, Buddy got into the plane too early and had to get out again to allow Peterson to climb across to his left-hand seat at the controls.

When everyone was settled, Dwyer slammed the door shut, then got into his car and drove to the control tower to watch their takeoff. He found the controller, Mr. Bryan, was already talking to Peterson over the radio. Dwyer's standing instruction to all his pilots was that they must file a flight plan with the tower before leaving the ground. Peterson had not followed this instruction, the controller told Dwyer, but had promised that he'd attend to it as soon as he was airborne.

The tower's open-air observation platform afforded Dwyer a good view of runway 17, where the Bonanza had been directed to take off. He remembered later that it sat at the end of the runway for a few minutes, then made a normal southward departure, breaking ground about a third of the way down the runway, leveling off around 800 feet, then making a textbook 180-degree turn and heading northwest for Fargo.

Dwyer went back into the control room and asked Mr. Bryan whether Peterson had yet filed his flight plan. But Peterson had not. The charter boss's later deposition clearly indicated that he was annoyed with his employee for this lapse, no doubt the result of Peterson's fascination with his famous passengers and desire to cut a dash in front of them. Dwyer asked Mr. Bryan to tell Peterson over the radio to file a flight plan for both his outward and return journeys without further delay. The controller tried several times, but was unable to get Peterson on the frequency on which they had previously spoken. After a few minutes, he ceased calling, but left his transmitter open in case Peterson had decided for some reason to change frequencies.

Dwyer went outside onto the platform again and watched the plane's white taillight dwindle away to the northwest. It disappeared as the Bonanza flew through a patch of cloud or fog, but after a moment or two Dwyer picked it up again. The runway's northerly edge was marked by two towers, each with a red light at the top. In relation to the two towers the Bonzana's taillight did not seem to be climbing but, in Dwyer's words, "drifting gradually downward." At the time, he thought this must be an optical illusion; that the light was not descending, just getting farther and farther away.

Beyond the runway lay infinities of Iowa farmland, the rich earth frozen rock-solid under the packed-down snow of months. The nearest house belonged to a farmer named Reeve Eldridge, who always left a light on in his front hall as an extra marker for departing planes. What farmer Eldridge heard around 1 A.M. he would later describe in an official deposition whose halting words evoke the wind-torn darkness and the impending catastrophe with peculiar vividness:

> Woke out of a sound sleep by motor roar. Sounded smooth, but pulling as though climbing. Couldn't see nothing because of darkness, but was low from sound. Strong wind blowing with a southeasterly direction. Woke my wife succenly [sic] & scared her & child.

Likewise the testimony of Eldridge's neighbor, farmworker Delbert Juhl:

> We got home about 10:15. The weather was pretty good, it was snow [-ing] a little bit now and then. We went to bed, then between 12 and 1 we heard a plane go over. To me the motor was working good and he had it going pretty good and that was the last we heard of it. To me I think the plane went somewhere near our place. It was pretty low and it [kept] right on going. The wind was blowing from the southwest.

Back in the control tower, Jerry Dwyer stood by as Mr. Bryan, the controller, continued his efforts to raise Roger Peterson on the radio. But still there was no response. Now definitely uneasy, Dwyer asked Mr. Bryan to send a teletype message to the Fargo airport, requesting to be notified the moment Peterson made contact with the tower there. Mr. Bryan also sent messages to the three other airports along the Bonanza's probable route, Alexandria, Minneapolis, and Redwood Falls, asking whether Peterson had contacted any of them. It was all that could be done for the moment, and at 1:30, Dwyer returned home, although not to sleep.

He telephoned Mr. Bryan at 2 A.M., but was told there still had been no word from Roger Peterson. Of the three airports contacted by teletype, only one had responded and it had not heard from Peterson either. At

3:30, half an hour past the Bonanza's estimated time of arrival in Fargo, the message was the same. Dwyer himself then placed a call to the Fargo control tower. The controller there said he'd had no contact with an incoming flight N3794N and did not expect one since the expected weather front had just hit and a heavy snowstorm was in progress.

Dwyer hung on the telephone until 4 A.M., interrogating his chief mechanic, Charles McGlothlen, "to see if he could give me any information as to where Roger might have gone," briefly clinging to the hope that the Minneapolis airport, with its vastly superior technology, might pick up the Bonanza where intermediate omni stations could not. But Minneapolis could find no trace of it either. At 4:10, Dwyer had no alternative but to ask Mr. Bryan to post the flight officially missing and tell Minneapolis air-traffic control to issue a general alert.

By 8 A.M., a bleary-eyed Dwyer was back in his office at the Mason City airport, staring at the wall map on which, a few hours earlier, three excited rock 'n' roll stars had traced how far they were from home. Finding N3794N was now the responsibility of the 10th Air Force Search and Rescue Coordination Center. But, rather than just sit and wait, Dwyer decided to roll out another aircraft from his hangar and follow Peterson's route to Fargo in the hope of finding some clue. He had barely cleared the runway when he spotted wreckage in the snow, four or five miles to the northwest. He radioed back to the control tower for the police and two ambulances, but did not land, thinking it more important to remain in the air and mark the spot for the emergency services.

The Bonanza had come down in a snow-covered stubble field, tearing off its right wing, then plowing 540 feet across the unobstructed terrain to finish, tail-up, against a wire boundary fence. The impact, at full speed —170 mph—had torn the red and white fuselage apart like paper, killing all four occupants instantly and flinging three of them into the air with the horrendous velocity of human cannonballs. J. P. Richardson's body lay 40 feet away from the wreckage, on the far side of the fence. Those of Buddy and Ritchie Valens each lay about 13 feet away, to the south and southwest respectively. Roger Peterson's was still inside the tangled remains of the cockpit. It could have happened no more than five minutes after takeoff.

In 1959, as now, few types of accident were more exhaustively investigated than those involving civil aircraft. But, despite a prompt and lengthy inquiry by the U.S. Civil Aeronautics Board, the cause of the crash was not established, and has not been to this day. Thirty-seven years on, it remains surrounded by a fog of rumors and theories, most far-fetched and illogical, all affording thousands throughout the Holly subculture much the same gloomy relish as picking endlessly at a scab that can never heal.

The one party that can be totally exculpated is the aircraft itself. Tests by a battery of CAB inspectors (including one with a surname of special poignancy to Buddy, Leo C. McGuire) confirmed the Bonanza to have been in perfect structural and mechanical order. The dashboard instruments had all been functioning normally, diligently clocking up their terrible readings in the final seconds until the impact stopped them dead: air speed, 165–170 mph; rate of descent, 3,000 feet per minute; attitude indicator stuck at 90-degree right bank and nose-down position. The Lear autopilot was switched off and the radio still tuned to Mason City's control tower.

The enduring mystery is why, just four or five minutes after his faultlessly executed takeoff, a pilot should have flown a well-maintained and mechanically sound aircraft at top speed straight into the ground. Most of the legends and rumors revolve around some alleged incident in the Bonanza's cockpit that fatally distracted Peterson's attention or even did him violence. One story has it that there were drugs on board; another that the Big Bopper was trying to change seats and toppled onto the pilot or upset the trim of the plane; another that four people and forty-two pounds of luggage were too heavy a load; another that the pistol Buddy carried in his overnight bag somehow went off, killing or wounding Peterson.

All can safely be dismissed as nonsense. None of the plane's passengers used drugs, nor were they in any mood for self-destructive rock-star horseplay. All three were exhausted, thankful to be liberated from their purgatorial tour bus, thinking only of reaching their destination, taking a hot bath, and tumbling in between clean sheets. Though certainly heavily loaded, the Bonanaza was within its weight limit. The idea that Buddy might have taken out his handgun and gratuitously waved it around contradicts everything we know of him. Getting four people into the Bonanza's small cockpit meant packing them together as tightly as sardines. Crossing or uncrossing one's legs was difficult enough; moving from the back seat to the front would have been impossible.

The only two conceivable causes of the crash were weather or pilot error, or a combination of both. Though the weather was not bad and visibility generally clear for the Bonanza's takeoff, Jerry Dwyer on the tower platform remembered seeing its taillight disappear into a patch of cloud or fog. Either would have been well below freezing, and it's possible even that short immersion made the Bonanza's wings ice up. A small plane can ice up within seconds, and the result is always the same: to obstruct the flow of air over the wings that gives it its lift. The plane heard by Delbert Juhl had sounded "pretty low," that is, lower than it should have when well clear of the runway. The "motor roar . . . pulling as though climbing" that awoke Reeve Eldridge and scared his wife and child could well have been the Bonanaza, with both wings perilously ice-crusted, unsuccessfully struggling to maintain height.

In light of what the CAB investigators subseqently discovered about Roger Peterson's flying record, pilot error would seem to have been, at the very least, a strong contributing factor. Overexcited by the company of his three musical heroes, chattering to Buddy on his right and Ritchie and the Bopper over his shoulder, Peterson was probably taken completely by surprise by the fog cloud, and in his confusion misread his instrument panel as he was so prone to do. Unfortunately, the instrument easiest to misread on that particular aircraft was the attitude indicator, showing the angle of its nose. The Bonanza was fitted with a Sperry gyroscope, which registered the nose angle in inverted form, descending when the plane was ascending and vice-versa. The only explanation for Peterson's stead-fast plunge to earth was that, habitually careless about instruments, he totally forgot the peculiarity of the Sperry gyroscope—that he believed he was climbing when in fact he was diving. This would explain the descending taillight that Jerry Dwyer mistook for an optical illusion. When a snowy stubble field suddenly rushed up out of the darkness, panic and vertigo overwhelmed Peterson, his sensory imbalance allowed his right wing to dip down, and the plane "got away from him."

Over the years, in common with many others, I've imagined the horror of those last few seconds inside the plunging plane. Now at last, in November 1995, I find myself sitting opposite the person who must have thought about it more than anyone: Buddy's widow, Maria Elena.

She admits that scarcely a day passes without a picture of that bleak Iowa night returning to her mind, along with the memory of the bad dream she and Buddy had shared just before he left. "I think how terrible it would have been, him going down—although I hear it was very fast—

him thinking of the condition that I was in, that he wouldn't see his child, that I'd be by myself. I still think about it, and it bothers me."

☆   ☆   ☆

The night on the bus to which Tommy Allsup's good sportsmanship had condemned him turned out a far less miserable one than he'd expected. Snuggled in the Big Bopper's new sleeping bag, stretched along the wide back seat, he slept soundly for most of the 400-mile journey to Moorhead. "When we got to our hotel, I was the first one off the bus," he remembers. "Right in the lobby there was a TV set with a picture of the Bopper on the screen. I thought it must be some kind of advertisement for the show at the Armory that night.

"So I go bouncing straight up to the guy at the front desk and say, 'Do you have reservations for the Crickets?' He says, 'Yeah, we got all you guys here.' I say, 'What room's Buddy in?' He says, 'Haven't you heard? Buddy Holly's been killed in a plane crash. It's on the news right now.'"

Dazed, Tommy went back out to the bus, where the rest of the "Winter Dance Party" troupe were returning to consciousness, yawning, rubbing their frozen hands and stretching their cramped limbs. Always a man of few words, the big Oklahoman did not lose his taciturnity even now. "Fellas," he said, "they didn't make it."

The story had broken with unusual speed thanks to a local ham radio enthusiast who intercepted Jerry Dwyer's message to the emergency services, then tipped off the Mason City media. By no means all of the radio and wire-service reports now chattering across the continent rated Buddy first in importance among the "three top rock 'n' roll stars" who had perished. "In order of bigness," one bulletin said, "that would probably be Ritchie Valens, then Buddy Holly . . ."

Initially there were reported to be five victims: Buddy, Ritchie, the Bopper, Roger Peterson—and Tommy Allsup. For Buddy had been carrying Tommy's wallet as the ID needed to pick up his registered letter from the Fargo post office. The first sifters of the plane wreckage calculated the death toll by the number of personal identifications they found, not the number of bodies. Still unaware of this, Tommy rushed to a phone to call his mother, tell her the dreadful news about Buddy, and reassure her that he was safe. "My mom hadn't heard a thing about it yet," he remembers. "But all the time I was talking to her on the phone, a neighbor of hers from down the street was trying to get through to tell her I'd been named as one of the dead."

Buddy's old friend and partner Bob Montgomery, now also a married man, had been away on a trip to central Texas with his new wife. On Tuesday, February 3, the Montgomerys were driving home to Lubbock, taking turns behind the wheel. "When my wife took over, I told her, 'Really be careful how you drive because I've got this bad feeling in the pit of my stomach, like we could be going to have some kind of an accident,'" Bob remembers. "I had that same weird feeling all the way back to Lubbock, that something just wasn't right. When we got home, I called Echo McGuire and the first thing she said was 'Isn't it awful? . . .'"

A thousand miles west in snow-free Los Angeles, the news devastated Buddy's close friends Eddie Cochran and Phil Everly, and Cochran's fiancée, the songwriter Sharon Sheeley. Sharon heard it over her car radio. "The shock hit me so badly, I had to stop the car and throw up. When I got back to my house, the phone started ringing. It was Phil Everly, just back from his Australian tour and full of life and fun. I'll never forget the awful silence down the phone line when I told him Buddy had gone."

For Eddie Cochran, Buddy's death was a blow from which he would never recover. "The two of them had been like brothers," Sharon Sheeley says. "And Eddie couldn't get it out of his mind that he'd almost gone on that tour with Buddy, but had dropped out to do *The Ed Sullivan Show,* which was supposed to be happening that very week. All the Sullivan people were at the airport waiting for Eddie—but he didn't get off the plane. He'd taken his station wagon and gone off into the desert by himself, to mourn."

After their unsuccessful attempt to reach Buddy at the Surf Ballroom, for whatever reason, J. I. Allison and Joe B. Mauldin had gone on working with Norman Petty until the small hours, then both had driven back from Clovis to Lubbock. Joe B. was awakened by a telephone call from his sister. He later recalled how he refused to believe what she told him until he'd dressed and gone out for a newspaper, even though he could have confirmed it by simply turning on the radio. Some early bulletins in the Lubbock area said Buddy's two fellow victims been "his group, the Crickets," and assumed that to mean Jerry and Joe B. For several hours, until the true facts emerged via national radio, the families of both were deluged by anxious calls from relatives and friends.

Petty himself had been told the news by a contact at a radio station in

Indiana. First to clock in at the Seventh Street studio compound that morning was Robert Linville of the Roses, the vocal trio whose churchy harmonies had so often been dubbed behind Buddy's voice. Linville found Petty and Vi up in their apartment, both sitting on the floor and weeping uncontrollably among their parchment-and-gilt lamps, Murano glass vases, and long-necked ceramic cats. Every few seconds, the telephone would ring and yet another grief-stricken voice would plead, "Say it isn't true."

Larry Holley was in Lubbock that morning, working on a tile job with the same absorption and perfectionism his kid brother had always brought to music. Stopping for lunch around midday, Larry drove over to the site where Travis, the gentle, quiet middle Holley brother, was supposed to be working. But the only sign of Travis was a scatter of tools, lying on the ground as if they'd been hurriedly dropped. Larry drove home, but could find no trace of his wife, Maxine, either, so in pique he decided to eat alone at a nearby café. "As soon as I walked in, the lady said, 'Isn't it terrible about those three boys getting killed!' I ran straight out and drove over to Daddy and Mother's place. I can still feel the sick feeling in my stomach when I saw all the cars parked outside."

L. O. and Ella Holley had begun the day alone and in usual harmony at their spotless house on 37th Street. Unsure quite where Buddy would be at this point, but confident he would call or write soon, they were loyally listening to his favorite radio station, KLLL. For them, the news did not burst like a bombshell but emerged by slow degrees, in the agonized tact of a telephone caller uncertain whether they'd heard it yet. "We got this call from a friend of ours, Niki Sullivan's mother," Ella recalled in an interview with Dutch television in 1988. Framed in pitiless closeup, she is by now a frail as well as tiny figure. Her quiet, steady voice, with its old-fashioned Western pronunciation, seems to belong to another century. But the indomitable strength and spirit that lifted her baby boy to the first rung of the ladder still shine out of her.

"[Niki's mother] wanted to know if we were were listening to the radio. I told her we were, and she said, 'Well, have you heard anything?' I said, 'I don't know what you mean. We're listening to music.' She said, 'There's been some news. Have you heard it?' I said, 'Why, no, I haven't. What are you talking about?' She said, 'Well, maybe I'd better find out some more about this, and then I'll talk to you later.'

"Then I told my husband and I said, 'Turn the radio on and see if there's some news.' And immediately we heard, 'There's been a small plane crash in Iowee.' And, just the minute I heard that, I knew what they were going to tell." After almost thirty years, her voice still breaks on the words; she looks down to hide her tear-filled eyes. "That's what came, just the minute we turned the radio on. 'There's been a small plane crash . . . up in Iowee . . .'"

In New York City, what snow there had been was already piled in sooty banks along the Greenwich Village sidewalks. Four stories above the junction of Fifth Avenue and Ninth Street, Maria Elena was still in bed, racked with another bout of morning sickness. For her, too, finding out was made all the worse by someone's efforts to break it gently. "I got a phone call from Lou Giordano, the young singer Buddy had been producing. He said, 'What are you doing?' and I said, 'I just woke up. As a matter of fact, I'm still in bed.' He said, 'Well, stay in bed; don't get up. I'm on my way right over. But do me a favor. Don't turn the TV on.' Well, of course, as soon as someone tells you not to do something like that, you do it right away. And at that precise moment, my aunt was on her way over to the apartment."

By early afternoon, disc jockeys across the nation were broadcasting tributes to the three fallen stars. Alan Freed's first act on stepping before the television cameras was to call for a minute's silence. One of the deejays quickest off the mark was Snuff Garrett, a friend of Buddy's at KLLL, Lubbock, now working for KSYD in Wichita Falls. Garrett followed his whole show that day with a special memorial program about Buddy, interspersing his records with telephone hookups to J. I. Allison, Joe B. Mauldin, and Norman Petty. Both J. I. and Joe B. were audibly struggling to hold back the tears. But, whatever Clovis Man's anguish earlier that day, he had completely recovered by the time he spoke to Snuff Garrett. His tone was as politely philosophical as if he'd merely been informed of some regrettable but unavoidable disaster continents away, an Indian famine or African coup d'état:

GARRETT: . . . I'm certainly sorry about it and I'm very sorry to bother you.
PETTY: Well, Snuff, things like this happen and there is nothing we can do to control them.
GARRETT: That's true.
PETTY: We often wonder why things like this happen but, of course, there is always bound to be a reason somewhere.
GARRETT: Uh, Norm, does Buddy have any more records in the can?

PETTY: He had two more, uh, that we did in New York. Do you know this last new one of Buddy's?

GARRETT: Paul Anka's? The Paul Anka tune?

PETTY: Right. We have two others that were done at the same time, and then I probably have some here in Clovis.

GARRETT: I see.

PETTY: He was supposed to go out for another session just next week.

GARRETT: Oh.

PETTY: However, the ones he did there and the ones I have here are the only ones we have left.

GARRETT: I see. I guess . . . uh, will you put most of these out? I hope you will, those last ones of Buddy's.

PETTY: It depends. There's bound to be some legal action, which we are not going to comment on. But I'm sure these last two from New York will be out.

Thanks to the five-hour time difference (six if you were in Iowa), Britain did not learn of the crash until early in the evening of February 3. There was, even so, ample time to make the two national television news bulletins, on BBC and ITV, and the sole national radio news bulletin on the BBC Home Service. But to none of these august organizations did even the highest rock 'n' roll tragedy rank as broadcastable matter. Fleet Street, the following morning, did rather better. The *Daily Mirror,* brashest of the country's two tabloid dailies, ran the story as its front-page lead, though still unable to avoid patronizing quotation marks: TOP 'ROCK' STARS DIE IN CRASH. The main picture was of the Big Bopper in his big Stetson, spreading his arms the width of the page. Buddy appeared as just a mug shot in the body of the text. I myself did not find out until early that evening, when I arrived at Ryde Pier Pavilion to play Buddy Holly numbers at my father's drafty and lackluster thrice-weekly rock 'n' roll dance. I can still see the acne-shiny face of my colleague, Alan Packer, as he showed me the *Mirror's* front page and said, "This is terrible . . ."

Despite the loss of its three headline attractions, and the traumatized grief of its surviving personnel, the "Winter Dance Party" troupe performed at Moorhead National Guard Armory on February 3 as advertised. Into the breach that night stepped a young Fargo group called the Shadows, whose fifteen-year-old vocalist, Robert Velline, was a better-than-average Buddy mimic. It was the beginning of big things for Velline who, renamed Bobby Vee, and managed by Buddy's friend Snuff Garrett, would lead the next generation of mimsy heartthrobs with Buddy-inflected, double-tracked songs like "Rubber Ball," "Take Good Care of My Baby," "Run to Him," and "The Night Has a Thousand Eyes." The Moorhead promoter ran true to type, first begging the depleted troupe not to disappoint the fans, then trying to pay them a reduced fee because their main performers had not appeared as per contract.

GAC showed the same hard-nosed attitude, informing them they must play all twelve dates remaining on the tour's wild interstate zigzag—Sioux City, Des Moines, and Cedar Rapids, Iowa; Spring Valley and Chicago, Illinois; Waterloo and Dubuque, Iowa; Louisville, Kentucky (the craziest detour yet); Canton and Youngstown, Ohio; Peoria and Spring-field, Illinois. To replace Buddy, GAC flew in Ronnie Smith, from Odessa, Texas, whose group had originally supplied drummer Carl Bunch—still languishing in the hospital with frostbite back in Michigan. Tommy Allsup and Waylon Jennings were promised that if they overcame their shock and grief, and backed Ronnie Smith for the rest of the tour, they could share the unpaid balance of Buddy's salary between them. For the remaining week and a half, Waylon played Buddy's Stratocaster, hugging it to him like a talisman that might summon its owner back from the snows.

The job of traveling to Iowa, formally identifying Buddy, and bringing him home for burial could only rightfully be done by the eldest brother who had always watched over him like a second father. Chartering a plane from the West Texas Aircraft company, Larry Holley left Lubbock on his heartbreaking mission on February 4, accompanied by his sister Pat's husband, J. E. Weir. But when they reached the Wilcox Funeral Home in Clear Lake, the tough ex-Marine who'd witnessed death wholesale in World War II "chickened out," as he self-deprecatingly puts it, and his brother-in-law made the identification for him. "When J. E. came out, he said, 'I'm glad you didn't see Buddy that way, Larry. 'Cause he was pretty beaten up.'"

They also drove out to the crash site, where the Bonanza's tangled wreckage was by now covered by several more inches of snow. Nearby lay what were perhaps the saddest bits of debris, the stage suits and shirts that had belonged to Buddy, Ritchie, and the Bopper and those they'd been carrying for their tour companions to be dry-cleaned in Moorhead. "There were beautiful, colorful clothes all piled up in a heap," Larry remembers. "I was asked if I wanted to take Buddy's things, but I said, 'No, get rid of them all. Burn them.' Then I spotted this little leather ditty bag, the one he carried his shaving kit in. I said, 'I'll take this. Just this.'"

The bag was missing the zip-up side compartment where Buddy carried his on-the-road earnings and his .22 pistol. He had been paid in cash after the Surf Ballroom show and so must have had something like $1,000 in the bag when the Bonanza took off. But no money was reported found, apart from what he, Ritchie, and the Bopper had in their wallets. Among the pathetic tally of personal effects—Buddy's black Faiosa glasses, a pair of dice, the Bopper's watch, engraved on the back with details of his record-breaking disc-a-thon—there was no .22 pistol either. That would not turn up until the winter's snows had thawed and the farmer who owned the field, one Albert Juhl, was plowing it up prior to spring planting.

When the pistol was handed over to the local sheriff's office, one of its five chambers was found to be empty. So was born the enduring legend of the crash's having been caused by horseplay or even violence. The truth proved rather more prosaic: Farmer Juhl later admitted that it was he who'd fired the .22, to see whether it was still working after its weeks in the frozen earth.

Having all but ignored Buddy in his lifetime, the Lubbock papers now could not honor him enough. LUBBOCK ROCK 'N' ROLL STAR KILLED was the evening *Journal*'s strident but oddly impersonal front-page banner on February 3. An adjacent story described how the Midwest's icy talons had reached down even as far as the Texas plains with a "killer storm" of snow and freezing sleet that had shut down schools and caused traffic chaos in the Odessa–Kermit area. SERVICES PENDING FOR BUDDY HOLLY, VICTIM OF IOWA PLANE CRASH, said the next day's headline; SINGING STAR'S BODY DUE HERE TODAY. A long feature inside proudly detailed some of the plans Buddy had been making: his album of "devotional music," his homecoming concert in Lubbock the following summer, and the European tour from which, it was said, he'd wanted to return by ocean liner, "just for fun."

By a horrible irony, the aircraft bringing Buddy's temporary coffin from Mason City ran into bad weather soon after takeoff and had to put down for an extended delay at Des Moines. Much as he wanted to stand watch over his brother on this last trip home, Larry Holley had to travel separately. "All the way back, I kept praying," he remembers. "But not for myself. I was saying, 'Please, Lord, let Daddy and Mother find the strength to live through this.'"

In New York, meanwhile, the shock and anguish that Maria Elena had suffered brought a second bereavement. Two days after losing Buddy, she also lost the baby that he was so sure would be a boy. By coincidence, the emergency room to which she was rushed happened to be St. Vincent's, the hospital where she'd once worked as a translator. The Puerto Rican doctor who treated her ("I can see his face now") was a colleague from those days.

Barely five weeks pregnant, Maria Elena was in no danger herself, and could return home after a few hours' observation. Weak and distraught as she was, she then caught a plane to Lubbock for Buddy's funeral. The Holley family, of course, did not even know she had been pregnant, and in the coming days of mourning—for reasons known only to her proud, defensive heart—Maria Elena did not mention her miscarriage. Consequently, there would afterward be wagging tongues (mainly in the Clovis area) that cast doubt on whether it had ever really happened.

The "killer storm" had melted away and normal Lubbock winter weather with temperatures in the mid-forties had returned by Saturday, February 7, when Buddy's funeral took place at the Tabernacle Baptist Church. The service drew 1,500 mourners, the largest congregation the church had ever seen, and far too many even for its cavernous premises to accommodate: a large number had to be content to pay their respects from the vestibule, some even from outside in the parking lot. In some Southern Baptist funerals, the coffin is left open to allow a formal farewell to the deceased, but the terrible injuries that Buddy had suffered made that impossible. His family was still palpably in shock, but as ever took strength from his mother, who remained composed and dignified throughout. The pallbearers were Buddy's original fellow Crickets Jerry Allison, Joe B. Mauldin, and Niki Sullivan, his teenage country music cronies Bob Montgomery and Sonny Curtis, and his close friend Phil Everly. Phil's brother Don, always considered the less serious of the duo, had found himself more affected by Buddy's loss than anything in his life before. "I couldn't go to the funeral," he says now. "I couldn't go anywhere. I just took to my bed."

Another notable absentee was Waylon Jennings, the musician who owed most to Buddy's generosity and unselfishness. As inducement to finish the "Winter Dance Party" tour, GAC had guaranteed Waylon time off to attend Buddy's funeral, even promising to pay his airfare back to Lubbock. That promise had now been conveniently forgotten, however, and Waylon was stuck on an icy bus somewhere between Iowa and Illinois, still wishing he could unsay his very last words to his mentor and friend.

The service was conducted by Ben D. Johnson, the same pastor who had performed Buddy's wedding to Maria Elena on that sweltering, impatient day just five months earlier. The ceremony included surprisingly little music in memory of one who had lived and breathed it. Nor were any of Buddy's records deemed fit, as yet, to be heard in his own church, even though he had created rock 'n' roll as purely joyful as any hymns. Instead, Bill Pickering of the Picks vocal trio sang a spiritual called "Beyond the Sunset." The congregation also listened to one of Buddy's favorite gospel records, "I'll Be All Right" by the Angelic Gospel Singers.

The casket was then carried to its resting place, just a mile or so from the simple wooden house where Buddy had been born and in the lee of the huge grain elevator which in the coming decades would mark his whereabouts like a Texas Taj Mahal. Sick with grief and still in pain from her miscarriage, Maria Elena did not feel equal to attending the funeral or visiting Buddy's grave. She has not seen it to this day.

EPILOGUE

CRYING, WAITING, HOPING

N orman Petty wasted no time in returning to practicalities. The day after Buddy's death, Petty wrote to Dick Jacobs at Coral Records:

Dear Dick:

The Crickets, Mr. Jerry Allison and Mr. Joe Mauldin, have asked me to authorize you to ask Brunswick Records to issue a new contract to the group known as THE CRICKETS. The boys will be able to use a new vocalist whenever they choose . . . with your permission of course. The new contract should be made payable to the Norman Petty Agency Inc., Box 926, Clovis, New Mexico.

This agency will receive all royalties due the Crickets consisting of Mr. Jerry Allison and Mr. Joe Mauldin, and will make payments to them when received.

This is your authorization by power of attorney invested in me to issue the new recordings of the above-named Crickets. The selections are "Someone Someone" and "Love'll Make A Fool Of You" [sic], the selections you are now holding on tape from us.

We are anxious to hear of your prompt action in this matter.

Best regards

The Crickets
Norman Petty
manager and power of attorney.

While desolation and disbelief put all around him into a state of sus-pended animation, Clovis Man calmly proceeded with the business of getting his own way, untroubled by any sense of timing or appropriate-ness. With Coral Records compliant, and no one else around to stand in his way, Petty was now free to register the Crickets' name as a business trademark encompassing two members only, J. I. and Joe B., and managed and administered solely by himself. In a further stroke of magnificent insensibility, the date on which he sent off the completed copyright regis-tration papers was Saturday, February 7, the day of Buddy's funeral.

With copyright documents filed, it was a simple matter to eliminate the second-edition Crickets, Tommy Allsup, Waylon Jennings, and Carl Bunch, whom Buddy had recruited to back him on the "Winter Dance Party" tour and who naturally, if naively, hoped to continue working under that name. For a time there was talk of turning Allsup, Jennings, and Bunch into another group, the Jitters, fronted by Ronnie Smith, the singer GAC had flown in to take Buddy's place for the rest of the tour. But that idea came to nothing, and four redundant Crickets were left to make their own dispirited way back from New York through the ice and slush to West Texas. The others remember letting Waylon Jennings out of the car on a windswept corner in St. Louis, Missouri, all blissfully un-aware that a future country music giant was walking away from them.

The sense of Buddy's being deeply and sincerely mourned was palpa-ble. In schools throughout both America and Britain, whole classes turned up for their lessons wearing black armbands. Yet the grief was curiously unfocused. Among his huge worldwide constituency, only an infinitesimal number had ever seen him perform or gained any but the vaguest impres-sion of his character. Grief was tinged with guilt, for not making more of him while he was around. Why hadn't one bought more of his records, learned more of his words, ferreted out his life story, fought one's way to a live concert of his by hook or by crook? The most specific shock came from belatedly finding out that this being who had encouraged, soothed, and reassured us had himself been only twenty-two. Even to a sixteen-year-old, accustomed to regard people in their early twenties as crusty adults, that seemed a horribly unfair moment at which to have to go.

The most hardened music industry opportunist did not dream at that point how Buddy's death would be the means of lifting his fame—and sales—into the stratosphere. It had never happened before. Previous famous casualties of popular music—the jazz cornetist Bix Beiderbecke, the bluesman Robert Johnson, the singer Billie Holiday, Buddy's own great country hero Hank Williams—all had been elevated to mythological status by early and unlucky death. All, too, had ceased to be regarded as commercial propositions from the moment they were lowered into the earth. Until Buddy, the accepted wisdom among record companies was that "stiffs don't sell."

But this was no longer old-time jazz or blues, with their familiar adult themes of pain and mortality. This was rock 'n' roll, the all-obliterating center stage of every worthwhile teenage life, a constantly unfolding social as well as musical melodrama whose players—like its audience—had hitherto been regarded as indestructible.

Buddy was the first white rock 'n' roll star to die in any circumstances whatever. That alone, in teenage eyes, was sufficient to bestow a glorious martyrdom. How or why he had died initially seemed less important than that the grim and gray real world had succeeded at last in plucking one of the music's foremost jewels from its gaudy crown. Strangers to pain, certain of their own immortality, young people have always been fascinated by the idea of sudden death, never more so than when it claims one of their own. By pulverizing his Porsche and himself, for no discernible reason, three years earlier, James Dean had become the first true icon of rock 'n' roll culture. But here was an end even more sudden, dramatic, and—one truly thought—glamorous. In the late fifties, in Britain at least, few young people had any direct experience of flying, and the news media did not report tragedy in the voyeuristic detail they do today. Few of those who grieved for Buddy could begin to imagine the terror he must have felt in his final moments, the sickening squalor of the wreckage strewn about that snowy cornfield, nor the horrific long, grieving twilight now faced by his family. It seemed an instantaneous and painless transition from life into legend.

The immediate commercial liftoff did not come from any belated appreciation of Buddy's talents, merely the piquant fact that the last single he'd released before his death had been called "It Doesn't Matter Any-more." With morbid hindsight, that seemed almost a comment from be-yond the grave on his recent unsuccessful struggle to get back onto the charts. The record had been available, and selling poorly since early January. But now the shadow of the Grim Reaper seemed to add an irresistible extra something to the pizzicato violins and lighter-than-air voice. Within days of Buddy's death, "It Doesn't Matter Anymore" leapt into the *Billboard* Hot 100, eventually peaking at No. 13. In Britain, it spent twenty-one weeks in the *New Musical Express* Top 20, reaching No. 1 on May 6.

Nowadays, the deaths of three major rock stars in such a plane crash would bring lawsuits against the charter company by the stars' respective spouses or families, calculated on potential future earnings probably run-ning into billions rather than millions of dollars. In 1959, such litigation was still in its infancy. The suits faced by Dwyer's Flying Service for that ill-fated midnight charter totaled just $3.5 million: $1 million each from Buddy's and J. P. Richardson's families and $1.5 million from Ritchie Valens's. A judgment in their favor would still have been more than enough to wipe out the business that Jerry Dwyer had already seen wrecked once by the vagaries of the Iowa weather. Fortunately for him, Iowa state law in those days put a ceiling of $50,000 on legal damages payable to any individual plaintiff. The Holley, Richardson, and Valen-zuela families each had no choice but to settle for that amount, and the $150,000 was paid by Dwyer's insurance company.

Although Dwyer's business survived the tragedy, his life was to be plagued by it forever afterward. The official report into the crash made no criticism of his personal conduct, which indeed had been thoroughly conscientious. What, clearly, would have been questioned if the lawsuits had reached court was his judgment in allowing Roger Peterson to take off that night with weather conditions as they were. In the following weeks, grief-stricken fans of all three dead stars reached their own intem-perate verdict: Dwyer received a deluge of hate mail, including several death threats.

As the years passed, and Clear Lake and the crash site became places of pilgrimage, the unlucky charter boss found himself an object of pitying or resentful fascination, endlessly pointed out as the Man Who Sent Buddy to His Death. Unable physically to hide, Dwyer was to take refuge in a gruff taciturnity, refusing to discuss the events of February 3, 1959, or to speculate what might have ailed Roger Peterson beyond a single cryptic sentence: "My pilot was indisposed."

The doomed aircraft itself, that once jaunty red and white striped Beechcraft Bonanza, was to suffer a similarly strange and tortuous fate. After the teams from the Civil Aeronautics Board had finished sifting through it, there was nothing to be done with its remains—now no longer the property of Dwyer's Flying Service—but to sell them off as scrap metal. The purchaser, in some weird approximation of nostalgia, was none other than Jerry Dwyer. For decades, the rumor among Clear Lake pilgrims was that Dwyer had the plane's carcass locked in a hangar at Mason City airport, and intended one day to have it broken into small pieces that he could then sell to Buddy fans as key-ring charms. Only recently has he disclosed that he had the remains of N3794N transported to a secret location in the Iowa wilderness and given decent burial.

Buddy had not filed a will, though his lawyer, Harold Orenstein, remembers that one had certainly been drawn up for him—indeed, it happened to be among the papers on Orenstein's desk the morning after the crash. New York law at that time prescribed that when a person died intestate, the first $50,000 of the estate went to the surviving spouse and the remainder was to be divided between the spouse and the parents of the deceased. Apart from Buddy's personal possessions and the $50,000 in damages from Dwyer's Flying Service, the main assets of his estate as it stood were the record royalties still being held back by the Norman Petty Agency. Even with Buddy dead, however, Petty continued to find reasons not to pay over the money. Maria Elena was obliged to leave the gentlemanly Orenstein and seek more aggressive legal representation, whereupon Petty finally disgorged what his books said he owed Buddy and what Maria Elena now describes as "a paltry sum," just over $35,000.

Paltry or not, it would have made the difference between struggling through the icy Midwest on a second-rate tour or staying safe and warm in the Brevoort, among the beatniks and coffeehouses. It was enough, in every sense, to have kept Buddy alive.

Petty's victory in disinheriting Buddy from the Crickets and cleaving them unto himself alone was, ironically, to bring him little satisfaction or profit. The group that he had reconstituted with vocalist Earl Sinks released only one single on Brunswick, "Love's Made a Fool of You" coupled with "Someone, Someone." In April 1959, J. I. Allison and Joe B. Mauldin followed Buddy's example in leaving Clovis Man—though, unlike their late friend, they took with them their share of recording royalties from the Holly hey-heyday. In Joe B.'s case, the payout was $10,000. "I was sure it ought to have been more than that," he says now. "But my accountant told me, 'Norman's books are in such a mess, you'd better take what you can.'"

The Buddy-less Crickets were to have a long if fitful history. J. I. and Joe B. had latterly been joined by Sonny Curtis, who had just missed being one of the original Crickets—and who'd come back into the group chiefly in the expectation that they were about to be reunited with Buddy. Sonny had himself developed into a talented songwriter, and was to be mainly responsible for tracks on the Crickets' first post-Buddy album that made Buddy seem almost still there: "When You Ask About Love"; "I Fought the Law" (subsequently a hit for the Bobby Fuller Four); "More Than I Can Say," co-written with J. I. Allison, which was to launch the career of Buddy's Fargo stand-in, Bobby Vee. As if in a gesture of condolence and support, the Crickets were then booked on an Australian tour as backup musicians to their old friends the Everly Brothers. Times had changed, indeed, since Don and Phil Everly first met Buddy, J. I., Joe B., and Niki, way back in 1957, when what had impressed the Kentucky brothers about the West Texans was their self-containment and independence as a performing unit.

Though J. I., Joe B., and Sonny would keep the Crickets going for an impressive number of years, and enjoy one or two minor Buddy-accented hits ("My Little Girl"; "Please Don't Ever Change"), they were never to find "a new guy" to fill the shoes of the one they had lost. Among the several replacement lead singers who would come and go during the next decade, only one could be seriously compared with Buddy—but not, alas, in vocal or instrumental ability. His name was David Box and in 1964 he, too, would die in a plane crash.

Coral-Brunswick were not slow to exploit the gusher they had tapped. *The Buddy Holly Story,* a compilation of Buddy's major tracks from the previous eighteen months, presented almost in the form of a Hollywood biopic, its cover adorned by the gentle face of the Bruno photographic session, went straight onto *Billboard*'s album chart, whither it would return intermittently over the next three and a half years. Maria Elena, meanwhile, had given Dick Jacobs the dozen or so new songs Buddy had put on tape in their apartment during the last weeks of his life. It being unthinkable to release any of these in their original form, with only

Buddy's acoustic guitar accompaniment, Jacobs's assistant, Jack Hanson, was given the job of dubbing instrumental backing onto them. Hanson's "sweetened" versions of "Peggy Sue Got Married" and "Crying, Waiting, Hoping" were later to be reviled by Buddy purists, but at the time they pleased and comforted his fans as much as had anything released during his lifetime.

Within the year, responsibility for producing and releasing all posthumous Buddy Holly material had been assumed by Norman Petty. It was an inevitable decision, since dozens of Buddy tracks still lay in the Clovis vaults, dating right back to the breezy version of Chuck Berry's "Brown-Eyed Handsome Man" he'd played for Petty by way of audition in late 1956. Though the Holley family were well aware of Buddy's battle with Petty at the end, they felt they had no choice but to cede him this absolute control. Innocents in the recording world that they were, it seemed preferable to deal with someone they knew personally. In any case, Petty had showed them consideration in the aftermath of Buddy's death, advising them on matters concerning his taxes and insurance.

Petty could now take sweet revenge on the Crickets by refusing to let them overdub the instrumentation onto new "unknown" Buddy tracks as he issued them. Instead, he brought in a young West Texas group called the Fireballs, giving their lead guitarist, George Tomsco, the awesome task of augmenting—sometimes even obliterating—Buddy's original Stratocaster riffs. For that arch-manipulator Clovis Man, it must have been the perfect consummation: a band of obedient boys out there in the studio and Buddy's voice to do with as he pleased, unhampered by Buddy's teeming ideas or Buddy's iron will.

The prayer Larry Holley had murmured to himself on the journey back from identifying Buddy's body seemed to have been answered. His parents not only survived their horrendous loss but were able to confront it with a fortitude which, to their good Baptist eldest son, appeared to come from a source outside themselves. Within a couple of weeks of Buddy's death, both L. O. and Ella could talk about him without breaking down, even play his records with equanimity. Among many personal keepsakes they kept at their house was the Ariel Cyclone motorcycle on which Buddy had blown $3,000 cash in Dallas that tornadoey May of '58. L. O. Holley took pride in maintaining the bike and, despite his advancing years, even went out for the occasional spin on it. There also were two dozen–odd pairs of high-fashion rock star shoes, too big to fit anyone in the family, so L. O. gave them to Jake Goss, the only barber who'd ever been able to sculpt Buddy's springy curls into a style that pleased him.

As more and more posthumous releases came out in Britain, fans would write to the music papers expressing doubts that this unquenchably alive and effervescent voice could really be Buddy's. One issue of the *New Musical Express* carried a letter from L. O. and Ella in Lubbock, thanking Buddy's British following for their loyalty and assuring them that they had not been deceived.

Larry himself received no divine help in coping with the loss of the kid brother he'd regarded as more like a son. For a good ten years after Buddy's death, Larry could not listen to any rock 'n' roll music or even bear to turn on a radio. Nor did he ever look under his bed, where he kept the brown leather overnight bag of Buddy's that he'd retrieved from the crash site.

Professionally, Buddy could be said not to have left a single enemy behind. "He never knocked nobody down in his life," runs a testimonial lyric by Sonny Curtis, one of countless friends in and out of the music business who were to mourn him as deeply, and for as long, as did his family. Joe B. Mauldin refused to accept that he was gone "for about the next two years . . . I kept thinking it might all have been just a publicity stunt . . . and one day he'd come walking down the street, and I'd see him." To Waylon Jennings's grief were added torments of guilt for having let the Big Bopper fly off with Buddy that night instead of himself. Don Everly refused to travel by plane for years afterward, and would not attend a funeral until the early 1990s, when his own father died.

Worst stricken of all was Eddie Cochran, the closest to an equal Buddy had as a guitarist or songwriter, and the only person to whom he'd confided his despair at the very end. At Cochran's next recording session, he had intended to record "Three Stars," the tribute song to Buddy, Ritchie Valens, and the Big Bopper recently composed by Tommy Dee. But the lyrics proved too emotionally charged. As Cochran spoke the line "Buddy Holly, I'll always remember you with tears in my eyes," his usually tough, blasé voice choked with distress. "When Eddie came back into the control room, he was in a terrible way," his fiancée, Sharon Sheeley, remembers. "He told his producer, 'If you ever release that song, I swear I'll never make another record again.'" So Dee's own version of "Three Stars" was put out instead.

Far from assuaging his grief, the passage of time seemed to make

Cochran still more deflated and morose. When he returned to Britain on tour with Gene Vincent in early 1960, he was taking tranquillizers for what today would be diagnosed as clinical depression. He also had become convinced that he was fated to die as prematurely, suddenly, and and violently as had Buddy. While appearing in northwest England, he even visited a gypsy clairvoyant on the Blackpool promenade, hoping to discover when and where he would meet his nemesis. "We were staying in Manchester or somewhere and Eddie woke up screaming in bed beside me," Sharon Sheeley remembers. "'My God!' he said. 'I'm going to die and there's nothing anyone can do to stop it!'

"From the day Buddy was killed, Eddie hadn't been able to listen to his music. But while we were in England, he sent me out to buy all of Buddy's records and he'd sit and listen to them over and over. I asked him, 'Doesn't it upset you, hearing Buddy this way?' 'Oh, no,' Eddie said. ' 'Cause I'll be seeing him soon.'"

On Easter Sunday, 1960, Cochran, his fiancée, and Gene Vincent were returning from the West Country by rented car to catch their return flight to America from Heathrow airport. Near Chippenham, Wiltshire, the car skidded out of control and hit a roadside lamppost. Its three passengers were rushed to the hospital with multiple injuries, Sharon's including a broken back and pelvis. When she regained consciousness and asked the doctors how Eddie was, they broke it to her that he was dead. In a further eerie replay of the Buddy Holly story, he, too, had left behind a new single whose title suddenly seemed all too grimly appropriate. It was called "Three Steps to Heaven."

☆   ☆   ☆

To the brand-new decade, with its thin-lapeled suits and goody-goody sounds, fifties rock 'n' roll appeared no more than a demented interlude whose flashy exuberance already seemed a hundred years out of date and whose principal exponents, one way and another, seemed to have come to the bad end so long prophesied for them.

Alan Freed, the movement's mellow-toned Pied Piper, had been broken both in fortune and health by the payola scandals. Jerry Lee Lewis's career had never recovered from the furor over his marriage to his thirteen-year-old cousin. Little Richard, now ostensibly studying for the ministry, had been beaten up by police after being caught loitering in a public toilet. Chuck Berry had received a two-year prison sentence for illegally transporting an underage girl across a state line. Even the angelic Everly Brothers had been brought low, canceling a tour of Britain after a suicide attempt by Don in his suite at the Savoy Hotel.

They survived only who renounced the faith: Elvis Presley with his conveyor-belt Hollywood movie musicals, Roy Orbison with his sobbing sub-operatic arias, Bobby Darin with his Sinatra-style revamp of Kurt Weill's "Mack the Knife." To be a teenage idol, you had to be called Bobby (if not Darin, then Vee, Vinton, or Rydell), sport a buttondown shirt and toilet-brush haircut, and look as though you wouldn't harm a fly. In all the world, the only place a rock 'n' roll song could still make the charts was Britain, and the only person who could put it there was Buddy Holly.

One remnant of 1950s music, at least, seemed to have no difficulty in adjusting to the new decade. In parallel to his doctoring and regular release of years-old Buddy Holly tracks, the career of Norman Petty as a manipulator of sounds and people continued to prosper. Petty's production of his own instrumental composition "Wheels," played by a group called the String-a-Longs, became an instant hit in 1961, reaching No. 3 in America and No. 12 in Britain. Two years later, he welded his Buddy Holly "ghost" backup group the Fireballs together with vocalist Jimmy Gilmer on a seemingly bland little song called "Sugar Shack." After the Fireballs had left the studio, thinking the track complete, Petty over-dubbed a piping Solovox organ riff that horrified them to the depth of their manly Texan souls. "Sugar Shack" went to No. 1 and became the biggest-selling American single of 1963.

"Sugar Shack" was Clovis Man's triumphant reply to the many—among his friends no less than his enemies—who had doubted he could ever again score a coup to compare with Buddy Holly. But his second wave of success with the Fireballs and other groups through the middle and late sixties tempted Petty into fatal hubris. In 1969, he closed down the little studio complex on West Seventh Street where so many Gold Records had been mined, exchanging his clumpy Altec board for a state-of-the-art control room in the auditorium of the old Mesa theater on Main Street. The key to the old studio's efficacy—not to mention its profitabil-ity—had been simplicity and improvisation. But at the Mesa theater, lavish ostentation prevailed. The stage, for instance, was fitted with steel curtains whose hundreds of individual strands had been dipped in 14-karat gold.

Thereafter, Petty's once acute, single-minded business sense became increasingly clouded by vanity, self-indulgence, and misjudgment. Nostalgic for his early years as a disc jockey, he started two radio stations, one AM, one FM. He opened a diamond store in downtown Clovis and acquired numerous other properties around the city, including a warehouse and part of an old church called the Citadel at West Seventh and Main. The Citadel was converted into living quarters for Petty, Vi, their animals, and vast collection of brass and colored-glass gewgaws. However, he kept the chapel area intact, and even spoke of making it available for weddings. A further lavish sum was spent in endowing his own place of frequent and ardent worship, Clovis's Central Baptist Church, with a magnificent pipe organ—though some whispered it was not his money, but Buddy Holly's, that paid for the instrument.

By the early seventies, Petty was in serious financial difficulties. The new studio at the Mesa theater, for all its 24-track board and 14-karat gold curtains, had not succeeded in turning out a single hit record. Both the new radio stations had signals too weak to carry their middle-of-the-road music programming to any but the most limited audience. The only unquestionably desirable asset that remained in his hands was the Buddy Holly catalog, administered by his Nor Va Jak company and containing evergreen songs for which he had so farsightedly appropriated half or one-third of the writer's credit all those years ago. Hence the 1975 sale of "That'll Be the Day," "Peggy Sue," and virtually every other worthwhile Buddy song to Paul McCartney's MPL company.

Hollywood's ludicrous 1978 version of the Buddy Holly story felt it unnecessary to mention that Buddy had ever met a man named Norman Petty or recorded in a place named Clovis, New Mexico. As well might one leave Colonel Tom Parker out of the Elvis Presley Story or Brian Epstein out of the Beatles'. Petty affected not to care about having been thus disinvented. But thereafter his claim to the credit for Buddy's success became noticeably more grandiose. Thanks to his habit of taping all his telephone calls, we can eavesdrop on him, around 1980, assuring a journalist, in that mellow, almost preacherlike voice, that he and Buddy used to write songs as "a fifty-fifty partnership . . . I worked on lyrics, Buddy worked on melodies. He didn't like to write bridges to songs, so on something like 'True Love Ways,' I'd do that . . ."

In the early eighties, Petty was stricken with leukemia, the same disease that had killed his elder brother Billy back in the thirties. Pinpointing the causes of leukemia is difficult as a rule. But in Petty's case, the disease may have been engendered by years of inhaling toxic fumes from the carbon tetrachloride he used to clean his studio equipment. His decline was swift and pitiable, the slim, stooping figure shrinking to bones inside its beige safari suit, the once blandly good-looking face aging far beyond its fifty-seven years. His last months were consumed with bitter regret for having ever left the original studio on West Seventh. His friend Jerry Fisher remembers him saying time and again how unique had been the atmosphere he had created there and how he'd never been able to re-capture it.

His final music project was an ironic one, considering with what deter-mination he had blanked Buddy out of his life in 1959. He was arranging and recording synthesizer versions of "That'll Be the Day," "Peggy Sue," and other tracks from their "fifty-fifty partnership" for a projected album to be called *Electric Buddy Holly*.

Norman Petty died on August 15, 1984—the twenty-sixth anniversary of Buddy's wedding. He predeceased his mother, the redoubtable Ma Petty who had been pumping gas in front of the studio the first day Buddy arrived there, and who had never ceased to dote on and coddle her Nor-mie. For the short remainder of her own life, Ma refused to believe he was gone; she would sit at the window, waiting for him to come home, cuddling a child's plastic doll as his surrogate.

His business affairs were found to be in chaos. The proceeds from selling Buddy's song catalog to McCartney had been frittered away, with little or nothing to show for them. Secretive to the last, Petty had taken no one into his confidence concerning the network of small corporations he had created over the years, the bank accounts he had set up in their name, and the numerous offices and hideouts all over Clovis to which he would periodically retreat to transact their mysterious business. His bewildered widow, Vi, now found herself in possession of an immense bunch of keys, with not the first idea how to find the locks they fitted.

Knowing Vi's inability to cope with the simplest business matters, Petty did not bequeath his estate directly to her. Instead, it was handed over to the two people he had come to rely on most during those painful final months. One was his financial adviser, Lyle Walker; the other was a former minister from Portales named Kenneth Broad. Walker and Broad were appointed joint administrators of Petty's studio and publishing inter-ests, and entrusted with responsibility for Vi's welfare.

During Petty's last illness, the old studio compound had sunken into disrepair and squalor. Norma Jean Berry, the Pettys' former bookkeeper, herself now in poor health, occupied the old guest suite at the rear; the echo chamber became silted up with empty boxes and broken furniture while Clovis Man's once spotless and orderly control room was reduced to a malodorous home for Vi's collection of thirty-six stray cats. Before the BBC documentary team came to Clovis in 1984, Petty's former associate Jerry Fisher volunteered to put the studio back in order. Fisher spent weeks of loving altruism on the job, restoring the single-track Altec board, which had soaked up Buddy's greatest musical moments, to its old pride of place on the veined work surface; stripping down and reassembling Ampex tape equipment corroded almost beyond recognition by cat urine.

The chief pleasure of Vi Petty's last years was the annual Clovis Music Festival, when friends from the old days, such as Jimmy Self and the Roses, would gather to perform and reminisce. In 1991, Vi died of a gastric ailment, compounded by years of self-neglect. The Petty estate then passed to Lyle Walker and Kenneth Broad. Some of those who worked with or for Petty in the glory days of the old studio are less than happy that it should now be under the control of such comparative newcomers. But, to their credit, Walker and Broad have preserved the place as a museum, accessible free of charge to groups of Holly pilgrims by appointment.

Even death was not to give Vi her husband's undivided company nor silence persistent rumors about the strange triumvirate that ruled so many years at 1313 West Seventh Street. With them under their headstone at Clovis city cemetery lies their ever-faithful amanuensis, Norma Jean.

☆　☆　☆

For two decades after Buddy's death, Lubbock maintained the seeming indifference it had shown him during his lifetime. The stream of fans who arrived to pay their respects were astounded by the grudgingness with which they found him commemorated by his hometown. In a land where civic honors and testimonial plaques are easily bestowed, Lubbock might have been expected to inaugurate a Buddy Holly Stadium, a Buddy Holly Freeway, at the very least a Buddy Holly Street. But what was given so readily in other places to individuals of far less moment failed to materialize in the City of Churches for its one and only modern hero. The single amenity that bore his name was the Buddy Holly Recreation Area, a small landscaped plot reclaimed from common land where, in former days, Buddy would park with his dates or write songs alfresco with Bob Montgomery.

As the years passed, Lubbock's City Council could not but recognize what an asset Buddy represented, both in international prestige and potential tourism and conference business. Various ideas were advanced for some more permanent memorial, such as a statue, but all fell by the wayside for one reason or another. Finally, as if exasperated by all this council-chamber dickering, the elements took a hand. In 1970, the worst tornado West Texas had seen in living memory tore through the center of Lubbock, completely demolishing the whole north side of Avenue Q. The subsequent extensive redevelopment included a new Civic Center plaza where, in 1980, an eight-foot-six-inch bronze statue of Buddy was at last unveiled.

The work of Texas sculptor Grant Speed, it shows Buddy with his Stratocaster, in the sidelong striding posture recognizable to anyone who ever saw him perform. Apart from innumerable classic photographs, the sculptor's main reference point was Travis Holley, the quiet introverted brother Buddy most resembled facially. Set about by beds of orange marigolds, framed at certain angles by an intrusive satellite dish, the statue may not be a particularly artistic or lifelike piece of work. But to the pilgrims who congregate around it with their cameras during the course of each year, Michelangelo's David could hardly be more beautiful or fulfilling. Below is a Walk of Fame, since augmented to honor other historic names in West Texas music: J. I. Allison, Joe B. Mauldin, Niki Sullivan, Roy Orbison, and Waylon Jennings.

"Buddy Holly contributed to the musical heritage of not only Texas but the entire world," runs his city's overdue encomium. "It is significant that this first plaque in the Walk of Fame bears his name. The citizens of Lubbock pay tribute to 'their native son.'"

The dearth of generally available background information about Buddy was to continue, mystifyingly, long after magazines like Jann Wenner's *Rolling Stone* had made rock journalism respectable—even fleetingly literate—and the rock 'n' roll era had become a legitimate subject for academic study. In the absence of illuminating books, films, or even articles, Buddy's fans had no option but to become researchers and investigators in their own right, expending what for many were substantial sums on traveling to Lubbock and Clovis to meet his family and former associates; in several cases starting magazines or newsletters to share their findings with hundreds of eager subscribers. Hardcore Buddy Holly enthusiasts as a result tend to be more competitively knowledgeable and fiercely proprietorial that any other species of rock fan, with the possible single exception of the Beatles'. For the still unconstituted Chair in Buddy Holly Studies, numerous worthy contenders exist, both in Britain and America. But none has shown more selfless dedication to the subject than Bill Griggs.

The son of two professional musicians, Griggs was born in 1941 and brought up in Hartford, Connecticut. As a rock 'n' roll–obsessed teenager in the late fifties, he saw every package show that ever played at Hartford's 4,000-seat State theater, eventually becoming such a fixture that the the-ater took him on as an usher. It was there that he first saw Buddy Holly and the Crickets on "The Biggest Show of Stars for 1957." He remembers vividly the several things about them that struck his soul awake with delight: the way they could reproduce the sound of their records onstage; the contrast of their dapper dark suits to the usual gaudy rock 'n' roll threads; above all, Buddy's stage presence and energy, and the good-natured way he devoted a few moments of his set to the bad seats at either end of the seventy-foot stage.

There was much more to Bill Griggs than just rock 'n' roll: he had intended to train as an astronomer, and had been a national drag-racing champion. But fifties music, especially that of Buddy Holly, inexorably took over his life. In 1976, realizing to his amazement that his idol had no American fan club, he founded one himself, naming it the Buddy Holly Memorial Society. Four years later, he moved his family from Connecticut to Lubbock, by chance settling on 56th Street, just a couple of blocks from Buddy's parents' last home. Since 1980 he has devoted himself to compiling a week-by-week—even day-by-day—dossier on Buddy's life, accumulating documents and memorabilia against the hoped-for day when Lubbock will build a museum in which they can be displayed.

The place where Buddy died has been rather more assiduous in com-memorating him than has the place where he was born. On the twentieth anniversary of his death, February 3, 1979, a memorial convention took place at the Surf Ballroom in Clear Lake, Iowa, his final port of call on the "Winter Dance Party." Despite Iowa's unmitigatedly inhospitable winter weather, the Clear Lake convention was to grow into an annual event, attended by delegates from all over America and Europe, with personal appearances by Buddy's family and close friends, and performances by musicians who owed him their careers: the Crickets, Bobby Vee, Mike Berry, and many more. The lake-bordering highway outside, from which an ever-optimistic young man took his last look back at colored lights and icebound water, has been renamed Buddy Holly Avenue.

The cornfield where the plane came down is still there, as is the same wire boundary-fence that brought it finally to a stop. A couple of feet inside the fence stands a simple metal memorial, the silhouettes of a guitar and three discs, one for each of the recording stars who perished. At convention-time, the memorial is usually buried under snow; in summer, it must be hunted for amid corn almost as high as an elephant's eye. The field's present owner does not mind anyone who treks across his land to visit it so long as they do no damage to his crops.

The cause of the crash continues to be argued over as hotly as ever. In recent years, a new voice has entered the controversy, that of an Iowa clergyman, the Reverend Jerry Miller, who claims that he alone knows the true reason why N3794N crashed so soon after takeoff, and that he has irrefutable proof in the briefcase he carries everywhere. Latterly, too, the charter boss Jerry Dwyer has begun to drop tantalizing hints that seem to link the sudden "indisposition" of his young pilot, Roger Peterson, with the .22 pistol Buddy carried on the flight. According to Bill Griggs, Dwyer has suggested that Civil Aeronautics Board investigators may have discovered a bullet hole through the back of Peterson's seat but that, for some reason, officialdom decreed that the matter be covered up. However, as Griggs drily remarks, "If you're three young guys just taking off at midnight in bad weather, who in their right mind is going to shoot the pilot in the back?"

The last days of L. O. and Ella Holley were clouded with anxiety, to add to their ineradicable grief. L. O. suffered a stroke that left his speech and mobility impaired—though he took pride in still having his hair cut by Buddy's old barber, Jake Goss. Handling their share of Buddy's increasingly valuable estate put the Holleys into a tax bracket that gave them as much worry as benefit. In 1982, they found themselves facing a hefty demand from the Internal Revenue Service, but with no reserves to meet it. As a result they were forced to sell to Paul McCartney's MPL company the "mechanical" (airplay) rights they held in "That'll Be the Day," "Peggy Sue," "Everyday," and a clutch of Buddy's other songs.

L. O. Holley died on July 8, 1985; the unfailingly courageous and dignified Ella followed him on May 20, 1990. Their equally modest tablets lie
in the grass next to Buddy's in the Lubbock city cemetery.

Maria Elena was never fully to recover from Buddy's death either. In
the sixties she met and married Joe Diaz, a Dallas toy manufacturer, also
of Puerto Rican background, and bore him two sons and a daughter. The
elder boy was named Carlos, the Hispanic equivalent of Buddy's real
Christian name, Charles. The marriage to Diaz did not last, and Maria
Elena spent some years in Florida, indulging her unexpected passion for
deep-sea fishing. Now sixty-three, she lives alone with two pedigree cats
in a suburb of Dallas and devotes her whole existence to guardianship of
the inheritance she wishes had never come her way. If people exploited
Buddy during his lifetime, Maria Elena is fiercely determined it shall not
happen now that he is dead: she personally approves and licenses all
commercial uses of his name and likeness, and has prevailed on the Texas
legislature to pass the so-called Buddy Holly Law, protecting him in his
home state as a trademark as sacrosanct as that of Disney or Coca-Cola.

Like Norman Petty all those years ago, many who have fallen foul of
Maria Elena, or failed to bend her to their will, consider her demanding
and difficult, but I have to say she did not seem so to me. Under an
admittedly tough, uncompromising exterior, I found a genuine eccentric,
warm and humorous, admirably courageous and self-sufficient, though
clearly rather lonely and still prone to clutches of grief for the young
bridegroom she lost thirty-seven years ago. As we drove through the
countryside near her house, Maria Elena gestured out the window. "Look
... a farm," she said with a wry grimace. "Buddy's plane came down on
a farm. And where do I end up living? Close to a farm!"

If rock 'n' roll stars were once regarded as pagan gods, they seem to
our modern age more like palpitant and preening patron saints whose
smallest possessions are as eagerly sought after and jealously cherished
as the holiest relics of medieval times. In the boom market for rock 'n' roll
memorabilia, Buddy has posthumously earned the price of his survival a
hundred times over. Sotheby's famous rock 'n' roll auction of 1992 saw
his gray wool stage jacket and French-cuff shirt go for $5,225, his high
school diploma for $3,300, and his birth certificate (on which the registrar
prophetically filled in his surname as Holly, not Holley) for $1,100. His
Gibson acoustic guitar, in the blue and black leather jacket he made for
it, went to Gary Busey, the actor who had portrayed him on screen, for

$242,000—a price tag that did not include the guitar's shoulder strap. The City of Lubbock recently spent $200,000 on acquiring his last Fender Stratocaster, stage clothes, shoes, and childhood mementos, including school notebooks, his slingshot, and Cub Scout badge. The wallet that Tommy Allsup lent him to show as ID at the Fargo post office now has pride of place on a wall of the Dallas Hard Rock Café. Tucked inside is one of the business cards Buddy had already had printed for his new Prism recording company.

His principal fan and archivist-in-chief, Bill Griggs, has amassed a remarkable personal collection of memorabilia, as the basis of that possible future Holly Museum. It includes Buddy's sunglasses, his movie camera, his fedora, the dice he loved to roll with Chuck Berry, a red polka-dot cravat from the set Maria Elena bought him to wear on the "Winter Dance Party" tour. A few years ago, Griggs visited Buddy's New York opticians, Courmetts & Gaul, to see whether his records were still on file and, if so, whether they contained any letters or documents signed by him. It turned out that Dr. Stanger, the optometrist who had treated Buddy, still worked for Courmetts & Gaul and that he had more on file than mere paperwork. Put away in a drawer was the second pair of Mexican Faiosa frames— these not black but tortoiseshell—that Buddy had left with Stanger as spares in the autumn of 1958. Griggs was able to buy them at face value, $72.

There is one memento, however, that even the tireless Griggs has been unable to track down. The simple wooden house on Sixth Street where Buddy was born ought by rights to be preserved as a shrine to a quintessential American hero. Instead, we are confronted by that mysterious empty grass plot between its former next-door neighbors. After the Holley family left it, the house gradually declined in fortune and, during the late seventies, was condemned as unfit for human habitation. It was scheduled to be demolished on February 3, 1978—ironically, the nineteenth anniversary of Buddy's death. Before the order could be carried out, an unknown party bought the condemned structure and had it lifted from its foundations and towed away, to be resited outside the jurisdiction of the public health authorities. It may well be there to this day, somewhere just beyond Lubbock city limits. Bill Griggs has mobilized search parties of up to fifty fans, armed with photo references of that covered front porch, and those distinctive window shutters with playing-card club shapes cut into them. But, despite all his efforts, the house continues to elude him.

When I last visited Lubbock, in January 1996, Griggs took me to see another remarkable Buddy Holly relic that had lately turned up just a stone's throw from his grave. Separated from the Lubbock cemetery by a traffic fly-over is a steel-fenced lot where hundreds of late-fifties Chevrolets stand row on row, gaudy and befinned, in the rattlesnake-haunted grass. The owner of the lot, a Chevy nut named Bill Clement, believes he has acquired the '58 Impala coupe that was Buddy's Christmas gift to himself in the euphoric December of 1957. It stands in Clement's yard, a crouching, eviscerated shell, its coral-pink body and white roof bleached almost colorless and eaten away by rust. But the serial number matches that of the vehicle whose Powerglide automatic transmission briefly gave trouble but was rectified for a $2 charge. And Buddy's brother Larry has confirmed it to be the same car.

Larry Holley is now seventy, a long-legged, boyish figure, still hale enough to work a full week in his tile business and have energy left over to ride dirt bikes on weekends. Larry is the one everybody comes to for stories about Buddy, and it shows in a slightly haunted and impatient manner. But the same slow smile always appears as he recalls the day Buddy came and coolly asked him for a thousand dollars . . . their trip down to San Angelo in the eighteen-wheel truck . . . the single-minded fourteen-year-old, doing leatherwork in the middle of Thanksgiving dinner . . . that cute little five-year-old, sawing away on his toy violin at the County Line schoolhouse, unaware that his big brothers had silenced his bow with grease.

Larry admits that he often has dreams about Buddy—dreams about their old companionship, from which he invariably awakens happy and calm. And, as ever, he is sustained by the simple, absolute certainty of his Tabernacle Baptist faith: "I know that Buddy's with the Lord, and that one of these days I'll see him again and put my arm around his shoulder, just like I used to."

A few years ago, Larry came to Bill Griggs with tears in his eyes and handed Griggs something wrapped in clear plastic. It was the brown leather overnight bag that Buddy had carried with him on his last journey. Since retrieving the bag from the crash site, Larry had kept it under his bed, never looking at it again. Now he said he wanted Griggs to have it, both as a mark of appreciation for Griggs's dedication to Buddy, and to ensure it a better home than some Sotheby's auction room.

Griggs treated this most poignant and intimate relic with almost religious reverence, taking out the contents, listing and photographing them, then replacing them, rewrapping the bag in its plastic cover, and promising himself never to open it again. I ask him to do so just once more, for the benefit of the Channel 4 film crew I have brought with me from London on this visit. He agrees, with deep misgivings, on condition that the camera crew and I shall be the only ones present.

The bag is unrolled from its plastic layers like a mummy's corpse being disinterred from its bandages. It is smaller than I expected, two feet long and perhaps eighteen inches wide. Back in 1959, one can see, it was an extremely stylish piece of kit, doubtless purchased from one of those swanky leather shops on upper Madison Avenue. You unzip it broadside, then snap the opening rigid, like the mouth of an old-fashioned Gladstone bag. On the handle is the neat binding of white adhesive tape with which Buddy had made it more comfortable to carry. The glossy vermilion leather is mounted on a quarter-inch steel frame whose misshapenness indicates with what terrible force N3794N hit the ground. Before opening the bag, Griggs turns it over to show the naked strip of plaid on its underside—all that remains of the severed compartment where Buddy kept his .22 pistol.

The contents are then lifted out reverentially one by one: a crushed and bent tube of Colgate toothpaste, a pink and yellow toothbrush, aspirins, suntan lotion, a lint brush, a hairbrush, and a black plastic comb. The lint brush is still clotted with the fluff that the fastidious Buddy had removed from his stage suits. The comb still has strands of hair caught between its teeth. Each dip into the bag coats Griggs's fingers with brown dust that he will be deeply reluctant to wash off afterward. For it is petrified Iowa soil from 1959: the very earth that took Buddy's life.

Griggs's one consuming regret is never having met and talked to Buddy, as he could easily have done back in 1957. But he feels that the omission may now have been partly rectified. Once or twice, while working alone at his office in Lubbock, he has sensed the nearness of Buddy's benign shade. "It always happens late at night, when I'm tapping on the computer. . . . I suddenly get the feeling someone else is in the room. It seems to me that Buddy's standing there near my desk. He's wearing black slacks and the gray V-neck sweater he had on his English tour. And he always says the same thing: 'Thanks for what you're doing.'"

Among Griggs's encyclopedic Buddy Holly photo albums is one he is reluctant to open, let alone show to anyone else. This contains the pictures of Buddy's body as it was found on that morning of February 3, 1959. "You can skip this book if you want to," Griggs tells me. But I've followed my one-time inspiration and friend all this way from the end of Ryde Pier. I can hardly stop now.

It is not, as I had feared, a shocking or gruesome picture. It is just terribly, terribly sad. Silhouetted against some burst-open luggage, a long figure in a pale coat lies face-down in the snow. I remember those light-hearted words of his very first hit, "That'll be the day . . . when I die." I realize he was a young man with everything he needed—everything except luck.

"He was an old soul," says Maria Elena. "He had a second passage in this world. Unfortunately, it was only a short one. If it's really true that they're out there somewhere and they can see down here, then he knows that people still appreciate his music, still love it. I say this all the time, every day. I say, 'I hope that, wherever you are, you can see and hear this happening for you and that it was not in vain that you died, because what you wanted has come true. Your music really does live forever.' "

Bill Griggs delivers what is perhaps the best epitaph, both to the man and his music.

"Whenever you mention his name, it always gets the same reaction. Everybody smiles."

INDEX

Nor Va Jak Music, Inc., 86, 92, 93, 102–3,
105, 120–21, 208, 221, 230, 266,
305
"Not Fade Away," 17, 23, 25, 86, 119–20,
123, 124, 127, 150, 154, 230
"Now We're One," 199, 213

O'Connor, Des, 184, 188
Off the Record, 191–92
"Oh Boy," 15, 86, 122, 123, 148–50, 157,
159–60, 168, 170, 178, 186, 230,
274
O'Keefe, Johnny, 179, 181
"Only the Lonely," 94
Ono, Yoko, 205, 221
"Ooby Dooby," 94
"Ooh, My Head," 262
Orbison, Roy, 67, 94, 98, 147, 304, 308
Orenstein, Harold, 232–34, 247–48, 263,
299
Oscar and Oscar, 132
Otis, Johnny, 65

Page, Frank "Gatemouth," 56
Parker, "Colonel" Tom, 71, 72, 76, 118,
173–74, 305
Parnell, Jack, 186
Parrish, Sue, 75, 78, 112
"Party Doll," 94, 120
Pastels, the, 192
"Patricia," 217
Paul, Les, 52, 91, 114
Payne, Jack, 191–92
Peer-Southern Music, 105–6, 119, 121,
176, 200, 201, 205, 208, 215, 227,
232, 237, 263
"Peggy Sue," 15, 22, 86, 87, 127, 131,
143, 147–49, 157, 158, 168, 178,
186, 230, 262, 274, 305, 306, 310
composition of, 121–24
on *Ed Sullivan,* 26–27, 151
as Gold Record, 176, 207
influence on other songs, 21
"Peggy Sue Got Married," 20–21, 242,
301
Penguins, the, 65
Penniman, Richard "Little Richard," 24,
66, 68–71, 81, 114, 139, 149, 168,
179, 216, 254, 274, 303–4
and Buddy Holly, 68–69, 140–41
image of, 118, 140–41
performing style of, 165, 178, 192
Perkins, Anthony, 237

Perkins, Carl, 24, 67, 76, 94, 112
Peter and Gordon, 23
Peterson, Roger, 271, 276–85, 286, 298–
299, 310
Petty, Norman
birth of, 89
on British tour, 179–80, 183, 187,
188
and Buddy Holly Week, 25
character of, 88–89, 95–96, 109–10
as Clovis Man, 87–88, 89, 95–96, 109,
126, 133, 153, 189, 208
and credits for music, 22, 93, 102–4,
116, 120–21, 123–24, 147, 154,
159, 181, 197, 226, 230, 250, 305
death of, 305–7
and death of Buddy Holly, 287–88,
289–90
described, 87–88, 95–96, 109–10
family background, 89–90
financial difficulties, 305, 306
frugality, 96, 111, 206
and legal action by Buddy Holly, 88,
232–35, 239–40, 244–52, 254–55,
263–66
as manager of Buddy Holly and the
Crickets, 132–33, 153–56, 175–
177, 179–80, 182–92, 206–8, 215,
226, 228, 263
marriage, 90–91, 92, 95, 125
and marriage of Buddy Holly, 208, 213,
220
musical ability of, 89–91, 123–24
Norman Petty Agency Inc., 234–35,
299
Norman Petty Recording Studios, 85–
87, 91–94, 97–102, 109, 111, 113,
120–24, 153–54, 176–77, 180–81,
196–97, 220–21, 232
Norman Petty Trio, 90–91, 92, 97–98,
103, 105, 110, 114, 147, 181, 184
Nor Va Jak Music, Inc., 86, 92, 93,
102–3, 105, 120–21, 208, 221,
230, 266, 305
post-Holly productions, 295–304
and posthumous releases of Buddy
Holly, 22–23, 300–301
and Prism Record Company, 219–20,
236, 244–45
and the Rhythm Orchids, 94
and Maria Elena Santiago, 206–8
secrecy of, 95–96, 110, 208, 306
technical ability of, 98, 114, 122

CONTINUED FROM FRONT FLAP

relevant reflections on various aspects experience, to show how a particular concept or theory developed, what he means, and how it can be justified. The present work not only does not assume prior acquaintance with philosophy, but should itself serve as an introduction.

There is no doubt, according to Dr. Koller, that in our own age we have put our very existence in jeopardy by allowing ourselves to remain ignorant of at least half of the world. Never has the need become greater to come to an understanding of all the peoples of the world. Consequently, upon the assumption that to understand what a people have done and what they are likely to do, it is necessary to understand their basic attitudes about life as reflected in their views about the nature of man, the good life, the nature of the universe, and the ways we can know reality—it is imperative that the philosophies of the Orient be studied and understood. Thus the two functions which this book is intended to serve—to introduce the reader to an understanding of the Asian mind and indicate different ways in which fundamental philosophical questions have been considered in the Orient—grow out of the same basic concern, the concern to maintain and improve human existence.

Dr. Koller is Assistant Professor of Philosophy at Rensselaer Polytechnic Institute. He has also taught at St. Thomas College (St. Paul), Chaminade College (Honolulu), and Colorado State University. Professor Koller received his A.B. from St. Thomas College, his A.M. from the University of Chicago and his Ph.D. from the University of Hawaii. He has studied at the University of Freiburg (Germany) and at Visva Bharati University (India). Professor Koller also completed a two-year residency at the Institute for Student Exchange, The Center for Cultural and Technical Interchange Between East and West, Honolulu.

Oriental
Philosophies

Oriental Philosophies

by JOHN M. KOLLER RENSSELAER POLYTECHNIC INSTITUTE

CHARLES SCRIBNER'S SONS · NEW YORK

1. Philosophy, Oriental
I. t

B-10.71 [MV]

Printed in the United States of America
SUL: 684-12721-0
TR: 684-10334-6
Library of Congress Catalog Card Number 70–99010

FOR CHRISTY

Preface

This book has been written with two basic aims in mind. First, it is intended to make possible an understanding and appreciation of Oriental thought and life. Second, it is intended to introduce the reader to certain fundamental and characteristic problems in philosophy as they are considered in the Oriental traditions. This is done in an attempt to make it possible for the reader to understand some of the answers given to the basic questions in life. The author is of the opinion that the traditions of Oriental philosophy are no less valuable and important than the traditions of Western philosophy. The assumption that a person can be introduced to philosophy only by considering the major thinkers and problems in the Western tradition is so obviously parochial that it is amazing that it continues almost completely unchallenged.

In the West philosophy is usually thought of in terms of the classical philosophers of the Western world. But in terms of understanding the nature of philosophy and philosophical problems there is no special advantage to studying philosophers who happen to have lived in the Western Hemisphere; geography is irrelevant here. Of course, there is an advantage in studying Western philosophers if the aim is not merely an understanding of the nature of philosophical activity and familiarity with certain philosophical positions, but also that of using the philosophical traditions as a means of understanding those ideas which have shaped the present condition of man in the Western Hemisphere. But by the same token, there is an advantage in studying the Oriental philosophers, for in addition to acquainting one with the nature of philosophy, one also gains understanding of the present condition of man in the Orient.

The reader who is accustomed to reading only Western philosophy will find it tempting to pigeonhole some of the material in this book as religion, or psychology, or even etiquette. He may dismiss certain areas of discussion (and the rest along with it) as "unphilosophical." But why should we force Western definitions of philosophy on the Orient? So far as I know, no one has ever demonstrated the superiority of Western concepts of philosophy over Oriental. And until this is done (if, indeed, it were possible!) Eastern thought should be studied within its own terms.

The important questions of life are no different for the Orient than for the West. Questions like, What is man? What is the nature of the universe in which man lives? In what does the good life consist? and, How can we know if the claims we make about the nature of man, the universe, and the good life are true? are basic philosophical questions, common to human beings the world over because they arise whenever and wherever man reflects upon his experience. Of course, these questions arise in different contexts and assume different forms for people living at different times and in different places, and the answers given may differ considerably. But these are the questions of man as man, arising out of the curiosity attending man's self-conscious nature and the innate urge to improve the conditions of his existence, and no human being can live without considering them. The question is not whether to answer or not answer these questions, but whether the answers will be explicit, thought-out, and well-argued, or whether they will be merely assumed, hidden, and implicit in the actions that constitute the history of a person.

On the easy assumption that an understanding of these questions as posed by philosophers and an analysis of the answers they have given will enable a person to understand and evaluate better the answers he or she gives to these questions, it seems obvious that it is important to know the forms and contexts of basic philosophical questions and answers, not just as they have appeared in the Western tradition, but as they have appeared in the whole philosophical tradition of man. This knowledge is needed to provide the imagination with the insights into man's experience which are required to provide an interpretation of experience that is worthy of the human animal. Ignoring the philosophical traditions of a majority of mankind and thereby depriving oneself of insights and knowledge needed for constructing a satisfactory philosophy of life is surely rash and unjustified.

The individual's need to construct for himself a philosophy of life is, I believe, imperative in our time. Therefore I have endeavored to make available to the lay reader some of the insights of the Oriental philosophers. To understand these ideas does not require any previous acquaintance with technical philosophy. Philosophical concepts and theories universally have their origin in, and depend for their justification and meaning upon, ordinary human experiences with which everyone is familiar. So it is possible, by tracing the relevant reflections on various aspects of experience, to show how a particular concept or theory developed, what it means, and how it can be justified. The present work not only does not assume prior acquaintance with philosophy, but should itself serve as an introduction.

These are among the reflections that have led to this attempt to provide an introduction to philosophy emphasizing the Oriental philosophical traditions. There is no doubt that in our own age we put our very existence in jeopardy by allowing ourselves to remain ignorant of at least half of the world. Never has the need been greater to come to an understanding of all the peoples of the world. Consequently, upon the assumption that to understand what a people have done and what they are likely to do it is necessary to understand their basic attitudes about life as reflected in their views of the nature of man, the good life, the nature of the universe, and the ways in which we can know reality, it is imperative that the philosophies of the Orient be studied and understood. Thus, the two functions which this book is intended to serve—to introduce the reader to an understanding of the Asian mind and to indicate the different ways in which fundamental philosophical questions have been considered in the Orient—grow out of the same basic concern, the concern to maintain and improve human existence.

Contents

INTRODUCTION

THE story of philosophy is the story of man's reflections on life. The problems of life are the source and touchstone of philosophy. If man's practical needs were provided for and his curiosity satisfied it is unlikely that there would be any philosophical activity in the world, for the two principal sources of philosophy are man's curiosity about himself and his surroundings and a desire to overcome all kinds of suffering. Man's practical needs and his theoretical curiosity lead to philosophical activity because it is his nature to be self-reflective. He not only has needs and is curious, but he is aware of himself having these needs and this curiosity. Seeing himself in the context of his surroundings as a being struggling to overcome pain and suffering and trying to uncover the mysteries of existence, man comes to examine the kind of being he is, the kind of world he lives in, and the sources of value and knowledge that are so characteristic of his existence. It is this self-reflective activity of man that constitutes philosophy, for philosophy is not to be identified with the problems of man, but with man's critical reflections on his problems.

To persons accustomed to hearing about the "deepness" and abstractness of philosophy it may appear difficult to see how any enterprise with its roots in the problems of human existence can be isolated from life. And perhaps true philosophy cannot be isolated from life. But the problems of getting food, shelter, and water are not philosophical problems. They are problems to be solved by technology, not by self-understanding and wisdom. And often the problems of the spirit, especially the problems connected with the meaning and value of life and the problem of death, are not recognized as the most basic and urgent of life's problems. It is when life is held over against death that the question "What is life?" arises. And if death and life are not understood, then what assurance is there that all of the rest of man's activities rest upon the right foundation? For all the other activities of man are aimed at preserving and making valuable life itself.

Theories about the meaning of life and death are caught up with speculation concerning how things come into existence and pass out of existence. As man reflects upon his speculations earlier theories come to be questioned. Alternative theories are proposed; these are questioned in turn and new ones proposed. Reflective persons consider the theories of others and reflect on their own experience as they attempt to find a philosophy that in its explanations accounts for all of man's experiences and assures him of the value and meaning of life.

In the process of working out satisfactory explanations, each formulation of the question and each aspect of the proposed solution must be examined from every side. Eventually the questions are raised, "Are things really the way we think they are? Is what we call *knowledge* really knowledge?" The philosopher, reflecting on what we know about our knowledge, may seem very far removed from the ordinary problems of life, though in reality he is not. It is not enough that he ask a question or propose a solution; he must also attempt to justify the proposed solution as a satisfactory answer to the original question. If he discovers that what he took to be knowledge was, in fact, opinion, perhaps mistaken opinion, his whole theory which seemed to explain the meaning and value of life may have to change. And when it does, the philosopher's orientation toward the good life—and his idea of the best means of achieving it—may also change. Could anything be more practical or closer to everyday life than that, even if it be abstract and subtle?

The charge is sometimes made that the philosophers dwell in ivory towers, that they concentrate on logical subtleties and minutiae, while ignoring the major concerns of life. They seem to hide in their abstractions. There is, of course, the possibility that the speculations of the philosophers may cease to be connected with the philosophy of the ordinary people. When this happens philosophy loses much of its relevance; it no longer serves the ordinary person in reflecting upon his own existence in the world, and fails to provide him with the materials needed for the construction of a personal philosophy of life. In the West we are accustomed, in large part, to thinking of philosophy as something apart from life.

In the East the gap between the philosophers and the ordinary people is not nearly as great. Oriental philosophers keep closely in touch with life, returning to the touchstone of human experience to test their theories. The ordinary people stretch beyond their day-to-day concerns and struggle to see their existence in perspective, to understand it in philosophical terms.

This difference between East and West, which is, to be sure, a matter of degree, is due in part to the Oriental insistence on the wholeness of life and knowledge. Unlike Westerners, Easterners dislike cutting up and compartmentalizing life and knowledge. The result is that they do not separate the various fields of philosophy, such as theory of knowledge, theory of being, theory of art, theory of action, theory of political organization, etc. There is no clear-cut distinction between Eastern philosophy and Eastern religion, between philosophy and psychology, or philosophy and science. One consequence of this is the Easterner's tendency to take philosophy seriously. Philosophy in the Orient is not an abstract academic matter with little or no relevance to daily life—it is regarded as life's most basic and most important enterprise.

In China, after Confucianism became the state philosophy, it was impossible to get a government job without knowing the works of Confucius. Chinese history tells of many kings, artists, and scholars who were philosophers. The Chinese regard thought and practice as inseparable from each other, as aspects of the same activity. The central problems of Chinese philosophy are reflected in the questions "How can man achieve a harmony with his fellow men?" and "How can man achieve a harmony with nature?" These two questions turn out to be closely related, because as philosophy developed in China, there was an increasing tendency to identify nature with human nature. To the extent that this identification took place, the problem of achieving harmony with nature was the problem of man being in harmony with himself. In turn, being in harmony with himself was regarded as the necessary basis for achieving a harmony with other men. Being in harmony with himself and in harmony with the rest of humanity is "the highest good" in Chinese philosophy. Because the basic nature of man is seen as essentially moral, the dominant concern of much Chinese philosophy has been with morality. The questions "How can I be good?" and "What is the basis of goodness?" are basic questions throughout the history of Chinese philosophy.

India is famous for the high regard it accords the seeker of wisdom and for its reverence and respect for wise persons. The accumulated practical wisdom of India takes the form of self-discipline (*yoga*) aimed at the total integration of life. In order that this discipline be available to all persons, it is channeled through the activities of worship and devotion, the activities of work, and the activities of knowledge and concentration. These paths of self-discipline are simply the philosophic wisdom of the ages being put into practice by the people. The source of this wisdom of self-discipline is to be found in that combination of deep, intense personal experience and highly abstract rational explanation which is so characteristic of the Indian mind.

Long before Jesus of Nazareth, the sages of India were pondering what man is in his deepest being, and what nature is in its ultimate reality. Pursuing these two questions the philosophers of the Upanishads came to the wonderful realization that man in his deepest being is one with the ultimate nature of reality. The immediate practical problem arising from this discovery was how to realize this inner Self and thereby identify with the very essence of the universe. The search for an answer prompted a variety of developments in *yoga* and religion as well as the construction of moral and social philosophies. The theoretical problems raised by this discovery centered around the difficulty of relating the multiplicity and diversity of experienced reality with the Upanishadic insight into the unity of all existence. Furthermore it was difficult to ascertain how knowledge of such an ultimate reality could be achieved. These problems—which can be formulated in terms of questions about the basis of morality, the nature and function of society, the means of valid knowledge, the principles of logic, and the relation between appearance and reality—all have a common basis in the practical question "How can man achieve the spirituality that is his true nature?"

In Buddhist Asia millions have embraced the teachings of the wisdom-seeking Guatama Siddhartha as the solution to all of life's sufferings. The central problem of Buddhism is that of overcoming suffering. The essential teachings of the Buddha revolve around the questions, What is suffering? How does it arise? How can suffering be eliminated? and, How should man live so as to achieve a suffering-less existence? These questions, however, cannot be answered without inquiring into the nature of the self that suffers and the nature of the world that constitutes a source of suffering for the self. The question, How is suffering caused? leads to a general theory of causation which shapes the theories of man and reality which constitute Buddhist metaphysics. The problems of justifying the claims made about the nature of the self and the nature of reality lead to a general theory of logic and knowledge. Thus, the eminently practical problem of overcoming suffering provokes the reflections that constitute the theoretical principles of Buddhist philosophy.

Despite the many differences between the philosophies of India, China, and Buddhist Asia, they share a common concern with living and being as well as with learning and knowing. Consequently, philosophy and the philosophers have primary importance in all Oriental cultures. In order to understand the life and the attitudes of the Oriental peoples, it is necessary to understand their philosophies. In order to understand their philosophies, it is necessary to look to the traditions wherein these philosophies were born and lived.

PART ONE

The Hindu Systems

Dancing Shiva. *The Metropolitan Museum of Art, Harris Brisbane Dick Fund, 1964*

DOMINANT FEATURES
OF INDIAN PHILOSOPHY

THE story of Indian philosophy is long and exciting. From its beginnings in the speculations of the Vedic seers about six thousand years ago to its present condition, Indian philosophical thought presents a richness, subtlety, and variety which constitute an almost awesome testimony to the human spirit. There is practically no insight or shade of speculation known to man that is not found in Indian thought. This richness and complexity makes it impossible to sum up Indian philosophy in clichés, slogans, or easy generalizations. Nevertheless, one can point out certain dominant features provided one keeps in mind that there are exceptions to every generalization. The following remarks must, therefore, be understood as an attempt to select those features of Indian thought which could be called dominant because of their endurance, their popularity with a considerable number of philosophers, or their widespread use in the lives of a majority of the people in India. In some cases, all three of these criteria apply.

Next to its richness and comprehensiveness, the most striking feature of Indian philosophical thought is its practical character. From the very beginning, the speculations of India's sages were aimed at solving life's basic problems. Their philosophy grew out of their attempts to improve life. Confronted with physical, mental, and spiritual suffering, India's early sages sought to understand the reasons and causes for this suffering. They attempted to improve their understanding of man and the universe because they wanted to uproot the causes of suffering and to achieve the best possible life. The solutions achieved—and the reasons for the conclusions underlying the solutions—constitute the philosophies of these early sages.

India's philosophies, then, responded to both practical and speculative incentives. Practically, there was the acquaintance with ordinary forms of pain and suffering—disease, poverty, starvation, and the knowledge that ultimately death would overtake the sufferer. Speculatively, there was the innate human curiosity to order and to understand human experience. Practical considerations led men to seek ways to overcome the various forms of suffering. Speculative considerations led them to construct explanatory accounts of the nature of reality and of human existence. These considerations were not undertaken separately. The understanding and knowledge derived from speculative curiosity was utilized in the attempt to overcome suffering.

The primacy of the practical considerations involved in Indian philosophies gives them substance, while the necessity of the speculative considerations determines their structure. Consequently, though the practical problems involved in determining the nature of the good life—including the social life—are always in the fore, the theoretical explanations—concerning the nature of self, reality, and knowledge—used to justify proposed solutions to the practical problems have great importance in Indian philosophies.

In all philosophy there are two fundamentally different approaches to the problem of suffering which are based upon and characterized by two different attitudes. Both approaches recognize that suffering is the result of a gap between what one is and has, and what one wants to be and wants to have. A man is poor; wanting the wealth he lacks, he suffers. A man desires deathlessness though he knows death is inevitable; fearing this inevitability, he suffers. If there were no difference between what one is and has, and what one wants to be and to have, there would be no suffering. When there is a difference, suffering is inevitable. This being the case, the solution to the problem is obvious: what is and what is desired must be made identical.

But how can this identity be achieved? One approach to the solution lies in adjusting what one is and has to what is desired. If a man is poor but desires wealth, he should endeavor to accumulate wealth. The other approach consists in adjusting one's desires to what one has. If one is poor and desires wealth, he can overcome the resulting problem by removing the desire.

It should be noted here that many shades of compromise between the two approaches are possible. If, theoretically, a pure form of each approach is possible, in practice there is always a compromise: the analyst can only observe how the emphasis falls upon one or the other. Basically it is the second approach that Indian philosophy has taken. India chose to emphasize control of desires. As a result, the philosophies of India tend to insist on self-discipline and self-control as prerequisite to happiness and the good life. Self-control rather than the satiation of desires is the basic way to eliminate suffering.

This need to regulate and control desires threw extraordinary emphasis on knowledge of the self: knowing and controlling the self could do far more than the sciences of nature to alleviate suffering. Consequently, the practice of Indian philosophy became, at best, the art of living in complete control of oneself.

The practical character of Indian philosophy is manifested in a variety of ways. The very word which is usually translated "philosophy" points to this. *Darshana* literally means vision. It is what is seen. In its technical sense it means what is seen when the ultimate is investigated. Thus the ancient seers of India, seeking the solution to life's sufferings, investigated the conditions of suffering and looked to the nature of man and the nature of the external universe to find the causes of suffering and the means for its cessation. What they found constituted their *darshana*, their vision or philosophy.

Of course it is possible to be mistaken in one's vision; one may not see things as they really are. Consequently, the philosopher must justify his vision by providing evidence of its truth. Historically, two methods of justifying philosophical visions are encountered. According to the first method, logical analysis is used to determine whether or not a particular view is justified. If the concepts and statements expressing the vision are inconsistent with each other the vision may be discarded as self-contradictory. For example, if according to the vision in question it is claimed that all things that are born must die, and if it is also held that man is born but will not die, then the vision contains two views which are incompatible with each other. Obviously, the vision cannot be accepted without somehow overcoming this internal inconsistency, for one cannot at the same time accept as true both the claim "all born things die," and the claim "not all born things die," for these claims are contradictory. Any vision which attempts to embrace both of these claims is self-contradictory and cannot be accepted.

But suppose that several visions, each consistent within itself, are mutually incompatible. For example, one vision consistently maintains that all born things die, and the other vision consistently maintains that nothing that is born dies. What reasons are there for preferring one over another? Logic alone is not enough to determine this, for the question is not primarily one of consistency.

The second method, in recognition of the insufficiency of logic alone, is pragmatic, finding the justification of views or theories in the quality of resulting practice.

Indian philosophers have always insisted that practice is the ultimate test of truth. Philosophical visions must be put into practice and life lived according to the ideals of the vision. The quality of the life lived according to those ideals is the ultimate test of any vision. The better life becomes, the closer the vision approaches complete truth.

The criteria for determining the quality of life are, in turn, derived from the basic impetus for philosophy: the drive to eliminate suffering. The vision that makes possible a life devoid of suffering is properly called a true philosophy. Degrees of philosophic truth are determined according to the degree of alleviation of suffering. Put in a positive way, views are true according to the extent they improve the quality of life.

Placing the positive emphasis for justification of a philosophy on experience rather than logic (though logic is not excluded) requires putting philosophy into practice. In India, this has meant the working-out of a way to the realization of the good life wherein suffering is eliminated. The path is part of the vision, and if the way to the realization of the goals of the vision cannot be followed the vision is itself regarded as inadequate. "Good in theory, but not in practice," is a remark that makes no sense when applied to Indian philosophies. Good in theory necessarily means good in practice. If a theory cannot be put into practice there is something wrong with it.

The identification of the way to the good life with the vision of the good life itself is the integrating factor between religion and philosophy in India. When philosophy is regarded as being concerned only with the *theory* of the good life, concern with the practical means of attaining the good life is not considered philosophical. The means of life may then be regarded as falling within the religious or economic spheres, but not the philosophical. When the good life is thought to be "at a higher level" than this ordinary life, the means of achieving it are usually thought of as religious. When a materialistic view of the good life prevails, the means of achieving it are often thought to be economic. In neither case does the matter lie within the philosopher's domain—if religion and economics are practical matters and philosophy is theoretical, the consequent differences of scope, goal, and approach will sharply delineate one approach from another. But in India a philosopher's theory of the good life had to be tested by practice, and the philosopher had to devise a means for achieving the good life in order to be a philosopher. No sharp distinction existed between theory and practice; philosophy and religion were not considered to be two separate activities.

The Indian insistence upon practice as a test of philosophical truth had another effect—it emphasized the introspective approach. To avoid suffering, the philosopher had to look into himself, into his life, and note what was happening. To see the changes taking place and to evaluate these changes it is necessary for the individual to continue his self-examination, to observe what he is and what he is becoming. This necessitates a constant subjectivity.

The subjective is emphasized in two senses in Indian thought. In one sense the subjective is considered as the opposite of objective; the criteria of truth are qualitative rather than quantitative. According to the other sense, subjective refers to the subject as opposed to the object. An object is anything that can be entertained or witnessed by a subject. The subject, however, is always witness or entertainer; never the witnessed or entertained.

Indian philosophy is concerned with the suffering of human beings, and the human subject is of greater importance than the objects that come within the experience of the subject. The self that suffers is always the subject. To treat it otherwise is to regard it as a thing, which places the consideration outside the immediate bounds of philosophy. The ultimate self of man is described in the philosophical literature as pure subject, or subject which can never become object—"The one without a second." It is the subjective or qualitative experience of the subject that is of primary concern.

The emphasis on the subjective, in both senses of that expression, tends to promote a synthetic attitude. The relevant philosophical criteria are not quantitative and public. They belong to subject as subject. Therefore it is impossible for one person to subscribe to one philosophy as alone being true and to regard the others as completely false. Truth in philosophy depends upon the human subject, and another's experience can be known only as an object. There is no knowing—according to ordinary ways of knowing, at least—the other as subject. Consequently, there is no rejecting the other's experience as inadequate or unsatisfactory. Recognition of this has led to a tolerant synthetic attitude which is commonly expressed by saying that while it may be that no vision, by itself, is absolutely true and complete, nevertheless, each vision contains some glimpse of the truth, and by assuming the viewpoints and experiences assumed by the various visions one comes closer to the absolute truth and the complete vision. Philosophical progress is not made by proceeding from falsehood to truth, but by proceeding from partial to more complete truth.

In addition to these features of Indian philosophy which stem from its practical orientation, there is a widespread tendency in Indian thought to presuppose universal moral justice. The world is seen as a great moral stage directed by justice. Everything, good, bad, and indifferent is earned and deserved. The impact of this attitude is to place the responsibility for man's condition squarely upon man himself. An individual is responsible for what he is and what he becomes. He himself has determined his past and will determine his future. In the sacred writings, the Vedas, the concept of *rita* (moral law) denoted justice as the ruler of the universe. As the duties of man in response to justice came to be emphasized, the concept of *dharma* as determined by the moral structure of the universe became dominant. The concept of *karma* came to refer to the relation between what one did and what he was, pointing, as it did, to the causal efficacy of human actions, standing for the self-determination of man.

There is also rather widespread agreement in Indian philosophical thought concerning non-attachment. Suffering results from attaching oneself to what one does not have or even to what one cannot have. These attached objects then become the causes of suffering insofar as they are not attained or are lost. Therefore, if a spirit of non-attachment to the objects of suffering could be cultivated the suffering itself could be eliminated. Thus, non-attachment is recognized as an essential means to the realization of the good life.

Because of the above features of Indian thought, the people of India have usually accorded the highest respect to the philosopher, and philosophy has been regarded as the highest knowledge and wisdom.

CHAPTER 2

HISTORICAL SURVEY
OF INDIAN PHILOSOPHY

INDIAN philosophy began before recorded history. The first bits of speculation which could be called philosophical date back over five thousand years, to about 4000 B.C. Since those beginnings, now dimmed and obscured by time, India has acquired a vast wealth of philosophical vision, speculation, and argument. It is difficult to approach Indian philosophy chronologically, however, as a history in terms of names, dates, and places is a most unsure thing. In India so much emphasis has been put on the content of the thought and so little on person, place, and time that in a majority of cases it is not known who is responsible for the particular philosophy in question. And when the author is unknown, the time and the place can be reckoned only indirectly. Because of this, time is usually reckoned in terms of centuries rather than years or decades, and authorship is attributed to schools rather than to individual persons. Nevertheless, it is possible to see changes in philosophical thinking occurring in a certain sequence. That is, it is possible to see the antecedents and successors of various philosophical problems and solutions.

The historical approach is facilitated by adopting a more or less arbitrary classification of periods in the development of the philosophical traditions in India. The Vedic period stretches from about 4000 B.C. to 700 B.C. The Epic period occurred between 1000 B.C. and 200 A.D. The

Sutra period lasted from about 400 B.C. to 500 A.D. The Commentary period commenced about 600 A.D. and continued until about 1700 A.D. The Renaissance period, which is still in progress, began around 1800 A.D.

THE VEDIC PERIOD: It was during the Vedic period that the Aryan peoples moved from Central Asia into the Indus Valley. The cultural traditions they brought with them mingled with the traditions and customs of the people they met, and what can properly be called Indian culture began to take shape, a growth nourished by the climates and conditions of two earlier cultures.

The philosophical fruit of this early period is contained in the collection of writings called the Upanishads, which represent the culmination of philosophical speculation of this first period, and in the earlier literature of the Vedic *Samhitas*, *Brahmanas*, and *Aranyakas*, which are, for the most part, religious. Finding themselves in a new land, in many ways cut off from their familiar routines of life, these early peoples formulated questions about the world around them and their place in it. What made the wind blow? What was responsible for the monsoon? And the sun, giver of warmth and light—who put it in the sky? And how is it that broad-bosomed earth brings forth these myriad life-forms? These are typical of the questions entertained in the early portions of the Vedic period—questions which at first received answers attributing all these things, both wonderful and terrible, to the gods.

Questions of how and why are the roots of philosophical speculation. At first men tried to answer these questions in terms of the human person, and they attributed events in nature to superhuman persons, or gods. This tended to encourage religious activity rather than specifically philosophical speculation. Inquiring minds, however, continued to probe into the why's of nature and man, so in addition to developing the Vedic ritual and worship found in the *Sama* and the *Yajur Vedas*, they also developed the cognitive inquiry which is the spirit of philosophy. This is attested to by the literature of the Aranyakas and the Upanishads. In this later literature a universal law of cause and effect called *rita* is important. So by the time of the Upanishads that most wonderful of all discoveries already had been made—the discovery that the ultimate source and power of all existence is identical with one's ultimate self.

The literature of this period (all of it termed *Veda*) can be divided into the following categories: *Rig-Veda*, *Sama Veda*, *Yajur Veda*, and *Atharva Veda*. Each of the first three Vedas contain hymns to the gods as well as various questions (the *Samhita* portion), arrangements of the *Samhita* portion for use in sacrifices (the *Brahmana* portion), interpretations of the rituals (*Aranyaka* portion), and speculations on the basic questions underlying religious practices (the *Upanishads*). Though all of this literature was composed prior to 700 B.C. it has exerted a very great influence on the people of India right up to our own times.

THE EPIC PERIOD: The wisdom of the Vedic literature was part of a sacred and jealously guarded tradition, often unavailable to many members of the society, or where available, beyond understanding. To compensate for this there grew up a folklore recited in stories and poems which managed to transmit many of the ideals of the sacred tradition to the majority of the people. The two most notable collections of materials constituting this literature are the *Mahabharata* and the *Ramayana*.

The *Mahabharata* is an epic of considerable length (the English translation runs to thirteen volumes). It tells the story of the conquest of the land of India and in so doing provides instruction for the various rules of life. It offers a guide to life in all its dimensions, including religion, philosophy, social science, politics, and even medicine. The single most influential part of the *Mahabharata* is the *Bhagavad Gita*, "The Song of the Great One." The *Gita* explains the nature of man and the universe, and from the explanation of matter and spirit are derived ways of life which will enable one to achieve the ultimately good life.

The *Ramayana*, a beautiful poem in four volumes, presents ideals for womanhood and manhood in the persons and lives of Sita, and her husband, Rama. The epic suggests an ideal order for society as a whole, and also an ideal ordering of the life of the individual.

During this period treatises on justice and righteousness—the *Dharma Shastras*—were compiled. These treatises were concerned primarily with regulating the life of the individual and the society in respect to specific codes of actions, which were presented along with their justification in the literature on *dharma*. The *Artha Shastra* of Kautilya justifies the need for and the importance of the various means of life and shows how they may be obtained. The *Manu Shastra* shows how justice and order may be secured in society by the king and the institutions of government. The *Shastra* of Yajnavalkya emphasizes justice and order in the life of the individual. The *Kama Shastra* (sometimes translated as *Kama Sutra*) of Vatsyayana deals with the attainment of pleasure. These are among the more influential of these treatises.

No doubt it was also during this time that the beginnings of the various systems of philosophy were established, for there are references in the *Mahabharata* to certain of the systems. But these systems did not receive definitive form until near the end of the Epic period.

THE SUTRA PERIOD: Toward the end of the Epic period, the beginnings of several systematic philosophical explanations of the world and man were established. These systems represent the first purely philosophical effort in India, for not only did they attempt to explain the fundamentals of life and the world, but they did so self-consciously and self-critically, arguing for the correctness of the answers suggested on the basis of reason.

The *Sutras*, or aphorisms, of Buddhism, Jainism, and Carvaka are designated *nastika*, or unorthodox, because their authors did not accept the pronouncements of the Vedas as true and final. Neither did they endeavor to justify their analyses and solutions by showing them to be in accord with the Vedas. The aphorisms expressing the philosophies of the Schools of Nyaya, Vaishesika, Samkhya, Yoga, Mimamsa, and Vedanta, on the other hand, all accept the authority of the Vedas.

Forest-dwelling Sages. *Reprinted by kind permission of Nancy Wilson Ross from* THREE WAYS OF ASIAN WISDOM (*Simon and Schuster, New York*).

These schools are all concerned to show that their analyses and solutions do indeed agree with the pronouncements of the Vedas. Consequently varying "orthodox" interpretations of the Vedas came about; each school's claim for its views was demonstrated by agreement with the "correct" interpretation of those teachings. These divisive claims especially affected the Vedanta philosophies.

The major division, however, is between Carvaka and the others: Carvaka is a completely materialistic system: all the others allow for spirituality—Nyaya is concerned primarily with a logical analysis of the means of knowing: Vaishesika analyzes the kinds of things that are known: Samkhya seeks to relate the self to the external world: Yoga analyzes the nature of the self and explains how the pure Self can be realized: Mimamsa concentrates on the criteria for the self-validity of knowledge, attempting thereby to establish the truth of the Vedic pronouncements: Vedanta begins with the conclusions of the Upanishads and attempts to show that a rational analysis of knowledge and reality will support those conclusions.

PERIOD OF THE GREAT COMMENTARIES: As generations of seers and scholars studied and examined the *sutras* of the various schools, they occasionally wrote commentaries on them. In this way the great commentaries of Guadapada (sixth cent. A.D.), Shamkara (eighth cent. A.D.), Bhaskara (ninth cent. A.D.), Yamuna (tenth cent. A.D.), Ramanuja (eleventh cent. A.D.), Nimbarka (twelfth cent. A.D.), Madhva (thirteenth cent. A.D.), and Vallabha (fifteenth cent. A.D.), came to be written on the Vedanta *Sutras* of Badarayana.

THE RENAISSANCE PERIOD: As a result of outside influences, especially the contact with the West, Indian philosophers began to reexamine their philosophical traditions. Beginning with the studies, translations, and commentaries of Ram Mohun Roy in the nineteenth century, the examinations have recently been carried on in especially notable fashion by Radhakrishnan and Aurobindo among others.

CHAPTER 3

RELIGION AND PHILOSOPHY—
THE VEDAS AND UPANISHADS

THE earliest recorded speculations about the nature of the world and the nature of man are found in the *Rig-Veda*. In the *Rig-Veda* there is no distinction between religion and philosophy, but the questions which give rise to both are asked at this time, and provide the structuring theme of the Vedic literature. Some of these questions— What makes the wind blow? Why does the monsoon come? Who put the sun, giver of warmth and light, in the heavens? and, How is it that broad-bosomed earth brings forth these myriad life forms?—would, according to present day classifications, belong to the sciences rather than to philosophy. Other questions such as, Who will save me from death? Who will protect me in time of danger? and, How will I be saved from the evils and misfortunes of life? might be thought to belong to religion. But six thousand years ago these distinctions did not exist, and all of these questions were the philosopher's concern. And there were yet other questions asked, questions that even according to today's classifications would be considered philosophical. These included such questions as, What is there beyond the gods? What, if any, is the relation between actions and their consequences? What knowledge, if any, does man have of himself?

Early attempts to satisfy curiosity about man's environment resulted in attributing all the wonderful and terrible things in it to the gods. The reason for this was simple: the questions *How? Why?* and *With what?* are appropriate when applied to human activity. Consequently, when these questions were asked of *natural* activity rather than *human* activity it was easy to assume personal forces behind the natural activities; then the questions were like questions about human activity and were answerable. Of course these personal forces were not thought of as similar to ordinary persons; they were regarded as "super" persons, or gods. The activity of fire was attributed to a god of fire, the activity of wind to a god of wind, etc. Nature, when thought of as a human person, was at least partially removed from the realm of the mysterious.

To the extent that the answers attributing natural activities to various gods were conceived to be ultimate answers, men endeavored less to understand nature than to control it. If the vital questions about nature, *How* and *Why*, were answerable in terms of *Who*, it is not surprising that men sought to control nature by influencing the gods with prayers, rituals, and sacrifices. Consequently it is not surprising that major portions of the Vedas are preoccupied with ritual and sacrifice.

But not all of the seers of the *Rig-Veda* were satisfied with religion as the way of understanding and controlling nature and man. Some could say;

> Who knows for certain? Who shall here declare it? Whence was it born, and whence came this creation? The gods were born after this world's creation: Then who can know from whence it has arisen? None knoweth whence this creation has arisen; And whether He has or has not produced it: He who surveys it in the highest heaven, He only knows, or perhaps even he may know not.[1]

They were the seekers of wisdom who searched beyond the gods to the rule that governs even the gods, to the reality that exists beyond the gods. They recognized that behind the regularities of nature and the gods stands an eternal and immutable law of order and justice. They called it *Rita*. In addition to providing for orderliness, this eternal law represented the unity of reality and man, for not only the activities of nature but also of man proceed from and according to *Rita*. *Rita* stands as order and justice directing the whole play of the cosmos; nothing happens except as directed by that eternal law.

Even the religious thinkers, however, concerned with ritual and sacrifice, could not be content with the assumption that nature was controlled by the gods, who in turn were subject to the appeals of prayer and sacrifice. The questions of how the gods controlled nature,

[1] *Rig-Veda*, X.129.6,7. Reprinted in Sarvepalli Radhakrishnan and Charles A. Moore, eds., *A Source Book in Indian Philosophy* (Princeton: Princeton University Press, 1957), pp. 23, 24.

and how man could influence the gods, resulted in theologies whereby these things were explained. While for the most part these explanations (which constitute the *Brahmana* portions of the Veda) were simply concerned with the elaboration of details of religious worship, occasionally they transcended the limits of the given answers and sought to explain the efficacy of sacrifice in terms of primordial principles more basic than the gods. In the *Shatapatha Brahmana*, the seer speculates as follows:

> Verily, in the beginning this (universe) was the *Brahman* [neut.]. It created the gods; and, having created the gods, it made them ascend these worlds: Agni this (terrestrial) world, Vāyu the air, and Sūrya the sky. . . . Then the *Brahman* itself went up to the sphere beyond. Having gone up to the sphere beyond, it considered, "How can I descend again into these worlds?" It then descended again by means of these two, Form and Name. . . . These, (Name and Form) indeed, are the two great forces of *Brahman*; and verily, he who knows these two great forces of *Brahman* becomes himself a great force.[2]

This is obviously an attempt to explain the religious in terms of the philosophical, transcending the religion of the time.

The Aranyakas, composed later than the Brahmanas, represent a move away from the ritualism of an earlier period and toward free intellectual inquiry into the nature of reality. Even though they accept the religious way, they tend to substitute meditation on aspects of nature for sacrificial objects. Gradually the meditation led to free speculation, and the contemplation which permeates the Upanishads came to replace ritualism. But the fact remains that while the early portions of the Veda—the *Samhitas, Brahmanas,* and *Aranyakas*—contain some philosophy, for the most part they are religious in content.

It is not a simple matter to distinguish between religion and philosophy. In the main, it can be said that philosophical thought is free. It is free to take man in whatever direction his total experience leads him, free from the restrictions of predetermined truth. The early portions of the Veda were philosophical to the extent that the persons' experiences and reflections led them to conclude that natural activities were due to the gods. But when this answer came to be regarded as absolute and final, men were no longer free to continue the quest: they were limited to the framework imposed by the attitude which regarded earlier answers as definitive.

---

[2] *Shatapatha Brahmana*, XI.2.2, trans. by Julius Eggeling, *Sacred Books of the East*, XLIV (Oxford: The Clarendon Press, 1900), pp. 27, 28.

Another feature of philosophical thought is that it is self-critical, ever aware that claimed answers depend for their truth upon the justifying evidence produced. Here again, the bulk of early Vedic thought appears non-philosophical, for the question of evidence for the truth of the various claims upon which the religious practices rested did not, for the most part, arise. And when the question did arise, men began to seek evidence through contemplation of and speculation upon nature and man, rather than through the way of ritual.

Another generic feature of philosophical thought is that it is concerned with fundamental and primary principles of existence and action; concerned not only with suppositions, but also with presuppositions. Thus, a great bulk of the early Vedic literature, which was devoted to descriptions of and elaborations upon rituals, could hardly be said to be philosophical.

The concluding portions of the Veda, the Upanishads, are much more philosophical than the preceding portions, for they are free from the restrictions of predetermined truth. They contain a recognition of the need to supply evidence for their claims, and they are concerned with the fundamental principles of existence. Nevertheless, even they are not fully philosophical in the current sense of that term, for they proceed without any formal analysis of the criteria of truth and the relation between truth and evidence. For the most part, personal experience of what is claimed is taken as sufficient evidence for the truth of the claim, but there is no attempt to show how it is that certain kinds of experience can count as evidence for claims about reality. And while there is general recognition that self-contradictory views cannot be true, it would be going too far to suggest that reason determined the truth or falsity of views, for there were no principles of logic or reason worked out. Consequently, the Upanishads tend to emphasize the content of the vision of the seer more that the means whereby the vision can be justified. The claims in the Upanishads are taken to be the reports of the experience of the seers, and not philosophical theories waiting to be justified. It is the experience of the seers that provides the evidence for the truth of the claims being made.

When man confronts his existence face to face and meditates on its beginning and end in an attempt to discover its meaning and value, he comes up against certain basic questions concerning the reality surrounding him. What is the nature of fundamental reality? How was the universe created? How is it controlled and regulated? How is it sustained? These are among the questions that gave rise to the speculations of the Vedas.

It was noted earlier that the first attempts to answer questions about the nature of external reality led to belief in the various gods of nature. Gradually the number of these gods decreased, as the functions of several lesser deities were attributed to a more powerful god. By this process it came to be thought that there was one single deity who was the creator and controller of the universe. By the time of the Upanishads it seems to be well accepted that there is a single reality which is the source of all external existence. But now the claim that this single reality is a deity is regarded as unsatisfactory and an attempt is made to discover just what this ultimate source is. Consequently the key question of the Upanishads with respect to external reality is, What is the one source and controller of all existence?

This question presupposes that there is a difference between what *appears* to be real and what is really real; appearance is not taken as being sufficient for its own existence, but is thought to be dependent upon some higher reality. The search was not for the world of space and time filled with sound, odors, colors, etc., which *appears* to man as his world, but for the *conditions* that make possible this appearing world.

The distinction is analogous to the distinction made between the colors one sees and the conditions which make possible the seeing of colors. One might say that what one sees are the various colors of the spectrum, taking the colors to be something that exist in the world. Someone else, however, might point out that colors as seen do not *really* exist, but that they *appear* to exist when certain wave-lengths of light pass through specified media before striking the retina. To talk about colors is to talk about the conditioned; to talk about wave-lengths and media is to talk about the sources of the conditioned which enable the conditioned to exist as appearance. Here the analogy breaks down, however, for the seers of the Upanishads were not seeking the specific conditions of any particular appearances, but were seeking that which conditioned or made possible existence itself.

These seers had no clear concept of what they sought; they simply knew that there must exist that by which all other things existed and which made them great. The name given to this "something" was *Brahman*, which means "that which makes great." It was a non-descriptive name; in fact it was a non-name, for it did not name anything definite, either abstract or concrete. The search for what *"Brahman"* named is recorded in the Upanishads as the search for the ultimate external reality. At first there was an attempt to identify that "something" with religious symbols and sacrifices, with natural objects, such as the sun and the moon, and with certain psychological functions of man. The difficulty with all of these attempts to state what *Brahman* is, was that they all presupposed limits on that power. But since they were seeking the ultimate power of existence it was impossible that it should be limited, for there could be nothing beyond it to limit it. As the seers began to realize more clearly that *Brahman* could not adequately be described by appealing to their experience of the world of appearance, they attempted to define this reality in a negative way.

According to Yajnavalkya in the *Brihadaranyaka Upanishad*, *Brahman* is not conceivable, not changeable, not injurable, etc. According to the *Katha Upanishad*, *Brahman* is inaudible, invisible, indestructible, cannot be tasted, cannot be smelled, is without beginning or end, and greater than the great. *Brahman* is described negatively in the *Mundaka Upanishad* as follows:

> Invisible, incomprehensible, without genealogy, colourless, without eye or ear, without hands or feet, eternal, pervading all and over all, scarce knowable, that unchangeable one whom the wise regard as being womb.[3]

Clearly it was felt that *Brahman* was not many and not material. But these characteristics are negative. The difficulty is that after regarding *Brahman* as that which makes possible time, space, and causality it was impossible to regard it as limited by them. Being prior to space, time, and causality means being beyond the characteristics of the empirical universe, and therefore beyond positive description. That which makes possible both conception itself and the conceptualized is not to be.caught with the net of the conceptualized world. But if that is the case then the nature of *Brahman* remains elusive and mysterious.

Despite the fact that for all of their concentration on *Brahman* they were unsuccessful in establishing the ultimate nature of external reality, the thinkers of the Upanishads were not completely stymied. Some of them, unlike the seers of the early portions of the Veda, were seeking an answer to a different question; a question about the ultimate nature of *man*. This second basic question of the Upanishads is the question, What am I, in my deepest existence?

This too, was a question about the conditions of appearance rather than about the appearances themselves. The question presupposes that the self is something more than meets the eye, for the bodily organism is not particularly elusive or mysterious. But the question of what

---

[3] *Mundaka Upanishad*, I.1.6, trans. by Paul Deussen, *The Philosophy of the Upanishads* (New York: Dover Publications, 1966), p. 148.

enables the bodily organism to exist is another matter. I may appear to be a bodily organism, but is that what I really am? Is the "I" that thinks the self to be a bodily organism also a bodily organism? And is not the "I" more properly the self than the body? These are the sorts of questions that occurred to these thinkers.

There is no doubt that the distinction between what the self appears to be and what it really is, was assumed by the thinkers of the Upanishads. Their search for the innermost essence of man is guided by the injunction:

> The Self (atman) which is free from evil, free from old age, free from death, free from grief, free from hunger and thirst, whose desire is the real, whose thoughts are true, he should be sought, him one should desire to understand. He who has found out and who understands that self, he obtains all worlds and desires.[4]

The question was, What is that wonderful and mysterious Self? Trying to answer that question, the seers of the *Taittiriya Upanishad* turned their attention to the various aspects and functions of the individual person as they searched for that ultimate Self. If the Self is thought to be the body then it is essentially food, they reasoned, for the body is simply digested food. But surely the Self is not to be identified with the body only, for it is something more; it is alive and moving. If the Self is not food, perhaps it is the life of food. But they saw that while this would serve to distinguish living from non-living matter it was not the ultimate Self of the person, for a person is more than simply living food. It sees, hears, feels, etc. Perhaps, the speculation continues, the Self should be thought of in terms of mind or perception. But this too seemed inadequate, for thinking and understanding are even more properly Self than perception. However, this too is rejected as inadequate, for there must be that which gives existence to thinking and understanding. As the Upanishad says, "Different from and within that which consists of the understanding is the Self consisting of bliss."[5]

This search for the ultimate Self was essentially a matter of going deeper and deeper into the foundations of human existence. Matter was regarded as covering for life, which in turn was a covering for the sensing self. And deeper than sensing was intellectual activity. But deeper still was the bliss of total consciousness. Consequently, the Self is not to be

[4] *Chandogya Upanishad*, VIII.7.1. In *The Principal Upanisads* ed. by Sarvepalli Radhakrishnan (London: Allen and Unwin Ltd., 1953), p. 501. Unless otherwise noted, all quotations from the Upanishads are from this work.
[5] *Taittiriya Upanishad*, II.5.1.

identified with any of the lower forms of the person exclusively, but is to be thought of as existing within the various layers of existence, giving them life while remaining distinct from them.

In the *Kena Upanishad* the search for the ultimate Self takes the form of a quest for the ultimate agent or doer of human activity. It is asked, "By whom willed and directed does the mind light on its objects? By whom commanded does life the first, move? At whose will do (people) utter this speech? And what god is it that prompts the eye and the ear?"[6]

In the very next paragraph these questions are answered by saying that there is a more basic Self that directs the eye to color, the ear to sound, the understanding to consciousness, etc. And this Self is said to be "other than the known and other than the unknown."[7] The question here is basically a matter of asking what makes possible seeing, hearing, thinking, etc. But the question is not about physiological processes; it it about the hearing subject, the seeing subject, etc. That is, I may be said to be a hearing, seeing, thinking thing; but by what do I do these things? I see the green colors in front of me when they are present to the eye; how is it that the eye is so directed? Must not there be an inner director, an agent directing the functions and activities of a person? The answer in the Upanishads is a most emphatic *yes*.

There remains, however, another question; What is that which directs all of the human activities? The answer to that question is that it cannot be known, for "there the eye goes not, speech goes not, nor the mind; we know not, we understand not how one can teach this."[8] The reason it is beyond the eye, beyond the ear, beyond the understanding, etc., is that what is seen, heard, understood, etc., is always an object known by the human subject. But the ultimate Self is the ultimate subject. Therefore it can never be an object of knowledge, and must remain beyond the grasp of ordinary knowledge. Nevertheless, since this Self is ultimate subject, it can be realized directly in total self-consciousness, where, so to speak, the knower stands illumined by its own illumination. Thus, though in one sense the ultimate Self cannot be known, in another sense, the sense of immediate experience, it can be known intimately and completely in the experience of total self-consciousness. In this sense it is known much more surely and completely than any object of knowledge. This is the certitude of one's own existence, beyond question or doubt.

[6] *Kena Upanishad*, I.1.   [7] *Ibid.*, I.4.   [8] *Ibid.*, I.3.

In the *Chandogya Upanishad* man's search for the ultimate Self is presented in the form of a delightful story in which Prajapati (representing the creative forces of the universe) instructs Indra (who represents the gods) and Virocana (who represents the demons) about the Self. As students seeking the wisdom possessed by the *guru*, or spiritual teacher, Indra and Virocana come, bearing fuel, to Prajapati for instruction. For thirty-two years they prepare themselves for Prajapati's teaching by practicing self-discipline. At the end of that time he tells them that the Self is what they see when they look at their reflection in a glass or a pan of water. They look and they see the physical form, clothed and adorned with jewels. Virocana, delighted with this knowledge returns to the demon-world and teaches that the body is the Self. Such is the teaching of the demons! But Indra reflects on this teaching and sees that if the Self is the same as the body, then when the body perishes so does the Self. This cannot be the immortal Self he is seeking, so he again asks Prajapati about the Self. This time Prajapati tells him that the dream-self is the real Self. But still Indra is uneasy. For although the dream-self is not absolutely dependent upon the body, nevertheless sometimes it too is subject to pain, suffering and destruction. So again he asks what the real Self is. And this time he is told that the self that is sound asleep, beyond dreams, is the real Self. At first this satisfies Indra, but before he has reached the abode of the gods he realizes that even though the deep-sleeping self is not subject to pain and destruction, nevertheless it cannot be the real Self—in deep sleep the self is not aware of itself; one might just as well be dead, he tells Prajapati. By this time Indra has spent a total of one hundred and one years disciplining and preparing himself for that highest knowledge (*paravidyam*) and now is ready to hear about the ultimate Self. Now Prajapati tells him that the Self being sought transcends all of the selves considered so far. It is true, there is a physical self, which some think to be the only self. And there is the self which is the subject that experiences dreams, a self recognized by some. And there is the self which experiences deep sleep, otherwise deep sleep would be the same as death. But the highest Self goes beyond all of these; it is that which makes possible the self of waking experience, of dreaming experience, and of deep sleep. Those selves are merely instruments of the highest Self, which is the very source of their existence.

The state in which one realizes the ultimate Self that gives existence to the selves of the waking, dreaming, and deep-sleeping selves is sometimes called the *turiya*, or fourth state. Unlike the condition of deep sleep this state is one of total self-consciousness and illumination. In the

Brihadaranyaka Upanishad it is said, "When one goes to sleep, he takes along the material of this all-containing world, himself tears it apart, himself builds it up and dreams by his own brightness, by his own light. Then this person becomes self-illuminated."[9]

Although ordinary knowledge, which presupposes the duality of object and subject, knower and known, is impossible in this fourth state, there is no doubt of the authenticity of its existence. The same Upanishad continues:

> Indeed, while he does not there know, he is indeed knowing, though he does not know [what is usually to be known]; for there is no cessation of the knowing of a knower, because of his imperishability [as a knower]. It is not, however, a second thing, other than himself and separate, which he may know.[10]

Thus, in the Upanishads, the question, What am I, in the deepest reaches of my existence? is answered by saying that the very foundation of existence is self-illuminating consciousness, which can be directly experienced by a person when one goes beyond identification with the false self of the objectified world. It is tremendously significant that the ultimate Self—the *Atman*—can be known directly and immediately as a matter of direct experience. For here there can be no doubts or lingering uncertainty. This is an answer which when realized provides for the total satisfaction of the individual.

The discovery of *Atman* is also significant in another way. The seers of the Upanishads who were seeking both the ultimate external reality (*Brahman*) and the ultimate internal reality (*Atman*) came to inquire into the relations or connections between these realities. The exciting discovery they now made was that *Atman* was none other than *Brahman*. There was only one ultimate reality which could be approached either by looking outside of man or by looking within man. Thus, though the search for the nature of external reality, or *Brahman*, had appeared to end in frustration because of the impossibility of saying anything about the ultimate object, it was now realized that *Brahman* could be known by the self-certifying experience of total conscious illumination, because *Brahman* was the ultimate Subject, or *Atman*. There was no difference between the ultimate subject and the ultimate object; ultimate subjective reality and ultimate objective reality were one and the same! It is hard to imagine a more exciting discovery. Seeking to understand what the world was and who he was, man had discovered that all

---

[9] *Brihadaranyaka Upanishad*, IV.3.9.   [10] *Brihadaranyaka Upanishad*, IV.3.30.

things existed within *Atman*; that he himself sustained all things in his deepest Self. One need only know the Self to know all. And the Self can be known in the surest way possible, for it is self-revealing in consciousness when the objects of consciousness that block out self-illumination are transcended.

The unity of *Atman* and *Brahman* is the greatest discovery made in the Upanishads. This unity above all is the mystery and sacred teaching (*upanisat*) that is so carefully guarded by the seers of the Upanishads, and that constitutes the basic message of these treatises.

The quest for the nature of *Brahman* and *Atman* and the discovery of the relation between them is well illustrated by the account of the five householders who studied with Ashvapati Kaikeya.[11]

Pracinashala Aupamanyava, Satyayajna Paulusi, Indradyumna Bhallaveya, Jana Sharkaraksya, and Budila Ashvatarashvi, famous householders, renowned for their learning and wisdom, got together to investigate what is self and what is *Brahman*. Consulting among themselves they agreed that since Uddalaka Aruni was at present studying this universal Self they would go to him.

But when they came, Uddalaka reflected; "These great householders and greatly learned in sacred lore will question me. I shall not be able to tell them all. Therefore, I shall direct them to another (teacher)." He said to them "Venerable Sirs, Ashvapati Kaikeya studies at present this universal Self, well, let us go to him." When they arrived, they announced their purpose saying, "At present, Sir, you know the universal Self. Tell us indeed about that."

Assuring himself that these persons were qualified to receive this sacred teaching, Ashvapati Kaikeya discovered that one of the householders regarded heaven as the universal Self. Another regarded the sun as the universal Self. A third considered space to be the universal Self. The fourth thought the Self was air, while the fifth householder regarded water as the universal Self. Uddalaka Aruni looked for the Self in the earth. Ashvapati Kaikeya told each householder that his knowledge was only partial and limited. He said to them, "Indeed you eat your food knowing this universal Self as if it were many. He, however, who meditates on the universal Self as of the measure of the span or as identical with the self, eats food in all worlds, in all beings, in all selves."

This teaching of Ashvapati Kaikeya is usually interpreted to mean that the universal Self is in each person and in each being without differentiation. The householders should realize the universal Self in themselves, for they are not different from that universal Self.

The *Chandogya Upanishad* also contains the famous teaching of Shandilya: "Verily, this whole world is *Brahman*. . . . Containing all works, containing all desires, containing all odors, containing all tastes, encompassing this whole world, without speech, without concern, this is the Self (*Atman*) of mine within the heart; this is *Brahman*."[12]

Because of the deep-seated ignorance that results in objectification of the world, and because of the resulting multiplicity, one is inclined to think of the ultimate reality as an other. But this is a mistake, for "in the beginning all this world was *Brahman* only. Whoever thus knows, 'I am *Brahman* (*Aham Brahman asi*)' becomes this All."[13]

Thus, the teaching received by the householders is that by knowing their deepest self they will know the universal Self; they will know all. This teaching is beautifully presented in the famous passage of the *Chandogya Upanishad* in which Uddalaka teaches his son, Shvetaketu about the ultimate reality, telling him that he is that ultimate reality ("*tat tvam asi, Shvetaketu*").[14] Shvetaketu had become a pupil at age twelve and for twelve years had studied the Vedas. At age twenty-four, thinking himself learned, he was arrogant and conceited. His father then said to him, "Shvetaketu, since you are now so greatly conceited, think yourself well-read and arrogant, did you ask for that instruction by which the unhearable becomes the heard, the unperceivable becomes perceived, the unknowable becomes known?" When Shvetaketu asks how such a teaching is even possible, his father responds, "just as, my dear, by one clod of clay all that is made of clay becomes known, the modification being only a name arising from speech while the truth is that it is just clay." The point of this is that the variety and plurality of objects in the world is only a disguise for the unified reality which underlies these objects. And that underlying reality is the reality of the Self.

The instruction then proceeds to the famous teaching:

> That which is the subtle essence, this whole world has for its Self (*Atman*).
> That is the true. That is the *Atman*. That art thou [*tat tvam asi*], Shvetaketu.

The "subtle essence" referred to is *Brahman*, the source of all existence. Thus, when Shvetaketu is identified with his deepest self, or *Atman*, and that in turn identified with *Brahman*, the mystic teaching has been imparted.

[12] *Chandogya Upanishad*, III.14.1,4.   [13] *Brihadaranyaka Upanishad*, I.4.10.
[14] *Chandogya Upanishad*, VI.

Of course, by understanding this teaching (in the sense of understanding the language in which it is presented) Shvetaketu does not
thereby come to know that Self, that subtle essence. His knowledge is
still of objects; the teaching itself is an object of instruction, whereas
what is to be known is pure subject. Yajnavalkya brings this out when
he answers Ushasta Cakrayana's request for an explanation of "the *Brahman* that is immediately present and directly perceived, that is the Self
in all things," by declaring: "This is your Self that is within all things."
When the question is put again, "Which is within all things?" the reply is,
"You cannot see the seer of seeing, you cannot hear the hearer of hearing,
you cannot think the thinker of thinking, you cannot understand the
understander of understanding. He is your Self which is in all things."[15]

This is the ultimate subject which can never become an object. Consequently, it cannot be known in the way that objects in consciousness
can be known, but must be realized directly in self-illuminating
experiences.

The advantages brought to the search for the ultimate Reality by the
nature of *Atman*-awareness as immediate and direct experience resulted
in providing for the establishment of the indubitable existence of
Atman. But this kind of knowledge carries with it also certain disadvan-
tages. Knowledge of objects is public in a way that direct experience is
not. It is open to anyone to examine the evidence for the knowledge-
claims about known objects. But one's immediate experience is available
only to oneself. Thus, while for the one with the experience there is
nothing surer than the experience itself, for one lacking the experience
there is little or no evidence for the claimed reality.

In this respect the knowledge of *Atman* is similar to the knowledge of
love. Only those experiencing love know what it is. Others might make
various claims about love, but they are obviously referring to certain
objective human relations, whereas the person who actually loves is
having subjective experience. For the person having the experience
nothing could be more sure than its existence, though a person lacking
this experience might very well be skeptical of the existence of love. In a
similar way, those without faith or experience might be skeptical of the
existence of *Atman* and the possibility of *Atman*-realization. But those
who have experienced the bliss of *Atman* know no other joy—they are
completely fulfilled.

---

[15] *Brihadaranyaka Upanishad*, III.4.2.

◊ | C H A P T E R 4 | ◊

SOCIETY AND PHILOSOPHY

SELF-REALIZATION

Because of the experiential nature of *Atman*-knowledge, three basic attitudes toward it were possible. The skeptics simply denied the existence of any such ultimate Subject on the grounds that they did not have any experience of it. Others were prepared to accept the existence and nature of *Atman* as a philosophical hypothesis to be established on the basis of reason. Still others, probably the great majority of people in India, were willing to accept the testimony of the sages and seers as adequate evidence for their belief in the existence and experiencability of *Atman*. For these people the major concern was to find a way to this wonderful realization.

This concern was not the privilege of a select few, but was shared by nearly all the members of society. A goodly number of the persons striving for *Atman*-realization could not, for a variety of reasons, share in the esoteric teachings and disciplines of the Upanishads, but had to rely on other means of instruction and achievement. Gradually a variety of fables, tales, poems, and codes were developed which gave the common people of India guides and ideals for the kind of life that would make possible the realization of *Atman*. This literature provides the chief vehicle for the transformation of the sacred teachings of the priests of the Vedas and the seers of the Upanishads into a way of life for the people. The early Vedic emphasis on the rituals of religion came to be combined with the philosophical monism of the Upanishads, with its

33

insistence of self-discipline and knowledge, in a way which tempered both the ritualism and the philosophical abstractness.

Rather than seeing the prayer, worship, and sacrifice of earlier traditions as incompatible with the Upanishadic emphasis on knowledge of *Atman* by enlargement of consciousness, this literature tended to synthesize these tendencies.

The most significant attempt at synthesis is the *Bhagavad Gita*, "The Song of the Supreme." In the *Gita*, which is a portion of the *Mahabharata*, the identification of the individual person with *Atman* and the identification of *Atman* with the ultimate reality of the universe are taken over from the Upanishads. But the *Atman* is here symbolized by God, and the divine teacher of the *Gita*, Krishna, describes himself as a finite form of the infinite, claiming to be both the god Vishnu of the earlier Vedas and the *Brahman* of the Upanishads. There is no contradiction here, for Vishnu is simply a form of *Brahman*, the ultimate Self, or *Atman*.

It is easy to see that the abstract philosophical discourses of the Upanishads would not find a ready acceptance by the majority of people accustomed to dealing with life in the concrete. But when the abstract *Brahman* is given concrete form in the person of Krishna, access becomes possible. Feeling in the depths of their being the surging of the infinite struggling to free itself from the bonds of the finite and concrete, the majority of India's people welcomed the symbol of the infinite made finite in Krishna. Here was a ray of light and hope, for if the infinite could reach down into the finite, then the finite could also reach up to the infinite. The gap between the finite and the infinite—between the empirical self and the *Atman*—could be bridged. This was the promise held out by the *Gita*, a promise giving hope and inspiration to hundreds of millions of people for thousands of years. The concrete forms of religious worship were a means to the realization of that ultimate Self taught in the Upanishads.

The *Gita* not only offered hope and inspiration but also provided a guide to life leading to the fulfillment of that hope and inspiration. The two important questions taken up by the *Gita* are (1) What is the relation between the ordinary empirical self and the ultimate Self (*Atman*)? (Or, looked at from the objective point of view, what is the relation between the ordinary empirical reality and the ultimate reality (*Brahman*)?) and (2) By what means can one come to realize or experience that ultimate Self, or Reality?

It is significant that these questions are considered in the context of a moral decision. As the *Gita* opens, Arjuna, representing Everyman, finds himself unable to determine the right thing to do, a situation known to every man. The specific question concerns the decision to fight or not to fight to regain the kingdom which rightfully belongs to him. The answer given by Krishna, disguised as Arjuna's charioteer, is given in general terms so that it can be adapted to any specific moral choice. The answer, occupying all but one of the eighteen chapters constituting this work, turns on the nature of man and the nature of the universe, and the resulting purpose, or end, of life.

The universe is regarded as ultimately unchanging and permanent, without multiplicity or plurality. Man's ultimate nature is also permanent, one and the same with the ultimate reality. The difficulty is that man is ignorant of his true nature, and mistakes himself for one complex changing individual among many, living in a world of many changing objects. Having identified himself with the impermanent and changing self, man seeks his satisfaction in the world of changing objects and desires, always without success, because the whole quest is fundamentally misguided.

But why does man make this mistake and engage in this misguided quest? The answer given is that it is due to the dual nature of man. On the one hand man is his empirical, or *guna-*, self. This self covers and obscures the spiritual and ultimately real self—the *purusha*, or *Atman*. The *guna*-self is the psycho-physical organism which the ignorant mistake for the real self. Thus Arjuna, who was suggesting that it would be wrong to engage in this war because of the destruction and killing that would occur, is instructed by Krishna, "The dweller (the *Atman*) in the body of everyone, O Bharata (Arjuna) is eternal and can never be slain."[1] The point of this instruction is that Arjuna had failed to take into consideration that the true Self, the *Atman*, or *purusha*, was essentially independent of the psycho-physical organism; he had mistaken the psycho-physical self for the ultimate Self. Consequently, he was concerned to seek satisfaction for that lower self of the *gunas*. But this is basically wrong. Krishna says "He who thinks that this slays and he who thinks that this is slain; both of them fail to perceive the truth; this one neither slays nor is slain. . . . He [the Self] is said to be unmanifest, unthinkable, and unchanging."[2]

But if the individual person mistakes himself for the *guna*-self because the real Self is obscured, how can the veil of the empirical be rent so that

---

[1] *Bhagavad Gita*, II.30, trans. by Sarvepalli Radhakrishnan (New York: Harper Bros., 1948), and contained in Radhakrishnan and Moore, eds. *A Source Book in Indian Philosophy* (Princeton: Princeton University Press, 1957), pp. 101–163.
[2] *Gita*, II.19,25.

the real Self might be seen? This is a question about the way to the realization of the *Atman*. In the *Gita* the answer rests upon the teaching that ultimately Self (*puruhsa*) and not-Self (*prakriti*) are independent. The short answer to this question is that the empirical self must be disciplined and brought under control so that it is no longer capable of confusing a person. But even though the short answer be accurate, it is insufficient, for the starting point on the path to *Atman*-realization is always occupied by the ignorant self who necessarily looks upon the empirical as real. The real task is to present ways or paths to the ultimate knowledge which begin where the individual actually is, but progressively lead him to higher and higher understanding, until gradually he is freed entirely from ignorance.

Thus, in the *Gita*, Krishna does not tell Arjuna that since activity proceeds from the world of the *gunas*, the not-Self, it should be abandoned. In fact he teaches that action is necessary, "for no one can remain even for a moment without doing work; every one is made to act helplessly by the impulses born of nature."[3] The crucial discipline is to engage in activity without becoming attached to the activity or to the results of the activity.

The *guna*-self is a combination of three different tendencies which combine in varying proportions. These tendencies, or *gunas*, are: *sattva*, which inclines one to intellectual activity; *rajas*, which inclines one to vigorous action; and *tamas*, which inclines one to devotional activity. These three *gunas*, in their varying combinations, account for the different personality types found among persons. The crucial thing, however, is that the personality type belongs to the psychophysical self, the self of *prakriti*, and as such constitutes the binding fetters of the true Self. Even though different persons are bound by different tendencies and personality types, nevertheless, they are all bound. Now, if individual A is bound by the chains of *sattva*, it is useless to try to achieve freedom by concentrating on the bonds of *rajas*, or *tamas*. And, individual B must concentrate on freeing himself from the bonds of *rajas* if this *guna* predominates in him, etc. Accordingly, the way of discipline will vary with the type of person.

The recognition that different individuals are bound by different forces led to the distinction of three basically different paths, or ways, that would take one to the realization of *Atman*. These three paths, which correspond to the *gunas sattva*, *rajas*, and *tamas*, were the paths of discipline in knowledge, discipline in work, and discipline in devotion re-

3 *Gita*, III.5.

spectively. What is common to the three paths is discipline, which is a matter of progressively freeing the real Self from the *guna*-self. These are the three famous disciplines, or *yogas*, taught in the *Gita*; the *yoga* of knowledge, the *yoga* of works, and the *yoga* of devotion. Because of the nature of the *guna*-self one cannot avoid engaging in activity. But it is possible to discipline oneself, no matter what kind of activity is involved, so that one can disassociate from the activity itself, which belongs to the *guna*-world. This is the essence of the non-attachment taught in the *Gita*.

According to the *Gita*, the two basic principles underlying the teaching of these three different paths of discipline are: (1) it is possible to realize one's essential independence of the *gunas*, and (2) in order to free oneself from the *guna*-self it is necessary to cooperate with and work through that *guna*-self, progressively transcending it.

This second principle, which is primarily an answer to the question of how an individual can realize *Atman* despite the *guna*-self, underlies a variety of practices and ideals characterizing the practical social life of the individual. Obviously, if the *guna*-self is capable of ensnaring the *Atman*, then the *guna*-self must be taken seriously if the attempt to realize *Atman* is taken seriously. And if this is the case, then the life of the empirical self in society must be taken seriously, for the kind of life the individual lives will determine the progress made in the quest for *Atman*, and it is obvious that human beings cannot live independently of society. Thus, the question arises, How can the life of the individual and the institutions of society be ordered so that progress can be made toward realizing one's true and ultimate Self? The question is based on a dual recognition—that there are differences between individual persons and between the various kinds of functions that society performs for the good of all persons A partial answer to the question is contained in the system of *varna*, or social classification.

SOCIAL CLASSES

Essentially, *varna* is a theory of social organization whereby the individuals in society are divided into different classes with different functions in society according to differing personal characteristics and different social needs. The theory is that the good of society will be furthered if there are different classes of individuals who will perform the different tasks requisite for a good life in society. Furthermore, this classification will be to the advantage of the individual in that it will prove easier to fulfill oneself and reach the true Self if one is engaging in those activities for which one is peculiarly well suited by temperament, disposition, and natural ability.

It is important to distinguish *varna*, or social class, from *caste*, or social *castes*. *Varna* refers to a system of social classification of individuals according to their qualifications, tendencies, and dispositions. This scheme of classification yields the four classes, or *varnas*, of *brahmana* (the intellectuals), *kshatriya* (military and administrators), *vaishya* (producers), and *shudra* (workers). *Caste* on the other hand, refers properly to a system of classification according to birth. There are only four classes, or *varnas*, recognized, but there are approximately two thousand *castes* in India. The castes are distinguished from each other not by qualification of the individual, but by heredity, dietary regulations, endogamy and exogamy, occupation, and place in the pecking order. The native word for caste is *jati*, which means birth. The word "caste" is modern. It is taken from "*casta*," a word the Portuguese applied to the practice of classification according to birth that they found upon coming to India. Caste, or *jati*, has existed for a long time in India, and for the most part has been regarded as an evil, except by a few persons near the top of the pecking order. *Varna*, on the other hand, is a theory of social organization that is very high ideal and has been so regarded in India.

The *brahmana varna* consists of the priests and teachers, who are, generally, the maintainers of culture. Their chief tasks have been the preservation of knowledge and culture, the satisfaction of the gods, and the safeguarding of justice and morality.

The *kshatriya varna* consists of the protectors and administrators of society. They have been the guardians of the rest of society, providing for their security, and enforcing the various rules required for the necessary social functions. According to the *Gita*, "heroism, vigour, steadiness, resourcefulness, not fleeing even in battle, generosity and leadership—these are the duties of a *kshatriya*, born of his nature."[4]

The *vaishya varna* consists of the traders and producers in society. The *Gita* says that engagement in agriculture, raising cattle, and trading are the duties of a *vaishya*, born of his own nature (*guna*-self).[5] His chief function is obviously to produce the various economic goods of life required in the society.

The *shudra varna* consists of the workers and servants in society. The *Gita* succinctly gives the duties of this class by saying, "the *dharma* [duty] of a *shudra*, born of his own nature, is action consisting of service."[6]

---

[4] *Gita*, XVIII,43.   [5] *Gita*, XVIII,44.   [6] *Ibid*.

According to the principle of *varna*, certain rights and duties accrue to an individual in virtue of belonging to a certain class in society. The duties and rights being determined for the four classes, the individual is in a position to be clear about his particular rights and duties in society when he determines which class he belongs to in virtue of his qualifications. The rights and duties of the four *varnas* do not exhaust the *dharma* of man, however, as there are certain privileges and responsibilities that belong to a person inasmuch as he is a human being and a member of society irrespective of class. Thus Bhisma, in the *Mahabharata*, says that all persons have the duties of controlling their anger, telling the truth, forgiving others, begetting offspring of their legitimate wife, pure conduct, avoidance of quarrels, the maintenance of dependents, and acting justly.[7] Non-hurting (*ahimsa*) and self-restraint are usually added to this list.

The duties of man as man and the duties of man as member of a particular class in society are grounded in the very order of the universe. The universe is regarded as essentially moral. Everything happens according to a rule, for the benefit of the whole. Each class of beings in the universe, by functioning as designed, contributes to the order and well-being of the whole. Man in society is no exception to this rule and therefore, in virtue of being human and occupying a particular place in the scheme of the universe, he has certain activities to engage in to maintain the well-being of the universe in general, and the well-being of society in particular. Sin and evil result when a person refuses to do those things over which he has choice and which are necessary for the well-being of the whole. The duties common to the several *varnas* are the actions one should perform or the rules of actions one should follow in order to avoid sin. The duties of the particular *varnas* issue from the rules to be followed if the social order is to be maintained, without which order man cannot make his contribution to the total order of creation, and without which man cannot realize his own nature. The content of the various duties is derived from the nature of the *gunas*. Krishna in the *Gita*, says, "The duties of *brahmanas*, *kshatriyas*, *vaishyas* and *shudras* have been assigned according to the *gunas* born of nature."[8]

LIFE-STAGES

Granted that the individual is to perform his duties according to his social class for the good of society, it is still possible to ask how the

[7] *Mahabharata, Shantiparva*, 60,7. (Poona: Bhandarkar Oriental Research Institute, 1927–54).
[8] *Gita*, IV,13.

individual should order his own life so that he can make the requisite contribution to the social order and also make the greatest possible progress in achieving self-fulfillment and self-realization. And in answer to this question the institution of *ashrama* was advocated. The institution of *ashrama* consists in a series of stages in life, classified according to the activities proper to each stage. The first stage is the student stage, the *brahmacarya ashrama*. The second is that of the householder in society, the *grihastha ashrama*. The third is a stage of retirement from the social world, the *vanaprastha ashrama*. After passing through these first three stages in life's journey a person enters into a life of contemplation and meditation in order that he might completely establish himself in perfection. This last stage is called *samnyasa ashrama*.

According to Manu, the stages in life are to be taken up successively, beginning with the student stage. He says, "Having studied the Vedas in accordance with the rule, having begot sons according to the sacred law, and having offered sacrifices according to his ability, he may direct his mind to final liberation. A twice-born* man who seeks final liberation without having studied the Vedas, without having begotten sons, and without having offered sacrifices sinks downward."9

The various duties laid down for the different *ashrama* follow from the debts contracted by birth into the world. Life in this world is regarded as an opportunity provided as a gift to man. It is an opportunity for the Self to free itself forever from the round of births and deaths. But the individual does nothing to warrant this opportunity. The gods present the gift of life in this world and therefore man has a debt to the gods. He also has a debt to his parents and ancestors, for without them life would not have been possible either. With his second birth, the birth into the world of culture and spirit, man incurs a debt to the seers and teachers who promulgate, preserve, and teach that which is worth knowing. These three debts could be satisfied by studying (debt to the seers and teachers), having children (debt to the parents and ancestors), and by offering sacrifice (debt to the gods). The three different kinds of life required to repay the debts correspond to the student, householder, and retirement stages respectively. Only upon satisfying these obliga-

---

* "Twice-born" refers to birth into the world of Spirit in addition to the world of nature. In ancient India there were elaborate rituals marking the initiation of young people into the cultural and spiritual life of the twice-born. Initiation into the ranks of the twice-born was considered a great privilege and was, at least in theory, reserved for those judged qualified.

9 *The Laws of Manu*, 6.34–37, trans. by G. Bühler, *The Sacred Books of the East*. XXV (Oxford: Clarendon Press, 1886).

tions to society and the gods was a person free to devote himself exclusively to meditation and concentration in his effort to experience the ultimate reality.

This emphasis upon satisfying one's debts through various kinds of social action reveals the importance attached to life in society and social organization in India. In fact, the very principles of life-stages and social classes are justified in terms of the importance of satisfying the empirical, or the *guna*-nature of man. This is clearly brought out in the concept of *purushartha*, which provides for the philosophical justification of the various forms of social organization advocated.

BASIC HUMAN AIMS

The word *"purushartha"* literally means "aim of a person." The four *purusharthas*, or human aims, recognized as basic in India are those of (1) *dharma*, or morality, (2) *artha*, or means of life, (3) *kama*, or enjoyment of the means of life, and (4) *moksha*, or realization of the ultimate Self (*atman*). These human aims are discussed by Manu and Kautilya, and are included in the *Mahabharata*. Furthermore they are presupposed by nearly all the literature which discusses life in society. They also underlie the social principles of life-stages and classes advocated in the *Gita*, for these forms of social organization are simply means to the achievement of these four human aims.

These four human aims are the aims, or goals, in life that every individual has or should have. The good life is defined in terms of these aims. Granted that man is a combination of the empirical and the spiritual, it is necessary to satisfy both the empirical and the spiritual needs in order to achieve the good life. In order to achieve the spiritual goal of *moksha*, it is necessary first to satisfy the empirical needs of the individual by providing the required means of life (*artha*) and by providing for the enjoyment (*kama*) of these means. For the regulation of the attainment and enjoyment of the means of life moral rules (*dharma*) are necessary.

Although the word *"dharma"* is used in a bewildering variety of ways there is a common notion of a *rule of action* running through the different senses of the term. The word is derived from the root *"dhri,"* which means "to support," or "to maintain," and the justification of a rule is that it maintains or supports. Consequently *dharma* came to mean that which one should do, for a rule of action is, essentially, a guide to action. The importance of *dharma* lies in the necessity of following rules of action in human conduct.

With respect to the individual, one's *dharma* may be one's moral duty. But with respect to society, *dharma* provides rules for settling disputes and possible conflicts between individuals, for only when conflicts of interest between individuals and groups are kept to a minimum can society be well maintained. Thus, *dharma* has a social sense and significance, for it represents possible rules for action in society which will enable the individual to fulfill himself and at the same time make a contribution to the self-fulfillment of others.

As man does not live by righteousness and justice alone, but requires also bread and bed, it is only natural that in addition to the human aim of *dharma* there should be the aims of means of life (*artha*) and enjoyment (*kama*).

Kautilya composed a treatise on *artha* as a guide to the acquisition of the means of life in the world. In it he explains the concept of *artha* as follows: "The sustenance of mankind is termed *artha*, the earth which contains mankind is termed *artha*; . . ." [10] The word "*artha*" is derived from the root "*ri*" which means literally, "that which one goes for." From this basic meaning which is, roughly, "aim" or "purpose," derives the meaning of "thing," "matter," or "affair," from which stem the meanings of "advantage," "wealth," "profit," and "prosperity."

The following statements from the *Mahabharata* and the *Panchatantra* will reveal the attitude taken toward *artha*. In the *Mahabharata* it is said, "What is here regarded as *dharma* depends entirely upon wealth [*artha*]. One who robs another of wealth robs him of his *dharma* as well. Poverty is a state of sinfulness. All kinds of meritorious acts flow from the possession of great wealth, as from wealth spring all religious acts, all pleasures, and heaven itself. Wealth brings about accession of wealth, as elephants capture elephants. Religious acts, pleasure, joy, courage, worth, and learning; all these proceed from wealth. From wealth one's merit increases. He that has no wealth has neither this world nor the next." [11]

The traditions of the common people as reflected in the collection of tales of wisdom known as the *Panchatantra* contain the following observations: "The smell of wealth [*artha*] is quite enough to wake a creature's sterner stuff. And wealth's enjoyment even more. Wealth gives constant vigour, confidence, and power. Poverty is a curse worse than death.

[10] *Kautilya Arthashastra*, 4.1, trans. by R. Shamasastry (Mysore: Sri Raguveer Press, fifth ed. 1956).
[11] *Mahabharata*, 12.8.11.

Virtue without wealth is of no consequence. The lack of money is the root of all evil."[12]

Artha, as one of the four basic aims in life, refers to whatever means are necessary for man's life. The emphasis is upon the means to biological and social life, but the means to spiritual life are not excluded, as it is recognized that biological and social life are conditions for spiritual life. The securing of material plenty is advocated as a goal in life subject only to the important restriction that no *artha* be pursued in violation of *dharma*.

Since accumulations of wealth or property are not valuable primarily for their own sake, however, but mainly for the satisfaction, pleasure, and enjoyment they make possible, the human aim of enjoyment, or *kama*, was included as one of the basic goals in life. The classic definition of *kama* is found in Vatsyayana's *Sutra*:

> *Kāma* is the enjoyment of the appropriate objects of the five senses of hearing, feeling, seeing, tasting, and smelling, assisted by the mind, together with the soul. The ingredient in this is a peculiar contact between the organ of sense and its object, and the consciousness of pleasure that results from the contact is called *Kāma*.[13]

Discussing the relations between *dharma*, *artha*, and *kama*, Manu says, "Some declare that the good of man consists in *dharma* and *artha*; others opine that it is to be found in *artha* and *kama*; some say that *dharma* alone will give it; the rest assert that *artha* alone is the chief good of man here below. But the correct position is that the good of man consists in the harmonious co-ordination of the three."[14]

The basic reason for regarding enjoyment as one of the basic aims in life is that the end of all activity is some presupposed good. It is the natural inclination of all things to strive after the satisfaction of the common desires for food, drink, and sex, and therefore these desires are not to be denied and frustrated, but are to be regulated and indulged. Consequently, the enjoyments of the satisfaction of regulated desires is reason for engaging in activity and is one of the basic aims in life.

The fourth basic human aim is *moksha*. The word derives from the root "*muc*," meaning "to release," "to free." In accord with the literal meaning of the word, *moksha* means emancipation, complete freedom. This aim reflects the emphasis put on the spiritual nature of man in

---

[12] *The Panchatantra*, trans. by A. W. Ryder (Chicago: University of Chicago Press, 1925), p. 210.
[13] *The Kama Sutra of Vatsyayana*, trans. by R. Burton and F. A. Arbuthnot (London: Panther Books, 1963).
[14] *Manu*, 2.224.

India. In accord with the teachings of the Upanishads, *Atman* is regarded as the power behind the powers of the universe. It is the ultimate power in the universe and the ultimate power in man, these being one and the same. In agreement with this conception of man, the ultimate perfection of man is seen to lie in his self-realization, in identifying himself with the ultimate source and power of his being. This realization will set man free, for this power, constituting the innermost and essential portion of his being, cannot be bound or limited by any other power. It is the ultimate power. There is, therefore, no power, not even the power of death, that can limit man because he is, in his deepest being and genuine Self, the highest power. So long as a person identifies himself with the lower powers he is bound by the higher powers and the lower powers as well. Consequently, the goal is to realize that one is not merely body, not merely biological life, not merely social organism, etc. This realization, in the sense of completely identifying oneself with the ultimate power, is the realization of *Atman*, or the true Self, and results in complete freedom, or *moksha*.

Thus, the basic presupposition of *moksha* is that man has within himself the seeds of his own perfection. But potential perfection implies actual imperfection. The problem is therefore one of moving from imperfect existence to perfect existence. Because of the integral view of man taken in India, to regard man as more than a social animal was not to deny that man is biological and social. Rather it was to assert that though man is social and biological he is something more. Consequently, it was held that the fulfillment of the biological and social were necessary, though not sufficient, conditions for the fulfillment of the something higher that man also is.

JUSTIFICATION OF SOCIAL ORGANIZATION

It is clear that the basic aims of man recognized in these theories require a fairly high degree of social organization, for the aims of *dharma, artha, kama,* and *moksha* cannot be realized in isolation. And since society can be successfully organized only when all of the different functions requisite for its maintenance are fulfilled, and this can happen only when personnel are provided for the different basic functions, it is easy to see that social classification is justified by the basic aims of life.

The principle of *ashrama* also finds its justification in the concept of the *purusharthas*. An *ashrama* is really a stage in life's journey, the goal of the journey being complete freedom, or *moksha*. It is the aim of *moksha* that provides the overall direction for the journey through life, the various stages being the means devised for the realization of this goal. But it is recognized that the traveller along life's highway is so constituted that in order to attain his goal of *moksha* he must first attain the goals of *dharma, artha,* and *kama.* That is, he must live a social life. Accordingly, the journey is divided into stages such that each of the basic aims can be satisfied or attained most efficiently, in a way most satisfactory to the individual.

The first life-stage, the student stage, enables the individual to learn about life in all of its various aspects. There he learns about his social and spiritual life, becoming familiar with the ideals according to which he is to live his life. It is here that one learns about social classes, life-stages, human aims, etc., and is introduced to the art of self-discipline. Having learned about the theory of life, the individual passes on to the next stage in life, where he continues to practice what he has learned in the first stage.

In the householder stage the individual looks after the society that looked after him in the first stage in his life and that will look after him in the last stages of his life. Now he must maintain and support society, maintaining the mores, the economic means, cultural values, living a righteous life of enjoyment amidst wealth, begetting and supporting children, and taking care of the old and the needy.

Having fulfilled his obligations to society, and having satisfied his biological and social needs, he now turns to a period of training in spiritual life. His training in righteousness and spirituality completed, his only concern will be with the attainment of *moksha.*

Thus the division of life into stages provides for the attainment of the basic aims of man. This is its justification. The institution of life-stages, in short, is designed to advise the individual of his various goals and to assist in the attainment of these goals by ordering his life in the best possible way. The *ashramas* are the stages in life in which one progressively realizes his true nature.

Having looked at the content of the concepts of social classes, life-stages, and human aims, it will now be helpful to look at the reasons underlying these three theories.

Turning first to the theory of the basic human aims, it can be seen that the function of the *purushartha* theory is to provide direction for human activity. The *purushartha* theory may be regarded as an answer to the question, What should man seek in life? or, alternately, How should man live? The answer embodied in the theory is that man should seek to be moral, to accumulate means of life, to enjoy himself, and eventually, to free himself from whatever binds. Looked at in this way, the concepts of *dharma, artha, kama,* and *moksha* are seen to be concepts embodying rules. They are normative concepts, providing directions for life's activities.

Now, if the concepts in question are considered to be essentially normative, that is, for the purpose of guiding human behavior, then each concept can be regarded as the embodiment of a rule or rules. And since the function of a normative rule is to guide behavior, it is reasonable to assume that the theory of human aims functions as an answer to the question, How should man live? Next follows the question, How should one act? which occurs in regard to a variety of circumstances and a variety of possible courses of action, so it is reasonable that there should be a number of rules. The theory of human aims represents an attempt to divide the basic rules concerning possible courses of action into four categories. Thus, the rules concerning how one should act with respect to other persons are included under the heading of *dharma.* The rules concerning how one should act with respect to wealth and material goods are included under the heading of *artha.* The rules concerning how one should act with respect to possible pleasures and enjoyments of the world are included under the heading of *kama.* Finally, the rules concerning how one should act with respect to realization of his inner nature are grouped under the heading of *moksha.*

Looked at in this way, the human aims are essentially answers to the question of how the good life is to be lived. Granted that it is the purpose of social organization to provide for the good life, the importance of considering the *purusharthas* for understanding the theory of social organization is obvious. For without understanding what the good life consists in, it would be most difficult to appreciate the means of social organization required to implement the good life in society.

Turning now to the theory of the life-stages, it can be seen that this also is intended as an answer to a question. The question in this case is, How should the individual so organize his life to most satisfactorily realize the good life? Thus, the *ashrama* theory, which holds that the life of an individual in society should be divided into four segments, or stages, is also normative for it provides direction for human activity.

The *ashrama* theory assumes the answer that the *purushartha* theory provides to the question, In what does the good life consist? It also develops an answer to the question, How can an individual in society best realize the good life? The answer proposed by the *ashrama* theory is that man should apportion his life so that part is spent studying and learning about the nature of self, society, and the good life, and in training for useful social activity; a part is devoted to the well-being of society by performing social service, to the begetting and rearing of children, and to sustaining the various social institutions, etc.; a portion of it is spent in establishing oneself in self-control and in meditation; and a portion is spent in concerted effort to shake off any binding fetters. Each stage has its own rules for the activities one must follow in order to realize the good life.

The theory of classes is similar to the theory of life-stages in that both presuppose the answer provided by the theory of *purusharthas* to the question, In what does the good life consist? Both theories provide direction for securing the basic goals in life, the attainment of which constitutes the good life. The two theories differ basically in that whereas the *ashrama* theory answers the question of how the individual life should be organized in order that the good life be realized, the *varna* theory answers the question, How should society be organized so as to provide for the realization of the basic goals of life for each member of society? The answer the *varna* theory provides to this question is that men should so organize society that its members are classified in such a way that the functions requisite for the proper functioning of society will be performed by those individuals best suited for the tasks they have to perform. The *varna* theory advocates distributing the labor required for a properly functioning society so that whatever is required will be performed, while at the same time each person will be doing only the work for which he is best suited. In this way social activity will be directly conducive to achieving *moksha*, the ultimate goal in life which lies beyond merely social activity. The rules for each class provide direction for the activities of the members of each class so that society will prosper and the individual will have the utmost opportunity to realize the good life.

The *varna* theory, then, proposes social classification according to a division of labor, the labor being distributed according to the special qualifications of the individual to perform the labor in question. It answers the individual's question, "What should I do to realize the good life?" by directing him to those social tasks for which he is best suited and which will, in the long run, be most conducive to the realization of his innermost nature.

The principles of Indian social philosophy can be further illuminated by considering certain objections that might be raised. One objection is that people are not, in fact, neatly divided or divisible into four distinct types, as assumed by the theory of *varna*. If people do not differ from each other in such ways that they can be classified into four distinct social groups with each group or class having different functions in society, then the *varna* theory, if put into practice, will result in certain individuals being arbitrarily saddled with jobs for which they are ill-suited, and which they would rather not do. Then social classification according to *varna*, instead of providing for the well-being of society and for individual self-fulfillment, would lead to the breakdown of society and would result in forcing individuals into doing those things for which they are ill-suited and which they are not disposed to do.

This objection possesses a certain validity which cannot be easily disposed of; for if a theory of social organization leads to the suppression of the individual and thereby contributes to the malfunctioning of society, it is an unsatisfactory theory. And if distribution of social tasks is made on the basis of supposed individual differences which do not, in fact, exist, it is possible that the individual will be forced to do precisely that for which he is least qualified, and the society as well as the individual might be the worse off for this.

Despite this core of truth in the objection, one can counter by considering that no society can function well without a division of labor within the society, for there are so many different functions that must be performed in order that society be adequately maintained. Surely there must be administrators, a military force and police, producers, and laborers within any society. The *varna* theory is based on a recognition of this basic fact. It is more than a mere recognition of this fact; it is an attempt to divide the labor required to maintain society in such a way that each person will do the type of work for which he is best suited. The assumption is that there are four fundamentally different types of activities required for the maintenance of society. Unless these activities are performed society either suffers or, in the extreme, becomes impossible. Therefore, since according to traditional Indian thought the good life is not possible without society, society must be maintained. Consequently the different requisite tasks must be performed, the different tasks being given to the individuals *best* (even though not perfectly) suited for the tasks assigned them.

Since, theoretically, classification into *varnas* is done on the basis of the qualifications of the individual being classified, it is difficult to see what more could be desired. It is doubtful that any society could function well if unqualified persons were performing vital functions, and the *varna* scheme is an attempt to ensure that only qualified persons would perform the various functions required in a good society. There may be questions about actual methods of classification, but these are questions about the implementation of the theory, which amount to questions about the practice of the theory, and not about the theory as such.

A second objection is that it is not practical to divide one's life into four separate stages, or segments. The weight of this objection lies in the implicit view that life is an integral affair, and, therefore, to attempt to live it in separate stages is to try to make of life something it is not. This would be a serious objection if the theory of *ashrama* did, in fact, require that life be divided into separate compartments or stages. To so construe the theory of *ashrama* is, however, to misconstrue it. As remarked earlier, the theory of *ashrama* constitutes an answer to the question, How can an individual best organize his life in order to realize the good life? Granted that according to the dominant thought of this period the good life was held to consist in the attainment of the four goals of *dharma, artha, kama,* and *moksha,* it was not held that these ought to be attained at separate stages of life.

All of the activities of one's life ought to be aimed at realizing the four basic aims. But as there is an order among these aims, so that before the final stage of *moksha* can be achieved the other three must be realized—and the aims of *artha* and *kama* are to be attained according to *dharma*—it follows that in order to attain all of the aims, special attention must be paid to each of them. Accordingly, it is held that the first task of an individual is to establish himself in *dharma.* Then he might attend to the aims of *artha* and *kama.* But, of course, one cannot live without *artha* and *kama,* and therefore it is not possible to ignore these aims at any stage in life. It is not the case that in each *ashrama* one pursues a different aim. According to the theory one pursues all the aims in each stage, though not necessarily with the same enthusiasm for each. The theory involves not a division of life, but an ordering of the activities of life. Thus, to argue that the *ashrama* theory requires that in one stage one realizes *dharma,* at the next *artha,* at the next *kama,* and then *moksha,* is to misconstrue the theory, for all the theory holds is that in order to attain all four of these aims it is necessary to concentrate on achieving each of them.

The objection that various of the *purusharthas* might come into conflict with each other overlooks both the nature of the *purusharthas* and the function of *dharma.* The theory of the *purusarthas* is that the good life consists in the attainment of these four aims. If, therefore, these goals should so conflict that the attainment of any one would become impossible, then it could not be the case that the good life consisted in the attainment of all four. So long as it is agreed that the good life consists in the attainment of these four goals, it cannot be argued that these four can conflict with each other. Furthermore, the function of *dharma* provides for the resolution of any conflicts of action. That is, the rules that make up the concept of *dharma* are rules for settling possible conflicts between courses of action that would interfere with living the good life. So long as *dharma* is included among them, conflict among the goals is impossible.

A fourth objection is that *varna* implies social immobility, restricting the freedom of the individual. In replying to this objection it is useful to distinguish between practice and theory. It may be that in trying to classify society according to *varna* there might occur a certain social immobility. It has often been said that this is what actually happened in India. But the question of whether or not the social classes of India did or did not become closed and whether they resulted in general social immobility is philosophically uninteresting. The interesting philosophical question is whether or not the theory of *varna* entails or implies closed classes and social immobility. The historical phenomena of India may be due to a lack of application of *varna* theory rather than to an application of it. And if the conclusion of the discussion of *varna* in this chapter be accepted, then clearly the theory of *varna* does not imply or entail closed classes or social immobility, for the principle of *varna* classification is the qualification of the individual. The individual belongs to the class for which he is best qualified and not to the class of his parents. Thus, according to the theory, an individual is free to move from one class to another if he has the requisite qualifications. There is nothing in the theory to prevent a scavenger's son from being a priest or teacher, and nothing to prevent the daughter of a priest from being a scavenger. In fact, the theory requires that if one is qualified for a certain *varna*, then that is the *varna* to which that person belongs, regardless of birth.

The objection that implementation of the *ashrama* scheme interferes with the freedom of the individual to live his life as he chooses also misses the mark. The *ashrama* scheme is essentially an arrangement to enable the individual to achieve the four goals that constitute the good life, and the individual is free to live his life as he chooses, in order to live the good life. The *ashrama* theory does not require that an individual spend a specific number of years in a given stage and then move on to the next stage, spend a specific number of years there and then move on, etc. The *ashrama* theory provides for an arrangement of life whereby the individual can, progressively, realize his potentialities; an arrangement providing for freedom rather than restricting it. One could argue that all this misses the point; if an individual is required to spend a part of his life studying and does not wish or choose to do this, then he is not free. One *could* argue that way, but then one could also argue that according to the *ashrama* theory one is being forced to live the good life, and is not free to live the bad life.

In conclusion, it might be remarked that the discussions making up this chapter reveal that traditional Indian social philosophy, as it involves the concepts of *purusharthas*, *varnas*, and *ashramas*, contains not only lofty, but theoretically plausible, ideals of social organization which may well serve to inspire social planners.

SELF AND THE WORLD:
SAMKHYA—YOGA

THE ethical, social, political, and religious philosophies of the epics, *Dharma shastras*, and the *Gita* presuppose certain relationships between the empirical self that is the social organism and the ultimate Self that is pure subject. This presupposition is obvious from the emphasis placed on the various prescriptions for life in society in order to realize *Atman*. Unless there were a connection between the empirical self and the *Atman*, the activities of the empirical self would be irrelevant to *Atman*-realization. The Upanishads appear to be so full of excitement over the discovery of the *Atman* that they are not, for the most part, concerned to analyze the nature of the non-*Atman* nor to analyze the relations between what is *Atman* and what is not *Atman*. It is not surprising then, that at a later time philosophical and critical minds should inquire into these matters and attempt to show what, if any, relations existed between Self and not-Self, between the ultimate and the empirical. The underlying question is, How can one be the self of flesh and bones and desires and habits and also be the *Atman*, unchanging and identical with the ultimate reality of the universe?

SUBJECT AND OBJECT

The oldest philosophical school to take up this question of the relation between the Self and the not-Self was the school of Samkhya. The teachings of this school suggest that it grew directly out of those portions of the Upanishads emphasizing the reality of the non-*Atman*, or the non-*Brahman*. In the Upanishads, *Brahman* is said to have created the universe and then entered into it.[1] The world of objects cannot be unreal, for it consists of *Atman*, which is object as well as subject. In the *Brihadaranyaka Upanishad* it is said that *Atman* entered into the universe "up to the fingertips, as a knife is hidden in its sheath, or the all-sustaining fire in the fire-preserving wood."[2] Such passages indicate two basic realities; that of *Brahman* and that of the objective world of empirical selves and things.

There is no doubt that for the most part the tendency in the Upanishads is to regard *Brahman* as "more real" than the empirical or objective world. Nevertheless, as seen earlier, knowledge of *Brahman* is not an ordinary kind of knowledge, and exclusive of *Brahman* knowledge, one has no choice but to take seriously the reality of the empirical self and the objective world, for there is no other reality in evidence. Furthermore, the empirical and the objective must always be the starting point for any investigation of reality, which means that at this level at least, the reality of the empirical must be acknowledged.

It appears that Samkhya, disposed to accept the reality of the empirical, perhaps partially on the basis of certain realistic remarks in the Upanishads, felt keenly the need to analyze carefully the relationship between the empirical and the ultimate realities.

The felt need to establish the relationship between the empirical and the ultimate arose from two considerations. On the one hand, the Upanishads had taught that realization of *Atman* would bring an end to suffering. Therefore, to find ways to realize this *Atman* and put an end to pain and suffering, it was necessary to discover the relationship between the empirical and the *Atman*, and to determine the sorts of things that would lead to the experience of *Atman*. Ishvara Krishna begins his discourse on Samkhya with the statement: "From torment by three-fold misery arises the inquiry into the means of terminating it. . . ."[3]

The other consideration is a matter of the basic human urge to know and render intelligible all human experiences by the exhibition of certain relationships inhering in them.

---

[1] *Taittiriya*, II.6; *Chandogya*, VI.3.2.

[2] *Brihadaranyaka*, I.4.7.

[3] *Samkhya-Karika*, I, ed. and trans. by S. S. Suryanaranyana Sastri (Madras: University of Madras, 1935), and reprinted in *A Source Book in Indian Philosophy* (Princeton: Princeton University Press, 1957), p. 425 ff.

Focusing attention on ordinary human knowledge and the ordinary world known by such knowledge, the Samkhya philosophers argue that the entire world that can be experienced is fundamentally of the same nature. That is to say, desires, feelings, intelligence, etc., are not basically different from colors, sounds, odors, etc., all of which are fundamentally like sticks and stones. But all of this—the world that can, in principle, be experienced—is of the nature of object (or potential object), or not-self, as opposed to the Self that is always experiencer, that is ultimately and finally Subject. It would seem that the ultimate Subject is of a different nature and order than the world, since what is ultimate Subject can never become object, and what is object cannot be ultimate Subject. The difference between Self and the world is fundamentally the difference between subject and object.

The starting point for any analysis of the world and the self must be the experience of the self and the world one has available for analysis. This experience reveals the existence of a knowing self in a changing world. Nothing is more obvious than that we and the world around us are changing. It is with this obvious fact that the Samkhya philosophers begin, and from which they derive the conclusion that all experience and all that is experienced is fundamentally of the same nature, though basically different from the ultimate experiencing subject.

CAUSALITY

The orderliness and regularity of the experienced world cannot be dismissed as the result of chance. Changes are caused. Whatever is or will be, is or will be due to various causes. The first important consequence of this is that human knowledge that comes to be must be caused. It is the effect of some prior cause. But since causality is unintelligible unless the dominant features of the effect be derived from the cause, it follows that the effect must be essentially like the cause. Therefore, our knowledge must be essentially like the world that is known. Since knowledge is the result of ordering experiences, the nature of experience must be basically the same as the world. Hence the claim that experience and the experiencable are fundamentally the same.

The analysis of causality provides the main reasons for the claims made about the world and the self by Samkhya. The theory of causality adopted is called *satkaryavada*, which means that the effect preexists in the cause. Now if it is admitted that nothing can occur without a cause and also that every effect has prior existence in the cause, it follows that in an important sense the effect does not provide any new reality, for it is simply a matter of making explicit what already existed implicitly.

The Samkhya theory of the nature of causation is summed up by Ishvara Krishna when he says: "The effect is existent (pre-existent): (1) because what is non-existent cannot be produced; (2) because there is a definite relation of the cause with the effect; (3) because all is not possible; (4) because the efficient can do only that for which it is efficient; (5) because the effect is of the same essence as the cause."[4]

The reason for claiming that effects exist is that the reality of the effect can be denied only upon denial of the cause, as a cause is a cause only to the extent it produces its effects. Therefore if there are no real effects then there are no real causes. Furthermore, the effect is as real as the cause, for the effect is simply a transformation of the cause. If one were to deny the existence of both cause and effect one would be forced to deny the whole starting point of one's analysis, which would make all the conclusions contradictory. Consequently, the existence of effects cannot be denied.

The claim that the effect is of the same essence as the cause is crucially important to Samkhya, for it is the main support of the claim that all objective reality is ultimately of the same nature, the connection being that all of objective reality is simply the result of various transformations of some one ultimate stuff.

To see the force of the Samkhya argument here it is helpful to consider some of the objections that might be raised against this theory of causation. It might be objected that the effect is a new whole different from the constituent parts, and not simply a transformation of them. Evidence is provided for this objection by the fact that no effect can be known before it is produced. But if it were essentially the same as its cause it could be known by knowing the cause prior to the production of the effect. According to Samkhya this objection is not valid, for it makes no sense to say that a whole is different from its material cause. Take the case of a table. The pieces of wood, which are the material cause of the table when arranged in a certain way, are not different from the table. If it were different, one could perceive the table independently of its parts. But this is clearly impossible. And to argue that the effect and the cause are independent and separate because they

4 *Samkhya-Karika*, IX.

are perceived as separate and independent is to beg the question. The Samkhya claim is that perceiving an effect is simply perceiving the cause in transformation. To go on from this to say, "and therefore seeing the effect is seeing a new entity," is not to present an objection at all, but to beg the question.

Another objection that might be raised is that if Samkhya is right in maintaining that causality is simply a matter of transformation and not the production of something new, then the activity of the agent, or efficient cause, would be unnecessary, for the effect was already in existence. But if the effect preexisted, then no efficient cause is required to bring the effect into existence. This objection is addressed by considering the assumption that the effect does not preexist in the cause. If the effect did not preexist in the cause, then causality would be the bringing into existence of something out of nothing. (Hence the claim, "What is non-existent cannot be produced.") If we look at some non-existent things, such as square circles, it will be discovered that no amount of exertion can bring them into existence. To claim that what is can be caused by what is not is not to provide an alternative view of causation but to deny causality completely. Furthermore, if you do not admit that the effect preexists, then you have to say that it does not exist until it is caused. This is tantamount to saying that the non-existent effect belongs to the cause. But since the effect does not exist there is really nothing to belong to the cause, for a relation of belonging is possible only between existing things. Thus, if the effect can be said to belong to the cause it must be admitted that it preexists in the cause. But then what of the objection that in this case no cause is needed? The answer is that the agent or efficient cause simply manifests or makes explicit what was implicit and unmanifest, and does not create something new.

Another reply to the objection that cause and effect are distinct entities is that the preexistence of the effect can be seen from the fact that nothing can be gotten out of a cause which was not in the cause. For example, curd is gotten from milk because it preexisted in the milk. It cannot be gotten from water or oil because it did not preexist in them. If it were not the case that the effect preexisted in the cause it would be possible for any effect to proceed from any cause. But this is obviously not the case; for example, you cannot produce iron from water.

Now if it is the case that only certain causes can produce certain effects, then obviously some causes are potent with respect to some effects, but not with respect to others. But this shows that the effect preexists in the cause; otherwise it would make no sense to say that a cause is potent with respect to a given effect. The reason is that the potent cause of an effect has some power related to the effect, and without the preexistence of the effect there is nothing for the power to be related to, and then it makes no sense to talk about potent causes or potentiality.

Another objection that might be raised is that to talk about manifestation and transformation is to smuggle the notion of causality, in the sense of production of new events and objects, back into the picture in disguised form. This is answered by showing that the nature of transformation has nothing to do with the cessation of preexisting attributes nor with the coming-to-be of a pre-non-existent attribute. Rather, transformation means the manifestation of an attribute or characteristic implicitly present in the substance, and alternatively, the relapse of the manifested attribute into the unmanifest condition.

To clinch the case, the Samkhya philosopher argues that the very concept of causal possibility requires the preexistence of the effect in the cause. Non-being, the non-existent, requires no cause. So if the effect were non-existent at any time there would be no question of locating its cause. But it does make sense to talk about the possibility of effects which do not yet exist and to try to determine what will cause these effects to come into existence. This, however, makes sense only upon the assumption that the effect preexists in some sense, for that which is absolutely non-existent has no possibility of coming into existence.

The foregoing are all arguments essentially designed to support the claim that causes and effects are essentially the same. Cause is here being considered in the sense of material cause—the stuff out of which something comes to be. No effect can exist in a place different from its material cause. Hence cause and effect are numerically the same. An example given of the essential sameness of cause and effect is the tortoise going in and out of his shell. The spread-out tortoise is the effect, the contracted tortoise, the cause (and vice versa). But this does not involve the production of something new. Another example is a piece of gold which can be pressed into many shapes and pieces. But changing its shape does not make the effect something totally new. The flower made of gold is basically gold, as is the tree that is made of gold; the difference involves only name and form, and not the stuff out of which they are made.

EVOLUTION OF THE WORLD

Having established that the causality that must be assumed to exist in order to make sense out of human experience is of the nature of *satkaryavada* (meaning that the effect necessarily preexists in the cause), the Samkhya philosophers proceed to argue that this implies some one ultimate principle, which as the result of its transformations is experienced in its effects as the objective world. This claim follows once one admits that the present world exists as the result of previous changes and that change is not the production of something radically new. If this is admitted, then in order to avoid ultimate infinite regress it must be admitted that there is some one ultimate material cause, which in its various transformations or manifestations constitutes the world of experience. From this it follows that the entire world of experience is of the same fundamental nature as this ultimate material cause, for everything is basically only a transformation of this first cause. In this way Samkhya comes to the conclusion that the entire experiencable world is of the nature of *prakriti*, which is the name given to the ultimate causal principle.

This conclusion brings to the fore another question, however. How does the pluralistic world of experience derive, through a series of transformations, from this basic reality called *prakriti*? Obviously, if there are no effects except those that preexisted in the cause, then all of the effects that constitute the experienced world must have preexisted in *prakriti*. Consequently, *prakriti* itself must be composed of different tendencies, or characteristics. Accordingly, *Samkhya* posits various tendencies: *sattva*, which is the tendency responsible for the self-manifestation and self-maintenance of *prakriti*; *rajas*, the tendency of motion and action; and *tamas*, the tendency of inertia. From the psychological standpoint, *sattva*, *rajas*, and *tamas* are the principles responsible for pleasure, pain, and indifference, respectively. By various combinations of these differing principles it is possible to account for the evolution of the whole world. The varying proportions of these embodied principles account for all the diversity found in the world.

But what caused the evolution of *prakriti*? If the world is looked at as evolving it is implied that there was a logical time when the principles constituting *prakriti* were in a quiet state of equilibrium. If this is the case, it is necessary to suppose another principle of reality in the world, a principle responsible for disturbing the equilibrium of the tendencies, and thereby setting in motion the evolution of *prakriti*. This second reality is called *purusha*, and it is considered to be of the nature of pure consciousness, being ultimate Subject. It is, in fact, the Samkhya version of the Upanishadic *Atman* or *Brahman*.

It is the existence of *purusha* that accounts for the evolution of *prakriti*. It is not that *purusha* actually has anything to do with *prakriti*, but simply because of the existence and presence of *purusha*, the equilibrium of *prakriti* is upset and the evolutionary process begins.

A summation of the arguments given for the existence of *purusha* is given by Ishvara Krishna as follows: "(a) Because all composite objects are for another's use, (b) because there must be absence of the three attributes and other properties, (c) because there must be control, (d) because there must be someone to experience, and (e) because there is a tendency toward "isolation" or final beatitude, therefore, the *purusa* must be there."[5]

Arguments (a) and (b) rest on the premises that (1) all experienced objects consist of parts, these parts being ordered in such a way as to serve the purposes of other objects or beings so that the whole of nature hangs together as an ordered whole, and (2) unless there is that which is not composed of parts for the sake of which those things composed of parts exist we are caught in an infinite regress. The conclusion is that the world of *prakriti*, which is the world of objects, exists for the sake of another, proving the existence of a principle other than *prakriti*. This principle is *purusha*.

Argument (c) assumes that material objects, the objects constituting the world of *prakriti*, could not work together, each being directed to its proper end, unless there be some principle of intelligence guiding this world. The conclusion is that *purusha* must exist in order that the world be ordered as it is.

Argument (d) claims that from the psychological point of view all the objects of the world are of the nature of pleasure, pain, or indifference. But pleasure and pain cannot exist without an experiencer. The conclusion is that the world of *prakriti* must exist for some experiencer, and therefore *purusha* as the principle of experiencer must exist.

Argument (e) claims that *purusha* must exist because of the desire of the individual to transcend himself. In an ordered universe it couldn't happen that the universal tendency toward the infinite—toward self-realization—would be self-frustrating. Consequently, the *purusha* must be there to be realized, since it is being sought.

---

[5] *Samkhya-Karika*, XVII.

But aside from arguments, the existence of *purusha* is put beyond question or doubt by the experience of those who have transcended the world of *prakriti*.

That *purusha* is regarded as being independent of *prakriti* is clear from the claim that "from the repeated study of the truth, there results that wisdom, 'I do not exist [as *prakriti*], naught is mine, I am not [*prakriti*],' which leaves no residue to be known, is pure, being free from ignorance, and is absolute."[6]

But if *purusha* is independent of *prakriti*, are not the questions of how they are related, and how the empirical self can realize the *purusha* within, even more enigmatic than ever? The clue to the reply is contained in the above quotation according to which it is wisdom that releases the *purusha* from *prakriti*. If the *purusha* were *really* caught up in the *prakriti* and constrained by it, then to say that the *purusha* is completely different from and independent of *prakriti* would be nonsensical. But the Samkhya view is that the relation between *prakriti* and *purusha* has its basis in ignorance. In this ignorance a tragic mistake is made, and *purusha* is confused with *prakriti*.

In order to explain how an illusory connection between *purusha* and *prakriti* can cause the real evolution of *prakriti* it is necessary to see how the mere existence and presence of *purusha* affects *prakriti*. Imagine that *purusha* were a shining light and *prakriti* a pool of water reflecting the light. Without *purusha* doing anything more than shining by its own light, the reflection in *prakriti* reflects on itself. But this is not the true light of *purusha*; it is a reflection in *prakriti* and therefore essentially of the nature of *prakriti*. Now in this reflection, which is the reflection of *purusha* in *prakriti*, *purusha* is lost sight of, and *prakriti* is taken to be the ultimate reality. Due to this mistake, the illumination of the empirical self which enables a person to see, hear, feel, think, desire, etc., is not recognized to proceed from the great light that is *purusha*. Consequently, as *prakriti* continues to evolve, *purusha* is not discriminated from *prakriti* but is identified with the evolutes of *prakriti*.

The order of evolution of *prakriti* sketched in the Samkya philosophy regards the first illumination of *prakriti* by *purusha* as *Buddhi*, or *Mahat*— the "great one." This reflection becoming aware of itself is the "I-Maker" (*ahamkara*) responsible for individuation in nature. From these evolutes proceed the mind and the organs of sensation as well as the organs of actions and the essences of the things that are sensed and acted

[6] *Samkhya-Karika*, LXIV.

upon. Finally the gross objects of the world evolved. In this way the origin of all of experienced reality is accounted for by Samkhya.

SELF-DISCIPLINE

The preceding account of the nature of the empirical self and world, and their relation to the *purusha*, or ultimate Self, provides a rational basis for the techniques of dicipline known as *yoga*. The practice of *yoga* is required to achieve the wisdom whereby the ignorance wherein the *purusha* is confused with *prakriti* is alleviated and the essential nature of the Self as *purusha* is realized.

The basic question of *yoga* is, How can that wisdom be achieved wherein the *purusha*, pure subject, recognizes itself for what it is; simply the spectator of *prakriti*, not actually a part of it or connected to it? When this wisdom is achieved there is no longer suffering, for the *purusha* is no longer mistakenly attached to the changing and suffering *prakriti*. Consequently, the afflictions of *prakriti* have nothing to do with *purusha*, and cannot cause suffering.

How the relationship between *purusha* and *prakriti* results in suffering, as explained by Samkhya, can be pictured by imagining a person in a room surrounded by audio-visual devices. These devices lead the person to identify himself with a person being picked up out of the sea, wafted to the peak of a jagged cliff high over the water, and plummeted down to be dashed against the rocks below. Time after time the process is repeated; each time the broken pieces are fused together again and the process commenced anew. For the person who has mistaken this image for himself there is the pain and suffering of a thousand horrible deaths. Nothing could be more wonderful than to escape this horrible fate. But when the person realizes that he has identified himself with a self created out of film and sound he recognizes that nothing that happens to that self has anything to do with him and he is free of the suffering with which he had identified himself. The point is that the person was really free from suffering all of the time, but ignorance prevented this realization. It was neither the audio-visual material in itself nor the person himself that caused the suffering. It was the mistaken identification of the one with the other that led to suffering. In an analogous way, neither *purusha* nor *prakriti* themselves are capable of suffering, but a wrong identification of *purusha* with *prakriti* leads to suffering. To overcome the suffering of the self something must be done to remove the ignorance leading to the mistaken identification of the pure Self with the not-Self.

To this end the *Yoga* aphorisms of Patanjali prescribes *yoga*, or self-discipline. The first four aphorisms indicate the nature and purpose of *yoga*: "Now the exposition of *yoga*. *Yoga* is the restriction of the fluctuations of the mind-stuff (*citta*). Then the Seer [that is, the Self] abides in himself. At other times it [the Self] takes the same forms as the fluctuations [of mind stuff]."[7]

What is here called "mind-stuff" corresponds to what in Samkhya is called the *Buddhi*, or *Mahat*, the "great one." The fluctuations or movements in *Buddhi*, or mind-stuff, lead to the identification with these fluctuations which are due to the not-Self, or *prakriti*. When the changes or fluctuations of the mind-stuff cease there is no foundation for the mistaken identification of *purusha* with *prakriti* and the independence of *purusha* is realized. But when the fluctuations occur they are mistaken for the real Self, the *purusha*. It is as though the light of *purusha* is caught by the rippling dirtied waters of the pool and is therefore regarded as changing and dirty. When the pool is calmed and the dirt allowed to settle, the light is no longer obscured. Accordingly, the important feature of *yoga* is the disciplining and controlling of the mind-stuff.

The eight aids to *yoga* indicate that since the mind-stuff has already identified with the ego, the mind, the senses, and bases of action, one restricts the fluctuations through self-discipline, by bringing under control the other aspects of *prakriti* that have evolved as empirical self—the habits, desires, physical self, etc.

The eight aids to the achievement of the goal of *yoga* are listed as: (1) abstinence from injury, falsehood, theft, incontinence, and the acceptance of gifts; (2) cleanliness, contentment, self-castigation, study, and devotion to the Ishvara; (3) stable and easy posture, accompanied by the relaxation of effort, or by a state of balance; (4) restraint of breath; (5) withdrawal of the senses; (6) not allowing the mind-stuff to wander; (7) focusing the mind-stuff, or contemplation; (8) concentration, wherein the object of contemplation is transcended and duality destroyed.[8]

The first five aids are indirect or preliminary steps in that they prepare the empirical self for the discipline of the mind-stuff that is taken up in the last three steps. Essentially, the discipline of *yoga* is a matter of bringing under control the various evolutes of *prakriti* as shaped by

[7] *Yoga Sutras of Patanjali*, I,1–4, trans. by James Haughton Woods, *Harvard Oriental Series*, XVII (Cambridge: Harvard University Press, 1914).
[8] *Yoga Sutras*, II, III.

mind-stuff, the reflected purusha. It is thus really the reverse process of the evolution of *prakriti*; the involution of *prakriti* back to the stage where the original mistake took place. When this occurs the *purusha* will no longer be regarded as constrained by matter and the Self will be realized in its pure subjectivity.

The explanation of the relation between the empirical and the ultimate by Samkhya, and the nature of the mistake causing bondage and suffering which is to be remedied by the discipline of *yoga*, is nicely summed up in an old and favorite Indian story. The story deals with a little tiger raised by wild goats who mistook himself for a goat and had to be instructed by a master and provided with the right kinds of experience in order to realize his true nature—that of a tiger.

The tiger's mother had died giving birth, and the infant was left all alone in the world. Fortunately, the goats were compassionate and adopted the little fellow, teaching him how to eat grass with his pointed teeth and how to bleat like they did. Time passed and the tiger assumed that he was just like the rest of the band of goats. But one day an old male tiger came upon this little band of goats. They all fled in terror, except for the tiger-goat, now about half-grown, who for some unknown reason felt no fear. As the savage jungle beast approached, the cub began to feel self-conscious and uncomfortable. To cover his self-consciousness he began to bleat a bit and nibble some grass. The old tiger roared at the little one in amazement and anger, asking him what he thought he was doing eating grass and bleating like a goat. But the little one was too embarrassed by all this to answer, and continued to nibble grass. Thoroughly outraged by this behavior, the jungle tiger grabbed him by the scruff of his neck and carried him to a nearby pool. Holding him over the water he told him to look at himself. "Is that the pot face of a tiger or the long face of a goat?" he roared.

The cub was still too frightened to answer, so the old tiger carried him to his cave, and thrust a huge chunk of juicy, red, raw meat between his jaws. As the juices trickled into his stomach the cub began to feel a new strength and a new power. No longer mistaking himself for a goat the little tiger lashed his tail from side to side and roared like the tiger he was. He had achieved Tiger-realization! He no longer took himself to be what he appeared to be in his ignorance, but realized his true nature, which had nothing to do with the world of goats.

CHAPTER 6

KNOWLEDGE AND REALITY: NYAYA-VAISHESHIKA

WHEREAS the Upanishads emphasized the ultimate nature of reality as an experienced unity, and the Samkhya attempted to show what reality must be like in order to make sense of both our ordinary experience and the claims of the Upanishads, the Nyaya philosophy centers on the nature of our *knowledge* of reality. The main question is not, What is reality like? but, What is our knowledge of reality like? What do we know about our knowledge? Accordingly, major portions of Nyaya philosophy are given over to consideration of the various problems of knowledge. Adopting the Nyaya analysis of the structure of human knowledge, Vaisheshika philosophy emphasized the nature of what is known, and came up with an atomistic picture of the structure of the universe.

The basic problem of knowledge is that of ascertaining whether or not what is claimed as knowledge is actually knowledge rather than just mistaken opinion. Does what is claimed as knowledge really reveal reality? Mistakes are easily made in matters of perception and inference. In the dim light the discarded rope appears to be a snake; it could cause someone to claim knowledge of a snake on the path. But if there were only a rope on the path obviously no one could have *knowledge* of a snake on the path. As examples like this are considered it becomes possible to speculate that perhaps what *appears* to us is always different from what really is there. It might be as though the eyes always present things as red, yellow, and blue, whereas all things are really orange, black, and green. The ear presents sounds differently from what they really are, and the other senses equally distort the reality with which they come in contact. Skeptical considerations of this sort push philosophers in the direction of trying to analyze what knowledge is.

In Nyaya the analysis of knowledge is taken up in terms of the knowing subject, the object to be known, the known object, and the means of coming to know the object. Analysis of claims to knowledge reveals that these four factors are involved in all knowledge, for there is no knowledge except when someone knows something. The one who knows is the subject, the something known is the object. The object is either the object to be known, or the object that is known. The whole point of coming to know things is to pass from ignorance, in which case the subject is separated from the object, to knowledge, in which case the subject, by various means, comes to be related to the object in certain ways. These relations constitute knowing the object. Consequently, anyone wishing to come to an understanding of what knowledge is must attend to (1) the knowing subject, (2) the object to be known, (3) the object as known, and (4) the means whereby the object comes to be known.

MEANS OF KNOWLEDGE

According to Nyaya, knowledge is essentially the revelation of an object, and the means of knowledge are distinguished according to the different causes responsible for the revelation of the object in knowledge. This principle of distinction yields perception, inference, analogy, and testimony as the four basic means, or sources, of knowledge. The principle for distinguishing between these sources is that a person is doing four basically different things in coming to know something in each of the different ways.

PERCEPTUAL KNOWLEDGE

Perceptual knowledge is defined as the true and determinate knowledge arising from the contact of the senses with their proper objects.[1]

---

[1] *The Nyaya Sutras of Gotama*, 1.4. trans. by Vidyabhusana in *The Sacred Books of the Hindus*, VIII (Allahabad: The Panini Office, 1930). Reprinted in *A Source Book in Indian Philosophy*, ed. by Radhakrishnan and Moore (Princeton: The Princeton University Press, 1957), pp. 358 ff.

It is known, by means of perception, that these words appear on a piece of paper, because of the contact of the eye with the marks constituting the words. If one were a considerable distance from the paper and perceived only dark spots on the paper, not knowing whether they were words, scribbles, or ants, it would not be a genuine case of perception, for the object perceived would not be determinate. If one were to mistake a rope for a snake it would not be a case of genuine perception either, for it would not be true knowledge, since there was no snake there to be perceived.

It may be asked, however, if in cases of perceptual illusions or mistakes there is not something actually perceived. It does not seem possible that the senses could reveal sensory objects without some external stimuli. Unless there were something with which the senses were making contact there would be nothing to be revealed. Furthermore, if it were the case that the senses could reveal something when there was no contact of any kind, it might turn out that all claimed perceptual experience was of this kind, and that in reality there was nothing in the world to be sensed. But this is self-contradictory, for the very claim itself rests on the assumption of real sensory contact.

But it still is necessary to explain how genuine perceptions of the kinds recognized as knowledge differ from and can be distinguished from perceptual mistakes. The Nyaya explanation of this point rests on a distinction between two kinds of perception. Determinate perception—perception of words on this paper—is preceded by indeterminate perception—sense contact with the marks on the paper prior to recognition and classification of them as words. To talk about a perceptual mistake in reference to the indeterminate perception doesn't make any sense, for there is nothing which is taken to be anything, and therefore it cannot be taken for something other than what it is. Indeterminate perception is simply the contact of the sense with its object. It is the most elementary sensory experience limited to precisely what is given by sense contact. But this is not classified as perceptual knowledge. Perceptual knowledge requires determinate perception in which basic sensory experience of the indeterminate perception is revealed as some kind of thing with various qualities and relations, being, in principle, nameable. There is thus a distinction between an immediate sensory experience and perception, though the latter always includes the former. Consequently there is also a distinction between ignorance and error. Ignorance may be due to a lack of either the immediate sensory experience or to a lack of determinate perception, but error results from mistaking what is given in immediate sensory experience for something other than what it is. In terms of the example of erroneously perceiving a snake instead of a rope, the immediate sensory experience reveals a darkish-colored, elongated and twisted color patch. But in perception this content of sensory experience is seen as a snake when it is in fact a rope and the result is the erroneous claim that a snake has been seen. From this is can be seen that true perceptual knowledge is the perception of what is perceived as it really is, and error is the perception of something other than what it really is.

But now the question may be raised as to how a particular perceptual judgment can be known to be true. Obviously it is impossible to *directly* test the correspondence between the perception and the reality being perceived, for this would mean knowing what is true knowledge by going outside of knowledge itself. But to know something outside of knowing it is impossible. If, however, the correspondence is tested within the framework of knowledge all we get is another knowledge claim about the claimed correspondence. And this can go on indefinitely without ever revealing anything about the actual correspondence between claim and reality.

Consequently Nyaya suggests that mistaken knowledge claims are detected, ultimately, in terms of the successfulness of practice. If one's perception of the finely granulated white stuff in the bowl on the table as sugar is erroneous because the bowl in reality contains salt, it will not help to take another dozen looks at it. Rather, it is necessary to take some action based on the perception and see how the action turns out. If the perception is non-erroneous a spoonful of the contents of the bowl will make the coffee a pleasant drink. If the perception is erroneous because the bowl contains salt, a spoonful in the coffee will make the contents of the cup undrinkable. Expanding this principle of verification of perceptual claims, the position is reached that whatever works—in the sense that it provides for successful activity, and eventually, human happiness and liberation—is true because it is seen to correspond to reality as attested to by the successful activity.

In this way the Nyaya philosophers define true perception in terms of correspondence to reality. But they advocate practice as the means of testing this correspondence.

Different kinds of perceptual knowledge can be distinguished according to the ways in which contact is established between the senses and their objects. Ordinary perception occurs when the eye sees color, the ear hears sound, the nose smells odors, the tongue tastes flavors, resistance is felt, or the mind comes into contact with psychical states and processes. The first five kinds of perceptual knowledge yield indeterminate perception, or merely the basic sensory experience itself. The sixth kind of perceptual knowledge, which is internal, is a matter of becoming aware of the sensory experiences and perceiving them to be something or the other. It corresponds to ordinary determinate perception.

In addition, Nyaya admits extra-ordinary perception. Analysis of our knowledge reveals that not only are there basic sensory experiences and perceptions of individual things, but also there are perceptions of natures of things. Visual experience of certain color patches is not simply perceived to be an individual thing that goes by the name of, say, Rama, but is perceived to be that *man*, Rama. Since the perception of the nature of the individual, by virtue of which the individual can be recognized as a member of a class (e.g., the class "man"), is not given in ordinary perception, it is regarded as one of the three kinds of extra-ordinary perception.

The second kind of extra-ordinary perception explains how what is proper to one sense organ can become the object of another sense. For example, it is often said that ice looks cold, or that flowers look soft, or fragrant. But coldness, softness, and fragrance are not the proper objects of sight. Consequently, these kinds of perceptual experiences are regarded as extra-ordinary.

The third kind of extra-ordinary perception refers to the perception of things in the past or future, or hidden, or infinitely small in size by one who possesses unusual powers generated by disciplined meditation, or *yoga*.

INFERENCE

Although perception is the basic kind of knowledge, there are three other means of knowledge recognized by Nyaya. Inference is regarded as an independent means of valid knowledge that is defined as producing a knowledge that comes after other knowledge.[2] For example, from perceptual knowledge it is possible to infer something about reality that has never actually been perceived. We know that dinosaurs existed because of certain fossil remains that have been seen. Inference proceeds from what has been perceived to something that has not been perceived by means of a third "something" called a *reason*, which functions

---

[2] *Nyaya Sutra*, I.5.

as a middle term in syllogistic reasoning. For example, in the syllogistic inference, "There is fire on the hill because there is smoke on the hill, and wherever there is smoke there is fire," the universal connection between smoke and fire is the reason (the third "thing") for affirming fire on the hill, even though the fire was not actually perceived.

A commonly used example of inference in its ordinary syllogistic form is as follows:

1. Yonder hill has fire.
2. Because it has smoke.
3. Whatever has smoke has fire, e.g., a stove.
4. Yonder hill has smoke such as is always accompanied by fire.
5. Therefore yonder hill has fire.

Nyaya distinguishes between reasoning to convince oneself and reasoning to convince another. When reasoning to convince oneself it is not necessary to set out the steps so elaborately as above, and either the first two or the last two steps can be eliminated. But when the inference is set down formally for the consideration of another, all five steps are insisted upon. The essential part of the inference in the above example is the coming to know that there is fire on the hill on the basis of (1) the perceived smoke and (2) the reason constituted by the invariable connection between smoke and fire.

In the above example, the first proposition represents the new knowledge claim. The second proposition gives the perceptual grounds for the new claim. The third proposition asserts the reason for making the move from a claim about smoke to one about fire. It is, so to speak, the inference ticket, enabling one to move on to the conclusion constituting the inferential knowledge claim. The fourth proposition asserts that the inference ticket is good for this trip, i.e., that the reason applies in this case. The fifth proposition repeats the claim, now not as a matter for testing, but as a valid knowledge claim, as established by the reasons provided.

Clearly, the most crucial part of the inferential process is establishing the reason (3), the invariable connection between two objects or events. Grant that it was observed on one or a hundred occasions in the past that fire was accompanied by smoke. Is this a guarantee that in the next case smoke will be accompanied by fire? After all, just because the first ten or one hundred persons who walked into the UN building were males does not mean that the next person will be male.

Nyaya philosophers regard the enumeration of individual objects

or events as an important part of the establishment of universal connections between events or objects. If ten black crows are seen and no
non-black crows, there is some probability that there is a universal
connection between being a crow and being black. But if thousands of
crows have been observed, all of them black, the probability is increased.
However, even if a million crows, all black, have been observed, and the
next crow observed is white, the probability that there is a universal
connection between being a crow and being black is zero, even though
we might want to say that the probability is very high that the millionth-
and-second crow will be black.

But if this is the case it would seem that no amount of confirming
instances would ever establish a necessary connection between events
or objects, for it would always be possible that the very next observed
case would refute the necessity of the connection. In light of this possibility, even though Nyaya places much emphasis upon presence of confirming experience and absence of unconfirming experience, the matter
is not left here. After all, they argue, there is a difference between claims
such as "Wherever there is smoke there is fire" and "Whatever is man
is mortal," on the one hand, and the claim "All crows are black,"
on the other. The difference is that there is nothing in the nature of
a crow that requires blackness. But there is something about the nature
of man that requires mortality. Usually that is expressed by saying that
smoke is *caused* by fire, and mortality is *caused* by man's nature as a
composite being.

Nevertheless, even if there is, in reality, a difference between these
cases, the question still arises as to how it is possible to determine that
in some cases the connection is universal and necessary because causal,
and that in others the connection is mere coincidence without any
causal basis. Since inference proceeds from perceptual knowledge, if
there is to be knowledge of a universal and necessary connection between
events or objects, it must be that this necessity is perceived, and not
inferred. Accordingly, Nyaya includes in perceptual knowledge the
perception of the class-nature in the individual. This is a kind of extra-
ordinary perception whereby the individual is perceived not merely to
be this or that particular thing or event, but as this or that particular
thing *and* one of a certain *kind*, or *class*, of things, the class-nature, or
essence, being perceived along with the individual characteristics of the
thing or event.

Those inferences involving universal connection are of either of two
kinds. Either (1) the unperceived effect can be inferred from the per-

ceived cause, or (2) the unperceived cause can be inferred from the perceived effect. All other inferences depend upon a non-causal and nonnecessary uniformity, and cannot be shown to be necessarily true.

To aid in avoiding certain common mistakes in drawing inferences, the Nyaya philosophers have listed a number of fallacies to be avoided. A fallacy is defined as that which appears to be a valid reason for inference, but which is really not a valid reason. In the inference "There is fire on the hill because there is smoke on the hill and where there is smoke there is fire," the inferred knowledge is that there is fire on the hill. The assertion "there is fire" is being made about the hill. Technically the term "fire" is called *sadhya*. The term "hill" is called *paksha*. The reason for the assertion—"There is smoke"—is called *hetu*. Unless what is taken to be a reason for connecting the *sadhya* with the *paksha* is really a reason, or *hetu*, the inference will be invalid. To insure that the given *hetu*, or reason, will really be a reason, several rules must be observed. (1) The reason, or *hetu*, must be present in the *paksha*, and in all other objects having the *sadhya* in it. (2) The reason, or *hetu*, must be absent from objects not possessing the *sadhya*. (3) The inferred proposition should not be contradicted by valid perception. (4) The reason, or *hetu*, should not make possible a conclusion contradicting the inferred proposition.

COMPARISON

The third means of valid knowledge recognized by Nyaya philosophers is knowledge by comparison based on similarity. For example, if someone knew what a cow was, and was told that a deer was like a cow in certain respects, he might come to know that the animal he met in the woods was a deer. This is different from being told what name to apply to a certain object. If, for example, one were to see a deer for the first time and he was told, "That is a deer," the knowledge would be due to testimony, not to comparison. Knowledge by means of comparison is attained when the association of the name of an unknown object is made by the knower on the basis of experiencing the similarity of the unknown object with a known object. The crucial aspect of this means of knowledge is the observation of the similarity. Nyaya thinkers hold that similarities are objective and perceivable. Accordingly, knowledge of the nature of a new object on the strength of its similarity to a known object constitutes a separate means of knowledge. While comparative knowledge involves both perception and inference, it cannot be reduced to either of them, and therefore is to be counted as a third means of knowledge.

The fourth means of valid knowledge recognized in Nyaya is technically called *shabda*. Literally, it means the word of a person, and it refers to the knowledge achieved as a result of being told something by a reliable person. Opinion is not the same thing as knowledge, for opinion might be erroneous, but knowledge cannot. Consequently, simply hearing the opinion of another is not a means of knowledge. But when the knowledge claims of another are heard there is genuine knowledge attained, if one understands the claim. The three basic criteria of knowledge based on the testimony of another are: (1) the person speaking must be absolutely honest and reliable with respect to what he is saying; (2) the person speaking must actually *know* that which he is communicating; (3) the hearer must understand exactly what it is that he is hearing.

Having analyzed the means of valid knowledge, the next step is to consider the objects of valid knowledge. Nyaya lists as objects of knowledge the self, the body, the senses and their objects, knowledge, mind, action, mental imperfections, pleasure and pain, suffering, and freedom from suffering.[3] These objects of knowledge all depend upon the relation between a knowing subject and a world of objects, for they have to do with the actions and passions of a subject. If one considers objects of knowledge from the viewpoint of their own independent existence they include the categories of the Vaisheshika system. These categories are (1) substance, (2) quality, (3) motion, (4) generality, (5) particularity, (6) inherence, and (7) nonexistence.[4]

These categories are the types of objects that correspond to the different types of perceived objects. Since perceptions are due to contact with objects by an experiencing self, the differences in perceptual objects must be due to different real objects. Thus, classification of objects of

[3] *Nyaya Sutra*, I.9.
[4] *Vaisheshika Sutra*, I.4, trans. by Nandalal Sinha, *The Sacred Books of the Hindus*, VI (Allahabad: the Panini Office, 2nd ed. 1923), Reprinted in *Source Book in Indian Philosophy*, pp. 387 ff. Actually, the seventh category, that of non-existence, was added centuries later than the others.

knowledge yields a classification of existing things, as differences in perception are due to differences in what is perceived.

The first kind of existing thing is substance. This refers to that which exists independently of other kinds of things, but which is the *locus* of existence for the other kinds of things. Real in itself, a substance can be thought of as the substratum of qualities and actions. The category of substance includes: (1) earth, (2) water, (3) light, (4) air, (5) ether, (6) time, (7) space, (8) self, and (9) mind. Earth, water, light, air, and ether are regarded as physical elements since each of them is known by a particular external sense; earth by smell, water by taste, light by sight, air by touch, and ether by sound.

These substances can be considered in two ways. First, they can be thought of as atomic, eternal, and indivisible. Secondly, they are the results of combinations of atoms, in which case they are temporal, composite, and destructible, being produced by the combination of atoms. That substances in the sense of composite things, such as this jar, are made up of atoms is known on the basis of inference. If the jar is broken it is reduced to several parts. Each of these parts can again be broken, being reduced to more parts. But no matter how long this process continues it is impossible that every part should be destructible, for that would mean it is composite. But if composite things exist it is necessary that their ultimate constituents be simple, or else composite things would never be produced. Therefore, the ultimate constituents of gross substances must be atomic. The substance space is inferred on the grounds that sound is perceived and since sound is a quality, there must be that in which it inheres or that to which it belongs, namely, space.

Space and time are known to exist because of our perceptions of here and there, far and near, and past, present, and future. Knowledge is a quality, and therefore it must exist in a substance called the self, which is the ground of consciousness. Mind is inferred on the grounds that feeling and willing are known, but since they are not known by the external senses they must be known by the mind. In addition there is that which directs the senses and collects their contacts into experience. That in which sense contacts reside as qualities is the substance known as mind.

The second category of known objects is that of quality. It refers to the various qualifications of the substances, and includes color, odor, contact, sound, number, measure, difference, connection, separation, long or short, far or near, knowledge, happiness, sorrow, volition, hatred, effort, heaviness, fluidity, potency, merit, and demerit. This list of qualifications is a way of saying that things or substances can be, e.g., red or blue, pungent or fragrant, touching or apart from, soft or loud, one or many, large or small, the same as or different from, separate or together, long or short, far or near, knowing or ignorant, happy or sorrowful, desiring to or desiring not to, loving or hating, trying or not trying, light or heavy, mobile or immobile, able or not able, and good or bad, respectively. There are many divisions of some of the qualities, but the above list is being taken as referring to the basic kinds of qualification of substances.

The third kind of basic and irreducible reality is motion. The different kinds of motion are (1) upward, (2) downward, (3) contraction, (4) expansion, and (5) locomotion. The kinds of motion are the kinds of reality that account for the changes substances undergo.

The fourth category is that of universal essences. It accounts for sameness found in substances, qualities, or actions. Four cows, four red objects, and four upward motions are each of them the same in that they are cows, reds, or upward motions. This sameness is regarded as objective, belonging to the individual things just as truly as do qualities. The reason that the four cows can all be recognized as cows is that they share in the same essence or nature. It is this essence which enables one to form class concepts and to classify individual things into various classes.

From a continuous field of sensing and mental activity particular objects are perceived. The ability to perceive particular and distinct objects is due to the category of particularity which belongs to the objects perceived. If things did not have the character of being different from other things there would be no reason why they should be perceived as different. But since they are perceived as different there must be some foundation for this difference in reality. Hence, particularity must exist in reality.

The category of inherence reflects the fact that different things, such as substance, quality, action, etc., appear as one whole. Thus, the size of the man, his color, his nature as man, and his particularity as this man, all appear so unified that we think of one thing appearing, rather than a collection of things appearing to us. Thus, the whole inheres in its parts; the jug in the clay, the pencil in the wood, etc. The basis for the unity of different categories must, like the other categories, have a foundation in reality, as different from other kinds of things. Otherwise it would appear as one of the other kinds of things, and not as separate. Therefore, the category of inherence is recognized as an independent kind of reality.

In addition to the above kinds of knowable objects there is non-existence. Although non-existence may seem to be a queer kind of reality it's existence cannot be questioned, for to question it is to suggest that it does not exist, which is to affirm the category of non-existence. Only by assuming non-existence does negation become possible.

In the way just outlined Nyaya and Vaisheshika come to their metaphysical view of reality. This list of the basic kinds of things that exist is a sketch of the ontological universe.

THE KNOWER

Considering the knowing subject, rather than the objects to be known, or the objects as known, Nyaya argues that the self is a unique substance. The qualifications of this substance are knowledge, feeling, and volition. Accordingly, the self is defined as the substance in which the qualities of desire, aversion, pleasure, pain, etc., inhere, for these follow upon knowing, feeling, and volition. Now, since none of these are physical qualities, since they cannot be perceived as physical qualities by any of the senses, it must be admitted that they belong to a substance other than a physical, or material, substance. Therefore the self must be distinct from physical objects, from sensations, from consciousness, and the mind, for the self experiences all of these. One may ask, who knows reality, who perceives, who is conscious, etc.? In every case the answer is given, "The self." Since everything else can become an object for the self, but objects—as objects—require a subject for which they are objects, it follows that the self cannot be an object, and therefore cannot be identical with anything that becomes an object, for it must be always subject.

Since the self is a unique substance and consciousness belongs to it as a quality, the self does not depend for its existence upon consciousness. In fact, according to Nyaya, ultimate liberation, or freedom, will also be freedom from consciousness. The reason for this is that consciousness is seen as consciousness of something or other. But that presupposes a duality between subject and object. And when there is duality there is possible suffering and bondage, for the subject can be bound by the object and caused to suffer. But to eliminate suffering and bondage duality must be eliminated. This can be done upon the elimination of consciousness. But if the self were essentially consciousness this would mean the extinction of the self. However, since consciousness is only a characteristic of the self, the self is not destroyed when consciousness is eliminated. All that can be said about the self in this state of liberation is that it simply exists as self.

CHANGE AND REALITY: VEDANTA

ALL the philosophies of India were very much influenced by the teachings of the Upanishads, including the philosophies of Jainism, Carvaka, and Buddhism, which did not accept the authority of the Veda. With the exception of these latter philosophies, all the philosophies of India took themselves to be in essential agreement with the teachings of the Upanishads. But as the canons of experience and reason were differently interpreted there came to be a variety of conclusions concerning the interpretation of the Upanishads, and some of these appeared to conflict with the conclusions of the Upanishads when these were taken literally. The Vedanta philosophers set out self-consciously to underwrite the main conclusions of the Upanishads with critical interpretations of reason and experience which did not conflict with those conclusions. As a result, the Vedanta philosophies turned out to be highly critical of some of the conclusions of the other systems. For example, the Samkhya claim that the world of the not-Self was eternally real and distinct from the Self, and the Nyaya, Vaisheshika and Mimamsa views of the world as real and pluralistic, being made up of different kinds of atoms, came in for severe criticism, since these conclusions appeared to deviate furthest from the emphasis on the sole reality of *Atman*, or *Brahman*, in the Upanishads.

The Nyaya, Vaisheshika, Samkhya, and Mimamsa systems of philosophy are unanimous in agreeing that our perceptions have a basis in reality. That basis can be expressed by saying that what is perceived exists independently of being perceived. Genuine knowledge occurs when the knower comes to see things as they really are. Philosophically, this position is known as realism, which simply indicates that the objective world revealed by experience is real and exists independently of being known. These systems also are pluralistic in that they agree that this objective reality is constituted by a variety of ultimately different objects. This view, pluralistic realism, is not a very startling view of the world. In fact, it is the view held by most people in the world. Philosophical proponents of this view have argued that whenever one's experiences are to be taken seriously as providing knowledge it is necessary that there be knowledge of *something*. If there is no something to be known there can be no knowledge. However, if something exists to be known, then there are objects that exist independently of perception even though they can be related to a knower in such a way that they come to be perceived and known. Therefore, it is logically necessary to admit the real existence of the world that is experienced unless it can be shown that there really is no knowledge. But to claim that one knows that there is no knowledge is absurd, for it is a claim that there is knowledge. And what basis other than knowledge is there for claiming that there is no knowledge of the world?

These are some of the difficulties faced by the Vedanta philosophers who felt that the realistic and pluralistic conclusions of the philosophers of the other systems were in direct opposition to the conclusions of the Upanishads. After all, the Upanishads taught the unity of reality and the identity of self with reality in passages such as the following: "All this is *Atman*."[1] "Atman being known . . . everything is known."[2] "There was only Being at the beginning, it was one without a second."[3] "All this is *Brahman*."[4] "This self is the *Brahman*."[5] "I am *Brahman*."[6]

The very fact that the unity of reality was thus taught in the Upanishads was sufficient reason for a Hindu to accept this view as true, for the Upanishads belong to the tradition of infallible literature. Nevertheless, for the critical mind it is important to show that this teaching does not conflict with reason or experience. A significant step in this direction

---

[1] *Chandogya Upanishad*, 7.25.2.
[2] *Brihadaranyaka Upanishad*, 4.5.6.
[3] *Chandogya Upanishad*, 6.2.1.
[4] *Mundaka Upanishad*, 2.2.11, and *Chandogya Upanishad*, 3.14.1.
[5] *Brihadaranyaka Upanishad*, 2.5.19.
[6] *Brihadaranyaka Upanishad*, 1.4.10.

could be taken simply by showing that opposing claims about reality were self-contradictory and implausible. Consequently the task of showing that the philosophies with conclusions at variance with the monistic teachings of the Upanishads were unsatisfactory became an important part of Vedanta philosophy. As a result, the critical analysis of the other philosophies came to be emphasized. But it was not sufficient simply to show that other systems were unsatisfactory. It was also necessary to show that the system of reality claimed by the Vedantic interpretation of the Upanishads was not subject to the same kinds of criticisms aimed at the other systems. In this way the Vedanta philosophies came to provide rational criticisms of the other philosophies and also to provide rational defences of their own interpretations and systems.

There are three principal schools of Vedantic philosophy, differing from each other in the way they account for the relations between persons, things, and ultimate Reality (*Brahman*). The oldest of these schools, that of non-dualism is often referred to as the Shamkarite school, being named after Shamkara, one of its important early philosophers who lived in the eighth century. The second school, that of qualified non-dualism, claims the eleventh-century philosopher Ramanuja as its principal figure, and is therefore sometimes called the Ramanuja school. The third school, the dualistic Vedanta, or Madhva, school has as its central figure the thirteenth-century philosopher named Madhva.

SHAMKARA'S NON-DUALISM

Shamkara's view of reality is that there is one absolute and independent reality which alone exists as real and unchanging. This reality is the *Brahman* of the Upanishads. This view rules out theories according to which the world is thought of as the product of material elements, or the transformation of unconscious matter that evolves, or the product of two kinds of independent reality, such as *Brahman* and matter.

According to Shamkara, *Brahman* is the reality that provides for the existence of the appearances that constitute the empirical world, but it is also beyond these appearances, not being exhausted by them. From the empirical and conceptual point of view, *Brahman* is in the world, or immanent. From the absolute point of view, *Brahman* transcends the world.

The nature and existence of *Brahman* cannot be proved from perception or reasoning, but is to be taken either on the basis of scriptural testimony (the Upanishads) or by direct and intuitive experience of the kind made possible by yogic concentration. Nevertheless, reason can be put to the use of justifying these means of knowing *Brahman*.

To reconcile the perceived plurality and objective reality of the world with the monistic conclusions of the Upanishads, Shamkara regards the world as appearance rather than reality, and perception as illusion rather than knowledge.

The individual self as pure subject, or *Atman*, is not different from *Brahman*.

By way of refuting conflicting claims about the nature of reality Shamkara considers first the Samkhya view and then the Vaisheshika view. According to Samkhya philosophy, the world is the result of the spontaneous evolution of unconscious matter, or *prakriti*, which is composed of the three *gunas—sattva, rajas*, and *tamas*. Samkhya includes within its view the existence of purpose in the world, for the world is such that it fits reborn selves and enables them to be liberated. But how can one suppose that the world, which is a harmonious system of related objects and ordered events as we experience it—and as claimed by Samkhya —could be the accidental result of an unconscious cause? To attribute purpose to unconscious nature is unintelligible according to Shamkara's analysis, and therefore the Samkhya view is untenable.

The Vaisheshika view is that the world is caused by the combination of atoms. But again, how can unconscious atoms produce out of their combinations the order that makes possible the moral law claimed by the Vaisheshika philosophers? Even if this objection is overlooked, Vaisheshika has not explained how or why unconscious atoms should first begin to move around and join together to produce the world. If atoms were incessantly in motion and joining together because of their very nature neither the beginning of the world nor its dissolution would be explicable. Therefore the Vaisheshika view is not satisfactory according to Shamkara's analysis, since it claims both production and destruction.

Thus, the explanations of Vaisheshika and Samkhya are seen to be inconsistent within the framework of their own assumptions. But their basic assumptions are not altogether satisfactory either. Nyaya, Vaisheshika, Samkhya, and Mimamsa all accept as a basic assumption the fact of real change and causation. That is, they all admit that various real changes occur in the world and that these changes are caused.

Concerning the relation between cause and effect only two views are possible. Either the effect preexists in the cause or it does not. If the effect does not preexist in the cause then the effect is totally new. This view is called *asatkaryavada* (non-existence of the effect). If the claim is that the effect preexists in the cause—this view is called *satkaryavada*—then two consequences may follow. On the one hand, it can be admitted that change and causality is a matter of making explicit what was implicit in the cause. Or it can be claimed that there is no difference between cause and effect. Nyaya and Vaisheshika held to *asatkaryavada*, as did some of the Mimamsa philosophers, on the grounds that effects are experienced as something totally new. Other Mimamsa philosophers and Samkhya philosophers held to *satkaryavada*, admitting change in the sense of making explicit what was implicit in the cause, but denying that effects were new realities.

Shamkara, in critically examining these views of causation, finds them both logically unacceptable. Nothing can show an effect to be different from its material cause. Clay pots are clay, gold rings are gold, etc. Furthermore the clay pot cannot exist apart from the clay, nor the gold ring apart from the gold. Consequently it is incorrect to say that an effect is something new that has been produced and that it did not exist before. In terms of its material cause it has always been there. From another point of view, it is argued that it is impossible to conceive of something totally new coming into existence. All that can ever be thought is the transformation of matter, never the coming into existence of matter.

Samkhya argues that if the effect were something new we would have the coming into existence of the non-existent. If this were possible, why not get non-existent oil out of sand? However, even though Samkhya may be right in claiming the theory of *asatkaryavada* to be unacceptable, the Samkhya philosopher does not realize that his own interpretation of *satkaryavada* is also untenable. If the effect already preexists in the cause, how can there be a genuine change of the material into the effect? If the effect is already there, then it is impossible for the material to become the effect, for that would be the coming to be of what already is, which makes no sense. If the Samkhya philosopher replies that though matter does not come into existence, the form does—a new form is produced—he is really admitting the existence of *asatkaryavada*, for he is admitting the effect as something that did not previously exist. But this contradicts his own arguments against *asatkaryavada*.

However, from the fact that the Samkhya philosopher has contradicted himself, it does not necessarily follow that something new does not come into existence. What follows is that either nothing new can come into existence, or that he was wrong in his argument and something new can come into existence. Consequently, it is still necessary for Shamkara to tend to the question of whether a change of form is a real change, for it cannot be denied that changes in form are perceived. Shamkara's solution is to show that though changes in form are perceived this does not imply a change in reality unless a form has reality of its own. But, of course, form has existence only in dependence upon matter, for there is no form except in formed matter. There is no form of a cup excepting the cup made of matter. Therefore, form has no independent reality. If a change in form were a change in reality, a person sitting down would be a different reality from a person standing up, since the form is different. But, of course, the same person standing up or sitting down is one and the same reality.

From another point of view, the argument is provided that if substances are distinct from their forms or qualities it would be impossible to explain the relation between the quality or form and the substance. If the form is distinct from the substance it cannot be related to the substance except in terms of a third reality which connects or relates them. But then, in order to relate this third distinct reality to the other two, another distinct reality is needed. And to relate this reality to the others, still another is needed. There would be no end to this process of multiplying entities to relate the form to the substance. But if there were no end to the process, then the form would be unrelated to the substance, making a change in reality impossible. If it is admitted that the form has no reality independent of matter then there is no change in reality.

ILLUSION

These arguments, if valid, lead to the conclusion that no changes are possible, for it has been shown that it is impossible for causation to bring about change. But on the other hand there is the perception of changes. Shamkara's solution to the dilemma is to suggest that since the perceived changes cannot be rationally accepted as real, they be regarded as similar to the perception of an illusory object.

If the objects constituting the furniture of the world are like the illusory objects of dreaming experience, it becomes possible to reconcile the existence of *Brahman* alone as the ultimate reality with the existence of the empirical world as unreal. The snake perceived in the dream *exists* in the dream, but is not *real*. That it exists must be admitted, for otherwise there would be no dream. But that it is real cannot be admitted for its unreality is what marks this particular experience as dreaming experience. In a similar way, the objects of the empirical world exist, for they are perceived. To deny the existence of the objects of the empirical world is to deny ordinary perceptual experience. But if there is an analogy between dream objects and the objects perceived in waking experience, then perhaps the objects of waking experience could also be said to be unreal, as compared with the experience of a greater reality. After all, as long as one is dreaming it is impossible to regard the objects of the dream as unreal. It is only possible to regard the dream objects as unreal when a different level of experience is attained. From the vantage point of waking experience the dream objects can be said to be unreal. But it may also be possible that from another level of experience—the experience of *Brahman*—the objects of ordinary waking experience could be seen to be unreal.

Thus, if the objects of ordinary waking experience were like dream objects in this respect it would be possible to reconcile the existence of the perceptual and empirical world with the sole reality of *Brahman*, in a way similar to the reconciliation of the existence of dream objects with their unreality.

If it is suggested that the whole world of ordinary experience is somehow illusory, it becomes important to understand the nature of illusion in order to see what sense this suggestion makes. An example considered in Vedanta is that of the rope that is mistakenly seen as a snake. The rope is said to be a snake because of ignorance of what really is there. If it were known that there is a rope there, there would be no illusion. But ignorance in itself is not enough to produce the illusion. After all, there are many things of which one is ignorant, but one does not say that these are snakes. The ignorance that produces an illusion must have two aspects. First, it covers up the reality actually present, e.g., the rope. Secondly, it actually distorts what is really there, representing it as something other than what it is.

Now, if the nature of the world is like an illusory object it must be that the world is also a product of ignorance, where the basic reality is not simply obscured and hidden from view, but is actually distorted into something other than what it is. In this way, the true reality, *Brahman*, as a result of ignorance, could be mistaken for the world of ordinary empirical objects. These objects are simply the concealing distortion of

Brahman, which alone is real. But, of course, it is only from the standpoint of the ignorant that there is any ignorance. It is only from this ignorance that the world proceeds, as it covers up the true nature of reality and causes us to see mistakenly something else in its place. Just as an illusion is produced when a magician makes one coin to appear to be many—though illusion exists only for the ignorant, not for the magician—similarly from the point of view of absolute reality there is no plurality of objects—no illusion. There is only the one true reality, just as for the magician there is only the one coin. For the wise, who succeed in seeing through the illusion of the magician, there do not appear many coins. Similarly, for the wise who experience *Brahman*, there does not appear a world of empirical objects as the ultimate reality.

It follows, if the empirical world is unreal, that there are no real changes in the world, for the changes have the same reality as the objects that are supposed to change. Consequently, the only theory of change possible is that of apparent change rather than real change. Real changes and causes are possible only if there are real objects and they really change. But if Shamkara is right, there can be no real changes and causes, for there are no real objects to change. This lends support to the Vedanta claims that the Nyaya-Vaisheshika and Samkhya theories of change are incorrect.

This theory of the nature of the empirical world also enable Shamkara to explain those passages in the Upanishads that speak of the world being produced out of *Brahman*. The world can be produced out of *Brahman* just as snakes are produced out of ropes and bent sticks are produced by water (by refraction). There is existence inasmuch as there are objects for experience. But there is no reality because the objects are illusory, being the result of ignorance.

This attempt on the part of Shamkara to explain the world as an appearance produced by illusory perception depends for its success largely upon showing that the analogy of illusory perception applies. This is done by analyzing carefully the notion of perceptual error.

Mimamsa philosophers argue that perceptual error is impossible. Immediate perception at least must be allowed to be valid, for it is the basis of all other knowledge. In support of their claim that perceptual error is impossible, the Mimamsa philosophers analyze alleged cases of perceptual error. They argue that in the case of perceiving a snake in a rope an error is made, but it is not a perceptual error. That erroneous knowledge is not simply one piece of knowledge, but a mixture of perception and memory, along with the failure to discriminate between the two. Thus, they argue that the perception itself is correct and the memory itself is correct, but that the two are wrongly conjoined. The error lies in failing to discriminate.

To this argument the Vedanta philosophers reply that the claim, "This is a snake," does not represent three pieces of knowledge—with the mistake being made in the third kind—but represents only one piece of knowledge. That memory is involved is not denied, but the claim that memory exists independently of the perception is challenged. Unless the memory combined with the perception to produce this one bit of knowledge there would be two claims: (1) "I perceive this," and (2) "I remember a snake." But in point of fact there is only one claim, "This is a snake." And this argues for positive identification, not merely a failure to recognize the difference between the perceived and the remembered. And, of course, if the Mimamsa reasons for their claim that no perceptual error is possible are unsatisfactory, then the claim need not be taken seriously.

The Nyaya-Vaisheshika view of error is that error is possible, but that it is really a matter of extra-ordinary perception. What happens when a snake is perceived in a rope is that this perception sets up the memory image of a snake perceived in the past so sharply that one becomes immediately aware of that image, mistaking it for the perceived object. The crucial part of this theory of error for Vedanta is the claim that error is taking something that really existed in the past for what is being perceived in the present. If this account is correct, then the notion that a perceptual illusion is possible is mistaken. The present perception of the world as an illusion makes sense only upon the assumption that a real world was perceived in the past and is being substituted now for the world presently being perceived. But this argues for the reality of the empirical world and not for the Vedantic view of the world as unreal.

The first objection to this theory of perceptual error is that it is not possible that something which existed at some other time and in some other place should be *perceived* now. What is perceived is *this*, and a memory is always of *that*, no matter how vivid. Thus, on the Nyaya account, the presence of the illusory object would be unexplainable. To suppose that a memory idea could actually transfer objects from one time and place to another is wildly implausible.

On other grounds it can be objected that the Nyaya view is unsatisfactory because what does not exist here now can appear to exist here now, and this is due to ignorance of what is here now. In the light of these objections it can be argued that a more plausible theory of error would hold that illusions are caused by the non-perception of the present object and the *construction* of another object which is substituted for the present object which is hidden by ignorance.

Of course, the illusory object must be present as an illusory object, being created by ignorance. However, it cannot be said to be real, nor can it be said to be unreal. In one sense, the snake is there: it is why one runs away and screams. It is not unreal in the way that a square circle or the son of a barren woman is unreal. But its reality lasts only as long as the ignorance lasts. When it is discovered that there is only a rope there, the snake no longer exists, so it cannot be said to be real. The difficulty of classifying the illusory object as real or unreal is comparable to Shamkara's difficulty in classifying the empirical world as real or unreal. In one sense it is real, for it is experienced. But in another sense it is unreal, for what is experienced is not what is really there but is the distortion of what is there. Just as in claiming that dream objects and events are not ultimately real one does not deny their existence, so Shamkara does not deny the existence of the empirical world, though he does deny its ultimate reality. In fact, Shamkara's analysis requires a more complicated classification of the reality of objects of experience than is usually found. On the one hand there is that which cannot exist at all, in any sense. These are the things that are logically impossible, such as square circles and children of barren women. Then there are the objects that exist in dreams and illusory perceptions, but which are repudiated by normal waking experience. Next come the objects of ordinary waking experience, which the realist takes to be the ultimate things of the universe. These objects are or can be repudiated by ex-perience of *Brahman*. Lastly, there is pure existence, *Atman* alone, the ultimate reality which in no way is unreal.

Thus, Shamkara does not really propose an alteration of our ordinary view of the world that consists in repudiating the existence of the universe. He does not suggest that the existence of any objects of experience be denied. Rather, he extends the nature of reality by claiming that in addition to the objects existing in dreams and in waking consciousness there is an ultimate reality. Whatever reality objects have they have; no one, not even Shamkara, can take that away. But to recognize that there is a higher view is to add a significant dimension to our notion of reality. It is only from this higher view that the rest of existence can be seen to be ultimately unreal. In this respect the matter is similar to waking and dreaming. Unless one wakes up it is impossible to regard dreaming objects as unreal. Within the dream they can only be regarded as real. But when one wakes up, the existence of dream objects is not denied. One simply now recognizes that dream objects were merely dream objects. They have the reality they have. Only now it is seen that there is a higher level of reality, namely, waking reality. In a similar way, one might wake up to the higher reality of enlightenment and discover that until now one has been having merely ordinary waking experience and not enlightened experience (*Atman*-realization).

Shamkara's view of the nature of reality provides explanations for both the reconciliation of the perceived plurality in the world with its absolute oneness and the identity of the self with this absolute oneness. He can say, "All this is that," when the "this" refers to the empirical world, and the "that" refers to *Brahman*, because the world is merely the misperception and the misconception of *Brahman*. It is like saying that the many coins of the magician are really the one coin displayed before performing the trick. But due to our ignorance we mistake the one coin for many, and *Brahman* for the world.

In an analogous way we mistake the psycho-physical self to be the true reality, whereas in fact that self is ultimately illusory and unreal. To say, "thou art that," is to say that "thou"—the self one takes oneself to be in ignorance—is, not in its appearance, but in its very basis, that *Brahman*. For the ignorant, of course, the self is only potentially *Brahman*, and this potentiality is realized by overcoming the ignorance. From the viewpoint of *Brahman*, however, it is not possible that the self is only potentially *Brahman*. It is one thing for the ignorant to regard the snake as potentially a rope, and quite another thing to suppose that from the viewpoint of what things really are a snake is a rope.

What happens in ignorance is that the individual self, which is really a composite of self and not-self, becomes the experience of the world because of this confusion. Experience is a strange phenomenon, because it requires that in a way the self become the other, though it must also remain the self and the other must remain the other. But unless other and self become one there is no experience. This shows that for experience to be possible, there must be a combination of the self and the not-self. But from the fact that the subject always remains subject—the self having the experience—it follows that the subject, or the self, is essentially independent of the object, or the not-self. Of course, this ultimate Self cannot be *looked* at as the true self, for to look at anything (either perceptually or conceptually) requires that it be an object of experience. But since the supposition is that the self is pure subject it follows that it cannot be known in any objective way.

The question might arise as to how this ultimate Self, which is identical with *Brahman*, is related to the empirical self, which is a combination of self and other. According to Shamkara, the self, or the "I," is so opposed to the not-self that they cannot really be related to each other. It is not a logically expressible relationship, for the not-self exists in ignorance, and the object of ignorance cannot be said to be either real or not real.

In this view becoming *Brahman* is a matter of the removal of ignorance which results in mistaking the appearance of the not-self for the reality of the Self. The fact of reality is the sole reality of *Brahman* and the identity of Self, or *Atman*, with *Brahman*. Ignorance veils this truth, but a practical realization of the ultimate Self will destroy the ignorance. There is no question of the theoretical knowledge of the ultimate reality. Such knowledge is ruled out by the fact that the ultimate reality is pure subject, one without a second. Knowledge of *Brahman* is practical knowledge; it is a matter of direct and immediate personal experience. Since ultimately the universe is identical with the Self, realizing *Brahman* is a matter of being completely oneself, and experiencing one's ultimate reality.

The real Self, the *Atman*, is not an appearance and is therefore not subject to the laws of appearances. The laws of causation apply to the world of appearance, not to the world of reality, or *Brahman*. There is consequently no saying that the Self is related to the appearance, for it is neither cause nor effect, these relations belonging only to the lower level of appearances. And if the *Atman* is not related to the appearances constituting the empirical world in any ways which are knowable, it becomes impossible to know *Brahman* except by an intimate experience that will be ineffable and incommunicable. This realization that one is the Self of pure consciousness, free from change and suffering, is certified by its own illumination. As Shamkara asks, "How can one contest the fact of another possessing the knowledge of Brahman, vouched as it is by his heart's conviction?"[7]

In conclusion, it can be said that for Shamkara the empirical world and the empirical self exist, but they are not ultimately real. The very basis of their existence is a higher reality than their appearance. This basis is pure existence, the very ground of experience and appearance. Consequently, when the individual takes the empirical world and the empirical self to be the ultimate reality he is confused, mistaking the appearance for the reality on which the existing appearance depends.

[7] *Shamkara Bhashya*, IV.I.15 trans. by George Thibaut in *The Sacred Books of the East*, vol. XXXVIII (Oxford: Oxford University Press, 1904).

That there is something beyond the existence that is perceived empirically can be seen by the fact that empirical things come into and pass out of existence, but their possibility of existence does not itself come into being and pass out of being. Of existence itself there is no coming into being or passing out of being, since it is prior to change, and presupposed by change.

Ramanuja agrees with Shamkara that ultimate reality is one rather than many. But he disagrees concerning the nature of the one. Ramanuja's view is that *Brahman* as the ultimate reality is not distinct from the empirical world, but that this world is a constituent part of *Brahman*. *Brahman* is a unity made up of the differences that constitute the experienced world as well as its basis. There is thus no distinction between *Brahman* on the one hand and the world on the other.

Basically, Ramanuja's differences with Shamkara are due to the former's position that pure identity is an abstract nothing. Identity and difference are correlative, and in existence are dependent upon each other. To posit one without the other is to posit an empty nothing. Unity or identity is the unity of different things; identity is an identity of parts. When the different things or parts are denied there can be no unity or identity. Consequently, the unity constituting *Brahman* is the union of the different selves and things making up the world. The identity is the identity of these parts in their substrata as existing.

Also, Ramanuja argues the self cannot be identified with knowledge, for knowledge requires a known and a knower. Where there is no known there is no knower, and so to regard the self as pure knower without a known is to regard the self into nothingness. Rather, it should be said that consciousness is the substratum of the self, wherein the self can come to know the unity of reality.

Thus, Ramanuja's view is that *Brahman* is an organic unity constituted by the identity of the parts. It is not abstract, but concrete, being made up of the various objects of consciousness as well as consciousness itself. This organic unity Ramanuja calls *Brahman*, or the Lord (*Ishvara*).

His view is that things and selves are distinct from *Brahman* in the way the body of a person is distinct from the self of a person. On this view unity of reality is maintained because the person is one thing, but plurality is also maintained because a person consists of both self and body. Furthermore, on this analogy *Brahman* is superior to selves and things just as a person's self is superior to his body, the body belonging to the self as the self's qualifications. The position is stated by Ramanuja as follows: "The supreme *Brahman* is the self of all. The sentient and non-sentient entities constitute its body. The body is an entity and has being only by virtue of its being the mode of the soul of which it is the body. The body and the soul, though characterized by different attributes do not get mixed up. From all this follows the central teaching that *Brahman*, with all the non-sentient and sentient entities as its modes, is the ultimate."[8]

According to this explanation reality is one, like a person, with the many things and selves in the universe constituting the body of reality, and *Brahman* constituting the self of reality. The body is real, although real not independently, but as a mode of *Brahman's* being. Thus, individual selves and individual things are the real qualities or modes of *Brahman*.

According to the metaphysics underlying this account of the relation of *Brahman* to selves and things, substance alone is independently real, and whatever exists as a characteristic or quality of a substance exists as a mode of that substance and can be identified with the substance of which it is a mode. The teaching "All is *Brahman*" should not be taken to affirm the existence of *Brahman* alone without qualification, for on that interpretation there is no "All" which can be identified with *Brahman*. Rather, the "All" should be taken to refer to the various things and selves in the world, because these are the real qualifications of *Brahman*. The mode of their existence is that of the body of *Brahman*. Just as a body does not exist except as the body of a self, so things and selves do not exist except as belonging to *Brahman*.

This view is supported by a theory of meaning according to which the terms referring to the qualities of a substance refer also to the substance which the qualities qualify. For example, if we say, "The teacher is white-haired," "white-haired" refers to the color of the teacher's hair, but it also refers to the teacher whose hair is white, for having white hair qualifies the teacher. But the reference does not stop there, for being a teacher is a qualification of the person who is the teacher, and thus "white-haired teacher" refers to a qualification of a person and to the person who is so qualified. Being a person, in turn is a qualification of matter and self, and so the term "white-haired-teaching-person" refers beyond merely the person to that of which

[8] *Vedarthasamgraha of Shri Ramanujacarya*, Para. 81, trans. by S. S. Raghavachar (Mysore: Sri Ramakrishna Ashrama, 1956), p. 67.

person is a qualification. Continuing in this way, the term "white-haired" is seen to ultimately refer to the absolute reality upon which everything else is dependent for its existence. This is, of course, *Brahman*, and therefore all terms refer ultimately to *Brahman*. If *Brahman* did not exist as the ultimate reality to which all terms refer there would be nothing for terms to refer to, just as if there were no ultimate substance there would be nothing of which qualifications would be qualifications of, and then there would be no qualifications. Thus, if there are qualifications—and this cannot be denied for qualities are the primary objects of perception upon which knowledge rests—there must also be *Brahman* as the possessor of these qualities. Ramanuja puts the point this way: "This is the fundamental relationship between the Supreme and the universe of individual selves and physical entities. It is the relationship of soul and body, . . . That which, in its entirety depends upon, is controlled by and subserves another and is therefore its inseparable mode, is called the body of the latter. Such is the relation between the individual self and its body. Such being the relationship, the supreme Self, having all as its body, is denoted by all terms."[9]

In this way Ramanuja maintains the reality of both selves and *Brahman* by admitting differences within the identity that is *Brahman*. Selves are real as differentiations *within* (rather than *from*) the ultimate reality.

DUALISTIC VEDANTA

A third school of Vedanta, that of Madhva, differs from the positions of the Shamkara and Ramanuja schools in claiming a fundamental dualism in the world. The world as empirically experienced, and its foundation as *Brahman*, are eternally and fundamentally distinct. The Self is regarded as distinct from both *Brahman* and the material things constituting the empirical world. The basic argument for this position is that perception is essentially a matter of becoming aware of the uniqueness of something. Since perception is the basis of all knowledge, and it depends upon realizing differences, to claim non-existence of differences is to repudiate the very basis of the arguments for the non-existence of difference. Objects are perceived as distinct from the self, and the basis of things and self is conceived to be different from either the things or the self. There is no possible evidence that these perceived differences are mistaken, as they constitute the very possibility of knowledge. Therefore these basic differences must be admitted.

[9] *Vedarthasamgraha*, Para. 95.

Furthermore, individual selves must be distinguished from *Brahman* if they are said to be caught up in suffering and bondage. Since it is with the individual suffering self that every attempt to achieve liberation must begin, the existence of individual selves cannot be denied. But if they are admitted, they must be admitted as different from *Brahman*. It will not do to say that as *suffering* the individual is different from *Brahman*, but that as released from suffering it is identical with *Brahman*, for two things that are really different cannot at *any* time be said to be the same. Being released from suffering does not change the nature of something, making it a something else. But if this is the case, and an initial difference is postulated, then individual selves and *Brahman* must remain eternally different. Madhva argues in the same way for the eternal difference between *Brahman* and matter. Along the same lines, arguing also for a real difference between selves and matter, between one self and another, and between one thing and another, he arrives at his "five differences." These are the differences between (1) *Brahman* and matter, (2) *Brahman* and selves, (3) selves and matter, (4) one self and another, and (5) one thing and another.

The epistemological basis for Madhva's claim that these five basic differences exist consists in his analysis of knowing as a simultaneous revealing of both the subject who knows and the object that is known. According to this analysis there is no denying that subject is different from object, for knowledge is always knowledge *of* something, and it is always knowledge *for* someone. Furthermore, to know one particular thing is to know it as that thing rather than another, and this is to be aware of its differences from other things. But if this is true, and the differences between subject and object and between one object and another are *known*, they must be revealed in knowledge. Thus, knowledge in its very nature reveals differences in reality. These differences cannot be called into question without calling into question the very basis and nature of knowledge. And if this is attempted within the limits of knowledge the attempt is self-defeating, for it requires rejecting that upon which a stand must be taken in order to do the rejecting.

Since knowledge reveals things to be different from each other and different from the self, and since it is acknowledged that both selves and things depend upon *Brahman* for their existence, Madhva maintains eternal difference between *Brahman*, selves, and things. Unlike Ramanuja, these differences are not accounted for in terms of the qualifications of *Brahman*, thereby maintaining the unity of reality, but are regarded as different substances. But if these are maintained to be different substances it is hard to see how things and selves—as ultimate substances —could be dependent upon a third substance, for a substance is complete in itself and independent. In fact, it is difficult to see why a third substance would be postulated as the ultimate reality. Of course, Madhva is reluctant to give up the dependency of selves upon *Brahman*, for then all traditional teachings about salvation must be given up. And if he gives up not only dependency, but also *Brahman* as the ultimate reality, he has given up the whole tradition!

These three schools of Vedanta represent the three basic ways of looking at the relations between the world and *Brahman*, and thus constitute the three basic interpretations of the Upanishads. According to Shamkara, *Brahman* alone is real, the world being mere appearance. Ramanuja claims that the world is real, but is not different from *Brahman*, since *Brahman* is the unity of differences that constitute the world. Madhva argues that the world and *Brahman* are eternally distinct. Reality is of the dual nature of *Brahman* plus the world, with *Brahman* always remaining distinct and different from the world of selves and things.

◊ | CHAPTER 8 | ◊

CONCLUDING REMARKS

At the beginning of this discussion of the Hindu systems it was said that a dominant characteristic of Indian philosophical thought was its practical character. This practical character was said to derive from the basic aim of philosophical activity which was to overcome suffering. Having followed the claims and arguments of the different philosophical schools and having noticed the heavy emphasis on logical consistency the reader may at this stage be skeptical of that original claim. However, the requirement of logical consistency does not rule out practicality. It might rule out every whim and fancy containing within itself the seeds of its own self-contradiction, but it does not rule out sound practice. Every one of the philosophical schools considered begins by observing that knowledge (of man and the universe) is required in the effort to improve life.

The Nyaya system, though primarily concerned with an analysis of the means of valid knowledge, begins by noting, in the first *Sutra* of Gautama, that supreme happiness follows upon the attainment of true knowledge of the various categories. Right knowledge will bring about the cessation of pain and death. The Vaisheshika system concentrates on analyzing the kinds of things that exist, but the *Sutras* of Kanada begin with the observation: "Now, therefore, we shall explain *dharma* (righteousness). *Dharma* (is) that from which (results) the accomplishment of exaltation and the supreme good." The Samkhya system, which provides an analysis of causality and a theory of the evolution of the world from a first cause, has for its first *Sutra* the statement: "From torment by the three-fold misery arises the inquiry into the means of terminating it:..." Yoga, concerned to show the true nature of the Self and to explain the functioning of the empirical self, has for its aim complete liberation. The concluding *Sutra* of Patanjali is: "Absolute freedom comes when the qualities, becoming devoid of the object of the *purusha* [Self], become latent; or the power of consciousness becomes established in its own nature." The Mimamsa *Sutras*, concerned to show the validity of the Veda, begins as follows: "Next, therefore, comes the enquiry into *dharma* (duty). *Dharma* is that which is indicated by means of the Veda as conducive to the highest good." Shamkara, in his commentary on the first statement in the *Brahma-Sutra*, observes that the enquiry into *Brahman* has for its fruit eternal bliss.

But not just any theory of the nature of man and the universe counts as right knowledge. And to find out which theories are inadequate it is useful to measure them against the yardstick of logic, which means, ultimately, against self-contradiction. It may be that reality, in its foundations, is beyond the reach of the logical net and that in the last analysis logic is irrelevant. But from the viewpoint of ordinary knowledge, expressible in conceptual and linguistic terms, it is nonsensical to say that logic is irrelevant. Logic is a basic presupposition of language and conceptual thought, and to dispense with it is quite impossible. What is self-contradictory cannot be known and—from the conceptual point of view (the only point of view from which self-contradiction is possible)—cannot exist. Philosophy is, at least in part, a conceptual matter, and insofar as it is a conceptual matter, respect for the principle of non-contradiction is an absolutely necessary condition of philosophical activity. Consequently, it is necessary to test theories of man and the universe against the measure of logic. What does not measure up must fall into the refuse pit of nonsense and self-contradictions. But, of course, measuring up to the yardstick of logic and being logically consistent does not guarantee the truth of the theory. For this it is necessary to go beyond the linguistic and logical to direct and immediate experience. Shamkara, for example, could regard his essential philosophical task as showing that claims about the nature of man and reality in opposition to the conclusions of the Upanishads were self-contradictory. After all, the claims of the Upanishads were the result of direct and immediate experience of man and reality and therefore could not be wrong.

It is not difficult to see how systems of thought can be practical insofar as they aim at eliminating suffering, and also be logically subtle and abstract. The various systems of philosophy can be seen as critical attempts to remove error from theories about the nature of man and the world by showing that the implications and assumptions of those theories lead to nonsense and self-contradiction. This is essentially an activity of logic and argument, though it is undertaken in order to secure a practical aim. This combination of respect for logic and respect for the testament of immediate experience has resulted in finding a place in philosophical theories for the practical and the ideal, the material and the spiritual. It would be a curious phenomenon for a culture to have no skeptics and materialists at all, but in India the view that knowledge and understanding is impossible, that there is nothing in existence except material things, and that the highest aim in life is pleasure, was considered so unsatisfactory that, though it was espoused by various individuals, it did not generate enough support to develop into one of the philosophical systems. The difficulty with materialism as a philosophy is that it ignores the demands of both logic and immediate experience. Consequently, the ground for this kind of philosophizing in India proved to be stony and barren.

The two most significant Indian philosophers in our time, Radhakrishnan and Aurobindo, looked to the ancient traditions for wisdom to guide modern man. Each emphasized the need for philosophy to encompass both logic and experience, the material and the spiritual.

RADHAKRISHNAN

Sarvepalli Radhakrishnan, the recent president of India, who has written scores of philosophical articles and dozens of philosophical books, is a champion and interpreter of the Shamkara school of Vedanta. He agrees with Shamkara that the empirical is not the ultimate reality, but he is aware that just as the criteria of logic and experience demand that philosophy admit an ultimate reality, so also do they require inclusion of the empirical and practical. For him there is no inconsistency in a philosopher actively participating in social and political affairs, for these are appearances of *Brahman*, and thus are means to be utilized in the effort to achieve the experience of the ultimate reality.

Recognizing that the experience of ultimate reality—*Atman*-realization—is the goal of human life, and seeing religion as the chief vehicle employed in man's quest for the absolute ground of all reality, Radhakrishnan's main philosophical problem consisted in working out a satisfactory philosophy of religion. The task of philosophy of religion is to develop a theory of the nature of things in the world, selves, and the ultimate ground of things and selves, that will exhibit the inter-relations between these three realities. This theory must account for the facts of religious experience and at the same time accommodate reason, for no attempt at explanation which is self-contradictory can be satisfactory. Consistency may not be enough, but it is a minimal necessity for any philosophy. Granted rational consistency, the theory must have its basis in religious experience itself. The experience and statements of religious persons must be explained—not repudiated or ignored—by a philosophy of religion.

Radhakrishnan's view of religion allows that theology, dogma, ritual, and various institutions are the external trappings of religion, not its essence. The essence of religion is the attempt to discover the ideal possibilities of human life. This quest is personal and necessarily in-volves the whole person. Experience which involves merely an aspect of a person, such as feeling, thinking, or volition, is not religious. What distinguishes religious experience from aesthetics, science, philosophy, and morals is that these are guided primarily by feeling, reason, and volition, respectively. Religion includes feeling, reason, and volition, but it goes beyond them to the innermost center of the person to the very source of these aspects of humanity, integrating these faculties and directing them from the wholeness that is their source, using it to transform the life of the person into something complete and whole.

This inner self which is the very source of the various limited aspects and faculties of man is referred to as Spirit, and the substance and essence of religion is experience of the life of the Spirit—not just as it is in man, or as it is in the world, but Spirit as it joins together self and other in a whole that is complete and perfect in itself, though utterly inexpressible. But though the experience itself is deeply inner and inexpressible there are clues to its character, for this experience takes form in the mani-festations of spiritual encounter which constitutes the essence of all religious life, and as such is attended by ritual, dogma, interpretation, and the varying institutions which provide forms that allow the ex-pression of contact with the Spirit in an intelligible and understandable way, and which serve to guide other persons to the direct experience of spiritual encounter.

These forms of religion may all change as culture and civilization change. In fact, as the forms of culture and civilization change, the forms of religion must change if they are to adequately manifest the immediate experience of spiritual encounter. Radhakrishnan says: "Theory, speculation, dogma, change from time to time as the facts become better understood. *Their value is acquired from their adequacy to experience.* When forms dissolve and the interpretations are doubted, it is a call to get back to the experience itself and reformulate its content in more suitable terms."[1]

Although a philosopher of religion could hardly proceed except by giving primacy to religious experience—that is, by considering the data of religious experience to be the basic material out of which one fashions a theory of religion—to do so is exceedingly complicated because of the great difficulty in describing religious experience. Religious experience is unlike the ordinary experience that provides the foundations for thinking and talking about ourselves and the reality around us. Our ordinary experience presupposes that the something experienced is always distinct from the experiencer; the subject is never the object, and vice versa. A person sees a stone or hears a bird; a person's reason is aware of a certain feeling consequent upon encountering a work of art, or one's feeling is aware of one's reason at work. In these cases we maintain the distinction between subject and object. But in religious experience the whole person is involved: there is nothing outside of the person, so the experience is radically different from ordinary experience. Because of this radical difference the distinctions that are usually made or presupposed between subject and object, between one faculty and another, are left behind and the claim is made that in religious experience the subject and object merge, becoming one, and the whole person, rather than just certain aspects of his being, is involved in the experience. But when the subject-object distinction is overcome all ordinary distinctions presupposed by thought are also left behind. Past, present, and future become so many abstractions that have no reality—there is only the *Now*, perfectly dimensionless. And there is no room for various locations in space; there is only the *Here*, without location.

Radhakrishnan explains religious experience as follows:

> It is a type of experience which is not clearly differentiated into a subject-object state, an integral, undivided consciousness in which not merely this or that side of man's nature but his whole being seems to find itself. It is a condition of consciousness in which feelings are fused, ideas melt into one another, boundaries broken and ordinary distinctions transcended. Past and present fade away in a sense of timeless being. Consciousness and being are

[1] *An Idealist View of Life*, Ch. 3 (London: George Allen & Unwin Ltd., 1929), and reprinted in *A Source Book in Indian Philosophy*, ed. by Radhakrishnan and Moore (Princeton: Princeton University Press, 1957), p. 616. Italics added.

there not different from each other. All being is consciousness and all consciousness being. Thought and reality coalesce and a creative merging of subject and object results. Life grows conscious of its incredible depths. In this fullness of felt life and freedom, the distinction of the knower and the known disappears. The privacy of the individual self is broken and invaded by a universal self which the individual feels as his own.[2]

Granted this view of religion and religious experience, what kind of theory of selves, things, and ultimate reality will serve to adequately accomodate, in a rationally acceptable way, the facts of religion? If the ultimate reality—Brahman—is taken to be alone real it is difficult to see how religion is possible, for the self struggling to realize Brahman would have to be regarded as unreal. And without a self struggling to achieve ultimate reality there can be no religion. On the other hand, if selves and Brahman are taken to be distinct and different realities, it is difficult to to see how the self could ever successfully identify itself with Brahman, without self-repudiation or self-annihilation.

Radhakrishnan's solution to this dilemma is to interpret Brahman not as static but as dynamic being. Brahman is the absolute reality, providing the ground of all existence and giving the universe unity. All things are united in Brahman which is the source and ground of all being. As the source and ground of all being Brahman is ever active, by its function expressing its substantial nature. It is this functioning of Brahman, which is not different from its existence, that manifests itself in the various things and processes that make up the universe of selves and things. Thus, things and selves are not unreal, for they are the expression of Brahman's functions. But as expressions of Brahman they are not totally distinct and separate from Brahman either. This explanation provides for distinctions between individual things and selves, for the functions of Brahman are dynamic, ever new. Since no one of Brahman's functions (nor aspect of the functioning of Brahman) totally exhausts the nature of Brahman, any given expression of Brahman's function lacks the total reality of Brahman wherein all functions and all expressions of those functions are united.

Proceeding with this interpretation of Brahman, Radhakrishnan goes on to regard man as the locus where Brahman, as absolute Spirit, and the world, as the functioning of this absolute Spirit, come together, for the person combines Spirit with matter. He makes this point by distinguishing between the empirical or lower self and the higher or spiritual self, which in its purity is one with the absolute Spirit. The

---

[2] *Idealist View of Life*, Ch. 3, reprinted in *Source Book in Indian Philosophy*, p. 618.

essence of the religious quest is now interpreted to be the lower self struggling to return to its source in the higher self. It is the movement toward transformation of self—never the annihilation or repudiation of self—in identification with its source, *Atman-Brahman.*

In explaining the relations between selves and things and both of these to *Brahman,* Radhakrishnan abandons the static substance view of reality according to which the world is thought to be made up of a great many independent beings or substances, each attended to by a greater or lesser number of characteristics or qualities. Instead, he views the world as constituted by processes. The structure of reality is not due to the relations qualities have to their substances, but to the inner structure of the activities making up reality. Thus, the world is essentially dynamic with all of the various processes interconnected. The various processes can be distinguished from each other according to the structure of their functioning. In this way, for example, living "things" can be distinguished from non-living, conscious from non-conscious, etc. They are similar in that they are of the nature of process, being essentially activities, but they differ according to the structure of the activities involved.

In explanation of the diverse structures found in the processes corresponding to the various gradations of existence, Radhakrishnan postulates unceasing activity of the absolute Spirit. Spirit is the source and ground of all the various grades of existence encountered on the empirical level. But these various distinctions do not imply absolute differences; they merely serve to mark out modes of spiritual activity. Even matter, finally, is spiritual activity. It is merely a different mode of the Spirit than consciousness or life. But regardless of the mode of manifestation, Spirit remains Spirit, and insofar as it is Spirit there is no denial of its reality. The various grades of matter and life are real and are expressions of *Brahman,* the absolute Spirit. But no one mode in itself is the totality of *Brahman,* and cannot be equated with the absolute reality.

Against this background, the main purpose of religion is to help a person realize that he can rise above the limits imposed by matter or life or consciousness to the realization that in his innermost being he is identical with the absolute Spirit and is in truth completely free from the limitations inherent in identification with simply one particular mode or function of Spirit. This realization is possible only in terms of practical activity; an activity of being rather than knowledge. It is the spiritual realization of Uddalaka's teaching to his son, Shvetaketu, "Thou art that [*Brahman*]."

Sri Aurobindo, the great philosopher-yogi of Pondicherry, studied and commented upon the ancient texts of the Veda and, in the early part of this century, was the leader of the movement for Indian independence. Emphasizing the ultimate spirituality of man, Sri Aurobindo recognized as the great problem of our times the transformation of the present lowly and ignorant man into the great spiritual being that he is potentially. To this end he worked out a theory of social organization not radically different from the ideals contained in the theories of *purusharthas*, *varnas*, and *ashramas*. His major works, *The Life Divine*, and *Synthesis of Yoga*, are attempts to show the type of life man can achieve by a total and comprehensive discipline, or *yoga*. The "life divine" is, of course, the life lived in full realization of *Brahman*, and the *yoga* is the means to this life. Sri Aurobindo emphasizes that the *yoga* must be practiced by present man in his present condition as a means to changing this condition, for therein lies the secret of the transformation into the Ideal Man.

Aurobindo's conception of the task of philosophy and the nature of reality is indicated in the following statement:

> The problem of thought therefore is to find out the right idea and the right way of harmony; to restate the ancient and eternal spiritual truth of the Self, so that it shall re-embrace, permeate and dominate the mental and physical life; to develop the most profound and vital methods of psychological self-discipline and self-development so that the mental and psychical life of man may express the spiritual life of man through the utmost possible expansion of its own richness, power and complexity; and to seek for the means and motives by which his external life, his society and his institutions may remould themselves progressively in the truth of the spirit and develop towards the utmost possible harmony of individual freedom and social unity.[3]

According to this view, the reality constituted by things and selves is the manifested power of the spirit. Spirit provides the unity of reality, and the manifested power of spirit provides the manifoldness of the universe. The various levels of existence—matter, life, mental life, supramental life—are distinguished insofar as the fullness of spirit emerges through these manifestations of its powers.

The main problem for Aurobindo is that of explaining how all the many things experienced—both at the conscious level of the empirical

[3] *Arya*, July 15, 1918, pp. 764–5; reprinted in *Source Book in Indian Philosophy*, p. 577.

and the rational, and at the supra-conscious level of mystic intuition—
came to be, and why they are different. His solution is to explain that the
absolute existence which makes it possible for anything whatsoever to
exist is itself pure existence, complete and perfect. This existence—*Brahman*—for no reason whatever, simply out of the sheer exuberance of its
being, manifests its *maya*, or power, in the manner of sport or play.
The manifestations of this power constitute the universe of existing
things. The universe exists therefore, as the play of pure existence. But
it is not simply capricious, for this play is directed by the Being-
Consciousness-Joy (*sat-chit-ananda*) that constitutes the absolute Spirit
of the universe. The evolution of the universe as a whole and of
particular species within the universe is seen as the returning of the
manifested powers of *Brahman* to their source. As these powers move
toward their source, evolution moves to higher and higher forms of life
and consciousness.

According to this explanation, the differences between levels of
reality are due to the evolution of spirit. As the spirit evolves higher
life-forms come into existence. But this is not the evolution of one
kind of thing to another *kind* of thing, such as matter becoming spirit.
Rather, it is the evolution of one thing—Spirit—from its many lower
forms and manifestations to its higher forms, the aim being to reach the
fullness of being, consciousness, and joy that constitutes Spirit. The
usual problems attending evolutionary accounts of existence, the problem of blind matter groping impossibly to evolve beyond itself, into
something quite other than itself, and the problem of blind matter
being lifted beyond itself by some other reality without any effort on
its own part, do not arise for Aurobindo. According to his explanation
the lower is ever evolving into the higher, but these are not absolutely
different. The higher is making itself felt in the lower, and the lower
is struggling to express itself according to the higher laws of the spirit
within, and this is the mutual effort that constitutes the play of *Brahman*
manifesting itself through its powers, but always remaining *Brahman*.

Seeing evolution as involving the mutual activity of both the lower and
higher forms of Spirit has important consequences for the life of man,
for it means not only that it is possible for man to evolve to a higher
kind of being than he now is, but also that he can, at least in part,
direct this evolution. The aim of man's existence—in its self-consciousness higher than the existence of matter and non-conscious life-forms—is
not to remain at its present level, but to transcend itself, moving on to
higher levels of existence just as previously lower levels of existence

moved up to the level of human existence. This is possible, Aurobindo points out,

> for the evolution proceeded in past by the upsurging, at each critical state, of a concealed power from its evolution in the inconscient, but also by a descent from above, from its own plane, of that power already self-realized in its own higher natural province. . . .[4]

How is man to direct his own evolution? Aurobindo's answer is that he must practice self-discipline (*yoga*) that is all inclusive, not ignoring any part of his being, and integrating the various aspects and faculties of his being, so that the lower comes under the control and direction of the higher, allowing man to gradually come to live according to the laws of the spirit dwelling within him, at the very center of his being. This requires, among other things, the material and social conditions that will enable man in his present state to successfully reach beyond himself, elevating his existence until it becomes the "Life Divine."

In his social philosophy, Aurobindo argued that justice and freedom are to be provided for and guaranteed by society as necessary conditions for the higher evolution of man. His view of the object of all society is:

> first to provide the conditions of life and growth by which individual Man— not isolated men according to their capacity—and the race through the growth of its individuals, may travel towards its divine perfection. It must be secondly, as mankind generally more and more grows near to some figure of it—for the cycles are many and each cycle has its own figure of the Divine in man—to express in the general life of mankind, the light, the power, the beauty, the harmony, the joy of the Self that has been attained and that pours itself out in a freer and nobler humanity.[5]

Clearly, in both Radhakrishnan and Aurobindo, as in the Vedas and Upanishads, the aim of philosophical activity is to make possible the realization of the Self that dwells within all beings.

[4] *Life Divine*, p. 859, reprinted in *Source Book in Indian Philosophy*, p. 604.
[5] *The Human Cycle* (Pondicherry: Sri Aurobindo Ashram, 1962), pp. 83–84.

PART TWO

Buddhist Philosophies

Serene Buddha. *The Indian Museum, Calcutta*

CHAPTER 9

BUDDHISM AND SUFFERING: BASIC TEACHINGS

No one who has lived in the world can be untouched by human suffering. Either in his own life or in the lives of those with whom he comes in contact there has entered injury, illness, misery, anxiety, death, or some other form of unwholesomeness and evil. Human existence is far from perfect. Even the most fortunate, the happiest people in the world have to admit a measure of unhappiness. Most people, in fact, recognize that life is not perfect. Either they simply shrug their shoulders and exclaim, "That is the way life is," or else they set about trying to reduce the imperfections in life. Ordinarily, when the latter attitude is adopted, effort is directed toward reducing poverty by increasing available wealth, reducing illness and premature deaths by extending sanitation or by promoting the practice of medicine, etc. But seldom is there a person who carefully and systematically directs his attention to the fundamental *causes* of suffering and the ways for the elimination of these causes. Gautama Siddhartha, the Buddha, was such a person, and the religious philosophy that issued from his teachings presents a systematic analysis of the nature and causes of suffering and provides a manifold of means for the overcoming of suffering.

Buddhism as a *Way of Wisdom* taught and practiced for the sake of improving the quality of life by removing the sources of suffering is, in its details, a complicated phenomenon incorporating a great many historical changes, but in its essence, as taught by the Buddha, it is a relatively simple teaching to grasp. One must hasten to point out, however, that understanding the outlines of a Way of Wisdom is quite different from following that Way. Following the Way is difficult. It is, indeed, so difficult that it has not yet been mastered by the discipline and self-control of the majority of mankind. Consequently, it should be kept in mind that there is all the difference in the world between *following* the Way and *talking* about following the Way. To follow the Way there is no substitute for practice. In fact, without practicing the Way, it is unlikely that one will even achieve a satisfactory intellectual understanding of what the Way is. Nevertheless, it is possible to achieve considerable knowledge about Buddhism by studying and analyzing the main features that constitute this Way of life.

THE BUDDHA

According to widely accepted legends concerning the life of the historical Buddha, Gautama received the immediate impetus for meditation and concentration on the problem of suffering by dramatic encounters with sickness, old age, death, and renunciation. His father, the ruler of a prosperous principality, had been told that if his son became acquainted with the evils of the world he would renounce his father's kingdom and become a great ascetic and teacher of men. Not wanting to lose his son in this way, the father resolved that everything would be done to seclude him from the cruel world. Accordingly the king provided him with all of the wealth and pleasures of life available to man—palaces, young and comely servants, entertainers, a beautiful wife—to protect him from experiencing the suffering of the world. The father was determined that Gautama should remain ignorant of the sorrows that beset mankind.

But one day, when the young Gautama was out riding in his chariot, the young lord saw an old man,

> as bent as a roof gable, decrepit, leaning on a staff, tottering as he walked, afflicted and long past his prime.[1]

Upon seeing him Gautama asked his charioteer why that man was not like the other men. The driver informed him that the man was old,

---

[1] This account of Gautama's encounter with suffering is found in *Digha Nikaya*, XIV. The quotations are taken from *Buddhism: A Religion of Infinite Compassion*, ed. by Clarence H. Hamilton (Indianapolis: Bobbs-Merrill, c. 1952), pp. 6–10.

but this word Gautama did not understand. He had no experience with old age. The driver explained that this man was nearly finished, he was soon to die. As understanding began to trouble his spirit, the young lord asked,

> "But then, good charioteer, am I too subject to old age, one who has not got past old age?"

The answer horrified Gautama; and from this time he began to think about the suffering of old age:

> "You, my lord, and we too, we all are of a kind to grow old; we have not got past old age."

Many days after this, he was once again setting out for the park, when Gautama encountered "a sick man, suffering and very ill, fallen and weltering in his own water, by some being lifted up, by others being dressed."

Upon seeing this, Gautama asked his charioteer what this man had done that he was not like other men. The driver explained that the man was ill, and that this meant that he was not far from being finished, that he might not recover. Gautama asked again,

> "But am I too then, good charioteer, subject to fall ill; have I not got out of the reach of illness?"

The answer that sent him back to his palace meditating on illness was,

> "You my lord, and we too, we all are subject to fall ill; we have not got beyond the reach of illness."

Many days later, when Gautama was again driving to the park, he saw "a great concourse of people clad in garments of different colors constructing a funeral pyre. And seeing this, he asked his charioteer, 'Why now are all those people come together in garments of different colors and making that pile?'"

Upon being told that this was because someone had died, Gautama demanded to view the corpse to discover what this thing called "death" was all about. When he had been told about death, he asked, as before,

> "But am I too then subject to death, have I not got beyond reach of death? Will neither the *raja*, [king] nor *ranee*, [queen] nor any other of my kin see me more, or shall I again see them?"

And once more the answer was,

> "You my lord, and we too, we all are subject to death; we have not passed beyond the reach of death."

Many days after seeing the dead man, Gautama was once again driving to the park. On the way he saw a shaven-headed man, a recluse, wearing the yellow robe. Upon learning from the driver that this recluse is one who is said to have "gone forth," Guatama was curious to learn what this meant. Approaching the recluse, he asked,

> "You, master, what have you done that your head is not as other men's heads, nor your clothes as those of other men?" "I, my lord, am one who has gone forth." "What, master, does that mean?" "It means, my lord, being thorough in the religious life, thorough in the peaceful life, thorough in good actions, thorough in meritorious conduct, thorough in harmlessness, thorough in kindness to all creatures."

Upon hearing this the lord Gautama bade his charioteer return him to his palace, saying,

> "But I will even here cut off my hair, and don the yellow robe, and go forth from the house into the homeless state."

Having been thus duly impressed with the *fact* of suffering, Gautama meditated on that *fact*, concentrating on discovering a way to the cessation of all suffering. After years of effort and discipline, including the most severe forms of asceticism, Gautama resolved that neither the extreme of over-indulgence in pleasures nor the extreme of excessive asceticism was conducive to extinguishing suffering. Adopting then a middle path between these extremes, Gautama, self-disciplined and purified, concentrated all of his energies on discovering the causes of suffering. As he concentrated the causes of suffering were revealed, and Gautama Siddhartha became the Buddha—the Enlightened One. Enlightenment as to the causes and the cessation of suffering were now his.

THE FOUR NOBLE TRUTHS

The content of this enlightenment constitutes the basic message of Buddhism. This message, in simplest form, consists in the Four Noble Truths and the Noble Eightfold Path. These truths are: (1) There is suffering; (2) Suffering is caused; (3) Suffering can be extinguished by eliminating the causes of suffering; (4) The way to extinguish the causes of suffering is to follow the Middle Way constituted by the Noble Eightfold path.

This teaching constituted the Buddha's first sermon after his enlightenment, delivered in the Deer Park at Benares. It was the teaching of the middle path,

> which leads to insight, which leads to wisdom; which conduces to calm, to knowledge, to perfect enlightenment, to Nibbāna [Nirvāna].

Concerning the First Noble Truth Gautama taught as follows:

> This, monks, is the Noble Truth of Suffering; birth is suffering; decay is suffering; illness is suffering; death is suffering; presence of objects we hate is suffering; separation from objects we love is suffering; not to obtain what we desire is suffering. In brief, the five aggregates which spring from grasping, they are painful.

Explaining the Second Noble Truth, Gautama taught that suffering

> originates in that craving which causes the renewals of becomings, is accompanied by sensual delight, and seeks satisfaction now here, now there; that is to say, craving for pleasures, craving for becoming, craving for not becoming.

Taking up the Third Noble Truth, he explained as follows:

> This, monks, is the Noble Truth concerning the Cessation of Suffering; verily, it is passionless, cessation without remainder of this very craving; the laying aside of, the giving up, the being free from, the harboring no longer of, this craving.

Coming now to the Fourth Noble Truth concerning the Path which leads to the cessation of suffering, he taught:

> It is this Noble Eightfold Path, that is to say, right views, right intent, right speech, right conduct, right means of livelihood, right endeavor, right mindfulness, and right meditation."

Having thus taught the essential truths about the fact of suffering, the Buddha concluded his first sermon by saying:

> This Noble Truth concerning Suffering I have understood. Thus, monks, in things which formerly had not been heard of have I obtained insight, knowledge, understanding, widsom and intuition.[2]

The First Truth, concerned with the existence of suffering, lists seven areas of suffering familiar to everyone. But these seven areas should not be taken as a definition of suffering; they are simply examples of suffering, examples obvious to anyone who has lived in the world. Suffering goes much deeper than those examples. It must be recognized that the

[2] The foregoing account is taken from Hamilton, *op. cit.* p. 29.

pleasures of one person are often the pains of another. And the pains of others are disturbing to one's own contentment. Thus, though it would seem that the wealthy captain of industry who has all of the goods of society at his disposal should be happy, this may not be the case. If he is truly a sensitive human being, the poverty of those workers in industry which is the direct counterpart of the captain's wealth might very well be the bitter dressing spoiling the enjoyment of all his wealth. To be aware that one's pleasures come at another person's expense is not to bring suffering only to the other; it is also to bring suffering to oneself.

In addition, even in those cases where one's pleasures are not tied to the sufferings of anyone else, they still are fraught with suffering. The pleasures that one enjoys bring with them an attachment to the objects and activities enjoyed. The anxiety resulting from the possibility of separation from the objects or activities in question is a hidden cancer in the pleasures, and thus a source of suffering.

Another feature of the suffering underlying the various pleasures of life concerns the fact that they are not only self-perpetuating, but that they are self-accelerating. Deriving pleasure from an activity or object does not diminish the drive for that pleasure, but rather serves to strengthen the drive. One becomes more closely tied to the conditions that provide pleasure as he derives more pleasure from his activities. The more pleasures one achieves the more he seeks. This cycle goes on unendingly, catching one up in its increasing tempo, with seemingly no escape. Granted that the achievement of pleasure does not bring complete happiness and contentment, but rather leaves one even more dissatisfied and unhappy, it appears that one is being led to even greater unhappiness by grasping at the pleasures of life.

This last point is tied in with a basic assumption of Buddhism which holds that the drive for pleasure is too shallow and insignificant to fulfill a person and bring true happiness. In the *Dhammapada* it is said, "One is the path that leads to worldly gain; and quite another that leads to *Nibbana*."[3] If this is the case, then the pleasures that one finds in the world, being shallow, are really factors producing unhappiness. In recognition of this, the observation in the *Dhammapada* noted just above, is followed by the advice:

> Understanding this, let not the Bhikku, the disciple of the Awakened One, delight in worldly honour but develop detachment instead.[4]

[3] *Dhammapada*, V. 75, trans. by Acharya Buddharakhita Thera (Bangalore, India: Buddha Vaccna Trust, 1966).
[4] *Ibid.*

Thus, not only do those seven examples given by the Buddha in his first sermon belong to suffering, but even those examples that would be given of the "good" side of existence are, at bottom, only disguised suffering. The basic illness that is responsible for suffering goes deeper than the examples given; it is the grasping of the aggregates or constituents of self.

The Second Noble Truth is the truth that suffering originates in craving. In one sense, suffering is caused by craving what one cannot have or craving to avoid what cannot be avoided. Thus, craving money when one is poor leads to suffering; craving health when one is ill leads to suffering; craving immortality in the face of the inevitability of death leads to suffering; craving extinction faced with the continuity of the stuff of which life is made leads to suffering, etc. But there is a deeper sense of craving. This is craving in the sense of a *blind compulsion to be or have a self*.

If the obvious forms of suffering are analyzed it will be seen that there are two basic factors involved. First, there is what might be called the existence of certain objective factors in the world. There is the fact that Jones has no money, that Smith's child just died, or that Singh's leg was cut off. But these objective facts in the world do not of themselves involve suffering. After all, who suffers when a boulder is split in two? Who suffers when a branch is cut from the tree? Who suffers when a young oak is broken in the wind? Probably no one would ever think of ascribing suffering to the boulder, or the trunk of the tree, or the "parent" oak. But probably everyone would attribute suffering to Jones, Smith, and Singh. The difference between these cases is obvious. Trees and boulders do not have selves; hence there is no one to suffer. But Jones, Smith, and Singh have, each of them, a self. And this self is aware of the suffering caused it by objective factors in the world. We think it makes sense for Jones, or Smith, or Singh to say, "I have lost my money, or child, or leg," but it does not make sense to think of the tree or boulder as saying, "I lost my part, or branch, or child." If this latter did make sense we should very well impute suffering to boulders and trees as well as to persons.

This points to the second factor involved in suffering; the existence of a self. There is no suffering until objective factors in the world are related to a self. When these objective factors are related to a self this self may crave them or crave to avoid them. And when what is craved is not had there is suffering.

But what is this self which constitutes the second basic factor involved in suffering? And does it make sense to attribute a self to a person?

What is this "I" to which reference is made when a person claims, "I have lost my child?" The truth of the origin of suffering is that *it is the craving of a self that gives rise to suffering*. Blindly, a person craves a self that though separate is attached to the factors constituting the person. This craving leads to the invention and projection of a self. This self, being attached to the factors making up a person, suffers when the identification is threatened by changes in the factors to which it is attached, whether these be the factors of that person, other persons, or other objects and activities in the world.

Analysis of a person reveals the existence of (1) the activities constituting what we call the bodily, or physical, self; (2) activities of sensing; (3) activities of perceiving; (4) impulses to action; and (5) activities of consciousness. But in addition to these five groups of activities nothing more is to be found. The self, as that to which the groups of activities belong, is a fiction, a fiction created by ignorant craving. And it is the craving for this fictitious self that underlies all suffering.

The third Noble Truth, that suffering can be extinguished, follows upon analysis of the causes of suffering. If selfish craving is the cause of suffering, then the cessation of suffering lies in the extinction of that craving. This is precisely what the Buddha recommended. In fact, the very goal of the Buddhist—*Nirvana*—has the meaning "be blown out." What is blown out—like a lamp—or extinguished, is selfish craving. When selfish craving is extinguished, suffering is pulled up by the root. Thus, the truth of the cessation of suffering is the truth that the extinction of craving will bring about the cessation of suffering.

It is a long way, however, from the recognition of what will bring about the cessation of suffering to the actual accomplishment of that cessation. And the Buddha, good physician that he was, did not stop with an analysis and diagnosis of the malady nor with the recognition of what was required for cure, but he prescribed a method of treatment which would destroy the illness. The prescription constitutes the Fourth Noble Truth, which teaches the famous "Middle Way" of Buddhism.

THE NOBLE EIGHTFOLD PATH

This Middle Way, which sums up the way of life that characterizes Buddhism as a practical philosophy, is built upon the eight principles constituting the Fourth Noble Truth. These principles are as follows:

1. Right views (*Samma ditthi*)
2. Right resolution (*Samma sankappa*)
3. Right speech (*Samma vaca*)
4. Right action (*Samma kammanta*)
5. Right livelihood (*Samma ajiva*)
6. Right effort (*Samma vayama*)
7. Right mindfulness (*Samma sati*)
8. Right concentration (*Samma samadhi*)

The various actions of life prompted by and expressing these eight principles should proceed more or less simultaneously, the aim being to achieve a completely integrated life of the highest order. The relationships between actions of life and the principles that underlie these actions can be seen by considering the three axioms of Ethical Conduct, Mental Discipline, and Wisdom, which underlie all principles and actions. The axiom of Ethical Conduct includes right speech, right action, and right livelihood. The axiom of Discipline includes right effort, right mindfulness, and right concentration. The axiom of Wisdom includes right views, and right resolution. The purpose of Ethical Conduct is to check the inflow of additional cravings. Concentration aims at destroying the already present cravings, and Wisdom is prescribed for living a sufferingless existence.

Understanding ourselves and the universe in which we live, action will be based upon a universal love and compassion. Accordingly, Ethical Conduct is based on love and compassion and springs from wisdom, or an enlightened mind. But to achieve wisdom and to cultivate love and compassion, discipline of the self is required. Thus, Ethical Conduct, Discipline, and Wisdom are the three axioms of the Good Life.

Wisdom includes both the correct understanding of things as they are and the resolution to act in accord with this understanding. Having right views consists in seeing things as they are. This includes, on a lower level, intellectual understanding of things. But intellectual knowledge takes place within a system, or network, of concepts and principles which reflect necessarily limited perspectives as underlying assumptions. Accordingly, intellectual knowledge is conditioned by the concepts and principles of the system and its truth is relative to the truth of the system in which it takes place. Consequently, intellectual knowledge is considered a lower kind of understanding than the understanding that results from seeing things just as they are by a direct

Wheel of Becoming. *Information Service of India. Photograph courtesy of Professor Grace E. Cairns. Reprinted from* RELIGIONS OF THE WORLD *by McCasland, Cairns and Yu.*

penetration. This direct seeing is the complete illumination of things just as they are in themselves and not as limited by concepts and labels. It is this direct penetration of things that is properly called Wisdom. It reveals the relative and conditioned nature of all things and shows suffering to be caused by selfish grasping.

Wisdom reveals the nature of things and the causes of suffering, but does not stop there. It also expresses itself in the resolution to overcome suffering by leaving aside all selfish cravings. This involves the resolve to cultivate a love universal in depth and scope that reveals itself in compassion and non-hurting. Selfish desires, ill-will, hatred, and violence are entirely given up when Wisdom is achieved.

Wisdom cannot be achieved without discipline, and therefore one practices right effort, right mindfulness, and right concentration. Practicing right effort includes (1) preventing evil and unwholesome states of mind from arising, (2) getting rid of such evil and unwholesome states of mind that may already exist, (3) bringing about good and wholesome states of mind, and (4) developing and perfecting good and wholesome states of mind already present.

Right mindfulness consists in being aware of and attentive to one's activities. This includes the activities of (1) the body, (2) sensing and feeling, (3) perceiving, and (4) thinking and consciousness.

To be aware of and attentive to one's activities means understanding what these activities are, how they arise, how they disappear, how they are developed, controlled, gotten rid of, linked together, and what they are in themselves.

Right concentration is essentially a matter of recreating oneself as an enlightened person. Ignorance and enlightenment and suffering and happiness have their root in one's mental activities. It is said in the *Dhammapada*:

> mind precedes all unwholesome states and is their chief; they are all mind-wrought. If with an impure mind a person speaks or acts, misery follows him like the wheel that dogs the foot of the ox. Mind precedes all wholesome states and is their chief; they are all mindwrought. If with a pure mind a person speaks or acts, happiness follows him like his never-departing shadow.[5]

If this is the case, it is entirely plausible to concentrate on purifying one's mental activities as a means of achieving happiness.

Ordinarily four stages of concentration are distinguished. In the first stage one concentrates on getting rid of lust, ill-will, laziness, worry, anxiety, and doubt. These unwholesome mental activities are replaced by feelings of joy and happiness. In the second stage one concentrates on seeing through and getting beyond all mental activities,

[5] *Dhammapada*, 1, 2.

although retaining an awareness of joy and happiness. In the third stage one goes beyond the mental activity responsible for the feeling of joy, and achieves an equanimity pervaded by happiness. In the fourth and final stage of concentration there is complete equanimity and total awareness, beyond both happiness and unhappiness.

Ethical Conduct is both a reflection of, and a condition for, Wisdom and Discipline. Only a wise person can be good, and only a good person can be wise. And both wisdom and goodness require discipline. Accordingly, one begins and ends with all three simultaneously. To act ethically means to be correct in speech, action, and means of earning a living.

Right speech means generally to avoid all talk that will lead to unhappiness and to use speech to bring about happiness. Its negative application includes: (1) no lying; (2) no slander, or character assassination, or talk that might bring about hatred, jealousy, enmity, or discord among other; (3) no harsh or rude talk, no malicious talk, no impolite or abusive language; and (4) no idle or malicious gossip, or foolish chatter. Its positive application teaches that one should tell the truth, speak in a kindly and friendly way, use language meaningfully and usefully. This includes knowing the time and place for which certain talk is appropriate. This implies that sometimes one should maintain "noble silence."

Right action means avoiding killing or hurting, and precludes stealing, cheating, and immoral sexual activity. Positively, it means that one's actions should aim at promoting peace and happiness for others and respecting the well-being of all living beings.

Right livelihood extends the principle of right action to one's chosen profession throughout one's life. Accordingly, it precludes professions that would harm others, such as trading in firearms, liquors, drugs, poisons, killing, sexual procurement, etc. Only those means of earning a living which promote peace and well-being are in accord with this principle.

It is obvious how the axiom of Ethical Conduct rests upon compassion and love for others. But further, this compassion and love is the natural result of a recognition of the conditionedness and relativity of things. If no things have independent being (*svabhava*), then all are dependent upon each other. But this leaves no foothold for selfishness. Consequently, ignorance and selfishness must be replaced by wisdom and compassion.

CHAPTER 10

HISTORICAL CONSIDERATIONS

T̲HE last chapter was concerned with the ethical-religious teachings which constitute the basic core of Buddhism as a way of life, and which probably reflect the main teachings of the historical Gautama. These teachings, aimed at inculcating the discipline and compassion that characterize the life and attitudes of a Buddhist, are not basically different today than they were twenty-five hundred years ago. On the other hand, the philosophies of Buddhism, which reflect the intellectual attempts to systematize the Buddhist way of life and to provide a rational basis for these ethical-religious teachings, have undergone considerable change and development.

The distinction between Buddhism as a way of life and Buddhist philosophies is the distinction between a way of living and the attempted justifications for that way. Thus, though Buddhists through the ages could agree on how to live, they could also disagree on the question of *why* they should live that way. If one is a Buddhist it follows that the Buddhist Way is accepted as the best way of life, for no person chooses an inferior way of life when he knows a superior way. But the question of justifying this acceptance is still open. Buddhism is sufficiently tough-minded and empirically inclined to rule out justification of the Middle Way by appeal to the fact that the Buddha said it was superior. In fact, appeal to faith as the only justification of the Middle Way was ruled out by the Buddha himself, as he encouraged his followers to examine the doctrine for themselves. Aside from an appeal to faith one could appeal to the consequences of following the Noble Eightfold Path. If this kind of life provided for goodness and happiness it could hardly be said to be an inferior way of life. But granting this kind of justification, and granting even that in a very important sense the results of a certain kind of life are the only justification for that kind of life, it is possible to raise the question of *why* that kind of life leads one out of suffering and provides for peace and contentment. It is this question that serves as a starting point for the *philosophies* of Buddhism. In the different answers to this question the different philosophies of Buddhism are to be found.

By way of providing a basic orientation to the cultural phenomenon of Buddhism and of seeing the historical relations between the religion and the philosophies of Buddhism, this chapter will be devoted to a brief historical account of the development of Buddhism.

PRE-BUDDHIST INDIA

The philosophical atmosphere of India in which Buddhism took its place in the sixth and fifth centuries B.C. was dominated by three attitudes. First of all there was the attitude that ritual and sacrifice were the principal effective means of securing whatever was desired. This attitude was connected with the belief—probably thousands of years old already by this time—that the creation and functioning of the world was due to, and controlled by, the effects of sacrifices and rites. The second attitude, reflected in the Upanishads, regarded the observable world and the observable self as mere "name and form." What was mere name and form was only temporary and passing, possessing no abiding reality. What was of abiding reality was the unchanging Self and the unchanging Real. This attitude was connected with belief in *Atman* as the abiding inner reality and *Brahman* as the abiding external reality, and with the identity of *Atman* and *Brahman*. The third attitude was skeptical. It was probably associated principally with the denial of the principal beliefs underlying the other two attitudes. Judging by various criticisms of the skeptical philosophy, it would appear that its adherents were the materialists, who denied physical, moral, and sacrificial causality, and who denied the possibility of knowledge.

The skeptical attitude obviously offered men no help in their struggles to overcome suffering because it consisted chiefly in denying the possibilities suggested by the other attitudes. The sacrificial and ritualistic attitude was at this time so involved with magic and taboos and with the cult and corruption of the priests that it also failed to offer any real hope in the perennial struggle against suffering. While the attitude reflected in the Upanishads was not as obviously helpless as the other two, its associations with philosophical abstractness and the underlying belief in the unchanging nature of the Real made it appear relatively unserviceable as the basis for a way to overcome or lessen suffering. Consequently, when the Buddha appeared teaching the causes of suffering and the way for ending suffering he found a ready acceptance.

BEGINNINGS OF BUDDHISM

Gautama Siddhartha was born about 563 B.C. at Kapilavastu, in what is today Nepal. Shielded by his father from the ugly scenes of suffering to be found all around, and happily married to a beautiful girl, Gautama led the easy pleasure-filled life of a prince of leisure until he was twenty-nine years old. Then, having been exposed to the sufferings of old age, sickness, and death, and having reflected that it would be well to discover some means for overcoming suffering, he left his palaces and family and took up the life of an ascetic. For six years he practiced the most extreme forms of self-discipline and self-denial. All to no avail. Finally, on the brink of death, he determined that the truth of the cause and cessation of suffering was not to be achieved by following the extreme of asceticism. Resolved now to follow a middle way between indulgence and asceticism, he soon achieved the enlightenment he was seeking. For the next forty years of his life the Buddha traveled around India teaching the Four Noble Truths and the Noble Eightfold Path. During these years of teaching the Buddha attracted many followers, and the Order of Buddhist Monks was already of good size when he died, in about the year 483 B.C.

The history of Buddhism after the death of the Buddha is a very complicated subject. Its early history can be viewed in terms of the changes in the Order prior to its split into two main movements, the more conservative movement characterized in the literature of the Theravada School, and the more liberal movement known as Mahayana. From that point on, Buddhist history is a matter of changes within each of these movements.[1]

---

[1] It must be noted that historical accounts of Buddhism are, for the most part, tentative because of insufficient evidence. The reader interested in the historical development of Buddhism would do well to turn to E. J. Thomas' *The History of Buddhist Thought* (London: Routledge & Kegan Paul Ltd., 2nd ed. 1951), which very carefully points out the kinds and amounts of evidence available for the various historical claims made. The reader is advised to construe this historical account as no more than "a likely account" of what took place historically.

THE BUDDHIST COUNCILS

The content of early Buddhism was contained not only in the actual teachings of the Buddha about suffering and its cessation, but also in the rules for living developed by the Order of Monks. In fact, it appears that clashes of opinion within the Order over interpretation of disciplinary rules occurred earlier than differences of opinion over the religious-philosophical teachings. Furthermore, these differences of opinion over disciplinary rules were considered more serious than other differences of opinion. So important was the matter of discipline that the early divisions in Buddhism and the formation of different schools were primarily the result of arguments over these matters. This is not surprising, of course, for after all the Buddha was concerned chiefly with getting rid of suffering. And getting rid of suffering is more closely tied up with how one lives than with theoretical teachings. Thus, the first three Buddhist councils were held for the purpose of discussing and resolving differences of opinion concerning interpretations of disciplinary rules.

The first council of Buddhists was held shortly after the death of the Buddha at Rajagaha. This council, attended by five hundred monks, resolved—in the face of a suggestion that since the Master was dead the monks could do as they chose   —that the rules were to be kept exactly as the Buddha prescribed, without either addition or deletion.

Probably about a hundred years after the first council there was a second council—the council of Vesali. Again the occasion of the council was a dispute over discipline. But this time it appears that the number of monks wanting a relaxation of the rules was relatively large. It was either at this second council or at the next council, that of Pataliputta, that the first main division took place. This division resulted in the Mahasanghika school being formed. It was followed by a series of further splits, both in the old order and within the Mahasanghika school. This development of differing schools can be pictured as in the diagram on the following page.

THERAVADA AND MAHAYANA

The exact teachings of each of these various schools, however, is a matter of considerable uncertainty. No doubt, these schools differed from each other on matters both of doctrine and disciplinary rules. But the exact nature of these differences is not known. Partially, the uncertainty in this area is due to the fact that by the fifth century of Buddhism, the major division was not that into these twenty schools, but

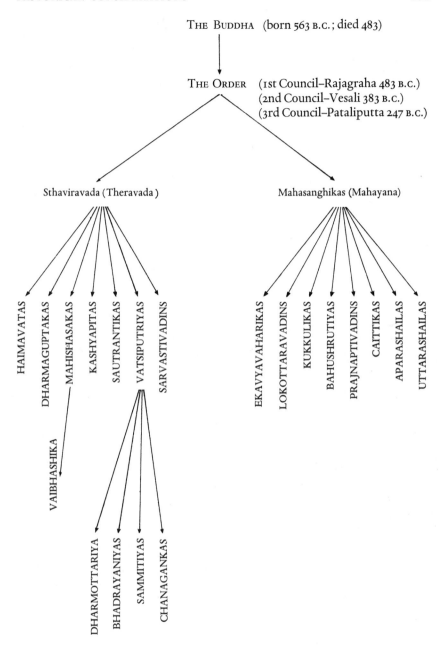

THE BUDDHA (born 563 B.C.; died 483)

THE ORDER (1st Council–Rajagraha 483 B.C.)
(2nd Council–Vesali 383 B.C.)
(3rd Council–Pataliputta 247 B.C.)

Sthaviravada (Theravada)

Mahasanghikas (Mahayana)

HAIMAVATAS

DHARMAGUPTAKAS

MAHISHASAKAS

KASHYAPITAS

SAUTRANTIKAS

VATSIPUTRIYAS

SARVASTIVADINS

VAIBHASHIKA

EKAVYAVAHARIKAS

LOKOTTARAVADINS

KUKKULIKAS

BAHUSHRUTIYAS

PRAJNAPTIVADINS

CAITTIKAS

APARASHAILAS

UTTARASHAILAS

DHARMOTTARIYA

BHADRAYANIYAS

SAMMITIYAS

CHANAGANKAS

HISTORICAL SKETCH OF THE EARLY DEVELOPMENT OF
BUDDHIST SCHOOLS

rather, the division into the Theravada and Mahayana schools, or sects. This was a division along religious lines, the chief differences being concerned with the interpretations of the Buddha's teachings concerning the attaining of *Nirvana*.

In Theravada there was great emphasis on self-discipline and individual achievement. The goal was *arhat*-ship, which symbolized the extinction of the fires of lust and craving in the individual, brought about by his or her own efforts. In Mahayana the goal was to become a *Bodhisattava*—a being whose only concern was with helping others extinguish suffering. The compassion shown by the historical Buddha was emphasized greatly, and as a result there came to be less reliance on individual effort and self-discipline, and more reliance on faith in the Buddha and *Bodhisattavas* who would provide assistance in overcoming suffering. In time these two different emphases in Buddhism came to be supported by different metaphysics. The emphasis on universal salvation represented by the Mahayana ideal of the *Bodhisattava* came to be underwritten by metaphysics of philosophical skepticism and absolutism. The emphasis on individual salvation represented by the Theravada ideal of the *arhat* came to be underwritten by a metaphysics of realistic flux, as formulated in the doctrine of momentariness.

PHILOSOPHICAL SCHOOLS

Thus, whereas from the religious perspective, the main division was into Mahayana and Theravada, from the philosophical perspective the division was into philosophies of realism as opposed to philosophies of idealism and absolutism. The philosophies of realism, which tend to be identified with Theravada Buddhism, are represented by the Vaibhashika and Sautrantika schools. The philosophies identified with Mahayana are (1) the "suchness" absolutism of Ashvaghosa, (2) the relativism of the Madhyamika school, and (3) the idealistic absolutism of the Yogacara school.

Before continuing with an historical outline of Buddhist schools of philosophy it must be pointed out that a division of Buddhism into religious and philosophical schools is somewhat arbitrary, and it is necessary to emphasize that the division is possible only from a certain perspective. In this case it is a perspective assumed primarily on the basis of the distinctions ordinarily made between religions and philosophies of the West. Buddhism as the living cultural phenomenon of the Orient is neither philosophy nor religion; nor is it really both religion and philosophy. It is simply Buddhism. The above distinctions do not apply. It might well be said that to look for philosophy in Buddhism is like looking for the tracks of birds in the air. Buddhism is essentially a way of life; it is not a philosophy about life. But granting this, it does not follow that Buddhism, as a way of life, does not presuppose a philosophy, or have an implicit philosophy. To be sure, it does rest upon certain views of man and the world, despite the common attitude that the philosophical analysis of those views is not essential to a Buddhist way of life. Nevertheless, the fact that Buddhism presupposes certain philosophical views means that one path to the understanding of Buddhism is through an analysis of these views. Thus, it is important not to mistake the metaphysical views found in the philosophies of Buddhism for the "Essence of Buddhism." The "Essence of Buddhism" consists in understanding and getting rid of suffering; not in theoretical views of man and the world. But an understanding of the views implicit in Buddhism can lead one to recognize the logical foundations of Buddhism and make possible a philosophical estimate of these basic foundations.

Probably the earliest of the philosophical schools was the Vaibhashika, as all of the other schools refer to the teachings of this school. The criticisms found in other Buddhist schools as well as in the Hindu schools reveal that the Vaibhashika held that the world is made up of atoms in continuous motion and also that this world can be directly perceived as it exists. But the individual philosophers belonging to this school are unknown.

The Sautrantika school may also be older than the schools belonging to the Mahayana, but the individual philosophers who are known to be connected with this school are contemporary with Madhyamika and Yogacara philosophers. Kumaralabdha, a contemporary of Nagarjuna, probably lived in the second century A.D. Probably he is not the first philosopher of this school, but he is the earliest known to us today. Other philosophers connected with this school are Vasubandhu, who composed the famous *Abhidharmakosha* as a summary of realistic philosophy, probably sometime in the fifth century A.D., and Yasomitra, who wrote a commentary on this work. One of the logicians of this school, Dharmottara, lived in the ninth century A.D.

The Madhyamika and Yogacara philosophies probably developed out of the insights present in the philosophies of Ashvaghosa and the

Lankavtara Sutra. Ashvaghosa formulated his philosophy of the "Thusness" of reality sometime in the first century A.D. This philosophy emphasized the role of consciousness in knowledge and understanding and pointed to the ultimate unknowability of reality. The *Lankavatara Sutra,* also emphasizing the activity of the mind in experience, is probably earlier than Ashvaghosa.

The Madhyamika school concentrates on the ultimate unknowability of reality by conceptual and perceptual means. It is thus a school of philosophical skepticism. It is not, however, a school of unqualified skepticism, for conceptual reality and conceptual activity are not regarded as the ultimate reality. The earliest and greatest of the Madhyamika philosophers was Nagarjuna, who should probably be placed in the middle of the second century A.D. His pupil, Aryadeva, commented on some of his works. Later philosophers of this school who attracted the attention of other philosophers in India and China were Kumarajiva, who lived in the fourth century A.D., and Buddhapalita and Candrakirti, both of whom flourished around the middle of the sixth century A.D.

The Yogacara school represents many of the tenets of the *Lankavatara Sutra,* as it emphasizes the activity of mind to the exclusion of everything else. It is the "Mind-only" doctrine of Vasubandhu of this school that attracted the most criticism from philosophers outside of this school. This is the same Vasubandhu who summarized the realistic philosophy of the Sautrantikas. He was converted from Sautrantika to Yogacara by his older brother, Asanga. And even prior to Asanga, there is a philosopher named Maitreyanatha, who belonged to this school.

With Dinnaga, a pupil of Vasubandhu, Yogacara philosophy took on an emphasis on logic that brought it closer to the Sautrantika school. Dinnaga, Dharmakirti, and Dharmottara are all logicians who seem to have a philosophy midway between Sautrantika and Yogacara. Sometimes this philosophy is referred to as Svatantra Yogacara. Later Yogacara philosophers are Shantarakshita and Kamashila.

After the ninth century A.D. Buddhist philosophies began to disappear from India. Although Buddhist philosophical activity did not disappear as Buddhism spread to China and other parts of Asia, there was never again to be the intense and critical philosophical activity in connection with Buddhism that was found during the first thirteen centuries of the Buddhist era in India. Whether it was because of a widespread feeling that the inadequacies of intellect for solving problems about ultimate reality had been so clearly shown by this time that no one wished to devote his life to the intellectual activity of philosophizing, or whether it was due to the more practical inclinations of the Oriental mind outside India, is hard to say. But though Buddhism as a way of life was as strong or stronger than ever, the heyday of Buddhist philosophy in India was over by 1000 A.D.

CHAPTER 11

THE NATURE OF THE SELF

T HE main philosophical implications of the ethical-religious teachings of Buddhism are contained in the doctrines of no-self (*anatta*) and impermanence (*anicca*). Both of these doctrines in turn are underwritten by the principle of dependent origination (*paticca samuppada*). The chief difference between the doctrines of *anatta* and *anicca* is that the former refers to the non-substantiality of the self, whereas the latter refers to the non-substantiality of things in the world. Both doctrines presuppose the theory of dependent origination.

As Buddhism developed, the principle of dependent origination underwent different interpretations. These different interpretations were then used to underwrite different theories of the non-substantiality of things and the self. The basic Buddhist philosophies can be studied by considering first the theories concerning the self, and then the theories concerning the nature of things in the world. In this chapter different views of the self will be considered.

BASIC PRINCIPLES

The Buddha's prescription for curing the ills of life follows upon his analysis of the causes of these ills. The Noble Eightfold Path was prescribed because it was what was needed to uproot the causes of suffering. No doubt, the religious genius of the Buddha is what made possible his diagnosis of the causes of suffering and the prescription for its cure. But both the discovery of the causes of suffering and the prescription for its cure are dependent upon the Second Noble Truth—that suffering is caused.

The recognition that suffering is caused reflects an understanding of the relations between events and things in the world. The Buddhist understanding of these relations is reflected in the theory of dependent origination (*paticca samuppada*) which holds, roughly, that whatever is, is dependent upon something else. The formulation of the theory is as follows: (1) If this is, that comes to be; (2) From the arising of this, that arises; (3) If this is not, that does not come to be; (4) From the stopping of this, that stops.

There are several features of this view of dependent origination that need to be noted before applying the theory to an analysis of the self. First, if whatever is, is dependent upon another, then any kind of "straight line" causality is ruled out. There are no independent beings who are responsible for the existence of dependent beings. For example, the theistic notion that one absolutely independent being—God—created the rest of what exists, and that this created universe depends for its existence upon God, makes no sense in the Buddhist view of dependent origination. Rather, whatever creates is also created, and the processes of creating and being created go on simultaneously without beginning or end.

Secondly, as a consequence of the mutual dependence of all beings, it follows that no beings are solely "other-created," but that all are mutually self-creating. The ongoing processes that make up the universe are co-dependent and mutually influencing. Each aspect of the process shares in the creation and the continuation of the other aspects of the process.

Thirdly, ordinary notions of space and time are ruled out by the Buddhist theory of dependent origination. Ordinary notions of space and time depend upon the location and duration of independent beings. Spatial characteristics are derived from the comparison of the location of one being relative to another. Temporal characteristics are derived by comparing the duration of one being to another. But according to the theory of dependent origination there are no beings independent of each other. There are only ongoing processes of mutually dependent factors. Reality is of the nature of process; *things* are merely abstractions. But ordinary notions of space and time depend upon these abstractions, and hence must also fall into the category of abstractions rather than realities. There are no beings; there are only becomings. And since a completion of becoming is never attained, being is never reached.

Fourthly, adequate definitions are impossible. If the universe is thought to consist of things, relatively complete and independent, it is possible to adequately define the things making up the universe. But when the universe is considered to be of the nature of process, definitions are not possible, for whatever might be defined would belong to past stages of the process and never to the present reality of the process.

DEPENDENT ORIGINATION AND THE WHEEL OF BECOMING

Avoiding linear notions of time and space, Buddhists ingeniously diagram the endless continuum of processes constituting reality by using the figure of a wheel. The wheel of becoming (*bhavacakra*) represents the major aspects of the continuous processes constituting what we ordinarily call a person. It is essentially an application of the theory of dependent origination to the processes constituting the self and represents an attempt to exhibit the causes of suffering. The stages of becoming constituting the suffering person are usually represented as in the diagram on the following page.

In the cycle of life depicted by the wheel, the suffering (*dukkha*) of man is symbolized by old age and death. It is not that *dukkha* is thought to consist solely in becoming old and dying, but rather, since these are two of the ills that are especially dreaded, they serve well as representatives of all the ills of life. Now it is asked, Upon what do old age and death depend? The answer is that it is upon the arising of birth that there is death, for death follows birth as surely as night follows day. Without birth there would be no death; and birth would not occur if there were no "becoming forces" (*bhava*) available to be born. In turn, the "becoming forces" depend for their existence upon grasping and clinging to life; grasping and clinging could not exist without desire; desires depend upon perception; perception follows upon sense impressions, which would not be possible without the six sense organs. The sense organs, in turn, depend upon the mind and body (*nama-rupa*), but the functioning of mind and body is dependent upon consciousness. And consciousness is dependent upon the impulses to action, for consciousness is clearly an activity, and without an impulse to action there could be no consciousness. All of these phases of the processes and activities constituting the life of the individual can belong to the self only upon the presence of ignorance. And ignorance, in turn, depends upon the preceding factors in the cycle. And so the cycle goes, without beginning and without end. Each phase or factor is relentlessly brought about by others, which in turn are brought about by still others; the

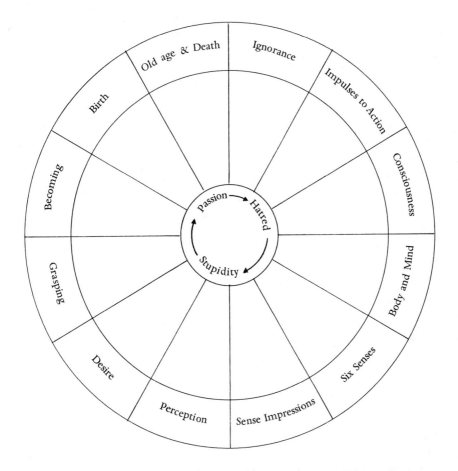

THE WHEEL OF BECOMING (*BHAVACAKRA*)

arising and the falling of the various factors of existence constitutes the
unending continuum of process that makes up reality. In this cycle man
is caught up, being born, suffering, and dying; being born, suffering, and
dying, *ad dukkham*. Life brings death and death brings life, as these are
no more than phases in the eternal process.

Although all of the factors constituting a being are intertwined
and interdependent, constituting one ongoing process, the factor of
ignorance is usually taken as the root-cause of the processes causing
suffering. Accordingly, the wheel of becoming can also be interpreted by
starting with suffering and then examining it in forward order. When

this is done the reflections are as follows: ignorance makes possible the impulses to action, which make possible consciousness; these factors together make possible the mind and body organism; given the mind and body, sensing is possible; and when sensing is provided for, then sense impressions are possible. Following upon sense impressions there is perception; when there is perception there is desire to achieve or avoid what is perceived. Desiring, in turn, makes possible grasping at and clinging to life in its various aspects; this, in turn, provides for the force of becoming, without which there would be no birth. And without birth of a self there would be no self to be suffering.

It is customary when commenting upon and explaining the wheel of life to divide the factors into those concerned with the present life, those concerned with the past, and those concerned with the future, so that ignorance and the impulses to action are regarded as the causes from the past, and birth and old age and death are regarded as effects to occur in the future, with the other factors making up the present existence of the individual. But this division into past, present, and future is somewhat misleading. After all, if the self is really of the nature of process, then there are no sharp lines between past, present, and future. Past, present, and future merely proceed from certain arbitrary perspectives which result from emphasizing the *thingness* rather than the process nature of reality. This can easily be seen by considering that what we call a person is no sooner born than he is dying; the process of aging which culminates in death is going on already at conception. But by the same token, the process of aging and dying is also part of the process of conception and birth. In fact, if a considerable over-simplification is allowed, it might be said that basically it is this ignorance of process and the consequent cutting of this process into segments, which are regarded as independent of each other, that underlies the grasping and clinging that inevitably leads to suffering. It means that the individual is constantly out of tune with reality.

The divisions of past, present, and future result from taking an arbitrary point of view which looks at reality as if it were cut up into distinct and separate pieces or things, rather than seeing it as an integral process. But the division of becoming into the twelve factors represented by the wheel of becoming also represents an arbitrary point of view, for in reality there are an unlimited number of factors that could be distinguished in the processes constituting an individual, with no clear lines of demarcation between them. Consequently this list of factors should not be taken as a true and complete list of the factors of reality.

Instead, it should be regarded as an attempt to effect a transition from an attitude which cuts up reality and makes possible clinging and grasping, to an attitude which is consonant with the flow of reality. The latter attitude cannot itself be adequately represented conceptually, for the whole conceptual approach rests upon the attitude that reality is of the nature of being rather than process. Concepts can adequately reveal only a static reality. However, they can point to (though not express) a different kind of reality.

Taking care that the picture of reality represented by the wheel of becoming is not taken to be the last word and truth about the subject, there are other traps one must avoid when reflecting on this symbol of the wheel. It would be easy to be misled into thinking that Buddhism is basically nihilistic if one seized a wrong interpretation of the causes of suffering and the way to their removal. If old age and death follow upon being born, and if birth were stopped, then old age and death would be stopped. And isn't this precisely what the Buddha taught? "Locate the factors upon which suffering is dependent and remove them, and this will bring about the elimination of suffering." It is true that the Buddha taught that removal of the causes of suffering will eliminate suffering. But it does not follow from this that he maintained that non-existence was the way to non-suffering. On the very face of it, the teaching that only non-existence would lead to non-suffering is absurd, for who could subscribe to this teaching as a way of deliverance? And history reveals that Buddhism has been embraced as a saving teaching by hundreds of thousands of persons for many, many centuries. If the Buddha did not teach nihilism, then what did he teach? Upon the non-existence of what would there be non-existence of suffering? To answer this question it is necessary to reflect on the Buddhist notion of what a person is.

STOPPING THE WHEEL OF BECOMING

Ordinarily when we talk about what a person is, especially when we talk about what we ourselves are, we assume that in addition to the bodily and mental characteristics constituting the individual there is also a self, an "I." Thus we say, "*I* will do that, *I* am doing this," etc. And the claim is made that various things, including our bodies and minds, belong to the person. We say, "It's *his* body." Or, "I'm improving *my* mind." It is this ego-self—this "I"—to whom suffering is attributed, as for example when we say, "It's terrible, the doctor just told me that

I am dying of cancer, and this is why I am suffering so." Clearly, if there were no ego-self, or "I", there could be no suffering, for suffering is always the suffering of a self; it always belongs to someone.

What foundation is there for the ordinary belief in the existence of an ego-self? This is the question underlying the Buddhist analysis of the self, undertaken to uproot the conditions upon which suffering depends. It is to the non-existence of the ego-self that the theory of *anatta* refers, and it is in overcoming attachment to the "I" that release from suffering is found. As the Buddha said,

> Therefore say I that the Tathagata has attained deliverance and is free from attachment, inasmuch as all imaginings, or agitations, or proud thought concerning an Ego or anything pertaining to an Ego, have perished, have faded away, have ceased, have been given up and relinquished.[1]

But surely it is paradoxical for anyone to claim that he does not exist. To say "I do not exist" obviously is not to make any claim at all, as the remark negates itself, since a non-existent being could not make the claim and an existing being would be asserting his own existence in making the claim. Consequently, the Buddhist claim that the self does not exist could not be a claim that there is no individual existence, that the person is non-existent. It seems more reasonable to regard a remark such as "I do not exist," as an attempt to get attention for another claim that is to be made. For instance, it might reasonably be claimed that I do not exist as a substance independent of the processes that constitute me. This is not a claim about my existence *per se*, but a claim about my existence as a "such and such." And these are quite different matters. The Buddhist claim about the non-existence of the self is a claim about the non-existence of the self as a being *in addition to*, or *apart from*, the various factors that are ordinarily said to belong to the self. It clearly is not a claim about the non-existence of the factors that make up the individual person. This is evident from the Buddha's reply to Vacchagotta's question concerning whether the Tathagata had any theories of his own (concerning the nature of the self). His reply was as follows:

> The Tathāgata, O Vaccha, is free from all theories; but this, Vaccha, does the Tathāgata know,—the nature of form, and how form arises, and how form perishes; the nature of sensation, and how sensation arises, and how sensation perishes; the nature of perception, and how perception arises,

[1] *Majjhima Nikaya, Sutta* 72, in H. C. Warren, *Buddhism in Translations* (New York: Atheneum, 1963) p. 125.

and how perception perishes; the nature of the pre-dispositions, and how the pre-dispositions arise, and how the pre-dispositions perish; the nature of consciousness, and how consciousness arises, and how consciousness perishes.[2]

This answer reveals that rather than considering various theories of the substantiality of the self, the Buddha took a long hard look at what a person is, and found no extra-mental or extra-physical thing to which the word "self" might refer. Rather, upon analysis it became evident that a person is constituted by a large number of processes. These processes can be grouped together, for the sake of convenience, in the way indicated by the Buddha's answer to Vachagotta's question. Schematically, this analysis of a person can be represented as follows:

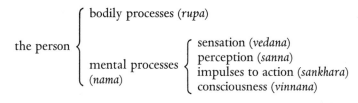

All of the various things that can be said of a person are about one or another of these processes. No person ever engages in any activities that do not belong to one or another of these five groups. But if the analysis of a person does not reveal anything other than these five groups of processes, then what foundation is there for claiming the existence of another component, namely, the self or the "I"? Ordinarily we say that the body, or the habits, or the thoughts of a person *belong* to a self, and thus suggest that there is, in addition to what is owned, also an owner of the processes. It is clear upon analysis, however, that this is simply a way of speaking, and cannot be taken as evidence that there exists a self in addition to the groups that make up a person.

It is now possible to become clearer about exactly what is meant by the theory of *anatta*, which denies the substantiality of the self. The *anatta* theory denies the existence of a self only when the word "self" is taken to refer to some thing in addition to the groups of factors making up a person. The *anatta* theory does not deny the existence of a self when the word "self" is taken to refer to only the five groups of processes constituting the person. Thus, it is the view that the self is a substance independent of the processes making up a person that is denied by the doctrine of *anatta*.

[2] *Majjhima Nikaya, Sutta 72.* Warren, p. 125.

With this explanation of the *anatta* theory in mind it is possible to see that the theory of dependent origination applied to the rise and fall of suffering in the wheel of becoming has nothing to do with nihilism. The ignorance that must be destroyed is the ignorance that consists in living as though the self exists over and above the groups of processes. The conviction that there is a substantial self is the root-cause of suffering, for this results in the attitude that underlies and makes possible the attachment of the various processes to a self. It is this ignorance that allows the attachment and thereby makes possible suffering.

It is important to note that the processes in themselves are not capable of suffering; it is only a self that suffers. Because of ignorance, a self is considered to exist and is attached to the groups. And now, when the groups change in relation to the self, there is suffering.

On the other hand, if the ego is not born there can be no attachment to the groups. The groups will continue their flow in conformity with the process nature of reality; there is no stopping this flow, even if one wished to do so. But the ego—the "I"—need not be born; it need not arise. It is from the arising of this ego that suffering arises. And upon stopping that ego from arising, the suffering will stop.

With this in mind, the wheel of becoming can be meditated upon as follows: old age and death come to a self because the self is born; a self is born because there is attachment to the becoming forces; there is attachment to the becoming forces because there is grasping; and there is grasping because there is desiring. Feeling leads to desiring. Feeling is possible because of attachment to the sense impressions; and because there is attachment to the sense organs impressions are received. Attachment to the sense organs follows upon attachment to the mind and body; this in turn follows upon attachment to consciousness, which follows from attachment to impulses to actions, which proceeds from ignorance.

Meditating on the wheel in forward order, reflection reveals that without ignorance there would be no attachment to the impulses to action, no attachment to the processes of consciousness, no attachment to mind and body, to the sense organs, to the sense impressions, to the feelings, to the cravings, to the grasping and clinging, to the becoming forces; and there would then be no ego to be born and no self to grow old and die.

It is important to notice that the various processes would go on without interruption; the removal of ignorance would not alter that. But the processes cause suffering only because of a wrong attitude toward them; an attitude that mistakes them for something other than what they are by cutting up reality and attaching this cut-up reality to a self which in ignorance is thought to exist. It is *attachment* to the groups and not the groups themselves that brings about suffering.

The difference between groups of processes and attachment groups is explained by Buddhaghosa (400 A.D.) as follows:

> "Groups" is a general term; while the term "attachment groups" specifies those which are coupled with depravity and attachment.[3]

Then, after indicating his intention to teach the difference between the five groups and the five attachment groups, he goes on to say:

> All form whatsoever ... belongs to the form-group. All sensations whatsoever, ... all perception whatsoever, ... all predispositions [impulses to action] whatsoever, ... all consciousness whatsoever, ... These, O priests, are called the five groups.

Distinguishing between the groups as such and the groups as attached to an ego he says,

> ... those groups which are in the grasp of attachment are attachment groups.[4]

Clarifying the distinction between the groups and the attachment groups, Buddhaghosa goes on to say:

> When there is form, O priests, then through attachment to form, through engrossment in form, the persuasion arises, "This is mine; this am I; this is my ego." When there is sensation, ... when there is perception, ... where there are predispositions, ... when there is consciousness, O priests, then through attachment to consciousness, through engrossment in consciousness, the persuasion arises, "This is mine; this am I; this is my ego."[5]

This distinction between the groups of existence and the attachment groups (attachment to the groups of existence) makes clear why the Buddhist teaching that to get rid of suffering the self must be rooted out has nothing to do with nihilism, but has to do only with the destruction of the product of ignorance. The groups of processes constituting existence are not to be destroyed. Only the falsely imagined self is to be destroyed. The reason why this false self is to be destroyed is that it is what makes possible the attachment to the groups which underlies all forms of suffering. Without this false ego-self, which is only a creation

---

[3] *Visuddhi-Magga*, Ch. 14, in Warren, *Buddhism In translations*, p. 155.
[4] *Visuddhi-Magga*, Ch. 14, in Warren. pp. 155, 156.
[5] *Ibid.* Warren, p. 157.

of ignorance, there would be no looking to the past, bemoaning what
has been lost, and no looking forward to the future lamenting over
what has not yet come about. Without this ego-self life could be lived
in the full richness of the present moment, without distinction, division,
or attachment. Consequently, once this ignorance is removed life will
be found complete and perfect just as it is.

This realization of the completeness and perfectness of life is beautifully expressed in a remark by a twenty-five year old girl by the name of
Yaeko Iwasaki, who achieved enlightenment after only five years of
discipline and meditation. In a letter to her master, Harada-*Roshi*,
dated December 27, 1935, she said:

> You can appreciate how enormously satisfying it is for me to discover at
> last, through full realization, that just as I am I lack nothing.[6]

The incompleteness and the insecurity and the feelings of aloneness
and estrangement that characterize the basic anxiety underlying the
mental suffering of most people proceed from the activity of the ego
attaching itself to various processes, clinging and grasping in a desperate
effort to claim existence. It is undeniably the mark of the ego that it
is a struggling-to-be; it is not a being already complete. Nor is it simply
an aspect of process. It is a striving-to-be and grasping-to-be which
seeks to collect and dominate all of reality. No wonder then that the
realization that the ego is unreal, that it is simply the product of ignorance, frees one from the basic causes of suffering. And this is why·
the doctrine of *anatta* is one of the fundamental principles of Buddhism,
for the belief in the reality of a self is incompatible with the extinction of
suffering at which Buddhism aims.

THEORIES OF THE NON-SELF

Despite agreement among Buddhist schools that the doctrine of
anatta was basic to the Buddha's teaching and central to the message of
Buddhism, there was considerable controversy concerning precisely
what it was that this doctrine of non-self did allow and what it did not
allow. Since the doctrine of *anatta* was, at least formally, a negative
theory denying a theory of self, and since a variety of theories of the
self are possible, it is not surprising that there should be disagreement
concerning just which theories of the self it was that the *anatta* doctrine
denied, and which theories it did not deny.

[6] The letter from which this is taken, along with seven other inspiring letters, are contained in
Philip Kapleau, *The Three Pillars of Zen* (New York: Harper and Row, 1967), pp. 269–291.

Consequently, even though Buddhists agreed that the doctrine of *anatta* was a basic and true teaching of the Buddha, there came to be considerable disagreement over who it was that could be saved by following the Way. The location of the five groups constituting the empirical individual, and the rejection of the supposed existence of a substance in addition to the groups, left open the question of what distinguished one set of five groups from another, and what connection there was between treading the Path and becoming enlightened. The problem presented itself as especially acute to the Buddhist mind, for unless there was a means of distinguishing one set of groups from another, there would be no basis for differentiating between one person to be saved and another. Furthermore, there would be no basis for distinguishing between the ignorant and the enlightened person unless there were some kind of identity or continuity within each set of groups. And if the latter distinction could not be made, it would follow that the Buddha is no different from the ignorant and suffering people to whom he addressed himself. And such a conclusion about the Enlightened One is not acceptable to any Buddhist.

SELF ANALYZED IN TERMS OF ELEMENTS

The earliest systematic reflections about the *dharma*, or teachings of the Buddha, are contained in the third portion of the orthodox collection (Pali canon) of Buddhist works known as the "*Abhidharma* basket." The main concern of the Abhidharma writers was not with the question of whether or not there were substances, or selves. They assumed that existence was not of the nature of substance, but rather consisted in the continuous flow of elements, called by the Abhidharmists, *dharmas*. The problem for the Abhidharmists was one of classifying these *dharmas* and of establishing their interrelations.

The basic Abhidharmist teaching on the nature of the self holds that at the core of individual existence, instead of a permanent and unchanging substance, or soul, there is a stream of continuously flowing discrete elements of sensation, consciousness, feeling, activity impulses, and bodily processes. These continuously moving elements give rise to the appearance of an enduring self. But this appearance is to be disregarded, for the individual is never anything more than these various elements in motion. Over and above these elements, which even though conditioned and transitory are regarded by the Abhidharmists as ultimately real, there is the element of *Nirvana*, which is held to be unconditioned and non-transitory. *Nirvana* is universally regarded as beyond description and definition, but when, from time to time, philosophers have felt constrained to say something about it, they have called it the indefinable essence of the various conditioned elements in a quiescent condition. The reasoning behind this is readily understandable even if the characterization is unintelligible; the teaching of the Buddha provides for the "quieting" of the elements of existence, and since it is impossible to regard total extinction as any kind of salvation, the philosophers postulated that salvation, or *Nirvana*, must consist in the quiescence of the conditioned elements.

There are numerous lists of the basic elements given in the Abhidharma literature showing the interrelations between them. The lists occasionally disagree with each other, and frequently overlap, but the lists all indicate that the fundamental elements, or *dharmas*, are of the nature of elemental forces rather than elemental substances. Using an analogy, it could be said that the *dharmas* are likened to elemental energy charges rather than to minute bits of solid matter; though devoid of spatial and temporal characteristics themselves, by their motions and combinations they give rise to the compounded elements or processes which can be located spatially and temporally. The individual is simply a combination of these impersonal forces in motion.

Concerning what the self is, the Abhidharma question is, How are the fundamental *dharmas* constituting the individual to be classified? Five groups, or *skandhas*, are taken as basic categories of the empirical self. These categories are then analyzed into constituent components, or *dharmas*. In this way lists such as the following are derived: (1) the group comprising the bodily processes (*rupa*) are constituted by the *dharmas* of eye, ear, nose, tongue, and skin, and the corresponding *dharmas* of color, sound, odor, flavor, and resistance; (2) the group comprising the processes involved in feeling (*vedana*) and, (3) the processes constituting perception, are left undivided at this point, but (4) the processes constituting the conscious and unconscious impulses to action (*sankharas*) are divided in such a way as to reveal the *dharmas* constituting perception and feeling as well. This division is as follows: (A) *constituents of mental activity present in consciousness*: feeling, perception, will, immediate sensation, desire, understanding, memory, attention, inclination, and concentration; (B) *constituents of virtue*: faith, courage, equanimity, modesty, disgust at objectionable things, non-greed, non-hatred, compassion, and mindfulness; (C) *constituents of vice*: dullness, doubt, sloth, carelessness, immodesty, anger, hypocrisy, envy, jealousy, deceit, trickery, hatred, and pride. (5) The group consisting of the activities of consciousness is divided into the elements, or *dharmas*, responsible for the three categories of consciousness: pure, impure, and indeterminate (capable of being either pure or impure). Altogether, these three categories of consciousness include eighty-nine elements, or *dharmas*, when they are associated with the various processes constituting the *sankharas*.

However, the division of the five groups of processes constituting the individual into these *dharmas* is not the end of the story, for all of these *dharmas* are conditioned, or made—that is, they are not independent; they have no existence in their own right, and are dependent for their being upon something else. So the question can be asked, Of what are these *dharmas* made? When this question is taken seriously, the *dharmas* themselves come to be divided into an indefinite (and potentially un-limited) number of components, or moments, which are regarded as the ultimate *dharmas* of existence. Each of these ultimate *dharmas* is by itself without characteristics of mass or duration, but all together they are responsible for the characteristics of things in the world.

What this analysis of the self accomplishes is to make human exist-ence a purely impersonal thing. Nowhere is there found a trace of ego, or self. Only impersonal elements are found, in constant con-junction and process, giving rise to the appearance of an enduring self. While this Abhidharma doctrine is in conformity with the Buddha's teaching that nowhere is there a self to be found, that all *dharmas* are without self,[7] and that enlightenment requires giving up all attachment to an ego,[8] it offered little assistance in understanding the continuity of the individual. Nor did it provide for an explanation of how the effects of actions of one person could possibly affect that person at a later time; but unless this were possible, the teaching that individual persons could overcome suffering would be wholly irrelevant. Now, it is true that a nominal explanation had been provided for these points in that it was held that the grouping of elements provided individual continuities. These individual continuities served the purpose of ex-plaining the enduring characteristic of the person by providing for endurance without permanence; they also provided for the distinction of one continuity from another. The difficulty with this view of personal continuities, however, is that there is no reason why the processes should

[7] *Dhammapada*, XX. 7, trans. by Acharya Buddharakkhita Thera (Bangalore, India: Buddha Vaccna Trust, 1966).
[8] *Majjhima Nikaya, Sutta 72, op. cit.*

form such continuities. Unless the *dharmas* contain something other than discrete impersonal forces, it is not necessary that these forces should combine into these personal continuities.

THE PERSONALIST VIEW

These difficulties with the Abhidharma interpretation of the *anatta* doctrine led Buddhists in the Vatsiputriya, Sammitiya, Dharmottariya, Bhadrayaniya, and Chanaganka schools to claim that in addition to the impersonal *dharmas* there was a person (*pudgala*) to be found. These Buddhists, known as Personalists (*Pudgalavadins*), sought an explanation of the *anatta* teaching of the Buddha that would square with the common belief in a self, and at the same time not violate the basic teachings concerning the alleviation of suffering.

The "person" claimed by the Personalists was recognized as something real in its own right that an enlightened person experiences. It is this "person" that accounts for individuation of processes so that individual persons and things can be distinguished from each other. It also makes possible the continuity within one distinct and continuous process, so that the effects of one person's activities accrue to that person and not to another. It is the "person" that provides the element of connection between the ignorant and the enlightened individual. This "person" is the agent of activities, and is responsible for coordinating the activities of the various mental processes involved in knowing and acting.

Even though the addition of the "person" to the impersonal realities catalogued by the Abhidarmists made it possible to stick to familiar and commonsense ways of talking about self and experience, the Personalists could not achieve a satisfactory theory unless they could show how this "person" was related to the impersonal elements, and also that their view was in conformity with the Buddha's no-self teaching. The difficulty involved in establishing both of these points proved insurmountable for the Personalists. To avoid a wrong belief in self, they could not identify the "person" with the groups themselves. Nor could they claim that the "person" was either inside or outside of the groups. If the "person" were to be identified with the groups nothing would be gained, for the "person" would appear and disappear when the groups arise and disappear. If it is distinguished from the groups, the "person" must be attached in some way to them. But this clearly violates the teaching of non-attachment, which all Buddhists accept.

What remains as a possibility for relationship between the groups and the "person"? According to the Personalists, the relation is one of *correlation*, which they contend cannot be further explained in terms of other relations. The difficulty with this claim is that only one of the correlatives is known, for by their own admission, the "person" is undefinable in every respect. But if one of two elements held to be correlated with each other is completely unknown, there is no basis for establishing either that there is a correlation, or what the correlation is, if it exists. Trying to avoid the difficulty, the Personalists resort to an example: the "person" is like the fire that is correlated with the fuel and the flame; though they are always found together, fire has a reality of itself, evident in its nature as heat; fire is not the same thing as fuel or a series of flames.

The difficulty with examples in general is that while they may illustrate a point, they do not prove the point. The difficulty with this particular example is that it is unclear in itself and consequently does not even serve to illustrate a point. As a result the Personalist theory, which comes closest of all Buddhist theories of the self to the ordinary commonsense point of view, is really nothing more than a rather dogged insistence that since we ordinarily talk and act as though there were a "person" in addition to the groups of processes constituting the individual, that "person" must exist, even though it is not possible to say what it is or how it is related to the processes.

SELF AS "SUCHNESS"

Dissatisfaction with the Personalist theory of the self led the Mahayana philosophers to seek other ways of solving the problems of personal continuity and enlightenment without invoking a theory of substances. For Ashvaghosa, the "person," or *pudgala*, of the Personalists came to be replaced by *tathata*, or suchness. For the Madhyamika philosophers it was *shunyata*, or emptiness, that took over the role of *pudgala*. It is important to note here that *suchness* and *emptiness* were not postulated as theories to explain the empirical continuity of an individual. As the Mahayana philosophers saw it, the problem had its roots in the attempt to understand the connection between the empirical individual and the enlightened one, between the ignorant self and the one who had attained *Nirvana* by achieving *Buddhi*. No problem arose in connection with empirical identity and continuity because it was universally accepted that what was empirical was compounded; was unreal; was transitory; was of the nature of *dukkha* (suffering); and was to be eradi-cated, not explained. But if those persons to whom the Buddha preached were to become enlightened, it must be the case that somehow, some-where, within the empirical world there must be that which is not of the nature of the compounded and is not inseparable from suffering. It would be this—whatever it is—that would constitute the nature of the enlightened person. The problem presenting itself here is not that of determining the essence of the ignorant empirical self, but that of understanding the essence of the enlightened self—the Buddha-nature itself. The almost impossible difficulty of this problem is compounded by the fact that it is the ignorant self who is trying to understand the enlightened self.

No doubt it was appreciation of the magnitude of the problem created by the ignorant self trying to understand the enlightened self that led the Personalities to say that the "person" is completely undefinable. But as the Mahayana philosophers point out, if this "person" is com-pletely undefinable it ought not to be called a *person*, for a person is something determinate and (at least roughly) describable. If the nature of the enlightened self is beyond the empirical and conceptual it cannot be named by the word "person" or anything else. In recognition of this, Ashvaghosa refers to it as *tathata*—"such as it is." In other words, the enlightened self is just what it is, and since nothing can be said of it as it is in itself, rather than trying to make it something determinate, it is better just to refer to it by using the non-name "suchness."

The Madhyamika philosophers also objected to attaching the name "person," or *pudgala*, to the enlightened self. The non-name they used for the enlightened self was *shunyata*, or emptiness. The clue to what the Madhyamikas were getting at is made obvious by the question that naturally follows a claim that something is empty, i.e., "Empty of what?" What the Madhyamika philosophers were claiming was that the *pud-gala postulated by the Personalists* was empty of reality. The argument behind this claim was supported by the position that whatever is de-termined perceptually and conceptually is of the nature of mind and not of reality. Perceptual and conceptual claims are based upon a cutting up of reality, and thus do not represent reality as it is. Hence these claims are empty of reality. The Personalist claim that there is a *pudgala* over and above the groups of processes is just an empty claim if it is about anything definite. On the other hand, if the *pudgala* claim is not regarded as a claim about anything definite, it is really not a claim about a reality. At best it could be regarded as a claim that since the theory of the groups is based on a cutting up of reality, this theory necessarily fails to establish the existence of the real self. This view would come close to the Madhyamika position, but there is no evidence that the Pudgalavadins ever advanced such a view.

The Madhyamika philosopher's own view about the nature of the enlightened self is really a non-view. Not claiming any views as his own, avoiding clinging to one theory as true and another as false, he understands that any theory of the self will be one-sided and incomplete. The achievement of enlightenment will directly reveal the peace and bliss of *Nirvana*. Thus, though he has theories about other theories, the Madhyamika has no theories about the enlightened self. In this area he remains a philosophical agnostic.

SELF AS CONSCIOUSNESS

The Yogacarins replace the Personalist's theory of a *pudgala* with the theory of *alaya-vijnana*, or "seed-consciousness." Their claim is that there is an extremely subtle and pervasive consciousness underlying ordinary consciousness, out of which ordinary consciousness evolves and into which it returns. This seed-consciousness provides the continuity between the activities of consciousness required to give continuity to the individual's mental activity. It also provides an answer to the question of the connection between treading the Path and being saved, for the essence of the self is contained in this seed-consciousness, and when everything impure and evil has been removed from this basic consciousness all *dukkha* is automatically eliminated and *Nirvana* is achieved.

That there must be a seed-consciousness can be seen by considering the nature of conscious activity, the Yogacarins argue. Building on the Abhidharma analysis, consciousness, or conscious activity, is reduced to a stream of moments, or points of consciousness. Sometimes this stream runs underground, and sometimes it surfaces, as when we are conscious of things and activities around us. Since consciousness could not come to the fore unless it were present in a latent, or seed form, it must be the case that there is a seed-consciousness. Into this seed-consciousness goes the residue of all past moments of consciousness, and from it comes the basis for the present consciousness.

This theory has the advantage of providing an explanation of *karma* (the retribution of effects of actions to the doer), rebirth (an individual is born and dies many many times), the distinction between one individual and another (different seeds), and the connection between treading the path and becoming enlightened (purification of the seed-consciousness).

The Yogacarins reject the Madhyamika criticism that all *dharmas*—including the *dharmas* of consciousness—are unreal because arrived at conceptually or perceptually by cutting up reality. Their argument is that if consciousness is taken as unreal, then the arguments whereby the Madhyamikas establish the unreality of all *dharmas* would also fall to the ground, since they are conceptual arguments, arising within consciousness. However, rejecting the unreality of all *dharmas* outside of consciousness, the Yogacarins are left without a basis for claiming the existence of other individuals, let alone distinguishing between them, since if the only reality admitted is that of my own consciousness, any other existence could be known only insofar as it existed within my own consciousness; whether there existed an objective counterpart to what was found in my consciousness would be forever unknown.

Aside from that difficulty, the Yogacarins are hard pressed to show that their theory of a seed-consciousness is correct. After all, there might be other theories that would also square with ordinary experience. It is one thing to suggest a probable theory of the self and another thing to show either that the theory is correct or that it is superior to every other theory. According to the seed-consciousness theory, ordinary consciousness arises out of, and exists in, a seed-consciousness. But out of what does the seed-consciousness arise? And in what does it exist? If something be postulated in response to these two questions, it appears that seed-consciousness is not the ultimate self, but simply an intermediary stage in the analysis. If, on the other hand, it is claimed that seed-consciousness is eternally existent and exists only in itself, it is difficult to see why the same thing could not be said about ordinary consciousness. A further and complicating difficulty is that it is only from the standpoint of ordinary consciousness that anything can be said about the seed-consciousness, and therefore claims about seed-consciousness itself are completely untestable.

The difficulties confronting these various theories of the self reveal some of the problems encountered in trying to provide a philosophically acceptable account of what a person is. It is clear that the Personalist and the Yogacarin views are both difficult to maintain without violating the principle of dependent origination. In addition, they face the various philosophical problems pointed out above. On the other hand, the views of Ashvaghosa and the Madhyamika philosophers, which provide the chief basis for the practices constituting the Mahayana Buddhist way of life, do not provide a definitive theory of the self. The Madhyamika philosophers, being complete relativists, appear to be most closely in accord with the principle of dependent origination. But this very fact prevents them from having any ultimate theory of their own, for they have no ultimates upon which to base such a theory. Even their claim that all views are relative is itself a relative claim.

It would appear that only the Madhyamikas interpreted the principle of dependent origination as applying to all conceivable existence. The realistic philosophers of the Abhidharma took the ultimate moments of existence as fundamental, or absolute, relating all other existence to these fundamental elements. The idealistic philosophers of the Yogacara school regarded the seed-consciousness as fundamental and absolute, relating all other existence to this fundamental reality.

Because they allowed exceptions to the principle of dependent origination both the realistic and the idealistic philosophers had a basis upon which to erect their theories of the self. The Madhyamika philosophers, however, did not interpret the principle in such a way that certain kinds of existence were exceptions, allowing for them to become the absolutes in a philosophical system. The price they paid for refusing to make exceptions is that they were unable to establish any view of their own, for they had no basis for any view. This, however, seemed a relatively small price to pay, for as seen above, the Buddha also professed to have no views of the self.[9] In fact, for a practicing Buddhist, having no views might well represent considerable progress along the Way, for this eliminates the possibility of clinging to purely conceptual entities, and thus marks non-attachment to the ego of ignorance that underlies suffering.

9 See above, p. 132.

CHAPTER 12

THE NATURE OF REALITY

AN OUTLINE OF DIFFERENT VIEWS OF REALITY

JUST as Buddhist theories of the self took shape according to their interpretations of the principle of dependent origination, so also different theories of the nature of external reality were influenced by this principle. As a consequence of sharing the common principle of dependent origination, Buddhist theories of the world and self have certain features in common. (1) Neither selves nor external things are of the nature of substance. (2) Both are constituted by processes of elemental forces. (3) Permanence is not found in either things or selves. (4) Space and time are not determining characteristics of either things or selves, since space and time are relative to the processes (which are already relative to each other). Nevertheless, despite this core of doctrine common to the different schools, there are many differences among their views of the nature of the external world which result from different interpretations of the principle of dependent origination.

The main differences in the teachings concerning the nature of external things can be summarized in terms of the views of the schools of Vaibhashika, Sautrantika, Madhyamika, and Yogacara. The first of these schools, the Vaibhashika, is associated with early or Theravada, Buddhism. Its view of the world is that the elements (*dharmas*) constituting the empirical world are what make up ultimate reality. These elements are presented directly in experience as the basic content of the experience, and are held to exist as real just as presented in experience. Since it is held that there are a great number of these ultimate elements, the Vaibhashika metaphysics can be called pluralistic realism.

The Sautrantika school, though often associated with Theravada Buddhism, is really a transitional philosophy, bridging the gap between Theravada and Mahayana. At first glance it appears that the Sautrantika view of the world is quite similar to the Vaibhashika view, for both hold a view that is both pluralistic and realistic. There is an important difference, however, as the Sautrantikas reject the notion that the basic features of ordinary experience constitute the ultimate elements of things. The Sautrantika view is that the empirical is conditioned. Whatever is experienced depends for its existence not only upon the experiencer, but also upon other elements which are not directly experienced. After all, the principle of dependent origination maintains that there are no beings, but only comings-to-be. And these comings-to-be are interdependent; no one of them has an independent reality of its own. But if this is the case, then the fundamental elements of experienced reality must also lack independent reality. Consequently, the Sautrantikas teach that the fundamental elements of reality are not known directly, but lie beyond the contents of experience, giving rise to the contents of experience and being represented by them.

The Madhyamikas give up pluralistic realism completely. Agreeing with the Sautrantikas that a correct interpretation of the principle of dependent origination does not allow the directly experienced "reals" claimed by the Vaibhashikas, they went further and claimed that the fundamental elements, or *dharmas*, claimed by the Sautrantikas were as good as no elements at all. Their argument is that by removing the ultimate elements from the realm of the experiencable, the Sautrantikas had really relegated them to the realm of nothingness. Supposedly the ultimate elements of things claimed by the Sautrantikas were represented by the contents of ordinary experience. But since there was no finding out whether or not they were represented correctly or whether in fact they were represented at all, the claim that they existed was really an empty claim. Consequently, the Madhyamikas stressed the relativity of the components of things. Their reasoning is that if whatever is, is dependent upon something else, then it is not possible to postulate some existents (*dharmas*) which exist first and are independent of other existents. The quest for ultimate elements, real in themselves, was a misguided seeking of a mere chimera. It was the result of a failure to penetrate the principle of dependent origination, for it belied a clinging to the erroneous substance view. Stressing the interdependence of elements upon each other and their essential relativity, the Madhyamika philosophers became famous for their theory of *shunyata*. The word *shunyata* means "devoidness," and the theory of *shunyata* holds that all elements are devoid of ultimate reality. That is, there is no existence in and of itself; all existents are dependent upon each other, and have reality only relative to other dependent existents.

The Yogacarins agreed that pluralistic realism was incompatible with the theory of dependent origination, and that no absolute and ultimate elements of existence could be claimed to exist in the world. The Madhyamikas were, therefore, correct in pointing out the essential relativity and interdependence that characterized all external reality. But the Yogacarins felt they went too far in characterizing *all existence* as relative and therefore unreal (i.e. possessing no independent reality), for if this claim were correct, it would follow that the existence of consciousness would also be relative and unreal, and if this were the case the results of consciousness would also be relative and unreal. Since the Madhyamikas arguments were the results of conscious activity they would be relative and unreal, and there would be no way to maintain their position. Consequently, the Yogacarins insisted that consciousness must be allowed to exist in its own right; it alone is independently real, and everything else has reality only relative to consciousness.

Here the Yogacarins had come full circle from the Vaibhashika point of view. The Vaibhashikas postulated the basic elements of external reality as absolute, with everything else having reality only relative to those fundamental *dharmas*. The Yogacarins regarded those elements as relative to consciousness, giving consciousness itself the position of the fundamental and absolute reality in the system. This view—that whatever exists, exists only relative to consciousness—is known as idealism. The basic difference between realism and idealism is that realism takes the reality of external things to be ultimate, and everything else, including consciousness, is relative to external reality. Idealism takes consciousness to be ultimate; everything else, including external things, is real only relative to consciousness. The Madhyamika view— that everything is devoid of reality—differs from both realism and idealism in that it does not regard either consciousness or external reality as ultimate. It is, therefore, a complete relativism, without an absolute. Consciousness and external reality are on the same ontological footing—both are real only in relation to each other. The dictum of this school is that whatever is, is relative.

PLURALISTIC REALISM

According to the interpretation of dependent origination underlying Theravada Buddhism, the processes constituting reality are comprised of an unlimited number of discrete and evanescent elements, or forces, in continuous motion. These elements, or *dharmas*, are the ultimate forces in the universe and are responsible for whatever exists. They exist independently in their own natures and everything else originates in dependence upon these ultimate elements. Though of extremely short duration, they are held to be ultimately real, for they have effects. The effects are the sticks and stones, tables and chairs, etc., that constitute the ordinary world of experience.

The relation between the fundamental *dharmas* and the world of ordinary experience is comparable to the relation between the modern scientific theory of the atomistic components of things and common sense perception. The common-sense view is that tables and chairs are stable and enduring things, as solid as you like. But the scientist informs us that what is called a table and thought to be a solid and permanent thing is really a collection of various forces and elements in constant motion. This is quite similar to the Buddhist view of *dharmas* as the ultimate constituents of things, for they too hold that the things of common sense turn out to be no more than collections of much more elementary forces in constant motion. For the Buddhist, as for the scientist, this way of looking at things does not mean the repudiation of the common sense world, nor the denial of any of its objects. The real world is out there, just as real as anybody thinks it to be. But its reality is constituted in a way different than usually imagined. It is, in fact, constituted by the combinations of discrete, evanescent elemental forces in constant motion.

In arriving at their metaphysical views the Vaibhashikas and Sautrantikas claimed the reality of the world of ordinary experience, but rejected the imposition of an abstract theory of substance on this reality. Experience is not denied. Whatever is experienced is real, otherwise it could not be experienced. However, a distinction must be made between the reality of the experienced world and the truth of a theory about that world. What common sense frequently does is to add to experience an interpretative framework. The data of experience are then clothed with the fabric of the theory, and the data of experience themselves are overlooked. The substance view of reality is a prime example of this sort of thing. Experience in and of itself never carries with it data of the identity and permanence of things. Identity and permanence, which are essential to a substance view of reality, are imposed on the data of experience as an interpretative framework. It is this framework that the Buddhist wishes to reject, for it is not given in the experience itself. The doctrine of *anicca*, or impermanence, is essentially a denial of the substance view of reality. But to deny the reality of substances in the world is not to deny the reality of the world. It is only a denial of the reality of the world *as substance*, and it leaves every other alternative open. Substituting process for substance, the Buddhist affirms the world that consists of process as real and denies only the world of substance.

The whole question of what process is, and how processes make up the world of everyday experience, is another matter. But it is clear that the reality of process is not denied. And it is because the reality of process is affirmed that the Vaibhashikas and Sautrantikas earn the name "realist." Furthermore, they are *pluralistic* realists because they hold that the processes constituting reality are made up of a great many discrete and interacting elements.

EXISTENCE

The main features of the metaphysics of the Vaibhashikas and Sautrantikas are determined by their rejection of the substance view of reality— a view that was held by many of the Hindu philosophers, especially those belonging to the Nyaya and Vaisheshika Schools. The substance view in metaphysics emphasizes the reality of being over becoming. Unchanging being is taken as fundamental, and change and becoming must be explained in relation to this reality in the best way possible. If it turns out that no theory of change can be found which is compatible with permanence and being, then change must be denied, as even more ancient thinkers of India (and Paramenides of Greece) had argued.

In order to see what metaphysics the Vaibhashikas and Sautrantikas were rejecting, it is necessary to examine the assumption inherent in the substance view. To assume a substance view of reality is to accept (1) permanence, (2) universality, (3) identity, and (4) unity as the basic characteristics of whatever really exists.

(1) Emphasizing permanence consists in stressing the stability and duration of things in the universe. In this view the unchanging rather than the changing features of reality are taken as basic. Changelessness

becomes the criterion of the real. The acceptance of permanence as a basic characteristic of existence is often accompanied by accepting the characteristic of identity.

(2) Identity refers to the sameness of things despite apparent changes in them. For example, stressing identity, one would say that though a puppy grows and becomes old, and though in the process every cell is replaced, nevertheless, it is still the same individual animal. Despite the various changes, the old dog is the same animal identical with the little puppy, except for age. The acceptance of identity is often accompanied by accepting universality.

(3) To regard existence as essentially characterized by universality is to view the differences in existing things as less basic than their similarities. For example, emphasizing similarities, various animals are lumped together into the category *dog* on the assumption that there is something important about each of them which is the same in all of them despite the differences between say, a poodle and a St. Bernard. This sameness is the essence of "dogness," and is taken to be the same for all times, in all animals, within a certain range. This essence is a universal, basically independent of space and time. Accepting universality as a basic characteristic of existence, it becomes possible to say that even though there are many different dogs, and even though the species is evolving, *what it is to be a dog* does not change. This "what it is to be a dog" is the universal found in all dogs at all times.

(4) The division of existence into distinct things which have a universal nature, which are permanent, and which are identical with themselves over a period of time, is usually accompanied also by accepting the unity of distinct things. For example, one particular thing, say, a dog, is made up of many parts. But though it is made up of many parts, it is still one thing. The assumption of many parts, or aspects, under the heading "one thing" is what is meant by the unity of a thing. Though flesh is not bone, and blood is yet a third thing, and all three of these are different from habits or appetites, and though a dog consists of all of these different things (along with many others), it is commonly assumed that they are all so related to each other that they form one thing, this dog. Sometimes this doctrine of identity is coupled with the doctrines of universality and identity, and it is held that the reason why the different parts of an organism are related in such a way that they form one thing is that they all belong to the same underlying thing, namely, the substratum of the dog. On this view the unity, identity,

and universality of things is attributed to an unperceived substratum in which the perceivable characteristics of things are thought to inhere.

Having in mind some of the main features of a substance view of existence, it is now possible to discuss the metaphysical views of the Vaibhashikas and Sautrantikas, who were, above all else, concerned to deny the substance view. Their main views are just the opposite of the permanence, unity, identity, and universality. The opposite of permanence is momentariness. The opposite of unity is conglomeration. The opposite of universality is particularity. And the opposite of identity is discreteness. In the Buddhist view, all existence is regarded as momentary, being made up of discrete particulars in various conglomerations. This view of existence is common to both Vaibhashikas and Sautrantikas. They also share the following views: (1) The discrete particulars which make up existence are "point instants" of force, or energy. (2) These "point instants" are in constant flux. (3) Arising and ceasing are inherent in existence. (4) The criterion for being real is the ability to have effects: only that can be admitted to be real which produces effects; that which does not produce effects could never be known to be real, for realities are known by their effects. (5) And of course, both of these schools accept the universal Buddhist doctrine that the order and regulation of the elements of existence is according to the principle of dependent origination (*paticca samuppada*), which is the law of arising and ceasing of elements of existence.

Before going into the arguments used to support the metaphysical views of these two schools, certain differences in their views need to be pointed out. The first difference concerns the duration of existence. The Vaibhashikas hold that the production of the succeeding moment in the sequence of becoming that constitutes reality would be impossible unless each moment existed in the past and the future as well as in the present. Unless it existed in the past it could not be affected by the moment of existence that preceded it most recently in the past. That it exists in the present is obvious. But it must also exist in the future in order to influence the next moment of existence which has not yet arisen. A considerably oversimplified picture of existence in this view would reveal each moment of existence having a small portion of its existence in the past and another small portion in the future, with the bulk of its existence in the present.

The Sautrantikas reject the view that the past and future constitute part of reality. They admit only the present as real on the grounds that

(1) *ultimate* moments of existence could not be further divided into past, future, and present moments if they were really ultimate, and (2) the past, by very definition, has passed on and no longer exists. And the future is not yet here; how then, could past and future be regarded as real?

The second difference concerns the nature of the ultimate elements, or moments, of existence. According to the Vaibhashikas these elements were the basic elements of the experienced datum. The most elementary features of the experienced datum constitute the ultimate moments of its existence. It does not appear that the Vaibhashikas distinguished between the features of the datum ("object") as it is in itself and the features of the datum as experienced. The Sautrantikas regarded the ultimate *dharmas*, or elements, as themselves not experiencable. They are outside the realm of time and space, for as constituting the basic components of existence they were the very conditions of space and time, and thus could not themselves be located in space and time. Thus, on the basis of distinguishing between the datum as perceived and the datum independent of perception, the Sautrantikas viewed the ultimate *dharmas* as the unexperienced and indescribable constituents of the perceived.

The third difference between Vaibhashikas and Sautrantikas concerns ways of knowing. The Vaibhashika is a direct realist, holding that what is, is perceived directly as it really is. Between what exists and what is perceived to exist, there is no difference. Perception conforms exactly to what is to be perceived. The Sautrantika is an indirect or representationalist realist, holding that we do not *directly* perceive things as they are in themselves, but that we perceive them only indirectly by means of certain representations. The data of experience, which are distinguished from the data experienced, are regarded as a means whereby the knower is acquainted with existence. A rough analogy can be made to a photograph. The photo is not reality itself, but it represents reality to us. If the photo is good, the datum photographed is not distorted and is presented as it really is. But nevertheless, the photo is not the reality; it is only a means for representing reality. Similarly, for the Sautrantika, the sensations and percepts of experience are only means for representing reality. Even though these are held to be adequate, in that ordinarily they do not distort reality, still reality is presented only indirectly through these means.

Turning now to the arguments used by the Vaibhashikas and Sautrantikas to support their metaphysics of flux and momentariness, we find that the overall argument is disjunctive in structure.[1] The basic assumption is that either the substance view of reality is correct, or else the opposite of that view—the flux view—is correct. Consequently, the major effort is directed toward showing the substance view to be untenable.

The arguments used to demolish the substance view of reality are arguments against (1) permanence, (2) identity, (3) unity, and (4) universals.

1. The arguments against permanence assume that the reality of something can be tested by determining whether or not it is a force capable of producing changes. Only that may be admitted to be real which can be known to have effects. The metaphysical support for this assumption is that the quest for ultimate reality is a quest for the causes of the experienced world. But since causes are causes only to the extent that they produce effects, it is not possible to have real causes that do not produce effects. Epistemologically, this assumption is supported by the fact that knowledge represents a change in the knower, and that nothing could be known which was not capable of producing a change in the knower. Therefore, it would be impossible to have knowledge of a reality which did not produce changes or have effects.

Assuming that action is the test of the real (for no changes can be caused except by bringing about a change), it remains to show that the permanent is not active. This can be done by showing that both terms of the following disjunction are false: either the action of causation is instantaneous and complete, or else it is temporally extended. The action of causation cannot be instantaneous and complete, for then all the effects would be produced at once and reality would, except for that moment, be static. Furthermore, if the action were instantaneous and complete, the question would arise as to whether or not the permanent exists after the first moment of change—if it does, then it should give rise to the same effects as it did in the first moment, and the same for each succeeding moment. But this is absurd, for it results in an infinity of complete universes. If the permanent continues to exist after the first moment of causation but not as a cause, then apparently it changed from a cause to a non-cause. But the changing is not permanent. Also, that would make the permanent two opposing things at the same time for it would have to be both cause and non-cause. Since it is not

---

[1] The following arguments are formulated historically by the Sautrantikas, but they are essentially the same as the arguments used by the Vaibhashikas. For fuller treatment of these arguments the reader might consult Th. Stcherbatsky, *Buddhist Logic* (Leningrad: Academy of Sciences of the USSR, 1932), Vol. 1, pp. 79 ff.

possible for a self-contradictory thing to exist, such a reality is not possible.

The alternative to instantaneous and complete causal action is temporally extended causal action. This view is untenable also, for if it were the case that the permanent cause produced first x, then y, and then z, etc., it could be asked whether or not y or z could have been produced while x was being produced. If the answer is affirmative, it would turn out that all the effects were producible at once, and this alternative would be indistinguishable from the first. But if the first cause could not produce effects y, z, etc. at any given time, say when x was being produced, it would be impossible for it to cause them at any later time, for what is not capable of producing a given effect at a given time cannot produce that effect at any other time, except by assuming other causal activty. For example, a barren woman cannot produce a son at this time. And for the same reason she cannot do so, she also cannot produce a son at any other time. An objection might be made to the Sautrantika argument on the grounds that while time itself does not produce a capability in the cause, nevertheless, time may allow for certain modifications to take place so that causation is possible. For example, sometimes a seed does not cause a plant, but sometimes it does. The reason is that time allows certain modifications in the conditions which enable the seed to cause a plant at one time, though not at another. But this objection begs the whole question of causation. If it is admitted that time itself does not cause things, then it cannot be admitted that time brings about modifications, for modifications are nothing other than changes or effects. Thus some other causality is required, and the same questions arise concerning the possibilities of this causation. Even if it is admitted that certain modifications in the cause are required, the Buddhist argument is successful, for this is an admission that the cause has changed. But if the cause has changed, then there are really two things; the cause prior to change and the cause after change. To admit that the substance changes as it produces effects is to deny permanence and to admit different existences at different moments. And this is in accord with the doctrine of momentariness which the Buddhists wish to support.

2. The arguments against identity proceed by trying to show that the identity of things is illusory. Advocates of a substance view of reality maintain that a thing remains identical with itself over a period of time by assuming that a thing naturally continues to exist unless destroyed or altered by outside and violent forces. But this assumption is false, for unless a thing were naturally subject to change and cessation,

nothing could bring about change and cessation with respect to that thing. For example, when forces such as a blow from a stick act upon a jar, the jar is destroyed. But one cannot say that the nature of a jar is to exist identical with itself without change unless acted upon by an outside force. After all, unless arising and ceasing belonged the the jar as part of its nature, nothing could cause or destroy a jar. If destruction was not inherent in the jar blows from sticks would mean nothing; the jar would continue to exist. But the nature of a jar is such that blows from sticks provide the occasion for its cessation. If it were not the blow from the stick then it would be some other occasion that would accompany the destruction of the jar, for the nature of a jar is not such that it can exist identical with itself forever.

The illusory quality of identity is quite clear in the case of the aging of a dog. It clearly is not the case that a dog goes along unchanging for several years, and then, at some precise time, begins to age. The process of aging begins when the puppy is conceived, and by the time it is born it has already aged considerably. Aging is simply change, which is a combination of cessation and arising of elements. The illusion of identity is based on certain arbitrary perspectives. When we fix on certain elements and notice their cessation we lament over the old age, decay, and death inherent in things. When we fix not on that ceasing of elements, but on the arising of elements, we rejoice over birth, life, and youth. But in reality, arising is always accompanied by ceasing, and ceasing is always accompanied by arising. Birth and death are parts of the same process, and it is simply the assumption of a certain attitude toward a part of the process that leads to revulsion and despair on the one hand, and to exultation and rejoicing on the other. The truth is that there is no identity. There is only the continuous arising and ceasing of elements.

3. The argument against unity is based on the impossibility of knowledge of a *whole*. According to the substance view, an object such as a table, though consisting of many parts, is held to be one whole. The Sautrantika argument against this view proceeds by showing that it is not possible to know the whole. For example, it is not possible to see the whole table. Only a small part of the table is seen. And only a small part can be touched, etc. Ordinarily this is explained by saying that it is one part of the whole table that is seen, and that by moving around to various perspectives one can consecutively come to see the whole table. But this explanation will not do, for even at best, all that would be seen would be the various *surfaces* of the table. It would not be possible

to see beyond the surface of the table, even though the table is assumed to consist of more than mere surfaces. But even if more than surfaces could be seen, the explanation would not be satisfactory, for the different visual perceptions attained from different perspectives do not of themselves also carry with them the perception that they are of the same whole. It is entirely possible that each different perception is the perception of a different thing. There is nothing in the perception itself to guarantee that it belongs to the same object as other perceptions. This being so, there is no basis other than that of fanciful mental construction for claiming that there are wholes made up of different parts. All that can be claimed is the object of perception, and since there is no valid basis for connecting these perceptions together into wholes, the supposed "oneness" of things must be illusory. Just as a movie is really no more than consecutive still pictures, so reality is no more than succeeding elements. But just as the consecutive passage of the still pictures gives rise to the appearance of one continuous whole moving picture, so does the incessant rise and fall of elements give rise to the appearance of the unity of whole things. In reality, however, the moments of existence are no more than "point-instants" of force, rising and falling in dependence upon each other.

4. The argument against universals claims the unknowability of such entities. The identity of one thing with another, such as the sameness of two tables, in virtue of their being tables, depends upon the supposition of a universal—tableness. Aside from the metaphysical difficulty of explaining how one universal entity could exist in many different entities widely separated in space and time, and be totally unaffected by what happened to the entities in which it existed, there is the problem of explaining how the universal is known. Since even the supporters of the substance view admit that perception is of particulars, the only way they can explain the perception of universals is to assume a kind of double perception, first perceiving the particular, and then perceiving the universal as a sort of timeless, spaceless duplicate of the particular. But there is no evidence of this kind of duplication in perception. Consequently the Sautrantikas take the position that the universals attributed to reality are nothing more than logical constructions placed on a reality that is in every respect particular.

In addition to arguing for their position indirectly by arguing against the opposite view, the Sautrantikas support their position by arguing that certain problems which arise as a result of trying to interpret reality systematically are more easily solved by taking a flux view of reality. Without doubt, the basic problem for a metaphysician is that of change. If change is admitted it would seem that permanence would also have to be admitted, for a change is always a change of something to something else, as when a green leaf changes into a red leaf. And the something undergoing change—the leaf—does not change, but some of its characteristics appear (red) and disappear (green).

The claim that a permanent reality exists is a difficult position to defend, as seen by the preceding arguments. On the other hand, if change is denied, the whole metaphysics is out of tune with our basic and immediate experience.

In order to maintain that reality is in complete flux, undergoing only change without any vestiges of permanence, the Buddhists obviously cannot think of change as the alteration of a permanent something underlying the various perceivable characteristics of things. In fact, they cannot accept any ordinary notions of causality, for nothing endures long enough to produce an effect. What they substitute for causality is the law of dependent origination, according to which entities and elements *replace one another rather than cause one another*. The law of dependent origination is a law of connectedness between moments, but it is not a law of causal connectedness. If it were a law of causal connectedness one moment in a sequence would be the cause of the next, and it would be necessary to attribute duration to the moments, as some of the Vaibhashikas did. But to attribute duration to the moments is to postulate a kind of permanence.

By replacing the law of causal connectedness with the law of dependent origination, the Buddhists are in a position to explain the appearance of continuity and duration that characterize the common-sense view of reality without giving up the momentariness of existence. There is continuous change without permanence because change is the *replacement* of one moment of existence by another, and not the *causing* of one moment by another. The replacement of moments occurs with a rapidity that looks like continuity and endurance—it is this false appearance that underlies the mistaken claims about permanence and identity. The mental constructions placed on the content of perceptions give rise to apparent unity and universals.

As a result of these various arguments, the Vaibhashikas and Sautrantikas hold a metaphysical position according to which reality is quite different from what those supporting the substance view claim. The substantialists hold that reality has more permanence that it appears to have: the Buddhists hold that things do not have the unity that they appear to have. The substantialists hold that there is less change in individuals than appears: the Buddhists hold that there is more. The substantialists hold that there is a greater amount of sameness (universality) in reality than appears: the Buddhists hold that there is less than appears. Thus, the Vaibhashika and the Sautrantika theory of reality is summed up in the view that reality consists of a numberless quantity of spaceless and timeless forces constantly arising and falling in dependence upon each other.

KNOWLEDGE

Turning now to the theories of knowledge underlying the metaphysical views of the Vaibhashikas and the Sautrantikas, it is found that they hold different and opposed views. Though they agree that reality can be known as it is in itself, and therefore are classified as realists rather than idealists, they disagree about how reality is known.

Concerning knowledge of reality two main views are possible. According to the first, external objects are known as they exist in themselves; there is no difference between what exists and what is known to exist. According to the other view, all that is ever known is the content of consciousness, and there is no way of showing that the contents of consciousness do or do not correspond to what really exists. This latter view, known as idealism, is rejected by the Vaibhashikas and the Sautrantikas, for they claim it allows no way of distinguishing (1) consciousness itself from the contents of consciousness, or (2) valid from erroneous consciousness.

The view that in knowledge objects are revealed as they exist in themselves has two major variations. The first variety is characterized by the claim that external reality is directly perceived to exist. The second variety is characterized by the claim that external reality is not known directly, but is inferred to exist from perceptual evidence. The first of these two views is held by the Vaibhashikas, who are therefore called *direct* realists, and the second view is held by the Sautrantikas, who are therefore called *indirect* realists, or representationalists.

The Vaibhashikas support their direct realism against the Sautrantika view by arguing that representationalism is an incorrect theory. According to the representationalist view, the ultimate elements of things are never directly perceived, but are inferred to exist, as they are *represented* by the perceptual experience. It is rather as if a man who has never seen Mt. Everest, but has seen photographs of it, can infer the existence of the mountain from the existence of the photos—for if there were no mountain, photographs of it could not possibly exist. In a similar way, even though the blueness present in the visual perception of a blue object is not the same as the blueness in the object itself, nevertheless it is a kind of copy of it, and enables the viewer to infer that there is really an independent blueness existing objectively in reality.

The difficulty with this view is that if nothing is perceived directly there is never any basis for inference. It is one thing to see Mt. Everest and then to see a photo of it and consequently judge the photo to be a good or bad likeness of the mountain. But if one saw nothing but photos and never experienced a mountain in reality, it would be impossible for him to judge whether or not the photos resemble the mountains. In fact, there would be no basis for even conjecturing, let alone knowing, that anything existed other than the photos. If a person were completely unfamiliar with an external object it is not possible that any content of perceptual consciousness should appear as the sign, or the copy, or the representation of that object.

The foundation of the Vaibhashika argument is the claim that inferential knowledge is necessarily a secondary knowledge, for the essential feature of inference is that it proceeds from prior knowledge. Without the prior knowledge there would be no inference. But if all perceptual knowledge is essentially inferential, what would be the source of the required prior knowledge? Since obviously there is no knowledge prior to perceptual knowledge it cannot be the case that perceptual knowledge is inferential, and it must be admitted that at least some perceptual knowledge is direct.

One of the main reasons for the Sautrantika's rejection of direct realism is that they hold that it conflicts with the theory of momentariness. Since moments of existence are without duration it is not possible for objects to be present at the time they are perceived. By the time they are perceived these objects have given place to succeeding objects. What happens in perception, according to the Sautrantikas, is that in its instantaneous arising and ceasing, the moment of existence leaves its mark on the perceiving consciousness. This mark is converted, in consciousness, into perception of the object. But by the time this occurs the original object has ceased to be, and has been replaced by another. What happens in inference, consequently, is that from the mark left on the perceiving consciousness the prior existence of the object is inferred. This explanation may be likened to the way we see a star. Since the star is so very far away the light waves from the star may reach us only after the star itself has ceased to exist. Still, even though it was not perceived directly, but only indirectly, through the light it gave off, from the mark (light) left on the mind by the star we can correctly infer that the star did exist.

In addition, the Sautrantikas urged that the Vaibhashika view does not readily allow for perceptual error. If what is perceived is perceived directly as it is, how is error possible? According to the Sautrantika view, a representation may be mistakenly attached to an object and thus result in erroneous knowledge claims. But the Vaibhashika view does not allow such an explanation of error.

IDEALISM

According to the idealism of the Yogacara school, reality is of the nature of consciousness. The existence of an extra-conscious reality is denied and consciousness alone is maintained to be real. The basic appeal of this position derives from the difficulty of maintaining the existence of a reality outside of consciousness. Since, by definition, whatever is known is known within consciousness, it is not possible to have knowledge of an existing reality except in consciousness.

The chief obstacle in the way of accepting this view is the common tendency to suppose that consciousness is always consciousness *of* something, and unless there were objects outside of consciousness there would be nothing for consciousness to be consciousness of, and then there could be no consciousness. Since this latter view is held by the realists, the Yogacarins directed many of their arguments against the Vaibhashika and Sautrantika views of reality.

In the first place, the realist view that there are objects external to consciousness can at best be regarded as a speculative theory designed to answer questions concerning the arising of consciousness and changes in consciousness. It cannot be regarded as a *fact*, for there is no direct evidence for it. It is not possible for anyone to experience an object outside of consciousness, for to experience something means to experience it in consciousness. Consequently, all the purported evidence and proofs for the existence of extra-conscious objects must come from consciousness itself. But clearly, the existence of objects within consciousness cannot be regarded as proof that objects exist outside of consciousness.

There is no possible direct evidence for the existence of objects different from the objects of consciousness. The Yogacarins argue that this can be seen clearly by considering the example of color. Often a distinction is made between the awareness of the color blue, and the color blue itself. According to the Yogacarins, however, this distinction is without basis, for the color blue is never perceived except in awareness of something blue. And since they are never perceived independently or separately, there is no possibility of assuming that the awareness of the color blue and the color blue itself are anything other than identical with each other. But if they are identical, the distinction between them disappears. And when this happens, the basis for claiming an extra-conscious reality disappears.

A kind of intuitive objection to the conclusion of the foregoing argument maintains that there must be a difference between consciousness of an object and the object itself, because nearly everyone feels that there is a difference for ordinarily the two are distinguished. This objection is countered by the Yogacarins with the example of dreaming. Most people dream, and while they are dreaming they assume that the objects of which they are aware have objective existence outside of their dream. Now, just as the assumption within the dream that there are objects existing outside of dreams does nothing to establish the existence of such objects, just so the assumption of people in a state of ignorance that objects of consciousness have an objective existence outside of consciousness does nothing to establish the existence of such objects.

Since the realism of the Vaibhashikas and Sautrantikas is not simply a matter of obvious fact, but is a philosophical theory about the nature of the world and knowledge, the Yogacarins could attempt to defend their view of "consciousness only" by demonstrating that realism rests on an untenable basis. To this end arguments were brought forth to show the impossibility of objective existence.

If objects exist independently of consciousness they must either be simple wholes, without any parts, or else they must be wholes composed of parts. Objective existence in the sense of a simple whole is ruled out by the nature of knowledge claimed by the realist himself, according to which knowledge consists in the revelation of relations. Since there are no relations unless there are parts to be related, there could be no knowledge of simple wholes. And if it is said that it is the simple wholes that are related to each other the difficulty remains, for now all the wholes together are taken as comprising a new whole, in which the simple wholes inhere in their various relations. But this is equivalent to the atomistic view of reality, according to which objects are composed of atoms or parts. And the problem with this view is that the atoms or parts in themselves are unknowable, but are simply postulated to account for the objects of consciousness.

According to the Yogacarins, the chief difficulty with trying to prove the existence of extra-conscious objects is connected with the inseparability of the object from knowledge. There is never the least shred of evidence for the existence of an object except when the object is known. But since the object is known only in consciousness there cannot be any evidence for the existence of objects outside of consciousness.

The Yogacarins reject the argument that the very existence of consciousness constitutes a proof for the existence of independent objects, inasmuch as consciousness is constituted by the activity of relating objects to each other and to a subject. For example, it might be said that in consciousness of a chair the existence of a chair is assumed; otherwise there would be nothing to be related to the self, and there would be no consciousness. Consciousness is always consciousness of something and any proof that there is no "something" is, by the same argument, proof that there is no consciousness. And just as the attempt to prove the non-existence of consciousness by the exercise of consciousness is absurd, so also the attempt to disprove objects of consciousness is absurd.

According to the Yogacara analysis, though consciousness cannot be denied since it is self-revealing, this does not provide evidence for the existence of objects, for it is the nature of consciousness to be self-existent. That consciousness does not require an object is clear from the example of dreams, where the dream objects are by none admitted as having objective existence, but by all admitted to have existence in consciousness. If this is the case with some instances of consciousness, it proves that consciousness can exist without the assumption of extra-conscious objects. It does not, however, prove that *in fact* consciousness either does, or can, in all cases, exist without the assumption of extra-conscious objects. Granted the impossibility of proving that there are extra-conscious objects and granted the possibility of consciousness without extra-conscious objects, as evident from dreams, the Yogacarins maintain that it is more reasonable to hold that the various objects of consciousness are simply the creations and projections of consciousness. The purported difficulty of accounting for the variety of objects and modes of consciousness disappears upon recognition that consciousness is itself a dynamic unfolding of its own inherent tendencies.

Supported by the foregoing objections to realism, the Yogacara position maintains that consciousness alone is real. Ideas are real, objects are not. The distinctions that are usually made between subject and object, between things and ideas, between existence and knowledge —these are really only distinctions within consciousness, and never distinctions between what is within consciousness and what is outside of consciousness. Consequently, the central theme of this school is that whatever is experienced is mind-wrought.

This position, which is supported by the arguments against realism examined above, is based upon psychological experience. The arguments against realism are not definitive, for they are relative to those views, and not independently valid. But the direct realization of absolute consciousness as the sole reality stands as irrefutable justification of the Yogacara position. For those who have not achieved such a direct realization there is still the evidence of consciousness in trance. On the assumption that someone who has disciplined and developed his powers of meditation and has concerted all his energies to discover the ultimate reality comes closer to reality than one who is distracted and scatters his energies in countless ways, the fact that a multitude of varied forms and colors can be directly experienced in trance is convincing evidence that objects are really only manifestations of consciousness. For those without even the experience of trance there remains the faith in the reports of the enlightened who have experienced ultimate reality. For others, there are the various arguments against realism, and the various explanations of the nature of consciousness to lend plausibility to the "consciousness-only" view of reality.

In order to show that the realist views are unsatisfactory it is not enough simply to argue that the arguments for their positions are unconvincing, but it is also necessary to show how the plausibility of the realist view depends upon a wrong interpretation of experience. Basically, this is a matter of showing that the belief in external reality rests upon a misinterpretation of inner experience or consciousness. The misinterpretation rests upon a failure to recognize the nature and functions of consciousness.

The Yogacarins distinguish between various levels of consciousness, all of them dependent upon an absolute consciousness called *alaya-vijnana*, or "seed-consciousness." By reference to this seed-consciousness it is maintained that consciousness can exist independently, and that the various conscious activities arise from its own potentiality. Furthermore, this consciousness is entirely self-determining and self-revealing. It is this consciousness that creates the objects believed by the ignorant to exist outside of consciousness.

At one level of consciousness there is the awareness of the various objects of the senses, accounting for the six consciousnesses of eye, ear, nose, tongue, touch, and mind. But at another level there is consciousness of these six consciousnesses. This is a kind of self-consciousness which underlies the other consciousnesses and gives them unity. These two levels of consciousness are within the realm of the experiencable. The third level of consciousness is not experiencable except in ultimate enlightenment. It is the seed-consciousness, which is the ultimate reality underlying all the other levels and modes of consciousness. It is not to be confused with what is experienced in the various modes of consciousness, but is entirely undifferentiated. From this seed-consciousness originate the other activities of consciousness, and to this seed-consciousness return the effects of those other functions of consciousness.

The nature of this seed-consciousness cannot be stated literally, for it is beyond all differentiations and distinctions. As a result, the relations between this fundamental consciousness and ordinary experience are indicated only in similies. For example, in the *Lankavatara Sutra* the following illustration is given:

> Consciousness, consisting of the *skandhas* [five groups], *dhātus* [elements of being], and *āyatanas* [sense fields], which are without a self or of anything of the nature of a self, arises from ignorance, *karma*, and craving, and it functions through being attached to grasping at things by means of the eye and all the organs, and makes the presentations of its store-mind [seed-consciousness] appear as bodies and vessels, which are manifestations of its own mind [the store-consciousness].[2]

As to be expected, since all reality is regarded as mind only, or consciousness only, the ultimate reality is equated with the fundamental consciousness, or seed-consciousness. As ultimate reality it is beyond differentiation and plurality, so there is no question of its being either one or many.

What then is to be made of the many distinctions ordinarily made, and assumed by the Four Noble Truths and the Noble Eightfold Path? According to the Yogacarins, a distinction must be made between absolute reality and absolute truth, and between relative reality and relative truth. From the perspective of the unenlightened the relative reality constituting ordinary experience can be conceived of as a manifestation of the absolute reality, evolving out of the basic seed-consciousness. It is seed-consciousness itself which manifests itself as touch, mental activity, feeling, perception, and choice. And it is seed-consciousness

---

[2] E. J. Thomas, *The History of Buddhist Thought* (London: Routledge & Kegan Paul, 2nd ed. 1951), p. 234.

itself that manifests itself as an underlying self-consciousness, and thus makes possible the heresy of a self. But all this is only from the standpoint of the unenlightened.

In ignorance the activities proceeding from the seed-consciousness are differentiated from that consciousness and taken to exist in their own right. This gives rise to the error of externality of objects. In ignorance of the truth that both object-consciousness and self-consciousness are nothing other than manifestations of seed-consciousness, the self-consciousness distinguishes itself from object-consciousness and relates itself to object-consciousness as subject is related to object. This is manifested in the constant grasping for objects characterizing the lower levels of consciousness. The grasping, however, is without real basis, for as Vasubandhu points out:

> The various consciousnesses are but transformations. That which discriminates and that which is discriminated are, because of this, both unreal. For this reason, everything is mind only.[3]

What this absolute reality of seed-consciousness is in itself cannot be said, but must be experienced directly. As Vasubandhu says:

> To hold something before oneself, and to say that it is the reality of mind-only, is not the state of mind-only, because it is the result of grasping. But when [the objective world which is] the basis of conditioning as well as the wisdom [which does the conditioning] are both eliminated, the state of mind-only is realized, since the six-sense organs and their objects are no longer present.[4]

According to the Yogacarins, the teachings of the Buddha reflect his skillfulness in distinguishing between the levels of consciousness and the corresponding levels of reality, and adapting his teachings to the condition of the hearer. For example, the principle of dependent origination, which underlies the basic Buddhist teachings, is perfectly valid on the plane of relative reality, and it is used by the Yogacarins themselves to explain the arising and ceasing of the appearances of externality and a self out of the fundamental consciousness. But at the level of ultimate reality, the principle of dependent origination is not itself taken to be real independently of consciousness.

RELATIVISM

Whereas the Sautrantikas and Vaibhashikas took the existence of the elements of external objects as the absolute basis for their theory

[3] *Source Book in Indian Philosophy*, ed. by Radhakrishnan and Moore (Princeton: Princeton University Press, 1957), p. 336.
[4] *Ibid.*, p. 337.

of reality, and the Yogacarins took the existence of fundamental consciousness as the absolute basis for their theory of reality, the Madhyamika philosophers regarded both external reality and consciousness as only relatively real. Because the Madhyamika philosophy recognized nothing in the conceptual realm as ultimately or absolutely real, it came to be known as the philosophy of *shunyata*, or relativism.

No doubt, all of the schools of Buddhism represent the attitude that peace and wisdom are not to be found in subtle conceptual theories, but can be realized only by a direct participation in the processes of reality. The Buddha-nature is the ultimate reality, regardless of how conceived, and is the ultimate basis of each person. Consequently, only participation in that Buddha-nature will bring illumination and an end to suffering. In Madhyamika philosophy, however, this attitude comes to be underwritten by a critical analysis of conceptual construction. No philosophical view escapes the criticism of the Madhyamika, and no conceptual absolutes are tolerated. According to Nagarjuna, the principal philosopher of this school, mistaking conceptual absolutes for ultimate reality lies at the heart of man's suffering.

Nagarjuna's philosophical position appears to recognize that the most basic and exciting fact about man is his quest to be. This quest to be—the most fundamental of all quests—manifests itself in the activity of creating a world out of the fundamental elements of experience. Man sees around him only the "other." In his quest to be, he cannot tolerate the other, for the other is not-self; it represents the being that man seeks. To make that other—that not-self—part of one's self is the challenge. The most obvious effort to convert the other into self occurs in knowledge, where there is a uniting of the other with the self in the act of knowing. In knowledge one can make the other self, for knowledge is a unity of the self and other. The thirst for knowledge is simply one manifestation of the quest to be, for in attempting to satisfy that thirst one attempts to make the world his own, to make it part of his being. In his knowledge he creates a world which is part of his own being.

The problem with this procedure is that it is temptingly easy for man to mistake the world he has created in his knowledge, which is merely a world of names and forms, for reality itself. When he succumbs to the temptation he fixes on the name and form of self, that he has created in his knowledge, as his own self. He identifies his own being with this construction of name and form. Then the real self, burdened by the ignorance resulting from mistaking the self of name and form and the world of name and form for the real self and the real world, gets overlooked in the struggle that ensues between the false self of name and form and the false world of name and form. The resulting bifurcation, which underlies this inauthentic existence in this inauthentic world, is responsible for the disease—the *dukkha*—that Buddhism wishes to overcome.

Distinguishing between reality and views of reality, Nagarjuna apparently desired to show the dangers inherent in regarding any one view of reality as being absolutely true. Views are conceptual constructions of name and form, and to claim any view as absolutely true is to refuse to recognize the insights of other views, and thus to rule out possible avenues of illumination.

The positive conception of Nagarjuna seems to be that while theories and views are constructions of name and form, and therefore could not be equated with reality itself, conceptual constructions can point to reality. Therefore a dialectic of views could provide a basis for insights into reality itself, although surely direct participation in reality is a matter beyond all views. Nevertheless, views constitute an invaluable aid to realization, if they are regarded not as absolute and independent, but as relative and complementary.

Historically, it appears that one of Nagarjuna's primary aims was to remove the sources of strife and differences found among the many different schools of Buddhism. This he attempted to do by providing a sufficiently broad base for the teachings of Gautama. Surely, since each of the schools clung to its own interpretation of the teachings of Gautama, and since Gautama clearly taught the need for non-clinging, these schools must be making a mistake. To exhibit the mistake was the job Nagarjuna set for himself. The task consisted in assuming the views (conclusions and arguments) of each Buddhist school of philosophy and showing that ultimately they were self-contradictory. The lesson drawn from the self-defeating views of the various philosophies is that a person should not cling to any one theoretical view, mistaking that view for the complete truth about reality.

The dialectic, which assumed the various conclusions and standpoints of the different philosophical systems and rigorously applied to them the canons of logic and reasoning that were accepted by their supporters, was itself not part of a philosophical system. It did not constitute or rest upon a view of reality. Rather, it was a method. Even as method it had nothing of its own to offer, for the critical analyses constituting the Madhyamika dialectic assume the principles and methods used by the supporters of the various systems. Concept after concept was taken up and shown to contain within it the seeds of its own contradiction; every system examined was shown to be inconsistent within itself. But the dialectic rested on the assumptions of the various systems and not upon assumptions accepted as true by the Madhyamikas. Every system-builder must erect his views on certain assumptions which are not, at least in his own system, questioned. The Madhyamikas, however, refused to accept any assumptions as undeniably true.

The critical aspect of Madhyamika thought, however, respresents only one side of its development within Buddhism. On the other side is found the customary Buddhist emphasis on meditation and direct realization. It is through the meditative practices that one can go beyond the emptiness of concepts and systems to the fullness of reality as it is in itself. Reasoning is a conceptual matter and always rests upon assumptions. Even though for his own methodological approach the Madhyamika philosopher does not regard the assumptions of his arguments as true, but only as accepted by his opponents, all the arguments can possibly do is to reveal something about the system in which the assumptions are located. They can never reveal the truth of things as they are in themselves, independent of conceptualization. Consequently, even the dialectic of the Madhyamika is not to be accepted as in itself valid for uncovering the nature of reality, and it too must be abandoned at some stage in favor of direct insight and realization.

Thus, even though it is Nagarjuna's view that clinging is the cause of conflict and suffering, and even though his dialectic is aimed at showing the futility of clinging to various conceptions of reality because of the complete relativity of all conceptual systems, still, in consistency with this relativity, he does not cling to relativity either. That is, it is considered just as perverse to regard relativity as the truth about reality as it is to consider any other view as the truth about reality. In fact, Nagarjuna says, "but if people then begin to cling to this very concept of Relativity, they must be called irreclaimable."[5]

Candrakirti, who wrote an extremely subtle commentary upon Nagarjuna's aphorisms, provides a quite unflattering comparison for those who insist on regarding relativity as itself absolute, and thus cling to non-clinging. "It is," he says, "as if somebody said, 'I have nothing to sell you,' and would receive the answer, 'All right, just sell me this—your absence of goods for sale!'"[6]

[5] Madhyamika Karika, XIII, 8, in Th. Stcherbatsky, The Conception of Buddhist Nirvāna (The Hague: Mouton & Co., 1965, originally published by the Academy of Sciences of the USSR, Leningrad, 1927), p. 49.
[6] Quoted by Stcherbatsky, Ibid., p. 49.

On the positive side of the Madhyamika philosophy lies the conviction that through practice in non-clinging and meditation a person can realize directly the reality he seeks for his own being. The primary function of philosophy is to lead a person to this realization, clearing away the tangles of conceptual knots and one-sided views that constitute the barrier to a direct participation in the reality man seeks. Both the formulation of systems of philosophy in an attempt to delineate the nature of this reality, and the critical attempts to show the relativity and incompleteness of such systems, are tasks secondary to that of encountering the unconditioned reality itself.

It needs to be emphasized that this underlying conviction of the Madhyamika is not itself regarded as a philosophical theory which requires justification. It is regarded as a fundamental insight issuing from an experience more basic than logic and reason. Logic and reason, though of considerable usefulness when properly understood and wisely used, are lower and secondary means for the realization of the unconditioned and undivided nature of reality.

When unwisely used, however, logic and reason themselves become barriers to this ultimate realization. The truth of *shunyata* is that no theories or views in themselves are complete and absolutely true. Concepts and systems of concepts are relative to each other. Thus, whatever truth is uncovered within concepts and systems of concepts is always relative to other concepts and other systems, and is at best only partial truth. This is the essential relativity of views that Nagarjuna attempts to demonstrate with his critical dialectic. This is done, however, not for its own sake, nor for the sake of destroying confidence in the ability to achieve a genuine encounter with reality, but for the sake of preparing a person for the higher way, the way of greater wisdom— the *Prajna-paramita*—that carries him beyond the limited wisdom concerned only with the conditioned and the relative.

As seen earlier, the Vaibhashikas and Sautrantikas taught that reality is of the nature of process, or becoming, and that it is made up of atomic elements in constant flux. These atomic elements were regarded as ultimate, not dependent upon anything else for their existence since they possessed *own-being*, or *sva-bhava*. This is, however, to teach a permanent reality, for the ultimate elements themselves are regarded as uncaused and unchanging in their own being.

The Yogacara school held that mind alone is real. External reality is declared to be unreal; it lacks *sva-bhava*. Mind, however, is totally existent; in no way is it non-being. Thus, Mind is absolute existence, possessing *sva-bhava*.

According to the Madhyamika, both the realists and the idealists have made the mistake of confusing the conditioned with the unconditioned. Neither realist nor idealist takes the middle path between *is* and *is-not*. Exclusive *is* and exclusive *is-not* are both mistakes. Exclusive *is* does not avoid the pitfall of eternalism and exclusive *is-not* does not avoid the pitfall of nihilism. Both kinds of view really regard the conditioned and the relative as the unconditioned and the absolute, and this is the basic mistake. The error lies not in recognizing that there is an unconditioned or absolute reality, but in taking what is conditioned and relative to be unconditioned and absolute. The Madhyamika also recognizes that there is an absolute, an unconditioned reality. But he does not fall into the trap of mistaking the conceptual for the unconditioned. For him the unconditioned is beyond views; i.e., it is the ultimate truth which cannot be grasped conceptually and which can only be realized by direct insight. As Nagarjuna says, "The teachings of the Buddha are based on two truths, the mundane and the ultimate. Those who do not know the distinction between these two truths do not understand the profound meaning in the teaching of the Buddha."[7]

The *Madhyamika Karika* is directed to pointing out the relativism and incompleteness of the various systems and the inadequacies of the concepts put forth as elucidations of reality. The method used in the *Karika* involves showing that when the various theories about reality which have been put forth as the ultimate truth about reality are carefully analyzed, according to the very logic of their construction, they are seen to be self-contradictory. The series of reductions to the absurd of the positions examined in the *Karika* should not be taken as establishing any positive view, but only as pointing out the fallacy of mistaking the conditioned and relative for the unconditioned and the absolute.

The first chapter of the *Karika* reveals the structure and the method of the work, and contains the examination of causality which underlies every theory of reality. To appreciate the fundamental importance of the analysis of causality, it must be recognized that assumptions about causality lie at the very heart of explanations of reality.

CRITICAL DIALECTIC

Every attempt to explain the nature of reality rests upon an assumption about the causal connectedness of reality. Philosophical and scientific theories are not exceptions. Unless a connectedness between events

---

7 *Madhyamika Karika*, XXIV, 8, 9.

in the world is assumed, there would be no basis for inferences from one observed "fact" to another. And without causal connections, knowledge would, at best, be nothing more than a chaotic collection of observations. Organization of observations presupposes a connectedness between the observations.

The inferences and deductions characteristic of both scientific and philosophical theories of reality are of a logical nature, dependent for their validity upon the nature of the concepts and theories wherein the various relations underwriting the inferences and deductions are given. The interest man takes in philosophical and scientific theories of reality rests upon the assumption that even though the inferences and deductions characterizing these theories are logical in nature, nevertheless, they have a foundation in the real world. This is the assumption that there is a correspondence between the connections made in theories about the world and connections within the world itself. This assumption must always remain an assumption, for to attempt to demonstrate its truth would only be to show the logical necessity of a theory or a concept, and would not say anything about reality (except on the chance that reality in fact corresponds to logic).

The important link between the connectedness of concepts and the supposed connectedness of reality itself is constituted by the concept of causality. Various theories of causality are possible, but they all have in common that whatever is or comes to be, is or comes to be in dependence upon something else. The search for causes is essentially the search for the conditions of the world that is experienced. Whenever the conditions upon which something depends for its existence, or coming-to-be, are known, then the conditioned—that which comes to be in dependence upon the conditions—is also known.

The assumption underlying all theories of causality is that experienced reality is not self-existent and self-explanatory. Its existence and its explanation are tied to various factors which are more fundamental than it, and these factors must be known in order to have full knowledge of the experienced reality itself. Where did it come from? Why is it shaped like this? How does it do that? etc., are questions asked by one desiring to know a reality being observed. And these are all questions about the conditions and causes of the item in question.

It is the purpose of the first chapter of the *Karika* to show that the assumptions about causality underlying the prevalent available theories of reality are shot through with inconsistencies, and are at bottom self-contradictory and untenable. If this can be done, it will have been shown—at least for the theories in question—that philosophical theories do not yield the ultimate truth about reality.

The first aphorism of the first chapter of the *Karika* states that "There absolutely are no things, nowhere and none, that arise (anew), neither out of themselves, nor out of non-self, nor out of both, nor at random."[8]

The claim being made here is that none of the four possible views of causation are tenable. These four views are: (1) whatever arises or is produced, arises or is produced out of itself; (2) whatever arises or is produced, arises or is produced out of another; (3) whatever arises or is produced, arises or is produced both out of itself and out of another; and (4) whatever arises or is produced, arises or is produced neither out of itself, nor out of another, nor out of a combination of itself and another. The first view is ruled out by the claim, "neither out of themselves." The second view is ruled out by the expression, ". . . nor out of non-self. . . ." The third view is ruled out by the claim, ". . . nor out of both. . . ." The fourth view is ruled out by the claim, ". . . nor at random."

As pointed out above, the arguments against each of these views of causality do not rest upon any claims made by the Madhyamika philosopher, but proceed by accepting the principles and conclusions adopted by the supporters of the view being examined. Consequently, the result of the argument is not to advance any independent claim about the nature of reality, but only to point out that the claim in question is untenable.

The first view of causality, that things are self-caused, is rejected on the grounds that identity of the cause and effect does not allow for causality. If things are their own cause, there is no difference between the cause and the effect. But if the cause and the effect are identical, then it does not make sense to talk of causality, for causality is possible only as a relation between two things, one of which is productive of the other. Identity, however, rules out the possibility of all relations, including the relation of causality, for it precludes real differences and genuine distinctions. Thus, to assume the complete identity of the effect and the cause is to rule out a causal relation between the supposed cause and the supposed effect. And if the cause and the effect are held to be identical only in certain respects and different in others, the problem still exists; for if they are identical in the aspects relevant to causation, the differences are irrelevant. But if they are different with respect to the aspects

8 Stcherbatsky, *The Conception of Buddhist Nirvana*, p. 71.

involved in causation, there can be no question of self-causation, for the thing as cause is held to be different from the thing as effect, and the view of causation is really one according to which things are caused not by themselves, but by another.

The second view, that things are caused by something other than themselves, is undoubtedly the ordinary view of causation. For example, when the potter is said to be the efficient (or agent) cause of the pot, and the clay is said to be the material cause, the cause is clearly being regarded as something other than the effect. This is the view according to which whenever something new is really produced, it is so because of the productive capacity and activity of other factors which are its causes. It is the view held by the Vaibhashikas and Sautrantikas, who agree that to assume self-causation is nonsensical, on the grounds that it postulates the prior existence of the thing in question and removes the basis of causation altogether by assuming the eternal existence of that thing.

Against this view of causation the Madhyamikas urge that it is the equivalent of claiming that being can be produced by non-being, which is to get something from nothing. If the cause and effect are different, what can the relation between them be? To say that they are related inasmuch as one is cause and one is effect is to beg the whole question, for the question at stake is the *reason* for calling one thing cause and another effect. Thus to say that cause and effect are completely different from each other except insofar as one is said to be cause and the other the effect is equivalent to saying that one is cause because it is called cause and the other is effect because it is called effect. But this would make sense only upon the assumption that saying that something is something else makes it that something else!

On the other hand, it has already been argued that to the extent that the effects preexisted in their causes, they were identical with their causes, and the identity of cause and effect destroys the notion of causation, as causation is a relation, and a thing cannot be in relation with itself. Thus, the realist can only argue that the cause and effect are, in all respects relevant to the question of causality, different from each other. But this means that the effect was totally non-existent before being produced. However, if production is taken to be the manifestation of a certain relation—a causal relation between cause and effect—it would seem that effects could never be produced, for what is non-existent cannot enter into relation with anything. Consequently, it is not possible for a non-existent effect to enter into a causal relation with the cause in order to be produced.

If no relation is assumed between effect and cause, it makes no sense to talk of causality, for then anything could be produced by anything else. That is, unless the causation of the sprout by the seed, or the curd by the milk, were due to certain relationships between seeds and sprouts, and milk and curd, there is no reason why gold should not be produced out of milk and sand out of seeds. The point is that the total lack of relationships between cause and effect leads inevitably to the abandonment of causality. And since the preexistence of the effect in the cause also leads to the abandonment of causality as superfluous, Nagarjuna says, "There absolutely are no things nowhere and none, that arise anew, neither out of themselves, nor out of non-self [another]. . . ."9

The next claim in the aphorism follows directly, for if the claim that things are produced out of themselves is untenable, and if the view that they are produced out of something else is also untenable then it follows that things cannot be produced out of both themselves and another, for the mere combination of two non-causes does not produce a cause.

The last claim of the aphorism—that things are not produced at random—requires no special refutation, because it is itself the abandonment of causality; it is a recognition of the lack of any relations between what is said to be cause and what is said to be effect.

The four views just examined represent a "strong" theory of causality according to which the cause represents a real creative power by means of which it produces the effect. The relationship between cause and effect according to this "strong" theory is rooted in this creative power of the cause. There is a weaker theory of causality according to which the relation between cause and effect is one of coordination rather than creative production. This is the view of causality Candrakirti puts into the mouths of the Buddhist realists, when he has them say,

> We are satisfied with establishing the fact that entities, such as sensation, arise in a certain coordination with (other entities), e.g., the organ of vision, etc. (This is all that we mean, when we assert that the existence of an organ of vision, etc. are the conditions under which a visual sensation, etc. can arise).10

According to this view there are certain conditions which are not in themselves causes, as for example, a blue flower. And there are other conditions, such as the eyes of a person, also in themselves not causes. But when these conditions are concomitant they give rise to a third

9 *The Conception of Buddhist Nirvana*, p. 170.   10 *Ibid.*

factor, the sensation of blue. When this third factor arises, the previous conditions, or factors of flower and eye, can be seen to be causes in the sense of conditions of the sensation of blue.

This weaker view of causation, or coordination, is also rejected by the Madhyamika philosophers. The difficulty with this view is that certain factors—the blue flower and the eye—are said to be conditions for the arising of a third factor—the sensation of blue. But if the sensation of blue has not yet arisen, how is it possible that it should have conditions? The eye and the blue flower would be non-conditions. But if the sensation of blue had already arisen, there would be no question of the conditions giving rise to it. So either it must be assumed that the sensation of blue always existed, or it must be assumed it came to exist dependent upon non-conditions. The former is implausible, and the latter makes nonsense out of dependent coordinations as an explanation of the arising of new factors.

The only possibility remaining is that though the factors of blue flower and visual perception are not themselves conditions for the production of the sensation of blue, they are the conditions for a concomitance which is a condition for the production of blue. This is the view that it is not the eye or the blue flower, but the concomitance of the two that is the causal condition. But to defend this view it must either be assumed that the concomitance of two things is something other than the simultaneous presence of two conditions and that this simultaneity is itself causally productive, or else that this simultaneity causes the non-conditions of blue flower and the eye to become conditions. But if simultaneity itself were a causal condition, then the concomitance of any factors should be sufficient for the production of a new factor. But the concomitance of a blue flower and an ear does not produce the third factor of a blue sensation. And if mere concomitance is not causally productive, how could it effect the change of non-causes into causes? Candrakirti puts the arguments against regarding concomitance as a causal condition as follows:

> This also won't do! Because this concomitant condition, concomitant with something which is not yet a condition, can be considered as a condition only if the other fact is (really) a condition. We are in this case faced by the same difficulty as before. Therefore this explanation cannot be accepted.[11]

If the Madhyamika attack on the examined views of causality is successful, and every view of causality is rejected, does it follow that

---

[11] *The Conception of Buddhist Nirvana*, p. 171.

there are no causes in the world, but only effects? Clearly, that cannot be, for effects are effects only of causes, and where there are no causes there are no effects. But if both causes and effects are denied, is not the existence of the world denied? And is this not one of the pits—the pit of nihilism—to be avoided, according to the Buddha?

The answer to this question is that it is only upon the assumption that reality is constituted by effects and causes that a denial of causes and effects implies a denial of reality. And since no sense can be made of an attempt to deny reality, it is clear that the implication of the Madhyamika arguments is to deny the assumption that reality is constituted of causes and effects. Lack of difference between cause and effect may well render the concepts of cause and effect empty and meaningless. It is a long way, however, from the emptiness of concepts to the emptiness of reality, and it is only by identification of concepts with reality that one would take the emptiness of concepts for the emptiness of reality.

The Madhyamikas distinguished between the world of concepts—a world of logical construction, a world outlined by philosophical theories of reality—and reality itself. The latter, as it is in itself, is entirely beyond views. The former cannot be the ultimate reality for it is shot through with contradiction and inconsistency. Nevertheless, the world of logical construction is based upon reality itself, even though it misrepresents it as something other than itself. It is similar to what happens in the mistaking of a shiny shell for a coin. The thing—the shell—is really there, but in ignorance the perceiver misrepresents it to himself as a coin. The coin is not real; it exists only as a construction in the mind of the perceiver. Still, it is not a construction of nothing, but is based on an existing reality—the shell—which is not seen for what it really is.

In a similar way, the world in which most people move is the world they have constructed in their mind. No doubt, there is a reality with which they come into contact and which provides a basis for the construction of the world of determinate entities and relations. But usually this reality is not seen for what it is in itself, but is mistaken for the world of names and forms which characterize the world constructed by the mind.

The constructed world created through the ignorance of its maker serves to veil the truth of the reality which underlies it. The essential furniture of this constructed world consists in (1) gross things, such as tables, chairs, persons and trees, (2) the constituent elements of the gross things, and (3) relational entities.

The gross things, such as tables and chairs, are the collections of perceptions designated by the expressions "chair," "table," etc. For example, curd is a gross thing constituted by resistance, smell, taste, and touch. Granted the combination of these entities produced by the mind in contact with something, there is produced the "thing" to which the name "curd" is applied. Curd in itself has no independent reality. It is like a forest, having no reality of itself apart from the individual things (trees) that make it up. The name "curd" is simply a conventional term applied to a collection of perceptual items in conjunction with each other. The subtle elements of existence, which are the constituents of the gross elements of the constructed world, are also conventional entities. When the perceptions of the mind, such as tables and curd, are subjected to logical analysis it is seen that they are constituted by simpler elements. The elements that are ultimate in such analysis are taken to be the subtle elements of the world, the elements taken as ultimately real by the Vaibhashikas and Sautrantikas. There is no basis, however, for regarding the results of the analysis of the conventional entities, such as curd, as themselves having any more than a conventional reality. After all, the name "subtle element" is merely imposed on what is conceived by someone to be the subtlest element constituting his experience. Since it is only by contrast with the "gross" entities that there can be "subtle" entities, and since the gross entities are seen to be merely conventional, it follows that the subtle elements, too, are merely logical constructions of the mind.

The third kind of entities in the constructed world include such things as length, weight, direction, time, and death, to name just a few. These are clearly relational entities, since they are derived by relating gross entities to each other and subtle entities to each other, and by relating the subtle elements to the gross elements. There is no length without shortness, no lightness without heaviness, no east without west, etc. The names of the relational entities are merely references to a comparison of the perceptions which give rise to the gross things of experience. There is no time except in the sense of duration of other entities. Death, too, has no being in its own right, but is simply a name given to a construction based on the comparison of certain changes to certain other changes.

The world referred to here as "the constructed world" is, of course, the world most of us take to be the real world. It is the world of ordinary things, such as people and cows, the world of the constituents of the ordinary things (such as atoms), and the world of relations between ordinary things and their constituents. But all of this is regarded by the Madhyamika as a world constructed by mind for the reasons just presented. The items in this world are constructed by the mind and analyzed by the mind. Mind is by itself incapable of dealing with anything other than what is mind-made. And what is mind-made is relational, for the nature of mental construction requires that one thing be in relation to another.

Philosophical views, just as all other items created by the mind, are constructions, and are therefore relative. There is no saying, from the perspective of any philosophical view, that what is constructed by the mind is of the nature of reality, or that it represents reality as it is in itself. Nor is there any saying that what is of the nature of the mind is unlike reality, that it distorts reality. The distinction between the relative world of mental construction and the ultimate reality of direct insight can only be based on direct insight. As in the case of mistaking the shell for a coin, it is only by seeing the coin for what it is that one can recognize that what he had perceived as a coin was in reality only a shell.

The dialectic, whereby the essential relativity of the mind-constructed world is demonstrated, reveals the non-ultimacy of the various views about this world, shows the conditionedness and dependent character of the entities of this world, and thus paves the way for a going beyond mere views of reality to a direct realization. But it does not, by itself, provide such a realization. Such a realization is necessarily entirely beyond the world of conceptualization.

With the realization of the complete relativity (*shunyata*) of the mundane world of mental construction, all basis for clinging to anything as absolute and ultimate will disappear. All distinctions, including the distinction between *Nirvana* and *samsara* (ordinary existence), will be seen to be only relative. With the abandonment of the ignorance and perverseness which insisted on taking the mind-made world as the ultimate reality, and with a direct participation in reality, it will be realized, as Nagarjuna says, "There is no difference at all between *samasara* and *Nirvana*." [12]

[12] *Karika*, XXV, 19.

CHAPTER 13

ZEN BUDDHISM

THE relativism of the Madhyamika philosophy continues to be an extremely influential philosophical persuasion right up to the present day, for it is the main philosophical conviction underlying the practices and teachings of Zen. Zen, of course, is Zen Buddhism—a way of life which has been practiced in China, Korea and Japan for the last twelve hundred years. Some of its components and aims are, no doubt, much older. The idea of *zazen*, the chief discipline of Zen, is basically the idea of *yoga*, which has a history of more than four thousand years. The idea of disciplining oneself as a sufficient means for overcoming suffering dates back to the historical Buddha, thirteen hundred years before the appearance of Zen. But these early forms of discipline and the early sects of Buddhism were not Zen, even though they contain the beginnings of this way of life. Zen (called *Ch'an* in China) appeared when scholasticized versions of Yogacara and Madhyamika which emphasized the theoretical and idealistic orientation of Buddhism met the realistic and practical mind of the Chinese. As a result of these two contributing influences, the methods and orientation of Zen tend to be characteristically Chinese, while the presuppositions underlying the practice tend to be more typically Indian.

Invariably, in discussing Zen, the question is raised as to whether it is a religion or a philosophy. Although historically the question has sometimes been answered one way and sometimes the other, I think it is a mistake to answer the question at all. If you do not accept the presuppositions that you are still smoking, or that you have just recently stopped smoking, then you will reject the question, "Have you stopped smoking yet?" rather than answer it. Analogously, if the presuppositions of the question, "Is Zen religion or is it philosophy?" are unacceptable, the question should be rejected rather than answered, for to answer the question is to accept the presuppositions of the question. In this case the presuppositions are not only that religion and philosophy can be satisfactorily defined, but that they can be clearly distinguished from each other, and that Zen must be either one or the other. Zen does not fit neatly into any of the popular definitions of a religious way of life, for it knows no gods, seeks no immortality, and has nothing to do with sin or soul. On the other hand, it does not seem to be philosophy for it is not concerned with reasons or arguments.

Not accepting the presuppositions of the question, and avoiding the categories of religion and philosophy, we can begin by characterizing Zen as a way of life. As such it incorporates certain aims, prescribes certain practices and rests upon certain presuppositions. Even though we may not, in the last analysis, be able to state what Zen is, we shall make some headway in understanding this phenomenon if we study its practices, aims and presuppositions. The first thing to note is that as a way of life, Zen is not so much a matter of beliefs, but of doing. What does a person do if he follows the Zen way? The core of his practice consists in training in the experience of seeing directly into his complete self in the fullness of the experienced moment without the mediation of intellect. Within the context of Zen experience this attempt at definition suffers the inevitable inadequacies of every attempt to comprehend things in a merely intellectual way. The reason for this is that the entire activity of conceptualization is inadequate for comprehending things as they are, because it rests upon the arbitrary and falsifying division of reality into subject and object. Zen emphasizes the integrity and completeness of the present moment of experience wherein there is no distinction between subject and object.

As opposed to the Zen emphasis on the completeness of the present moment there are other ways of life that insist on living in the moments of the past, either wishing to regain the past or to avoid it. There are also ways of life which insist on living in the future. Here the emphasis is on tomorrow. Tomorrow we will change the world by clearing the slums, invading other galaxies, unfreezing and curing yesterday's cancer patients, and so on. From the religious perspective adopted by Christianity, Islam and Judaism, tomorrow is the big event. Tomorrow will see us, if Divine providence works in our favor, enjoying the king-dom of God.

What this attitude of looking so hard to the future that the present is virtually ignored can do in the economic spheres is well known from our understanding of the Middle Ages in Europe. But what this attitude can do to the emotional and spiritual self is not so well understood. It is possible to get a glimpse of the dangers inherent in this attitude when we see the threats and fears resulting from taking seriously the claim, formulated recently by Nietzsche, that God is dead. What the death of God means in the religious sphere is that the source of life and value in the universe has disappeared, for creation and endowing value are the main functions of God. But for those who take seriously the death of God, the belief in God as the source of value and meaning in life must now be seen not only as an illusion—the fulfillment of the wish for a powerful father image—but also as a delusion, for no God exists. But if God, who created the world and bestowed value upon it, no longer exists, then what is the source and guarantee of value in the universe?

The recent answer to this question is that man himself is the source of value in the universe. But notoriously, this has left man with an uneasy feeling. He is too much aware of his own inadequacies to assume the role of God. But at the same time he is too completely caught up in the presuppositions of God's existence to be satisfied without the fulfillment of God's functions. When man relies upon himself he must face his own incapacities and inadequacies. The transformation of the world through knowledge is one of modern man's noblest ambitions. But the large gaps in his knowledge and understanding rightly leaves man with doubts and anxieties about the outcome of the transformation. The effect of the philosophies of Kant and Hume in the West, and Nagarjuna and Shamkara in the East, was to draw attention to the limitations of reason. In this century faith in the power of reason was severely shaken when it was discovered in mathematics—the very darling of reason—that the completeness of mathematical systems could not be attained. And Heisenberg's indeterminacy principle was an unpleasant dose of medicine for those confident that modern physics would completely lay bare the organized structure of the universe. In short, the universe shows no signs of being the completely rational structure in which reason would feel completely at home.

Despite the fact, however, that the inadequacies of reason are being felt at this time, the projections of life still presuppose the older goals of reason—the complete understanding of life and reason through rational means. Man has not adjusted to the inadequacies of reason. He still proceeds—though more uneasily of late—as though reason were the adequate guide to a complete and satisfying life. Thus he continues to see himself existing in one moment, but reaping the fullness of that existence in a future moment. But underneath the plans for achievement in the future lies an awareness—sometimes so dim and murky that it passes unnoticed, and sometimes so disturbingly acute that it is frightening—that there is no existence and life except in the present moment. The future moment belongs to the future, which belongs not to life, but to forms of understanding.

What Zen does, rather than postponing the complete life to that chimerical moment in the future when we will have the complete rational knowledge required to provide for that kind of life, is to make the most of the present moment, finding therein the wholeness of self and the completeness of life. It is the quality of experience here and now, and not precision of reason, that assumes paramount importance for the Zen Buddhist.

The Zen emphasis on the immediacy and completeness of the present moment shows up in the underlying principles of Zen practice, in the quality of enlightened life, and in the teachings underlying Zen. Of these three basic features of Zen—practice, enlightenment and teachings —it is practice that comes first. Enlightenment depends upon practice, and teachings support and are determined by practice and enlightenment. It is fitting, therefore, that we should turn now to a description of the practice of Zen.

Zazen, the chief discipline of Zen practice, is taken up in order to achieve the optimal conditions for seeing directly into oneself and discovering in the purity of one's own existence the true nature of all existence. This discipline requires assuming complete control and regulation of the hands, feet, legs, arms, trunk, and head. Next breathing must be regulated so that the activities of the mind can be brought under control. Through a series of special forms of concentration the activities of the mind are brought together, unified and stilled. The emotions and volitions are also brought under control and harmonized with intellect. Having attained the foregoing, it remains to cultivate what is usually called a deep or profound silence in the deepest recesses of one's being.

The question might be raised, Why engage in the discipline of *zazen*? The answer is contained in the immediate presuppositions of Zen. Zen presupposes that the ordinary person is caught up in a maze of crisscrossing ideas, theories, reflections, prejudices, feelings and emotions such that his every experience is cut up into a variety of segments. These segments are then taken as parts of experience which can be synthesized into a whole. Thus, the ordinary person does not really experience reality, but only the network of ideas and feelings he has about reality. These ideas and feelings always stand between the individual and the reality he confronts, mediating the experience. The aim of *zazen* is to free the individual from this mediating network and allow him to enter directly and fully into the reality he confronts.

There are three basic aims of *zazen*. The first is to increase the powers of concentration by getting rid of all distracting factors and all dualities. The second is the awakening of enlightenment, or the achieving of *satori*. This is the seeing into one's ultimate self and discovering the ultimate nature of reality and the completeness of existence in the realization constituting *satori*. The enlightenment may come like a flash, but it presupposes intensive training for most people. The *koans*, or problems, and the questions and answers that are commonly used in the large sessions in the monasteries and in the private sessions between master and disciple are famous as devices for triggering enlightenment. For example, the famous Zen master, Dogen, who had been doing *zazen* for many years had heard his master say on numerous occasions that in order to realize enlightenment body and mind must fall off. But one day when he heard this his mind and body dropped off and he was enlightened. That is, he had now reached the level of concentration and insight wherein he became empty of the conceptions of mind and body. The third aim of *zazen* is to incorporate the complete enlightenment of the total self into all the daily activities. Thus every action and every moment is an action and moment lived in enlightenment.

In addition to *zazen*, *koans*, or problems, are often used in practice. They serve both to teach the aspirant and to test him. Used as a test they reveal whether or not the *zazen* efforts have succeeded in reaching a given level of concentration and enlightenment. As teaching devices, *koans* represent expressions apt for leading a person beyond the bifurcations of intellect to the direct and immediate participation in the living, whole, and complete reality. One of the most famous *koans* is known, by way of the answer, as the *mu-koan*. A monk, in all seriousness, once asked master Joshu, "Has a dog a Buddha-nature?" Joshu replied, immediately, "Mu!" Now, what is ordinarily meant by Buddha-nature is that the nature of everything is such that it can become enlightened.

This is a common Mahayana teaching, and is found in many texts. But Joshu refused to say yes. No doubt he would have been right in refusing to answer affirmatively if he had suspected that the monk was thinking that there was some *thing* called the Buddha-nature, hidden somewhere within beings. Joshu's refusal to answer yes or no was more radical. He saw that the question not only presupposed the conceptions *Buddha-nature* and *dog*, but worse, in asking if a dog has or has not a Buddha-nature, it presupposes the dichotomy between *is* and *is not*—between being and non-being. This shows that the question is merely conceptual, and that the questioner has not got outside the confines of intellect. Since it is the aim of Zen to go beyond the limitations of merely intellectual understanding Joshu says *Mu!* That is, he said nothing (but said it immediately!). This is the main point about *koans*—they have no intellectual answers. They appear to be problems only upon the assumption of certain bases and conceptions which are to be left behind. Once a monk asked the master, "What happens to our thought systems when being and non-being are not distinguished?" The master laughed heartily and drank tea. And of course this was the only answer! No answer to the question would have done, for it would have required accepting the distinctions making possible the question, in this case the distinction between being and non-being.

The enlightenment (*satori*) at which Zen aims requires going beyond all distinctions, including the distinction between *is* and *is not,* upon which all thought systems rest. Consequently, no statement is possible of what enlightenment is, except negatively, by way of pointing out what it is not. But even this presupposes *is* and *is not*, and fails to provide much understanding of this important aspect of Zen. Short of practicing Zen and achieving some measure of enlightenment, perhaps the only way to get a feeling for the experience of *satori* is to talk with or read the biographies of people who have achieved *satori*. What impresses one when this is done is the almost unanimous reference to the overcoming of distinctions, and the beauty and perfection of the world just as it is—without any distinctions. This, of course, fits in with Nagarjuna's observation that between *nirvana* and *samsara* there is no difference at all.

Turning to the teachings of Zen, it must be pointed out that the actual teachings of Zen are primarily teachings connected with the practice of *zazen*, *koan*, and question-and-answer sessions. That is, they are practical teachings, directed to fostering the way of life that Zen is. Nevertheless, these questions, as well as the practices to which they are essentially connected, have certain philosophical presuppositions. These presuppositions can be seen in the Mahayana philosophies of the Yogacara and Madhyamika schools.

As the Yogacara philosophy developed it came to regard the empirical world—the world of intellectual consciousness—as the world of *Mind-only*, since what was known thereby was only consciousness. But a reality beyond this was presupposed. It was, of course, beyond reason, but could—by practicing the Noble Eightfold Way—be experienced. Most importantly, to experience this reality would be to put an end to suffering. This ultimate reality is referred to variously as the "pure mind," and "undivided being," and the "Buddha-nature." Buddha-nature, or the pure mind, as the ultimate reality is a basic teaching of Mahayana Buddhism, and underlies the practical aim of becoming one with the all-illumining Buddha-consciousness. To achieve enlightenment is to go beyond seeing everything as mental phenomenon, or of the nature of consciousness, to seeing reality as whole, undivided and without distinction.

This teaching is important for Zen, but the texts containing the teachings about this point are quite confusing, because the expression "mind" is used in different ways. The word is used in two quite different senses, sometimes even in the same passage. We need to ask, "What is meant by mind?" The one sense of mind found in Mahayana is the ordinary view of mind as consciousness engaged in differentiating things. The other Mahayana notion of mind is something else. It is called variously *Buddha-nature, the Enlightened mind, Emptiness, No-mind, Mind-only,* and *Suchness*. These expressions all refer to the same reality, which is the very basis of human reality. The discriminating consciousness is just one expression of this reality. Feelings, emotions, and volitions are other aspects. One could go on indefinitely enumerating aspects of this reality. But the important thing to note is that this enumeration, and every assumption of a perspective which makes possible an aspect is just another activity of discrimination. In other words, all aspects and characteristics exist only as the result of discriminatory activity.

So far there is no problem. But the damage is done when this discriminatory activity, usually called intellectual or rational activity, presents itself as the ultimate judge of truth—the God's eye point of view which contains all perspectives and all truths. The result is that the perspectives of intellect are taken to be ultimate and absolute when they are only partial and dependent. The chief activity of intellect is to divide reality and to isolate the divided aspects, representing these aspects as objects or activities existing independently of each other. Furthermore, when intellect is taken as ultimate the division between subject and object—between *I* and the *that*—is taken as absolute. The result is that the individual is set apart from the reality in which he lives.

Now when the world consisting of the objects of our knowledge is described by saying "all this is mind only," the reference is clearly to the world differentiated by intellect, which means it is indeed the product of consciousness only. But this does not mean that there is nothing other than this consciousness. It means only that the world of which we are intellectually conscious is a world represented from merely one perspective: the perspective of lower discriminatory consciousness, and it should be recognized for what it is—the result of intellectual differentiation. I think it can be seen now that, at least in part, the thrust of the mind–only teaching is to call attention to the fact that we are ignoring the deeper basis of human existence by mistaking one aspect or expression of that basis for the whole reality.

The limitations of the rational consciousness are well illustrated in reason's eldest and most highly honored child, philosophy. It is well known that in any attempt to understand the world intellectually there must be a seeing of the relations between the parts that make up the whole. And these parts must themselves be understood. But to understand the parts or things that make up the world it is necessary to come to see them as they are in themselves. In order to get at things as they are in themselves there is an attempt to leave aside the personal and subjective elements in experience. This is greatly emphasized in scientific laboratory procedures where objective measurements, relying primarily on counting devices, are regarded as the key to objectivity. But what is overlooked is that the whole question of objective versus subjective is itself subjective. It is the subject's awareness of the object that must be considered. Nothing can be considered by reason except in conscious awareness. But are the objects represented in the subject's consciousness at all the same as the reality that exists outside of human consciousness? In science this question is ignored, basically because of the great confidence we have in intersubjective agreement as a guarantee of objectivity. But as soon as this attitude is stated its inadequacy is obvious.

Philosophers, in their preoccupation with this problem, have resorted to the notion of a noumenal reality, a thing-in-itself. The noumenal reality cannot itself be an object of knowledge, but it is what makes possible whatever becomes an object of knowledge, for it is the basis of the object's existence in consciousness. What is known is supposedly the noumenon only as affected by the mind. But since things are known only in consciousness, there is no way of telling whether what is present in consciousness is in any way similar to the noumenal reality. And if this is the case, then the noumenal reality postulated to explain the relation of knowledge to reality is itself totally mysterious and entirely without explanatory power. According to the Yogacara analysis, this result is not at all surprising. The whole concept of noumenal reality, which is the final result of the intellectual search for the underlying principles of ultimate reality, is simply an abstraction arrived at to solve a problem arising out of the ignorance of the limitations of the viewpoint assumed by reason.

The emphasis in Yogacara Buddhism on the mental nature of the world known in consciousness served to de-emphasize reason as the vehicle for attaining absolute truth and wisdom. When reason was assigned a secondary role the "thatness" of things achievable by reason also became secondary. Primary now was the "suchness" of things, and the immediate seeing into things just as they are. As a result, the development of techniques for experiencing the suchness of reality assumed greater importance than attempts to define and state what reality is. This resulted in the emphasis on practice so characteristic of Zen, and which precludes defining it as a philosophy. But Zen carries with it a mistrust of reason which suggests that the Yogacara philosophy is taken seriously.

Despite the importance of the Yogacara analysis of consciousness for Zen, it is the Madhyamika philosophy that provides the most adequate foundation for this way of life. This philosophy emphasized the inability of reason to solve the basic problems it sets for itself with respect to subject and object and existence and non-existence. But rather than regarding this as a cause for despair, it was taken as evidence for a higher way of truth. This higher way, the way of wisdom, is the seeking by the complete person for the ultimate reality. This way consisted in going beyond all clingings by seeing the relativity of all things and rising above limited perspectives. It was especially the development of relativism in the Madhyamika philosophy that made it suitable as a basis for Zen, for as shown in the previous chapter, this philosophy left no room for theoretical absolutes, and made way for the development of practical techniques related to the circumstances of each person.[1]

[1] See pp. 166–179.

But there are serious difficulties in attempting to provide a philosophical basis for Zen. Such difficulties can be seen clearly in Nagarjuna's attempts to point out the bankruptcy of reason and the importance of a more basic encounter with reality. His middle-way philosophy claims that all philosophical views are untenable because they are ultimately self-contradictory. Furthermore, the negation of all views opens up the way for a direct apprehension that transcends mere thought and unites man with the real.

The difficulty with this argument is that the rejection of all views as self-contradictory presupposes the classification of all views, and this presupposes the validity of the principle of excluded middle in exhaustively classifying all systems. It also presupposes the principle of non-contradiction for purposes of rejecting views. But these two principles themselves belong to the thought systems of reason. So the Madhyamika philosopher is in a bind. If he wishes to reject philosophical systems he must embrace the very principles upon which they rest. This position, however, gives him a view subject to his own criticisms. The alternative is to give up the principles of excluded middle and non-contradiction. But then he is without the means for rejecting any views as inadequate.

Aware of this dilemma, the Madhyamika philosophers maintain that they have no view at all; the self-conscious awareness of all points of view, or of reason itself, is not another view. It is the transcending of all systems of thought. The Madhyamika position is that the direct apprehension of reality emerges when the obstacles of reason have been overcome. This seems a difficult position to maintain, however. How can it be known that what is directly apprehended is the real, and that it is being apprehended as it really is? Just because reason does not enter into this activity does not mean that the activity warrants itself. Nor does the fact that Madhyamika does not question the ontological status of this directly apprehended reality prove that it is not being distorted in being apprehended. After all, many philosophers have been without doubts that the reality they outlined in their theories was the true reality, but no Madhyamika philosopher would allow their confidence to serve as a guarantee of the truth of their views. But on what grounds can the Madhyamika philosopher disallow these claims? He cannot make any reply without contradicting his own position.

From a philosophical point of view then, we are left with the claim that since reason leads us into blind alleys, producing antinomies, there must be a means for getting in touch with reality higher than reason.

But this disjunction itself is the work of reason, so should not be allowed. Furthermore, even if the disjunction is allowed, the claim could be maintained only if it were shown that reality is, in its essence, understandable somehow—if not by reason, then by something higher than reason. And if this is not allowed, then we can challenge the second assumption of the Madhyamika, which maintains that there is a reality other than the ordinarily experienced reality. Obviously, reason cannot demonstrate this claim. But if this claim is not maintained then there is no basis for maintaining the distinction between the ultimate reality and the experienced reality. And without that distinction the Madhyamika philosopher has no basis from which to criticize the world of reason.

It would seem that there is nothing more for the Madhyamika philosopher to say. He cannot even say, as he did say historically, that all this just proves his point that reason is an inadequate means for investigating reality. However, just because there is nothing more for the philosopher to say it does not follow that there is nothing more for the Buddhist to do. Faced with these antinomies, he can resolve to practice Zen. The silence forced on the philosopher can be the beginning of a seeing into reality that goes beyond thoughts and words, and that does not leave behind any aspects of the person.

But to practice Zen is not to do philosophy, and success in Zen practice, no matter how much it improves or appears to improve the quality of life, does not constitute an argument for the correctness of any philosophical point of view. It would seem, therefore, that rather than trying to say what kind of philosophy Zen is we should conclude that it is a way of approaching reality that constitutes an alternative to the intellectual way. The rational and philosophical approach, so well known to the West, is one approach. The existential meditative way of Zen is another. The two do not exclude each other unless such exclusion is founded within a point of view assumed by one or both of these ways.

CHAPTER 14

BASIC CHARACTERISTICS
OF BUDDHIST CULTURE

THE religious-philosophical teachings of Buddhism outlined in the preceding pages have left their mark on much of Asian civilization. Buddhism, much more so than most religions, has permeated the cultures with which it has been associated. Consequently, in Ceylon, Burma, Cambodia, Thailand, and Laos, where Thervada Buddhism has held sway, and in Tibet, China, Korea, Japan, and Vietnam, where Mahayana Buddhism has been influential, we find rather distinctive Buddhist cultural traits. Prominent among these cultural characteristics are the following: (1) emphasis on the dignity of man, (2) an attitude of non-attachment, (3) tolerance, (4) a spirit of compassion and non-violence, (5) an inclination to meditation, and (6) a practical orientation.

THE DIGNITY OF MAN: In Buddhist cultures man has not been subordinated to things and machines. Man is regarded as self-creative, as the determiner of his fate by his own efforts. What greater dignity can be bestowed upon man than to recognize that he is the master of his own life and destiny? In theistic religions man is usually subordinated to his God, and is regarded as a thing fashioned by this God to suit His own aims. In a materialistic culture man is often subordinated to things in the world external to himself, and sometimes subordinated even to his own artifacts. But according to the teachings of Buddhism these alternatives represent the projection of, and ensnarement by, man's own ignorance. It is entirely up to man whether he will or will not subordinate himself to God or nature.

NON-ATTACHMENT: As a result of his conviction that there are no enduring selves or things in the world, the Buddhist does not attach himself either to his ego or to things in the world. Recognizing that impermanence is the mark of this world of suffering existence, he refuses to cling to absurd conceptions of permanence. As a result, he is unruffled by change, and faces the future with equanimity, and does not lament over what has gone by. Thus, a spirit of ready acceptance of life marks the Buddhist as a result of his non-attachment to permanence.

TOLERANCE: Buddhism is a way of practical realization of the truth of non-suffering attainable by self-discipline and mental purification. It is not based on the commands of jealous gods and is not affected by claims to exclusiveness that grow out of such jealousy. Consequently, it is tolerant both of other religions, and of differing individual interpretations of Buddhist teachings. Despite the many differences found among the Buddhists of the different countries of the world, they all recognize each other as Buddhists. Furthermore, they do not look upon non-Buddhists as inferior, without a hope of happiness, and for whom salvation is impossible because they live outside the fold of Buddhism. The sickness and suffering that dogs man accrues to the individual person, and it is the individual person who must make the Way from suffering to peace and happiness. This recognition lies at the bottom of the respect for individual differences in all spheres of life that is so characteristic of Buddhist cultures.

NON-VIOLENCE: In the twenty-five hundred years since its beginnings, Buddhism has spread throughout Asia and has made its way even to the other continents, claiming over four hundred million followers at the present time. During this time no wars have been fought and no blood shed in the propagation of the teaching. Violence is absolutely contrary to the teachings and practice of Buddhism. It is a common conviction of Buddhists everywhere that anger and violence only provoke more of the same, and that anger and violence are only appeased and removed by kindness and compassion. The compassion demonstrated by Gautama as he travelled around the countryside teaching the causes and cessation of suffering has permeated all of Buddhism, and in Mahayana occupies the central place in the religion, in the form of the *Bodhisattava* ideal. It is a relatively easy thing to say, "Love thine enemies," but a much more difficult thing to do in the face of the enemies' anger, hatred, and violence. Nevertheless, the Buddhist record on this score is excellent, as is seen by the relative lack of war, revolution, or violence of any kind in predominantly Buddhist cultures.

MEDITATION: As a result of the Buddhist emphasis on self-discipline and self-purification, it is common practice for Buddhists everywhere to concentrate on emptying themselves of everything impure and conducive to suffering. The meditative techniques involved in these practices, despite the great variety of forms or degrees, are all essentially a matter of self-cultivation and self-discipline. Their aim is to enable a person to participate directly in reality without the intermediaries of false selves, desires, and ambitions estranging him from reality. The mark of these meditative practices in Buddhist lands is a calm peacefulness that characterizes the majority of the people.

PRACTICAL ORIENTATION: Practice in meditation produces an attitude that strikes an observer as very practical and down-to-earth. No doubt, this is due, at least in part, to the Buddhists' ability to immerse themselves in the activity of the present moment. When one is at peace with himself and not pulled by a thousand desires and nagged by ten thousand doubts he can freely and completely engage in the activities at hand. For example, a Buddhist does not ordinarily regard eating, working, and playing as simply activities to be gotten over with in order to get on to the "real business of life." Rather, these are counted as among the activities of which life is constituted. Consequently, these things are regarded as important, and participation is whole-hearted, occupying the total attention of the person. Yet they do not cling to these things and become long-faced and heavy-hearted when there is not quite enough to eat, or the work is hard.

Learning from the past and planning for the future are, of course, essential for improving the quality of life in all spheres. But learning from the past and planning for the future are themselves activities of the present moment, and should not be confused with living in the past or the future. There can be no real happiness in brooding over the future which has not yet come. Nor can happiness be found in lamenting the past. The Buddhists' recognition of this fact and, in consequence, their relatively complete engagement and immersion in the activities of the immediate present results in an attitude that strikes an "outsider" as extremely practical.

PART THREE

Chinese Philosophies

Portrait of Confucius. *Courtesy of the Field Museum of Natural History*

BASIC CHARACTERISTICS
OF CHINESE PHILOSOPHIES

CHINESE civilization and culture rest upon a philosophical basis shaped primarily by the principles of Confucianism, Taoism, and Neo-Confucianism. These three philosophies have guided and shaped the lives and institutions of the Chinese people for more than twenty-five hundred years. Stressing the importance of preserving, cultivating, and making great human life, Chinese philosophy has been closely connected with politics and morality and has assumed most of the functions of religion. Consequently, the study of Chinese philosophy is valuable not only because of its intrinsic merit, but also because of the insights into the Chinese mind that it makes possible.

The basic aim of Chinese philosophy has not been primarily that of understanding the world, but primarily that of making man great. Although the various Chinese philosophies share this common aim, they differ considerably as a result of different insights into the source of man's greatness. Thus, in Taoism, the emphasis is upon becoming great by becoming one with the inner way of the universe. On the other hand, in Confucianism, the emphasis has been upon developing man's humanity by cultivating human-heartedness and the social virtues. Neo-Confucianism combines these emphases.

Being great has a double aspect in Chinese thought. First of all, it involves *inner greatness*, which is a magnitude of spirit reflected in the peace and contentment of the individual in his completeness. Secondly, it involves *outer greatness*, which is manifested in the ability to live well practically, dignifying the social context of one's ordinary day-to-day existence.

This twofold greatness is basic to both Confucianism and Taoism, the philosophies which provide the foundations and inspiration for the later Neo-Confucian philosophy. Lao Tzu says that unless one knows and lives according to the inner laws of the universe, which he calls the "invariables," he ends up in disaster. According to this mystic sage:

> To know the invariables is called enlightenment. He who knows the invariable is liberal. Being liberal, he is without prejudice. Being without prejudice, he is comprehensive. Being comprehensive, he is vast. Being vast, he is with the Truth. Being with the Truth, he will last forever, and will not fail throughout his lifetime. Not to know the invariable and to act blindly is to go to disaster.[1]

For Confucius the most basic thing was to cultivate one's human-ness and to regulate all activities in accord with this developed human-ness. According to one of the chief texts of Confucianism,

> The ancients who wished to manifest their clear character to the world would first bring order to their states. Those who wished to bring order to their states would first regulate their families. Those who wished to regulate their families would first cultivate their personal lives. Those who wished to cultivate their personal lives would first rectify their minds. Those who wished to rectify their minds would first make their wills sincere. Those who wished to make their wills sincere would first extend their knowledge. The extension of knowledge consists in the investigation of things. When things are investigated, knowledge is extended; when knowledge is extended, the will becomes sincere; when the will is sincere, the mind is rectified; when the mind is rectified, the personal life is cultivated; when the personal life is cultivated, the family will be regulated; when the family is regulated, the state will be in order; and when the state is in order, there will be peace throughout the world.[2]

This pervasive aim of becoming great internally and manifesting this greatness externally has tended to make Chinese philosophy inclusive of all aspects of human activity. Philosophy is not divorced from life, and practice is considered inseparable from theory. There have been very few professional philosophers in China. Nearly all of China's great philosophers have held administrative positions in government or

[1] *Tao Te Ching*, Ch. 16. All references to, and quotations from, this work are taken from *The Way of Lao Tzu*, trans. by Wing-Tsit Chan (Indianapolis: Bobbs-Merrill, 1963).

[2] *The Great Learning (Ta-Hsüeh)*, in *A Source Book in Chinese Philosophy*, trans. and compiled by Wing-Tsit Chan (Princeton: Princeton University Press, 1963). pp. 86–87.

have been artists. And the assessment of philosophers in China depends, in the last analysis, upon their moral character. It is not conceivable that a bad man could be a good philosopher, or that a good philosopher could be a bad man. The real test of a philosophy is its ability to transform its advocates into greater persons.

Since greatness of persons is the basic concern, considerations for people come first in China. The world of man is primary; the world of things is of secondary importance. In Confucianism this characteristic is manifested in the emphasis on social humanism. In Taoism it is evident in the mystical ontological unity of man and the universe.

Emphasis on man's greatness leads naturally to emphasis on ethics and the spiritual life. The spirit of man rather than the body, is the most important aspect of being human. This spirit must be nourished and cultivated in order that it might develop according to its capacities. And for this development the moral life is a first prerequisite. This is a very obvious characteristic of Confucianism, where there is really no distinction between the moral and the spiritual, and where man is defined as a moral animal. But it is also a characteristic of Taoism, which stresses the quality of life and aims at a higher level of human existence.

Putting greatness into practice led to emphasis on the familial virtues, especially the concept of filial love, which provides the very cornerstone of Chinese morality. The immediate environment surrounding infants in a civilized society is a social structure constituted by the family. Here the child's moral and spiritual character is shaped and molded. Here the beginnings of smallness or greatness are established. Only through great love and respect within the family can greatness be cultivated in persons.

Turning to methodology, it can be seen that the emphasis on inclusiveness of views has been a primary consideration. Rather than seeking truth by excluding various alternative views as false, Chinese thought has tended to look for truth in the combination of partially true views. This leads to a spirit of synthesis and harmony which results in tolerance and sympathy. Persons, practices, and views that are different are to be tolerated and considered sympathetically in order to appreciate their value. It is characteristic of Chinese philosophy that it emphasizes complementariness rather than contrariness. Often views and principles can be seen to be not only different, but also opposed. But, of course, if they are opposed it is necessary that they have a common basis. In Chinese thought it is this common basis that is emphasized, and the differences are regarded as complementary rather than contrary.

The differences are viewed as completing each other, thereby constituting a whole. Instead of thinking, "*A* and *B* are opposed, therefore one must take either *A* or *B*," one thinks, "*A* and *B* are opposed, therefore both are needed for the whole." For example, one does not choose between practice and theory, but chooses *both* theory *and* practice.

This emphasis on complementariness in Chinese philosophy is reflected in a synthetic attitude which sees harmony in apparently conflicting theories and modes of life and fuses them together into a new whole. For example, there are basic differences between Taoism and Confucianism, and Buddhism does not appear to have a great deal in common with either of these philosophies. Yet Buddhism found a welcome home in China, and more than a thousand years ago these three philosophies contributed the materials required for the imposing edifice of Neo-Confucianism. In addition, this synthetic attitude leads to tolerance for the thoughts and actions of others, and promotes sympathy and appreciation for what is different.

This summary of basic characteristics of Chinese philosophy indicates a rich and complex philosophical heritage. The emphasis on the greatness of man and the preference for methodological inclusiveness suggest that this tradition should be considered in its own context and in terms of its own merit, for it does not fit neatly into European intellectual categories, which have resulted from an emphasis on the greatness of the external world, and a preference for methodological exclusiveness.

HISTORICAL PERSPECTIVES

CHINESE philosophy as a critical investigation of man and his environment has its beginnings in the sayings of Confucius and Lao Tzu. Although this means that Chinese thought prior to around the middle of the sixth century B.C. is pre-philosophical, it does not mean that the philosophies of Confucius and Lao Tzu can be understood without investigating China's pre-philosophical tradition. On the contrary, since both Confucianism and Taoism are critical reactions to earlier theories and practices, it is imperative to have a picture of pre-philosophical China in mind in order to give these philosophies the context required for their understanding.

Although there is evidence of advanced civilization in China in very ancient times, actual recorded history begins in relatively recent times, with the Shang dynasty, in the fourteenth century B.C. Available evidence indicates that this was an advanced civilization. For example, art from this period is quite sophisticated, even according to modern standards. This dynasty ended with the invasion by the more primitive Chou people, who according to tradition established the Chou dynasty in 1122 B.C. Although more primitive artistically and culturally, the Chou were a powerful and determined people. They conquered huge portions of China by sheer force and might. Not having the means to administer all of the conquered territory as one central state, the Chou delegated administrative power to friendly chiefs and nobles, providing parcels of land in exchange for the friendship and cooperation of these newly endowed landholders. Apparently this feudal system worked quite well during the early Chou period, as each vassal had considerable freedom and power within his own territory, and this seemed well worth the taxes and military conscription owed the king in return for these privileges. Although there is nothing to indicate that the first half of the Chou period was anywhere nearly as advanced as the earlier Shang period, it was a time of relative peace and security within the structure of the new feudal system. And because of this peace it came to be regarded later on as a "golden period" in China's early history.

This peace was relatively short-lived, however. It was only the might of the Chou kings that prevented the vassals and the oppressed serfs from rebelling. As time went on, it was recognized that the kings did not really have the strength to control all of the conquered land, even through the device of feudalism. There came to be greater and greater unrest in the country. Feudal lord turned against feudal lord, and serfs rebelled when they thought the lords sufficiently weak and ineffectual. As neighboring states became weakened by war and strife they were attacked by larger and more remote lords. By 770 B.C. things had degenerated to the point where a coalition of feudal lords were able to launch a successful attack on the Chou capital in the west. They killed the king and usurped his power. From this date on the Chou kings were puppets controlled by the coalition of feudal lords who happened to be in power at the time. Power was constantly shifting hands, and war and strife were the order of the day during the two centuries immediately prior to Confucius' birth. Violence and intrigue characterized the political scene and expediency took the place of morality. Cheating and trickery provided the basis for the intrigues that functioned in lieu of political government. The costs of these intrigues and the resulting wars in terms of poverty, suffering, and death is almost unimaginable.

It is in the context of this severe crisis crippling China in the centuries immediately preceding the birth of Confucius and Lao Tzu that these philosophers must be viewed. And granted this context, it is not at all surprising that they should both be reformers. For Confucius, born in 551 B.C., it was obvious that the problems of the people stemmed from sovereign power exerted without moral principle and solely for the benefit of sovereign luxury. Small wonder, then, that he urged social reforms that would allow government to be administered for the benefit of all the people. This could be done, he urged, if the people in government were of the highest personal integrity, understood the needs of the people, and cared as much for the welfare and happiness of the people as they did for themselves. "Do unto others as you would have done unto you," represents a brilliant and daring principle of reform in the context of the pre-Confucian China just outlined. It is a principle resulting from reflections on the conditions required for an ideal society. The attitude underlying these reflections regards knowing man as more important than knowing nature. If man cannot know and regulate man, how can he hope to know and control all of nature? Furthermore, Confucius did not look for the basis of human goodness and morality outside of man. Within man himself was to be found the source and structure of human goodness and happiness. It is this attitude that makes Confucianism a humanism rather than a naturalism.

Confucius lived from 541 to 479 B.C., but some of the ideas of Confucianism are derived from earlier times, and other ideas are not developed until later. According to tradition, Confucius drew inspiration from the Five Classics, and the expression of his thought is contained in the Four Books. The Five Classics are as follows: (1) *Book of Poetry* (*Shih Ching*), a collection of verses from the Chou period; (2) *Book of History* (*Shu Ching*), a collection of records, speeches, and state documents from 2000 to 700 B.C.); (3) *Book of Changes* (*I-Ching*), a set of formulae for explaining nature, widely used for purposes of divination (this work is traditionally attributed to Wen Wang, 1100 B.C.); (4) *Book of Rites* (*Li Chi*), a collection of rules regulating social behavior. This was compiled long after Confucius, but may well represent rules and customs from much earlier times; (5) *Spring and Autumn Annals* (*Ch'un Ch'iu*), a chronicle of events from 722 to 464 B.C.

The Four Books are: (1) *Analects of Confucius* (*Lun Yu*), which are sayings of Confucius to his disciples, collected and edited by them; (2) *The Great Learning* (*Ta Hsueh*), teachings of Confucius containing his suggestions for governing. This work reflects Hsun Tzu's development of Confucius thought; (3) *Doctrine of the Mean* (*Chung Yung*), teaching attributed to Confucius concerning the regulation of life; (4) *Book of Mencius* (*Meng Tzu*), an elaboration of some Confucian principles by Mencius, an early commentator of Confucius.

The essence of the Confucian teachings contained in this literature is expressed in the teaching that by developing the humanity within him, man can become great both in his personal conduct and private life, and in his relations with others. When all individuals do this, goodness will abound and happiness will be achieved.

In addition to the development of Confucianism by Mencius (ca.

371–289 B.C.), further elaborations on the teachings of Confucius are found in the *Hsun Tzu*, attributed to Hsun Tzu (ca. 320–238 B.C.). Hsun Tzu emphasized the need for the Confucian virtues by pointing to the inherent badness of human nature. Thus, whereas Mencius emphasized the need to practice the virtues of humanity, righteousness, and filial piety in order to preserve man's goodness, Hsun Tzu claimed that they must be practiced to root out the evil in man and replace it with goodness.

The desperate conditions of the times also provide an explanatory context for the rise of Taoism, which emphasized the need to look beyond the promises and treaties of man for a source of peace and contentment. Lao Tzu, born late in the sixth century B.C., urges a simple and harmonious life, a life in which the profit motive is abandoned, cleverness discarded, selfishness eliminated, and desires reduced. In the context of a China in which greed and desire were bringing about nearly unimaginable hardship and suffering, a philosophy emphasizing the need to return to nature's way to avoid the viciousness of man's way would understandably find a ready following. Yang Chu's (ca. 440–ca. 366 B.C.) claim that he would not exchange even a single hair for the profits of the entire world makes sense against the background of graft and corruption that resulted from preoccupation with profit. Lao Tzu, who is earlier than Yang Chu, felt that so long as human actions were motivated by greed and avarice there was no hope for peace and contentment, and so he advocated the principle that only those actions which were in accord with Nature should be undertaken.

Taoism, the philosophy of the natural and the simple way initiated by Lao Tzu, received a foundation of metaphysical monism from Chuang Tzu (fourth century B.C.). This philosopher also sharpened the emphasis on the natural way as opposed to the artificial and contrived way of persons. In fact, it was a revival of Chuang Tzu's development of metaphysical doctrines of naturalism that provided the common meeting ground for Taoism and the Buddhism that developed in China during the fourth and fifth centuries A.D.

Although Confucianism and Taoism were to become the most influential of the early philosophies of China, they were by no means the only philosophies of the day. Mohism, which received its main direction from Mo Tzu (468–376 B.C.), shared the Confucian interest in advocating the increased welfare of man, and also agreed that the measure of man's welfare was man himself rather than Nature or the Spirits. But Mo Tzu felt that the Confucian emphasis on cultivating humanity was too vague and general for actually bringing about an improved human condition. He argued that the way to improve man's condition was to tend to the immediate welfare of the people. The slogan of the school became "promote general welfare and remove evil." The criterion advocated for measuring human happiness was utility. Ultimately, according to Mohism, value was to be measured in terms of benefits to the people. Benefits, in turn, could be measured in terms of increased wealth, population, and contentment.

Although Mo Tzu saw himself in opposition to Confucius, probably thinking of himself as a practical reformer and Confucius as an idealistic dreamer, the long-run effect of his philosophy was to strengthen Confucianism by adding external sanctions and criteria to the internal sanctions and criteria advocated by Confucius. The result was a humanism with a utilitarian flavor and a greater practical emphasis. The special strength of this combination was due to the moralistic emphasis of Confucianism which served as a corrective to utilitarianism, while utilitarianism added a practicalness to the moralism.

The School of Names had its early development in the work of Hui Shih (380–305? B.C.) and Kung-sun Lung (b. ca. 380 B.C.). The main interest of philosophers of this school was in the relationship between language and reality. Their motivation appears to have been primarily theoretical, as these logicians were interested in knowledge for its own sake rather than for its utility. This interest in knowledge for its own sake makes the school unique, and caused it to be the source of ridicule for members of the other schools. But despite the opposition between the logicians and the other philosophers of China at this time, the investigation of the relations between words and things, and the concern with knowledge for its own sake served as an important antidote to the excessive practicalness of the other philosophers. It served to keep alive an interest in theory, and the studies in the relations between words and things became useful later in both Taoism and Confucianism as they sought a metaphysical basis for their social philosophies.

The Yin-Yang school, concerned with cosmogony and cosmology, also was influential in the time of early Confucianism and Taoism. Since no individual philosophers connected with this school are known it is not possible to provide specific dates. But most likely this school goes back to late Shang or early Chou times in its beginnings, and continues to be important until long after Confucius.

The beginnings of the *yin-yang* speculation apparently are contained in a natural curiosity of the people about the workings of nature on all sides of them. For an agrarian people living very close to nature and feeling the rhythms of her workings, nothing could be more natural than to speculate about the principles, or "inner workings," of nature's functions. There were two questions implicit in this early curiosity about nature. On the one hand, there was the question about the structure of the universe, What is the organization or plan of the universe? On the other hand, there was the question about the origin of the universe, Where did the universe come from, and how did it originate?

The theory of the Five Elements is essentially an answer to the question about the structure of the universe. The *yin-yang* theory is essentially an answer to the question of the origin of the universe. According to early versions of the Five Elements, or Agents, theory, the five powers of the universe that control the functioning of nature are symbolically represented by Wood, Fire, Metal, Water, and Earth. The combinations of these powers determine the workings of the universe. For example, when the power represented by Wood is dominant it is spring. When the power of Fire dominates it is summer. Autumn represents the ascendancy of Metal, and winter results when Water is dominant. In late summer Earth is dominant. The important thing about the Five Elements theory is that it was an attempt to explain the functions of nature by appeal to inner principles, or powers, which are really the forces responsible for the manifestations of nature.

According to the *yin-yang* theory, the universe came to be as a result of the interactions between the two opposing universal forces of *yin* and *yang*. The existence of the universe is seen to reside in the tensions resulting from the universal force of non-being, or *yin*, and the universal force of being, or *yang*. Whatever is experienced simultaneously has being and lacks being; it comes into being and passes out of being. But this is just to say that it is being pulled between the forces of *yin* and *yang*. The changing world that is experienced—that is characterized as nature—can exist only when there is both being and non-being, for without being there is no coming-into-being, and without non-being there is no passing-out-of-being. Hence *yin*, the negative, and *yang*, the positive, are required as a source of nature.

Both the Five Elements theory and the *yin-yang* theory were influential in the rise of Neo-Confucianism. In the formulations of various later thinkers these theories underwent metaphysical interpretation and found their place in a general theory of existence.

The other early school of considerable importance is that of Legalism. The most important philosopher of this school is Han Fei Tzu (d. 233

B.C.), though the school itself is several hundred years older. The basic presupposition of this school is that man is basically evil, and consequently the authority of laws and the state are required for human welfare. Although this school is opposed to the Confucian inasmuch as Confucius emphasized morality and goodness over laws and punishment as a means for promoting human happiness, and the Legalists advocated law and authority, the long-term effect of the Legalist emphasis was to add to morality a dimension of legality, making the law a vehicle for morality. In this way the Legalist school added a considerable measure of strength to Confucianism.

In early medieval times, Hui-nan Tzu (d. 122 B.C.) a relatively late Taoist, developed a cosmology according to which the unfolding of *Tao* produced successively space, the world, the material forces, *yin* and *yang*, and all the things. According to this theory *yin* and *yang* become the principles of production and change among all the things in the world. Tung Chung-shu (176–104 B.C.), a late Confucianist, also referred to the *yin* and *yang* as the principles of things. According to him, all activities are due to the forces of *yin* and *yang*, which manifest themselves through the five elements.

That the Taoist Hui-nan, and the Confucianist Tung Chung-shu, should both make use of the *yin-yang* and Five Elements theories shows that these philosophies were coming closer together at this time and finding a common ground of explanation. The revitalization of both of these philosophies as a result of their meeting and the resulting cross-fertilization had to wait for many centuries, however, until the catalyst of Buddhism had been introduced. In fact, it was not until around 900 A.D., with the rise of Neo-Confucianism, that the meeting of Confucianism and Taoism prepared by Hui-nan Tzu and Tung Chung-shu bore fruit in the form of a vigorous new philosophy.

Part of the reason for the long delay is due to the fact that Tung Chun-shu was successful in getting Confucianism adopted as the state ideology. This of course meant that Taoism was out of official favor, and removed most of the critical challenges required for a vigorous and healthy philosophy. For nearly the next thousand years after being adopted as the state ideology, the philosophy of Confucianism was to see little development, as most of the emphasis was upon putting the philosophy that had already been developed into practice, rather than on developing further the philosophy itself.

Although Buddhism was introduced into China from India prior to the end of the first century A.D., it remained almost entirely without influence until after the fifth century. All of the different Buddhist schools of philosophy were introduced into China, but only those which could be reconciled with the principles of either Taoism or Confucianism became forces in shaping the future development of the Chinese mind. The realistic philosophies of Vaibhashika and Sautrantika which supported Theravada Buddhism failed to take hold in China because of their insistence on the momentary and fleeting character of reality. The idealism of the Yogacara philosophy did not suit the practical emphasis of the Chinese temperament, and the skepticism of the Madhyamika proved too radical for a pragmatic people.

The Buddhism which was accepted by the Chinese and which has been influential right up to our own times was a modified version, adapted to the inclusive and synthetic tendencies of the Chinese mind.

The Buddhist school of uncompromising idealism, emphasizing the reality of "Consciousness-only" and the causality of ideas only, found its counterpart in the Hua-yen school of Chinese Buddhism. But here ideational causation became a universal or total causation, according to which all the elements of reality are perfectly real and reflect each other, being at the same time simple and complex, pure and impure, subtle and gross, conscious and unconscious. In this way, far from distinguishing between conscious and unconscious reality and denying reality to the latter, this school of Buddhism held that the universe is a grand harmony of conscious and unconscious, pure and impure, simple and complex. The Indian disjunction, "either conscious or unconscious," had become the conjunction, "both conscious and unconscious." The Grand Harmony was the harmony of all opposites in the universe and the harmony was possible because each of the ultimate elements of which the universe is composed contained within itself all of the differing aspects and tendencies in the world.

The T'ient-t'ai school of Buddhism, which has its beginnings around the beginning of the seventh century A.D., evolved what it called the "Round Doctrine." The school began with the teaching of the non-being of all reality. From this doctrine of the Void, wherein things are held to be unreal, they moved to the position that things have temporary existence. From the temporary existence of things, they moved to the position that things in their temporary existence represent the true state of Being. The "roundness" of the doctrine consists in the fact that these three—the void, the temporary, and the true—constitute the fullness of existence, and they are all three identical.

The other two schools of Chinese Buddhism that flourished are the Pure Land school, which is mainly religious, and the Ch'an (Zen) school. The Ch'an school is really a method of meditation rather than a philosophy, but it is underwritten by the philosophical attitude that through the negation of being, being is affirmed in its true nature. The meditation involves negating both production and extinction; arising and ceasing; annihilation and permanence; and unity and plurality. But this negation is simply an aspect of affirming the presence of the Buddha-nature in all things. The enlightenment marked by coming to see the presence of the Buddha-nature in all things is the aim of the Ch'an meditation.

The tendency to synthesize opposing features of metaphysical views so clearly evident in Chinese Buddhism was the most significant factor in the rise of Neo-Confucianism. Chinese philosophers had tended to be highly critical of Buddhist philosophies ever since their introduction to China. They objected to the emphasis on overcoming suffering and death, which to them seemed little more than selfish escapism. The monastic aspect of Buddhism which involved the renunciation of the family and society seemed wrong-headed, since it was clearly impossible that man, a social being, could ever escape society so long as he lived, even though he desert family and friends. They were also critical of the Buddhist emphasis on metaphysics which led to the denial of being, on the grounds that to regard all things, including food and clothes, as unreal and yet to depend on them was contradictory. But perhaps the deepest difference between the Chinese philosophers and the Buddhist schools that were introduced to China was due to the emphasis on society as the primary metaphysical reality by the Chinese, as opposed to the emphasis on the non-social by the Buddhists.

Granted these differences and the critical attitude of the Chinese philosophers toward Buddhism, the rise of Neo-Confucianism is not hard to understand. It represents the attempt of the philosophers from the tenth century A.D. on to counteract Buddhism with a more comprehensive and superior philosophy. And granted the synthetic tendency of the Chinese philosophers, it is not difficult to predict that the new philosophy would incorporate features of Buddhism along with features of Taoism and Confucianism. Furthermore, granting the preoccupation with social reality that characterized earlier Chinese philosophy, it is not surprising that Confucianism should have the primary role in this reconstruction.

Although the beginnings of Neo-Confucianism can be traced to Han Yu (768–824), it was not until Sung times that a comprehensive and definitive formulation was achieved. It was during the Sung period (960–1279) that the school of Reason of the Ch'eng brothers (Ch'eng Hao, 1032–1085, and Ch'eng Yi, 1033–1108) arose, and the great synthesis of Chu Hsi (1130–1200) was achieved. The school of Mind, which leaned in the direction of idealism, also originated during this period. The two most illustrious philosophers connected with this school are Lu Chiu-yuan (1139–1193) and Wang Yang-ming (1473–1529). The third phase of the development of Neo-Confucianism is represented by the Empirical school of the Ching period (1644–1911).

The key concept in the Reason school of Neo-Confucianism is that of the Great Ultimate (*T'ai-chi*). This Great Ultimate is the ultimate reality and underlies all existence. It is the reason or principle inherent in all activity and existence. Through activity it generates *yang*. Upon reaching its limit, activity becomes tranquil, and through tranquillity the Great Ultimate generates *yin*. When tranquillity reaches its limit, activity begins, the one producing the other as its opposite. This reversal of opposites is a notion of Taoism, where it is held that reversal is the way of the Great Way, the Tao of the universe. Through the interaction between *yin* and *yang* the five elements are produced, the ten thousand things in the universe are produced, and the seasons run their course. The Great Ultimate, which produces all things and determines their functions, is a combination of matter (*ch'i*) and principle (*li*). The nature of things is the result of what they are and how they function. The stuff of which they are made is their matter, or *ch'i*, and their function is their principle, or *li*. When *ch'i* and *li* are in harmony, things are in order and there is a grand harmony. Since the Great Ultimate represents a harmony of *ch'i* and *li*, order is the law of the universe. It remained for Chu Hsi to observe that the Great Ultimate is nothing but the principle of ultimate goodness, to transform this pervasive metaphysics into a groundwork for a social philosophy.

The Reason school was dualistic in positing matter (*ch'i*) and reason (*li*) as the ultimate realities. Wang Yang-ming (1472–1529) was monistic in his emphasis, holding that mind alone was ultimately real. He did not deny the reality of things external to the mind, but emphasized that it is only through consciousness, or mind, that a person becomes aware of things. Thus mind is the primary reality. The essential character of mind, according to this philosopher is its capacity for love. In its pristine goodness the mind of man forms a unity with heaven and earth and consequently the ideal man views all things as one and extends a universal love to all things. This universal love becomes the basis for all existence and all relationships. In the Ch'ing period (1644–1911), Wang Yang-ming's idealism came to be tempered with the empiricism of the Empirical school of Neo-Confucianism. Chu Hsi had emphasized the superiority of principle, or reason, over matter. Tai Chen (1723–1777) objected to this emphasis on the grounds that neither matter nor principle could be considered superior to the other, since reality could not be cut up in this way. In reality, there is no distinction between principle and matter. In the transformations of matter, principle is manifested, and the orderliness of transformations is due to principle. But there is no transformation without order, and there is no order without transformation. At best these two—matter and principle—are just two different ways of looking at reality, the basis of which is *jen*.

In the Empirical school, there is a return to the empirical and the particular, a greater concern with the position of the individual in society, and less interest in speculative metaphysics. In this respect, the third phase of Neo-Confucianism is closer to earlier Confucianism.

The development of philosophy in China in contemporary times is a subject which is not susceptible to analysis for a variety of reasons, chief of which is the lack of communication between the Chinese and the Western world.

In summing up the development of philosophy in China it could be said that Confucianism represents the *yang* of Chinese philosophy whereas Taoism represents its *yin*. Philosophy, as everything else, has its *yin* and *yang*, and finds perfection in the Grand Harmony of these two opposing principles. In China it was Neo-Confucianism that sought the harmony of all principles, drawing upon the various earlier philosophies.

CHAPTER 17

CONFUCIANISM

CONFUCIUS

Iᴛ has already been noted that the times of Confucius were marked by political and social disintegration and a widespread breakdown of morality. Granted these conditions, it was natural that Confucius should turn his attention to the reform of society. Having been introduced to hard work, suffering, and responsibility at an early age, he knew from personal experience the poverty, political abuse, and hardship that affected the lives of the ordinary people. No doubt his background aided his understanding of both government and the problems of the ordinary people.

At an early age Confucius found himself with a position in the government of his native state of Lu. There he could not only observe the inadequate administration of the kingdom of Lu, but could also, in a small way, do something about this administration by properly carrying out his own duties. He thus got a taste of practical politics, and this probably was a factor in his decision to turn his attention to the problems of government. From a background where he could see the misery of the people and the bad administration of the rulers, a person of Confucius' humanistic bent would naturally set himself to thinking about the correction of society.

Recognizing that his times were not all they should be, what was Confucius to do about it? How could a new order (or, what comes to the same thing, an old order) in society be established? In short, how is the well-being of society to be achieved? Confucius' answer to this question is his philosophy, a humanistic social philosophy. It is obvious that if Confucius' philosophy is a social philosophy it is about man and his society rather than about nature and man's knowledge of nature. But what does it mean to say that this is a *humanistic* social philosophy?

The most significant feature of humanism is the conviction that man is ultimate. To say that man is ultimate has a special meaning, as can be seen by contrasting humanism with naturalism and supernaturalism. According to naturalism it is nature—the non-human world—that is taken as ultimate. Here the principles for human action and life are taken from nature. Man should act in certain ways because the world is what it is. Discovering how human beings should act is a matter of discovering how nature acts, so that man's actions can be in accord with those of nature.

According to supernaturalism, a force or power other than man or nature is taken to be ultimate. This supernatural force is seen as regulating both nature and man, making them subordinate to this supernatural and superhuman power. The supernatural may be regarded as creating both nature and man and determining their behavior. According to this view, discovering how humans should act is a matter of discovering how this supernatural power intended them to act. In a theistic religion this might be seen as a matter of knowing and doing God's will.

Humanism becomes possible when man rather than nature or supernature is taken as ultimate. When man is taken as ultimate there is nothing superior to man as a source of human principles. Man does not look to either nature or supernature for norms of life and action; rather, he looks to himself to find the principles that provide for goodness and happiness. Thus, to call Confucianism a humanism is to note that it is a philosophy that answers the question "How can goodness and happiness be achieved?" by pointing to the principles of action found within man himself. The source of these principles is what makes human beings human. In Confucianism, that which gives human beings their humanity is called *jen*, and it is the source of all human actions and principles. Consequently, the first principle of Confucianism is to act according to *jen*. When all human relations are properly ordered according to *jen*, happiness will be achieved. *Jen* is the source of human actions and human relation, but *li* (order) is needed for their regulation and control. These twin concepts of order (*li*) and humanity (*jen*) constitute the basis of Confucianism.

It is recorded that one day, after a ceremony, Confucius heaved a great sigh, and upon being asked why he was sighing, replied, "Oh, I was thinking of the Golden Age and regretting that I was not able to have been born in it and to associate with the wise rulers and ministers of the three Dynasties." [1] As Confucius went on to explain how and why this was such a golden age, he remarked that the founders of the Great Dynasties

> were deeply concerned over the principle of *Li*, through which Justice was maintained, general confidence was tested, and errors of malpractice were exposed. An ideal of true manhood, *Jen*, was set up and good manners or courtesy was cultivated, as solid principles for the common people to follow. . . . [2]

The importance Confucius attached to *li* is also seen by his remark that "*Li* is the principle by which the ancient kings embodied the laws of heaven and regulated the expression of human nature. Therefore he who has attained *Li* lives, and he who has lost it, dies." [3]

What is this principle of *li*, to which Confucius attaches so much importance, and how is it related to good conduct and good government? No brief answer to this question can be satisfactory, because *li* is all pervasive, being the very basis, the *sine-qua-non*, of government for Confucius. *Li* represents an entire social and moral philosophy, which rests upon the principle of harmony in essential human relationships.

The word "*li*" means many things. It means religion; it means the general principle of the social order; it means the entire body of social, moral, and religious practices taught and rationalized by Confucius. It also means ritual and ceremony. It means a system of well-defined social relationships with definite attitudes toward one another, love in the parents, filial piety in the children, respect in the younger brothers, friendliness in the elder brothers, loyalty among friends, respect for authority among subjects and benevolence in rulers. It means moral discipline in man's personal conduct. It means propriety in everything.

Thus, the concept of *li* is seen to include many notions, more or less closely related, and while it is true that the concept of *li* is basic to Confucian philosophy it must be realized that in the sense that *li* provides the basis for Confucius' philosophy it is general, being constituted by several rather more specific concepts, such as *jen* (human-heartedness), *yi* (righteousness), and *hsiao* (filial piety). Consequently, an understand-

---

[1] *Li Chi*, Ch. IX, trans. by Lin Yutang, in *The Wisdom of Confucius* (New York: The Modern Library, 1938) p. 227.
[2] *Li Chi*, in *The Wisdom of Confucius*, p. 229.   [3] *Ibid.*

ing of *li* in the broad sense is to be achieved by first understanding the rather more specific virtues that make up *li*.

Since *li* is of such importance in Confucian philosophy it is appropriate that it be explored both from the point of view of its history and from the point of view of its content.

The earliest notion of *li* is of religious character, where *li* is concerned with rites regarding religious performances. It soon came to denote other rites, such as marriage, military, festival, government, etc.

This sense of *li* coincides with a more or less elaborate set of rules and convention which demand strict observation in carrying out various activities, mainly religious or social in character.

The second notion of *li* refers to a customary code of social behavior. In this sense *li* is the customary law, or common morality. *Li*, in this sense, takes the place of written law, although it differs from written law in that it is positive rather than negative ("do this," rather than "don't do this"), it does not bring with it automatic punishment, and it generally is assumed to refer to the behavior of the aristocracy rather than ordinary persons.

The third, and extended, meaning of *li* is anything which is reasonable, anything which has a rational basis. It is this third sense of *li* that is of most importance for understanding Confucius, although Confucius uses the term "*li*" in all of its meanings. This is not surprising, since the meanings of "*li*" are all related. This third sense of *li* is more basic and more nebulous in character than the first two, and it will be easier to make clear the character of *li* in the third sense by analyzing the concepts contained within it, rather than attempting a summary statement.

The most important virtues comprising *li* are *hsiao*, *yi*, and *jen*. It has been said that *yi* is the essence of *li*. It has also been said that *hsiao* is the foundation of all the virtues, and it is commonly said that *jen* is the key to Confucian philosophy. What are the concepts embodied in each of these virtues?

Hsiao, usually translated "filial piety," is the virtue of reverence. First of all, the parents are revered because life itself is generated from them. In showing reverence for parents it is important to protect the body from harm, since the body is from the parents. Therefore, to protect the body is to honor the parents. But even more, reverence should be shown for parents by doing well and making their name known and respected. If it is not possible to bring honor to the name of one's parents, at least they should not be disgraced. Thus, *hsiao* does not consist merely in giving one's parents physical care, but also in bringing them emotional and spiritual richness. And, equally important, after parents are dead, their unfulfilled aims and purposes should be the aims and purposes of the children. This is even more important than offering sacrifices to the departed spirits of deceased parents.

But *hsiao* is not merely a family virtue. Originating in the family, this virtue influences actions outside the family circle. It becomes, by extension, a moral and social virtue. When children learn respect and reverence for their parents they can have respect and love for their brothers and sisters. And when they have accomplished this, they can respect and love all mankind. And when all actions are directed by love of mankind they are acting according to their humanity, or *jen*. Thus the beginnings of *jen* are found in *hsiao*.

Yi, often translated "righteousness," refers to a moral disposition to do good. It is the recognition of what is right and proper, and also refers to something like a moral sense, an ability to recognize what is right and good. What is according to *yi* is unconditional and absolute. Some actions must be performed for the sole reason that they are right. A person ought to respect and obey his parents because it is morally right and obligatory to do so, and for no other reason. Other actions ought to be performed for the sake of something valuable they bring about. Such actions, done for the sake of attaining something else, are performed for the sake of profit. They are to be contrasted with actions performed according to *yi*, for these actions are performed only because they are right, and not because of what they produce. When a person does all actions for the sake of *yi*, or because they are the right things to do, he is not far from *jen*. To practice *jen* is to act out of a love and respect for humanity for no other reason than that it is the right, or human, way to act.

Jen, translated "benevolence," "human-heartedness," "true manhood," etc., is remarked by both Confucius and Mencius to be *love of man*. It represents the relation that should exist between two men, a relation of love and harmony. To practice *jen* is to love man as man. It includes the universalization that whatever is undesirable is undesirable for everyone, and whatever is desirable is desirable for everyone. *Jen* refers to the seed of humanity present in all persons. The cultivation of *jen* refers to the development of this seed until it becomes the sole principle of action in man. Only when all actions issue from a person's humanity and are for the sake of humanity has one achieved *jen*.

It is the concept of *jen* that supports and makes possible the famous Golden Rule of Confucius, which expresses the notion that man is the measure of man. When a person has developed his humanity he will be able to use himself as a "measuring square," and do to others what he wants done to him, and avoid doing to others what he does not wish done to him.

Hsiao, jen, and *yi* are the characteristics of the superior man, the man who has developed his humanity and who is morally cultivated and aware. This superior man is opposed by the small, or inferior, man who is morally uncultivated, who acts on instinct and for profit.

It is the conviction of Confucius that the cultivation of *jen* through *hsiao* and *yi* will lead to a personal embodiment of virtue which will result in a well-ordered society, because the well-ordered society is based on virtue, which is rooted in *jen.* There is no sharp distinction here between ethics and politics. If man is true to himself, having good faith or sincerity, then he will embody the various virtues. And if every man does this, good government and a happy social order will be assured.

The idea of government by virtue, or goodness, rather than by law may sound rather strange to Western ears, but government by virtue is exactly what Confucius was hoping to achieve. Before questioning this utopia, the various relations between the virtues embodied in *li*, especially those aspects of *li* known as *jen* and *hsiao*, need to be examined.

The most comprehensive statement of the Confucian philosophy is contained in the *Great Learning*. There, after observing that true greatness consists in manifesting the great virtues, loving the people, and achieving the highest good, eight ethical-political items are enunciated as means of achieving greatness. The text reads as follows:

> The ancients who wished to preserve the fresh or clear character of the people of the world would first set about ordering their national life. Those who wished to order their national life, would first set about regulating their family life. Those who wished to regulate their family life would set about cultivating their personal life. Those who wished to cultivate their personal lives would first set about setting their hearts right. Those who wished to set their hearts right would first set about making their wills sincere. Those who wished to make their wills sincere would first set about achieving true knowledge. The achieving of true knowledge depended upon the investigation of things. When things are investigated, then true knowledge is achieved; when true knowledge is achieved then the will becomes sincere; when the will is sincere, then the heart is set right; when the heart is set right, then the personal life is cultivated; when the personal life is cultivated, then the family life is regulated; when the family life is regulated, then the national life is orderly, and when the national life is orderly, then there is peace in this world.[4]

4 *The Great Learning (Ta Hsueh)*, trans. by Lin Yutang, *The Wisdom of Confucius*, p. 139.

The last statement in this quotation—"When the national life is orderly, then there is peace in the world"—is an expression, maybe utopian, of what most people would expect from government. Peace within a particular social entity and peace among neighboring social entities depends upon a great many factors, such as enough to eat, a place to sleep, security against disease, self-expression etc., all of which may be reduced to the factors of material and spiritual sufficiency. Sufficient material wealth and ample means and opportunity for spiritual development and expression (art, education, religion, etc.) are necessary (though they may not be sufficient) conditions of peace. A pervasive morality may also be needed to regulate competition and to prevent strife and conflict.

It is to be seen therefore, that the task given to government by Confucius is gigantic, because so utopian. According to him, it is the business of government to insure that material and spiritual sufficiency exist and that people act morally in order that peace be achieved. Granted that this is very nice and very idealistic, but isn't it terribly impractical? After all, how can the government take care of all the material needs, to say nothing of the spiritual needs, of every individual? Is not morality a matter for individuals rather than the province of government? Besides pointing to the fact that the goal of government for Confucius was very high, such questions point to the way in which Confucius regarded government. One way of regarding government is to take the attitude that the obvious means to material and spiritual plenty, if provision of these is to be regarded as the function of government, are the passing of laws, the raising of taxes, the building of schools, churches, museums, etc., and the regulation of production and labor so that enough will be produced and each person will get his share of the production. Putting this into action would, of course, require great bureaus with much paper shuffling, and hordes of government workers.

However, in the Confucian ideal state the main functions of government are carried out at a local rather than national level, in the communities and the families. The national governor is something of an overseer. The actual government is effected not really by government workers, but by each citizen observing his proper relations to other individuals. When proper relations exist between all persons in society the aim of government will have been achieved.

Obviously, the Confucian concept of government is that of a moral system. When all individuals act morally in all of their relations with other persons there will be no social problems. This is why Confucius can say that to achieve world peace it is necessary and sufficient to set right one's heart, cultivate his personal life, and regulate family life properly. When these three things are done *jen* will be cultivated and morality and goodness will prevail.

The above quotation, concerning the way to world peace, reflects not only the idea that education (investigation of things) is a basic element of Confucian social philosophy, but suggests also a certain philosophy of education, in the sense that it is most important to come to know man. For man's good it is necessary to know both what man is and what things are, so that man's life may be ordered in a way conducive to his welfare, making the best use of things in the world. Confucius says, "The principles of the higher education consist in preserving man's clear character, in giving new life to the people and in dwelling (or resting) in perfection, or the ultimate good."[5] Only through education will man know himself and the world. Without this knowledge it is very difficult to order life so that it will be in harmony with things of the world; only when life is in harmony with the world is there peace and happiness.

According to Confucius, "true knowledge" ensues when the root, or basis, of things is known. An example of what it is to have true knowledge is afforded by Confucius when he says, "In presiding over lawsuits I am as good as anyone. The thing is we should make it our aim that there not be any lawsuits at all, . . ."[6] In other words, one should remove the evil by removing the causes of the evil. Knowing the basic causes is primary in the rectification of malfunctions. So, if one has true knowledge, i.e. knowledge of the basic causes, of crime, then it may be possible to do away with crime itself, thereby eliminating lawsuits.

Man's most important knowledge, however, is self-knowledge rather than knowledge about external things such as social conditions and institutions. "Having knowledge" is above all knowing who and what one is, and this means knowing the principles upon which he acts. Accordingly, true knowledge is had only when there is self-knowledge, for in Confucianism it is always the moral and social self that is taken as ultimate.

When it is said that the will becomes sincere when there is knowledge, the reference is to self-knowledge, and the point is that one who has self-knowledge will not deceive himself about the motives and principles of his actions. Thus it is said, "What is meant by making the will

[5] *The Great Learning (Ta Hsueh), op. cit.*, p. 139.   [6] *Ibid.*, p. 143.

sincere is that one should not deceive himself."[7] A person should not try to deceive himself that if he does something in private no one will know and therefore it is all right. The wrong action will be known to himself immediately, and soon the effects will be known not only to himself but to others as well. Corruptness of private character does not remain purely private—a person does not live in isolation—but affects, and is affected by, the whole community of men.

When a person is upset by worries and cares, or is overcome with joy or passion, then his heart is not right. Then he is hardly in position to make fair and just decisions concerning any matters, personal or public. If his decisions are unjust, those persons affected by his decisions may be adversely affected. When on the other hand "the heart is set right," one avoids the excesses and defects that affect one's ability to make good decisions, or according to the Confucian statement, "The cultivation of the personal life depends on setting one's heart right." If one has the proper attitude toward the things of life he will remain calm even in joy and sorrow and will be able to live a good personal life.

If the parents are morally upright there can be a family in which the proper relationships exist. If the father, himself a good man, is respected and obeyed, and the mother, a good woman, is loved and cherished, harmony can exist in a home. And if there is harmony in every home, then there is harmony in the whole country.

This emphasis on proper familial relationships is one of the most important ideas of Confucius and is worthy of some elaboration. Suppose children are born into a family where love and goodness abound. These children will grow up seeing parents loving and respecting each other and will have a model on which to develop their own sense of respect and love. Here the children see their parents respecting other adults, the various offices and officials of government, morality and law. Not only is it possible for the father to rule properly in this family, but respect and obedience are natural to the children.

Psychologists, with good evidence in support of their remarks, report that the first five years of human life are the most important for establishing basic attitudes and behavior patterns. This being so, what better way of insuring respect for law, government, and people than by good education of the child in his early years? Since, except in unfortunate cases, the first five years or so are spent in the home, the education

[7] *Ibid.*, p. 144.

must take place in the home. There is no question here of educating or not educating a child from birth to say, five years. Education will take place, based mainly on imitation of a model, and the question is whether the education will be good or bad, which reduces to the question of whether the parents provide the proper model for their children or not.

Suppose that children, maybe unwanted in the first place, are born into a family where little love or respect is shown one parent by the other and where fighting is part of the daily fare. If also the parents show no respect for anyone or anything else, what will the situation in the home be like? Where will the children learn to respect themselves and other men and the institutions of men? Statistics offered by sociologists suggest that this latter kind of family situation produces criminals, or at best, maladjusted persons.

It is hard to think of anything more important for good government and peace than proper family relationships, where this means the kind of familial relationships that enable children to grow up with respect for authority, love for their fellow men, and a sense of the propriety of things. A nation is only a collection of individuals which have joined together for their common good, agreeing to the rule of the few for the good of the many. The good of the many is the good of many individuals. Since government is for the sake of the individual, and it is the individual who benefits or suffers from government, it would seem only natural to study means and ways of government from the point of view of the individuals concerned. Put in other words, the study of government ought to start with man, not institutions. This is precisely what Confucius is doing. He begins with man in his fundamental relationships with other men. And where is the best place to begin with man? Begin with the beginning of man! A man begins in a family where he is born. If education is the key to good society education must begin when man does, and this is in the family when the man is born. The family is the basic stable unit of society, and traditionally the most influential unit socially. Larger units of government can easily be imagined as "merely larger families."

With the individual and the family viewed in this way it is easy to understand why Confucius stressed the virtue of hsiao, and regarded it as basic to all the virtues. Nothing can be more important than that a child should develop the proper attitudes to the rest of the family. If he doesn't come to have respect and love for his parents and brothers and sisters, and from them learn respect for other men and institutions of men, and if within the familial situation he does not learn respect for himself, it is hardly to be expected that upon becoming an adult he will become a model citizen.

It is now easy to see that certain aspects of Confucius' analysis of social structure might illuminate problems of our own times. What is uncommon is the role that goodness is expected to play in government. Goodness, for many people today, is something for philosophers to talk about, or a subject for religion. Government based on goodness or virtue is almost unthinkable; yet this is what Confucius was suggesting, and is what Mencius, a follower of Confucius, taught even more clearly. It is important to see how Confucius, in all seriousness, could suggest as a basis for government that which today seems, at first glance at least, completely impractical and impossible.

It is not so much that Confucius had a different view of the basic nature of man than that commonly held today, but rather that Confucius had quite a different idea concerning the aims of education and government than we have today. While Confucius nowhere explicitly affirms that man's nature is basically good, still, it is implicit in his view of government and education, and it is explicitly stated by Mencius that man is basically good. Now it is not uncommon for people today also to hold that man is basically good, and needs only to develop this goodness. But it is also commonly held today that at bottom man is the kind of being Hobbes saw, selfish and demanding, using other people to serve his own end. It makes little difference which of these views is held—in either case goodness will be claimed as an impossible basis for government. The need to develop laws and to punish infractions will always be one of the necessary conditions of government, and one of its most basic tasks. If people are good it will be easier to carry out the laws, in the sense of enforcing them, but it will never make law unnecessary.

There is an important reason for this attitude in our own times. Today, in the Western world, whether man is regarded as basically good or basically evil, the purpose of his education is regarded as the mastery of a skill or trade that may enable him to obtain sufficient material goods. Young people are urged to go to college so they can get a good job; once enrolled at a university or college they are advised how best to prepare themselves for the professional labor market. If this observation is slightly exaggerated, it nonetheless points toward a fundamental difference between our contemporary philosophy of education and the Confucian purpose of education as the development of man's moral character. Confucius tells us that "the only way for the superior man to civilize the people and establish good social customs is through education. A piece of jade cannot become an object of art without chiselling, and a man cannot come to know the moral law without education."[8]

One cause, perhaps, for this difference in aims of education is that for Confucius the final good, or happiness, of man (in this life at least, if another be assumed) is thought to be spiritual in nature, not material.

If, without enforced positive law (in the relevant sense), there is to be peace and well-being, it is necessary that everyone act appropriately, or practice the virtue of *li*. To act appropriately one must respect and care for others, or practice the virtue of *jen*, and this respect for men is learned early through respect for the parents, or by practicing the virtue of *hsiao*. This will produce a true moral self, a "real man." So it is that if the true moral self is to be realized there must be education at all levels. Each individual must take seriously his responsibility for guiding those whom he influences. When the true moral self is achieved then the person is in harmony with all things and there is peace and fulfillment.

The character of and means to good government should now be clear. Here is how a modern student of Confucianism sums it up:

> To be kept stable, society must have leaders who can be trusted; that the only leaders to be trusted are men of character; that character is to be developed through education acquired both from others and through self-discipline; that no man is a safe leader who goes to extremes; that the right cultivation of his own character must be the chief concern of every leader; that no parent, teacher, or public officer has the right to take lightly his responsibilities for guiding, through percept, rules and example, the conduct of those who are under him.[9]

This is the conviction of Confucius, a conviction that by cultivating his human-ness (*jen*) man can perfect this society and achieve happiness.

The main question of Confucius is, What should our conduct be with respect to other human beings? The one and only answer given by Confucius, though taking many forms and assuming many details, is that actions should proceed from *jen* and be regulated by *li*.

The Confucian philosophy outlined so far probably represents primarily the thought of Confucius, though it is extremely difficult to keep separate and distinct the various streams of thought contributing to Confucianism. There is no doubt that the realism of Hsun Tzu and

---

[8] *Book of Rites (Li Chi)*, trans. by Lin Yutang, *The Wisdom of Confucius*, p. 241.
[9] D. Willard Lyons, as quoted by Clarence Burton Day, in *The Philosophers of China* (New York: The Citadel Press, 1962), p. 43.

the idealism of Mencius were influential in the development of Confucius' thought into Confucianism. While Confucius emphasized *li* and regarded *jen*, *yi*, and *hsiao* as necessary for a well-developed and regulated individual and for a well-ordered society, he did not attend to the question of *why* man should practice these virtues. He simply assumed that if man wanted to be happy he *should* act this way. Mencius and Hsun Tzu, on the other hand, were very much concerned with the question of *why* man should live in accord with *jen*, practicing *yi* and *hsiao*. Mencius held that it was because of the original goodness of human nature that man should practice the virtues stressed by Confucius. Hsun Tzu, on the other hand, took the view that it was because of the original evilness of human nature that man should practice these virtues. The direction given to the development of Confucianism by these two philosophers was determined by their answers to the question of *why* man should practice *jen*.

MENCIUS

Mencius agreed with Confucius that *jen* is basic, that it is the source and foundation of all goodness and virtue. And he also agreed with Confucius that *li*, or rules for proper behavior, was required for the development and manifestation of *jen*. In addition, *hsiao* was recognized to be the beginning point for goodness. But Mencius gave a more important role to *yi* than did Confucius. It is *yi*, or righteousness, that above all else contains they key to the development and cultivation of *jen* according to Mencius.

The reason for the emphasis on *yi* is due to a recognition by Mencius of the distinction between goodness and rightness. *Jen* refers to the goodness that is basic to man's nature. But *yi* refers to the rightness of human actions. The need for the distinction is due to the fact that although all men possess *jen*, or humanity, not all men act in the right way. For Mencius, who claimed that *jen* was an actual beginning of goodness present in each person, the problem was to explain how the evil that everyone recognizes could be present in the world. Explaining as he did, that evil was due to wrong actions, it was necessary to distinguish between the rightness of actions and the goodness of human nature, or the presence of *jen*. Despite the presence of goodness in man it is possible that man should occasionally act in a wrong way and thus bring about evil in the world. Because this is so, it is necessary to emphasize *yi*, or the correctness of action, in order to rid the world of evil. But, of course,

Mencius did not hold that a distinction between *yi* and *jen* was equivalent to claiming that they are totally different and do not meet. Rather, he held that if *jen* is completely developed, *yi* will naturally follow. And if all actions are in accord with *yi*, *jen* will come to be developed. But it is easier and more successful to begin with the correction of the actions of persons than with developing the natures of persons. Hence *yi* comes first.

The two most significant points of difference between Confucius and Mencius are their views about the nature of man, and the relation between goodness and rightness. Confucius claimed that man has a *potential* for goodness, and Mencius claimed that man possesses an *actual goodness* as part of his nature. Confucius regarded goodness and rightness as the same, but Mencius distinguished between them.

Mencius did not simply state that man possesses an innate goodness, but presented arguments for this view. The first argument runs as follows: (1) All men are alike by nature; (2) the sage, who is good by nature, is a man; (3) therefore all men are good by nature. According to the second argument, the goodness of man is evident in the virtues of *jen*, *yi*, *li*, and *chih* (moral wisdom). All men possess the beginnings of these virtues as can be seen by the universality of the basic feelings that constitute the beginning for them. Compassion is the beginning of *jen*. Any person would have compassion for a child who had fallen in a well, and would attempt to save the child. Shamefulness is the root of *yi*. Any person who robs another person and thereby causes the death of that person will feel shame and try to make retribution. Reverence is the beginning of *li*. The universality of this beginning can be seen in the fact that all children have a natural reverence for their parents, and in the presence of superiors all people feel their own shortcomings and are modest and reverent. If one were to simply throw the body of a parent in a ditch instead of burying it, and later were to come and see the birds and beasts preying on it, a natural reverence would cause one to hurry and bury the body. The knowledge of right and wrong is the root of the virtue *chih*. Since every person draws his or her ideas about the rightness and wrongness of actions from reflections in his or her own mind, it follows that these innate ideas of right and wrong must be found in every person.

The conclusion of these arguments is that man is a moral animal, for because of his innate goodness he knows right and wrong, has compassion, reverence, and modesty, and knows shame, and consequently can distinguish between right and wrong.

But if this innate goodness of man be granted, how is one to account for the presence of evil in the world? According to Mencius, evil in the world has three sources. First, evil is due to external circumstances. Although man is by nature good, still his nature is distorted by the externals of life. Society and culture are responsible for the presence of wrong actions and evil in the world. Secondly, evil is due to the abandonment of self. Man abandons his innate goodness. Rather than allowing his nature to manifest itself in goodness he forsakes this goodness and determines to do evil. Thirdly, evil is due to the failure to nourish the feelings and the senses. That is, though the intentions are good, one is incapable of doing the right things because of a lack of knowledge on which to make the correct decision.

Upon accepting Mencius' arguments for the innate goodness of man and agreeing with his explanation of the source of evil in the world, it follows that the reason why man should live according to *jen*, *yi*, and *li* is that through acting correctly one's humanity is developed, and thereby human behavior will become well regulated. Furthermore, to regulate one's actions by *li* is to live according to the innate goodness that is man's basic nature. In brief, man should live the way Confucius said he should because it is his nature to do so.

HSUN TZU

The views of Hsun Tzu on this point are diametrically opposed to those of Mencius. According to Hsun Tzu, human nature is originally evil. It is through social institutions and culture that man becomes good. Although man is said not only to lack the beginnings of the four virtues claimed by Mencius, but to actually possess the beginnings of evil in that he has an inherent desire for profit and pleasures, it is held to be possible for every man to become a Sage, for what every man does possess is intelligence, and through the employment of intelligence goodness is brought about. Mencius said that man is born good; Hsun Tzu says that man is born evil. Mencius said that society and culture bring about evil; Hsun Tzu says that society and culture bring about goodness. Whereas Mencius says that anyone can become a Sage because of his innate goodness, Hsun Tzu says that anyone can become a Sage because of his innate intelligence and educability.

The problem for Hsun Tzu is to show how it is that if man is born evil he can become good. He argues that goodness comes about as the result of social organization and culture. Social organization and culture come as the result of (1) the drive to live better, and (2) the need to overcome other creatures. The arguments are (1) man cannot provide the goods needed to live, let alone to live well, except through the cooperation of other persons, and (2) man cannot make himself secure from the various creatures and forces of nature without mutual cooperation. And without security, the structures of society required to improve the quality of life are not possible.

Since it is clear, for these two reasons, that man requires social organization, the question is that of how social organization brings about goodness. Hsun Tzu's answer is that social organization requires rules of conduct, which bring about goodness. His theory is that man is born with desires, some of which are ordinarily unsatisfied. When desires remain unsatisfied man strives for their satisfaction. When many persons are striving for the satisfaction of their conflicting desires without rules or limits there is contention and strife which brings about disorder. This is harmful to everyone. Accordingly the early kings established rules of conduct regulating the activities involved in attempting to satisfy desires: in this way the various rules required for social living came about. Within this line of reasoning, goodness is brought about as a result of the regulation of human conduct required for social living.

Hsun Tzu also argues for the creation of goodness through the employment of intelligence. He observes that it is not the absence of hair or feathers on this two-legged creature that distinguishes man from other animals, but it is the ability to make distinctions. Man's intelligence is displayed in his making of social distinctions. Since it is the making of social distinctions and the resulting social relationships regulated by li that distinguish man from the birds and the beasts, man ought to act according to li in order to preserve and manifest his nature.

Both lines of argument given by Hsun Tzu emphasize that goodness is the result of human creation through the employment of intelligence and the making of distinctions in the social sphere. He differs from Confucius in distinguishing between goodness and intelligence and in stressing the actual evil present in the nature of man. Through their attempts to support the social philosophy of Confucius by providing an answer to the question, Why regulate life by li, and, why develop jen by practicing yi? Hsun Tzu and Mencius strengthened the philosophy considerably. What happened historically was that neither of these philosophers was rejected in the favor of the other, but rather, both the idealism of Mencius and the realism of Hsun Tzu were added to the philosophy of Confucius, thus rounding out the philosophy of Confucianism. From

Mencius was taken the emphasis on determining the correctness of action as a means to the development of man's humanity, and from Hsun Tzu, was taken the emphasis on following rules of behavior for developing man's nature. By adopting both views, Confucianism favored equally respect for internal sanctions, using the internal feelings as guides to behavior, and the external sanctions, using social rules as guides to behavior. This is roughly equivalent to employing both the internal criteria of conscience and the external criterion of law to determine how one should live.

Through his emphasis on the utility of rules, or *li*, for guiding conduct Hsun Tzu was able to add to Confucianism the insights of the Utilitarians (Mohists) and through his emphasis on social rules and external sanctions he was able to add the insights of the Legalists, or positivists, to Confucianism.

MO TZU

The Utilitarian school of Mo Tzu was a strong and popular school in ancient times. Mo Tzu was critical of the Confucian emphasis on goodness as the key to successful social organization on the grounds that it was not sufficiently practical. He was also critical of the traditional institutions, charging that they were not sufficiently useful for achieving the well-being and happiness of the people. The key principle of this school is that the correctness of actions can be determined by reference to their usefulness in producing benefits for man. This principle derives from a theory of the origin of society according to which the social institutions of man were established to obtain benefits for the people and eliminate their hardships, to enrich the poor and increase the population, to replace danger with security, and confusion with order.

Since Hsun Tzu had a similar view of the origin of society, it was possible for him to adopt Mo Tzu's utility principle as a criterion for determining both the goodness of government and the correctness of actions without denying that *jen* and *li* were the foundations of happiness and goodness.

HAN FEI TZU

The Legalist school, which is best represented by Han Fei Tzu, a student of Hsun Tzu, advocated the establishment of infallible laws designed to meet the needs of the time. Prior to Han Fei Tzu it was common to regard history as something essentially static, with the same things happening over and over again. In this context it was natural enough to expect that traditions, institutions, and customs that had served earlier generations would be adequate for the present generation. Han Fei Tzu, however, regarded history as essentially a matter of change. Consequently, he argued that as times changed the institutions and practices of the past became inadequate for solving present problems. This view, though commonplace today, was quite revolutionary, and by no means widely accepted at the time. Consequently, his proposal that laws be created to deal with current problems, and that authority be established to administer these laws, was viewed with considerable skepticism at first.

The key principle of the Legalist school was that rewards and punishments could be used to regulate and make good the actions of people. It was not necessary to wait until the people became good to have good behavior; good behavior could be produced through a system of law to which were attached rewards and punishments as sanctions. Although this principle is opposed to the Confucian principle that goodness and order in society can be produced only by cultivating the moral nature of man, the philosophy of Hsun Tzu made it possible to combine these two views by the twin processes of legalizing morality and moralizing legality. Thus through the philosophy of Hsun Tzu, the significant dimension of law came to be added to Confucianism.

On the other hand, Mencius' emphasis on *yi* led to greater emphasis on *hsiao*, or filial piety, and provided greater support for the attitude that regarded the family as the basic social structure. It thus directly led to increased moral training in terms of example and guidance at a very early age in the family. This insured a secure basis for *li* in later life, for it tended to encourage respect for laws and superiors. Consequently, people were inclined to act morally both because they felt it was the right thing to do and because various rules of society required such action.

Even though Confucianism, as a result of the influence of various other schools and the contributions of Mencius and Hsun Tzu, had various external criteria available for determining the correctness of actions, it continued to be the case that the primary stress was on the humanity that each person possessed within himself. A person knows what to do here and now because all men have within them a measure for determining whether or not to do something, because everyone possesses *jen*, or humanity. All that is required is that the Golden Rule be applied. If it is not something you would like done to you, then do not do it to anyone else. It is probably this humanistic measure of goodness that constitutes the timeless essence of Confucianism. Confucianism as a thoroughgoing humanism with respect to the conduct of life and society is something not merely of historical, antiquarian interest. Rather, it is a permanent social spirit that will exist as long as men have respect for themselves and their fellow men—as long as men are truly men.

TAOISM: THE METAPHYSICS OF NATURE

Taoism, in contrast to Confucianism, seeks its principles and rules for human life not within man himself, but within nature. Consequently, instead of emphasizing man and society, this philosophy emphasizes the metaphysical foundations of nature.

The story of Taoism can be told in two installments. The first part of the story deals with the philosophy developed in the classical work known as *The Treatise on the Way and its Power (Tao Te Ching)*. This is traditionally regarded as the philosophy of Lao Tzu. The second part of the story is concerned with the Taoism of Chuang Tzu, who drew out the epistemological and mystical implications of this philosophy.

LAO TZU

Taoism, just as Confucianism, has its beginnings in a philosophical protest against the conditions of the times. The times of Lao Tzu were approximately the times of Confucius, and Lao Tzu's charges that poverty and starvation were caused by bad rulers, that greed and avarice resulted in wars and killings, and that desires for wealth, power, and glory were bringing about the destruction of society, reveal that his philosophy is inspired by a concern with the deplorable social conditions of the times. However, despite having this inspiration in common, the two philosophies developed in quite different and even opposing ways.

Whereas Confucianism stressed the moral goodness of man as the key to happiness, the Taoists stressed the harmony and perfection of nature. The Taoist attitude is that the contrivances and artifacts of man lead to evil and unhappiness. To find peace and contentment man must follow the Way, or *Tao*, of the universe, and achieve a oneness with this *Tao*.

In Confucianism the complex and well-developed life is taken to be the ideal. Lao Tzu, however, considered the ideal life to be simple and harmonious. A simple life is one which is plain, wherein profit is ignored, cleverness abandoned, selfishness minimized, and desires reduced. This last feature of the simple life serves well to contrast Lao Tzu and Confucius. Confucius advocated rites and music so that the desires and emotions might be developed and regulated, for therein lay the development of *jen*, or humanity. To Lao Tzu, efforts to develop and regulate the desires and emotions seemed artificial and tended to interfere with the harmony of nature. Rather than organize and regulate things to achieve perfection, Lao Tzu would let things work to their perfection naturally. This means supporting all things in their natural state, allowing them to transform spontaneously. In this way no action is needed, no regulations required, and yet everything is done and all things are regulated. It is not the case that the contrast between Confucius and Lao Tzu is that between action and inaction, or doing and non-doing. Rather, it is between holding that man is the measure and source of all things, and holding that nature is the measure and source of all things.

In Confucianism man and nature are differentiated, and goodness and well-being are considered to proceed from what belongs to man rather than nature. Taoism sees man and nature as a unity and does not differentiate between the two. According to this philosophy, the basis of man's being is not of his own making, but is contained in the being and the function of the totality of the universe. Consequently, in its critical and negative aspects, Taoism analyzes the deficiencies and evils confronting man and concludes that they stem primarily from a wrong view of man and the universe. The Confucian views on the nature of man and the universe are criticized as inadequate and incapable of providing for a solution. Constructively, Taoism is concerned to provide more adequate views of man and the world. Here Taoism offers a picture of the universe and man as a unity. Man's knowledge transcends the limits of percepts and concepts. It is direct and immediate, not being dependent upon a false duality between the knowing subject and the known object. The principles that are to guide life and regulate the actions of man are the principles that regulate nature. Life is lived well only when man is completely in tune with the whole universe and his action is the action of the universe flowing through him. The institutions of society are regulated by allowing them to be what they are naturally; society, too, must be in tune with the universe. The task of philosophy is to lead man to a unity with the universe by illuminating its *Tao*, or Way. The word "*Tao*" refers to a path or a way, and in Taoism means the source and principle of functioning of whatever exists. When the *Tao* of man and the *Tao* of the universe are one, man will have realized his infinite nature.

The ethical and social teachings of Taoism represent a constructive attempt to preserve and make great human life. To preserve life is to protect it from threats to its very existence. Making life great assumes the preservation of life and consists in improving the quality of life. It is above all else the attempt to provide a *Tao*, or Way, to a completely satisfying and fulfilled life that motivates the Taoist philosopher. Lao Tzu's teachings concerning the *Tao* of human life in society can be summed up in the following nine principles:

(1) People generally act to fulfill their desires.

(2) The result of many individuals attempting to satisfy their desires is competition and conflict.

(3) In order to provide peace and harmony among individuals struggling to satisfy their desires, standards of human rightness and morality are devised.

(4) Obviously the erection of moral standards does not solve the problem, for competition and conflict remain. Rules are broken and new rules are devised to protect the old rules. But new rules and old rules are broken and desires remain unsatisfied while wrongdoing and evil are fostered.

(5) Since devising moral standards does not solve the problem, the solution lies in giving up moral standards.

(6) However, standards can be abandoned only when desires as sources of action are given up.

(7) Actions arising out of desires can be given up only when people adopt the "easy way" of action.

(8) The "easy way" of action presupposes being in tune with the universe and acting in accord with the universal *Tao*.

(9) Regulation of society and government of the people should be according to the easy and natural way and should foster the natural way in the people.

In attempting to rectify the social evils present in his society Lao Tzu recognized the necessity of understanding the basic causes of these evils. For this it is important to know the sources and guides of human actions. As he turned his attention to these matters it appeared obvious to Lao Tzu that the choices and actions of most people proceed from their desires, and are guided by the satisfaction of these desires. Accordingly, the most basic regulatory principle of action is the fulfillment of desires.

Now if people act in order to fulfill their desires, and if different persons desire the same things, and if there aren't enough goods to go around, there will be competing and conflicting actions. It is, of course, notoriously the case that people are never able to satisfy all of their desires and that they often desire the same things. Consequently, they compete with each other and conflicts arise. When competition is unregulated and conflicts are settled through the use of power and force the whole fabric of society is threatened. Therefore, to regulate competition and reduce conflicts moral rules are introduced as guides to human behavior.

The primary function of moral rules and social institutions is to regulate the actions of the people in order to provide for a maximum satisfaction of desires for everyone. Lao Tzu has no quarrel with the aims of morality; rather, he questions the possibility of achieving this aim through the regulation of competition and conflict. Observing that when the great Tao prevailed there was no strife and competition, he remarks, "When the Great Tao declined, the doctrines of humanity and righteousness arose."[1] The doctrines of humanity (jen) and righteousness (yi) are the basis of the Confucian morality, and have as their object the satisfactory ordering of all human actions and social institutions. Lao Tzu's remark, however, reveals that he considers morality an inadequate solution, for it comes about only as a result of the decline of the great Way of nature.

Undoubtedly, Lao Tzu saw the failure of Confucian morality to achieve ideal social conditions as a sign of the inadequacy of the moral approach. Morality does not attack the problem at its root. By allowing desires

---

[1] *Tao Te Ching*, Ch. 18, trans. by Wing-tsit Chan, *The Way of Lao Tzu* (Indianapolis: Bobbs-Merrill, Inc., 1963).

to function as legitimate sources of human action, morality could not remove competition and strife. The best it could do was to regulate the competition and reduce the strife. But this simply complicates the matter of satisfying desires in accord with the moral rules, and leads to rule breaking, thereby bringing about immorality. It does not remove the competition and does not provide for the complete satisfaction of all desires. Hence Lao Tzu said, "Therefore when *Tao* is lost, only then does the doctrine of virtue arise. When virtue is lost, only then does the doctrine of humanity arise."[2]

Since morality is incapable of providing for peace and happiness, it should be regarded as an unsuccessful solution to the problem of achieving the ideal society and abandoned in favor of a different solution. But morality cannot be abandoned without changing the conditions which inevitably lead to the regulation of action by moral rules. These conditions, a world of competition and strife where the powerful subdue the weak at their pleasure, are the result of acting for the sake of satisfying desires. Since acting to satisfy desires brings about the conditions requiring morality, morality cannot be abandoned until desires as source of actions are abandoned. The reason why acting out of desires leads to evil is that it is contrary to the Way, for the great *Tao* is always without desires. The good is accomplished not by action driven by desire, but by inaction inspired by the simplicity of *Tao*, according to Lao Tzu. He says, "Simplicity, which has no name, is free of desires. Being free of desires it is tranquil. And the world will be at peace of its own accord."[3]

Advocating giving up desires as sources of action, the important question for Lao Tzu is, How then should people act? His answer, in brief, is that people should adopt the "easy way" of *Tao*, not inflicting their desires upon nature, but following her. With regard to society, he advocates a government of the people which is in accord with the easy and natural way of *Tao*, and which fosters the natural way in the lives of the people.

To understand this answer of Lao Tzu, it is necessary to turn to his conception of *Tao* and its manifestations, *te*. Prior to Lao Tzu the principles of *yin* and *yang* were known. They were regarded as opposites, and all of the things in the world were considered to be the production of the interaction between *yin* and *yang*. But *yin* and *yang*, opposed as light and dark, cold and warm, being and non-being, etc., being opposite,

---

[2] *Tao Te Ching*, Ch. 38.   [3] *Ibid.*, Ch. 37.

could not of their own nature either produce themselves or interact with each other. A third something providing a basis and a context for the interaction of yin and yang was required. The great contribution of Lao Tzu was his recognition of Tao as the source of both being and non-being—of yin and yang—and the function of Tao as the basis for the interaction of yin and yang.

As the absolutely first principle of existence, Tao is completely without characteristics. It is itself uncharacterized, being the very source and condition of all characteristics. In this sense it is non-being. But it is not simply nothing, for it is the source of everything. It is prior to all the existing things, giving them life and function, constituting the oneness underlying all the diversity and multiplicity of the world. Lao Tzu says, "The Tao that can be told of is not the eternal Tao; the name that can be named is not the eternal name. The Nameless is the origin of Heaven and Earth; the named is the mother of all things."[4]

The reason Tao cannot be named is that it is without divisions, distinctions, or characteristics. It is unified, like an uncarved block, being without change, knowing neither beginning nor end. But if Tao cannot be named, what is named by "Tao"? Lao Tzu's point in saying that the Tao is beyond all names is that the fundamental source and principle cannot be named, for it is the very source of names and descriptions. Consequently, "Tao" is a non-name; it does not refer to any one thing. Rather it points to that which enables things to be what they are; it is that which gives them existence and allows them to pass into non-existence. When it is said that Tao is the source of all being, and non-being, the word "Tao" functions very much like the word "that" when it is said "the 'that' from which being and non-being proceed."

The importance of Tao lies in the recognition that there is something which is prior and anterior to the various particular things that exist in the world, something which gives unity to all the existing things and which determines the very existence and function of everything that exists. What that something is cannot, of course, be said, for whatever can be talked about is limited and determined, whereas it cannot be said that the source is limited and determined, for it is the very condition of limits and determinations.

Although what Tao is cannot be said, but can only be pointed to, a feeling for what Tao is can be achieved by considering the functioning of Tao. Strictly speaking the function (te) of Tao cannot be stated or

---

[4] *Tao Te Ching*, Ch. 1.

observed, but since it is the function of *Tao* that supports all things in their natural state something of the function of *Tao* can be seen, at least partially, by looking to nature. The function of *Tao* is manifested in the workings of nature, for what individual things possess of *Tao* is the *te*, or function, of *Tao*. *Tao*, as a source, provides for the very existence of things, but the function of *Tao* provides for their distinctness. Examining the working of things in their natural conditions, Lao Tzu observes that no-action (*wu-wei*) is what they inherit from *Tao* as their function. He says, "*Tao* invariably takes no action, and yet there is nothing left undone."⁵ What he means by "taking no action" is not straining and contriving to accomplish, but letting things be accomplished in a natural and spontaneous way. Thus, immediately after the remark quoted above he says, "If kings and barons can keep it, all things will transform spontaneously."⁶ The reference here is to *Tao*. If the ruler will keep to the way of *Tao*, government will proceed in a natural and spontaneous way. There will be no need for harsh laws, conscriptions, punishment, and wars.

Lao Tzu's advice to the rulers is that they should govern as little as possible, keeping to the natural way, letting people go their own way. He suggests that the people are difficult to rule because the ruler does too many things. What the ruler should keep in mind is that "ruling a big country is like cooking a small fish." In cooking a small fish one must take care not to handle it too roughly for too much handling will spoil it. In ruling a country care must be taken not to push the people around, forcing them to rebel. When the people are satisfied there will be no rebellion or wars. Therefore the easy way of governing is to give the people what they want and make government conform to the will of the people rather than trying to force the people to conform to the will of the government.

When Lao Tzu suggests that the ruler should know the mystic *Tao*, and in his ruling emulate the function of *Tao*, he has in mind that the perfection of all things lies in expressing the *Tao* they possess. The job of the ruler is to let the *Tao* operate freely, rather than trying to resist and change its function. What *Tao* is, and how it functions, is revealed in the fourth chapter of the *Tao Te Ching*, where Lao Tzu says:

> *Tao* is empty (like a bowl).
> It may be used but its capacity is never exhausted.
> It is bottomless, perhaps the ancestor of all things.
> It blunts its sharpness.

⁵ *Tao Te Ching*, Ch. 37.   ⁶ *Ibid.*

It unties its tangles.
It softens its light.
It becomes one with the dusty world.
Deep and still, it appears to exist forever.

To say *Tao* is empty is to note that it is without characteristics; it is empty of all particularity, for it is the possibility and source of all particularity. Even though it is empty of particular things it is the most useful of all things. Just as the most useful thing about a house is its emptiness—its space—so the most useful thing about *Tao* is its emptiness of characteristics, for this means it has infinite capacity. Thus the emptiness of *Tao* is synonymous with its being the infinite source of all things. The functioning of *Tao* is eternal and recurrent, producing all things and directing their activities. Comparing the functioning of *Tao* to blunting sharpness, untying tangles, and softening light draws attention to reversal as the movement of the *Tao*. The lesson the Taoists drew from nature is that when a thing reaches one extreme, it reverses and returns to the other extreme. Thus, the advice is given that if one would assist the ruler with *Tao* he does not use force and violence, for this would bring about a reversal.[7] When it gets very cold, reversal sets in and it begins to get warm. When it gets very warm, reversal again sets in and it begins to get cold. This is the way of nature as seen in the passing of the seasons. In similar fashion, when a person becomes extremely proud and conceited, disgrace and humility will follow. To know the reversals that constitute the functioning of *Tao* and to adapt oneself to these movements is the way to peace and contentment. Just as one does not dress lightly in winter and suffer in the cold, and does not dress warmly in the summer and suffer in the heat, but dresses warmly in the winter and enjoys the cold, and dresses lightly in the summer and enjoys the warm weather, so one should not resist the natural way, but should act in accord with the Way of the Great *Tao* in all things.

To recognize that *Tao* becomes one with the dusty world is to understand that *Tao* is not transcendental, but immanent. That is, *Tao* does not remain aloof from the world, directing it from afar, but functions through the world, and is indistinguishable from the functioning of the world. *Tao* is not to be found aside from life, but within life in the world.

When the ruler knows the *Tao* and its *te* he knows how to stay out of the way of the people and serve them without intruding. Thus, Lao

---

[7] *Tao Te Ching*, Ch. 30.

Tzu says that the people "are difficult to rule because the ruler does too many things."[8] In accord with the function of *Tao*, Lao Tzu says, "Administer the empire by engaging in no activity." Supporting this advice, he notes that "the more taboos and prohibitions there are in the world, the poorer the people will be," and, "the more laws and orders are made prominent, the more thieves and robbers there will be."[9]

By giving up desires and letting the *Tao* enter and pervade oneself, life will rise above the distinctions of good and evil. All activity will proceed from *Tao*, the very source of existence, and man will be one with the world. This is the solution Lao Tzu brought to the problem of evil and unhappiness in man's life. It is a solution that depends ultimately upon achieving a unity with the great inner principle of reality, and is therefore, basically mystical.

CHUANG TZU

Although the positive foundations of Taoism are mystical, there are good reasons for seriously considering this way of life, as Chuang Tzu points out. Chuang Tzu (ca. 369–286 B.C.) developed a philosophy not basically different from Lao Tzu's, though he does develop further the concepts of the total spontaneity of nature, the incessant activity of things, and the underlying unity of all existence. He emphasized that man's ultimate freedom lay in identifying with the *Tao* of reality, where this means transcending ordinary reality. The most valuable contribution of Chuang Tzu, however, lies in the *arguments* he provided for rejecting other ways of life and accepting the Taoist Way.

The philosophy of Chuang Tzu is based on the conviction that true happiness is dependent upon transcending the world of ordinary experience and cognition and identifying oneself with the infinity of the universe. This conviction appears quite clearly in his description of the man who has achieved complete happiness. Of the happy man, the true sage, the perfect man, Chuang Tzu says, "Suppose there is one who chariots upon the normality of the universe, rides upon the transformation of the six elements, and thus makes excursions into the infinite, what has he to depend upon? Therefore it is said that the Perfect Man has no self; the Spiritual Man has no achievement; the Sage has no name."[10]

[8] *Tao Te Ching*, Ch. 25.   [9] *Tao Te Ching*, Ch. 57.
[10] As quoted in Fung Yu-Lan, *History of Chinese Philosophy*, trans. Derk Bodde (Princeton: Princeton University Press, 1952), vol. I, p. 243.

This remark is intended to suggest that the ordinary cognitive scheme wherein one distinguishes between self and other, between doing and not doing, and between names (words) and realities (things) is inadequate. It is claimed to be inadequate because of its limitations; its finiteness. Consequently, in the *Book of Chuang Tzu* it is suggested that the finite point of view (the ordinary cognitive point of view, which is dependent upon perception and conception) should be exchanged for an "infinite," or "transcendent," point of view. This infinite point of view is regarded as becoming one with *Tao*, the essence (normality) of the universe.

Not infrequently the aspects of his philosophy just referred to are regarded as evidence that Chuang Tzu was a Chinese mystic. Being so labeled, Chuang Tzu could be dismissed from further philosophical consideration. But such dismissal is unfortunate, for Chuang Tzu does not merely suggest that the finite point of view should be exchanged for the infinite. He argues, quite ingeniously, for the acceptance of the infinite point of view by trying to show that the finite point of view (the ordinary cognitive scheme) is inadequate.

The arguments against accepting the ordinary cognitive scheme, which constitute Chuang Tzu's arguments for an infinite point of view, can be classified as (1) the argument from the relativity of distinctions, (2) the argument from the complementariness of opposites, (3) the argument from perspectives, and (4) the argument from general skepticism.

1. The first argument, the argument from the relativity of distinctions, would have it that judgments about values and matters of taste are subjective and therefore relative. A particular sauce may be sour to *A*'s taste, but sweet to *B*'s taste. Thinking about the relativity of distinctions may be good for *X*, and bad for *Y*. This relativity is taken to hold for all distinctions. Chuang Tzu says, "Let us take, for instance, a large beam and a small beam, or an ugly woman and Hsi-shih [famous beauty of ancient China], or generosity, strangeness, deceit, and abnormality. The Tao identifies them all as one."[11] He also says "There is nothing in the world greater than the tip of a hair that grows in autumn, while Mount T'ai is small. No one lives a longer life than a child who dies in infancy, but P'eng-tsu (who lived many hundred years) died prematurely. The universe and I exist together, and all things and I are one."[12]

---

[11] In Wing-tsit Chan, trans. and compiler, *A Source Book in Chinese Philosophy* (Princeton: Princeton University Press, 1963), p. 184.
[12] *Ibid.*, p. 186.

The basic reason for regarding all distinctions as relative is that it is held that the characteristics attributed to things or events in the making of distinctions are generated by the mind, which is regarded as independent of the so-called characteristics of things generated by it. Chuang Tzu says, "A road becomes so when people walk on it, and things become so-and-so [to people] because people call them so-and-so. How have they become so? They have become so because people say they are so. How have they become not so? They have become not so because [people say] they are not so."[13] The argument from the relativity of distinctions is intended to prove the triviality of knowledge. If the possibility of knowing what is good, or big, or sweet is claimed, and it can be shown that the concepts of good, big, and sweet are relative, it follows that the knowledge claimed is relative, and therefore can be regarded as trivial or unreal.

This argument is directed primarily against the Confucianists and Mohists, both of whom claimed they had genuine knowledge of right and wrong, but who disagreed on nearly every point. Chuang Tzu says, "There have arisen the controversies between the Confucianists and the Mohists, each school regarding as right what the other regards as wrong. . . ."[14] The Mohists were pragmatists, accepting practice as the criterion of knowledge. Their view was that knowledge is possible, for in the main, man lives in such a way as to avoid a lot of unpleasantness. Now, since on pragmatic or utilitarian grounds the rightness and wrongness of actions is determined by the amounts of pleasantness and unpleasantness respectively, right and wrong can be known simply by looking to the pleasantness and unpleasantness brought about by actions. The Confucianists, on the other hand, maintained that knowledge of right and wrong proceeded immediately and intuitively from an internal moral sense.

Chuang Tzu uses the argument from relativity to show that pleasantness and unpleasantness are relative concepts, and though people appear to get on well in this life, this may be a mere appearance and not the case at all. Furthermore, it is not clear how practice can serve as a criterion of knowledge, and it may be possible that there is no way of knowing whether or not practice is an adequate criterion of knowledge, for practice itself is relative. For the Confucianist, the problem lies in showing that the moral sense, which is supposed to provide knowledge of right and wrong, is any less relative than any of the other senses.

[13] *Ibid.*, pp. 183–184. (Brackets are Chan's.)   [14] *Ibid.*, p. 182.

Both the Confucianist and the Mohist would agree, though for different reasons, that we can have genuine knowledge of the fact that it is wrong to kill. Employing the relativity argument of Chuang Tzu, however, it can be seen that this is not absolute knowledge, but only relative knowledge. From another perspective it might turn out to be mistaken opinion. Suppose it is claimed that it is wrong to kill. Now if a man is starving and the only way to escape death is to kill a hare, all would agree that it is right to kill the hare. But someone might suggest that though in need it is right to kill animals, it is always wrong to kill a man. If, however, the only way to prevent the death of his wife and family is for a man to kill the attacker, it would again be conceded that in this special case it would be right for a man to kill, but only because of the special circumstances. Somewhere along the line it could be suggested, by someone using Chuang Tzu's argument, that there can never be any real knowledge of the wrongness of an action such as killing, because right and wrong are purely relative. Everything depends on who is doing the killing, who the considering, and what the circumstances are. There can be no absolute right and wrong because rightness and wrongness are relative to the circumstances of the actions in question. And if this is the case there is no real knowledge of rightness and wrongness, for one might always be mistaken in thinking he knew that a particular action was right or wrong.

Of course, it might be argued against Chuang Tzu that if all knowledge is purely relative, then so is this knowledge; namely, the knowledge that all knowledge is relative and trivial. But Chuang's suggestion is that because of the relativity of knowledge you could never really know that that bit of knowledge is trivial. It will not do to return the compliment by claiming that he can never really know either that that, or any knowledge, either is or is not trivial, because the point of Chuang Tzu's argument from skepticism is precisely this: to maintain the impossibility of certain, indubitable knowledge.

Chuang Tzu's position is clear. If it is certitude of knowledge that is doubted, indubitable knowledge is impossible without begging the question. And there seems no way, other than by knowing, of ascertaining that there is indubitable knowledge. Thus, Chuang Tzu's argument, on these grounds at least, is unanswerable.

2. The second argument, from the complementariness of opposites, suggests that any concept logically implies its negation, and that without its negation, or opposite, a concept could not exist. The argument is intended to show that affirmation and negation are simply different

ways of looking at the same thing. If A is A, then A is not *not-A*. Or, the negation of A is the affirmation of *not-A*. In a similar way, right and wrong are the same thing looked at differently. If A is right, then A is not-wrong. If there were no right, there would be no wrong (and vice versa). For if A is right, then A is not wrong, implying a wrong that A is not, and in virtue of which A is, or can be, right. In other words, *what is* involves *what is not*, and opposites, from this point of view, turn out to be complementary. Chuang Tzu says, "Nevertheless, when there is life there is death, and when there is death there is life. When there is possibility, there is impossibility, and when there is impossibility there is possibility. Because of the right, there is the wrong, and because of the wrong there is the right."[15] He also says, "There is nothing that is not the "that" and there is nothing that is not the "this." Therefore I say that the "that" is produced by the "this" and the "this" is also caused by the "that."[16]

Chuang Tzu appears to be thinking in terms of pairs of correlative terms. For example, if there were no concept of up, there could be none of down, and the same holds true for left and right, right and wrong, self and other, etc. For such pairs of concepts, the existence of one presupposes the other and the removal of one is the removal of the other. It might be objected that it is by no means clear that all concepts can function only as correlatives. In fact, if one avoids adjectival concepts and concentrates on substantive concepts, it is by no means clear that a concept is possible only if it is opposed by another concept. By what concepts need the concepts *man, house, dog*, etc. be opposed in order that they can function as concepts?

According to Chuang Tzu's argument, however, even a concept such as *dog* involves, at least implicitly, the concept of *not-dog*, for if there were no concept of *not-dog*, the concept of *dog* could not be used discriminately. That is, it would be impossible to decide what to call and what not to call a dog. And if a person could never properly use a concept in a discriminatory fashion this would be sufficient evidence for claiming that he did not have the concept at all. But a necessary condition of using a concept properly is being able to discriminate between what the concept refers to and what it does not. Thus, in terms of the present example, having the concept *dog* involves knowing what is not-dog, or of having the concept of *not-dog*. The same line of reasoning can be used with any substantive concept, for having a concept of anything

[15] *Ibid.*, p. 183.   [16] *Ibid.*, p. 182.

presupposes an ability to discriminate between that to which the concept refers and that to which it does not, and this involves knowing what the concept is not. In this way it is seen that a concept of something is always relative to what that something is not. Thus, Chuang Tzu says, "the 'this' is also the 'that'," and, "when 'this' and 'that' have no opposites, there is the very axis of *Tao*."[17]

The question could be asked, Which is the essential feature of knowledge, the not-dog or the dog? According to Chuang Tzu, the answer is neither, since both are necessary. Coupled with the argument from skepticism, this argument implies neither that there is no real knowledge nor that real knowledge is impossible, but that we can never know (i.e. be certain) either what this or that knowledge really consists in, or whether or not we really have knowledge.

3. The third argument, the argument from perspectives, presupposes the previous two arguments. It is obvious that the same thing appears differently to different people if their perspectives are different. Or, the same thing appears different to me if I change my perspective. If my organs of sensing were different, no doubt I would perceive things differently. The point of this is that the same thing has many appearances, depending upon the perceiver. Which of the appearances is the correct or true appearance? Is what the worm or the cat perceives the same as what a person perceives? Is what is perceived now the same as what was perceived a minute ago?

Chuang Tzu's point is that these questions cannot be answered. Each thing is just what it is and not another and it is what it is independent of how it appears to anything or anyone. It is contained in itself, in its own perspective, and the only way to get at it is, is to transcend our own perspective and view the other as a totality, from its own perspective. The claim is that everything in the world is a self-sufficient unit with a perspective of its own. Everything has a view of itself and has a function. From its own point of view everything is a totality. But if everything is a totality from its own point of view and no other, then it appears that morality and knowledge are purely relative. And if everything is looked at from its own point of view, right and wrong disappear. This is exactly what Chuang Tzu recommends: obtain the transcendent point of view from which everything is seen in its proper perspective, from its own point of view. Then there will be unity with the universe; there will be enlightenment; the *Tao* will be found in every-

[17] *Ibid.*, p. 183.

thing. According to Chuang Tzu, "Things do not know that they are the 'that' of other things; they only know what they themselves know."[18] And, "Only the intelligent knows how to identify all things as one."[19] The point is illustrated with the butterfly story:

> Once I, Chuang Chou, dreamed that I was a butterfly and was happy as a butterfly. I was conscious that I was quite pleased with myself, but I did not know that I was Chou. Suddenly I awoke, and there I was, visibly Chou. I do not know whether it was Chou dreaming that he was a butterfly or the butterfly dreaming it was Chou.[20]

Going further, Chuang Tzu advises giving up a particular perspective and adopting a universal perspective:

> We say this is right or wrong, and is so or is not so. If the right is really right, then the fact that it is different from the wrong leaves no room for argument. Forget the passage of time (life and death) and forget the distinction of right and wrong. Relax in the realm of the infinite and thus abide in the realm of the infinite.[21]

Here the point of the argument is that we can never really know what a thing is in itself. To make this point, the argument *assumes* a transcendent point of view, for by its own premises, ordinary experience could never show anything about things as they are in themselves, as totalities with their own perspectives. Only by assuming a transcendent point of view can it be known that there are things in themselves, locked within their own perspectives and not accessible to ordinary means of knowledge. To assume a point of view is not the same thing as to argue for a point of view. The argument for a transcendent point of view depends on showing that the ordinary cognitive point of view leads to skepticism, and because of this the argument from skepticism is relevant at this point.

4. Chuang Tzu's fourth argument, the argument from skepticism, advances the claim that the question, Is that really so? can never be answered. Suppose, for example, that it is claimed that X is red. The retort is, "But how can it be shown to be *really* red?" The difficulty in proving that the claim is true is that the claim cannot be compared with what is actually the case, because any claim about what is actually the case would be subject to the same doubts as the original claim. What is needed is a standard to judge the first standard, a standard to judge the second standard, etc., *ad infinitum*. But it appears that choosing

---

[18] *Ibid.*, p. 182.   [19] *Ibid.*, p. 184.   [20] *Ibid.*, p. 190.   [21] *Ibid.*

even a third standard is impossible, for if *A* and *B* have opposite views, a standard acceptable to *A* would be unacceptable to *B*, and a standard acceptable to *B* would be unacceptable to *A*. And if the standard is acceptable to no one, it is of no use. Therefore is would seem impossible to defend the claim that *X* is really red.

On one occasion Chuang Tzu presented the skeptical argument in the form of the following question: "How can it be known that what I call knowing is not really not knowing and what I call not knowing is not really knowing?"[22] On another occasion he presented the argument in the form of a different question: "For knowledge depends on something to be correct, but what it depends on is uncertain and changeable. How do we know that what I call nature is not really man and what I call man is not really nature?"[23]

This skepticism is pushed even further in the following statement:

> Suppose we make a statement. We don't know whether it belongs to one category or another. Whether one or the other, if we put them in one, then one is not different from the other. However, let me explain. There was a beginning. There was a time before that beginning. And there was a time before the time which was before that beginning. There was being. There was non-being. There was a time that was before that non-being, and there was a time before the time that was before that non-being. Suddenly there is being and non-being, but I don't know which of being and non-being is really being or really non-being. I have just said something, but I don't know if what I have said really says something or says nothing.[24]

Chuang Tzu, in suggesting that it is impossible to know whether what is called man is really man or whether it is really nature, or that it is impossible to tell whether it is Chuang Tzu dreaming he is a butterfly or a butterfly dreaming it is Chuang Tzu, is obviously assuming the skeptic's role. Taking the butterfly example, it can be seen that Chuang Tzu's problem is that of ascertaining whether he was dreaming or being dreamed. Chuang Tzu can find no indubitable criteria that can be used to distinguish between being awake and dreaming, and no indubitable criteria to distinguish being dreamed from dreaming. Hence he cannot be sure that he does not exist merely as a character in a butterfly's dream.

The obvious answer to this kind of skepticism is that the doubts expressed make sense only within a certain cognitive scheme, in this case a cognitive scheme wherein individuals such as Chuang Tzu and

---

[22] *Ibid.*, p. 187.   [23] *Ibid.*, p. 191.   [24] *Ibid.*, pp. 185–186.

Sage in Meditation. *The Metropolitan Museum of Art, Rogers Fund, 1923*

butterflies can be identified and differentiated. When Chuang Tzu goes on to use this cognitive scheme to reject this identification and differentiation he is rejecting the very conditions in terms of which it makes sense to question such identification and differentiation. In this way he rejects the grounds which make possible the first doubt and which are needed to make sense of his skepticism. For unless Chuang Tzu could accept "Once I, Chuang Tzu, dreamed I was a butterfly" he could not go on to doubt whether he dreamed or was dreamed.

Though the above answer may be sufficient to refute skepticism generally, it will not refute Chuang Tzu's general position. To see this, recall that Chuang Tzu is arguing for a transcendent point of view. His arguments are negative, in the sense that they are aimed at refuting a finite point of view. Suppose for a moment that Chuang Tzu's only argument is the skeptical one, and that the above argument adequately refutes the skeptical argument.

Has Chuang Tzu been refuted by the above argument? Not at all. In fact, his position has been strengthened. The reason for this is that Chuang Tzu is arguing that the ordinary cognitive framework is inadequate, and that a new cognitive framework, a universal cognitive framework, must be adopted in order to escape the limitations of the limited cognitive scheme ordinarily employed. It is for this reason that the fact that though thorough-going skepticism is self-contradictory in terms of a conceptual framework which is limited in the relevant ways (e.g. a conceptual framework that is essentially spatial-temporal), this is not an argument for the rejection of thorough-going skepticism, but is an argument for rejecting the limited cognitive scheme.

Does recognition of the limitations of ordinary cognitive schemes and adoption of a transcendent perspective mean rejecting the ordinary and mundane world? The answer is no, for to interpret Lao Tzu and Chuang Tzu in this way is to ignore their concern with social rectification, the concern inspiring their philosophies. Kuo Hsiang, a later commentator on Chuang Tzu, puts the matter as follows:

> To cry as people cry is a manifestation of the mundane world. To identify life and death, forget joy and sorrow, and be able to sing in the presence of the corpse is the perfection of the transcendental world . . .

He then goes on to point out that the true sage, the person who is fully able to transcend the mundane world, finds his happiness in the mundane world. He says,

> There has never been a person who has roamed over the transcendental world to the utmost and yet was not silently in harmony with the mundane world, nor has there been anyone who was silently in harmony with the mundane world and yet did not roam over the transcendental world. Therefore the sage always roams in the transcendental world in order to enlarge the mundane world. By having no deliberate mind of his own, he is in accord with things.[25]

In the sage the transcendental and the mundane meet, for here the *tao*, or way of man, is identical with the *Tao* of the universe. Man's will is in accord with nature and his actions are spontaneously produced by *te*.

[25] *Ibid.*, p. 330.

CHAPTER 19

NEO-CONFUCIANISM: THE GRAND HARMONY

THE third major indigenous philosophical movement in China is that of Neo-Confucianism. This philosophy represents a harmonizing of the underlying principles of Confucianism and Taoism, in an effort to reduce the influence of Buddhism in China. The introduction and development of Buddhism in China provided a strong catalyst in the philosophical milieu during China's middle ages. But Neo-Confucianism also is indebted to developments in Neo-Taoism, the School of Names, and the metaphysical developments in the *Yin-Yang* interactionist school. Without all of these elements it is unlikely that the Ch'eng brothers and Chu Hsi could have reinterpreted the principles and concepts of Confucianism in such a way as to include and coordinate the apparently conflicting principles of the other schools of philosophy in China.

In 221 B.C. the state of Ch'in succeeded in subduing all of the states of China: for the first time China was a unified country. But despite the Confucian teachings that government should proceed according to moral principles, and the Taoist teachings that government should leave the people alone as much as possible, not interfering in the lives of the people except when necessary for their own well-being, the unification of China came about as the result of military power and economic control. However, this event, though brought about by means

contrary to both philosophies, did not refute either Taoism or Confucianism. In fact, in the long term it tended to confirm them both,
for the excessive regulation of the people coupled with the harshness
of the rule and lack of concern for moral qualities led to rebellion against
the Ch'in dynasty, and by 206 B.C., just fifteen years later, the Han
dynasty controlled the country. The Han dynasty lasted for more than
four hundred years, its longevity being due, at least in part, to its attempts to provide for political unity and to construct a new social order
along the lines of the Confucian philosophy.

From the point of view of Neo-Confucianism, the most significant
feature of the unification of China was the adoption of Confucianism
as the state philosophy. It was primarily the work of Tung Chung-Shu
that was responsible for making Confucianism the national philosophy
of China, to the exclusion of other philosophies. This was possible
because of the close relation between politics and philosophy in China
which permitted the foundation of a civil service examination system
designed by Tung Chung-Shu to be based on the Confucian texts. In
addition to this, Tung Chung-Shu helped found the Imperial University,
where the Confucian texts were the basis of all education. Although
these programs secured the continuation of Confucianism it did not
preserve the Confucianism of Confucius and Mencius in its purity, for
Tung Chung-Shu had interpreted the Confucian texts in the light of his
systematization and amplification of the *yin-yang* and the Five Elements,
or Five Agents, theories, into which he had incorporated certain aspects
of Taoism.

From an objective philosophical point of view, the most serious
effect of adopting Confucianism as the state philosophy and excluding
the philosophies of Taoism, Mohism, Legalism, and the School of Names
was that without the challenges of different philosophical perspectives
and positions there was really very little philosophical development.
Instead of undergoing further philosophical development, Confucianism
was allowed to remain essentially static, since the main effort of Confucian scholars was to put into practice this philosophy rather than
develop it further philosophically. But, of course, a system of philosophy
cannot remain static. If it is not subjected to criticism and analysis it
not only fails to develop further, but it becomes empty and hollow,
being little more than a concatenation of names and formulas. Consequently, since the other schools of philosophy had been officially
silenced and therefore never became sufficiently influential to attract
the kind of intellectual attention they needed for fuller development,

and since Confucianism was relatively lifeless and static, there was little indigenous philosophical development in China from around the beginning of the Christian era until the beginnings of Neo-Confucianism.

During this same period, however, Buddhism was introduced into China, and underwent considerable development and became quite influential. In fact, all of the Neo-Confucian philosophers took considerable pains to discuss the weaknesses of Buddhism in an attempt to decrease the influence of Buddhism and increase the importance and influence of Confucianism. Part of the reason for the growth and development of Buddhism in China was due to the fact that all of the different schools of Buddhism were brought to China and there was, therefore, the stimulation of mutual criticism right from the beginning. In addition, Buddhism represented a systematic explanation of the world and man in which practical living was defined by reference to theoretical principles, such as the nature of causality, the nature of Buddhahood, and the nature of consciousness or the mind. Indigenous philosophies of China had not managed to combine systematic completeness with detailed prescriptions for living. In Taoism the base was sufficiently broad, but the philosophy remained too abstract to be practical. In Confucianism there was a wealth of detailed rules for the guidance of life, but no theoretical and systematic foundation for these prescriptions. By contrast, therefore, Buddhism immediately appeared attractive, and won sufficient attention from Chinese scholars and intellectuals to ensure translation not only into the Chinese language, but also into Chinese philosophical concepts and practice. As it turned out historically, many of the Buddhist schools were too theoretical in their emphasis to catch on in China, and the Buddhist philosophies that did take hold underwent modifications that increased their concern with morality and politics and gave them a more practical bent. But despite the extent to which schools such as the Hua-yen, Chen-yen, T'ien-t'ai, Ch'an, and Ching't'u became modified by the Chinese scholars responsible for their development, they continued to be regarded as foreign and extraneous philosophies, and among the Confucian scholars there was an increasing concern to replace these foreign philosophies with something having roots in China's ancient past. Since Confucianism was still officially the state philosophy and the civil service and university systems were based on this philosophy, it is natural that it should be regarded as the basis from which a philosophy could be derived which would prove superior to the Buddhist philosophies. In this way Buddhism proved the critical catalyst in Confucian studies that produced Neo-Confucianism.

Neo-Confucianism begins with an attempt to find a metaphysical explanation of the universe that is as comprehensive as the Buddhist, but which is completely affirmative, being built upon the supremacy of the individual person and the particular thing, and which emphasizes the moral features of the universe and provides for the achievement of moral goodness among the people. Granting this metaphysical accomplishment, the ethical and social philosophies of Confucianism could be recast, putting them upon this new basis. In effect, this new basis would allow for a synthesis of Taoist, Buddhist, and Confucian principles and tendencies, and give expression to the practical philosophies of Taoism and Confucianism. Buddhism was very influential in China from around 800 A.D. to 1200 A.D. After that period, however, from about the beginning of the thirteenth century, when Neo-Confucianism came into its own, Buddhism was on the decline, and the next eight hundred years of Chinese philosophical history are clearly Neo-Confucianist.

CHOU TUN-I

It was Chou Tun-i who was directly responsible for laying the foundations of Neo-Confucianism. He was born at a time when the ascendancy of Buddhist philosophies in China was viewed by government officials as a threat to the social organization of the country. These officials feared that the negative attitude of the Buddhists toward life in the world and their preference for retreating from active social life into monasteries would undermine the ancient forms of Chinese social organization.[1] Ou-yang Hsiu (1007–1072 A.D.) tried to cast this concern into a program by suggesting that Buddhism could be opposed by displaying the indigenous philosophies of China, showing them to be superior to Buddhist philosophies. The difficulty of achieving what Ou-yang Hsiu proposed was due largely to the fact that the various Buddhist philosophies could boast a complete philosophy of life wherein practical considerations rested upon solid metaphysical principles. The Chinese philosophies, on the other hand, were not systematically complete. Chinese philosophers had tended to be concerned only with things at hand and did not concern themselves with the elegance of complete systems. Consequently, though they had maxims and rules for living, they were not in a position to justify these rules and maxims by appeal to a comprehensive philosophy.

The problem, therefore, in opposing Buddhism was that of having to

[1] The point here is not that the Buddhist philosophies are life-negating and unconcerned with practical social matters, but that they were so regarded by the Chinese officials in question.

construct a systematic philosophy of man and the world which would show the relations between man and nature and between man and man, and which would, of course, be completely life-affirming, emphasizing the importance of particular things and individual persons.

Han Yü was expressing a prevalent criticism of his day when he said, "But now the followers of Lao-tzu and the Buddha who talk about rectification of the mind ignore this world and their native land and reduce the normal duties required by heaven to nothingness. Following the ideas of Lao-tzu, a son does not have to consider his father as a father, nor does a man have to regard the king as a king. He does not even have to discharge his duties as a subject."[2] He went beyond mere criticism, however, and urged a return to Confucius. As he saw it, this meant a return to an all pervasive love as the common basis for all human activity. This universal love proceeds from the basic nature of man, for it represents the humanity (jen) of man. In addition to jen, human nature is constituted by propriety, sincerity, righteousness, and wisdom. Three grades of persons can be distinguished on the basis of how these five virtues constituting human nature are practiced. If one of these—jen—is the ruling virtue and if the other four are also practiced the person is superior. If no one of these is perfected and they are practiced only sometimes and in impure form the person belongs to the medium grade. When jen is rejected and actions are not in accord with the other four the person is inferior. This system of three grades, usually acknowledged to be an original contribution of Han Yü, emphasizes the priority he gave to the moral principles of Confucianism.

It would appear that Han Yü's objections were primarily due to the excessive interest in metaphysical things in Taoism and Buddhism at the expense of practical things. Therefore he argued that the Tao (Way) of life consists in loving the people and observing the proper human relationships. This concern for practical things and the belief that Confucianism was fully the equal of Buddhism and Taoism is also clearly evident in Li Ao, a pupil of Han Yü. Li Ao says, "Everybody has joined the schools of Lao-tzu, the Buddha, Chuang-tzu and Lieh-tzu. They all believe that the Confucianist scholars were not learned enough to know about nature and the heavenly order, but that they themselves are. Before those who raise this hue and cry I do my best to demonstrate the opposite."[3]

In his attempt to demonstrate the adequacy of Confucianism, Li Ao

[2] Carsun Chang, The Development of Neo-Confucian Thought (New Haven: College and University Press, 1963), p. 96.
[3] Carsun Chang, op. cit., p. 109.

argued that human nature is originally good, but failure to control and quiet the feelings, or emotions, leads to corruption. The Confucian virtues are required to regulate the feelings. But apparently he did not distinguish clearly between the Confucian virtues and the Buddhist (ch'an) way of overcoming desires and cravings, for when he was asked how man can return to the original goodness of his nature, he replied, "As long as there is no deliberating and no thinking, one's emotions are not in action. When emotions are checked one has the right way of thinking. Right thinking means no deliberating and thinking. In the *I-Ching* it is said: 'Where evil thoughts are cleared, truth will be kept.'"[4]

Although Han Yü and Li Ao did not succeed in their attempts to revive Confucianism as a powerful rival of Buddhism, they did pave the way for the first attempt to provide a theoretical basis for Confucianism by Chou Tun-i.

By bringing together and reinterpreting concepts from a variety of philosophies, Chou Tun-i managed to construct a metaphysical basis broad enough for all existence. The notions of *yin* and *yang*, as negative and positive concepts of reality respectively, were familiar to Chou Tun-i. The idea that these two principles were not absolutely first was also familiar to him, for the Taoists had argued that *Tao* was prior to all things, and was the source of being and non-being, or *yang* and *yin*. The difficulty with the Taoist notion, however, was that *Tao* itself was regarded as non-being, and therefore the whole philosophy tended to have a negative character. But if the source of the principles of *yin* and *yang* were positive instead of negative there would be a basis for a philosophical explanation which could emphasize the ultimacy of the particular, while at the same time having a principle for explaining the particular. This is precisely what Chou Tun-i achieved by regarding the Great Ultimate (*T'ai-chi*) as the source of all things. He regarded the Great Ultimate as productive of *yin* and *yang*. In turn, the interactions between *yin* and *yang* produce the Five Elements of Water, Fire, Wood, Metal, and Earth. By further interaction, all of the rest of reality is produced.

Describing the production of *yin* and *yang* from the Great Ultimate, Chou Tun-i says, "The Great Ultimate through movement generates *yang*. When its activity reaches its limit, it becomes tranquil. Through tranquillity the Great Ultimate generates *yin*."[5] His explanation of how

---

4 *Ibid.*, p. 110.
5 As translated by Wing-tsit Chan in *A Source Book in Chinese Philosophy* (Princeton: Princeton University Press, 1963), p. 463.

the *yin* and the *yang* are produced from the Great Ultimate leans heavily on the Taoist notion of "reversal as the movement of the *Tao*." According to the Taoists, reality is the manifestation of the reversing of *Tao*, as it goes from one extreme back to the other. Thus, he goes on to say, "When tranquillity reaches its limit, activity begins. So movement and tranquillity alternate and become the root of each other, giving rise to the distinction of *yin* and *yang*, and the two modes are thus established."[6]

Having thus provided a basis for the principles of *yin* and *yang* in the Great Ultimate, Chou Tun-i explains that through the interaction of these two principles and their resulting mutual transformation the powers or principles of particular things came to be produced. He says, "By the transformation of *yang* and its union with *yin*, the Five Agents of Water, Fire, Wood, Metal, and Earth arise."[7] These Five Agents, or Elements, are taken to be the material principles of things. They are not themselves regarded as things, but as *principles* of things. For example, as principle of direction, Wood is east, as principle of the seasons, Wood is spring, as principle of the body, it is liver, and as principle of color, it is blue. Because these Five Agents are not conceived of as things, but as principles, they can be considered to be the common basis of all things.

Given the Great Ultimate and the two principles of *yin* and *yang* along with the principles of the material forces of the universe, it remains to explain how these can act on the unproduced and non-existent and bring it into existence. Chou Tun-i explains this as follows:

> When the reality of the non-ultimate [non-existent] and the essence of *yin*, *yang*, and the Five Agents come into mysterious union, integration ensues. Ch'ien (heaven) constitutes the male element, and K'un (earth) constitutes the female element. The interaction of these two material forces engenders and transforms the myriad things. The myriad things produce and reproduce, resulting in unending transformation.[8]

The model for production is the symbolic male and the symbolic female, for male and female are readily understood as principles which by their union bring into existence what was previously non-existent. The union between the non-existent and the principles of *yin* and *yang* and the Five Agents is said to be mysterious, for it is not clear how what exists can be related to what does not exist. Yet if some relation were not possible how could the non-existent be brought into existence? The particular things that are brought into existence through this

6 *Ibid.*   7 *Ibid.*   8 *Ibid.*

mysterious union possess their own modes for reproduction, and consequently there is the ceaseless productive activity of things.

In this part of his explanation of the Great Ultimate, Chou Tun-i has managed to give a metaphysical picture of the origin of things, tracing them to the Great Ultimate. To complete his explanation he needs to show how man and the practical affairs of man fit into this picture. This he does in the following words:

> It is man alone who receives (the material forces) in their highest excellence, and therefore he is most intelligent. His physical form appears, and his spirit develops consciousness. The five moral principles of his nature (humanity or *jen*, righteousness, propriety, wisdom and faithfulness) are aroused by, and react to, the external world and engage in activity; good and evil are distinguished; and human affairs take place.[9]

The point of this description of man's place in the total order of the universe is that the principle of the sage, or perfect man, is one with the principle of the Great Ultimate, and therefore man, in his perfection, forms a harmony with the universe. The beginnings of sagehood are received from the Great Ultimate, just as are the beginning of everything else that exists. In man these beginnings are the moral principles of his nature, which are listed as humanity (*jen*), righteousness, propriety, wisdom, and faithfulness. To become a sage and be in harmony with the universe man must be true to these moral principles. This is what Chou Tun-i means when he says that *Ch'eng* is the foundation of the sage, for *Ch'eng* (faithfulness, or sincerity) means being true to one's nature.

In this way the moral principles advocated by Confucius come to be put on a metaphysical foundation by Chou Tun-i. The reason man must act in accord with the fundamental moral principles is that these constitute man's fundamental nature as produced by the Great Ultimate.

PHILOSOPHY OF PRINCIPLE

Although it may be said that Neo-Confucianism received its foundation from Chou Tun-i, it was the brothers Ch'eng Hao (1032–1085) and Ch'eng I (1033–1107) who gave Neo-Confucianism its enduring structure. This they accomplished by making principle (*li*) the basis for their philosophy. Building upon the work of Chou Tun-i, who had been their teacher for one year, the Ch'eng brothers replaced the concept of the Great Ultimate—which impressed them as being too abstract and excessively Taoistic—with principle. The main philosophical reason for the

[9] *Ibid.*

substitution was to put the perfection of human nature on a secure basis. Chou Tun-i was concerned primarily with a metaphysics of reality, and found in the concept of the Great Ultimate the key to the overarching unity of things. The Great Ultimate was entirely too vague and abstract, however, to provide a foundation for a practical philosophy of morality, which was the chief concern of Ch'eng Hao and Ch'eng I.

The Ch'eng brothers could concentrate almost exclusively upon the philosophy of human action because Chou Tun-i had already provided an explanation for the metaphysical unity of reality and had laid the basis for a complete philosophical explanation of man and reality. Concentrating on explaining how human nature could be perfected so that every person could become a sage, and all persons could live harmoniously together, the Ch'eng brothers realized the need to have a first principle that is operative in every thing, person, and action. It must be more than simply a source from which all proceeds, for otherwise the connection of the particular person and the particular action with the ultimate source of everything would not rest on a secure basis. Consequently, they substituted principle for the Great Ultimate, regarding principle not only as a source of things, but also as the law of being inherent in every being, giving it existence and directing its function. Because they regarded the principle from which all things proceed to be the same as the principles inherent in particular things, the difference being only one of manifestation or embodiment, they conceived of all things as forming a unity with respect to principle. When principle is realized and exhibited in all actions, the perfect harmony will be achieved.

Ch'eng I says, "That which is inherent in things is principle," and:

> Principle in the world is one. Although there are many roads in the world, the destination is the same, and although there are a hundred deliberations, the result is one. Although things involve many manifestations and events go through infinite variation, when they are united by the one, there cannot be any contradiction.[10]

Ch'eng Hao, discussing principle as the unifying factor in reality, says, "The reason why it is said that all things form one body is that all have this principle, simply because they all have come from it."[11] He also says, "There is only one principle in the world."[12]

These remarks by the Ch'eng brothers reveal that they regarded principle both as a source of things and as the directive force within

---

[10] Ibid., p. 571.   [11] Ibid., p. 533.   [12] Ibid., p. 534.

things. That is, although principle was regarded as one, the source of all, it is also regarded as many, for it is inherent in all of the many things that have proceeded from the source. How can principle be both one and many? To answer this question it is necessary to understand both the concept of principle generally, and the specific concept of principle that the Ch'eng brothers used.

From the fact that the Ch'eng brothers considered the production of things to be dependent upon material force (*ch'i*) and principle, plus the fact that principle was regarded as the determination and manifestation of specific things out of material force, it appears that they considered principle to be the inner working of nature through things. It is obvious that different things are different; apples are not trees and trees are not men. To what is the difference due? The Ch'engs' answer is that it is due to form and function. Apples do not function or behave the way trees or men do. They do not give off the same colors, odors, sounds, flavors, etc. The reason they appear different in color, odor, sound, taste, shape, etc., is because of their different principles. If this is the case it is clear that the general concept of principle is that of *the reason why something is just what it is rather than something else.* Since there are differences between things, and since these differences can be explained, it follows that there are reasons for the differences, and reasons are possible because things are distinguished according to their principles. That is, in the last analysis, the reasons for distinguishing between any two things consist in identifying the principles of those things; the reasons reveal the principles.

The Ch'eng brothers extended this notion of principle to the totality of what exists. Everything that exists—heaven and earth and "the ten thousand things"—exists due to principle. That is, there is a reason for the existence of things. Furthermore, this principle of the universe is not really different from the principle in any particular thing, for the particular thing exists only as a manifestation of the supreme principle. Things are distinguished according to the *embodiment* of principle, not according to principle as such. What makes a particular thing what it is, is the principle embodied and manifested in a certain way in material force.

It would appear, therefore, that principle in the philosophy of the Ch'eng brothers referred to the reason, or law, operating within things which gives the universe its order. The importance, therefore, of making principle the basis of their philosophy is that it provided them with an ordered universe. Thus, the order in society that issues from the ordering and rectification of the individual was held to have a foundation in the very structure of the universe. This concept gave to Neo-Confucianism the metaphysical basis for its social philosophy it had been lacking.

With this general idea in mind of the kind of concept principle is, and the function it served in the philosophy of the Ch'eng brothers, it is possible to turn to the writing of Ch'eng Hao and Ch'eng I for a more detailed analysis of principle, and the application of principle to the practical affairs of man.

Once someone asked Ch'eng I if in investigating things in order to gain understanding that would allow one to become a sage, a person should be concerned with internal things, such as feelings and thoughts, or with external things, such as natural happenings. His reply was "It does not matter. All that is before our eyes is nothing but things, and all things have their principles. For example, from that by which fire is hot or water is cold to the relations between ruler and minister, and father and son, are all principle."[13] This answer makes clear that the principle of a thing is regarded as the source of that thing's essential activity, for the essential activity of fire is to produce heat, and it is said that that from which fire is hot is principle. But it is also clear that it is not the multiplicity of detail that is to be investigated, but only the principles operating through the detailed manifestations of things. Thus, in answer to the question, "If one investigates only one thing, does he understand only one thing or does he understand the various principles?" the answer is, "We must seek to understand all. However, even Yen Tzu [a wise man referred to in the *Analects* of Confucius] could only understand ten points when he heard one. When one finally understands principle, even millions of things can be understood."[14] Obviously, millions of things in their details could not be understood, so the meaning is that millions of things could be understood in terms of their basic principle. For example, when the correct relation between father and son is understood the relations between fathers and sons in millions of particular cases are understood. When once the love a mother has for a newborn child is understood, then the love of millions of mothers for their newborn is understood even without investigating the particular cases. The reason is that one knows the principle involved. This is why Ch'eng I says, "All things under heaven can be understood in the light of their principle. As there are things, there must be specific principles."[15]

[13] *Ibid.*, p. 568.   [14] *Ibid.*, pp. 568–569.   [15] *Ibid.*, p. 563.

On another occasion he said, "A thing is an event. If the principles underlying the event are investigated to the utmost, then all principles will be understood."[16] It would appear, therefore, that the principles of specific things, or specific kinds of things—*qua* principle—are the same, although with respect to their embodiment and manifestation in material force they differ. For example, the principle of a dog is different than the principle of a man. If this were not the case one could not distinguish between the two. But this difference is due to the embodiment of principle in the particularizing material force, and does not proceed from the nature of principle as such. By analogy, in comparing pieces of china one might notice that cups differ from saucers. It might be suggested that this is due to their different principles. But both cup and saucer are the same insofar as they are constituted by the kind of stuff called bone. It must be admitted that the bone embodied in the cup and the saucer is not different in the two cases. Likewise, it could be said that the great principle participating in the ten thousand things is not different in each case, though the embodiment is different.

The questions that arise from this analysis are: (1) What is the nature of the principle that is responsible for the substance and the function of the universe? (2) How is the principle of the universe related to man? and (3) Is man's mind different from this principle, or one with it? The answers to these questions are revealed in the practical philosophy advocated by the Ch'engs.

According to Ch'eng Hao, "The student must first of all understand the nature of *jen*. The man of *jen* forms one body with all things without any differentiation. Rightness, propriety, wisdom, and faithfulness are all (expressions) of *jen*."[17] The reason why the student must first understand *jen* is that *jen* is principle. In other words, the nature of principle in man is *jen*. But since principle is the same in nature as it is in man, the cultivation of *jen* is at the same time the establishing of a unity with all things. As Ch'eng Hao points out, "There is no difference between Nature and man."[18] Thus, to know *jen* is to know principle, and to know principle is to know (in a way) all things and to be in harmony ("form one body") with all things.

Ch'eng I points out that knowing *jen* is not a matter of having information about it, but is a matter of having experienced this principle. He explained this point as follows:

> True knowledge and ordinary knowledge are different. I once saw a farmer who had been wounded by a tiger. When someone said that the tiger was

16 *Ibid.*, p. 552.   17 *Ibid.*, p. 523.   18 *Ibid.*, p. 538.

hurting people, everyone was startled. But in his facial expression the farmer reacted differently from the rest. Even a young boy knows that tigers can hurt people, but his is not true knowledge. It is true knowledge only when it is like the farmer's. Therefore when men know evil and still do it, this also is not true knowledge. If it were, they would surely not do it.[19]

So, when Ch'eng Hao says that the student must first of all understand *jen*, he is really saying that he must first of all cultivate his own humanity, living according to the principle of *jen*. This, of course, is the most important and most difficult of all tasks, for it is the task of becoming a Sage.

Ch'eng I notes that in the school of Confucius there were three thousand pupils, but only one—Yen Tzu—was praised as loving to learn. The reason Yen Tzu was singled out is that he alone concentrated wholeheartedly on learning the way of becoming a Sage. Becoming a Sage is the highest goal, for the Sage represents the perfect person, and in a philosophy where the reality of the person is regarded as the highest reality, the perfection of a person represents perfection of the ultimate reality.

But is it possible for man to learn to become a Sage? Ch'eng I answers this question in the affirmative.

From the essence of life accumulated in Heaven and Earth, man receives the Five Agents (Water, Fire, Wood, Metal, and Earth) in their highest excellence. His original nature is pure and tranquil. Before it is aroused, the five moral principles of his nature called humanity, righteousness, propriety, wisdom, and faithfulness, are complete. As his physical form appears, it comes into contact with external things and is aroused from within. As it is aroused from within, the seven feelings, called pleasure, anger, sorrow, joy, love, hate, and desire, ensue. As feeling becomes strong and increasingly reckless, his nature becomes damaged.[20]

Having thus postulated the original goodness and purity of man and having attributed the evil in man to a disturbance of this original goodness due to uncontrolled feelings, it is possible to suggest that one can learn to become a Sage by learning to control the feelings and thereby return to the original principle in its purity. Accordingly, Ch'eng I said, "The way to learn is none other than rectifying one's mind and nourishing one's nature. When one abides by the mean and correctness and becomes sincere, he is a Sage."[21]

These statements reveal that for the Ch'eng brothers principle is the inner law of a thing's nature which is received from the inner law of the universe. Man also receives the law of his being from the inner

[19] *Ibid.*, p. 551. [20] *Ibid.*, p. 548. [21] *Ibid.*, p. 548.

law of the universe, and therefore is in union with the universe with respect to principle. Since mind refers to the original essence of man, it turns out that mind is identical with principle. Man's nature—his principle—is that of a moral being, and since morality issues from *jen*, it follows that man's nature is *jen*. Since this is the original principle of man's being, to realize his perfection he must be true to this principle (practice *ch'eng*, or sincerity) and cultivate it. For this the virtues of propriety, wisdom, and righteousness are also needed.

CHU HSI

The problem of how *jen* (humanity) can be cultivated and perfected is the central problem for all Neo-Confucianists. The chief obstacle to be overcome in solving this problem is that of the relation between good and evil. Chu Hsi's importance in the Chinese mind (he is considered to be in the same league with Confucius and Mencius) is due primarily to his ability to reinterpret and synthesize the philosophies of earlier Neo-Confucian thinkers in such a way that he was able to construct a complete and systematic philosophy in which he reconciled the presence of evil with the basic goodness of human nature. This he was able to do along the lines suggested by Confucius and Mencius by incorporating the metaphysical philosophies of earlier Neo-Confucian philosophers. This enabled him to achieve a systematic completeness that Confucius and Mencius had lacked, while providing a more detailed practical philosophy than his Neo-Confucian predecessors had managed. In Chu Hsi's philosophy the problem of the relation between good and evil is considered in terms of the relation between man and nature and in terms of the relation between man's basic nature and his feelings.

For both Confucianists and Neo-Confucianists the central concern of philosophy was the cultivation of *jen*, rectification of the basic human relationships, and development of the constant virtues. The five basic relations between persons are those between ruler and subject, between father and son, between husband and wife, between elder and younger children, and between friends. The constant virtues are righteousness, propriety, sincerity, and wisdom. The three activities of philosophy, cultivation, rectification, and development, are all the same essentially, for when the relations are rectified and the virtues developed, *jen* will be cultivated. And when *jen* is cultivated, the virtues will be developed and the relations will be rectified. And when these three are accomplished, evil will have been removed and peace and goodness will reign supreme in the world.

The difficulty encountered in advocating and supporting this philosophy stemmed from the problems encountered in trying to explain the sources of good and evil and the relations between them. The difficulty was felt already prior to Mencius, who attempted to resolve the problem by claiming that man's nature is essentially good, but is corrupted by society and culture. Hsun Tzu, on the other hand, tried to resolve the problem by arguing that man's nature is essentially evil, but through education and culture this evil can be rooted out and replaced with goodness. Neither of these theories proved satisfactory, however, for if man's nature is essentially good, as Mencius would have it, then how can society and culture, which proceed from man, be evil and corrupting? On the other hand, if man's nature is essentially evil, as Hsun Tzu would have it, how can what proceeds from man's nature—in the form of culture and education—be good, and opposed to man's evil nature?

During the centuries following the Mencius–Hsun Tzu controversy it was generally agreed by Confucianists that man is basically good, but no satisfactory theoretical support for this position was worked out. Han Yu, a pioneering figure in the Neo-Confucian movement, suggested that man's nature was of three kinds, good, bad, and good and bad mixed. But there was no satisfactory explanation of how human nature could be all three simultaneously. Consequently, the need for a philosophical theory of the nature of good and evil continued to be keenly felt by the Neo-Confucianists, for without it their emphasis on the removal of evil by the cultivation of jen would be unsupported.

Chang Tsai made a significant step forward when he distinguished between the essential nature of man and the physical nature. But since he failed to establish a satisfactory relationship between the two his theory was deficient. The Ch'eng brothers also made an important contribution to the problem with their theory that principle and human nature were identical. But it was left for Chu Hsi to show how the basic nature of man was identical with the supreme principle of the universe, and therefore of the nature of pure goodness, while the secondary nature of man, created by the association of principle with material stuff (ch'i) was impure and the source of evil. According to this explanation the source of goodness was man's basic nature. But man is also a concrete being with body, and feelings, as well as mind; man's embodied nature gives rise to evil, for from the feelings come those passions that obscure the original goodness, that deviate from *jen*, the supreme principle of man.

Distinguishing between principle in itself and principle as embodied in concrete things, Chu Hsi says: "What exists before physical form is the one principle harmonious and undifferentiated, and is invariably good. What exists after physical form, however, is confused and mixed, and good and evil are thereby differentiated."[22] This statement is the key to Chu Hsi's solution to the problem of how the presence of evil can be reconciled with the goodness that is man's basic nature. The distinction he makes is between the goodness of principle and the evil-producing material stuff of which particular things are composed. In man, as in all things, principle combines with material stuff, and therefore goodness is mixed with evil. But man's fundamental, basic nature is identical with principle, which is of the nature of *jen*; the material stuff constitutes a secondary nature. Since *jen* is the basic nature of man and this is good, the removal of evil depends upon the cultivation and development of *jen*, or the basic nature, over the secondary nature.

This distinction between basic and secondary natures on the basis of the distinction between principle and material stuff requires a general theory of the nature and source of things as an explanatory context. According to Chu Hsi, all things are the result of a combination of material stuff (*ch'i*) and principle (*li*). He says, "Man and things are all endowed with the principle of the universe as their nature, and receive the material force of the universe as their physical form..."[23] That there is principle is obvious from the fact that things are what they are rather than something else. That man is different from dog is due to different principles. However, differences in principles are not merely differences in principles, but also involve differences in matter. Nothing whatsoever is found that does not involve both principle and material stuff, and the manifestation of principle is regulated by the material stuff while at the same time principle determines the material stuff. When Chu Hsi was asked for evidence that there is principle in material force he replied, "For example, there is order in the complicated interfusion of the *yin* and the *yang* and of the Five Agents. Principle is there. If material force does not consolidate and integrate, principle would have nothing to attach itself to."[24]

In explanation of what principle and material stuff are and how they are related Chu Hsi said:

---

[22] *Ibid.*, p. 597.   [23] *Ibid.*, p. 620.   [24] *Ibid.*, p. 635.

> Throughout the universe there are both principle and material force. Principle refers to the Way, which exists before physical form [and is without it] and is the course from which all things are produced. Material force refers to material objects, which exist after physical form [and is with it]; it is the instrument by which things are produced. Therefore in the production of man and things, they must be endowed with principle before they have their nature, and they must be endowed with material force before they have physical form.[25]

It would appear from this explanation that principle is prior to material stuff in two senses, for principle is the essential reason for the being of something, and principle is also the knowable characteristic of a thing. Thus principle is first in the order of being and in the order of knowledge. But despite this priority, it remains the case that nothing exists except through the combination of principle and material stuff.

Still, the things that exist have a source from which they receive their natures, and for Chu Hsi's explanation to be complete he must relate principle and material stuff—as the determinants of things—to their source. This he accomplishes by integrating Chou Tun-i's concept of the Great Ultimate into his system. His view is "The Great Ultimate is nothing other than principle."[26] In other words, principle is the ultimate source of all things. As such it gives a unity—a unity of principle—to the manifoldness of reality and serves to integrate all of reality into a harmonious whole. In Chu Hsi the Great Ultimate is regarded as "the principle of heaven and earth and the myriad things."

> With respect to the myriad things, there is the Great Ultimate in each and every one of them. Before heaven and earth existed, there was assuredly this principle. It is the principle that "through movement generates the yang." It is also this principle that "through tranquillity generates the yin"[27]

And, of course, through the activity of yin and yang the Five Agents came about and by their power produced the ten thousand things that make up the concrete reality surrounding us. Thus, Chu Hsi has provided for a systematic explanation of the origination and nature of things through his discovery of principle and material stuff and the relation between them.

Applying this explanation to the problem of evil in human nature Chu Hsi said, "The Great Ultimate is simply the principle of the highest good. Each and every person has in him the Great Ultimate and each and every thing has in it the Great Ultimate."[28] The importance of this

---

[25] Ibid., p. 636.   [26] Ibid., p. 638.   [27] Ibid., p. 638.   [28] Ibid., p. 640.

view is connected with the priority of principle over material stuff. If principle is more fundamental than material stuff, and if there is the Great Ultimate in man as the principle of his mind, then this will be prior to the material stuff. On the strength of this it can be claimed that the basic nature of man is principle, though the secondary nature is the embodiment of principle in material stuff. Because man possesses the Great Ultimate it follows that *jen* is the basic nature of man. Chu Hsi shows this by pointing to the two essential relationships involved. First, after identifying mind with the basic nature of man, he says, "The principle of the mind is the Great Ultimate."[29] Secondly, he says, "*Jen* is man's mind."[30] These two statements together mean that the Great Ultimate is identical to *jen*. Chu Hsi supports this view in his treatise on *jen*:

> In the production of man and things, they receive the mind of Heaven and Earth as their mind. Therefore, with reference to the character of the mind, although it embraces and penetrates all and leaves nothing to be desired, nevertheless, one word will cover all of it, namely, *jen* (humanity).[31]

Granted that *jen* is man's basic nature—"the principle originally inherent in man's mind"[32]—the question of greatest importance is how to realize *jen*. According to Chu Hsi's philosophy, there are two equally important practices essential to the realization of *jen*. On the one hand, since *jen* is already there as the basic nature of man, one must concentrate on preserving one's true nature. On the other hand, the nature of man is learned and realized through its function: understanding of the function of anything depends upon empirical investigation to discover the nature of principle.

> The mind embraces all principles and all principles are complete in this single entity, the mind. If one is not able to preserve the mind, he will be unable to investigate principle to the utmost. If he is unable to investigate principle to the utmost, he will be unable to exert his mind to the utmost."[33]

The twin doctrines of preservation (of goodness) and investigation (of principle) rest upon the distinction between substance and function. Substance refers to what something is, and function refers to how something operates. The distinction itself goes back as far as Lao Tzu, who distinguished between *Tao* (the substance) and *te* (the function of *Tao*), but in Chu Hsi the distinction is applied to principle. Thus man's basic nature, or principle—the character of his mind—as substance is *jen*.

29 *Ibid.*, p. 628.   30 *Ibid.*, p. 594.   31 *Ibid.*, pp. 593–594.   32 *Ibid.*, p. 633.
33 *Ibid.*, p. 606.

But the function of man's mind is love. In other words, the function of humanity is love. Love, as the function of *jen*, comprises the other virtues and is the basis for the proper human relations. Chu Hsi puts the matter as follows:

> The moral qualities of the mind of Heaven and Earth are four: origination, flourish, advantages, and firmness. . . . Therefore in the mind of man there are also four moral qualities—namely *jen*, righteousness, propriety, and wisdom—and *jen* embraces them all. In their emanation and function, they constitute the feeling of love, respect, being right, and discrimination between being right and wrong—and the feeling of commiseration pervades them all.[34]

The nature of something provides for its function, and its function expresses its nature. Therefore *jen* provides for the function of man, namely, acting in accord with the moral qualities, and functioning in accord with the moral qualities is the expression of *jen*.

> If we can truly practice love and preserve it, then we have in it the spring of all virtues and the root of all good deeds. This is why in the teachings of the Confucian school, the student is always urged to exert anxious and unceasing effort in the pursuit of *jen*.[35]

This, then, is the foundation Chu Hsi provides for the practical philosophy of Neo-Confucianism which can be summed up in his own words as follows: "To be sincere, empty of self, courteous and calm is the foundation of the practice of love . . . To love others as we love ourselves, is to perfect love."[36]

WANG YANG-MING

The distinction between principle and material force enabled Chu Hsi to recognize both the reality of the mind and the reality of things external to the mind. In philosophical terminology, he was rationalistic to the extent he emphasized principle, but empiricistic to the extent he emphasized the investigation of things. He was idealistic to the extent that he emphasized that the Great Ultimate is both the basic nature of all things and the essence of mind, but he also insisted that without material force to embody principle there could be nothing.

After Chu Hsi, however, developments in the school of Principle through the work of Lu Hsiang-shan and his pupils led to the identification of principle with mind in the philosophy of Wang Yang-ming.

[34] *Ibid.*, p. 594.   [35] *Ibid.*, p. 594.
[36] As quoted by Clarence Burton Day in *The Philosophers of China* (New York: The Citadel Press, 1962) p. 209.

According to him "there are neither principles nor things outside the mind."[37] A philosophy built upon such a principle is quite sharply opposed to Chu Hsi's, for only when a distinction is made between what belongs to mind and what is outside of mind can the investigation of the things be emphasized as the key to the cultivation of *jen*, and investigation of things is one of the two pillars upon which Chu Hsi's philosophy rests. The other pillar—preservation of the original mind—was perfectly acceptable to Wang Yang-ming, but it was not emphasized by Chu Hsi's followers.

Among the reasons for the ascendancy of Wang Yang-ming's idealism during the Ming dynasty (1368–1644), two stand out. First, from 1313 on, Chu Hsi's interpretation of the Confucian classics enjoyed the status of being the official state philosophy in China. In addition to discouraging other philosophies, this meant that the civil service examinations were based on his interpretations.

As so often happens, the security attending such entrenchment led to the decline of Chu Hsi's philosophy. Without the need to establish itself against other strong systems of thought there came to be increasing attempts to consolidate and refine translations and definitions, and there was too little attention given to reexamination and rethinking of basic principles and arguments. Such a lack is, of course, fatal to a philosophy, for philosophy cannot be done once for all time. It it is rather like loving someone. Just because someone in the past established a happy relationship based on love does not mean that love has been established in the world. Love is something that must be experienced by every individual in every generation. When it is not it is lost. In a similar way, a philosophy is a kind of overview fitting together the various aspects and activities of life and providing a secure ground for the meaning and value of the activities of life. And this is something that each person in each generation must do for himself. If it is not done the person is shallow and life is hollow. Now, since Chu Hsi's interpretation of Confucianism had, as Wing-Tsit Chan points out, "degenerated into trifling with what Wang [Yang-ming] called 'fragmentary and isolated details and broken pieces'"[38] it did not provide an adequate basis for assisting the people in forming a satisfactory philosophy of life. Consequently, there was a ready reception for a fresh and vigorous philosophy such as Wang Yang-ming proposed.

Secondly, following Chu Hsi's emphasis upon investigation of things,

---

[37] See *Source Book in Chinese Philosophy*, p. 673.   [38] *Ibid.*, p. 654.

but slighting his emphasis on preserving the original mind of man, his followers got further and further away from the moral emphases that were the distinguishing characteristic of Confucian thought. When Wang Yang-ming turned his attention almost exclusively to moral matters it was greeted as a welcome return to the central concern of philosophy.

Wang Yang-ming's philosophy is characterized by its preoccupation with moral values. It rests upon the principles of the all-inclusive character of the mind and the unity of knowledge and action. These two principles give rise to the doctrine of the extension of the innate knowledge of the good (*chih liang-chih*). These features of his philosophy are all reflected in the following statement: "The learning of the great man consists entirely in getting rid of the obscuration of selfish desires in order by his own efforts to make manifest his clear character, so as to restore the condition of forming one body with Heaven, Earth, and the myriad things, a condition that is originally so, that is all. It is not that outside of the original substance something can be added."[39]

There is here no appeal to the investigation of things as an essential part of learning or cultivating *jen*. Knowledge is not distinguished from action, for true knowledge is action that proceeds from the love that constitutes the humanity of man. In Wang Yang-ming's words, "Knowledge is the beginning of action and action is the completion of knowledge. Learning to be a sage involves only one effort. Knowledge and action should not be separated."[40] The basis for the unification of knowledge and action is Wang Yang-ming's emphasis on will or choice rather than reason or knowledge. Intellectual or discursive knowledge of the kind characteristic of the sciences can, of course, be separated from choice and morality. But practical knowledge of the value of things has no significance apart from the activity of choosing and acting. When what a person does is regarded as more fundamental than what he knows or says, then the kind of knowledge required for making choices becomes more important than theoretical knowledge. Furthermore, a person's choices are revealed in the action taken and this shows the combination of knowledge and action. This is why Wang Yang-ming can claim that the learning of the great man consists in getting rid of selfishness and in manifesting his good character. The general point involved here is that action is more basic than knowledge and all knowledge is for the sake of action. In the language of classical philosophy, this means that Will is higher than Reason.

[39] *Ibid.*, p. 660.   [40] *Ibid.*, p. 674.

Wang Yang-ming's philosophy is most clearly revealed in his interpretation of the *Great Learning* (*Ta Hsueh*), a classical Confucian text
that served as an inspiration to many of the Neo-Confucian philosophers.
The text of the *Great Learning* consists in a statement and explanation
of "three major chords" and "eight minor wires." The three major
chords are (1) manifestation of the clear character, (2) loving the people,
and (3) abiding in the highest good. Asked about manifesting the clear
character, Wang Yang-ming replied, "The great man regards Heaven
and Earth and the myriad things as one body. He regards the world as
one family and the country as one person. As to those who make a
cleavage between objects and distinguish between the self and others,
they are small men."[41] The thinking behind this claim is that all things
really form integral parts of one whole, just as the children and the
mother and the father really are one family. In the family it is the bond
of familial love that proceeds from human-ness of the individual person
that creates the unity of one family. In the world it is the bond of great
love proceeding from the *jen* of the universe that creates a unity. In
the great man the *jen* of the universe is identified with the *jen* of the
individual and there is a unity of all things ("forming one body").

When he was asked why the learning of the great man consists in
loving the people, Wang Yang-ming replied, "Manifesting the clear
character consists in loving the people, and loving the people is the way
to manifest the clear character. Therefore, only when I love my father,
the fathers of others, and the fathers of all men can my humanity really
form one body with my father, the fathers of others, and the fathers of
all men."[42] The explanation behind this is that by "clear character" is
meant the original purity and goodness of man's basic nature or mind.
According to Wang Yang-ming, this original goodness consists in love
—a pervasive and universal love which both forms and proceeds from
the basic principles of all things. When things are in accord with this
love they are perfected. When man is in accord with this love he too is
perfected. This can be seen in the fact that when the clear character of
love is manifested the constant virtues are perfected and the human
relations are rectified. Thus, Wang Yang-ming goes on to say that when
his humanity forms one body with the fathers of all men, then the
clear character of filial piety will be manifested. And when his humanity
forms one body with the brothers of all men, then the clear character
of brotherly love will be manifested. And in sum,

[41] *Ibid.*, p. 659.   [42] *Ibid.*, p. 660.

Everything from ruler, minister, husband, wife, and friends to mountains, rivers, spiritual beings, birds, animals, and plants should be truly loved in order to realize my humanity that forms one body with them, and then my clear character will be completely manifested, and I will really form one body with Heaven, Earth and the myriad things.

When he was asked why the learning of the great man consists in abiding in the highest good, Wang Yang-ming replied,

The highest good is the ultimate principle of manifesting character and loving people. The nature endowed in us by Heaven is pure and perfect. The fact that it is intelligent, clear, and not beclouded is evidence of the emanation and revelation of the highest good. It is the original substance of the clear character which is called innate knowledge of the good.[43]

All things are present in *jen*, which is the basis of man's nature. Therefore to realize his perfection man must cultivate this basic nature. But nothing external is required for this task, since this nature is pure and perfect of itself. To know the good is to do the good, and knowledge of the good is already contained in man's basic nature as *jen*. Therefore, what is required is the extension of this innate knowledge of the good into all spheres of action. As Wang Yang-ming puts it, "This is what is meant by 'manifesting the clear character throughout the empire.' This is what is meant by 'regulation of the family,' 'ordering the state,' and 'bringing peace to the world.' This is what is meant by 'full development of one's nature.'"[44]

After Wang Yang-ming, Neo-Confucianism underwent a movement away from the emphasis on principle that characterized the philosophy of the Ch'engs and Chu Hsi, and away from the introspective idealism of Wang Yang-ming. The emphasis in this new movement was on things and feelings.

TAI CHEN

Neo-Confucian philosophy through Wang Yang-ming had emphasized the principles of things over their material constitution and elevated the "fundamental mind" over the feelings. In the seventeenth and eighteenth centuries there was a reaction against this rationalism and idealism, and the empirical came to be emphasized more and more, both in the studies of man and in the studies of things. An objective study of things characterized by detailed and analytical investigations

[43] *Ibid.*, p. 661.   [44] *Ibid.*, p. 661.

of things came to be regarded as the path to truth, and the feelings of persons exhibited in day-to-day living came to be regarded as the real source of man's actions. According to Tai Chen, generally accepted as the greatest of the empiricistic Neo-Confucian philosophers, "A thing is an affair or event. When we talk about an event, we do not go beyond daily affairs such as drinking and eating. To neglect these and talk about principle is not what the ancient sages and worthies meant by principle."[45]

This remark clearly indicates the empiricist's impatience with metaphysical speculation and idealistic introspection. Tai Chen was concerned with the principles that could be discovered empirically in things, feelings, and actions; abstractions were useless. It is not the case that Tai Chen rejected the concepts and principles of earlier philosophers of the Sung period, but rather that he reinterpreted them in such a way that the concrete and particular were not overlooked. This, of course, gave a balance to Neo-Confucianism, bringing the metaphysics down to an empirically verifiable level. This was, by the same token, a paving of the way for the empirical sciences of physics and psychology which were to come later. In fact, much of Tai Chen's work is often regarded as scientific rather than philosophical because of his minute investigation of particular things.

The emphasis during this later period of Neo-Confucianism continued to be on the nature of man, however, and the nature of man continued to be regarded as a source of morality. Consequently, the primary objects of investigation continued to be the actions of human beings, and the categories used in this investigation were primarily moral. This means that instead of classifying and investigating the relations between the components of external things, human actions and relations between persons were classified and investigated. When external things are investigated it is important, for example, to know what neutrons, protons, and electrons are, and how they are related to each other. But when the moral nature of man is being investigated the virtues of humanity, righteousness, sincerity, propriety, and wisdom must be known, and the relations between these virtues in terms of the principal relations between persons must be investigated.

Throughout the earlier Confucian tradition it was man as moral agent and society as moral institution that were regarded as the primary objects to be known. In the Neo-Confucian tradition there was an

[45] *Ibid.*, p. 713.

attempt to provide metaphysical support for this view that held morality to be the subject of ultimate concern. To Tai Chen it appeared that some of the Neo-Confucianists had allowed the metaphysics of morality to become the subject of primary importance. This he was concerned to rectify, for clearly the moral relations between persons and the moral virtues are of primary concern, and the metaphysics of morality is secondary, being merely for the sake of a theoretical defense of morality.

CHAPTER 20

MAO TSE-TUNG

Even as the emphasis on investigating particular things that characterized Tai Chen's empiricistic philosophy began to become influential, there were signs of a revived interest in metaphysics and in the
rationalism of the Ch'eng brothers and Chu Hsi. The movement back
to a philosophy of principle was slow in developing, however, and as a
result of the political and social upheaval in China during the nineteenth
and twentieth centuries, never matured beyond infancy. After the
British defeated China in the Opium war of 1840–42 the people found
themselves not only poor, hungry, and oppressed, but forced to admit
tremendous loss of face. It was now exceedingly difficult to maintain
the two-thousand-year-old tradition of the world's superior and only
civilized people. Of course, a people finding themselves in such circumstances are not likely to pay nearly as much attention to working
out satisfactory philosophical explanations as they are to trying to rem-
edy things at hand. It appeared that the political situation was beginning
to improve with the establishment of the Chinese Republic in 1912.
Within a decade, however, it became clear that this government was
not the answer to China's problems. Before a new solution could be
tried Imperial Japan controlled the country. Since the removal of Japan,
China has been preoccupied with internal revolution, and only since the
establishment of the People's Republic of China under the dominance
of the Communist Party has there been any climate at all conducive to
philosophy. And since the Central government has encouraged only

Marxist-Leninist philosophy, Mao Tse-tung is regarded as the most important philosopher in China today.

In the troubled years between Tai Chen and Mao Tse-tung are found the beginnings of a number of attempts to turn philosophy from the empiricistic preoccupation with concrete things to a consideration of the underlying principles of things. K'ang Yu-wei (1858–1927), who in 1914 attempted to get Confucianism adopted as the state religion in the new Republic, emphasized love as the basis of humanity. He held that the love which makes human beings human is also, in its cosmic aspect, what makes anything what it is. He advocated a return to the reforms of humanity that he considered Confucius to have initiated in order that a higher order of society might evolve. Chang Tung-sun (1886–1926) combined his understanding of the traditional Chinese philosophies with his understanding of classical Western philosophies—especially Kant and Dewey—in advocating a philosophy based on a critical pragmatic theory of knowledge which views philosophical concepts as historical social creations. Fung Yu-lan (1895–) has been greatly influenced by Taoism and Neo-Confucianism, and under the influence of Western rationalism reconstructed the various Taoist and Neo-Confucian ideas into a systematic rational philosophy. Hsiung Shih-li (1885–1968) revived Wang Yang-ming's idealistic philosophy, putting it on the basis of his reinterpretation of the Buddhist Consciousness-only philosophy, thereby providing a basis for both the unity and plurality of the world.

These philosophers, along with others less well known, have written extensively, and their philosophies are more carefully worked out in terms of analysis and arguments than the classical Chinese philosophies. In terms of their content these philosophies are deserving of careful and detailed study. But they have not had much influence on the people, being confined mostly to the circles of professional philosophy. They never came to direct and regulate the lives of the people the way Taoism, Confucianism, Buddhism, Neo-Confucianism, and Maoism did.

Mao Tse-tung's philosophy is influenced greatly by Marx and Lenin, but is not basically out of tune with the principles and attitudes of traditional Chinese philosophies. Probably his most important philosophical work is the lecture delivered in 1937 entitled "On Practice." In this lecture he explained the relation between theory and practice, showing how theory originates in practice and returns to practice for its justification and fulfillment. This approach to the relation between theory and practice grew out of Mao's practice in reconciling the differences among the people as leader of the revolutionary forces. It is not a theory worked out for its own sake, but for the practical purpose of establishing the Great Harmony—the age-old Chinese utopia.

To see the practical aims presupposed by Mao's theory of the relation between practice and theory it is helpful to consider the address commemorating the twenty-eighth anniversary of the Communist Party of China. In that address Mao outlined the aims of Communist practices in China as follows: "When classes disappear, all instruments of class struggle—parties and the state machinery—will lose their function, cease to be necessary, therefore will gradually wither away and end their historical mission; and humanity will move to a higher stage."[1] The concluding phrase—"human society will move to a higher stage"— reveals Mao's concern for the human condition. Of course, improving the human condition has always been the foremost consideration among Chinese philosophers. It was the hope of the Confucians and Neo-Confucians that when *jen* was made to prevail the Great Harmony would be achieved. That Mao sees the aim of Communist practice to be the achievement of the Great Harmony is clear from his remark that the Party's function is that of ". . . working hard to create the conditions in which classes, state power, and political parties will die out very naturally and mankind will enter the realm of the Great Harmony."[2]

To accomplish the task of achieving the Great Harmony, Mao considers it necessary to understand the conditions which regulate the growth and development of man and the world generally, so that the natural processes of growth and development can be assisted in arriving at their final goal. Probably the most important principle to be understood in this connection is that "all processes have a beginning and an end; all processes transform themselves into their opposites. The stability of all processes is relative, but the mutuality manifested in the transformation of one process into another is absolute."[3] No doubt, this principle is the central feature of the dialectic of Marxism, but it also restates the Taoist principle that "reversal is the way of Tao," and that "all things have their opposites." It is a restatement of the Neo-Confucian explanation of the source and structure of all things that has its initial expression in Chou Tun-i's concept of the Great Ultimate, which generates all things through the interaction of the opposites *yin* and *yang*. Mao is quite aware that he is here well within the mainstream of traditional Chinese thought, for he remarks in the same paragraph, "We

[1] *Mao Tse-tung: An Anthology of His Writings*, edited with an introduction by Ann Freemantle (New York: The New American Library, 1962) p. 184.
[2] *Ibid.*, p. 185.   [3] *Ibid.*, p. 237.

Chinese often say, 'Things opposed to each other complement each other.'"4

According to the dialectical relation between knowing and doing that Mao presents in his lecture "On Practice," knowing begins with practice, moves to the stage of theory, and is completed in doing. Theory represents the half-way house of knowing. Taking seriously the principle that the great dialectic of nature is "reversal of opposites," and holding that the dialectic of any particular thing is also according to this principle, Mao is concerned with the opposites of theory and practice. His concern, of course, is with the successful democratic socialization of the People's Republic. This process, like any other process, proceeds according to its inner dialectic, and for the sake of successful practice Mao is concerned to understand the dialectical relation between practice and theory, for these are the two primary opposites in the Communist program.

This problem—the relation between knowing and doing—has nearly always been of central concern to Chinese philosophers. Mao's solution to the problem is in agreement with traditional solutions, for he holds that knowing and doing form a unity. His theory of knowledge maintains that "human knowledge cannot be separated the least bit from practice, and repudiates all incorrect theories which deny the importance of practice or separate knowledge from practice. . . ."5 Verification of knowledge is had only when the anticipated results are achieved in the process of social practice. The principle is that "if man wants to achieve success in his work, that is, to achieve the anticipated results, he must make his thoughts correspond to the laws of the objective world surrounding him; if they do not correspond, he will fail in practice."6

In attempting to show the plausibility of the claim that social practice is the only criterion of truth, Mao argues that all knowledge has its beginnings in practice, in the activity of changing the world. "If you want to know the taste of a pear you must change the pear by eating it yourself."7 This is the first stage in acquiring knowledge, the stage of perception. The next step consists in "making a rearrangement or a reconstruction; this belongs to the stage of conception, judgment, and inference."8 Conception, judgment, and inference constitute rational, as opposed to merely perceptual knowledge, and as such provide for theories about the things perceived. But the acquisition of knowledge does not stop here. Just as perceptual knowledge leads to rational knowledge and is incomplete without it, so rational knowledge

---

4 *Ibid.*, p. 238.   5 *Ibid.*, p. 203.   6 *Ibid.*, pp. 201, 202.   7 *Ibid.*, p. 205.
8 *Ibid.*, p. 207.

remains incomplete until it is applied in practice. As Mao points out, "What Marxist philosophy regards as the most important problem does not lie in understanding the laws of the objective world, thereby becoming capable of explaining it, but in actively changing the world by applying the knowledge of its objective laws."[9]

Knowledge is nothing but meaningless words and empty ideas until it gets embodied in experience. Only in the changing of the person and the changing of the reality encountered in practical activity does knowledge become real. From practice comes theory, and from theory practice proceeds. But theory and practice are not two different things. They are simply the dialectical opposites of one process—living in the world. The advance of knowledge is dialectically coupled to the advance of practice. The development of democratic socialism in China can ignore neither theory nor practice, but must combine them if the cause is to advance. Mao urges that "... the development of things should be regarded as their internal and necessary self-movement, that a thing in its movement and the things around it should be regarded as interconnected and interacting upon each other. The basic cause of development of things does not lie outside but inside them, in their internal contradictions."[10]

This is remarkably similar to the Neo-Confucian theory that through the interaction of the opposed principles of *li* and *ch'i* individual things develop and grow, and the universe as a whole is a cosmic dynamic structure of *li* and *ch'i*. The universe as a whole—as the Great Ultimate— functions through the opposites of *yin* and *yang*. The universe is a unity of all things and man participates in this unity. This unity is regarded as dynamic rather than static, being of the nature of process. The process is constituted by the relative processes of particular things. This metaphysical conception of the universe is described by Mao as follows: "... In the absolute, total process of the development of the universe, the development of each concrete process is relative; hence in the great stream of absolute truth, man's knowledge of the concrete process at any given stage of development is only relatively true. The sum total of innumerable relative truths is the absolute truth."[11]

It would appear, therefore, that in his metaphysics and epistemology Mao carries forward the traditional attitude which sees a unity in particular things and which sees knowledge as inseparable from practice. Consequently, his philosophy also places the traditional emphasis on the unification of humanity through improved practical living.

[9] *Ibid.*, p. 209.   [10] *Ibid.*, p. 216.   [11] *Ibid.*, p. 212.

Suggestions for Further Reading

Glossary of Oriental Words

Index

Suggestions for Further Reading

The following books have been chosen as being among those most likely to be of assistance to readers wishing to continue their exploration of Oriental philosophies. The brief description of each item is intended to furnish clues to the kind of subject matter and treatment found in the book. Many of the books listed contain quite excellent bibliographies, and the reader is encouraged to use these to supplement the list of titles provided here.

I. SOURCE MATERIAL

There are two excellent collections of primary philosophical texts from the Indian and Chinese traditions. *A Source Book in Chinese Philosophy*, translated and compiled by Wing-tsit Chan (Princeton: Princeton University Press, Princeton paperback edition, 1969), contains nearly eight hundred pages of the most important Chinese philosophical texts arranged in a chronological order. The readability of the translations, the choice of materials and the explanations of difficult passages provided by Professor Chan combine to make this an exceedingly useful aid for the study of Chinese philosophy. *A Source Book in Indian Philosophy*, compiled and edited by Charles A. Moore and Sarvepalli Radhakrishnan (Princeton: Princeton University Press, Princeton paperback edition, 1967), contains standard older translations of selections from the major philosophical texts of India. Hinduism, Buddhism, Cārvāka and Jainism are all represented in this anthology which contains the *Bhagavad Gītā* and *Dhammapada* in their entirety. The introductions to each section are very useful.

Buddhism, as it developed in different Asian countries, is well represented in its religious and practical aspects as well as its theoretical aspects by the basic texts collected in *Buddhist Texts Through the Ages*, edited by Edward Conze, I. B. Horner, David Snellgrove, and Arthur Waley (New York: Harper and Row, Torchbook edition, 1964). Japanese Buddhism is well represented in *Sources of Japanese Tradition*, compiled and edited by Wm. Theodore de Bary (New York: Columbia University Press, 1958). This anthology also contains source material from the non-Buddhist sources of Japanese culture. The other two anthologies edited and compiled by Wm. Theodore de Bary, *Sources of Indian Tradition* (New York: Columbia University Press, 1958) and *Sources of Chinese Tradition* (New York: Columbia University Press, 1960), are not as good on the strictly philosophical texts as the source books by Chan and by Radhakrishnan and Moore, but have the advantage of containing excellent selections from the literary traditions of these cultures.

Three Ways of Thought in Ancient China, by Arthur Waley (Garden City, N.Y: Doubleday & Company, Anchor edition, n.d.), contains excerpts from Mencius, Chuang Tzu and Han Fei Tzu arranged and introduced by Waley so that the reader feels himself taking part in a discussion. Although it also contains some of his political and military thought, *Mao Tse-tung: An Anthology of his Writings*, edited, with an Introduction, by Ann Freemantle (New York: The New American Library, Mentor edition, n.d.), contains Mao's most important philosophical thinking. The classic Vedāntic text, *Vedārthasaṁgraha* by Śri Rāmānujācārya, English translation by S. S. Raghavachar (Mysore: Sri Ramakrishna Ashrama, 1956) presents an excellent introduction to the problem of the relations between selves, things and the ultimate reality based on Rāmānuja's interpretation of the major Upaniṣads. (This little book is available through Ramakrishna or Vedānta centers in the U.S.A. and Canada.)

II. SECONDARY MATERIAL

An Introduction to Indian Philosophy by S. C. Chatterjee and D. M. Datta (Calcutta: Calcutta University Press, 1960) is an extremely well organized and lucid introduction to the philosophies of India which focuses on the central aspects and problems of the various systems. The reader who is interested in the historical development and continuity of Indian thought might well turn to *Outlines of Indian Philosophy* by M. Hiriyana (London: George Allen & Unwin, 1964). This book combines the historical approach with a sharp focus on philosophical concepts and arguments, but avoids becoming overly technical. For the reader who wishes to go beyond these two books there is the excellent detailed scholarly two-volume work by S. Radhakrishnan, *Indian Philosophy* (London: George Allen & Unwin, 1962). Karl Potter's recent book,

Presuppositions of India's Philosophies (Englewood: Prentice Hall, 1963), is helpful in showing how certain basic concepts determine the structure of the various philosophical systems. For the reader interested in getting a feel for Hinduism as a living philosophy, guiding and directing the lives of the majority of India's peoples, there is Radhakrishnan's *The Hindu View of Life* (New York: Macmillan, 1964).

One of the most helpful books available for understanding Buddhism as a complete way of life is *What the Buddha Taught*, by Walpola Rahula (New York: Grove Press, Evergreen edition, 1962). This is a simple but masterly introduction to the basic features of Buddhism by a practicing Buddhist Monk who is an excellent scholar. The emphasis is on Buddhism as a way of life rather than either a philosophy or a religion. A more technical account of the main features of Buddhism is found in *The Essentials of Buddhist Philosophy*, Junjiro Takakusu (Honolulu: University of Hawaii, 1947). *Buddhist Thought in India* by Edward Conze (Ann Arbor: The University of Michigan Press, paperback edition, 1967) is an excellent study in the basic concepts of Buddhism as they developed historically. *The Central Philosophy of Buddhism* by T. R. V. Murti (London: George Allen & Unwin, 1955) and *Nāgārjuna's Philosophy*, Venkata Ramanan (Rutland, Vermont: Charles E. Tuttle Company, 1966) focus on the Mādhyamika philosophy, and from the point of view of this central school of Buddhism give excellent accounts of Buddhist philosophy. Both are scholarly works, containing much critical analysis of concepts and arguments while remaining sympathetic to the Mādhyamika philosophy. Zen, which represents the practical rather than the theoretical aspects of Buddhism, is presented in an extremely fascinating and illuminating manner by Philip Kapleau in *The Three Pillars of Zen* (New York: Harper and Row, 1967). Instructions for practice and autobiographical statements describing the achievements of Zen adepts accompany the explanations of principles underlying this form of Buddhism, providing for a many-faceted look at Zen. *Zen Buddhism: Selected Writings of D. T. Suzuki*, edited by William Barret (Garden City, N.Y.: Doubleday & Company, Anchor edition, 1956), contains selections from four of Suzuki's earlier works on Zen. The essays in this volume, by the Japanese Buddhist who gained a reputation as the foremost interpreter of Zen to English-reading peoples, aim at tracing the development of Zen Buddhism and explores the practical meanings of the central concepts of Zen. Comparisons with the West are usually based on deep insight and are extremely illuminating.

H. G. Creel's *Chinese Thought from Confucius to Mao Tse-tung* (New York: New American Library, Mentor edition, n.d.) is an extremely lucid account of the main trends in Chinese philosophy. This is a history of the outlines of the historical development of Chinese thought designed for the non-specialist. *A Short History of Chinese Philosophy* by Fung Yu-lan (New York: Macmillan, Macmillan paperback edition, 1960) is an excellent scholarly account of the development of Chinese philosophy, written by one of China's outstanding contemporary philosophers. The *Short History* is a shorter version of the two-volume work by Fung entitled *A History of Chinese Philosophy* (Princeton: Princeton University Press, second printing, 1959–60) which is generally acknowledged to be the most comprehensive and authoritative survey of Chinese philosophy available. For the reader interested in studying neo-Confucian philosophy there is the excellent two-volume study by Carsun Chang, *The Development of Neo-Confucian Thought* (New Haven: College and University Press, 1963). Wing-tsit Chan's *Religious Trends in Modern China* (New York: Columbia University Press, 1953) focuses on the practical aspects of Chinese thought, providing a basis for reflections about the future of China.

Finally, for the reader interested in comparing concepts of different cultures, East and West, there is the excellent collection of essays on the nature of man in *The Concept of a Man: A Study in Comparative Philosophy*, edited by S. Radhakrishnan and P. T. Raju (London: Allen & Unwin, 1969).

Glossary of Oriental Words

In order to facilitate pronunciation of Oriental terms and names a phonetic spelling has been provided as a guide. No indications have been provided for accenting syllables because according to native grammarians Sanskrit and related languages place equal emphasis on each syllable. However, since in practice pronunciation without accenting a particular syllable is extremely difficult, the rule generally adopted by modern grammarians and linguists is to accent the last syllable containing a long vowel.

The glossary is organized so that the first column gives the term or name as it appears in the text. The next column provides the usual scholarly transliteration wherever this differs from the form given in the first column. In cases where Sanskrit and Pali terms are sometimes used interchangeably the correct transliterations for both languages are given. The letter *P* next to a word indicates that it is the Pali form; the letter *S* next to a word indicates that it is the Sanskrit form. The third column gives a phonetic pronunciation of the name or term. The fourth column provides information about the items in the first column.

WORD AS IT APPEARS IN THE TEXT	SCHOLARLY TRANSLITERATION	PHONETIC PRONUNCIATION	EXPLANATION
Abhidharma		ah bee dar mah	Collections of advanced reflections on *dharma*
Abhidhar-makosha	Abhidharmakośa	ah bee dar mah ko shah	A systematic treatment of Abhidharma philosophy from the Sarvāstivādin viewpoint by Vasubandhu
Agni		ugh nee	Vedic fire god
Aham Brahman Asi		ah hum brah mun us ee	"I am Brahman"
Ahamkara	Ahaṁkāra	ah hum kah rrah	In Sāṁkhya, the principle of individuation. (Lit. "I-maker.")
Ahimsa	Ahiṁsā	ah him sah	Non-hurting
Alaya-Vijnana	Ālaya-Vijñāna	ah lye ah vih gnyah nah	Source of consciousness
Anatta		ah not ah	No permanent self
Anicca		ah nee chah	Impermanence of all existence
Aparashailas	Aparaśailas	ah pah rah shy lus	A Mahāyāna school of thought
Aranyaka	Āraṇyaka	ah rahn yah kah	A portion of the Veda containing reflections on sacrifice
Arhat		are hot	In Theravāda Buddhism, a person enobled by becoming perfect
Arjuna		are joo nah	Leader of the Pāṇḍavas to whom Kṛṣṇa conveys the teachings of the *Gītā*
Artha		are tah	Means of life
Artha Shastra	Artha Śāstra	are tah sha strah	Treatise on politics by Kauṭilya.
Aryadeva	Āryadeva	are yah day vah	Mādhyamika philosopher who was a pupil of Nāgārjuna

WORD AS IT APPEARS IN THE TEXT	SCHOLARLY TRANSLITERATION	PHONETIC PRONUNCIATION	EXPLANATION
Asatkaryavada	Asatkāryavāda	ah sot kar yah vah dah	The theory that a cause brings some new being into existence
Ashrama	Āśrama	ahsh rah mah	A stage in life; a place to "do one's thing"
Ashvaghosa	Aśvaghosa	ahsh vah gho shah	Buddhist philosopher who emphasized the "thusness" of all existents
Ashvapti Kaikeya	Aśvapti Kaikeya	ush vup tee kye kay ah	A much respected sage referred to in the *Chāndogya Upaniṣad*
Atharva Veda		ah tarh vah vay dah	The fourth Veda, representing ancient popular Indian religion
Atman	Ātman	aht mun	The innermost self
Aurobindo	Aurobindo Ghose	oro been dough	Twentieth-century Indian philosopher who championed the spiritual nature of man and the world
Ayatana	Āyatana	i ah tah nah	Basis of sensation
Badarayana	Bādarāyaṇa	bah dah rah yah nah	Author of the *Vedānta Sūtra*
Bahushrutiyas	Bahuśrutīyas	bah hoo shroo tee yahs	An early Mahāyāna school
Bhadrayaniyas	Bhadrāyaṇīyas	bha drrah yah nee yahs	One of the Sthaviravādin schools, most likely an offshoot from the Vātīputrīyas
Bhashya	Bhāṣya	bhosh yah	Commentary on a text
Bhaskara	Bhāskara	bhosh kah rah	Ninth-century Vedānta philosopher
Bhava		bah vah	Becoming
Bhavacakra		bah vah chock rah	Wheel of becoming
Bhikku		bhih koo	Buddhist monk
Bhishma	Bhīṣma	beesh mah	One of the heroes of the *Mahābhārata*

WORD AS IT APPEARS IN THE TEXT	SCHOLARLY TRANSLITERATION	PHONETIC PRONUNCIATION	EXPLANATION
Bodhisattva		boh dhee sah twa	An enlightened and compassionate being
Brahmacarya		brrah mah cha rree yah	Student stage of life
Brahman		brrah mun	The ultimate reality
Brahmana	Brāhmaṇa	brrah muh nah	A member of the priestly class; the ritual portion of the Veda
Brihadaranyaka	Bṛhadāraṇayaka Upaniṣad	brrih had dah rahn yah kah oo pah nee shod	One of the oldest Upaniṣads
Buddha		boo dhah	Enlightened; honorific title given Gautama
Budila Ashvatarashvi	Buḍila Aśvatarāśvi	boo dill ah ahsh vah tah rahsh vee	One of the five householders who sought Self-Knowledge from Aśvapti Kaikeya in the Chāndogya
Buddhaghosa		boo dha gho shah	Buddhist philosopher of the Theravāda tradition, fourth century A.D.
Buddhi		boo dhe	Enlightenment
Caittikas		chye tih kahs	One of the early Mahāyāna schools
Candrakirti	Candrakīrti	chan drrah keer tee	A Mādhyamika philosopher, sixth century A.D.
Carvaka	Cārvāka	char vah kah	A materialistic and skeptical Indian philosophy
Ch'an	Ch'an	chaan	The Chinese school of Buddhism which in Japan came to be known as Zen
Chanagankas		cha nah gahnk us	A Theravāda school, most likely a branch of the Vātsīputrīya school
Chandogya Upanishad	Chāndogya Upaniṣad	chun dogh yah	One of the earliest Upaniṣads

WORD AS IT APPEARS IN THE TEXT	SCHOLARLY TRANSLITERATION	PHONETIC PRONUNCIATION	EXPLANATION
Chang tsai		jung tzie	Neo-Confucian philosopher of the eleventh century A.D.
Chang tung-sun		jung doong soon	Twentieth-century Chinese philosopher
Ch'eng		jheng	Sincerity
Ch'eng hao		jheng how	Eleventh-century Neo-Confucian philosopher
Ch'eng I		jheng ee	Eleventh-century Neo-Confucian Philosopher
Chen-yen		jhen yen	Chinese Buddhist school
Ch'i		jhee	Material force; concrete thing
Chih		chee	Moral Wisdom
Chih liang-chih		chee lang chee	Doctrine of the extension of the innate knowledge of good
Ch'in		chin	The Chinese state from which the name "China" derived
Ching-t'u		jing too	Pure Land school of Buddhism
Chou Tun-i		chou toon ee	A pioneer of Neo-Confucianism (1017–1073)
Chuang Tzu		jwung dzuh	Taoist philosopher of the third or fourth century B.C.
Chu Hsi		jhoo she	A major Neo-Confucian philosopher (1130–1200)
Ch'un Ch'iu		choon chew	Spring and Autumn
Ch'ung Yung		jhoong yoong	Doctrine of the Mean
Citta		chih tah	Mind-stuff
Darshana	Darśana	dahr sha nah	Vision
Dharma		dhahr mah	Righteousness; duty as determined by righteousness

WORD AS IT APPEARS IN THE TEXT	SCHOLARLY TRANSLITERATION	PHONETIC PRONUNCIATION	EXPLANATION
Dharma Shastra	Dharma Śāstra	dhahr mah sha strah	Treatise on dharma
Dharma-guptakas		dharh mah goop tah kahs	A school of Theravāda Buddhism
Dharmakirti	Dharmakīrti	dhar mah keer tee	A Buddhist logician of the sixth century
Dharmottara		dharh moh tah rah	Ninth-century Buddhist logician of the Sautrāntika school
Dharmottariyas		dharh moh tah rree yahs	A school of Theravāda Buddhism
Dhatu	Dhātu	dah too	Element of existence
Dinnaga	Diṅnāga	dingh nah gah	A Buddhist logician, pupil of Vasubandhu
Dukkha		doo kah	Suffering, unwholesomeness
Ekavyava-harikas	Ekavyava-hārikas	eh kah veeah vah ha rree kahs	A Mahāyāna Buddhist school
Fung-yu-lan		foong you lon	Twentieth-century Chinese philosopher
Gaudapada	Gauḍapāda	gwad ah pah dah	Early Vedāntic philosopher
Gautama Siddhartha	Gautama Siddhārtha	go tom ah sid darh tah	The founder of Buddhism
Grihastha	Gṛhastha	grrih hah stah	Householder stage
Gunas	Guṇas	goo nahs	In Sāṁkhya, the material constituents of things
Guru		goo roo	Spiritual teacher
Haimavatas		hye mah vah tahs	Early school of Theravāda Buddhism
Han fei tzu		hun fay dzuh	Early Chinese philosopher identified with the Legalist school
Han yu	Han yü	hun yewh	One of the earliest Neo-Confucianists (768–824)
Harada-roshi		hah rah dah row she	Twentieth-century Japanese Zen master
Hetu		hay too	Reason (for something)
Hsi-shih		she she	Legendary beauty of ancient China

WORD AS IT APPEARS IN THE TEXT	SCHOLARLY TRANSLITERATION	PHONETIC PRONUNCIATION	EXPLANATION
Hsiung shih-li		shoong she lee	Twentieth-century Chinese philosopher (b. 1885)
Hsiao		showe	Familial love
Hsun tzu	Hsün tzu	shoon dzuh	Naturalistic Confucian philsopher (third century B.C.)
Hua-yen		whah yen	School of Chinese Buddhism
Hui Shih		hoo she	Chinese logician, fourth century B.C.
I-ching		ee jhing	Book of Changes
Indra		in drrah	Vedic god of the heavens
Indradyumna Bhallaveya	Indradyumna Bhāllaveya	in drrahd youm nah bhah lah vay ah	In the *Chāndogya*, a householder seeking Self-knowledge
Ishvara Krishna	Īśvara kṛṣna	eesh vah rah krish nah	Sāṁkhya philosopher, author of the *Sāṁkhya Kārikā*
Jana Sharkarakshya	Jana Śārkarākṣya	john ah shar kah rahks yah	In the *Chāndogya*, a householder seeking Self-knowledge
Jati	Jāti	jah tee	Birth; class determined by birth
jen		wren	Humanness of a person
joshu		jah shoo	Buddhist monk to whom the mu-koan is attributed
Kama	Kāma	comma	Pleasure
Kama shastra	*Kāma Śāstra*	comma shah strah	A treatise on the pleasures of love
Kamashila	Kamaśīla	comma she la	A Yogācāra philosopher, probably eighth century
Kanada	Kaṇāda	kah nah dah	Vaiśeṣika philosopher, author of the *Vaiśeṣika Sutra*, probably third century B.C.
Kapilavastu		kah pih lah vus too	Birth place of the Buddha

WORD AS IT APPEARS IN THE TEXT	SCHOLARLY TRANSLITERATION	PHONETIC PRONUNCIATION	EXPLANATION
Karma		car mah	Action; effect of action
Kashyapitas	Kāśyapītas	kahsh yah pee tahs	School of Theravāda Buddhism
Katha Upanishad	*Kaṭha Upaniṣad*	Kah tah oo pah nih shod	One of the older Upaniṣads
Kena Upanishad	*Kena Upaniṣad*	kay nah oo pah nih shod	One of the older Upaniṣads
Koan		cone	Problem set for a Zen pupil
Krishna	Kṛṣna	krrish nah	An incarnation of the ultimate reality, Arjuna's teacher in the *Bhagavad Gītā*
Kshatriya	Kṣatriya	kshot ree yah	Class of the protectors of society
Kukkulikas		koo koo lih kahs	An early school of Mahāyāna
Kumarajiva	Kumārajīva	koo mah rah jee vah	Mādhyamika philosopher, probably fourth century
K'un		koon	Earth; hexagram representing earth
Kung-sun Lung		koong soon loong	Chinese logician, fourth century, B.C.
Kuo Hsiang		Kwo shang	Third century Neo-Taoist philosopher
Lankavatara	Lankāvatāra	lahnk ah vah tah rah	The *Lankāvatāra Sūtra* is one of the very early Mahāyāna texts.
Lao Tzu		lao dzuh	Early Taoist philosopher, probably fifth century B.C.
Li		lee	Principle
Li Ao		lee ow	Eighth century philosopher instrumental in reviving Confucianism
Li Chi		lee chee	Book of Rites
Lokottaravadins	Lokottaravādins	loh koh tah rah vah dins	Early Mahāyāna school
Lu		loo	Native state of Confucius

WORD AS IT APPEARS IN THE TEXT	SCHOLARLY TRANSLITERATION	PHONETIC PRONUNCIATION	EXPLANATION
Lu Chiu-yuan	Lu Chiu-yüan	loo choo yoon	Neo-Confucian philosopher (1139–1193)
Lun Yu	*Lun Yü*	loon you	Analects or sayings of Confucius
Madhva		mudh vah	Dualistic Vedānta philosopher
Madhyamika	Mādhyamika	mah dhyah mee kah	Relativistic school of Buddhist philosophy
Madhyamika Karika	*Mādhyamika Kārikā*	mah dhyah mee kah kah ree kah	One of the main critical works of Nāgārjuna
Mahabharata	*Mahābhārata*	mah ha bha rah tah	One of two main long epics of India
Mahasanghika	Mahāsanghika	mah ha sangh hee kah	The large group of Buddhist monks who split off from the rest of the order in the third century B.C.
Mahat		mah hot	"The great one"
Mahayana	Mahāyāna	mah ha yah nah	One of the two main groups of Buddhists
Mahishasakas	Mahīśāsakas	mah hee shah sah kahs	An early school of Theravāda Buddhism
Manu		mun ooh	Indian social philosopher, probably fourth century B.C.
Mao Tse-tung		Mao dzuh doong	Chinese communist leader
Mencius		muhn shoos	Idealistic Confucian philosopher, fourth century B.C.
Mimamsa	Mīmāṁsā	mee mahm sah	Ritualistic school of Vedānta
Ming		ming	Destiny
Mohism		mo izm	Utilitarian school of philosophy named after Mo Tzu
Moksa	Mokṣa	moke shah	Liberation
Mo Tzu		mo dzuh	Utilitarian Chinese philosopher of the late fifth century B.C.
Mu-koan		moo kone	One of Joshu's famous answerless Zen questions

WORD AS IT APPEARS IN THE TEXT	SCHOLARLY TRANSLITERATION	PHONETIC PRONUNCIATION	EXPLANATION
Mundaka Upanishad	*Muṇḍaka Upaniṣad*	moon dah kah ooh pah nih shad	One of the early Upaniṣads
Nagarjuna	Nāgārjuna	nah gar joo nah	Mādhyamika philosopher, second century
Nama-rupa	Nāma-rūpa	nah mah roo pah	Mind-body complex
Nastika	Nāstika	nah stee kah	Unorthodox schools of Indian thought
Nibbana	Nibbāna (S. Nirvāṇa)	nee bah nah	The Buddhist goal of sufferingless existence
Nyaya	Nyāya	nyah yah	Indian school of logic
Paksha	Pakṣa	pahkh shah	Minor term of a syllogism
Panchatantra	*Pañcatantra*	pah cha tahn trah	Collection of Indian fables and stories
Paravidya		pah rah vih dhyah	Higher wisdom
Pataliputta	Pāṭaliputta	pah tah lih puh tah	Place of the third Buddhist council
Patanjali	Patañjali	pah tahn jah lee	Author of the *Yoga Sūtras*
Paticca Samuppada	Paṭicca Samuppāda (S. Pratītya Samutpāda)	pah tee cha sah moo pah dah	Dependent origination
P'eng-tsu		peng dzuh	Legendary Chinese Methusala
Pracinasala Aupamanyava	Prācīnaśāla Aupamanyava	prra chih na shah lah oh pah mah nyah vah	In the *Chāndogya*, one of the Householders seeking Self-knowledge
Prajapati	Prajāpati	prah jah pah tee	Hindu Lord of Creation
Prajnaptivadins	Prajñaptivādins	prah gnyahp tee vah dins	Early school of Mahāyāna
Prakriti	Prakṛti	prah krrih tee	In Sāṁkhya, the source of the material universe
Pudgala	(P. Puggala)	puhd gah lah	Substratum of personality
Purusha	Puruṣa	puh roo shah	In Sāṁkhya, the source of spirituality
Purushartha	Puruṣārtha	puh roo sharh tah	Aim in life

WORD AS IT APPEARS IN THE TEXT	SCHOLARLY TRANSLITERATION	PHONETIC PRONUNCIATION	EXPLANATION
Radhakrishnan		rah dah krrish nun	Twentieth-century Indian scholar, philosopher, statesman
Raja	Rāja	rah jah	King
Rajagaha	Rājagha	rah jah gah hah	Place of the first Buddhist council
Rajas		rah jus	The active element in existence
Rama	Rāma	rah mah	Main hero of the *Rāmayāna*
Ramanuja	Rāmānuja	rah mah noo jah	Theistic Vedāntic philosopher of the eleventh century
Ramayana	*Rāmāyana*	rah mah yah nah	One of India's two major epics
Ranee	Rāni	rah nee	Queen
Rigveda	*Ṛgveda*	rrig vay duh	One of the four Vedas making up the ancient Indian vedic literature
Sadhya	Sādhya	sahd yah	Major term of a syllogism
Sama Veda	*Sāma Veda*	sahm vay duh	One of the four Vedas making up the ancient India vedic literature
Samhita	Saṁhīta	sahm hee tah	Portion of the Veda containing hymns of praise and speculation
Samkhya Karika	*Sāṁkhya Kārikā*	sahm khyah kah ree kah	A basic Sāṁkhya text by Īśvara Kṛṣṇa
Sammitiyas	Sāṁmitīyas	sahm ih tee yahs	A Theravāda school, probably an off-shoot of the Vātsīputrīyas
Samnyasa	Saṁnyāsa	sahm nyah sah	Stage in life devoted to complete spiritual realization
Samsara	Saṁsāra	sahm sah rah	Round of births and deaths
Sankhara	Sankhāra (S. Saṁskāra)	sahn kah rah	Impulses to action
Sanna	Saññā	sah nah	Perception

WORD AS IT APPEARS IN THE TEXT	SCHOLARLY TRANSLITERATION	PHONETIC PRONUNCIATION	EXPLANATION
Sarvastivadins	Sarvāstivādins	sahr vah stee vah dins	Realistic Buddhist philosophers, including Vaibhāṣikas and Sautrāntikas
Satkaryavada	Satkāryavāda	saht car yah vah dah	Theory that effects pre-exist in their causes
Satori		sah tory	Zen enlightenment
Sattva		Saht twa	One of the three guṇas constituting all material things
Satyayajna Paulishi	Satyayajña Pauluṣi	soh yah yah gnyah paw loo she	In the *Chāndogya*, one of the householders seeking Self-knowledge
Sauntrantikas	Sautrāntikas	saw trahn tee kahs	A critical school of Buddhist realists
Shabda	Śabda	shahb dah	Word; testimony
Shamkara	Śaṁkara	shum kah rah	Non-dualistic Vedāntic philosopher, eighth century
Shandilya	Śāṅḍīlya	shahn deal yah	Indian sage referred to in the Upaniṣads
Shantarakshita	Śantarakṣita	sah tah rahk she tah	A later Yogācāra philosopher
Shatapatha Brahmana	*Śatapatha Brāhmaṇa*	shah tah pah tah brrah mun ah	Vedic text explaining the significance of various religious practices
Shih Ching	*Shih Ching*	she jhing	Book of Poetry, one of the Five Classics
Shudra	Śūdra	shoo drrah	Laboring class
Shunya	Śūnya	shoon yah	Empty
Shunyata	Śūnyatā	shoon yah tah	Emptiness
Shurya	Śurya	shoo ree yah	Indian sun god
Shvetaketu	Śvetaketu	shveh tah kay too	In the *Chāndogya*, the recipient of the famous "tat tvam asi" teaching
Sthaviravada	Sthaviravāda	shtah vee rah vah dah	"Teachings of the Elders." The early followers of the Buddha

WORD AS IT APPEARS IN THE TEXT	SCHOLARLY TRANSLITERATION	PHONETIC PRONUNCIATION	EXPLANATION
Sung		soong	Chinese dynasty (960–1279)
Sutra	Sūtra	soo trrah	aphorism or collection of aphorisms
Svatantra		Swa tahn trrah	A Buddhist school midway between Sauntrāntika and Yogācāra
Svabhava	Svabhāva	swah bah vah	Independent existence
Ta Hsueh	*Ta Hsüeh*	dah sheeh	Great Learning
Tai-chen		dye jhen	Chinese empirical philosopher of the eighteenth century
Tai-chi		dye jhee	Great ultimate
Taittiriya Upanishad	*Taittīriya Upaniṣad*	tye tee ree yah oo pah nee shod	One of the early Upaniṣads
Tamas		tom us	One of the three guṇas making up all things
Tathagata	Tathāgata	tah taah gah tah	"Thus gone." Honorific title of Gautama Siddhārtha
Tao		dow	The way of ultimate reality
Tao Te Ching		dow day jhing	Basic text of Taoism, attributed to Lao Tzu
Tathata	Tathāta	tah taah tah	The "thusness" of things
Tat Tvam Asi		tut twum us ee	"Thou art That"
Te		day	Virtue; power
Theravada	Theravāda	tehr rah vaah dah	The more conservative branch of Buddhism
T'ien-t'ai		dee en die	School of Chinese Buddhism
Tung Chung-shu		doong choong shoo	Confucian philospher responsible for making Confucianism the state ideology (second century)

WORD AS IT APPEARS IN THE TEXT	SCHOLARLY TRANSLITERATION	PHONETIC PRONUNCIATION	EXPLANATION
Turiya	Turīya	too ree yah	The fourth stage of consciousness wherein the real Self is discovered
Uddalaka Aruni	Uddālaka Āruṇi	oo dah lah kah ah roo nee	The sage in the *Chāndogya* who teaches his son "tat tvam asi"
Upanishads	Upaniṣads	oo pah nee shods	The concluding portion of the Vedas, containing reflections about ultimate reality
Upanishat	Upaniṣat	oo pah nee shot	Secret; the secret about ultimate reality
Uttarashailas	Uttaraśailas	oo tah rah shy lus	An early school of Mahāyāna
Vacchagotta		vah cha go tah	Man who questioned the Buddha about the nature of the self
Vaibhashika	Vaibhāṣika	vy bah she kah	School of Buddhists who are direct realists
Vaisheshika	Vaiśeṣika	vy shesh ee kah	Hindu system of philosophy that is realistic and pluralistic
Vallabha		vah lah bah	Fifteenth-century Vedantic philosopher
Vanaprastha	Vānaprastha	vaah nah prrah stah	Third stage in life according to the āśrama theory
Varna	Varṇa	vahr nah	Class
Vasubandhu		vahs oo bahn dhoo	Sautrāntika and Yogācāra philosopher of the fifth century
Vatsiputriyas	Vātsīputrīyas	vaht see put rree yahs	Early school of Theravāda Buddhism
Vatsyayana	Vātsyayāna	vaaht see ah yaah nah	Author of the *Kāma Sūtra*
Vayu	Vāyu	vaah yoo	Ancient Indian god of the wind
Vedana	Vedanā	vay dah nah	Sensation or feeling

WORD AS IT APPEARS IN THE TEXT	SCHOLARLY TRANSLITERATION	PHONETIC PRONUNCIATION	EXPLANATION
Vedanta	Vedānta	vay daahn tah	The system of philosophy with its basis in the Upaniṣads
Vesali	Vesālī	veh saah lee	Place of the second Buddhist council
Vinnana	Viññāna (S. Vijñāna)	vih naah nah	Consciousness
Virocana		vee row cha nah	A chief demon in Hindu mythology
Wang Yang-ming		wang yang ming	Idealistic Neo-Confucian philosopher (1472–1529)
Wu-wei		woo way	No artificial action
Yajnavalkya	Yājñavalkya	yaah gnyah vul khyah	Famous sage in ancient India
Yajur Veda		yah joor vay dah	One of the four Vedas or sacred texts of Hinduism
Yamuna	Yāmuna	yaah moo nah	Theistic Vedāntic philosopher of the tenth century
Yang		yang	Active principle of the universe
Yang Chu		yang choo	Early Taoist philosopher who emphasized self-preservation
Yashomitra	Yaśomitra	yah show mih trah	A Sautrāntika philosopher of the sixth century
Yi		yee	Righteousness
Yin		yin	Passive principle of the universe
Yin-yang		yin-yang	Theory of the interaction between yin and yang as a cause of all things
Yoga		yoh guh	Discipline
Yogacara	Yogācāra	yoh guh cha rah	Idealist school of Buddhism
Zazen		za zen	Zen discipline
Zen		zen	Form of Buddhism developed and practiced in China, Korea, and Japan

Index